THE ONE IS
JACK HURLEY

Volume One

Son of Fargo

By John Ochs

Foreword by J Michael Kenyon

RhythmMaster Publishing, LLC
Seattle, Wa, USA

Copyright © 2017 by RhythmMaster Publishing, LLC

All rights reserved. No part of this book may be reproduced or transmitted in any form by any means, electronic, or mechanical, including photocopying and recording, or by any information storage and retrieval system, except as may be expressly permitted by the 1976 Copyright Act or by written permission from the author. Requests for permission should be made in writing to: RhythmMaster Publishing, LLC.

ISBN # 978-1-5323-0636-5 (hardback)
978-1-5323-0637-2 (paperback)
978-1-5323-0638-9 (e-book)

Printed in the United States of America

Front cover photo: Square-off photo for Russie-LeRoy fight in Fargo, March 12, 1922,. Left to right: Bobby Ward, Jack Reddy, Leo Kossick, Russie LeRoy, and Jack Hurley

Back photo: Billy Petrolle (left) and Jack Hurley (right)

Spine photo: Jack Hurley, c. 1930

Permission to use photographs in this volume has been granted by the Hurley family, North Dakota State Library, Wayne State Museum (Michigan), Mercer County Historical Society (North Dakota), John Salvator II, Museum of History and Industry (*Seattle Post-Intelligencer* photo collection), Jake Wegner, Willis Miller, Karen Richter, John Ochs, and Steve Gorman, Jr. Other photos are from the author's collection of public domain photos including pre-1978 published wire photos for which copyrights were never filed and/or renewed and pre-1978 newspaper press photos which pre-date the originating newspapers' adoption of copyright-filing-and/or-pre-1964 renewal procedures. The publisher has made every reasonable effort to trace the copyright status for all the photographs in this book. Any errors in this regard can be forwarded to the publisher in care of johntochs@comcast.net.

RhythmMaster Publishing, LLC
Seattle, Washington

To my parents

*Casimir Joseph Ochs
and
Margaret Susan Erpelding Ochs*

*who gave me everything they had,
including a close connection
to the Upper Midwest*

Contents

	ACKNOWLEDGEMENTS	*i*
	FOREWORD	*iv*
	PREFACE	*vi*
1 –	THE PREACHER AND THE KID	1
2 –	LESSONS FROM A FAMOUS PROFESSOR	21
3 –	GOOD FIELD, NO HIT	44
4 –	PRIVATE HURLEY COMES LIMPING HOME	56
5 –	JUST IN TIME FOR BOXING'S BOOM TIME	79
6 –	HURLEY'S MAN FROM MOTLEY, MINNESOTA	99
7 –	"WE'LL BE ROBBED!!"	117
8 –	EXILE AND REDEMPTION	132
9 –	THE BEST $35 HURLEY EVER SPENT	159
10 –	FIGHT FANS, NOW HEAR THIS	181
11 –	GO EAST (AND WEST), YOUNG MEN	201
12 –	PINKEY'S TALE OF A SORE TOE	225
13 –	WHO WAS THAT MASKED MAN?	244
14 –	FINDING THE GREAT WHITE WAY	267
15 –	ARRIVING, VIA 'DELAYED KNOCKOUT'	289
16 –	OUTDOORS, IN A BALLPARK	312
17 –	NEXT STOP: DULUTH AND A POLISH KILLER	334
18 –	THE FARGO EXPRESS STALKS A TITLE	360
19 –	HURLEY AND LEROY BURY THE HATCHET	382
20 –	JACK'S KIND OF TOWN, CHICAGO IS	416
21 –	BUMPY RIDE ON THE GRAVY TRAIN	446
22 –	MA AND THE MANASSA MAULER	482
23 –	AN OLD EGYPTIAN JINX	514
24 –	THE DYNAMITER FROM DULUTH	557
25 –	FIRST ENCOUNTER WITH A BOY BANDIT	582
26 –	AN ATTRACTIVE, DARK-HAIRED WOMAN	618
27 –	HOW'S THE GAS WITH YOU, BILL?	646
28 –	THE OLD MAN REACHES THE END OF THE LINE	683
	AFTERWORD	710
	BIBLIOGRAPHY	711
	INDEX	715

ACKNOWLEDGEMENTS

I would be criminally remiss if I did not put my wife, Pamela Bradburn, at the top of this list. In addition to serving as my final copy editor, she endured 11 years of late meals, distracted dinner conversation, unwashed pots and pans in the sink, and unfolded laundry in the living room as I worked my way through the project. Even during times of relative normalcy, her deliverance was temporary, as these ever-escalating cycles were repeated 53 times, once for each chapter. Also beyond the call of duty was her willingness to adapt our vacation plans to include multiple visits to Fargo, Minneapolis/St. Paul, and Chicago.

My mentor has been J Michael Kenyon, celebrated sportswriter, columnist, newspaper editor, publicist, promoter, radio broadcaster, researcher, world-class grammarian and all-around free spirit. Without his help these volumes would not have been nearly as readable or thorough as they are now. A legend throughout the Pacific Northwest and among sports historians everywhere, and a pro in the best sense of the word, J Michael spent countless hours teaching, suggesting, researching, fact checking, editing, prodding, and otherwise encouraging me throughout the project, all of which he shrugs off as just part of "the service" he so selflessly provides to his stable of aspiring and established writers.

Since the main sources of information for these books derived from newspapers located in cities where the events occurred, kudos are owed to the Seattle Public Library staff which gathered newspaper microfilm from libraries all over the country and guided me in the use of at least three generations of microfilm reading equipment. Meriting special mention are Dona Bubelis and Elizabeth Walsh in Periodicals, Newspapers, and Government Publications; Doris Johnson and John LaMont in Geneaology; and Martin Burgess, first in Periodicals, et al. (1999-2009) and then in Interlibrary Loans (2009-2015).

An early out-of-town stop was Fargo's public library where Steve Hubbard ferreted out background information about the city's early days and its contributions to the country's World War I effort. Steve phoned Carol Bradley Bursack, then librarian at Fargo-Moorhead's *The Forum*, who promptly delivered the newspaper's Hurley clipping file to me, thus saving countless hours tracking down articles after Jack left Fargo. Especially helpful was a 1951 questionnaire he filled out. It opened the door to information about his World War I record and his 1932 marriage.

On the same trip, I met Don McAllister, who purchased Hurley's Religious Goods store from Jack's brother Hank in the 1970s. Don took time to show me some Fargo landmarks, including Holy Cross Cemetery where Jack is buried. Steve Gorman, Jr. and his wife Mary K. also welcomed me and shared memories and photos about Steve's father and the

Grand Recreation Billiard Parlor. The late Robert Diemert, a past Fargo resident, fleshed out the Grand Rec story with a description of its floorplan and the services it offered.

The two surviving branches of Hurley's family filled in gaps about Jack's childhood and marriage. My first contact was in Minneapolis with Carol Olson, daughter of Jack's elder sister Margaret, and her husband Richard. They introduced me to Carol's cousin Gail Hafner, daughter of Jack's younger sister Abigail, and her husband Yates, who happened to be visiting from Detroit. Particularly memorable was an evening with the family of the Olsons' son, Paul, who found time in a busy schedule to host a last-minute dinner guest.

My introduction to the Hafners led to a rendezvous at the home of Gail's nephew, John Conmy III, and his wife Diane in River Forest, a Chicago suburb where Abigail's family had settled. They graciously hosted me for four days while I commuted on the "El" to do research at a library in Chicago. John III also arranged a visit with his father John Conmy II and his uncle Brian D. Conmy, who shared memories about their Uncle Jack. Since John III's home was the designated repository for Jack's artifacts, I was able to inspect a crate of pictureboards which had once hung on the walls of Jack's gym in Duluth and to make Xerox copies of newspaper clippings Hank had collected about Jack over the years.

One of my most fruitful contacts was made in St. Paul with John Salvator II, son of boxing promoter Johnny Salvator, one of Jack's closest friends. Fortunately, as an only child, John accompanied his parents everywhere. It was his memories as a nine-year-old flyspeck on the wall which furnished an account of Jack's 1932 courtship with his wife Rachel (also known as Reggie). John also provided the only photo of her I could find and offered the most complete explanation of why she and Jack separated in 1949.

Seattle boxing manager and promoter George Chemeres, who died in 2002 at age 87 three years before I began writing, sensed I was serious enough about the topic to follow through so he gave generously of his time during his last few years by answering questions, telling stories, and even taking me through a short course of his teaching methods. George's son, John, who worked with many of his father's boxers, was kind enough to proofread the section summarizing his father's life before he met Hurley.

Since most of the participants in Hurley's early and mid-life are now dead, I relied heavily on relatives for source material. Cena Anderson, daughter of Ingomar, Montana fighter Billy Seward, provided a motherlode of information and photos when she forwarded photocopies of her father's boxing scrapbook as well as additional photographs. Gary Marquart, nephew of boxer Billy Marquart, filled me in on Billy's family background and pre-boxing life. Connie Urresti, niece of Boise boxing promoter Al Berro, located a photo of her uncle with Jack Dempsey. Nephew James

Robert Ullman and daughter Sharon Harbourne likewise provided beautiful photos of St. Paul fighter Babe Daniels. In similar fashion, Sheri Clayton Spomer, came through with photos of her great great uncle, Omaha promoter Max Clayton.

With the help of Larry Buck, I interviewed the late Harry (Kid) Matthews twice prior to his death in 2003. Happily, Hurley's last fighter, Boone Kirkman, is still hale and hearty. He kindly reviewed the chapters dealing with his career and suggested a few changes to improve the manuscript's accuracy. Former *Seattle P-I* sports editor John Owen and reporter Paul Rossi, both now deceased, also provided details about Jack's life in Seattle.

Boxing memorabilia collector and dealer John Gay and I visited the late Hall of Fame historian Hank Kaplan at his Miami home over a five-day period. Hank permitted me to make copies of his Hurley clipping file and introduced me to the late Jack Kearns, Jr., who furnished information about his father, which I used in the first volume of this series.

The project would not have been so rich in photos without the help of Bill Gonzalez at Durham Museum, Omaha, Nebraska; Michelle Gullett of the *Omaha World-Herald*; Deborah Rice at the Walter P. Reuther Library, Wayne State University; John Hallberg at the North Dakota State University Archives in Fargo; Lani Meyhoff at the Mercer County Historical Society in Beulah, North Dakota; Marie Koltchak at the *Seattle Times*; and Carolyn Marr, Librarian, and Howard Giske, Curator of Photography, at the Museum of History and Industry in Seattle, Washington.

The late boxing film collector Tony Fosco, a true pioneer in the field of film preservation and research, provided videotapes of the film clips of Billy Petrolle's second fights with both Jimmy McLarnin and Tony Canzoneri and of complete versions of Harry (Kid) Matthews' fights with Bob Murphy, Danny Nardico, Rex Layne and Don Cockell (second fight), and the Floyd Patterson-Pete Rademacher heavyweight title contest.

I also have received encouragement from friends at the International Boxing Research Organization (IBRO) and elsewhere, most particularly Clay Moyle, James Johnston, Jake Wegner, and Steve Compton, who all made helpful suggestions. Steve used his computer wizardry to help design the cover and improve the quality of some images. Jake provided photos of the Hudson Arena and of Babe Daniels. Thanks also to David Bergen who furnished copies of several photos from his extensive archive and to James Dickson who forwarded the photo of Jack Dempsey, Max Baer, and Ancil Hoffman.

FOREWORD

John Ochs set out to tell us the story of a fascinating life spent in boxing. He has succeeded, and in admirable fashion. But the finished product is far, far more than just the long-overdue biography of a legendary boxing manager and promoter.

It is a veritable encyclopedia of the sport's halcyon era, as measured by the span of years between America's participation in World War I – Jack Hurley was among the millions of doughboys shipped to France – and Vietnam.

These were Hurley's adult years. It was a time when boxing was always a major sport, when the media attention it received was always on a par, and often exceeded, that devoted to baseball and football.

Consider this: over the more than 16 years John Ochs devoted to researching and writing this biography, Jack Hurley – a member of boxing's World Hall of Fame – did not have a Wikipedia page devoted to his remarkable life. In fact, as this is written, there still isn't one.

Perhaps, at a glance, it is understandable. None of Hurley's fighters ever won a title, although they always were knocking on the throne-room door. His best fighter, by far, was Billy Petrolle, the popular and remarkable "Fargo Express," but he was gone from the fistic stage more than 80 years ago. And, alas, Hurley always seemed to encounter more than his share of hard luck.

Almost invariably, after his wily stratagems had succeeded in building a fighter into a budding, box-office sensation, the fates chose not to be kind.

Like most boxing men, Hurley spent much of his managerial career in quest of a championship-caliber big man. He sent a succession of heavies into battle, seeking to take away the laurels of every title claimant from Jack Sharkey to George Foreman – but every foray ended shy of the mark.

After Petrolle, Hurley's next best fighter may have been a young welterweight named Vince Foster. He died young, and tragically, before realizing his potential. Nowadays, scarcely anyone recalls the name of Vince Foster, all the more so because it was usurped by a political suicide that tormented the Bill Clinton administration.

Jack Hurley grew up so Roman Catholic he could never tell his mother he had married a Jewish woman. He first aspired to be a first baseman, but was bedeviled by curve balls. The people he admired most as a youth were boxing men, a curious breed of carnival hustlers and poor man's Pied Pipers.

And, he quickly surmised, they didn't have to get up early in the morning to go to work.

Hurley thought late hours and a lot of independence just might be the thing for him. As so often would be the case for across his 75 years, he turned out to be correct. Hurley returned from the Great War to become a trainer, a manager, a corner man, a promoter, a publicist, a gym operator, a matchmaker, a booking agent – you name it, and he did it ... and did it well.

So good was he at ballyhoo, Abe Saperstein hired him as advance man for the Harlem Globetrotters' greatest player, Wilt Chamberlain. Hurley wound up scarcely mentioning basketball, and instead had sportswriters wondering what Chamberlain might achieve as a heavyweight boxer.

Unlike so many of his pugilistic brethren, Hurley developed a philosophic set of ideals and morals from which he seldom, if ever, wavered. He sealed deals with a proverbial handshake, never turned down a friend in need and was always true to his word. Above all, he treated fighters with a dignity and honesty that not too many others of his craft exhibited.

All the twists and turns of a whirlwind life spent barnstorming the rails and flight paths of America are meticulously detailed here. John Ochs, with a fervor seldom displayed by biographers, has chronicled, absorbingly and charmingly, the life of this singular and intriguing man who wound up being called "The Deacon."

Damon Runyon said he had only ever known two honest fight managers: "One is Jack Hurley, and I forget the name of the other one."

Here, in these action-packed pages describing the glory years of boxing and one of its most colorful disciples, you'll discover what Runyon had in mind.

– J Michael Kenyon

PREFACE

My fascination with boxing manager Jack Hurley dates from my pre-teens when I devoured the sports sections in the Seattle newspapers and watched Friday-night fights on TV. I horsed around at boxing, but was more interested in playing baseball and basketball. Even then, I realized boxing took the meaning of competition to a new level, where the cost of being mediocre was too high for my taste and ability. Even so, the sport captivated me, and local boxers I saw in the 1960s and '70s remain my heroes to this day.

Since I attended a parochial high school across town, I took a city bus to and from school. The ride was not a one-stop trip. On days I was not busy with after-school activities, I sometimes used the extra time on my bus transfer to visit one of my regular downtown haunts. Some days, I might literally run four blocks east up Pike Street to the Mohr Bookstore past 7th Avenue where Mr. Mohr was holding a variety of sports books for me, including used copies of *The Ring* magazine for 15 cents each. Other days, I might sprint full tilt eight blocks south along Second Avenue to the Cherry Street gym to see boxers train. In each case, I had about an hour before my transfer expired.

Fighters I saw included world-class boxers like Eddie Cotton, Fraser Scott, Larry Buck, and Boone (Boom Boom) Kirkman. Already a legend, Hurley lived in Seattle at the time and was usually at the gym overseeing Kirkman's training, but I never approached him. All told, I must have seen him 20 times, and we never exchanged a word. I retain a picture in my mind, however, of him peering balefully at me over the top of his spectacles, as if suspicious of my reason for being there. As well he might have been. Little did either of us know one day I would write his life story.

I initially went to the gym to see Cotton, who remains to this day the most finished fighter I have ever seen in the flesh. Watching Eddie go through his warm-up paces, I noticed that even before entering the ring, he began every workout by dancing back and forth and gliding from side to side, practicing his footwork with hands dangling at his sides, all within a rectangle his mind's eye had marked out on the gymnasium floor. After a while, he would add shadow boxing to the mix and pitch a few punches in sequence. Later, when I began watching Kirkman, I noticed he started his workouts the same way.

In writing these volumes, I came to understand that these workout rituals were the very same ones Hurley learned while watching Mike Gibbons train fighters during Jack's season at St. Paul in 1922-'23. When I first saw Cotton, his trainer was George Chemeres who learned his methods observing Hurley's work with Harry (Kid) Matthews. Cotton had already learned to box from Frisco McGale, but Chemeres still made Eddie follow the routine George learned from Jack, a building-block type of regimen I try to describe in chapter nine of the first volume in this series. Little discoveries like this made during my research have made my connection to the topic particularly meaningful.

My father was not a fight fan per se, but he grew up in Canby, Minnesota and knew well the story of St. Paul's famous Gibbons brothers, Mike and Tom. Unfortunately, he had a stroke which affected his speech when I was 14, so after I became interested in boxing, we were unable to have any in-depth discussions. Somehow, however, I learned that when my dad moved to Minneapolis in 1928 he lived in a boardinghouse owned by Mike Malone, the father of one of St. Paul's most celebrated fighters, Jock Malone, who had studied with Mike Gibbons. The Malone house became my dad's home base in the Depression, and he resided there most of the time until 1937.

At the time, Jock was at the end of a long and distinguished pugilistic career. As best I can determine, my father was living at the house in March 1930 when Malone was training for his last St. Paul fight against Gorilla Jones. It may have been then my dad saw Jock fight in the gym. I have a distinct recollection of my father mimicking Jock's ability to slip punches and then smiling and shaking his head at the wonder of it all.

For a time in 1934, Jock managed Lee Savold, who also happened to be from Canby. Savold hung around the boardinghouse at the time, and my father connected with him there. Lee was four years younger than my dad but had been a Canby classmate of my dad's brother, Andrew, who was later my godfather. Years later, while reading an issue of *The Ring*, I learned Savold had won the British version of the world heavyweight title in 1950. When I shared this exciting insight with my dad, he promised to introduce me to Lee if he ever visited Seattle. Unfortunately, Savold died in 1972 before I could meet him. My dad was never one to boast or force himself on people, so he must have known Lee pretty well.

My father also knew all the stories about Hurley and his fighter, Billy Petrolle, the Fargo Express. The mention of Hurley's name for some reason always elicited a chuckle. Dad was living with the Malones on February 1, 1931, when Jock and his father came home from the Petrolle-King Tut fight at St. Paul where Tut kayoed Billy in 34 seconds. Jock was upset because he was still getting settled in his seat when the critical punches landed.

Although I had been hanging around the Cherry Street gym for a couple of years, the first live boxing show I ever attended was the Eddie Cotton-Roger Rouse fight in November 1966. I was 16 and fresh from my first summer job, so I had money enough to pay $10 for a first-row ringside seat directly behind the press section. The fight was Cotton's first after having almost won the world light-heavyweight title from Jose Torres a few months earlier. Cotton and Rouse were rated as the division's leading contenders, and Eddie was fighting for the right to face Torres again. Cotton, who by then was over 40 years old, just didn't have it that night, and Roger won a close decision to become the No. 1 contender.

I never knew my father to attend live boxing shows while I was growing up. Even watching the Friday-night fights on television was a rare event for him. Consequently, I was surprised when he agreed to accompany me to the Boone Kirkman-Bowie Adams fight in January 1967. Kirkman had turned pro under Hurley's management in 1966 after winning the 1965 national AAU heavyweight title. Boone already had won six out-of-town fights, and the Adams go was his pro debut in Seattle. I think my father went with me because of his interest in Hurley.

Kirkman stopped Adams in two rounds, and Boone was on his way. In the next seven months, he had three fights at the Seattle Coliseum, and I was part of the roaring throng which cheered him on. The memory of hearing the rhythmic rumble of 14,000 mostly bass-pitched voices spontaneously chanting in perfect unison the mantra of "Boom – Boom – Boom" as Kirkman made his way up the aisle still sends chills up my spine.

Kirkman suffered a series of training injuries which set his career back a couple of years, and the duty fell upon Hurley to keep his name before the public during this dry period. I naturally followed all his stratagems in the newspaper. When Boone finally earned his big chance against George Foreman at Madison Square Garden in November 1970, I was one of thousands who saw the fight on closed-circuit TV at the Seattle Center Arena. Foreman was virtually unbeatable during this period, and he kayoed Kirkman in two rounds, just as he did Joe Frazier two years later while winning the heavyweight title.

My involvement with boxing lagged during my college, post-graduate, and career days, but I maintained an interest in the sport's history. I collected 8mm and 16mm fight films before the VHS, DVD, and YouTube eras and provided entertainment at local gatherings honoring ex-fighters. At these events, I was lucky enough to meet and become friends with many of my heroes, including several who helped me with this project.

Hurley died in November 1972, but I persisted in reading everything I could find about him. Even after his death, famous writers like W. C. Heinz, Red Smith, Jimmy Cannon, and Jim Murray continued to extol his virtues. Heinz, five-time winner of the E. P. Dutton Award for the year's best magazine story, wrote: "Of all those I came to know in sports nobody else ever fascinated me as did Jack Hurley." Locally, *Seattle P-I* sports editor Royal Brougham, looking back in 1976 on a 65-year career, echoed Heinz's opinion by placing Jack at the top of his list of the "most fascinating people" he had ever met.

Despite these ringing endorsements, no one stepped forward to write a biography about this man who enchanted so many of the world's best journalists. In my own case, I knew a lot about his 22 years in Seattle, but what of his earlier years? Hurley never had told anyone the full story of his days in Fargo, Duluth, New York, and Chicago. Moreover, the likelihood of anyone digging so deep was becoming increasingly remote since Jack was rapidly being forgotten even in Seattle, the site of his most recent accomplishments.

I was fortunate enough to be able to take an early retirement from my day job. Seven years in anticipation of the event, I began ordering newspaper microfilm on a variety of topics which interested me through the Interlibrary Loan program at the Seattle Public Library. Soon, my orders were focusing on newspapers from Fargo, Duluth, New York, and Chicago during the years Hurley roamed the streets in each of those cities.

When the big day finally happened in April 2005, I had accumulated three stacks of Xeroxed newspaper articles, each stack piled seven feet high. In those pre-flash-drive days, it took six months to organize the articles into binders and files before I could begin fully digesting the information in preparation for putting fingers to the keyboard.

Being a person who likes to plumb the depths of any topic which interests me, I had become disenchanted with multiple biographies about familiar figures featuring the same old rehashed set of facts. In my relatively small library of haphazardly accumulated boxing books I have 12 biographies of Muhammad Ali, eight each of John L. Sullivan, Jack Johnson, Jack Dempsey, and Joe Louis, as well as multiple biographies of many other boxing figures. To me, the depth of research in some of these endeavors seemed to be lacking, and they failed to add to the pool of accessible information. Helpful, I suppose, to readers new to the topic, but not to veteran readers like myself.

And so, I decided to throw my hat in the ring, so to speak, as a writer. I had time to learn the craft, earn some standing on the issue of quality research, and have a try at producing a high-quality boxing book. In Hurley, I had a well-respected figure whose professional life coincided with the most exciting and transformative period in boxing history and whose popularity with writers left behind a long trail of quotes which would bring the fascinating aspects of his character to life.

It took a few years of writing to realize no rational individual would choose to devote so much time writing a narrative about anyone less than a major world figure. Still, I forged ahead. For better or worse, I had partnered with Jack Hurley to prove I could write a book which met the expectation of my own ideals and accomplish something meaningful on my own terms, and it had to be completed, whatever the cost.

As I followed each thread of the Hurley saga to its logical conclusion, the story evolved into something much greater than that of just one man. His life was of such scope that an entire history of boxing from a promoter's viewpoint unfolded. Little did I know when I began that the frail old man I saw in the 1960s had helped topple boxing's most powerful regime at New York in the 1930s and set up Mike Jacobs as the sport's most effective czar ever. Nor did I suspect he was Chicago's foremost promoter in the 1940s or that he led the way in bringing the IBC's worldwide boxing monopoly to its knees in the 1950s.

What emerged is a tale unlike any other I am aware of, a detailed study of big-time boxing's 20th-Century glory years told through the life experience of one of its greatest sole practitioners. Hurley's life, more than that of any other figure, personifies boxing's journey out of the backrooms and bars of the 1900s, to the arenas and stadiums of the 1920s, '30s, and '40s, and into the parlors and family TV rooms of the 1950s and '60s.

As I complete the third and final volume of this project, I look back upon a revolution which has occurred during my 18 years of research and writing. It is no longer always necessary (but still essential for accessing newsprint not yet on-line) to plan an extended campaign by placing long-term continuing orders for each target newspaper with a local library and then waiting for the microfilm rolls to dribble in via the U. S. Postal Service. Now, through a variety of subscription websites, back issues of more than a thousand newspapers are immediately accessible at the touch of one's home computer.

One result is that more people than ever are writing books. Sometimes, the research is taken mostly from secondary-source magazine articles or from national wire service reports rather than from local newspapers not yet on-line. Wire reports are valuable for the version of the facts contained therein and as a first look at the event, but there still is no substitute for going back to the original accounts of the local papers. Those articles include pre-and post-event coverage, and even more importantly, contain observations of local reporters with inside knowledge about the event and its participants.

There still is much work to do in the trenches – the heavy lifting of scrolling through the microfilm of local newspapers. As I write, many of the country's post-1922 papers are not yet on-line, due partly to copyright considerations. They include solid work from unheralded writers who deserve an audience. It is the researcher's privilege to search the field and pull out the undiscovered gems so we can all enjoy them.

In time, however, all newspapers will be available on the worldwide web. My hope is that as they become more accessible, some authors will use the time saved by the advances in research technology to better integrate information with thoughtful narrative. There is a place for the quick dissemination of raw information, but there is also a need for more and better narratives to organize the flow of history for the reader.

These have been my thoughts as I reflect on the journey of that naive person who began to formulate this story so many years ago. What started out as a compulsion to follow a specialized interest evolved into a mission to tell a comprehensive story about boxing's most interesting era, and finally became a desire to contribute to the process of advancing the quality of research in the sport. It is my hope this work has inched that process along.

– John Ochs

CHAPTER 1

THE PREACHER AND THE KID

It's a hot night in 1951, and Hurley and I are coming out of Memorial Stadium after watching Billy Graham preach at the crusade he was holding in Seattle that summer. Jack asked if I wanted to go, and I thought, "What the heck, why not?" Billy was in town for six weeks, and the revival drew almost a half a million people. It was a big deal for the city, you know, and Hurley was great for wanting to see things like that.

Graham, you know, could put over a show. There must have been 15,000 people there. Admission was free, but Billy's people passed the plate that evening, and the amount they collected was way more than they could have made selling tickets. On our way back to the car, I suggested to Jack how great it would be to fill a place like that for a fight, and he looked at me kind of funny like.

Hurley didn't say anything for a while, but then he told me when he was a kid in Fargo, Billy Sunday came to town for six weeks. Jack was raised Irish-Catholic, you know, and to see a Protestant preacher he had to sneak out of the house because his mother was afraid he'd be swayed. But he wanted to see what the fuss was all about, so he went anyway.

Jack said Sunday took a break halfway through and asked the people to keep quiet while money was being passed. As the plates went around, the only sound being made was the clinking of coins. When the collection was over, you know, the plates were full. The coins were poured into three large bags, which the preacher's assistants took up front.

After intermission, Sunday went back to preaching and at the end the congregation went wild. When he finished, you know, hundreds of people walked up front and pledged themselves as believers. After shaking their hands, Billy again asked for silence.

*When the crowd settled down, Sunday said he was going to pass the plate once more. Only this time, he wanted a **real quiet** collection. The plates were passed, and the only sound heard was the faint rustling of paper. When the collection was over, the plates were full again, but this time with **clean, crisp bills**. Billy's assistants sorted the bills, and again the bags were delivered to the podium.*

When he finished, Hurley paused awhile before he finally looked over at me and said, "You know, George, I think we're in the wrong racket." [1]

– George Chemeres

****

---

[1] Told to the author by George Chemeres in a conversation October 1998.

John Cornelius Hurley's pale blue eyes first saw light of day on December 9, 1897, at Moorhead, Minnesota, just across the Red River from Fargo, North Dakota. Although fall still had 12 days to go, the city's 20-degree weather and its bitter wind would have been considered mid-winter by the measure of anywhere else in the United States.

Indeed, though it was late in the year, the region barely had recovered from the ravages of the prior spring thaw. A combination of a heavy winter snowfall, ice jams in Canada, and a late but rapid snow melt in the Dakotas had caused the Red River to overflow its banks.

Damage to the Fargo-Moorhead area was dramatic. Flooding began on April 1, 1897, but the river did not begin its slow retreat until finally cresting six days later. By then, nearly all the region's business and residential areas were covered by a deep blanket of water, which stretched 150 miles long by 30 miles wide, leaving 50,000 people homeless.

As the flooding continued, some residents awakened in the middle of the night to find their bedrooms awash in three feet of water. For others, the water came up so quickly during the night that livestock were already found drowned the next morning. In the Island Park area of Fargo, people were forced to board rescue boats from their second-story windows.

Water lifted houses from their foundations and propelled them downriver like runaway houseboats. Resourceful owners anchored their homes with cables to keep them from drifting away. Fargo's streets and sidewalks, consisting of wooden blocks, literally headed downstream to Canada. A big cable was pulled across the river north of town to collect the blocks and pull them back to the riverbank.

Other incidents were more bizarre. Some citizens, concerned that an abandoned grain elevator would wash away, set it on fire before it could do any damage to a downstream bridge. To the dismay of onlookers, as soon as it was burning nicely the elevator did indeed break loose, ran into the bridge, and set it ablaze.

In another incident, desperate homeowners armed with pickaxes and shovels stormed a section of Great Northern railroad track bed because it was causing water to back up into their homes. When the railroad became aware of the situation, the company eventually sent a crew to remove the blockage so water in the southern part of the city could drain.

The flood provided opportunities to a few entrepreneurs endowed with a little ingenuity. The pilot of the steamboat 'Sloppy Slocum' cashed in by delivering customers to and from their submerged homes and businesses in his vessel. In waters high above street level, the boat started at Moorhead and continued east along the Front Street Bridge to Fargo. It then took a right and traveled six blocks up Broadway to Northern Pacific Avenue. It finished its circuit by taking another right turn back to Moorhead.

According to the *Fargo Forum*, hundreds of families were forced to leave their homes for prolonged periods. A network of charitable and city-sponsored organizations provided for the immediate needs of the most unfortunate citizens. However, when federal aid was offered, Mayor R. A. Johnson of Fargo declined to accept assistance, and a controversy ensued.

Those opposed to federal aid asserted the government's offer was so small as to be "a pittance" and funds for rebuilding could be more easily obtained if Fargo maintained a "reputation in the eastern money centers of caring for its own poor." Those in favor of assistance held the opinion that "neither the mayor, the council nor the whole city full of well-to-do people had any right to decline this gift to the poor," especially since those "destitute people – the beneficiaries of the act – have not been consulted."

After the flood abated, the city slowly began repairing its streets, sewers, and sidewalks. The projects were financed, not by Eastern banks, but by a series of assessments levied on landowners. Judging by assessment dates, the streets were rebuilt first, followed by the sewers, and then the sidewalks. By the third round of assessments in November 1897, notices of "inventory close-out sales," "receiver's sales," and "sales of land for unpaid assessments" appeared in the *Forum* with increasing frequency.

As an unforeseen consequence of the flood, the city council was forced to hire a special attorney to defend against lawsuits brought by citizens injured on the as-yet-unrepaired sidewalks. The decision to spurn federal assistance was proving far more costly to the city, and a far greater hardship on its citizens, than the city fathers had anticipated.[2]

And so, during a typically cold December in 1897, John Cornelius Hurley, the first son and second child of John Albert Hurley and Julia Agatha Healy Hurley, arrived into a self-sufficient community fully engrossed in renewing itself and recovering from a natural disaster.

At birth, there was little need for discussion about his Christian name. As the first-born male in a traditional Irish Catholic family, he naturally inherited his father's first name, and his middle name was chosen to honor his maternal grandfather and great-grandfather. From the beginning, to avoid confusion in the family, almost everyone called him Jack.

---

[2] "Nearing the Limit," *Fargo Forum*, April 5, 1897, p. 1. "Barely Rising," *Fargo Forum*, April 7, 1897, p. 4. "Does Fargo Beg?" *Fargo Forum*, April 9, 1897. Letter to the Editor from "One Who Escaped" dated April 15, 1897, *Fargo Forum*, c. April 15, 1897. Summaries of Fargo city council meetings (discussions of lawsuits, claims, and attorneys), assessment notices, and advertisements for distressed sales of real property, all of which appear in the May through December 1897 issues of the *Fargo Forum*. Hurley, Jack, "Ring Rations," *Fargo Forum*, January 7, 1934, sports section. University of Minnesota Extension Service, "Red River Valley Flooding During 1800s Was as Serious as 1997 Flooding," (University of Minnesota Extension Service, October 1997) Piehl, Mark, Clay County historian, interviewed by Dan Gunderson, "*The National Weather Service Predicts Red River Will Rise to 37.5 Feet in F-M*," (Minnesota Public Radio, April 1997).

Jack's parents married on November 18, 1895, at St. Leo's Catholic Church in Casselton, North Dakota. John was 32, and Julia was 25. Their first home was at Devil's Lake, North Dakota, where John worked for the Northern Pacific Railway Co. They still lived there on September 11, 1896, when Margaret Eleanor, their first child, was born.

Prior to Jack's birth in 1897, the Hurleys moved to Moorhead on the Minnesota side of the North Dakota-Minnesota border the city shared with Fargo. The family's relocation to a town which was home to one of the Northern Pacific's major terminals corresponded to the advancement of John's career. By 1907, John had become a switchman.

When a third child, Abigail Mary, arrived in 1901, the family resided in Fargo. The move across river was a logical one since it was the area's business hub, a booming town of 10,000 where alcohol was illegal. By contrast, Moorhead, with a population of 3,000, was a rowdy railroad town with a thriving red-light district. John and Julia likely felt setting up house in Fargo trumped Moorhead's less family-friendly environment. Later, they would have two more children, Katherine M. in 1908 and Henry J. in 1910.

John Albert Hurley, was born June 6, 1863, in Canada to Irish immigrants who moved to Morton, Minnesota around 1869 or '70. The surname of Hurley was derived from the Gaelic O'hUrthuile, and his parents may have come from County Cork where the name remains prevalent. Little is known about John's family except he had two sisters, neither believed to have married, who once lived in St. Cloud, Minnesota.

Julia Healy Hurley's parents also came from Ireland. Her father, Cornelius Healy, was born June 15, 1834, in Kenmare, County Kerry. The 1860 U. S. census identified him as a laborer living in Manchester, New Hampshire. He became a U.S. citizen at Manchester in 1866. Cornelius' wife, Margaret Scannell, was born April 2, 1846, near Black Rock Castle, County Cork. She was 15 years old when she emigrated in 1861.

Cornelius Healy and Margaret Scannell, Jack Hurley's maternal grandparents, were married while still living in Manchester in 1864. About a year later, their first child, Timothy, was born. In 1867, the family moved to St. Paul, Minnesota, where Cornelius took a job as a surveyor for the Northern Pacific. A second son, Daniel, was born the next year, with Julia – Jack's mother – following on December 1, 1869.

In 1871, Cornelius' work caused him to pull up stakes.

The United States Congress in 1864 had created the Northern Pacific Railway and authorized it to construct the northernmost tier of the transcontinental railroads. Under its charter, the Northern Pacific was to lay track from Lake Superior in the east to the Puget Sound in the west, a distance of 2,000 miles; in other words, from Duluth, Minnesota to Seattle in the Washington Territory. To fund construction, Congress granted the Northern Pacific rights to some 60 million acres along the proposed route.

Construction began at Carlton, Minnesota – 25 miles west of Duluth – in 1870. Railroad planners had heard about an Indian tradition which told of past years in which the Red River had flooded, covering the entire valley in water. Armed with this intelligence, the railroad sent a scouting party to find a bridge site with high embankments on each side of the river. After an extensive search, they chose a venue located slightly south of the 44th parallel, the present locale of Moorhead and Fargo.

After the land for the bridge was secured, progress on laying tracks on the eastern side of the river was rapid. It was about this time, in early September, 1871, that the Northern Pacific dispatched Cornelius Healy with his young family to western Minnesota where his talents were needed to help survey the grade at the Buffalo River, just east of Moorhead.

According to family lore, the trip from St. Paul was made in a prairie schooner drawn by horses, mules, and oxen. All five family members lived and ate in the covered wagon, procuring food along the way, and cooking and keeping warm with campfires. For lighting at night, they used tallow dips, which they made by soaking a rag in a saucer of melted fat and allowing the rag to burn until the tallow was gone.

The Healys crossed the Red River from Minnesota to North Dakota on September 30, 1871, and set up camp in a tent city which already was home to about 50 people. The family found a spot next to a cave close to the river bank and was able to use both their tent and the cave as a dwelling. Cornelius' surveying continued until the track reached Moorhead on December 31 in minus-28-degree weather. Thereafter, bridge construction began and proceeded through the winter and into spring.

In the spring, high water drove the family from their make-shift home. The bridge was completed June 6, 1872, and on that day the first train crossed the river and into the new city of Fargo, North Dakota. Later that same year, Cornelius and Margaret purchased a lot from the railroad where they built their first home in Fargo. According to family tradition, the lot was the first to be sold, and the house the second to be built in the city.

The building originally stood on the property where the future Washington School would be erected, but it was later moved to 4th Street North across the alley from the plot where Christianson Drug Store subsequently would be built. The house was made of wood, framed with 12-foot-high posts, which measured 1-1/2 stories tall and which had a floor space of only 16 by 24 feet. It had a shingle roof, four windows, front and back doors; and was heated with a cast iron wood stove.

The family quickly settled into Fargo community life. Jack's uncle Timothy recalled attending a school opened by three Catholic nuns as a six-year old in 1872. The nuns taught reading, writing, arithmetic, penmanship, and spelling. Cornelius was one of six aldermen elected in 1875 to serve under Fargo's first mayor, George Egbert.

Margaret and Cornelius had four more children in Fargo before they sold the house in 1878 and began farming on a homestead twenty miles to the north near Sheldon, North Dakota. Timothy recalled that the family used old-fashioned machinery drawn by horses, mules, and oxen to work the farm. At the time, mules were popular in the region because they lived longer, withstood more hardship, and took less feed than horses and oxen.

In 1884, the family moved to a farm near Argusville, North Dakota. At Sheldon and Argusville, Margaret and Cornelius parented their final three children who survived to adulthood. In 1892, they moved back to Fargo.

Three years later, in December 1895, their eldest daughter Julia married John Albert Hurley and moved to Devil's Lake where the new couple started the family into which Jack Hurley would be born in 1897.[3]

****

Jack's pre-teen years were typical of many boys in small-town America in the early 1900s. Entering the first grade in 1903, Jack attended Longfellow Grade School in Fargo until his eighth-grade graduation in 1912. A hangout of Jack and his pals was Art Ross' candy store on Front Street where they read the day's funny papers posted in the window. On Saturdays, they often attended a downtown theater matinee, enjoying the films of silent-era stars John Bunny, Maurice Costello, and Flora Finch.[4]

In summers, Jack and his pals swam in a pond next to the Milwaukee Railroad tracks west of town. Some Sunday afternoons, they perfected their marksmanship shooting rats with their .22 gauge rifles at the local dump.[5]

Jack on occasion would tease his younger sister Abby. Years later, she would tell her daughter Gail she was afraid of the water because Jack had thrown her in before she learned how to swim. Abby, who had beautiful auburn hair, also told Gail she had been moved to tears as a little girl on more than one occasion as a result of "Jack telling her that she was adopted because she was the only one in the family to have red hair."[6]

Young Jack also had his share of fights, often over his given names. Gail recalled that he "didn't like the name John and he didn't like his middle name Cornelius, either." According to his brother Hank, "Jack hated that name John. Oh, how many fights he got into in school when somebody

---

[3] Healy, Thomas, unpublished manuscript tracing Healy family lineage beginning with marriage of Cornelius Healy (b. June 15, 1834) and Margaret Scannell (b. April 2, 1846). The foregoing paragraphs pertaining to the Healys were based on information from this manuscript.

[4] O'Keefe, Vince, "Early Day Look at a Famous Curmudgeon," *Seattle Times*, October 22, 1972, p. D-10. Hurley, "Shadow Boxing," *Fargo Forum*, October 28, 1933, sports section. Hurley, "Ring Rations," *Fargo Forum*, July 6, 1930, sports section.

[5] Hurley, *op. cit.,* October 5, 1930 and January 25, 1931 sports sections.

[6] Story related to author by Gail Conmy Hafner.

Jack, 8, with sisters Margaret (left), 10, and Abigail (center), 6.

Jack's mother Julia, early 1900s.

Julia with mother Margaret Healy.

Abigail & Margaret, c. 1915.

called him Johnny ... Jack would fight at the drop of a hat when he was a kid, but the trouble was he couldn't stay on his feet."[7]

From age 10, Jack operated an early morning newsstand in partnership with his friend, Jack Williams, selling the morning edition of the *Fargo Daily News-Courier* before school began. The stand's location, at Broadway and Northern Pacific Avenue, was the choicest corner in downtown Fargo, and the two Jacks on occasion had to fight off other newsboys in order to protect their territory.[8]

If anything stands out about young Jack Hurley during these years, it was his fascination with sports. From the day he learned to read, he pored over the local sports pages and frequented the town's barbershops, pool halls, and cigar stores to learn the latest news and read sporting journals like the *Police Gazette*, the *Sporting News*, and *Sporting Life*.

This all-consuming interest subsequently led Jack to try his hand at every type of sport. Even while still playing pick-up games with friends, he was courting older athletes. During his grade school years, he traveled as a mascot with the Fargo high school football and basketball teams. He had no money so the players hid him from the train conductor. They put the backs of two coach seats together and pushed Jack under the seats. Then they threw a couple of overcoats across the seats and placed an equipment bag on the floor to hide his feet and make him invisible to the conductor.[9]

A few years later, Jack became the first batboy for the Fargo-Moorhead Graingrowers baseball club of the new Northern League. The team was managed by ex-big leaguer Bob Unglaub and owned by the Cantillon brothers who also owned the Minneapolis Millers of the American Association, a league just a step below the majors. The Northern League's season ended early, and the Millers would bolster their roster for their annual run at the pennant by calling up some of the Graingrower players.

Several of the Northern League players had either played, or would later play, in the big leagues. Jack's association with these local heroes increased his stature among his growing circle of friends. Endowed with an apparently easy-going and forthright manner, Jack willingly shared with his buddies the experiences and stories overheard from these older men. They began to look to him as a leader, organizer, and teacher.[10]

While Hurley was growing up, Fargo, a town of little more than 10,000, hosted an array of barnstorming troupes, baseball teams, vaudevillians, wrestlers, boxers, billiard players, musicians, clergymen, actors, and just

---

[7] Heinz, W. C., *Once They Heard the Cheers*, (Doubleday & Company, New York, 1979), p. 155 (first quote). Lund, Bob, "Boxer and Manager Were Well Known, Respected," *Fargo Forum*, September 2000, sports section (second quote).

[8] Hurley, *op. cit.*, January 28, 1930, sports section.

[9] Hurley, "Shadow Boxing," *Fargo Forum*, September 16, 1934, sports section.

[10] "Fargo Gets Team in Northern League," *Fargo Forum*, September 9, 1913, sports section.

Jack's youngest siblings, Kathleen & Hank, c. 1917.

Jack at Longfellow School, 1908.

Kathleen and Hank, c. 1920.

Jack and Hank, c. 1915.

plain interesting hustlers. The appearances of these performers were the result of local entrepreneurs and promoters trying to make a buck in the time-honored tradition of small-time capitalists everywhere.

Some of these performers were artists and lecturers imported by schools and organizations to present concerts devoted to the appreciation of the arts. Others were athletes and entertainers hired by fraternal organizations, such as the Masonic Lodge, the Elks club, or the Knights of Columbus.[11]

And then, there was the Commercial Club, incorporated in 1902, which had its offices and on the second floor of the Odd Fellows building located on the northeast corner of Broadway and First Avenue North. It was a kind of early day chamber of commerce, which, in the words of its promotional literature, boasted membership of 200 "live merchant and professional men who are building a better and bigger Fargo."[12]

Club members took their mission to boost the civic welfare seriously. An early project, in 1906, was the financing and construction of the racetrack, covered grandstand, and associated structures which would for the next 60 years comprise the site for the annual North Dakota Interstate Fairgrounds. A few years later, in 1914, the club would undertake an equally challenging project by arranging for construction of the Fargo Auditorium, which became the city's major indoor venue for cultural and sporting events.

The fairgrounds covered the three blocks between 17th and 19th Avenues North and from University on the west to Broadway on the east. Besides the grandstand and racetrack, there were six buildings showcasing cattle, pigs, poultry, domestic crafts, farm machinery, and trade show merchandise. The annual July fair featured a week chock-full of automobile, horse, and harness races; livestock and trade shows; carnivals; band concerts; drill teams; fireworks displays; acrobatic exhibitions; and vaudeville routines.

It was the fairgrounds which hosted annual visits by circuses, wild-West pageants, and wild animal shows. Ringling Brothers made its inaugural appearance at the fairgrounds in 1906. Barnum and Bailey brought its first show to Fargo in 1907. The two circuses alternated their annual appearances until merging in 1919.

As an avid newspaper reader and a precocious boy-about-town, young Jack no doubt followed the circus parades and attended the Interstate Fairs regularly throughout his childhood. As a young teenager, he talked a trainer at the fair into letting him ride a horse, named "Little Chubby," in one of the races. Jack did well enough that the trainer offered him a job riding in other fairs throughout the state.

---

[11] "This City Will Be Mecca of Hundreds Early in December," *Fargo Forum*, November 1, 1913, p. 1 (cited as only one example among the many famous artists who appeared in Fargo. This particular article discusses an appearance by the famous pianist Paderewski, sponsored by Dakota Conservatory of Music.).

[12] Double-page paid advertisement by Commercial Club, *Fargo Forum*, November 1, 1913.

Money was scarce in the Hurley household, and Jack rushed home to break the news to his mother. Julia, however, did not share her son's enthusiasm and instead sent word to the trainer, threatening to set the law on him. To emphasize her point, she grounded Jack for two weeks.[13]

For sheer showmanship and hype, nothing compared to the excitement generated by a circus in the early part of the 20th Century. For weeks in advance, local newspapers carried advertisements, photos, and press releases trumpeting the wonders of the big top.

Announcements heralding the Ringling Brothers Circus were calculated to inspire anticipation in every heart, young or old: "The only big circus coming to Fargo this year ... 89 railroad cars loaded with 1,000 all new wonders ... more than 1,350 people, 735 horses, 82 camels, 41 elephants and 108 dens of wild animals ... In addition to the circus, the Ringling Bros. bring here the massive spectacle of Solomon and the Queen of Sheba which ... was the marvel of the engagement in Chicago this spring."[14]

Not to be outdone, Barnum and Bailey advertised a "world premiere season," featuring an exotic new menagerie "of over fifty specimens, hitherto unknown to any other zoo in the world." The grand finale of the show was "Jupiter the Balloon Horse, standing like a statute ... carried by a balloon high in the dome of the tent: at the highest point in the air a battery of fireworks will be ignited, completely surrounding Jupiter and his rider in a fountain of fire, yet the horse will show no signs of nervousness."[15]

The Commercial Club and the fairgrounds also hosted the smaller Barnes Wild Animal Circus and the Sells-Floto Circus on alternate years, both laying claim to specialty acts which trumped those on offer from their two mega-circus competitors.[16]

Circus pomp and hyperbole provided a fertile training ground for a youngster who was a quick study of events and human nature. It is fairly easy to imagine Jack watching peoples' reactions and assessing whether the claims had been justified or instead had overreached the bounds of belief.

Beyond doubt, the Commercial Club's most extravagant promotion was the appearance of revivalist Billy Sunday at Fargo in 1912. The duration of his visit and its news coverage far surpassed any spectacle Fargo had ever witnessed. The turmoil generated by the revival's pre-event negotiations ended up straining relations both between, and within, the religious and business communities like no other episode in the city's history. Not surprisingly, the affair made a lasting impression on a young Jack Hurley.

---

[13] Hurley, "Shadow Boxing," *Fargo Forum*, August 5, 1934, sports section.
[14] "Ringling Circus Will Be Here Tomorrow," *Fargo Forum*, July 28, 1914, entertainment section.
[15] "Five Special Trains Will Be Used to Bring Barnum and Bailey Circus to Fargo," *Fargo Forum*, June 29, 1911, entertainment section.
[16] "Barnes Circus Here Tomorrow," *Fargo Forum*, June 5, 1914, entertainment section. "Sells-Floto Circus Coming," *Fargo Forum*, May 25, 1914, entertainment section.

Sunday first came into prominence in 1883 as an outfielder for the Chicago White Stocking baseball team. Known for blazing speed, he ran the bases in 14 seconds and set a season record by stealing 84 bases in 117 games. In 1886, he converted to Christianity after hearing a Chicago street preacher. Five years later, while still in his prime as a player, he gave up his $480-a-month baseball salary to devote himself to Christian service. His first job was as a teacher for the Chicago YMCA earning $84 a month.

Beginning in 1893, Sunday worked as an advance representative for evangelist J. Wilbur Chapman, until Chapman tired of traveling and accepted a pastorate. Sunday then campaigned on his own as an evangelist beginning in 1896. He was officially licensed as a preacher by the Presbyterian Church in 1898 and ordained a minister in 1903.

Until 1907, Sunday limited his preaching to smaller towns in Illinois and his home state of Iowa. The tour was called the "Kerosene Circuit" because most of these meetings were held in churches, tents, auditoriums, and opera houses without electricity. As he grew more popular and these structures were no longer able to handle the crowds, he required his sponsors to erect large wooden "tabernacles," built to strict specifications.

Since there was no amplification, a huge, shell-shaped device was hung above the platform and baffles were built in the ceiling to project the speaker's voice. The floors were covered with sawdust to deaden the sound of footsteps. For the "sound system" to work, anyone who could not refrain from making noise was politely, but firmly, directed to the nearest exit.

At the end of every meeting, Sunday would invite his listeners to leave their seats and proclaim their commitment to Christ. Because the floors were blanketed with sawdust, this practice of going up the aisle became known as "hitting the sawdust trail."

Sunday was flamboyant in word and deed. While preaching, he would prance from one end of the stage to the other like an eccentric dancer, waving his hands and kicking his legs to emphasize his message. Criticized for his rough vocabulary he replied, "I want to preach the gospel so plainly that men can come from the factories and not have to bring a dictionary." Impatient with false piety, he warned, "Going to church doesn't make you a Christian any more than going to a garage makes you an automobile."

His teachings were wide-ranging and hard to categorize. He spoke against divorce, dance halls, evolution, cigarettes, Unitarianism, gambling, and movie-going. He supported women's suffrage, argued for an end to child labor, and included African-Americans – then known as "coloreds" or "Negroes" – in his revivals, even in the Deep South. His strongest rhetoric, however, was saved for the evils of demon rum. Saloons often were voluntarily closed during his revivals to avoid being targets of his wrath.

After 1907, Sunday's fame gradually spread to larger communities, but it was the revivals in Canton, Ohio and Wheeling, West Virginia which

Billy Sunday's entourage on its way from Terra Alta, West Virginia to Wheeling, the evangelist's last stop before Fargo.

Billy Sunday in action.

first earned him nationwide acclaim. The Canton revival took place from December 1911 to February 1912, during one of the coldest winters on record. In sub-zero temperatures which lasted the entire six weeks, Billy's 5,000-seat tabernacle was filled to capacity at every service.

By the second week at Canton, overflow crowds waited and listened outside in the cold. Some worshippers even scaled the rooftops and listened through ventilators. On the final day of the crusade, 20,000 people attended the final four services while 10,000 were turned away. Another 10,000 sang gospel songs at the depot as the party's train departed. Crowds continued unabated throughout the next six weeks at Wheeling.

Fargo was the Sunday party's next stop after Wheeling. Although preparations for the revival in Fargo had been in the making nearly two years, the publicity generated in Ohio and West Virginia had raised interest in the Sunday revival to a fever pitch. Every day the Fargo papers reported not only on the Canton and Wheeling revivals but also on the progress of the tabernacle construction and the planning meetings in Fargo.

In early March, Billy Sunday's advance agent, B. K. Gill, took a room at the Gardner Hotel to meet with Fargo's executive committee and finalize arrangements. The executive committee comprised some 20 clergy and businessmen. The revival was set to begin April 7 and last through May 12.

Final negotiations, however, hit a snag. At a planning meeting with participating clergy, Mr. Gill referred to those who did not support the Sunday revivals as "hypocrites" who would be "unmasked." In response, one of the clergy, Dr. R. A. Beard of the First Congregational Church, took issue and said not all those who failed to take part in the Sunday campaign deserved such vilification. Indeed, Dr. Beard told Gill, many of his most respected parishioners disagreed with the revival's methods.

The next evening, Mr. Gill replied by giving the Commercial Club 30 minutes to raise $6,000 – in addition to the amounts already advanced – or the crusade would be called off. After several hours of frantic negotiation, the parties were able to reach agreement.

A few days later, in letters to the newspapers, Dr. Beard withdrew his support from the revival, and resigned from the committee. The following day, eight more ministers from various churches in Fargo and Moorhead signed a statement joining Dr. Beard in his opposition to the appearance of the Sunday crusade.[17]

That very same day, Sunday replied from Wheeling it was the "rule of his life" that the churches must unite 100 percent behind his revivals or he would not appear. He was therefore canceling his appearance in Fargo. His decision was "absolutely final."[18]

---

[17] "Beard Opposed to Billy Sunday," *Fargo Forum*, March 11, 1912, religious section. "More Ministers Back Up Beard," *Fargo Forum*, March 12, 1912, p. 1.

[18] "Billy Sunday Will Not Come to Fargo – Wires the Decision Is Final," *Fargo Forum*, March 12, 1912, p. 1.

The next day, on March 13, Sunday wired he had reconsidered. He had learned the "whiskey gangs" in Fargo and Moorhead were the true instigators of the opposition. His wire stated he "had never taken the count for that bunch of moral assassins yet" and he would "come as agreed and will give the devil and his cohorts the best run for their money they ever had. All sing 'There Will Be a Hot Time in the Old Town Tonight.'"

The *Fargo Forum* reported that the news Billy was still coming "was received with great rejoicing in Sunday booster circles in the city." Prayer meetings were held in churches throughout the Fargo-Moorhead area. Members of the tabernacle building committee were instructed to meet at the YMCA offices to resume construction of the tabernacle being built at the corner of Fifth Street and Second Avenue North.[19]

The Sunday team inundated the Fargo daily newspapers with letters of endorsement from purported community leaders throughout the Midwest. The *Forum* reported receiving "dozens of letters in each mail ... telling what great things Billy will do when he gets here." The paper published these letters almost every day for the following three weeks.[20]

The discord the revival caused among Protestants must have fascinated most Roman Catholics in Fargo, including the Hurley family. Although both religions professed to follow the teachings of Jesus Christ, each viewed the other with suspicion and even outright distaste. Protestants disputed Catholics' rigid devotion to a pope who they believed had strayed from the correct interpretation of the Bible. Catholics, for their part, felt that in renouncing the Pope, Protestants had deserted the one true church.

A young Jack Hurley likely monitored the entire episode and subconsciously absorbed its lessons. The similarities between the devices used by Sunday's team in Fargo and those used later by Hurley to promote his fights are striking. A leading precept throughout Jack's life was that the public needed a reason to attend a fight. To accomplish this, he often would invent a controversy, much as Sunday did prior to the Fargo revival.

An instance of this occurred when Hurley handled Billy Petrolle in his classic, three-bout series against Jimmy McLarnin in 1931. Sensing public interest was lagging for the third fight, Jack launched an attack in the press questioning McLarnin's courage. This so incensed his fans they turned out in droves to see him lick Billy.

At other times, Hurley would quietly arrange for the opposing camp to fire the opening salvos by attacking either Jack directly, or demeaning the ability of his fighter. Wayne Thornton and his manager, Pat DiFuria, were willing accomplices in this type of ballyhoo in 1968 when they wrote disparaging letters to Seattle newspapers while Jack was trying to drum up

---

[19] "Sunday Is Coming to Fargo," *Fargo Forum*, March 13, 1912, p. 1.
[20] "Says Sunday 'Got My Goat,'" *Fargo Forum*, April 4, 1912, religious section.

Exterior of Fargo's tabernacle built to Billy Sunday's specifications. Photos this page courtesy of North Dakota State University Library.

Interior view of the Fargo tabernacle.

interest in a bout between Thornton and Hurley's fighter, Boone Kirkman.[21]

Another device to which Jack was first introduced during the revival was Sunday's use of endorsement letters to tout his coming. Later, Jack would become an avid correspondent, and he regularly sent articles written about himself and his boxers to writers all over the world. These clippings served as endorsements for whatever point he wanted to make. In the 1950s, when a newspaper cost five cents and first-class postage three cents, his annual budget for stamps, stationery, and newspapers approached $10,000.[22]

Along with the clips he sent, Hurley would enclose a cover letter asking the reporter to forward a copy of any article he wrote using information from the clippings. Jack thus would compile a library of articles endorsing his position, all of which might derive from a single incident.

If the articles Hurley received in reply were especially good, he would have photo-static copies made and send them out for another round of supposedly new publicity. In this way, he "pyramided" one event into many apparently newsworthy events. This was the tack taken in his 1951-52 campaign against the International Boxing Club (IBC), which Jack claimed refused to give his fighter, Harry (Kid) Matthews, a lucrative match.

Sunday's Fargo revival ended as scheduled on Sunday, May 12, 1912. The *Fargo Courier News* reported total attendance of 240,750 people during the crusade's 36-day run, including a full tabernacle of 6,500 at each of the last day's three services. The total amount collected was not disclosed, but the final day's offerings were reported as a robust $5,028. Spiritually as well, the revival was a success. A total of 3,738 converts stepped forward to walk the sawdust trail during the revival's duration.[23]

A month later, on June 13th, Jack completed his studies at Longfellow Grade School as one of 166 students to graduate from the eighth grade in the Fargo school system. A few weeks after that, he packed his belongings, said goodbye to his friends and relations in Fargo, and moved with his family to a new residence in Rainy River, Canada.

Sometime before the 1912 school year ended, Jack's father had quit the Northern Pacific and taken a job as a Canadian Northern Railway switchman. It seems likely John went to Rainy River ahead of the others, and that Julia and the five children joined him as soon as school was out.

---

[21] Owen, John "Shame on You, Gullible Fight Fans of Seattle," *Seattle Post-Intelligencer*, March 24, 1968, sports section. Owen, John, "House That Jack Built," *Seattle Post Intelligencer*, May 24, 1968, p. 23.

[22] Watson, Emmett, "Now That Jack Hurley Has a New Man to Move, Look Out, Cassius Clay," *Seattle Magazine*, August, 1966, p. 43.

[23] "Many Thousands Bid Revivalists Farewell," *Fargo Courier-News*, May 13, 1912, p. 1. Obviously, the attendance figures were swollen by repeat visitors. For example, one person attending every meeting would have counted as over 50 since there was a minimum of one meeting every day of the revival's run and as many as three on weekend days. The same would hold true for the convert count, as well.

Rainy River is a township in the province of Ontario located on the Canadian side of the Rainy River, just southeast of the Lake of the Woods, and across the U.S.-Canada border from Baudette, Minnesota. The town, first called Beaver Mills, was founded in 1898 to support the Beaver Mills Lumber Company and a small fur trading industry.

In 1901, Rainy River became a terminal for the Ontario and Rainy River branch (O&RRR) of the new Canadian Northern Railway. This terminal served as the railway's connection with Fort Frances to the west and Port Arthur to the east. The construction of a bridge across the Rainy River from Beaver Mills to Baudette connected the Canadian and U. S. rail systems.

In 1904, the town incorporated and changed its name to Rainy River. Bolstered by a thriving lumber industry and the arrival of the railroad, the town boomed, and by 1910 it boasted a population of 4,500. But prosperity was short-lived. That year, the region experienced the driest summer on record. In October, a forest fire started in Minnesota, swept through the area, and destroyed the town. The conflagration, later called "The Great Fire of 1910," wiped out the region's timber industry and killed 43 people.

The town was re-built, but its economy came to rely entirely on the railroad. Its population shrank to about 1,000, a number which has remained relatively steady to this day. By the time the Hurleys arrived in 1912, most of the reconstruction after the fire had been completed.

Leaving behind relatives, friends, and the familiar sights and sounds of Fargo likely was a shock to Julia and the children. Certainly, the social and cultural amenities of Rainy River did not approach those of Fargo. As for Jack, his parents apparently decided the best course of action was to keep him busy. When he arrived at Rainy River, he had two jobs awaiting him – one as call boy for the Canadian Northern and the other as a laborer in a stave factory forming wood slats that went into making barrels.[24]

Although making staves was little more than a repetitive factory job, the post of call boy was an entry-level position requiring a certain degree of tact. In the era before the telephone became a universal appliance, a call boy had to find and inform train crew members when and where to report for work to handle an outgoing train. A call boy was needed because the traffic of incoming freight trains was erratic and often unscheduled.

Typically, a call boy would ride his bicycle to the home, hotel, or boarding house where a crew member was staying, and remain there until the man was awake and had his shoes on. This might involve waking the crewman up from a sound sleep, or interrupting a late night card game, or some other nocturnal endeavor. Obviously, to be good at his job, a call boy had to exercise ingenuity and initiative in tracking down the crewman and tact in dealing with whatever situation he might encounter once he did.

---

[24] Hurley, "Shadow Boxing," *Fargo* Forum, March 4, 1934, sports section.

It is likely John Hurley made the arrangements for the Canadian Pacific to hire Jack at the same time John took the post as switchman. Apparently, John and Julia decided Jack's best prospect for a job, at least in the short term, was to follow in his father's footsteps. The elder Hurley had worked as a railroad man for most of his adult life, and the best way he knew to help his son was to find him a job in the same industry. As for any advancement, Jack would have to work his way up through his own efforts.

Along with that of a brakeman, a switchman's job was the most perilous in a rail yard. Although the industry was changing to a system where rail cars were joined by automatic couplers, many cars still were connected by inserting a steel pin into an iron link, and a switchman standing between the cars could easily be crushed if they moved. Most insurance companies refused to insure the lives of switchmen, and those that did rated their life expectancies 20 years less than the general population.[25]

In 1912, an average railroad worker averaged ten hours a day six days a week. Switchmen worked an extra two hours a day, and cases were reported where they worked 14 and even 15 hours a day, seven days a week, causing them to fall asleep and lose their jobs, either because of lapses in attention or because they failed to wake up for work on time. For this, the top pay for a foreman in 1910 was reported as 38 cents an hour.[26]

On September 3, 1912, the law of averages caught up with the Hurley family. The *Northern News* reported that "while attempting to cut off a car to make a switch in the Canadian yards at Rainy River ... John Hurley, a switchman ... missed his footing and fell to the track ... and before he had time to extricate himself was caught by the following car and ground under it, the wheels passing over the right leg below the knee crushing the latter and splitting and slivering the former a distance of five inches."

The accident occurred in the afternoon, and John was taken to the hospital in Spooner, Minnesota by train engine and placed under the care of Dr. J. E. Corrigan. Due to his critical condition and the severity of the shock he suffered, the doctor decided to delay an operation until the elder Hurley's condition stabilized. Unfortunately, his condition worsened, and at nine o'clock that same evening, John Hurley died.

His body was taken to Weeks' Undertaking in Spooner where arrangements were made for transportation to Luger Undertaking in Fargo. On September 6, the *Fargo Forum* reported "the sad death of the late Mr.

---

[25] Morgan, James, *The Life Work of Edward H. Moseley in the Service of Humanity,* (Macmillan Company, New York, 1913), p. 357. Marshwood School District and Old Berwick Historical Society, "Hike Through History, the Lure of Trains: Harry Ernest Adlington, Section 2.4.

[26] Staff of Kheel Center for Labor Management and Archives at Cornell University, Abstract of Switchmen's Union of North America Arbitration Arbitration Proceedings, 1910. Kheel Center for Labor-Management Documentation and Archives, Martin P. Catherwood Library of Cornell University, Collection No. 5406mf.

Hurley will be received with keen regret by his many friends in this city, many of whom will attend the funeral service tomorrow morning." The article also noted "the deceased was 47 years old and is survived by a widow and five children ... His widow was formerly Miss Julia Healy."[27]

According to family lore passed down to Jack's niece, Gail Hafner, from her mother Abigail, the railroad personnel summoned Jack to the scene of the accident, where he saw his father in the railroad yard while he lay injured. When Jack arrived, the elder Hurley was still conscious, and he instructed Jack to take care of the family if John should die.

The funeral was held at 9 o'clock on Saturday morning, September 7, 1912, at St. Mary's Catholic Cathedral. The burial was at Holy Cross Cemetery in the Hurley family plot.

After the funeral Julia and the family moved back to Fargo. Her two older brothers and their families still lived there, and most of her other siblings resided in nearby North Dakota communities. There was no reason for the family to remain in Rainy River.

Back in Fargo, Julia retained an attorney and filed suit in July 1913 alleging the accident was caused by the negligence of the Canadian Northern Railway. After negotiations, the suit was settled in April 1914 for $3,500. According to family lore, Julia was grateful at the time, but she never received any further payment or pension. Exactly how much she received after deducting attorney's fees and other costs is not known.[28]

At this late date, there is no way to know what Jack's plans were before his father died. All his siblings continued their educations after grade school, so it seems likely he might have done the same eventually. If this was his plan, however, John's death radically altered things. Instead of continuing his studies, the next few years would see Jack trying his hand at whatever jobs a young teenager in Fargo could find to help his family out.

As for his free time, Jack would look to sports for relief from the pressures of his new obligations, and to local sports heroes as mentors to replace the father he no longer had. Over the next few years, he would have ample opportunity to test his strengths and weaknesses and experiment with a future which best suited his own unique lifestyle and temperament.

---

[27] "Fatal Railroad Accident in Rainy Yard," *Northern News* (Spooner, MN), September 6, 1912. "The Hurley Funeral," *Fargo Forum*, September 6, 1912.

[28] Canadian Northern Railway Claim File no. 82-55, Central Regional Law Department – Personal Injury Claim of Julia A. Hurley of the State of Minnesota for Damages for the Fatal Injury of John A. Hurley; currently available from the Library Archive of Canada, Finding Aid No. 30-51, System Control No. FIND030/14431, Mikan No. 1544526. Author's conversations with Hurley nieces Gail Hafner and Carol Olson together with their husbands Dick Olson and Yates Hafner October 5 and 6, 2007.

CHAPTER 2

LESSONS FROM A FAMOUS PROFESSOR

I was a ten-year-old boy trying to sell newspapers on street corners in Fargo when I first learned I was different than everybody else. I couldn't sleep at night and I couldn't stay awake in the daytime.

I hated getting up early in the morning, so I knew I'd have to find a job where I could work nights, or at least not have to go to work until noon. I tried being a fighter. I wasn't any good. Then I tried baseball. No good at that, either. One night, I saw a stage play, and I tried acting, but I couldn't act. Boxers work at night and sleep during the day. I gave boxing a try, but found I was better at teaching, so I became a fight manager.

You know, I almost gave my life for my country during the First World War before ever getting to the front. Imagine. They had me getting up at 5 a.m. and going to bed at 10 p.m. By the time I was discharged I was almost a basket case.[1]

– Jack Hurley

****

Pro boxing in Fargo prior to 1912 was a hit-and-miss affair. Since boxing was technically illegal, advance publicity was largely by word of mouth. Sometimes, a match would occur without any mention at all in the local press. In other instances, an out-of-town fighter might publicize his presence in Fargo by appearing at the office of a local newspaper. The paper would print a simple annoucement that the fighter was in the city and desired a match with a particular opponent.

Alternatively, a visiting fighter might write a letter to the paper, challenging a local boxer to a match. In either situation, the local man would respond, also by letter, accepting the challenge. A few days later the paper would proclaim the bout was assured and that the two fighters would settle their differences within a short time.

The phrases "short time" or "the match is assured" served as code words that the fight would place in the next day or so and, if the reader wanted to see it, he had better find out when and where from a local sportsman in the know. In this way, the newspaper protected itself from claims of aiding and abetting an illegal event. It also made it difficult for the local authorities to learn when or where the event was occurring. The next report might not appear until a few days after the bout. The story might simply state the bout had occurred without incident and that one boxer or the other had won. In other instances, it might give a four or five paragraph account of the event.

---

[1] Kehborn, Hank, "Staff Roundup," *St. Paul Pioneer Press*, November 28, 1951, p. 18. Johnson, Bob, "My Nickel's Worth," *Spokane Daily Chronicle*, December 1, 1961, p. 13.

Just as often, the article might disclose the fight had not taken place at all because local authorities had found out about it and raided the location. In such a case, the press frequently would report a few days later that "the two battlers were getting ready" again and "that very little publicity would be given the affair" this time. The match would then take place without further notice at a different location than originally planned.

The authorities were not particularly worried about moral or even legal objections to the sport. Their concerns were more pragmatic. If there was no controversy surrounding a bout, and no cries of outrage from clergymen, the fight would likely occur without interference. On the other hand, if there were rumors the outcome was pre-arranged, that the parties were not evenly matched, or that the affair was shaping up as a brutal "prize fight" rather than an exhibition of science and skill, they would likely stop the contest.

The unpredictability of this "system" made life difficult for a promoter. He had little control over the rumors which circulated either before or after a fight. If he was fortunate enough to present an exciting match, his next show might be shut down by moralists who claimed boxing was brutal. If he was unlucky enough to stage an unsatisfactory fight, he might lose customers or face stoppage of future promotions by the police.

The obstacles faced were so diverse as to make one wonder why anybody wanted to stage boxing shows at all. A promoter's sole assets were the newsmen who, despite the limitations noted, influenced opinion by emphasizing the scientific nature and lack of brutality in a particular bout. In this way, they provided "cover" to a promoter against the moralists who, even if they didn't attend fights themselves, did read the newspapers.

Reporters also took care to point out when the fighters promised to compete on a "winner-take-all" basis, or to make side bets at ringside prior to the fight. Such undertakings by the combatants were portrayed as guarantees of honesty, designed to allay the fears of skeptical patrons and thereby enhance their attendance at the event.

It took a local hero to end serious opposition to boxing in the Fargo area and to bring the sport from out of the backroom and into the parlor. The hero was Leo Kossick, a Moorhead native born April 4, 1890, who began his professional boxing career in Fargo early in 1909. Leo first had become interested in the sport at the Fargo YMCA where he took boxing lessons from Professor Sigismund Kirkenburg in the fall of 1908. He turned pro in 1909, and by the end of 1911 had engaged in 30 bouts without a loss.

By early 1912, Kossick was dominating local opponents so completely that he and his manager, Moorhead barber and restaurateur George Saumweber, set out for the Saskatchewan province of Canada to look for bigger game. In just a few months, Leo took the Canadian prairie by storm, beating such men as Charles Lucca, Ben Cornish, Mickey McIntyre, and Tommy Kilbane, brother of world featherweight champ Johnny Kilbane.

The first of his several Canadian tours established Kossick as one of the Northwest's top lightweights and welterweights. Unimpeded by legal considerations, Fargo papers reported Leo's Canadian successes in much greater detail than they had his local victories. Their articles praised his clean living habits, his gentlemanly demeanor, and his winning personality.

Between trips to Canada, Kossick returned to Fargo to defeat Jimmie Potts, generally regarded as one of the best lightweights in the Northwestern states; and Labe Safro, similarly viewed as a top welterweight. As a result, Leo claimed regional championships in both classes and became the area's best hope for world title honors.

Fargo fans at first had been slow to adopt the Moorhead native as their own, but his success in Canada, along with his aggressive style and pleasing smile, won them over. Before long, Kossick was being mentioned as a possible foe for such world-class ringsters as Ad Wolgast, Packey MacFarland, Battling Nelson, and Freddy Welsh.

Kossick's appearance on a card guaranteed action. Fans abandoned their reservations about boxing and left fight shows happy and exhilarated. Leo's popularity, even among church-goers, quieted the moralists. Law enforcement officials relaxed. Reporters abandoned their circumspection and expanded their fight coverage. By the end of 1912, a match featuring Kossick was an event eagerly awaited by sports fans who previously had not given boxing a second thought.[2]

It was to this exciting scene the young sports enthusiast Jack Hurley returned after four eventful months in Rainy River, ready to immerse himself fully in whatever activities might hold his attention and help him overcome the past summer's trauma.

While his pals attended high school, the Hurley family's circumstances precluded such a course for Jack. With his father's last words ringing in his ears, he set out to find work which would satisfy his obligation as the family's oldest male and at the same time offer something more than the drudgery of an ordinary job. Jack had seen where 14-hour days of mind-numbing work had led his father, and he was keen to avoid the same fate.

During the next year, Jack tried his hand at no less than six different jobs without finding his niche. By the end of 1913, his resume already would include posts as an usher at the Bijou and Grand theaters, a bellhop at the Gardner Hotel, a batboy for the baseball team, an elevator operator at a downtown apartment building, and a soda jerk at a drug store.[3]

---

[2] Summary of Fargo fight scene is based on the author's review of all the local boxing articles published in the *Fargo Forum* and *Fargo News-Courier* between 1911 and 1913. Leo Kossick's boxing instructor, Sigismund Kirkenburg, was known more widely to the Fargo sporting world under his ring name of "Jack Broad." Hurley, Jack, "Ring Rations, *Fargo Forum*, February 21, 1932, sports section.

[3] Hurley, *op. cit.* December 28, 1930 (usher at Bijou); March 1, 1931 (bellhop at Gardner Hotel); September 13, 1931 (elevator operator at Improvement Building); May 15, 1931

In a 1930 interview, Julia Hurley recalled her frustration at Jack's lack of interest in the jobs he found, and his penchant for walking off whenever he felt like it. "I often wondered if he'd ever get any kind of a job," she said. "It was always so hard to get him up in the morning." The article concluded: "Carrying baseball bats held more lure to his wanderlust nature than the most secure desk job."[4]

The last comment referred to the desertion of his post as elevator operator at the Improvement Building on First Avenue North and Roberts Street. The building had only one elevator and consisted of residential apartments above first-floor shops. To accommodate the tenants, the operator was on the job from early morning until 11 p.m.

One day Jack was unable to find a substitute for an afternoon shift. He was supposed to be a batboy at a Fargo-Moorhead Graingrowers baseball game. Rather than miss the game, he vacated his post, taking care to lock the elevator door, and hurried over the Red River Bridge to Moorhead. Needless to say, the absence of elevator service caused no little inconvenience to the building's residents.

Afterward, Jack told Julia the elevator malfunctioned and dropped precipitously from the fifth floor all the way to the basement. She was shocked and told him not to return to the elevator job. Jack was ecstatic at the prospect of not having to work for a while. He could, after all, make more money in an afternoon as a batboy than working a regular job. His mother, however, thought baseball was a waste of time. The next day she went out and found him another job.[5]

Hurley's inability to focus on any one activity unless it involved sports was to be a source of concern to his mother and other family members for a long time. This tension would continue until he finally convinced Julia he could follow his own path and earn a decent living in boxing.

In 1912, however, Hurley's future was not at all clear. It is possible his father's death may have affected his perception of work. He may even have associated arising early in the morning for work with the tragedy. If so, his avoidance of an ordinary job may have been a way to keep from reliving that shocking experience.

For sure, Jack was not shy about answering to his love of sports even as he experimented with traditional employment. One of the first things he did upon returning to Fargo in September 1912 was to enroll in the YMCA's

---

(batboy); April 12, 1931 (usher at Grand). Wood, Wilbur, "Odd Lure in Fight Managing," *New York Sun*, August 17, 1934, sports section (soda jerk).

[4] Fairbanks, Ruth M., "Mother Aids Jack Hurley," *Fargo Forum*, December 28, 1930, 1930, sports section.

[5] Fitzgerald, Eugene, "Eugene Fitzgerald – Hurley Quit Elevator Job," October 7, 1968, sports section. Hurley told the story about his elevator job to *Forum* sports editor Fitzgerald who had known Jack since the teens. The occasion of the recollection was the demolition of the Improvement Building during his visit to Fargo in 1968.

gymnastics program. By March 1913, he had become proficient enough to perform at the semi-annual YMCA Gymnastics Carnival.[6]

Hurley also bowled for the YMCA and was touted in the *Courier-News* as the boy most likely to win a medal. His team, the Blizzards, tied for first place with the Cyclones in the Windy League for 14-year olds, although they lost the play-off. His single game score of 155 was the season's second highest among 16 bowlers, surpassed only by a score of 186.[7]

The activity which Hurley pursued most aggressively was not sponsored by the YMCA, however. As described previously, excitement about the fistic exploits of Leo Kossick was rampant. Jack had grown up watching Kossick play baseball for the amateur and semi-pro teams around town, but his new popularity as a boxer piqued Hurley's interest.

Kossick and his manager, George Saumweber, had opened their own gym in 1911 as a matter of necessity. After Leo gained stature as a pro, he was barred from the YMCA in Fargo and had no place to train. As a solution, Saumweber outfitted the basement below his Moorhead barbershop into a state-of-the-art training facility.

The gymnasium, described in the *Forum* as "elegant," was equipped with a real ring, a large wrestling mat, pulleys, a sandbag, and a number of lighter punching bags. The facility, named "Kossick's Gym," was managed by Leo himself and served as the main training quarters for all the area's pro boxers and wrestlers.[8]

Sometime between September 1912 and January 1913, Hurley ventured across the Red River Bridge to Moorhead to see firsthand what the fuss about Kossick was all about. Jack was 15 years old and weighed 120 pounds when he walked into the gym and saw Leo training alongside such grizzled ring veterans as Ted Childers, Kid Johnson, Kid Bruny, Leo Stokes, and Submarine Smith. His experience as a mascot to older high school and professional ballplayers, as well as his stint as a railroad call boy, had given him a degree of self-possession far beyond his tender years.

Having joined the YMCA a few months earlier, Hurley was also familiar with the inside of a gymnasium. He felt comfortable among these older men who sought to earn unconventional livings solely by dint of sheer physical prowess. He made himself useful around the gym and, after a while, Kossick and the others welcomed him as a regular.[9]

---

[6] "The Big Night at the YMCA," *Fargo Forum*, March 28, 1913, sports section.
[7] "Athletic News from the "Y," *Fargo Forum*, December 27, 1912, sports section. "Cyclones First in Windy City League, *Fargo Courier-News*, March 19, 1913, sports section. "Bowling," *Fargo Courier-News*, March 13, 1913, sports section. "Windy City League Is Tied at the Top," *Fargo Courier-News*, March 16, 1913, sports section. "Cyclones First in Windy League," *Fargo Courier-News*, March 19, 1913, sports section.
[8] "Kossick Gets Place to Train," *Fargo Forum*, October 14, 1911, sports section.
[9] Heinz, W. C., "The Man Who Makes Fighters," *Esquire Magazine*, May, 1952, p. 100.

Hurley watched the fighters and practiced what they did in front of a mirror at home. The moves came naturally, and pretty soon he was demonstrating what he learned to anyone who would watch. He also listened to the handlers tell stories about their own ring experiences and about fights they had seen and boxers they had known.

One fighter they discussed was Luther McCarty, whose name had been in the papers a lot. McCarty had lived in Fargo for six months, and everyone at the gym considered him a personal friend. Leaving the area in October, 1911, Luther had made a name for himself in the boxing centers on both sides of the North American continent, and it was rumored he would return to Fargo for an exhibition at the end of January, 1913.

Indeed, McCarty had succeeded beyond the wildest dreams of even his most ardent admirers. A strapping, 6-foot-4, 205-pounder, Luther was still three months shy of his 21st birthday when he scaled the heights by kayoing Al Palzer January 1, 1913, to win recognition as the "white hope heavyweight champion of the world."

The term "white hope" referred to the search by managers and promoters for a white man to defeat Jack Johnson, the true heavyweight champion. Johnson, the first black man to win the title, had a penchant for being his own man and flouting the conventions of white society. Under federal indictment for allegedly violating the Mann Act, "Little Arthur," as he disparagingly was called, had been barred from leaving the United States and was boycotted by promoters in the U. S., Great Britain, and Australia.

Many writers then believed that, as a result of these problems, Johnson would never defend his title again. By January 1913, some already had dropped the adjective "white" and were referring to McCarty in unqualified terms as "the heavyweight champion." Certainly, the Fargo papers Hurley was reading did not hesitate to give Luther full credit as world champion.[10]

McCarty was born March 20, 1892, in Wild Horse Canyon, Nebraska, on a homestead near Driftwood Creek. After nine years of raising Luther to enjoy life on the open range, his father, Aaron P. McCarty, and his stepmother sold the ranch. They adopted new identities as Chief White Eagle and Marguerite White Eagle and organized a traveling medicine show.

The troupe featured a snake charmer as well as a strong woman and a strong man who bent heavy steel bars and broke iron chains. The company traveled in a painted wagon pulled by two spotted ponies, followed by two shaggy dogs. Its main source of income was the sale of "rattlesnake oil" which Dr. White Eagle sold between shows. The concoction was advertised as a cure for gout, toothache, headache, aching muscles, rheumatism, and, as the "doctor" claimed, "most anything in the way of ordinary ills."[11]

---

[10] "Luck's Next Go Important One," *Fargo Forum*, November 12, 1912, sport section.

[11] The story of Chief or Dr. White Eagle is likely true since it was verified by interviews with McCarty's father himself, *Fargo Forum, January 15, 1913*, and with interviews from

Young Luther, or "Lute" as he was known almost everywhere except in Fargo, alternated between staying with relatives in Colorado Springs and touring with his parents. He also spent winters with them when they were unable to travel. While with his family, Lute's duties included caring for the diamondback rattlers his father used to help advertise the snake oil. In early 1907, the McCartys moved their home base to Sydney, Ohio, where young Lute worked as a window washer, a street paver, and a sewer digger.

In Sydney, Lute met Rhoda Wright, the daughter of a prosperous Ohio farmer. They married in May 1908, just two months after his 16th birthday. The couple lived in Sydney until 1910 when they moved to Michigan where he was employed on freight boats. After a short while, they made their way to Saskatoon, Canada, where Lute scrounged work as a cook and a cowboy, and learned to rope cattle and work a lariat.

In the spring of 1911, Rhoda went home to Sydney for a visit while McCarty drifted south of the Canada-U. S. border looking for work. After finding a job in Fargo, Lute sent word to Rhoda and their infant daughter, Cornelia, to join him there. His ultimate goal, however, was not to eke out a living doing odd jobs, but to pursue a boxing career. According to his father, Lute always had been "daffy" about prize fighting. He had several pro fights before the move, but these were only rough and ready affairs.[12]

Former heavyweight champion Tommy Burns had seen one of these fights in Canada and told McCarty that he could go far in the game, but only if he sought professional instruction. Luther found out about Kossick's Gym, and that sealed his decision to settle in Fargo.[13]

The McCartys resided in Fargo for about six months during 1911. "Luck," as he came to be known around the city, worked for Alex Stern and Co. as a cleaner and apprentice tailor, at Peterson's Livery Barn as a

---

other sources in Piqua, Ohio, *Fargo Forum, January 22, 1913*, and Peoria, Ill., *Fargo Forum, February 10, 1913*. According to an article in the January 1966 issue of *Frontier Times*, Luther's mother died while giving birth to a stillborn brother in 1893. Sometime later, Aaron P. McCarty married a woman named Marguerite, who traveled with the medicine show under the name of Marguerite White Eagle. One newspaper article published after Luther became famous claims Marguerite died after a bite from one of the troupe's rattlesnakes. The *Frontier Times* article does not mention Marguerite at all, but it does say Aaron married Miss Caroline Emma Wolford in 1904. *Fargo Forum, January 15, 1913 and January 22, 1913*.

Also, there is confusion about the first name of Luther's father. Contemporary sources variously refer to him as Aaron P, *Fargo Forum, January 22,* 1913; as Anton P. *Fargo Forum, January 15, 1913*; as Abner, *Fargo Courier-News, December 19, 1912*; and as John, *Fargo Courier-News, December 11, 1912*. In the text, the author has opted for the apparently more thoroughly researched *Frontier Times'* version of Aaron P. Riley, Paul D., "Sod House Frontier Boxing Champ," *Frontier Times, January 1966, pp. 26-7*.

[12] "'Good-Natured Kid' Says Wife," *Fargo Forum*, January 3, 1913, sports section.

[13] "Luck McCarty in His Old Home," *Fargo Forum*, January 15, 1913, sports section ("daffy"). "Luck M'Carthy (sic) in Limelight," *Fargo Forum*, June 17, 1912, sports section (spotted by Burns).

groom, and at the Broadway Cigar Store as a general helper. More importantly, Luck met Kossick who introduced him to his first gym workouts and taught him how to condition himself.[14]

McCarty had two pro bouts in Fargo against Al Withers in the spring of 1911, winning both by knockout with Kossick in his corner. In October, he fought in Fargo for the last time, knocking out Tommy Crawford in one round. The very next day, feeling he was ready for bigger things, McCarty set out for the big city and, hopefully, the big time in Chicago.[15]

Now, in January 1913, having achieved his dream by winning the "white hope" title, McCarty was returning to Fargo for an exhibition. The return of "our Luck" was a matter of pride to Fargoans and a homecoming for Lute. During his absence, Rhoda remained behind in Fargo-Moorhead, washing dishes at Armstrong's Dairy Lunch and waitressing at Howard's Café.

Though McCarty's support of Rhoda after leaving was meager at first, he had sent home a substantial sum after his two most recent bouts. On this trip, Luck hoped to reach an agreement with his wife about their future and square accounts with the creditors he had left behind earlier.[16]

Fifteen-year-old Jack Hurley was likely one of the admirers who greeted McCarty's party on the Oriental Limited at the Great Northern Depot in the morning, and then followed the group to the Gardner Hotel for a reception on the afternoon of January 27, 1913.[17]

That evening, Hurley left his job at the Bijou Theater early and wheedled his way past the turnstile to see McCarty's exhibition at Pirie's Hall, causing his mother, who waited up late for him, no little anxiety. The *Fargo Daily-Courier* reported that Luther wore elaborate Wild West regalia and toted a "six-shooter which looked more like a rapid-fire battleship gun." Luck also gave a demonstration of lariat throwing, which showed he was "not yet as adept as he has been pictured" but that "he is learning fast."

After changing into his boxing togs, McCarty ran through a routine which included tossing a medicine ball, shadow boxing, and sparring with Fred Fulton for four rounds, "livening things up in the final round." Luther "made his opponent miss many times during the short bout and showed that he has a rapid-fire right uppercut which might stow anyone who comes in contact with it. He fights in a crouching position and sends out straight rights and lefts which are very tantalizing if not dangerous."

---

[14] Hurley, Jack, *op. cit.*, January 11, 1931 (Alex Stern), and April 20, 1930 (Peterson's Livery Barn). Hurley, "Shadow Boxing," February 10, 1935 (Broadway Cigar Store). All from the *Fargo Forum* sports sections.
[15] "Kossick Is Given Great Notices in East," *Fargo Courier-News*, March 18, 1913, sports section (verbatim from an article published originally in the *Philadelphia Evening Times*).
[16] "'Good-Natured Kid,'" *op. cit.*
[17] "Large Audience Saw McCarty in Action," *Fargo Forum*, January 28, 1913, sports section.

Two poses of "white hope" heavyweight champion Luther McCarty.

McCarty demonstrates his straight left to manager Billy McCarney.

The performance concluded with movies and a lantern slide show, personally narrated by Professor Billy McCarney, Luck's famous handler. The film showed the boxer's life as a cowboy, his boxcar trips, his rise to fame, and ended with his recent kayo of Al Palzer.[18]

Sometime during the course of McCarty's visit, Kossick introduced Hurley to McCarney. Their friendship, which endured until the older man's death in 1948, was to impact Jack's future in a way he could not have imagined at the time. Indeed, it is not going too far to say that Billy would become for Hurley the father figure he had just lost. Conceivably, but for their fortuitous meeting, Jack might not have pursued boxing as a career.

Meeting McCarney was Hurley's first experience with that unique, vagabond breed of sportsman who did business "out of his hat" and made decisions "by the seat of his pants" – namely the old-time fight manager. In Billy, Jack encountered a perfect role model, a kindred spirit whose best attributes mirrored those for which he himself would later be admired.

McCarney was known as an affable, witty, eloquent, and honest man in a business where such qualities were in short supply. Along with these traits, he was a master storyteller who blended a wee bit of old-world blarney with a keen grasp of facts. Added to the mix, Billy was a rarity for the era, a boxing man with a college degree. Born in Philadelphia's Irish quarter in 1872 and son to a saloon keeper, he graduated from La Salle College, boxed a little there, and studied law. Bored with his studies, he left school and took a job as sportswriter for a local paper.

Before long, McCarney opened a fight club in Philadelphia and soon was managing boxers all over the country. During the next 50 years, he would handle such boxers as Unk Russell, Ad Wolgast, Carl Morris, Dick Hyland, Frank Moran, Young Erne, Nate Brown, Charlie Weinert, and Steve Dudas.

In the mid-1920s, McCarney would form a partnership in New York with Joe Jacobs and share with him in the management of flyweight champ Frankie Genaro, light-heavyweight champ Mike McTigue, and heavyweight champion Max Schmeling.

Over the years, McCarney developed a specialty organizing training camps and arranging theatrical and exhibition tours for many of the world's most famous boxers. Training camps served the dual purposes of conditioning well-known fighters for important bouts and functioning as hospitality centers for thirsty and hungry sportswriters. In the era before TV, exhibition tours were a major source of income for successful boxers, affording fans in remote localities a chance to see their heroes in the flesh.

---

[18] Hurley,, "Ring Rations," December 28, 1930, sports section. "McCarty to See Old Friends Here Monday," *Fargo Courier-News,* January 26, 1913, sports section. "McCarty Proves to Fans That He's Real Champ," *Fargo Courier-News,* January 28, 1913, sports sections.

McCarney organized tours for such renowned pugilists as Jim Jeffries, Genaro, Max Baer, and Schmeling. Billy's last major effort before his death was to arrange a post-World War II tour in the Philippines for then heavyweight champion Joe Louis.

Dubbed variously "the Professor" and "the old Carpetbagger" by writers for his sagacity and gypsy-like lifestyle, McCarney first met McCarty in December 1911 shortly after Lute left Fargo for Chicago. Billy was down on his luck and was seeking a way to reverse his fortunes. He had invested heavily in the motion picture rights to the Jack Johnson-Jim Jeffries fight, and the film's distribution had been a bust.[19]

McCarty was training at Bill O'Connell's gym in Chicago under the tutelage of Sig Hart. The latter was not impressed enough by Lute to bother signing him to a contract. When Hart's boxer, Walter Monahan, bowed out of a fight with Joe Cox due to an injury, Sig asked McCarney to accompany Luther to Springfield, Missouri, where he was substituting for Monahan.

At the time, McCarty had never traveled by paid fare. He arrived at the train station decked out in tight pants with trouser legs stopping four inches short of his ankles. He wore an ill-fitting overcoat that hung around his shoulders like a sack and had sleeves extending beyond his fingertips. On top of his head he wore a little round hat with a short brim that was a size too small. All in all, he had the appearance of an over-sized scarecrow.

Professor McCarney took one look at McCarty and, except for the fact Billy himself was nearly destitute, almost changed his mind about the trip. He figured that even if Lute could fight twice as well as he dressed, he still didn't stand a chance against Cox.

After a series of embarrassing incidents on the train, the travelers arrived in Springfield to learn Hart had failed to wire ahead that Monahan was not able to appear. The promoter accused McCarney of passing off McCarty as Monahan and threatened to cancel the show. Billy, who had never seen Luther fight before, assured him Lute would put up a good fight and the promoter himself could decide how much to pay after the fight was over.[20]

Much to everyone's surprise, especially McCarney's, Luther stopped Cox in the sixth round. The Professor, however, was not so taken aback that he neglected to obtain Luther's signature on a contract. From that day until Lute's tragic death a year and a half later, the two Macs were inseparable.

Springfield's reception was so enthusiastic the new team stayed on for six months. After two early setbacks against seasoned opposition, Lute

---

[19] Daniel, Dan, "McCarney Mourned for Wit, Friendship," *Ring Magazine*, December 1948, pp. 26-7, 41.
[20] McCarty did in fact identify himself as Walter Monahan and continued to hold himself out as Monahan until McCarney confessed Luther's real name to a *Springfield Republican* reporter in a story published December 24. "Drops Name of Monahan; Is Now M'Carthy," *Springfield Republican*, December 24, 1911.

McCarty greets his father, Dr. A. P. (White Eagle) McCarty and his stepmother.

Billy McCarney, circa 1905.

An older Professor McCarney dispenses advice, circa 1942.

settled down and scored five straight wins, including three knockouts, to become the region's biggest drawing card.

McCarney kept the results of these fights quiet by not sending out reports over the wire services. As a result, Billy lured Carl Morris, then a leading heavyweight contender, to Springfield for a bout on May 3, 1912. McCarty disposed of Morris in six rounds. This time, Billy circulated reports all over the country, and Lute became an overnight sensation.[21]

Aterward, McCarney initiated an intense ballyhoo campaign. As if McCarty's background as an authentic cowboy, medicine show trouper, and rattlesnake keeper was not enough, Billy invented a new history for Lute which inflated many of his prior achievements and totally invented others.

According to this new narrative, Luther left home on a freight train at age 11, worked as a cornhusker in Kansas, a bill poster in St. Louis, a messenger boy in Omaha, and an itinerant laborer in Los Angeles. Making his way to Boston at age 12, he shipped out as an able-bodied seaman. His ports of call over the next three years were said to include Buenos Aires, Cape Horn, Norway, China, and Japan.

Returning to dry land near Mobile, Alabama, McCarty allegedly worked at a lumber camp in Pine Hill and a coal mine near Blue Creek. After stints at dairy work and bridge building in Nashville, he drifted to North Dakota where he drove cattle and lived among the Sioux Indians on a reservation.[22]

More important than McCarney's overblown rhetoric, however, was McCarty's performance in the ring. Although at first sportswriters were skeptical about his boxing ability, Billy made sure Lute was not overmatched and received proper instruction. During the next seven months, he kayoed Jack McFarland, Al Kaufman, and Fireman Jim Flynn.

It was the victory over Flynn, who had just lost to Jack Johnson in a heavyweight championship battle and who later would kayo a young Jack Dempsey in a single round, which led to the fight with Al Palzer on January 1, 1913, when McCarty won the white hope championship.[23]

And so, when Hurley met McCarney in 1913, he was meeting a man at the height of his career, managing one of the most popular fighters in America. Jack was suitably impressed at the time, but he had no way of knowing just how important Billy would be to his future.

When Hurley decided to pursue a career in boxing it was the Professor who became his model, sponsor, advisor, and friend. It was no accident that when Jack briefly moved his base of operation from Fargo to the East

---

[21] Hurley, *op. cit.*

[22] "Luck McCarty in Limelight," *Fargo Forum*, June 17, 1912, sports section. This creative part of Lute's background was apparently McCarney's work because it appeared shortly after the win over Morris. The tales were not repeated afterward, and were inconsistent with later accounts by McCarty's wife and father.

[23] Fleischer, Nat, *1943 Ring Record Book*, (Ring Book Shop, New York, 1943), p. 304.

McCarty wins the "white hope" heavyweight title from Al Palzer.

McCarty lands a right that sends Palzer reeling.

Palzer starts to fall.

McCarty – Winner and new champion!

Coast in 1925, his first choice was Philadelphia, McCarney's home base. It was also no coincidence that when Hurley first invaded New York in 1926, it was Billy who paved the way for Jack to operate freely in the community of fight entrepreneurs which was usually closed to outsiders.

Typically, in those Prohibition days, a visiting manager would be forced to sell or give at least part interest in his fighter to a local manager with underworld connections before obtaining a match in New York. Such an arrangement invariably took away the out-of-town manager's control of his boxer and made him a tool of that amorphous entity known as "the mob." With Billy's help, Hurley was able to avoid these entanglements and retain his independence at the stage in his career when he was most vulnerable.

McCarney introduced Hurley to reporters and, more importantly, to managers, promoters, and other behind-the-scenes operatives. Billy's backing left him free to negotiate directly with these powerbrokers and avoid local politics. Without the Professor's help, the fierce independence which became the hallmark of Jack's reputation might have been muted, and his career as an honest and courageous boxing man stillborn.

The exploits of McCarty and McCarney continued to captivate Fargo fans throughout the 1912-'13 indoor boxing season. News about the two Macs appeared in one or the other of the two Fargo papers almost daily.

Leaving Fargo, the McCarty party traveled through Chicago on January 31, 1913. On the stopover there, McCarney told the press Lute would not fight again until July because of theatrical engagements booked through that date. Billy was hoping Luther's exhibition tour would allow them to cash in on his new title without requiring him to risk it in the ring.[24]

Unfortunately, the tour fell short of McCarney's expectations. On February 17, Luther told Pittsburgh reporters he was "disgusted with stage life and ... has had enough of it." He was quoted, "I'm going to take on all the heavyweight aspirants ... I'm not going to pose as a champion and refuse to give the others a chance to wallop me."[25]

Responding to his fighter's wishes, McCarney left for New York and met with Madison Square Garden promoter Billy Gibson. Gibson offered Billy $10,000 for McCarty to box British heavyweight champion Billy Wells at the Garden. McCarney counter-offered, asking for $10,000 with an option for 40 percent of gross receipts, or else a flat $15,000 with no option. Finding the Professor's counter-proposal too rich, Gibson instead signed Gunboat Smith to fight Wells for a lesser sum on March 14.[26]

McCarney's rejection of Gibson's offer was a serious miscalculation. Smith easily knocked out a totally ineffectual Wells in two rounds. Besides

---

[24] "Luck and Mac on Way to St. Louis," *Fargo Forum*, February 1, 1913, sports section.
[25] "McCarty to Quit Stage to Fight," *Fargo Courier-News*, February 18, 1913, sports section.
[26] "To Let McCarty Take on Wells," *Fargo Courier-News*, February 17, 1913, sports section.

losing the purse, McCarty had lost a chance to increase his popularity before the most influential boxing experts in the world, the New York press corps. Instead, Smith became the sensation in New York. Obviously, he was a far more serious threat to Luther's laurels than Wells.[27]

No one was more disappointed about this turn of events than McCarty himself. In an interview, Luther "sorrowfully admit(ted) that his manager made a mistake when he let $10,000 slip by in the Wells affairs in New York." Lute also conceded "he is not the attraction on the stage that he thinks and he will have to fight to be popular."[28]

Sensing McCarty's lack of action was losing him favor, McCarney changed his strategy, canceled all theatrical engagements, and signed Luther for three fights in five weeks, each for a flat $5,000 guarantee. To prepare for these matches, he sent Lute to Chicago to train with Harry Gilmore, one of the era's great boxing teachers. Billy's plan was to use these bouts to reburnish McCarty's stature as the champion white hope and to set the stage for a July 4th title showdown against Smith or Jess Willard.[29]

McCarty easily won his first two bouts against tough competition. On April 15, he defeated Fireman Jim Flynn via a six-round newspaper decision at Philadelphia. Fifteen days later, reporters awarded him a 10-round verdict over Frank Moran in New York.[30]

The last of the bouts in the Professor's plan was expected to be the easiest. McCarty was matched to fight Arthur Pelkey in Calgary, Alberta May 24, 1913. Former world heavyweight champ Tommy Burns was the promoter. It was Burns who had staged Lute's second pro fight in Calgary two years earlier and encouraged him to pursue a ring career.

Pelkey was a well-proportioned, six-foot-tall, 200-pounder, who at age 28, had come late to the boxing game. Arthur possessed a fair punch, but experts thought he was too slow and to give McCarty much trouble. Lute was favored to win at 5 to 1, but even at those odds there was not much Pelkey money wagered.[31]

Despite these predictions, Fargo sports fans were shocked to their heels when they woke up on May 25 to read the headline emblazoned on the front page of the *Fargo Courier-News*' morning edition: M'CARTY KILLED IN CALGARY PRIZE RING!

---

[27] "'Gunboat' Smith," *Fargo Forum*, March 21, 1913, sports section.
[28] "M'Carty Is Not Stage Success," *Fargo Courier-News*, March 18, 1913, sports section.
[29] "M'Carty to Have Four Big Bouts," *Fargo Courier-News*, March 24, 1913, sports section. The article actually mentions four proposed bouts, but one of them subsequently fell through. "Luck to Take Boxing Lessons," *Fargo Forum*, February 25, 1913, sports section.
[30] "M'Carty Wallops Flynn with Ease," *Fargo Forum*, April 20, 1913, sports section. "Luck Disappointing," *Fargo Forum*, May 9, 1913.
[31] Daniel, "McCarney Mourned for Wit, Friendship," *Ring Magazine*, December, 1948, p. 26.

Only four months after his triumphant return to Fargo as heavyweight champion, Luther McCarty, "Our Luck," was dead. It seemed only yesterday that he first arrived in town broke and hungry with only his wry, good-natured grin and a strong, willing back to offer in trade. It couldn't be true. But it was. Only two months past his 21st birthday, he was killed when Pelkey landed a seemingly light left jab to the jaw, followed by a right to the heart, after just one minute and 45 seconds of fighting in the first round.

According to reports, McCarty died only eight minutes after referee Ed Smith finished his ten-count. At first, the cause of his death was said to be "from heart failure super-induced by the (second) blow." An autopsy showed otherwise, however. The coroner's physicians found "McCarty's death resulted from a dislocation of the neck" which pressed against a blood vessel and caused internal bleeding. It was later revealed Lute had complained of neck pain when he fell off a horse not long before the fight.[32]

A coroner jury's inquest which convened immediately after the bout exonerated the participants. The Calgary prosecutor, however, set aside the verdict the day afterward and charged Pelkey, McCarney, promoter Burns, and referee Smith with manslaughter. The prosecutor's reasoning was that the coroner's jury was made up almost entirely of friends of Burns. All except Pelkey were released on bond pending trial. That same day, a fire mysteriously broke out and destroyed the arena where the fight was held.

In Fargo, McCarty's wife, Rhoda, received the news with surprising calm. She admitted to the *Courier-News* that although she and Lute "never openly quarreled, they were rendered unhappy when together by incompatibility of temperament." Earlier, when he visited Fargo, she had refused his offer of $2,000 for a quiet divorce. Lute had agreed, however, to send monthly payments of $100 as support for their daughter, Cornelia.

The article noted that of the $100,000 which McCarty's fights grossed in the prior 18 months, his estate retained about $30,000, all of which Rhoda and their daughter stood to inherit. The reporter observed that McCarty's wife, while appearing "naturally shocked over the news of Luther's death ... did not assume a false semblance of a grief she did not feel over her husband's demise; nor, in fact, was she overly bold about her affairs."

Asked what she would do with the money, Rhoda gave a partial reply before deciding to end the interview: "Oh, I think I will come back to North Dakota and settle down – but there, I don't want to say any more."[33]

There was at least one person whose grief was real enough, however. Over 30 years later, McCarney discussed Luther's death with a *Ring*

---

[32] "M'Carty Killed in Calgary Prize Ring," *Fargo Courier-News*, May 25, 1913, p. 1. "Fighter Left Snug Fortune," *Fargo Courier-News*, May 27, 1913, sports section. Daniel, "Tommy Burns Tells Inside on McCarty," *Ring Magazine*, February 1949, p. 30.

[33] "Fighter Left Snug Fortune," *Fargo Courier-News*, May 27, 1913, pp. 1, 5. "Fight Promoters Will Be Tried," *Fargo Courier-News*, May 28, 1913, sports section. "Says M'Carty Left $30,000," *Courier-News*, May 29, 1913, non-sports section.

Pelkey and McCarty prior to their tragic bout May 24, 1913.

McCarty grins while squaring off minutes before being hit by the blow that killed him.

Famous photo of sun forming a kind of halo as McCarty was counted out. Eight minutes later, he was pronounced dead.

A doctor tries to revive McCarty as McCarney looks on with hands clasped behind his head.

Magazine reporter. "I never got over the death of McCarty," Billy said. "I liked that kid as if he were my own son. He was such a grand guy. Not like so many others I was hooked up with, phonies. When I saw him lying there in the Calgary ring, dead, I shed bitter tears."

McCarney conceded some people might suspect his anguish was false, but he insisted such was not the case. "I always have been a sharp-shooter," Billy told Daniel, "and you might say, 'Why not cry? You were losing your meal ticket.' But, so help me, I said [when he died], 'Why did it have to be this kid? Why not me?'"[34]

The Professor's actions supported his words. Instead of returning home to Philadelphia after the fatal fight, he took charge of transporting Luther's body from Calgary to its final resting place near his father's home in Piqua, Ohio. Enroute, the train stopped in Fargo, where Rhoda climbed aboard.

Sensing Rhoda was distressed by questions from the press, Billy acted as her spokesman, fielding questions put to her at a stop-over in St. Paul. After the funeral in Piqua on June 2, he accompanied her to Springfield, Missouri, where he assisted in her application to the probate court for an appointment to administer her husband's estate.[35]

McCarty's death left McCarney not only emotionally drained, but in doubt about his future livelihood. At the time, he vowed "I will never manage another prize fighter, nor attend another bout." Although he did, in fact, manage others, he never found another fighter like Luther McCarty.[36]

McCarney did what he could to help McCarty's wife cope with Luther's death, but he could never put the tragic event behind him. For years afterward, he visited Lute's grave in Piqua annually and paid a caretaker to maintain it throughout the year. Writing in 1934 to Jack Hurley, by then an old friend, while on one of these Piqua pilgrimages, Billy explained: "It is good to the eye, to see its wonderful condition and a mental treat to me to be so close to him and recall our wonderful friendship."[37]

Even as the teen-aged Hurley was reading about this tragedy, he was preparing for his first season in a real baseball league. In this endeavor he was by no means alone. At the end of every winter season, virtually every athlete in the Fargo-Moorhead area with any ability at all put aside other sports to play baseball. Included in this category of athletes were boxers. Even established pros like Leo Kossick, Jack Doyle, and Kid Benson hung up their boxing gloves until fall in exchange for baseball mitts.

Indeed, Hurley himself was good enough to later be forced to choose between baseball and boxing. After returning from World War I, he was given a tryout with the Louisville Colonels in the American Association.

---

[34] Daniel, p. 26.

[35] "M'Carney Quits Ring Forever," *Courier-News,* May 30, 1913, non-sports section. "Will File Claim for M'Carty Estate," June 3, 1913, sports section.

[36] "M'Carney Quits Ring Forever," *Courier-News,* May 30, 1913, non-sports section.

[37] Hurley, "Shadow Boxing," *Fargo Forum,* April 24, 1934, sports section.

When he failed to make the team, Jack decided he was at best a good glove, no-hit, prospect, and his real future lay in boxing as a manager and promoter. In 1913, however, Hurley had been swinging a bat longer than punching a bag, and he remained more devoted to baseball than boxing.[38]

That spring, the Fargo YMCA established the Collegiate Baseball League for 15-year olds. The league's teams were named after four ivy-league colleges: Harvard, Yale, Cornell, and Princeton. Not surprisingly, Jack was elected captain of one of the teams. The teams played one another in doubleheaders every Saturday morning throughout the spring.

The doubleheader on May 16 was the only series of the season reported in the papers. Princeton's game against Cornell was covered in the *Forum*:

> "The second contest was really the closest and most exciting of the two. The participants were Princeton and Cornell. Taking an early lead of four runs in the first inning John Crowders and his Cornell men finally captured the contest by the score of 4 to 5. Jack Hurley's Princeton team made only one run in the first inning and tied the score in the next to the last inning. At this time, things were extremely exciting and though Murphy of the Princetons, after two were out, with a nice hit managed to get around to third, he was too anxious to score and was thrown out trying to steal too far away from third base. The games next Saturday will be between Harvard and Cornell and Princeton and Yale."[39]

After the 1913 baseball season, Hurley enrolled in the YMCA's fall/winter gymnastics program, just as he had the prior year. Now an experienced gymnast, Jack traveled to neighboring communities to take part in competitions and demonstrations. He also participated again in the "Y's" annual gymnastics carnival held in Fargo at the end of March 1914.[40]

Unlike the prior winter, however, Hurley decided against supplementing gymnastics with bowling. Instead, he gave the theater a try. On December 1, the St. Mary's Cathedral Dramatic Society presented a full vaudeville bill in the Cathedral auditorium at 604 Broadway Avenue. Sandwiched between such acts as "Fifi from Paris," the "Famous Florodora Girls," and "Pickaninny Ballads," Jack, just a week shy of his 16th birthday, starred in a one-man skit entitled "A Rube from Wild Rice."

In its review, the *Forum* noted that "Hurley is another promising young actor. His part was well taken and his make-up only added to the merriment which he was capable of creating. His remarks, which were mostly of an

---

[38] Houston, Robert, "Hurley: One of Boxing's Great Figures." *Sunday World Herald Magazine*, January 13, 1952, p. 10-G.
[39] "Baseball – Opening of Season," *Fargo Forum*, May 17, 1913, sports section.
[40] "'Y' Boys to Give Gym Exhibition," *Fargo Forum*, March 28, 1914, sports section.

original nature, brought down the house repeatedly." Despite the positive response, Jack's performance must have been his last theatrical venture since he was not listed in the society's next production.[41]

At about this same time, Jack began working out at the Cathedral Club's newly out-fitted gym in the cathedral's basement. Although he had previously been a hanger-on at Kossick's Gym, the use of its facilities was reserved for professionals. The Cathedral Club, on the other hand, was a multi-purpose facility that included space for amateur athletes to train.

Bishop John Shanley, Fargo's first Roman Catholic bishop, founded the club in 1905 as a place for young men to get "acquainted, find recreation, and be in a good clean moral atmosphere." Its facilities included pool and billiard tables, a gymnasium, showers, a library, and an auditorium with a seating capacity of 600. One of the club's attractions was that the young men organized their own activities and managed its business affairs.[42]

During that same season, Hurley found time between his gymnastic and stage performances to help arrange the boxing and wrestling bouts for the Cathedral Club's amateur smokers. The highlight of the season was to be the club's inaugural athletic carnival set for February 4. A well-publicized appearance of Leo Kossick boxing a four-round exhibition against Ted Childers was scheduled as a feature attraction.[43]

Jack no doubt was disappointed when Leo's appearance was abruptly canceled. On the day of the event, the club's board of directors passed a resolution barring professionals from appearing at the club.[44]

Before long, Hurley was boxing in smokers both at the Cathedral Club and elsewhere against foes from other clubs around the state. His mother told a reporter in a later interview that Jack sometimes traveled to matches "riding the blinds" on the front platform of a passenger train baggage car. On the return trip home, he would travel in style by purchasing coach fare from the tranportation fee he received for the bout.

It was only after Hurley came home from one trip battered and bruised that she learned he was boxing. Until then, he had always told her he was participating in "an exhibition." Julia, having in mind Jack's YMCA activities, had always assumed the event he was attending was nothing more than a gymnastics demonstration.[45]

---

[41] "Amateurs Make a Great Hit," *Fargo Forum*, December 2, 1913. Jack's cousin, Margaret Healy, also participated as a Florodora girl. In the interest of providing context and full disclosure, it should be added that the reviewer was equally positive about all the performers that evening. "Cathedral Club Play Tonight," *Fargo* Forum, February 23, 1914, sports section.

[42] "Interesting Facts about Well-Known Cathedral Club," *Fargo Forum*, September 27, 1915, local news section.

[43] "Cathedral Club Athletic Meet," *Fargo Forum*, January 30, 1913, sports section.

[44] "Wrestling Match at Big Carnival," *Fargo Forum*, February 5, 1913, sports section.

[45] Fairbanks, "Mother Aids Jack Hurley," *Fargo Forum*, December 28, 1930, 1930, sports section. Fortunately, Mrs. Hurley's confusion of boxing with gymnastics exhibitions dates

In early 1914, Hurley went to work at his first full-time job as a press feeder for the Knight Printing Company, located at 619 Northern Pacific Avenue. He obtained the post as a result of his friendship with Fred W. (Fritz) Schroeder who was employed there in the same capacity and whose family was well connected in the industry. Jack stayed with Knight for about a year before accepting a position in the same capacity from its chief competitor, Pierce Printing Company, located at 1019 First Avenue North.[46]

The position's rigid hours made it hard for Jack to play on an organized team during the spring/summer baseball season of 1914. Additionally, now that he was 16, he was too old to play for the YMCA and too young to play on the adult teams. As a solution, Jack established his own team, the Fargo Juniors, so he could schedule his own games and practices.

The Juniors, or "Toddlers" as the *Courier-News* called them, established itself as the city's premier 16-year-old team, winning 10 of 11 games. The team's best players were Jack and Schroeder, who shared pitching and catching duties as well as filling in at other positions. While the mound work of each was noted several times, it was Fritz's "pegging to second" to catch "nearly every runner who tried to steal" that merited special praise.[47]

The following report, from the June 23rd edition of the *Courier-News* is probably the earliest surviving example of a Jack Hurley press release:

> "In two days the Fargo Juniors, champion kid ball players of the city have won six games, almost a world record. Sunday they broke the Sabbath into some 100 pieces and came out ahead in four bouts. Yesterday they took the Irish Picketts and the Eighth Street Whirlwinds into camp, 14 to 2 and 3 to 0 respectively. The Juniors want games with any 16-year-old team in the city. Telephone Jack Hurley, 1954J."[48]

Jack's participation in the Cathedral Club smokers with reasonable accuracy. We can be relatively sure that Jack concluded his gymnastics career at the Y's final demonstration on March 29, 1914. It is therefore likely that his participation as a boxer at the Cathedral Club occurred sometime not long before that date and the beginning of baseball season in June.

[46] Unpublished *Fargo Forum* Biography Questionnaire filled out by Jack Hurley on May 12, 1951. *Fargo-Moorhead City Directories of 1913, 1915, 1916, 1917*, published in separate volumes by Pettibone Directory Company. Fred W. (Fritz) Schroeder is listed as a "feeder" in 1915 and as a "pressman" in 1916 employed by Knight Printing and as an "employee" of the Newspaper Union in 1917. Fritz's father, Fred W. Schroeder (whose personal residences are the same as Fritz's in 1915, 1916, and 1917), is listed as a "bookbinder" in 1913 and 1915 (employer not referenced), as a "pressman" in 1916 and as a "foreman bindery" employed by Knight both of those years. The Schroeders are not listed in the directories after 1917. Hurley also mentioned in his syndicated column that Cecelia Schroeder worked at Knight Printing. "Ring Rations," *Fargo Forum, December 1, 1935, sports section.* As of January 2014, Knight Printing was still in business, and Pierce Printing still had a skeleton website on the worldwide web with a forwarding email address.

[47] *Fargo Daily Courier-News*, various articles, June 11, 12, 13, 15, 19, and 23, 1914.

It is probable Hurley's stint as newsboy for the *Courier-News* helped obtain coverage for the Juniors since there is no mention of the team in the rival *Fargo Forum*. The effect of the release may, however, have been contrary to Jack's original intent, since the *Courier-News* reported no further games by the Juniors that year. The incident likely taught Hurley a lesson valuable to his future career as a boxing manager, namely to not toot his fighter's horn so loudly as to scare away his next intended victim.

After baseball season ended, both Jack and Fritz trained at the Cathedral Club during the 1914-'15 fall/winter indoor season and boxed in amateur smokers throughout the region. Gradually, after losing a few bouts, Jack realized that while he had a talent for mimicking and learning boxing moves, he lacked the physical equipment to be a successful fighter.[49]

Soon, Hurley was boxing less and teaching more. He began to tutor Fritz and work in his corner. "It was so easy," he later said. "I'd look at another fighter and the next day I could imitate him ... and I'd pass it on to my fighters ... It's just an ability I have. There are guys who've never seen a piano before who can walk in and sit down and fool around with it for a few minutes and then play something. I could sit at a piano for three years and I wouldn't be able to play *Home, Sweet Home*, but I can figure fighters."[50]

By the time Hurley turned 18 on December 9, 1915, he had discovered a lot about himself and already walked a few steps along the path he would follow the rest of his life. Although he took a job to please his mother, he knew punching a clock was not for him. He was quick to grasp how people did things and liked describing and mimicking them to his friends. He tried acting, but was more comfortable showing others the things he had learned on a one-to-one basis rather than projecting them on stage to an audience.

Jack enjoyed sports, and the sports he liked best were baseball and boxing. He didn't have the physique to be a boxer, but he still hoped to make it in big-league baseball. He had a gift of gab and an ability to make listeners believe the things he said even when he was not sure if he believed them himself. He also had a knack for analyzing boxing styles and imparting his knowledge to his fellow amateurs.

He was not sure what the future held or how he would earn his living, but by a gradual process of elimination he was narrowing the field to a short list of acceptable options. His next step was to wait for an opportunity to dip his foot a little deeper into the waters of the sports world and see whether he would sink or swim.

---

[48] "Fargo Juniors Are Making Clean Sweep," *Fargo Courier-News*, June 23, 1914, sports section.
[49] Hurley, *op. cit.*, December 30, 1934, sports section.
[50] Houston, *op. cit.* Heinz, *op. cit.*

CHAPTER 3

GOOD FIELD, NO HIT

The man I still consider the greatest prospect I ever had is Fritz Schroeder. He was my first, in 1916, and he would have been great. He was better as a beginner than Billy Petrolle.

He left Fargo and moved to Portland, Oregon soon after 1916, wasn't the kind who forced himself in for attention, and gradually dropped out of the boxing game.

What a prospect Schroeder was! He punched so sharply he'd knock boys out in the gym, and he didn't mean to. He still lives in Portland (in 1951) where he is a pressman at the Journal of Commerce."[1] – Jack Hurley

****

The highlight of the 1915-'16 indoor boxing season in the Midwest was the legalization of fisticuffs in Minnesota and the opportunity it afforded fans throughout the region to once again see their great St. Paul boxing hero, Mike Gibbons, in a Minnesota boxing ring.

Gibbons began boxing in 1908 with lessons from George Barton at the St. Paul YMCA. After eliminating local competition, Mike invaded New York and created a sensation by kayoing Willie Lewis on February 23, 1912, in two rounds. Over the next three years, he defeated most of the world's top middleweights to earn recognition in the East as the division's best fighter. Champion Al McCoy, however, refused to meet Mike in a title match, and he was never achieved official recognition as champion.[2]

Known as "the Phantom" for his defensive skill, Gibbons was famous as a pioneer of the St. Paul school of boxing. Boxers using this style uniformly held their hands low at the waistline, rejecting the accepted "on guard" stance taught by most experts at the time.

A St. Paul stylist relied on footwork, proper judgment of distance, and movements of the head and waist to avoid punches rather than blocking them, thus freeing his fists to deliver counter-blows. As he "slipped" or "side-stepped" a blow in this manner, he would shift one or both of his feet to place himself in position to counter his foe's missed punch with a

---

[1] L. H. Gregory, "Greg's Gossip, *Oregonian,* April 30, 1951, sports section. The quote has been re-arranged to fit the context. In other interviews, Hurley said Schroeder's career ended when he suffered a non-boxing related injury. A possible explanation may be that he suffered an injury that temporarily suspended his boxing and before he could resume he moved to Portland. The exact circumstance that ended his career is not critical here.

[2] Gibbons, Mike, "My Eighteen Years in the Ring" (series), *Boxing Blade,* July 5, 1924 through August 22, 1925. Mike told his life story in 37 chapters for this publication. The middleweight weight limit at the time was 158 pounds on the day of the fight. Now it typically is 160 pounds the day before the fight.

counter-blow or combination of his own. Ideally, this shifting of weight was to a balanced position that enabled the counter-blows to be delivered with maximum leverage.

When a St. Paul boxing move was perfectly executed, the counter-blow's impact was magnified by the opponent's forward momentum generated by his missed punch. In the style's most refined form, a Gibbons' exponent would purposely leave an apparent opening for his foe, lure him into making a move, shift his feet, slip the blow, and counter with a well-leveraged punch which had been carefully worked out in advance.[3]

Gibbons, who was something of an intellectual when it came to boxing, would become a driving force behind making boxing instruction an integral part of the U. S. Army's hand-to-hand combat training program. Mike enlisted for service in World War I in July 1917, and was installed as boxing instructor at Camp Dodge, Iowa on October 29. At the time, boxing was thought to be valuable only as a recreational activity for the soldiers.

At camp, Gibbons studied bayonet fighting with Sergeant Major Hinsley, a British army expert. After a few lessons, Mike was struck by similarities between boxing and bayonet fighting, and he became convinced boxing should be taught as part of a soldier's training.

Gibbons noticed that the moves used by a St. Paul fighter were especially adaptable to bayonet fighting. Most other systems of boxing instruction emphasized a raised guard that featured parrying, blocking, retreating footwork as methods of defense. In bayonet fighting such strictly defensive maneuvers left the combatant out of position for counter-attack and vulnerable to an opponent's further aggressive thrusts.[4]

The St. Paul style, however, with its emphasis on lowered guard, judgment of distance, and side-stepping, employed maneuvers similar to bayonet fighting. Additionally, repetitive drills designed to teach the proper positioning of the feet and body to achieve balance and leverage were applicable to both forms of combat.

Working with the camp's bayonet teacher, Gibbons drew up a course of boxing exercises and submitted them to his commanding officer. The officer was impressed and made boxing a required part of bayonet training at Camp Dodge. The lessons were published in eight installments from March 15 through May 25, 1918 in the Camp Dodge newspaper.

The course was so well received that U. S. War Department athletic chairman Joseph Raycroft summoned Gibbons to Washington, D.C. Raycroft ordered Mike to write up a course incorporating boxing into the U. S. Army's hand-to-hand combat regimen. After completing this task, the manual was made part of the Army's general orders for basic training.

---

[3] Gibbons, Mike, *How to Box*, Gibbons Athletic Association, pp. 51-58.
[4] Gibbons, "My Eighteen Years in the Ring," *op. cit.*, "Soldiers Start Boxing Course under Gibbons," *Camp Dodger,* November 2, 1917, sports section.

From Fort Dodge, Mike reported August 12 to Camp Gordon in Georgia where he was placed in charge of a special corps organized to train all the Army's bayonet and boxing instructors before they were assigned to other camps. The men he trained at the camp comprised an all-star list of the era's greatest boxers, including Johnny Kilbane, Benny Leonard, Packey McFarland, Jimmy Barry, Tommy Gibbons, Tommy Ryan, Jack "Twin" Sullivan, Jeff Smith, Johnny Griffiths, Johnny Coulon, and Willie Ritchie.

Gibbons remained at Camp Gordon until the war's end when the school was discontinued. He was honorably discharged December 12, 1918.[5]

On January 18, 1916, Gibbons was scheduled to box Young Jake Ahearn, the European middleweight titleholder, in a ten-round bout at St. Paul. Since boxing had previously been illegal in Minnesota, it was Mike's first fight in his home state in five years. Out of frustration born of champion Al McCoy's refusal to afford Gibbons a chance at the world crown, the newly established Minnesota boxing commission permitted the promoter to advertise the bout as a world championship affair.

Excitement generated by the bout spread across the Midwest. As an added attraction, Leo Kossick was returning to ring action after a two-year layoff to box Jeff (Buff) Seidel on an undercard bout set for ten rounds.[6]

The chance to see Kossick in action again was itself a big event for Fargo fans. Just three years earlier, Leo seemed destined for greatness. After Luther McCarty's Fargo exhibition in January 1913, Kossick joined McCarty's troupe and headed east in search of fame and fortune. Serving as a sparring partner and trainer for Luther on the latter's theatrical tour, Leo left the group in Billy McCarney's home base of Philadelphia and stayed behind to try his luck against eastern boxing talent.

Since McCarney was then busy promoting McCarty's career, Kossick was placed under the management of Billy's friend, Bob McClusker. Leo won newspaper decisions in two preliminary bouts, with both performances being well received by the press. However, severe nosebleeds and influenza, both attributed to the sudden change in climate, necessitated cancellations of several important bouts. Homesick, Leo returned to Moorhead in early April after only two months in Philadelphia.[7]

Back home, Kossick regained his health and returned to the ring to win three bouts during the spring and summer months of 1913. At the time,

---

[5] Gibbons, *op. cit.* "Boxing Instructions for Soldiers" (series), *Camp Dodger,* March 15 through May 25, 1918, August 16, 1918, December 13, 1918, sports sections.

[6] "Gibbons-Ahearn Card Spiciest Event for Years in Northwest," *Fargo Courier-News,* December 1, 1915, sports section. The fight was set for December 10, but was delayed due to Gibbons' flu. "Leo Kossick Slated to Meet Buff Seidl on Next Capital City Card," *Fargo Forum,* December 31, 1915, sports section.

[7] "Kossick Is Given Great Notices in East," *Fargo Courier-News,* March 18, 1913. "Leo Kossick Is Home," *Fargo Forum,* April 7, 1913. Hurley, Hank, "Leo Kossick Has No Desire to Live over Ring Days of 1900s," *Fargo Forum,* April 28, 1935.

Jack Dempsey & Leo Kossick.

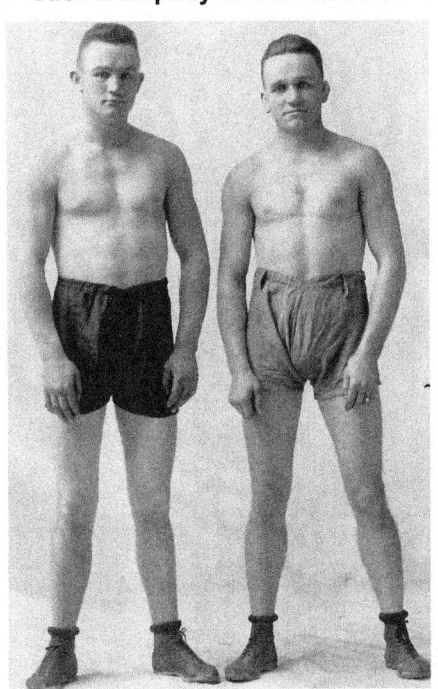

Middleweight Mike Gibbons.

Gibbons brothers, Tom & Mike.

Mike Gibbons' snarling smile.

Gibbons (No. 9) at Camp Gordon with his corps of instructors. Top (left to right): D. R. Scanlon, Billy Rodenback, Packey McFarland, Jack (Twin) Sullivan, George Blake, Tom Gibbons, Al Williams, Lankow, W. R. Williams, Tommy Ryan, Wyatt, Jeff Smith, Fred Dyer, Willie Ritchie, and Johnny Griffiths. Bottom: A. W. Wrenz, Jimmy Barry, Johnny Coulon, Mike Morrison, Johnny Kilbane, Lieutenant Albernese, Captain Brown, Colonel Getty, Captain Leslie, Gibbons, Eddie Hanlon, Charlie Leonard, Benny Leonard, Billy Armstrong, and Billy Sandow.

GOOD FIELD, NO HIT 49

Gibbons demonstrates several uses of the right hand for the boxing course he developed for the Army's World War I training program.

Gibbons counters with a left to the body.

The similarity between an uppercut in boxing and a butt strike in bayonet fighting.

Freddie Welsh, lightweight champion of Great Britain, was touring Canada and the U. S., taking on all comers in an effort to land a shot at the world title. Freddie had defeated Willie Ritchie at Vernon, California in 1911 before Ritchie won the title, and now Welsh had returned to the U. S. from his home in Wales to pursue the champion on his home turf.[8]

As a stepping stone to the title, "the Welsh Wizard" agreed to fight Kossick at Billings, Montana October 13, 1913. Leo stayed a full 12 rounds with Freddie, but according to news reports "accepted a world of short arm punishment in doing so." Even though outclassed, Leo showed great courage and was never in any danger of being knocked out.

After the fight Welsh told a writer, "Kossick ... is not quite as fast as he might be, but he has a hard punch, and he can stand punishment. Also, I like the way he trains. He keeps himself in the pink of condition all the time. In my opinion, he is one of the best little boxers in the Northwest. I have had eight fights since I started on this trip in May, and he is one of the best men I have met." In less than a year, Welsh would realize his dream and win the world's lightweight title from Ritchie by a 20-round decision.[9]

After a six-month break, Kossick returned to a Fargo ring on March 18, 1914, against Labe Safro, whom he had defeated the prior year. This time, Safro, with an eight-pound weight advantage, kayoed Leo in two rounds. Kossick, admitting he was foolish to give up so much weight, asked Labe for a rematch at the "even weight" of 140 pounds. Labe politely refused and said he would be happy to fight others at 145 pounds but "Kossick is a tougher proposition than a second-round knockout would indicate."[10]

Kossick's bad luck continued when a car struck his motorcycle in May 1914 while he was crossing the Fargo-Moorhead bridge. Thrown into a railing, he was "rendered insensible for a time besides suffering bruises on his leg and ankle." Kossick was idle until the early part of 1915 when he began to fight his way back into shape with a series of exhibitions against his stablemate Ted Childers. The bout with Buff Seidl on the Gibbons-Ahearn card was his first official fight since the accident.[11]

Over 60 fans made the trip from Fargo to St. Paul to see Gibbons stop Ahearn in one round. The bout was less than a minute old when Mike trapped "the English Bearcat" and landed a crushing right to the jaw. On the

---

[8] "The Style Was a Big Handicap, *Fargo Forum*, May 21, 1913, sports section. "Result Was a Draw," *Fargo Forum*, July 25, 1913, sports section. "Kossick Easily Defeats Schultz," *Fargo Forum*, September 24, 1913, sports section.

[9] "Kossick Stays Twelve with Welsh Champion," *Fargo Courier-News*, October 14, 1913, sports section. "Kossick Good Mans Says Welsh," *Fargo Forum*, October 15, 1913, sports section.

[10] "Kossick Out with Defy for Safro," *Fargo Courier-News*, March 20, 1914, sports section. "Safro Says Kossick Is Tough Proposition," *Fargo Forum*, March 21, 1914, sports section.

[11] "Kossick Has Battle in District Court – Purse Is for $2,000," *Courier-News*, January 12, 1916, sports section. "Boxing Match in Dilworth Tonight," *Fargo Forum*, March 4, 1915, sports section.

undercard, Kossick overcame a slow start to win his bout. Leo, obviously rusty from his lay-off, hit his stride in the seventh round and was in complete command when Seidl quit in the eighth due to an arm injury.[12]

Eighteen-year-old Jack Hurley was one of the fans at the bout. He likely also saw Gibbons' other two bouts at St. Paul in 1916 – against Jeff Smith on March 17 and Jack Dillon on November 10. Hurley years later told writer W. C. Heinz that, after he met Gibbons, Jack spent a lot of time in St. Paul watching Mike train and asking questions. "He was a nosy punk," Heinz wrote of Hurley. "He'd watch fights and lift a move here and a move there, and that's the way he started building up his library of punches."[13]

At about this same time, Hurley left Pierce Printing and took a job as a shipping packer for the Ford Motor Company's assembly plant at 505 Broadway. The plant was the company's distribution center for the Upper Midwest. It was also Fargo's largest factory, employing 300 workers.[14]

Hurley landed the job as a result of his friendship with Joe Kossick, Leo's brother, who was assistant plant manager. Jack later told the *Omaha World-Herald*'s Robert Houston it was "damned hard work." He would be there until he enlisted in the army in July 1917.[15]

The 1916 baseball season began auspiciously for Hurley as the manager of his own semi-pro team, the Fargo Cubs. According to Jack's May 9th press release, the team had practiced three weeks and been issued new uniforms. The team boasted "some of the fastest semi-pro and amateur baseball players in the city" and had "already scheduled games with some of the strongest out-of-town teams in the state and Northwest, including Wahpeton, Buffalo, Sabin, Wheatland, Barnesville and others." The release ended: "… other out-of-town teams wishing games should communicate with Mgr. Jack Hurley, care Ford Motor Co., Fargo, N. D."[16]

By June 23, Hurley had attracted enough attention to earn a tryout with the Fargo-Moorhead Graingrowers, the team for which Jack had been batboy earlier. Before leaving, he arranged for the Cubs to join forces with another semi-pro team, the Fargo Red Sox. The new team retained the "Cubs" name, but leadership was delegated to Red Sox manager Jack Williams, Hurley's former street-corner partner selling the Courier-News.[17]

---

[12] "Sixty Fargo-Moorhead Fans to See Big Battle Tonight," *Fargo Forum*, January 18, 1916, sports section. "English Bearcat Put to Sleep by Mike Gibbons in First Round at St. Paul," *Fargo Forum*, January 19, 1916, sports section.

[13] Hurley, Jack, "Shadow Boxing," *Fargo Forum*, March 4, 1934, sports section. Heinz, W. C., "The Man Who Makes Fighters," *Esquire Magazine*, May 1952, p. 100.

[14] "Fargo Forum Biography Questionnaire," filled out by Jack Hurley on May 12, 1951. "Ford Motor Company to Build Big Local Plant," *Courier-News*, July 16, 1914, p. 1.

[15] Hurley, *op. cit.*, May 25, 1930, sports section. Houston, Robert, "Hurley: One of Boxing's Great Figures," *Omaha World-Herald Sunday Magazine*, January 13, 1952, p. 10-G.

[16] "Fargo Cubs Are Lined Up for the Year," *Fargo Forum*, May 9, 1916, sports section.

[17] "Fargo Cubs and Red Sox Join Forces," *Fargo Forum*, June 23, 1916, sports section.

Regrettably, Jack's tryout was short-lived. A review of both Fargo papers fails to uncover his name in a single Graingrower box score. By July 15, he was back with the Cubs, but only as a left fielder, not as manager. The season ended September 25, with Hurley going one for four at the plate and stealing a base, as the Cubs lost to cross-town rival, the Fargo Athletics, 3 to 2. For Jack, it was the end of an up-and-down summer, and he no doubt was hoping for better luck during the coming winter boxing campaign.[18]

The start of the 1916-'17 boxing season marked a shift for Jack from the role of aspiring pugilist to rookie boxing manager. In later years, he would recall that Fritz Schroeder was the first boxer he ever managed. In a technical sense, this was true. In practice, however, his first try at managing was more like sharing an adventure with a pal than entering into an arm's-length business arrangement. Their relationship was a natural outgrowth of two close buddies sharing similar interests, but possessing diverse talents.[19]

Of the two, Fritz was undoubtedly the better athlete. Jack, on the other hand, had gifts of analysis, communication, and promotion. Just as they had pooled their talents to best advantage playing baseball, it was only natural they would do the same in boxing. When Fritz began boxing for money, he asked Jack to advise and train him inside the ring and to tend to the business details with the promoters outside.

In a later interview, Hurley claimed Schroeder had about nine pro fights, at least two of which were in Fargo. The only Schroeder match reported in the Fargo press took place on January 19, 1917, on a card at the Fargo Auditorium featuring a six-round exhibition between Mike Gibbons and his brother Tommy. In a preliminary bout, Fritz fought a four-round draw with veteran Fargo welterweight Submarine Smith.[20]

In his syndicated newspaper column years later, Hurley recalled that Schroeder also met Charlie Jennings at the Elks Hall in an unreported fight for members only. It is likely this bout or others like it happened sometime before Jack's 19th birthday on December 9, 1916, since on several occasions he insisted he was only 18 when he managed his first pro boxer.[21]

Although most of Fritz's other fights probably occurred in neighboring towns, Hurley and his charge were serious enough to take a trip to New York looking for action. Whatever else happened, however, the journey was more memorable as a learning experience than a triumph in fisticuffs.

---

[18] "Fargo Cubs-Moorhead Red Men Contest Big Attraction Tomorrow," *Fargo Forum*, July 15, 1916, sports section. "Boardman Wins Pitching Duel," *Fargo Courier-News*, September 25, 1916, sports section. Although Hurley did not appear in any local box scores for the Northern League team, he apparently made the roster for a short time because the *Forum*'s July 15th article refers to him as "formerly with the Fargo-Moorhead leaguers." Out-of-town box scores generally were not reported in the Fargo papers.
[19] Zimmerman, Paul, "Just Country Boy, Claims Jack Hurley," *Los Angeles Times*, June 29, 1958, sports section.
[20] "Boxing Carnival a Success," *Fargo Forum*, January 20, 1917, sports section.
[21] Hurley, "Ring Rations," *Fargo Forum*, May 17, 1931, sports section.

A rare smile from Jack (center) with friends, circumstances unknown.

Jack in his Fargo Cub baseball uniform with brother Hank, 1917.

Jack squares around to bunt.

Again, the only surviving details about their tour come from an apocryphal story Jack wrote for his syndicated column in the 1930s.

Hurley recalled that, during a stopover in Chicago, he jumped off the train and bought a new blue suit at clothing shop near the railway station. He was pleased with his purchase and thought it looked "pretty snappy," especially as the price had been very reasonable. The only problem was that by the time he returned to Fargo the suit had faded to such a washed-out purple people mistook him for a mail carrier.

In New York, a sleazy looking operator beckoned from a doorway and showed them a book featuring pictures of public figures and local monuments. The vendor took a piece of transparent glass and held it over the pictures, and Grant's tomb was transformed into a scantily clad bathing girl. At four bits, Jack figured he had a bargain, so he agreed to the sale.

Rushing to his room, Hurley applied the glass to the pictures and found that while the collection included images of President Wilson and General Pershing, the glass produced no bathing beauties. Other bargains included the purchase of a wrist-watch with no inner workings for $1 and a red umbrella for $1.50 that leaked color and ruined another suit when it rained.

The travelers returned to Fargo just before the start of the 1917 baseball season. Even before the opening game, however, there was talk the season might have to be cut short. In February, German submarines had initiated a series of attacks on American merchant ships which threatened to bring the U. S. into a war in Europe which had raged since 1914. In response, President Woodrow Wilson cut off diplomatic relations with Germany and issued an edict arming merchant ships with naval personnel and equipment.

It was under this cloud of uncertainty that Hurley again took the field with the Fargo Cubs. Newspaper reports of the team's games were intermittent and short on detail for the most part, but Hurley is listed as the starting second baseman for an April 28th pre-season exhibition game against the Northern League's Fargo-Moorhead Graingrowers. However, the game was postponed twice due to heavy rains and wasn't rescheduled.[22]

The Cubs played most of their games in towns like Sabin, Baker, Pelican Rapids, Wahpeton, and Barnesville. Of the results reported, the Cubs won four and lost one in an abbreviated season. On July 9, the Cubs posted an 18-5 win against Harwood in their last game of the year. By then, war against Germany had been declared, and most of the players already had registered for the military draft scheduled on July 20.[23]

---

[22] "Fargo-Moorhead Meets Cubs in Practice Game," *Fargo Courier-News*, April 29, 1917, sports section. "Rain Prevents Practice Game for Local Nine," *Fargo Courier-News*, April 30, 1917, sports section. "Practice Game with Fargo Cubs Is Called Off," *Fargo Courier-News*, May 4, 1917, sports section.

[23] "Cubs Beat Sabin," *Fargo Forum*, May 7, 1917, sports section. "Cubs Swamp Baker Line," *Fargo Forum*, May 14, 1917, sports section. "Cubs to Wahpeton," *Fargo Forum*, May 30, 1917, sports section. "Fargo Cubs Lose 5-1 to Pelican Rapids," *Fargo Forum*, June

The period between the fall of 1915 and the summer of 1917 brought an increasing sense of self-awareness to Jack Hurley. Although his tryout with the Graingrowers was unsuccessful, he was not ready to give up on his dream to play baseball. The Graingrower players were all older than Jack, and he still hoped he might improve enough to join their ranks. In addition, he had proven his mettle as a team organizer and publicist, and the contacts he had made in the Fargo sports community might someday come in handy.

On the boxing front, even though Hurley's weak physique forced him to surrender forever any notion of becoming a boxer, his field trips to see Mike Gibbons in St. Paul increased his own boxing knowledge and gave him confidence to teach what he had learned to those of his friends who still held fistic dreams. Jack's time on the road with Fritz Schroeder gave him a taste for travel and further whetted his appetite to give managing a try.

Despite his desire to explore these options further, world events were evolving so rapidly that he soon would be setting aside his personal aspirations to join over two million other Americans on an expedition far bolder than the one from which he had just returned. In six months' time, Jack would find himself being sent across the Atlantic Ocean as a soldier on a passenger ship with 13,500 others to fight the German army on the Western Front. And there would be nothing quiet about it.

25, 1917, sports section. "Fargo Cubs Defeat Harwood 18 to 5," *Fargo Forum,* July 10, 1917, sports section.

CHAPTER 4

PRIVATE HURLEY COMES LIMPING HOME

It was 1917, the last time I crossed the Atlantic – and I didn't do it because I wanted to, either. Ocean? I'd never seen an ocean, and I didn't much care to. But there we were, thousands of us, in New York, and they took us to the dock and showed us this transport. Looked as big as Coulee Dam, and I guess it pretty near was at that. Had been called the Vaterland, when the Germans had her. Then we got her, and she became the Leviathan.

So they herd us aboard, and pretty soon they start handing out assignments. I draw a dandy. They take me away down into the guts of the ship some place, and they show me this watertight door, and beyond the watertight door is a compartment where maybe 300 or 400 men are supposed to sleep. "Hurley," they tell me, "you mount guard here. Anything happens to this ship on your watch, you got to see those 400 men get out through this door; then, when the last one's out, you close it."

"Anything happens to this ship," they tell me. What can happen to this ship? Everything can happen. What do I know? I'm on deck the first day out, talkin' to a sailor. "How come we got no escort?" I ask him. "Huh – we don't need no escort," he tells me. "How come?" I say. "Because," he says, "we're so fast, no escort can keep up with us." "But, how about submarines?" I ask. "Huh," he says again. "Don't worry about submarines. The best gunner in the United States Navy, we got him aboard the Leviathan."

"The best gunner," he tells me. So how do I know the best gunner in the United States Navy is gonna be on watch when a submarine picks us up? How do I know the best gunner in the United States Navy can even hit one of these submarines? I'm a green punk, and the first night I go on guard by that watertight door, I'm scared.

The only light is a little blue light over the door. It don't give enough light to see anything. And all the time, deep inside me, I'm scared, and I don't dare let anyone know it, for fear they'll ride me the rest of the way. But I know what I'll do if anything happens to the ship. I'll holler through that watertight door, "Last guy out, close this door, and then I'll beat it up on deck. So, what happens? I don't sleep for the five days and five nights it takes to cross the ocean, and I don't sleep for the five days and five nights it takes us to come home later on. Man, that ocean – you can have it.[1]

– Jack Hurley

****

---

[1] Boni, Bill, "Writing Out Loud," *Spokesman-Review*, November 7, 1952, p. 14.

As was the case for most young adult American males, the life of Jack Hurley was taken out of its owner's control on April 6, 1917, when President Woodrow Wilson requested that the United States Congress declare war against Germany. By the time the U. S. entered World War I, the Allied Powers, led by France, Russia, Italy, and the British Empire, already had been battling against the Central Powers of Austria-Hungary, Germany, Bulgaria, and the Ottoman Empire for almost three years.

Initially in 1914, Germany quickly advanced deep into France, coming within 40 miles of Paris. At the same time, Russia mounted an offensive on the Eastern Front and diverted German forces intended for use in France to the east. The Central Powers were forced to fight the war on two fronts. As a consequence, the Allied Powers successfully halted the German advance east of Paris in September 1914 at the First Battle of the Marne.

The lull resulting from the diversion of German troops to the east gave each side time to dig a web of ditches along the Western Front. For 2-1/2 years, both sides relied upon this vast tangle of trench work to serve as an impenetrable defense against the other. The introduction of barbed wire, hand grenades, artillery, poison gas, and machine guns made crossing open ground between trenches a nightmare. Neither side was able to gain any tactical or strategic advantage even though casualties were huge.

The specter of a protracted, industrialized war with no end in sight took its toll. Senseless attempts at frontal assaults on entrenched German troops proved costly to Great Britain and France, both on the battlefield and politically at home. In one day, at the Battle of Somme in 1916, the British suffered 57,470 casualties and 19,420 dead. By the end of the battle, the French army, which had borne the brunt of the German attack for two years, was on the brink of collapse.

From 1915 to 1917, the Allied Powers incurred far more casualties than the Germans. Troop morale was at low ebb in 1917. As news of the Russian Revolution spread along the battlefield, sympathetic red flags were raised in the allied encampments. French troops openly revolted against their officers' orders to "go over the top" into the "no man's land" between the trenches – to meet certain death. At the peak of the mutiny, 40,000 French soldiers rebelled against their officers.

A British naval blockade was effective in keeping ships from reaching German ports. The lack of provisions virtually halted Germany's offensive war effort and devastated its economy, resulting in famine and starvation.

As a response to the British blockade, Germany instituted a policy of "unrestricted submarine warfare" in January 1917. This approach was an attempt to break the blockade and cut the supply lines between the United States and Great Britain. The German leaders realized that the U. S. would soon enter the war. Germany was wagering it could re-open its own supply lines and strangle those of Great Britain before the United States could train and transport a large army to cross the Atlantic Ocean.

Although 128 Americans lost their lives when a German submarine attacked the British passenger liner Lusitania May 7, 1915, negotiations between the United States and Germany averted U. S. entry into the war.

President Wilson maintained diplomatic relations with Germany until February 1917. Up until then he had hoped to stay out of war. Indeed, Wilson felt ill at ease in the presence of military men and had avoided developing specific mobilization and strategic plans prior to the declaration of war. He believed contingency planning tended to compromise the objectivity of decision-makers and predispose them to war. Consequently, the U. S. was as unprepared for war in 1917 as at any time in its history.[2]

Early in 1917, Germany, as it had warned, resumed its submarine attacks and sank three American merchant ships. On April 6, the U. S. House of Representatives approved the president's war resolution, 373-50, and the Senate followed suit, 82-6. The nation's late entry into the war and the precarious condition of the Allied Powers in Europe created a sense of urgency throughout the country. This eagerness to help its European allies was nullified, temporarily, by the by the nation's lack of readiness.

It was the world's first mass, industrialized conflict. Never had humanity encountered a war which consumed human and material resources at such a rapid and voracious rate. The United States had little idea how to train, arm, and equip the millions of men needed to prosecute such a war. The country lacked manufacturing facilities to produce the machine guns, armaments, and heavy artillery required at the Western Front.

After war was declared, the U. S. sent military planners to Britain and France to engage in a crash course on the logistics of trench warfare. Under the National Defense and Selective Service Acts, the War Department created a large infantry. By war's end, four million Americans had served, with two million sent overseas. Of these, 13 percent joined as volunteers, ten percent as National Guard enlistees, and 77 percent as draftees.[3]

The first draft under the Selective Service Act occurred July 20. All males between 21 and 30 were required to register in advance. Men under 21 and over 30 were not subject to this draft. The act also provided that as of August 5, "all members of the National Guard" would be automatically "draft(ed) into the military service of the United States."

---

[2] Cooper, Jerry, *Citizens As Soldiers, A History of the North Dakota National Guard*, (The North Dakota Institute for Regional Studies, North Dakota State University, Fargo), p. 184. Cooper's book has been an invaluable aid to the author in providing information about the motivations of the military in general and about the various reincarnations and troop movements of Fargo's Company B in particular. All interviews with Wesley Johnson, Boyd Cormany, the 41st Division War Diary, as well as the any unattributed quotes which appear in this chapter have come from Cooper's book.

[3] Cooper, pp. 184-5.

To be eligible to enter the Army as a unit, a National Guard company was required to recruit enough enlistees to reach full company strength of 150 men before the August 5th cut-off. Any company short of the minimum on that date would have to find additional recruits from the pool of men under 21 and over 30 or risk not being drafted as a unit.[4]

Company B of the First Regiment, North Dakota National Guard, representing Fargo, was one of the units which found itself in the unenviable position of being at less than full strength. As of July 20, the company was still 50 recruits short of the minimum.

In an interview with the *Fargo Forum*, recruiting officer Captain Reginald Colley emphasized that enlisting in Company B would allow local volunteers the opportunity to serve alongside their friends and townsmen "instead of waiting for [another round of] the draft which will place them in ranks where they are strangers."[5]

With the help of intense publicity campaigns by Fargo's two newspapers and the support of its business community, Company B was able to muster enrollment of 156 recruits, just over war strength, by the end of July. Among those who enlisted prior to the August 5th deadline was 19-year-old Jack Hurley. Unlike those drafted on July 20, he was still two years under the draft age and was therefore a true volunteer. Years later, Jack would say he enlisted because "he was afraid he would miss something."[6]

On August 5, the automatic drafting of all members of the National Guard into the United States military was duly implemented. Company B

---

[4] Cooper, pp. 185, 192-3.

[5] Cooper, p. 193.

[6] Hollis, John, "The Best of Colorful Jack Hurley," *Houston Post*, January 6, 1965, sports section. "32 Recruits from Co. B Bring List Close to Point Required by U. S.," *Fargo Forum*, July 25, 1917, p. 1. Hurley's actual enlistment date was July 23, 1917.

As part of the campaign to swell the ranks of Company B, Leo Kossick fought in a benefit six-round exhibition bout on June 11 against his stablemate Ted Childers. The crowd was entertained prior to the bout by the regulars of "Company B (who) did a bit of bally-ho work in front of the auditorium in the way of drills." Over $250 was raised for the company's permanent improvement fund.

The exhibition proved to be Kossick's swan song as a boxing contestant. Since his match with Buff Seidl in St. Paul, Leo's pro career had been winding down. Except for a few exhibitions, he had engaged in only two fights in the preceding year and a half, both against Roy Coquil of Cody, Wyoming, one a ten- round draw at Billings, Montana and the other an eight round decision win in Jamestown, North Dakota. After World War I, Kossick remained active as a referee until the 1920s during which he officated at some of Billy Petrolle's most important bouts in Fargo. In the 1930s he served as matchmaker for amateur boxing cards sponsored by the Fargo Elks club. He also took a short fling at promoting pro wrestling and boxing at Fargo in 1935. Leo became a community leader in Moorhead. He operated a poolroom and confectionary shop in Moorhead for years. He was a founding member of the Moorhead Rotary Club in 1921. As a merchant, he generously sponsored sports teams and other events long after his own athletic career ended.

of the First Infantry Regiment, North Dakota National Guard, and Private Jack C. Hurley were in the army now.

The ability of researchers to delve into the personal history of any particular American soldier's participation in World War I became especially difficult after 1973 when a fire at the National Personnel Records Center in a St. Louis suburb destroyed almost all the army records for the period. Hurley himself left no diary or journal, and any letters he may have written were lost in the mail or else not preserved by the family.

Fortunately, articles in the *Forum* and surviving letters and journals from a handful of soldiers who served in the same regiment as Hurley preserve a picture of what life as a National Guard soldier was like. Entries by Major James Hanley and Privates Wesley Johnson and Boyd Cormany describe their experiences going overseas. Even more helpful is a diary kept by Private Frank Last, whose assignments after training camp were nearly identical to those of Jack, including the time he spent in the trenches.

According to the *Forum*, the men of Company B reported to the National Guard Armory in the basement of the Fargo Auditorium immediately after enlistment. The War Department had planned to send all Guard regiments to training camps at warmer locations in the southern United States in early August. Unfortunately, the department's preparations for outfitting the camps fell woefully behind schedule. Instead, fully 2-1/2 months passed before Company B received orders to proceed to camp where they would connect with the First Infantry Regiment's other North Dakota companies.

Initially, recruits accepted the life of waiting in a crowded basement with good humor. The *Forum* reported on July 25, they "are taking kindly to the 'mess' being served at the armory, declaring that the food is plentiful and well prepared. 'We had young chicken this morning,' one of the privates said today in telling of the good 'grub,' 'only it was in the form of eggs.'"[7]

By August 10, however, "the monotony of constant drill with none of the excitement of camp life [was] beginning to tell on the morale of the soldiers." Other than light drills, the men did nothing to advance their combat skill during the hiatus. Wesley Johnson recalled that during the delay, "we had a few guards, a few inspections, light drill during which poker occupied a good part, and a few maneuvers." The wait was especially trying because, while many had families in walking distance, they were unable to live or work at home.

In addition to time wasted, all units in the regiment experienced a lack of equipment. One officer's report on mobilization day concluded, "This Company short knives, forks, spoons, meat cans, haversacks, canteens, cartridge belts, entrenching tools, cook stove and utensils, also tents and rifles, bayonets and bayonet scabbards, in fact all ordnance."

---

[7] Cooper, pp. 184-186, 192-195. (Title unavailable), *Fargo Forum*, July 25, 1917, p. 1.

Hurley with his sister, Abigail, shortly after he enlisted.

New recruit awaiting his orders.

Private First Class Jack C. Hurley, Company B, 164th Infantry.

The problem was that, while the Army had secured the men, it was not ready for them. The nation's sudden declaration of war, coupled with its lack of readiness, gave rise to a "hurry up and wait" syndrome which reverberated throughout the military system. As a result, while the War Department strove to do everything at once – implement the draft, build camps, purchase supplies, organize its training programs, and countless other things – new enlistees everywhere, such as those in Company B, had nothing to do but wait.[8]

Orders for the First Infantry Regiment to report to the divisional training camp at Camp Greene, Charlotte, North Carolina finally came through on September 19, 1917. On the morning of September 29, Private Hurley and the rest of Company B joined a parade arranged by the Fargo Rotary Club and marched through downtown Fargo from the armory at the corner of Broadway and First Avenue South to the Great Northern depot. Amid enthusiastic fanfare, the men boarded a special train bound for Charlotte.[9]

At Camp Greene, they remained together for the time being, but under the War Department's new re-organization plan individual companies such as Company B were eliminated, and the entire First Infantry Regiment was rechristened as the 164th Infantry Battalion of the Army's 41st Division.

The War Department had originally planned for each division to spend at least four months in basic training before sending troops to Europe. This plan was jettisoned as the situation in France became desperate and the need for America's presence there escalated.

Instead of four months, the division remained at Camp Greene a month and a half. Although officially credited with nine days' target practice, Johnson wrote that "each man only shot two hours during the entire time on the rifle range." Equipment shortages, including machine guns and mortars, hindered drills, as did a lack of uniforms. In addition, the division's diary noted that training was upset by "lack of adequate space for drilling (and) by time lost in readjusting the old units to the new organization."

On November 16, the 164th Infantry Battalion departed by train to Camp Mills, Long Island, New York. Before leaving, Private Hurley and his fellow soldiers were treated to a dance at the Selwyn Hotel in Charlottesville. On the eve of their departure, the 164th Infantry football team challenged and defeated the regulars of the 39th Infantry.

Conditions at Camp Mills were miserable. "It was a hell hole," Boyd Cormany wrote, "and the weather was really cold." The tents were rotting and full of holes. To warm themselves, the soldiers tore down derelict buildings and used the wood as fuel for "those miserable little camp stoves

---

[8] Cooper, pp. 194-195. "New Uniforms Arrive for Men of Company B." *Fargo Courier-News*, August 10, 1917, p. 2.

[9] Cooper, pp. 199-201. Moline, Melva, *The Forum First Hundred Years*, (Fargo Forum, 1978), p. 105.

– one to a tent." Twelve to 16 men lived in eight-man tents. Latrines "were merely burlap sides hung on wood poles."

Due to cold weather, "we drilled spasmodically," Johnson remembered, adding that his company awoke one morning "to find a flood of water over all our section of the camp. That meant that all of our clothes were soaked or had floated away." During this same period, the 41st Division's diary recorded: "The division was under canvas at this camp and suffered from the severe cold weather, all water pipes being frozen at times."

On December 6, the 41st Division was moved to Camp Merritt in Tenafly, New Jersey, where it spent a few days in relative comfort at a wooden barracks, awaiting transport. On December 15, Hurley and his mates boarded the SS Leviathan in Hoboken, New Jersey, for the voyage to Great Britain. They were being sent across the Atlantic Ocean to face one of the greatest military machines in history without yet receiving any real combat training. Jack had just marked his 20th birthday six days earlier.[10]

The Leviathan was a giant German steamship, formerly the Vaterland, which the United States seized upon entering the war in April. First launched as a passenger liner on the Hamburg-America Line in 1913, the ship had been docked in Hoboken since July 1914 when it had been unable to return to Germany because of Britain's domination of the seas. Onboard for the December 1917 crossing, which was the vessel's first voyage under American colors, were 13,000 passengers, including 500 Red Cross nurses.

It was a tense journey. Years later, Jack told columnist Emmett Watson that he was on pins and needles the entire time as a result of his lifelong fear of the water. He also related the situation of the Allied Powers was so urgent that the Leviathan sailed before a convoy could be arranged to protect it from submarine attack. At the time, Jack told Watson, the likelihood of a successful crossing was thought to be such a long shot that "Wall Street was quoting 50 to 1 against safe passage."

Hurley recalled he was assigned special duty on the trip. "They put me to guarding a water-tight compartment," he said to Watson. "Four days and four nights I am down in the bowels of that vessel, waiting for a torpedo to hit. If they'd known how scared I was they'd have given me the Congressional Medal or maybe the Croix de Guerre."[11]

Despite Jack's fears, the ship reached port safely at Liverpool, England on Christmas Eve. The following day, Private Hurley and his fellow soldiers traveled by train to Camp Winnall-Down at Winchester where they

---

[10] Cooper, pp. 210-203.

[11] Watson, Emmett, "England Still Is an Island." *Seattle Post-Intelligencer*, November 2, 1951, sports section. The Congressional Medal of Honor is a military decoration which the United States bestows on its military heroes. Likewise, the Croix de Guerre was a medal which France bestowed on Allied war heroes.

recuperated and were fed a Christmas dinner of English rations, which Private Frank Last mentioned in his diary as "not very good."[12]

To Johnson, Liverpool was a "dismal port." Camp Winnall-Down was cold and wet, and many of Johnson's fellow soldiers came down with measles and scarlet fever. Boyd Cormany felt that the British troops "had no use for us" and "we were damned glad to leave Merry Old England." Major James Hanley agreed with Last that "the food was poor," and added that most of the British officers were unpleasant. "As a rule, I did not like the English officers very much," Hanley diaried. "They seem cads."

From England, the next move for the 41st Division was to cross the English Channel into France. Private Hurley was among the men in the first of five detachments to make the crossing. Jack's group left Southampton, England on the evening of December 31 and arrived at Le Havre, France, on New Year's Day. Cormany recalled the trip was made in "a cattle boat" which "smelled like a pig pen." For food, the men were given coffee and a sandwich of cold, fat mutton to be eaten on the trip.[13]

Frank Last, who also was in the first detachment with Hurley, described the crossing in his diary. "The channel was very rough and the ship was tossed about like a cork," noted Last. "We were all seasick. The boat was very crowded and there wasn't standing or sitting room and there were no pathways either, as they were filled with soldiers who were lying over seasick. Naturally, those who happened to be in back of several others didn't 'make the railing' and quarters were anything but pleasant."[14]

The soldiers, tired and sick, landed in France well before dawn's early light New Year's morning, but were not allowed to disembark until 6:30 a.m. They received two rations of English hardtack and a piece of cheese for breakfast before marching through the town of Le Havre to camp.

The sight of doughboys in France was still very much a novelty in the winter of 1918. Except for a relatively small number of career regulars in the First Division who were sent over earlier in 1917, the soldiers of the 41st Division were the first American infantrymen to set foot in Europe. In contrast to their cool reception at Liverpool, the Americans were greeted warmly by the French people. While hiking through Le Havre, they encountered an old man and woman who hoisted the American flag as they

---

[12] Last, Frank (edited by Rick Riehl), "My War Diary," Entry One, webpage: fylde.demon.co.uk/riehl.htm,. Last's diary is a fascinating account especially valuable in tracing Hurley's movements and experiences. Last also was in the army by virtue of his service with the North Dakota National Guard. He served in the same Infantry battalions and performed the same duties as Hurley until Jack was disabled in late February or early March 1918. The sights, sounds, and smells Last describes are virtually the same as those which Jack experienced from about October 1, 1917, until he was disabled.

[13] Cooper, p. 204. Unpublished *Fargo Forum Biography Questionnaire* filled out by Jack Hurley on May 12, 1951. Hurley gives the date of his arrival in France as "Dec. 31, '17."

[14] Last, Entry One.

Troop ship S. S. Leviathan on which Hurley voyaged to Europe during World War I.

Doughboys on the Leviathan awaiting the opportunity to disembark.

passed. The couple was so excited they had trouble accomplishing this simple task but, when they finally succeeded, the passing troops raised a spontaneous cheer that lasted for some minutes. The two raised the French flag beside the American flag and the marching soldiers cheered again.

Although the language difference prevented direct communication, the couple's obvious pleasure made the soldiers feel better. After walking for several hours in the fresh air, everyone felt pretty good until they arrived at camp just before lunchtime. The men were told they were not expected and that there would be no rations available until the next day. Private Last recalled the soldiers were assigned the usual eight men to a tent, but that the tents were empty with neither ground covering nor cots with them.[15]

Finally at 10 p.m., the hungry doughboys received some food, but it was burned so badly most couldn't eat it. They were issued two blankets and told to sleep on the ground. The weather was cold; there was no fuel for fire, and it rained all night. Few slept well. For breakfast, they ate leftovers from dinner and a few hardtack biscuits and pieces of cheese.

The next day at noon, Hurley and his comrades were loaded onto "40 and 8" boxcars and sent off to La Courtine, a town near the Western Front. The trip lasted three days, with the men subsisting on rations of canned meat and hardtack. Most of the cars had holes in the floor where horses had kicked the boards loose. The air was fresh because the boxcars had missing doors which let in the frigid outside. The men were desperately cold the entire trip, partly because they were packed so tightly they had no room to move about and stay warm.[16]

The troops arrived at La Courtine on the night of Saturday, January 5. They were quartered in stone barracks which at one time housed Napoleon's army. For the next two days, they were able to rest and clean up a bit, even finding time to sightsee and buy a few trinkets.

On Tuesday, the men learned the 164th Infantry Battalion, 41st Division was being phased out, and they were leaving the next day to join the First Division regulars already at the front. They also learned that their officers were not being transferred with them.[17]

These orders signaled a definite change. The American Expeditionary Force (AEF) hierarchy originally intended to keep all divisions intact. This plan called for putting each division through a four-month instruction cycle. The cycle would have alternated training in a rear area with short intervals of service at the front alongside veteran French troops. The

---

[15] Last, Entry Two.
[16] Last, *op. cit.* The boxcars were dubbed "40 and 8s" because while they originally had been designed to haul eight horses, for the war effort they were used to haul 40 men from Le Havre to the Western Front.
[17] Last, Entry Two. The American Expeditionary Forces (AEF) was the official name and acronym bestowed upon the American troops serving in Europe during World War I.

Troops disembarking from the Leviathan at the landing stage in Liverpool. The ship's stacks are seen in the distance to the left.

The "40 and eight" cattle cars, originally designed to hold 8 horses, but used to transport 40 U. S. troops to the Western Front in France.

division would then have been re-united behind the front lines to conduct field maneuvers before assuming responsibility for a sector by itself.

The 41st Division never even launched this program. The AEF's General Headquarters failed to consider the First Division's needs resulting from attrition. As a result, instead of being groomed to hold a sector at the front on its own, the soldiers of the 41st were sent in as replacements for the First Division, which had been in France since June 1917 and had lost troops to accidents, sickness, and combat. As his part in the new plan, Hurley was assigned to Company D, 18th Infantry Battalion, First Division.[18]

On Wednesday January 9, 1918, the new contingents of the First Division bade farewell to their hometown officers, jumped into the same 40 and 8 boxcars which had brought them to La Courtine, and headed for Heudicourt, a town in the St. Mihiel sector of France. Again, they subsisted on rations of hardtack and canned meat while they huddled together to stay warm in the boxcars. Two days later, they arrived at Heudicourt, about 70 kilometers (43 miles) southwest of the France-Belgium border.[19]

There followed a short layover which would have a lasting impact not only on Private Hurley the soldier, but also on Hurley, civilian boxing manager and trainer. It was during these three days that Jack and his fellow troops received their first serious combat training. From January 12 to 14, the 18th Infantry drilled in close order in a wood on the side of a little hill facing the German army, dug in five kilometers (3.1 miles) away.[20]

Hurley's instructor was a British Sergeant Major named Cassidy, who taught the 18th Infantry how to use bayonets. Cassidy's skill was a revelation. "He was a miserable S.O.B., but he knew his business," Jack told W. C. Heinz later. "He would stand there unarmed, with his hands down at his sides, and he'd say: 'Stick me.' You'd have your rifle with the bayonet fixed and you'd make a lunge at him and you'd miss. Maybe the next time your rifle would go flying up in the air, or you'd get the butt of it under the chin.

"I used to go and see this guy at night," Jack added. "His stuff fascinated me, so one night I said to him, 'This puts me in mind of boxing.' He said, 'The bayonet manual was taken from boxing. If you're standing in the on-guard position and I take the rifle out of your hands, you're standing like a boxer. Now I put the rifle back in your hands and at the command of long point you make a left jab. Now you move your opponent out of position and you come up to hit him with the butt. Isn't that the right uppercut?'"

The aspect of Cassidy's craft which impressed Hurley most, however, was footwork. The sergeant would take hold of his rifle in a classic bayonet

---

[18] Cooper, pp. 205-206. Heinz, W. C., "The Man Who Makes Fighters," *Esquire Magazine*, May 1952, p. 100.
[19] Last, *op. cit.*
[20] Cooper, p. 207. Last, *op cit.*

stance, and by shuffling his feet just a few inches either way, would avoid the forward thrusts of anyone who tried to strike him. Responding to Jack's inquiries, Cassidy agreed the same footwork would work in boxing. "If a boxer would master this shuffling style," he said, "he'd save thousands of steps. He'd be just as safe as I am, and he'd save all those fancy steps."[21]

Ironically, at virtually the same time Hurley was learning about the relationship of boxing to bayonet fighting in Northern France, Mike Gibbons was making the same discovery at Camp Dodge in Iowa. Even though Gibbons' boxing lessons before the war had prepared Jack to see these similarities, the uses to which they would put their new insights would in effect be reverse-mirror images. For even as Mike was using his knowledge of boxing to teach soldiers how to use a bayonet, Jack was making plans to use his knowledge of bayonet fighting to teach his boxers.

When he returned to civilian life, Hurley would master the art of teaching boxing based on the bayonet manual. The "shuffling style," with hands held low and body crouched slightly forward, would become a trademark of all his fighters. Indeed, after the success of Billy Petrolle in the 1930s, the words "Hurley style" would become a common phrase in the sport's lexicon to describe Jack's particular approach to boxing.

On Tuesday morning January 15, the newest members of the 18th Infantry left Heudicourt to join their new battalion. The regular soldiers in the First Division had been fighting in the trenches alongside their French counterparts for six months, but they had not yet been assigned their own area to defend along the Western Front. Their North Dakota replacements were arriving just soon enough to join the division as it departed for the Toul sector to guard its own section of trenches for the first time.

The Allied Powers had learned that the Germans were preparing to carry out a massive offensive in hopes of ending the war before the bulk of the American forces arrived. In response, the French, who were still in overall charge of tactics, were adopting a new defensive strategy. Instead of placing the bulk of their forces in trenches close to the enemy, they decided to add further rows of trenches behind the battle line so the Germans couldn't simply punch through without encountering further resistance.

Although the British and the Germans had been using this type of defense for a while, it was the first time France had implemented the system. The change caused major planning problems for First Division officers since it came when they were still in the midst of establishing basic systems in anticipation of overseeing their first sector. Any arrangements to teach the new replacements last-minute details about trench warfare prior to their deployment were put on hold because all soldiers not actually guarding the front were put to work digging the new rows of trenches.

---

[21] Heinz, pp. 100-103.

The 18th Infantry was one of the battalions chosen to occupy the trenches as the First Division assumed control over the Toul sector for the first time on January 18, 1918. According to prior procedure, the rotation called for each soldier to serve eight or nine days in the trenches and then another eight or nine days on reserve while men from other units took their places. Hurley, as a new arrival, likely was held back a few days to dig the new system of fall-back trenches before taking his first turn on the front line.

The First Division guarded the Toul sector for two months until it was relieved in March by the Second Infantry Brigade. Although no major battles occurred during the period, both the Germans and the Americans pulled off raids resulting in casualties to each side. Other hostile actions included artillery bombardments and gas attacks. Even during quiet times, however, sniper attacks and random shellfire remained constant threats.

The 18th Infantry's most significant action during the period was defending against a dawn attack brought by 220 German soldiers at Bois de Remieres on March 1, 1918. Major George C. Marshall, then acting chief of staff for the First Division, was stirred to write afterward that the U. S. troops "fought beautifully and viciously, and covered themselves with glory," and that the Germans "were badly cut up."

Though little more than a skirmish, the event was noteworthy as the first hostile action by the Germans against an American battalion in the war. President Georges Clemenceau of France himself thought it was important enough to make a trip to division headquarters at the front to pin the Croix de Guerre on the men who distinguished themselves in battle.[22]

Whether or not Private Hurley participated in this attack, life for an infantryman in the middle of winter was at best uncomfortable, and at worst dangerous. Disease from rat, lice, nit, beetle, and even frog infestation was commonplace. Again, the diary of Frank Last, who like Jack was with the 18th Infantry in the Toul sector, offers a graphic image of the subtle challenges which even off-duty time at the front presented.

"I had not been accustomed to having rats crawl over me when I was asleep," Last wrote, "[but] I saw a great many of them. They were quite tame and came close to me ... [and] were a lot larger than the ordinary rat that we have in this country, also a lot darker and their fur longer. They looked very much like our muskrats. Whenever I got a chance to sleep or lie down in the night after this, I often felt rats walking across my body. I have even felt them on my face. I have laid almost rigid when they were on me."[23]

---

[22] Last, Entries Two and Four. Horton, Blaine A., "A Most Efficient Officer In Every Respect – George C. Marshall in World War I (1916-1919)," Shepherd College, Winner of the 2003 WFA-USA Phi Alpha Theta Undergraduate Essay Award, webpage: wfa-usa.org/new/geomarshall.htm. pp. 9-10.

[23] Last, Entry Three.

American troops looking toward the Germans and "No Man's Land.

And this, the German view.

Another view of the trenches from the American side.

More prevalent than disease from infestation were injuries resulting from exposure to the cold. The most common of these injuries was foot trauma, which usually occurred in two forms known colloquially as "trench foot" and "frozen feet." Trench foot, or "immersion injury," occurs when tissue is exposed for a long time to temperature lower than needed to maintain the body's blood flow to affected areas. This injury does not require freezing temperatures. Severe damage to tissue can result from standing in cold water or from extended contact with cold, wet socks or shoes.

Frozen foot injury, also known as "frostbite," occurs in temperatures below freezing. Damage to the tissue is caused not only by restricted blood flow but also by formation of ice crystals inside and outside the cell walls.

Although permanent injury can result from trench foot, it is far more likely to occur in cases of frozen feet. Trench foot and frozen feet were in the nature of an epidemic at the beginning of the war. In 1917, the British began supplying their soldiers with rubber boots and introducing wooden "duckboards" into the trenches for them to stand on. These simple innovations substantially reduced the number of reported cases.[24]

The defense of the Toul sector was the first American exposure to winter warfare in the 20th Century. Division officers hadn't yet absorbed the British methods of coping with the challenges the cold weather provided. The U. S. Army's newest arrivals were neither trained nor equipped to deal with winter in the trenches. The sudden infusion of men and the hasty excavation of new trenches left the Americans short of rubber boots, duckboards, and other equipment necessary to cope with cold weather.

Men on night watch in the trenches were especially at risk for traumatic foot injury. This duty required a soldier to remain perfectly still all night at his "listening post" so he could hear and report any movement by the enemy without being detected. After several motionless hours, a rookie soldier could find his feet virtually paralyzed from the cold.

Last's description of his first night in the trenches paints a vivid picture of what Hurley's own experiences must have been like. "The Lieutenant tried to explain just what our duties were," wrote Last, "and said, 'Listening post means just what it is named; you are out there to listen, and when you hear anything that doesn't sound right, let someone know about it.' He also told us that we were not to make any noise – the Boches were to make the noises and we were to hear them."

"On the way to the front lines, in the communication trench, we had to go through a great deal of water," Last continued. "Quite naturally we got wet feet and limbs, as for quite a distance we walked through water up to our hips. Shells were falling quite rapidly all around us so we didn't notice

---

[24] Paton, Bruce C., *Medical Aspects of Harsh Environments, Volume I: Chapter 10 – Cold, Casualties, and Conquests: The Effects of Cold on Warfare* (Office of the Surgeon, Department of the Army, United States of America), p. 326.

A panoramic view of trench fortifications on the American side.

Troops standing in mud in trenches. Note absence of duckboards.

U. S. troops receive Croix de Guerre for repelling the March 1st 1918 German attack at Bois de Remieres. Note the snow on the ground. It was around this time Private Hurley suffered from frozen feet.

the water. When I got to my listening post I tried to follow orders as best I could. I didn't move a muscle and doubt whether I even blinked an eye.

"I stood there with my rifle ready for action. I also realized that Fritz was not coming around with a brass band. When he came, he was going to also be as quiet as he could be. There was a barbed armament out in front of me. I was sure that the posts of it were walking around and the more I stared, the faster they would bob around.

"Every now and then a flare would go up and I could see my post there – as dead as ever. I was 'seeing things.' Ask some of the boys who have been on this assignment and see if they haven't seen posts walking around too.

"I stood still so long without getting a chance to move that I almost froze that way and commenced to think I couldn't do anything if I had to. My feet being wet were almost stiff. I was suffering, but up to now I hadn't had time to notice it. It seemed as though I could stand it no longer. I had ... my eyes steadfast on No Man's Land..."[25]

As best as can be determined from the sketchy outline of Hurley's military record in the *Official Roster of Soldiers* published by the North Dakota legislature, his assignment as an infantryman at the front lasted about six weeks. Sometime in late February or early March 1918, he was taken to the battalion aid station at the 18th Infantry's headquarters in Beaumont, suffering from frozen feet. It is likely that from Beaumont he was transported by ambulance to a field hospital at the First Division's headquarters in Menil-la-Tour.[26]

The wounds resulting from a case of severe trench foot or frostbite can be quite gruesome. At first, the skin in the involved area becomes hardened and feels woody. A day or two after being warmed, severe blisters filled with blood appear. If the nerves, blood vessels, muscles, or tendons have been involved, the use of the affected part may be lost temporarily, or in especially severe cases, even permanently.

In the first weeks of recovery, Hurley, as a frostbite patient, would have been at risk for gangrene and infection both because of the wound's large size and the circulatory problems inherent in the injury. After a few days, a dull ache would have increased to a throbbing pain. The pain would have lasted anywhere from several weeks to several months as his circulatory system worked to supply blood through damaged blood vessels.

The extent of disability and tissue loss resulting from a cold injury is difficult to predict in the first weeks of recovery. In most cases, it takes

---

[25] Last, *op. cit.*

[26] Legislative Assembly of North Dakota under direction of Brigadier General G. Angus Parker, *Official Roster of North Dakota Soldiers, Sailors, and Marines in the World War, 1917-1918, Volume 2*, (Bismarck Tribune Company, 1931), p. 1,456. Cass County, North Dakota, *The Honor Roll in the World War—1917-1918-1919*, (Buckbee-Mears Co., St. Paul, Minnesota, 1919), p. 75. Ireland, Major General M. W., *The Medical Department of the United States in the World War* (Washington Government Office, 1925), pp. 292-293.

several months to determine the extent of damage. Any necessary surgery to amputate toes or tissue is often delayed up to four or five months. Even in cases of no permanent disability, long-term sensitivity to cold usually persists indefinitely. Under the treatment practices at the time it is likely, at the very least, Hurley would have been bed-ridden for several months.

After Hurley's injury, the First Division deployed to Cantigny in March to help the British resist the German offensive against Amiens. In July, the division was sent to the Soisson sector where the Allied Powers conducted a successful offensive attack against the German front line, advancing 11 kilometers. Meanwhile, it was determined that Jack's injuries were severe enough to prevent him from returning to the front. By July 25, 1918, he had recovered sufficiently to have been sent back to the United States.[27]

In September, the First Division participated in the first all-American operation of the war at St. Mihiel. Under General Pershing, it was one of nine divisions which joined together in the newly constituted First Army Corps to win a complete victory over the Germans and capture 16,000 prisoners, 443 artillery gunnery, and 240 miles of territory.

Beginning in late September, the men of the First Division were among 1.25 million First Army soldiers who took part in the final push at Meuse-Argonne. From October 4th until the armistice, the First Division engaged in non-stop attack against the western flank of German forces which had been solidly entrenched in the well-fortified Argonne forest for three years. In mid-October, the First Army successfully completed its first objective of the campaign by clearing the forest and breaking the German line.

On November 1, the First Army continued its offensive beyond the Argonne to the Meuse River on the forest's northern border. On November 5, the First Division reached the hills overlooking the Meuse. The division then was ordered to attack the Germans at Sedan, which lay on the northern side of the river. By November 7, the First Division, led by Hurley's former 18th Infantry Battalion, had routed the Germans to advance 35 miles beyond Sedan and come within striking distance of the German border.

By this time, the entire German Army was in total disarray and the German monarchy of Kaiser Wilhelm in a state of complete collapse. On November 9, a new provisional government in Germany declared the country to be a republic and conveyed its intent to surrender.

---

[27] Since virtually all personnel records from World War I were destroyed by the fire at St. Louis in the early 1970s, the history of Hurley's service during his convalescence in Europe and after his return to the United States is not available. It seems likely that upon returning to the U. S., he would have been given leave to go home for a while if he was well enough. He also may have been stationed for a time in North Carolina at Camp Greene, which was the mobilization station for North Dakota National Guard units in World War I, or else at Camp Dodge in Iowa, which was the U. S. Army camp closest to Fargo. Information regarding whether he was hospitalized or assigned to clerical or other limited duties between his return to the U. S. and his discharge in January 1919 is also not available. Surviving family members also had no information about this.

Wounded soldiers in bunks coming home on the Leviathan.

Hurley convalescing at home.

Awaiting his 1919 discharge.

At 11 a.m. on November 11, 1918 – at the 11th hour of the 11th day of the 11th month – the armistice was signed, and the war was over. In a little over a year, the First Division had lost 5,516 troops to death, over 17,000 to injury, 170 reported missing, and 124 taken as prisoners; totals almost equaling the division's strength at full force. Of the 2,051 soldiers from the North Dakota National Guard's original First Infantry Regiment, 278 had been killed and 650 injured; numbers adding up to more than 45 percent of those who served. Illness and non-combat injuries, of the type suffered by Hurley, were not included in the casualty statistics.

Wounded soldiers who already had returned to the U. S. were sent to hospitals in the same areas of the country where they were inducted. The government's plan was to not discharge any man unless he was as close as possible to being as fit as when he entered the service. For his final evaluation, Hurley likely went to Fort Des Moines Hospital at Camp Dodge in Iowa, which was the base hospital nearest Fargo.[28]

Every soldier had to undergo a physical examination before discharge. Any person whose condition could benefit from further treatment was assigned to a development battalion for curative training or medical care. Each soldier whose condition was not as good when he entered the service and who could not benefit from treatment was to have his impairment evaluated and rated according to the degree of permanent disability.[29]

Private Jack C. Hurley was honorably discharged at Camp Dodge on January 12, 1919. For the injury to his feet, he was given a Surgeon's Certificate of Disability of 10 percent.[30]

Hurley returned to Fargo knowing he had served his country honorably, even if without notable distinction. He enlisted believing he could make a difference, only to return knowing his confidence was misplaced. Failing to provide him the training necessary to make a genuine contribution, the government had squandered his investment. Instead of allowing him to serve in a regiment with his townsmen as promised, the military command had shuffled him from one unit to another, finally sending him to serve as a replacement at the front without adequate preparation.

Even so, he had no reason for bitterness. Having lived through the experience, he saw firsthand the logistical problems which a nation so long

---

[28] The preceding paragraphs discussing the participation of the First Division in World War I were taken primarily from two sources: Stewart, Richard W., *American Military History, Volume II* (Center of Military History, United States Army, Washington, D.C., 2005); and Coolidge, Calvin, "Patriotism in Time of Peace" (speech presented on October 4, 1924 dedicating the monument to the First Division A.E.F.). Statistics of casualties for North Dakota National Guard First Regiment were taken from Cooper, p. 211.

[29] "Wounded Yanks to Be Located Near Families," *Camp Dodger,* December 13, 1918. "... Needy Cases – Consider Home Needs," *Camp Dodger,* December 20, 1918, p. 1.

[30] Parker, Brigadier General Angus G., "Official Roster of North Dakota Soldiers, Sailors, and Marines in the World War, 1917-1918 – Volume 2 (Legislative Assembly of North Dakota, printed by Bismarck Tribune Co., 1931) p. 1456.

at peace had faced gearing up for war. Besides, he was one of the lucky ones who lived to tell the tale. Except for the rheumatism in his feet which would plague him the rest of his life, he had emerged intact. Ironically, his inexperience and lack of training, along with the inadequacy of his equipment, had allowed him to escape the battlefield before he was killed.

Nonetheless, Hurley would never again view the world with quite the same innocence or optimism as before the war. If nothing else, the experience reinforced the lessons he learned from the early deaths of his dad and his hero, Luther McCarty, namely life was too short to be chained to a job he hated. More than ever, he resolved to follow his own star rather than do what others expected of him. From this time on, Jack would shed the shackles of convention and blaze his own trail – wherever it might lead.

CHAPTER 5

JUST IN TIME FOR BOXING'S BIG BOOM

Tex Rickard is rated the greatest promoter of all times and is given credit for lifting the boxing game from the saloon into the present day amphitheatre. Rickard is a businessman, a gambler and has wonderful foresight. He seems never to become riled or excited, and no task is too big for this man of steel nerves.

The Tunney-Dempsey championship fight at Philadelphia last September was Rickard's biggest achievement and the way in which the crowd of 120,000 people was handled was unbelievable. I was around Rickard's headquarters most of that afternoon and to look at him, one would never know that he was connected with the show, or had a worry in the world. He succeeds where others fail and he is worthy of all of his success.

****

Jack Kearns has again distinguished himself as the greatest manager of all times. When the Dempsey-Carpentier match was being made, Kearns demanded a guarantee of $300,000 for Dempsey to box Carpentier and he was immediately branded as insane. Kearns insisted that the bout would draw $1,000,000 and his critics were sure he had lost his mind. However, Dempsey got the '300 grand' and the show drew $1,600,000.

Kearns made Dempsey and himself rich through his uncanny management and nerve. Anyone can demand unheard of guarantees, but collecting them is another question.

****

I got Billy Petrolle as a cub and I brought him up the right way. Petrolle came in bobbing, weaving, and slashing like Jack Dempsey and many people figured he was just a slam-bang club fighter. In fact, he was polished and clever with the courage of a lion but also remarkable skill, science and judgment.

He'd walk straight in and you'd think he was stepping right into the fire; but it only looked that way. Petrolle really walked to the edge of the blaze, where he could go to work, but not into the flame itself. Billy's style is a composite of Mike Gibbons, Dempsey, and one or two others. One can't make Petrolles of every fighter." [1]

– Jack Hurley

---

[1] Hurley, Jack, "Ring Rations," *Fargo Forum*, July 6, 1930, sports section. Hurley, "Broadway Breezes," *Fargo Forum*, March 27, 1927, sports section. Gregory, L. H., "Greg's Gossip," *The Oregonian*, April 30, 1951, sports section. Payton, Ralph, "The Fargo Express," *Boxing Illustrated*, May 1959, p. 33. Quotations are edited to fit the context.

****

Even as World War I raged in Europe, and Jack Hurley was awaiting his discharge in the United States, events were taking place in the boxing world which would dramatically affect the nation's view of the sport in general and the future of Hurley's professional life in particular.

A fighting hobo from Utah and two gamblers nurtured in the raucous gambling houses of the Alaska Klondike were masterminding a revolution which would take boxing out of the mining camps and backrooms of the early 1900s, and move it into the sports palaces of the Roaring '20s. The concerted action of these men, propelled by the social changes resulting in the aftermath of World War I, would redefine an enterprise which until then had straddled the murky borders between legal and illegal activity.

Together these men would defuse the objections of boxing's severest critics, and present to the world, as new, an old sport, freshly washed and re-coated in a veneer of the era's most up-to-date showmanship and hype. Under their guidance, boxing would be accepted as a valid spectator sport suited for rich and poor, man and woman, working person and aristocrat alike. Before they finished, boxing would not only be legal, but embraced as an essential element in the whole cloth of American sporting life.

The hobo was William Harrison (Jack) Dempsey, and the gamblers were George (Tex) Rickard and Jack (Doc) Kearns. Their first of several joint enterprises was a collective assault to wrest the world heavyweight championship from Jess Willard. The date of their conquest was July 4, 1919, at Toledo, Ohio. On that day Rickard, the promoter, would stage a prizefight in which, Dempsey, the challenger, fighting under the direction of Kearns, his manager, would attempt to win the title from Willard.

Willard, a white man, became champion by knocking out Jack Johnson in the 26th round April 5, 1915, in Havana, Cuba. The heavyweight division had been largely dormant in the U. S. since Johnson's exile in Europe the prior three years. True, the "white hope" tournament had provided some activity, but the American public's interest in boxing had nonetheless suffered during Johnson's absence from the U. S. scene.

Known as "the Pottawatomie Giant," Willard was a towering 6-foot-7-inch 230-pound, well-proportioned, pleasant-looking man. Experts thought he would rejuvenate the sport but, in fact, the opposite occurred. Rather than defend the title, he chose to cash in on his new status with stage, movie and circus appearances. In four years as champion, he fought just once, against Frank Moran in a ten-round no-decision bout, which in reality was not a true test since Jess could lose the title only if he was kayoed.

Willard's ring inactivity was not the only reason he was unpopular. Early in his reign, he dismissed the advisors who had guided him to the title so he would not have to pay them a share of his earnings. During World War I, he limited his activities to a couple of short, unprofitable exhibitions while other champions engaged in real fights and donated portions of their purses to war-related charities. As the war continued, other fighters served as soldiers and boxing instructors while Jess retreated to his farm in Kansas.

Possessing something less than a winning personality and hiring no one versed in public relations to advise him, the press turned on him: "Willard is the most unpopular champion we ever had ... He antagonized people at every turn with his clumsy money-making mania. Willard owes everything to the public. He made a fortune as a public entertainer, yet he apparently has no consideration for his friends. Big Jess gave nothing for nothing – when he owed everything ... The army and navy have no use for him."[2]

As time passed, Willard's relationship with the press grew even more contentious. By war's end, boxing was sorely in need of a new face to capture the public's fancy.

****

Tex Rickard was one of those rare individuals who backed up an immense capacity for visionary foresight with purposeful action. At first glance, he was not remarkable. He talked sparingly, as if afraid to betray his lack of formal education. One associate remarked: "Tex was a man who never had two sentences to rub together in his life."[3]

Closer study, however, revealed that, though he rarely looked directly at anyone, neither word nor deed escaped his wandering gaze, and behind those calculating, blue eyes lay an intellect which allowed him to size up people, analyze situations, and react appropriately when the need arose.

It was the big things he did and the way he did them, rather than force of his personality which attracted attention and respect. He had common sense, an intrinsic loyalty to his own ideas, and a way about him which convinced others of his sincerity. His word was his bond. His reputation for honesty went a long way to making big things happen. Anyone he made a deal with knew that his seemingly impossible plans were not just idle dreams, but were instead events which would actually take place.

George Lewis Rickard was born January 2, 1870, at Kansas City, Missouri. Shortly afterward, his parents moved the family to Sherman, Texas. As a young man, he worked in Sherman as a cowboy and became its city marshal. In 1895, he left Texas for the Alaska gold fields to make his fortune. He worked a claim at Bonanza Creek for a year, decided the weather was too cold and the work too hard, and sold the claim for $60,000. His plan was to leave Alaska, return to Texas, and buy a ranch.[4]

While waiting in Circle City for a steamer to take him up the Yukon River and out of the gold fields, Rickard met a man named Tom Turner.

---

[2] "Jess Willard Is Most Unpopular as Title Holder," *Camp Dodger*, October 11, 1918, p. 4.

[3] Samuels, Charles, *The Magnificent Rube* (McGraw-Hill Book Co., Inc., 1957), p. 46.

[4] Depending on the source, the date has variously been given as 1870 or 1871 and the location as Kansas City, Missouri or Kansas City, Kansas. Hurley, Jack, "Shadow Boxing," *Fargo Forum*, January 3, 1937, sports section.

Turner had just left Dawson and was excited about how the town was booming. He told Tex that anyone who had enough cash to start up a gambling house there could make a fortune. Rickard, who had worked at a gambling shack for a short while after his arrival in Alaska, was intrigued.

The two men pooled their resources and opened "The Northern" in Dawson. From the start, the partners did a land-office business. One night, however, a half-dozen prospectors came in and started playing the roulette. They placed their bets on the same numbers all evening and before the night was over, in Rickard's own words, "We rolled ourselves right out of house and home." Tex had lost his first fortune.

For the next 15 months, Tex worked as a bartender, faro dealer, and front man at various gambling emporiums in Dawson. Most of his meager earnings were gambled away at the faro tables in his own futile attempts to raise a stake. While working as a bartender at the Club Monte Carlo, he was joined behind the bar by a robust, 21-year-old, 6-foot-3-inch Wilson Mizner, the black-sheep son of a U. S. diplomat and aristocrat.

When they met in 1897, Mizner already had seen enough adventure for a lifetime. Raised in Guatemala, he had worked with a medicine show in Oregon, performed as a singer in San Francisco, run a string of prostitutes on the Barbary Coast, and experimented with opium. Later, he would sell fake Guatemalan relics in New York, manage fighters, write hit plays on Broadway, run a gambling den in Long Island, mastermind a series of million-dollar land swindles in Florida, and write Hollywood screenplays.

Even though they came from opposite ends of the social spectrum, Mizner and Rickard hit it off immediately. As Rickard's biographer Charles Samuels wrote, "The best talker in the Western Hemisphere had met the perfect listener, a young man who hung on every word he uttered and never interrupted ... except to go to the men's room."

Not long after meeting Rickard, Mizner talked the Monte Carlo management into letting him promote prize fights in its dance hall. Tex had never even seen a legitimate boxing match at the time, and the shows were his introduction to boxing promotion. In addition, Wilson's knowledge about the lifestyle of the socially elite gave Tex a valuable perspective into a way of life he had never experienced. This knowledge would serve him well later on when he moved on to promote boxing shows in New York.

After his stay in Dawson, rumor of a gold discovery beckoned Rickard to Nome, Alaska. With $21 in his pocket and an idea in his head, Tex met up with a miner named Jim White who had a small stake and a huge tent. Begging recycled wood for a floor in exchange for a promise of future repayment and offering to store a vendor's alcoholic beverages under the tent for the privilege of retailing them, the two men opened "The Great Northern" saloon and gambling house beneath the canvas cover.

While Rickard's subsequent boxing shows would make him famous, the establishment of "The Great Northern" was arguably his most remarkable venture. As luck would have it, gold was discovered on the beaches of Nome just a few blocks away, only days after the opening. Within a year the saloon earned the partners $100,000. When Tex sold his interest four years later, the business had netted $500,000. In less than five years, he had parlayed a $21 investment into a business which generated half a million.

After the excitement in Alaska ended, Rickard followed his star south to the country's next Gold Rush boomtown, Goldfield, Nevada. In February 1905, Tex and two friends opened a new "Northern" saloon, which was an immediate success. The three men settled right in and soon joined a committee of local businessmen dedicated to promoting the sale of the area's mining stocks and to bring more business to the town.[5]

The committee's idea was to stage a boxing match in Goldfield on September 2, 1906. Based on his Klondike experience, Rickard was appointed to oversee the details of the project and see if the show could at least break even. At this point, the possibility of making a profit by staging a prize fight in the middle of the desert in a small Nevada town during the hottest part of the summer never even entered anybody's mind.

Initially, Rickard had trouble convincing anyone he was serious about the match. His first overture, a telegram to featherweight champ Terry McGovern offering a hefty $15,000 guarantee, was dismissed as a pipedream by McGovern's manager, Joe Humphreys.

A $30,000 offer to lightweight champ Joe Gans and challenger Battling Nelson, however, was not. After confirming the proposal was legitimate, the two sides readily agreed to the fight. Promoter Rickard, to show good faith, arranged to have the money displayed in the window of the John S. McCook Bank in the form of freshly minted $20 gold pieces.

The window display proved to be a sensation. Photographs of the gold coins appeared in the sports pages of nearly every city in the country. City editors of the major newspapers throughout the country dispatched their ace sports reporters to Goldfield to report about the fight and to interview this novice promoter who no one had ever heard of.[6]

Rival San Francisco promoter Sunny Jim Coffroth, who had lost out in bidding for the fight, refused to believe the money displayed in the window was real gold. He sent his associate and well-known referee, Ed Graney, to Goldfield to prove the coins were only "stage money." When the money was proved genuine, the reporters had a field day and the story was the lead article in sports pages throughout the country.

Billy Nolan, Nelson's obstreperous manager, generated even more pre-fight publicity. Nolan had ruthlessly and, in the minds of most reporters unfairly, insisted on every possible advantage prior to the bout. Among

---

[5] Samuels, pp. 50-52, 57-59, 66-79, 93.
[6] Samuels, pp. 90-91, 97-101.

Tex Rickard (left) and two Goldfield businessmen pose with a teller and the $30,000 in gold coins displayed at McCook Bank to publicize the Gans-Nelson fight in Goldfield, Nevada, 1906.

Tex Rickard, 1928.

Dempsey's massacre of Willard July 4, 1919 set the stage for Tex's great triumphs in the '20s.

other things, Nolan demanded that challenger Nelson receive twice the amount of money as the sepia-skinned champion.

In addition, Gans was having trouble making the 133-pound weight limit. Nolan insisted that the fighters weigh in at ringside rather than three hours before the fight. Customarily, the time of the weigh-in was the champion's prerogative. Weighing in at ringside would give Gans no time to recover from the ordeal of getting down to the required weight.[7]

The fight's outcome was dramatic and satisfying to almost everyone. Joe Gans, a great lightweight champion, displayed mastery over Nelson until the challenger was disqualified for a low blow in the 42nd round. Spectators who thought Nelson had taken unfair advantage of Gans were jubilant.

Financially, too, the affair was an overwhelming success. The show in the middle of nowhere sold out every seat in the specially built 8,000-seat arena. The national publicity generated surpassed Goldfield's wildest expectations. Receipts of almost $70,000 were the highest ever realized for a boxing match up to that time. Unbelievably, the venture which had begun as a loss-leader realized a $13,000 profit for investors.[8]

It was the contest's improbability which made it such a triumph. The neophyte promoter staging such an unlikely event in a location so remote had captured the imagination of the public. The experience taught Rickard that a promotion impossible enough to generate publicity by virtue of its own improbability was well on its way to success. People would pay for the chance to feel a part of something special. It was a lesson he never forgot.

Rickard would go on to promote just two more bouts before World War I. The most famous would be the 1910 heavyweight title match in which

---

[7] Samuels, pp. 114-119. The Nelson camp could extract these concessions from Joe Gans, even though he was reigning champion, because of fallout from Gans' match with Terry McGovern at Chicago in 1900. It was widely rumored and generally accepted that Gans had taken "a dive" and had allowed McGovern to knock him out in the second round. Motion pictures of the fight seem to bear this out.

Without going into socio-economic treatises on race relations and gambling in 1900, suffice it to say that the opportunities of even successful African-American boxers to make a living were circumscribed by the mores of the time. Consequently, Gans was a target for both gamblers' promises of financial gain and threats of bodily harm. Unfortunately for Gans, his income opportunities became even more limited after his fight with McGovern and continued to be limited even after he won the lightweight championship in 1902.

Gans agreed to fight in Goldfield because his opportunities for such a large purse were non-existent elsewhere. In addition, Gans was using the Goldfield fight as a vehicle to rehabilitate his image in the eyes of the American sporting public. As a result, he was willing to suffer the indignities forced upon him by Nelson's manager Billy Nolan rather than to lose the match altogether. Gans' victory in the face of the overwhelming adverse circumstances did, in fact, help return him to public favor.

Gans' change in fortune was short-lived, however. Two years later he lost his championship in a re-match to Nelson at San Francisco. He died of tuberculosis at the age of 35 on August 1, 1910, at his home in Baltimore, Maryland. After his death it was disclosed that he had been suffering from the disease at the time of his fights with Nelson.

[8] Samuels, p. 126.

ex-champ James J. Jeffries would fail so miserably in his attempt to "wipe that golden smile off" Jack Johnson's face and thus redeem the championship for the white race. The other contest would be the Jess Willard-Frank Moran heavyweight title fight at New York in 1916.

However, it was his Goldfield experience, more than the others, which persuaded Rickard to become a full-time boxing promoter when boxing became legal in New York in 1920. Without Goldfield, the Golden Age of Boxing in the 1920s might never have happened.

****

If Rickard was the supreme visionary, then Jack (Doc) Kearns was the consummate opportunist. Though each had a nose for a fast buck and an ability to gauge the public's gullibility for the outrageous, their approaches to turning a profit differed according to their talents and values.

In contrast to the taciturn promoter whose major assets were extraordinary foresight and a reputation for square dealing, the slick, fast-talking Kearns prided himself as a sharp-shooter and con man. Rickard's skill was an ability to recognize and develop a chance for profit. Jack's forte lay in attaching himself to a lucrative situation and using whatever means at hand to exploit it for all it was worth.

John Leo McKernan was born on a farm near Waterloo, Michigan on August 17, 1882. Seven years later, his family moved to Seattle, Washington, where his father set up a small grocery business. In 1898, Jack stowed away on a freighter, "the Skookum," bound for Skagway, Alaska to earn his fortune in the Klondike gold fields.

Before long, Kearns made his way to Rickard's saloon, "The Great Northern," in Nome. Like Tex, Jack fell under the spell of Wilson Mizner who had followed Tex to Nome. Kearns later related: "Wilson was a gambler with little luck, an author and playwright who detested the labor of writing, and, variously, scamp and opportunist. He seldom had much for long, but when he had it he was a high-roller. He had a mousetrap mind and a scalpel tongue ... Mizner dazzled me and had a lifelong effect on me."

Kearns described himself as Mizner's "volunteer errand boy, messenger boy, and all-around flunky." Before long Wilson, through his friendship with Great Northern owners Rickard and Tex's partner, Billy Wallace, landed Kearns a job at the gambling house, first as a waiter and later a scale-tender of gold. The scaler had the important job of weighing the gold dust proffered by the customers as payment for their drinks.

Mizner taught Kearns a scaler's trick of spilling gold dust onto a carpet. After a week's time the carpet would be burned and the gold dust retrieved from the ashes. A variation had the scaler pouring the dust into his hands before weighing it and then wiping the residue from his hands into his well-oiled hair. The dust in the hair would be retrieved later in a wash basin.

JUST IN TIME FOR BOXING'S BIG BOOM 87

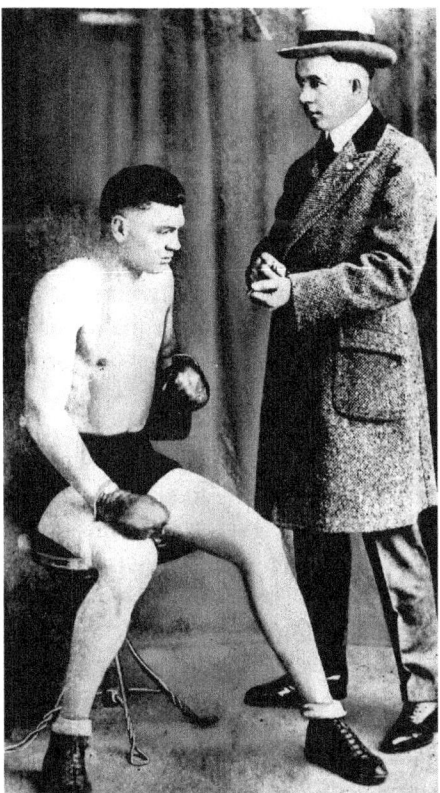

Jack (Doc) Kearns (right) and Jack Dempsey, circa 1917, before Jack became champion.

Dempsey & Kearns shortly after Jack won the heavy title in 1919.

Dempsey and Kearns, c. 1924.

Doc living high with middleweight champ Mickey Walker in 1927.

Kearns' position as a scale-tender gave the young hustler time to drum up friendly conversations with the clientele, including such passers-by as lawman Wyatt Earp, and writers Rex Beach, Robert W. Service, and Jack London. Although Doc and Rickard had a nodding acquaintance, Kearns at this early date was just another employee to Tex.[9]

Returning to Seattle around the end of 1899 "with a few hundred dollars and an education at the hands of Mizner," Kearns learned another lesson, this one more painful than in Alaska. To pick up a little spending money he took part in rowing ashore Chinese laborers who had illegally entered the country by ship from Vancouver, B. C. Despite working under the cover of darkness, Jack was arrested in Puget Sound by the revenue cutter service.[10]

The authorities told Kearns they were not interested in his small part in the smuggling, and he would be freed if he admitted his guilt. He complied, was convicted and then sent to a reformatory. He later told his son, Jack, Jr., the experience taught him a lesson – never admit anything to anybody.

Apparently, it was a lesson well learned. Kearns never saw the inside of a prison again, even though he later became popular as a "person of interest" to testify before the various committees which investigated organized crime in boxing during the 1950s and '60s.[11]

Leaving Seattle, Kearns drifted east and began boxing in mining camps and bars in Butte, Montana and Pocatello, Idaho. He eventually ended up in San Francisco and hooked up with Dal Hawkins, one of the era's great featherweights, whose career was winding down. Hawkins befriended Doc, and according to Jack was "among the finest and most decisive influences of my life. It was he ... who turned me irrevocably to boxing ... sheltered me, guided me and taught me all he knew, which was considerable."[12]

Bolstered by the knowledge acquired from Hawkins, Kearns returned to the mining towns of the western mountains and toured with several different troupes of boxers. Typically, they would show up in town, present themselves to a saloon owner, and offer to stage a boxing show in whatever building would hold the most people. The fighters would rotate from show

---

[9] Kearns, Jack (Doc) and Fraley, Oscar, *The Million Dollar Gate,* (The Macmillan Company, 1966), pp. 21-23, 27-31.

[10] Kearns and Fraley, pp. 36-39, 57-59. Kearns' biography tells a different version. The book version admits Kearns transported Chinese workers from their ships to shore, but attributes his incarceration to an arrest after a street fight. The version presented here was related to the author by the late Jack Kearns, Jr. The younger Kearns explained that he provided much of the information in the book to collaborator Oscar Fraley and did the final reviews for accuracy himself since his father was very ill during the venture and died before the book was finished. He explained that the differences between his descriptions and those appearing in the book were editorial judgments made by the publisher. The author is grateful to the late Hall of Fame boxing historian, Hank Kaplan, for the introduction to Jack Kearns, Jr.

[11] Nagler, Barney, *James Norris and the Decline of Boxing* (Bobbs-Merrill Co., Inc., New York, NY, 1964), p. 136-137.

[12] Kearns and Fraley, pp. 44-49.

to show, serving as seconds in one show and participants in another.

Gradually, Kearns found himself boxing less and devoting more time to handling fighters and arranging shows. Around 1907, he assembled a stable and set out for Los Angeles. On the way, he stopped in San Francisco and spotted William Brady, the famous theatrical impresario, having dinner in a cafe. Brady managed fighters as a hobby, and in the process had made fortunes for two out of the then three most recent heavyweight champions, James J. Corbett and Jim Jeffries.[13]

Kearns approached Brady and was invited to join him for dinner. The encounter had a profound influence on the young manager's life. He told Brady about his plans to assemble a stable of fighters and asked if he had any pointers. Luckily for Jack, the "great man" was in an expansive mood.

"Young man, just remember that you must be a showman every minute," Brady advised Kearns. "Dress the part and talk the part. You must be a salesman and an actor as well as a manager, because your personality is your fighter's best advertisement.

"The fighter's job is in the ring, so keep him in the gymnasium as much as possible. Make certain his living quarters are off the beaten track. Don't, for goodness sake, let the public see too much of him – unless it is paying for the privilege, that is. Once they know him as just an ordinary man, the illusions vanish. And remember, above all, box office appeal is all illusion. Remember, you're selling color, color, color. Sometimes you'll have to make your own, but with showmanship you can always put it over."[14]

From then on, Kearns became a manager and publicist to the exclusion of all else. For the next decade, he would travel across the U. S. and two other continents beating the drum for whatever set of world-beaters he could muster. He would ply his trade as "a dealer in adult fairy tales." He would sell himself and his boxers by spending lavishly and cultivating friendships with sportswriters everywhere.

And, wherever he went, he would always be on the lookout for a pugilistic prodigy worthy of his increasingly refined promotional prowess.

****

Apart from viewing footage of his fights, the most striking evidence of Jack Dempsey's radical impact on boxing is contained in a text entitled *Championship Fighting – Explosive Punching and Aggressive Defense*. Dempsey himself wrote the book with assistance from writer Jack Cuddy.

This little volume is an abrupt departure from the conventional methods of teaching boxing both at the time Dempsey fought and ever since. In the book's early chapters, Dempsey writes generally about his early contests

---

[13] Kearns, "Life Story" (Syndicated Column for Hearst, 1926, copyright The Christy Walsh Syndicate), Chapter 3.

[14] Kearns and Fraley, pp. 63-65.

and how he picked up pointers about fighting here and there "from a long parade of guys." In Chapter Six, entitled "You're the KO Kid," he begins actual instruction. In the first two paragraphs he makes this promise:

"To protect yourself with your fists, you *must* become a knockout puncher ... within three months, if you're a normal chap... you should be able to knock out a fellow of approximately your own weight, with either fist, if you follow my instructions exactly and practice them diligently. And in six months or a year, you may be able to knock out fellows a lot bigger and heavier than you are."[15]

Early instructional chapters are full of expressions entirely foreign to the traditional boxing lexicon, like "shoulder whirl," "upward surge," "power line," "falling step," "three-knuckle landing," and "relaying and exploding." Basic topics like "stance" and "footwork," in most texts introduced in the first chapter, do not appear until chapter 11.

Relegated to the back of the book, and preceded by a chapter titled "Punch Ranks First" are chapters called "General Defense and Blocking," "Deflection," and "Evasion," all topics usually appearing much earlier in boxing "How to" books.

Missing altogether are chapters on "the left jab," "the right cross," "the left hook," heretofore thought to describe the most basic punches in the sport. Any distinctions between blows delivered by right and left hands are ignored. In their places we have "the straight jolt," "hooking," and "straight punching from the whirl."

Tried and true methods of boxing instruction are either ignored or rejected outright as proof that "self-defense is being taught wrong nearly everywhere." The left jab, generally thought to be the most important part of a boxer's arsenal and the first punch a student should master, is dismissed as a "tap" and "defensive hokum" used only by a "sap."[16]

Under Dempsey's pen, the manly art of self-defense becomes the art of assault and battery. We are left not so much with a book on how to box but rather with a roadmap on how to fight in a backroom or alley. In this little volume, Jack has left for posterity his personal codification of how boxing was practiced in the mining camps, barrooms, and dance halls of 1915.

Kearns always took credit for transforming Dempsey from a conventional stand-up boxer "with a passion for throwing his right hand" to a bobbing and weaving fighter with a knock-out left. Doc claimed that, but for his promotional genius, no one ever would have heard of Dempsey.

Dempsey, for his part, acknowledged Kearns was a great publicist, but always maintained that, except for a few light touches, his rough and ready

---

[15] Dempsey, Jack and Cuddy, Jack, *Championship Fighting – Explosive Punching and Aggressive Defense*, (Nicholas Kaye, London, 1951), p. 24.

[16] Dempsey and Cuddy, pp. 18-19, 26-27, 41, 50-51, 68, 78, 120, 134, and 141. Dempsey does refer to the left jab, the right cross, and the left hook in later chapters in the context of defending against their use by conventional boxers.

Dempsey squares off with Andy Malloy at Durango, Colorado, 1915.

A young Dempsey in Colorado, circa 1916.

A cold, killer Dempsey in 1919.

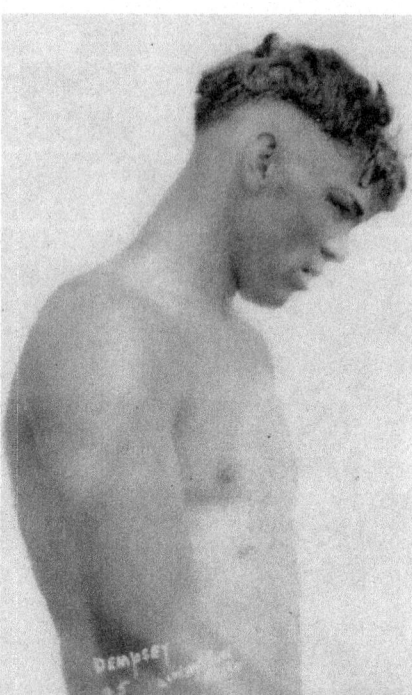

Jack with trainer Jimmy DeForest.   A serious Jack before Willard go.

Dempsey steps in the ring to face Willard. Kearns is on the apron in striped shirt. Sparring partner Jock Malone with striped shirt and backward cap follows Dempsey.

fighting style was already fully developed when he and Doc met. Dempsey also believed it was his own ability and hard work, more than Kearns' ballyhoo skills, which contributed to their success in the 1920s.

In truth, neither Kearns nor Dempsey were able to scale the heights without the other. And, it is also true that, without Rickard, neither could have achieved the acclaim and level of success each ultimately reached.

****

The end of World War I signaled to Rickard the country was ready to forget the horrors of war and indulge its long-suppressed passion for entertainment by supporting a heavyweight title fight. In Tex's mind, Willard's unpopularity only added fuel to the fire. The trick was to find an opponent who could capture the public's imagination.

He had heard about a hobo fighter from Utah by the name of Jack Dempsey. Since the clever Kearns became his manager in April 1917, Dempsey had beaten virtually every heavyweight of note.

Tex, however, had trouble believing a man of Dempsey's size, not much over 180 pounds, stood stand a chance against Willard, who now tipped the beam at 245. He feared the public would agree and not bother to attend. Even so, he was committed. He had guaranteed the champion $100,000 to defend the title against a foe of Rickard's choice. And now, because of his record, that choice had to be Dempsey, whether Tex liked it or not.[17]

As a result, much of Rickard's ballyhoo was devoted to minimizing the size differences of the two men. Tex built special elevated platforms for photographers above the ring where Jess trained so he would appear smaller in the photos. Pictures of Dempsey, on the other hand, were taken at upward angles near ringside so to make him look larger. Tex also made sure photographers took plenty of pictures displaying Dempsey's back, shoulder, and arm muscles to emphasize his extraordinary strength.

Rickard's decision to stage the match in Toledo, Ohio was driven by necessity rather than choice. Tex would have preferred New York, Los Angeles, Chicago, or Philadelphia, but in 1919 boxing legislation was still restrictive in most states. New York and Illinois outlawed the sport altogether. California limited its fights to four rounds while Pennsylvania allowed only six-round no-decision bouts, both too short for title contests. Only a handful of states allowed decision bouts of 10 rounds or more.

Toledo was a major railroad center and one of the few cities close to the eastern population centers where boxing was unrestricted. In selecting Toledo, Rickard was relying on the railroad to transport fight fans to the arena. He placed tickets for the fight on sale at every major railroad station in the country and scheduled the bout to take place over the three-day

---

[17] Roberts, Randy, *Jack Dempsey, the Manassa Mauler,* (Louisiana State University Press, 1979), p. 50.

Another look at the Dempsey-Willard Toledo massacre.

The new champion relaxes.

Jack Dempsey, man-about-town.

Fourth of July weekend. In this way, Tex hoped to make it as attractive and convenient as possible for fans from the big cities to make the trip to Ohio.

For a time, ticket sales at these offices were brisk. Then came the shock of Rickard's life. Government orders for the transportation of troops and supplies required the railroads to notify civilian customers that special charter trains would not be available during the summer. As a result transportation to Toledo for the big fight could not be guaranteed.

With this announcement, Rickard's plans to sell out the 80,000-capacity outdoor arena he was building flew out the window, and his dream of the first million-dollar gate evaporated into thin air. Ticket-holders who returned their tickets were given a full refund. He had staked his all, and now it was doubtful whether he would even make expenses. Nonetheless, even as he faced financial ruin, Tex remained outwardly calm.[18]

On July 4, 1919, slightly less than 20,000 fans paid $452,522 for the privilege of seeing a superbly conditioned, brown-skinned, 24-year-old panther named Jack Dempsey crash a slightly pudgy and soft-looking 37-year-old Jess Willard to the canvas seven times in the first round. Dempsey continued his vicious assault for two more rounds until Willard's handlers threw in the towel at the end of the third round.

After paying expenses of $315,000, taxes of $40,000, a $31,500 donation to a Toledo charity, and undisclosed amounts to an untold number of local politicians, Rickard and his partner Frank Flournoy realized only a small profit. Even so, Tex finally was able to breathe a sigh of relief. Despite the close call, the show had been worth while. He had overcome a disastrous stroke of bad luck and survived financially. He also had maintained and even enhanced his reputation as the world's foremost sports promoter.[19]

More importantly, he had acquired, in heavyweight king Jack Dempsey, an attraction whose popularity would surpass that of all prior sports stars.

The Toledo experience emphasized the difficulties which had kept boxing from becoming a major sport. The cost to a promoter of building an arena and the cost and inconvenience of travel and lodging to fans made it impossible to stage fights at remote sites like Toledo on a steady basis. To thrive, boxing needed a stable environment in a major metropolitan area. For this to happen, it would be necessary to legalize the sport in states with permanent facilities big enough to hold large numbers of people.

Until 1920, religious leaders were largely successful in preventing boxing's legalization in large eastern cities. These leaders had urged boxing was inherently immoral and "a refuge to crooks, thieves, and cheats."[20]

This stance became hard to defend after World War I. Governmental and

---

[18] Dorgan, Ike, *Building Up Big Fights* (Syndicated, Copyright 1931), Chapters 29-31.
[19] Samuels, pp. 212-213.
[20] Daniel, Daniel M., "Fowler Tells Inside Story of Walker Law," *Ring Magazine*, July 1949, p. 20.

Jack Dempsey, a studio pose of the then new world's champ.

military leaders alike had endorsed boxing as a centerpiece of combat training for all soldiers. Men returning from the war formed a ready-made audience for boxing. The war changed the whole world. Man's inhumanity to man had shaken confidence in long-held beliefs. The Roaring '20s would host a profound social and cultural conflict between the progressive ideas of the post-war era and the traditional values which preceded it.

Women who had worked in wartime jobs formerly held by men were reluctant to automatically return to positions of domesticity. New technologies developed during the war, a huge post-war influx of immigrants, and the migration north of thousands of workers, mostly black Americans, all contributed to re-energizing a society that eagerly accepted novel ideas and sought out new ways of self-expression and entertainment.

Sensing the time was right, James J. Walker, then minority leader of the New York State Senate, introduced legislation in January 1920 to legalize boxing. The bill provided for a commission with disciplinary powers and authority to license promoters, managers, and boxers. It also provided for two judges and a referee to decide the winner of each bout.

After contentious debate by the state Legislature, Governor Al Smith reluctantly signed into being the "Walker Law" on May 25, 1920. Less than 60 days later, Tex Rickard entered into a ten-year lease to rent and operate the famous Madison Square Garden at the unprecedented rate of $200,000 per year. For the first time in his nearly 15 years as a promoter, he had the law, and the place, to conduct boxing on a full-time basis.[21]

From the start, the promoter from way-out-west demonstrated an East Coast instinct for success. In January 1921, Rickard donated the use of the Garden for one night to the daughter of the renowned financier J. P. Morgan. With Tex's help, she staged a boxing match between lightweight champion Benny Leonard and leading contender Ritchie Mitchell to raise money for her pet charity, the American Friends of France.

The event drew a black-tie audience to the Garden and raised $75,000 for Ms. Morgan's charity. The cream of society attended, including members from the country's wealthiest families: the Vanderbilts, the Rockefellers, the Biddles, the Goulds, and the Astors.

Flushed with the success of the evening and eager to reinforce his new image as a philanthropist, Tex pledged ten percent of his profits for the year's fights to Mrs. William Randolph Hearst's Free Milk Fund. In the ensuing years, Tex would frequently promote special shows which contributed large portions of gate receipts to a wide variety of charities.[22]

Rickard's belief in Dempsey as a star attraction would prove correct. With the help of a little ballyhoo, Jack's kayo punch would capture the

---

[21] Daniel, pp. 20, 46. Durso, Joseph, *Madison Square Garden, 100 Years of History* (Simon and Schuster, 1979), pp. 115-117.
[22] Durso, pp. 122-123.

public's imagination and enable Tex to realize his dream of a million-dollar gate five times for a combined total of $8,605,764. In addition, over a ten-year period Rickard would promote over 250 boxing shows at Madison Square Garden, realizing additional receipts in excess of $11,200,00.[23]

Rickard's success in New York caused boxing's critics throughout the country to reluctantly acknowledge the sport was here to stay. By courting wealthy and influential members of New York's social registry and donating large amounts to charity, he outflanked boxing's foes and overcame arguments that boxing was without redeeming social value.

The sheer number of Rickard's promotions meant that news about his fights was reported daily in newspapers across the nation. Soon, sports fans everywhere were reading about his shows and becoming comfortable with the idea of boxing as a core sport. Before long, they came to believe that if legalized boxing worked in New York, it would work in their hometowns as well.

In the mid-1920s the legislatures of California, Illinois, and Pennsylvania all passed laws legalizing decision bouts over championship distances. By the end of the decade, live professional boxing was being seen at arenas in almost every state in the union. It had been a long, hard road from the hot Nevada desert to the concrete jungle of New York, but the battle for the universal recognition of boxing as a lawful enterprise had been won.

****

Jack Hurley's decision to hitch his star to boxing could not have come at a better time. The Roaring '20s would host one of the biggest sports booms the United States ever experienced. Hurley would be an active participant in, and benefactor of, that boom.

Hurley would follow the trail blazed by Rickard, Kearns and Dempsey, who each excelled in a unique aspect of the boxing business. He would pick up bits of knowledge from each of them and from others along the way. Within a few years, he would regard them not only as models, but also as peers. Before long, he would build on what they taught him and carve his own niche alongside them as an iconic figure in boxing history.

---

[23] Durso, pp. 91-96. Fleischer, Nat, *Nat Fleischer's Ring Record Book and Boxing Encyclopedia*, 1961 Edition (Ring Book Shop, 1961), p. 91. The five million dollar gates were: Dempsey v. Carpentier – $1,789,238; Dempsey v. Luis Firpo – $1,188,603; Gene Tunney v. Dempsey I – $1,895,733; Dempsey v. Jack Sharkey – $1,083,530; and Tunney v. Dempsey II – $2,658,660. The figures of Madison Square Garden receipts were compiled by adding the totals from Rickard's receipts listed in the Ring Record Book and then subtracting receipts from fights known by the author to have occurred at sites other than the Garden. Any mistakes in math and in misidentifications of these non- Garden shows are the author's. The statistics are not offered as absolutely accurate, but only to give a close idea of the volume of Rickard's Garden business. The figures include promotions at the third (which ceased operation in January 1924) and fourth (which commenced operation in December 1924) Garden buildings. Rickard's tenure ended with his death in 1929.

CHAPTER 6

HURLEY'S MAN FROM MOTLEY, MINNESOTA

Hurley was something else. A great actor, truly a tragedian who lived at the right time, but lived too long. Fate is really unkind. Hurley should have passed out in front of a crowd, orating, exhibitioning, conning his audience. And watching out of the corner of his eye to see the suckers' response.

I guess I was his one of his first partners. I came to Fargo, North Dakota from Chicago. When I first went into the business of promoting fights with him, I moved into the Hurley house. I had a chore: his mother gave me the job of getting him up for last Mass every Sunday. I pulled him, I pushed him, insulted him and finally got him up in time to stagger to church and save us both our saintly souls.

He was truly Irish. He hated the Establishment but knew he had to work with people who worked for a living, a chore he despised and stayed away from all his 75 years. Someone should have sealed off his room at the Olympic Hotel in Seattle. You could have found a thousand stories, all funny, all tongue in cheek, all mocking those who paid.

Yesterday's newspaper stories – I wish somebody was left to mourn the last small-town P. T. Barnum. How great he would have been in commerce! What a J. Paul Getty or H. L. Hunt he might have been – what a nickel-and-dime robber baron he actually was!

Jack had only one rule – the price you paid for your ticket did not entitle you to know how the fight was going to come out. He never deviated from his Hurley Law. I still see him in a barber shop, taking a boxing stance, showing everybody how the guy who was going to fight his next "champeen" was an honestly tough opponent.

We were fortunate we knew the guy.[1]

– Phil Terk

****

On February 26, 1919, the U. S. S. President Grant docked in Hoboken, N. J., carrying the last batch of North Dakota National Guard doughboys home from Europe. By this time, Jack Hurley had already been back in Fargo enjoying his mother's home cooking for at least a month-and-a-half. Two weeks later, he was one of several ex-soldiers who served as a welcoming honor guard when these troops finally arrived home at the Fargo train depot. The occasion marked Jack's last duty as a World War I soldier.[2]

---

[1] Sherrod, Blackie, "Jack Re-called," *Dallas Times Herald*, November 1972, sports section.
[2] "Fargoans Offer Many Ideas for Grand Welcome to Returning Men," *Fargo Forum*, February 26, 1919, p. 1. Jack's participation in this event is a likely scenario.

A civilian once again, he turned to what he knew and loved best – sports. The opening of the 1919 season found Fargo without a pro, or even a semi-pro, baseball team. The Northern League had disbanded at the start of the war, and the city's semi-pro teams were slow to organize. Fargo-Moorhead would not have another minor league team until 1933 when the Twins would become a founding franchise in a new Northern League.[3]

Instead of waiting for a team to be assembled in Fargo, Hurley headed west to pitch and play infield for the Grace City Buckos in Foster County, North Dakota. Jack was eager to see if his feet had recovered sufficiently from frostbite to support his skinny frame. Going out of town gave him a chance to test his skills before playing in front of the hometown folks. He also had been without a job since his discharge and needed to take some money home.

The Buckos' season extended from May 24th to early July and ended with a record of nine wins and two losses, the best ever posted by a Grace City nine. In the only game reported by the *Grace City Gazette* with a full box score, "the old vet (Hurley) was put in" as a relief pitcher in the fifth inning. He came in with the Buckos trailing 9 to 5 and was able to hold on until his team came back to win 14 to 12.[4]

After Grace City's season ended, Hurley jumped north and played a month for Cooperstown in nearby Griggs County. The Cooperstown team posted a record of seven wins, four losses, and one tie. He joined the team as "a ringer" in time to help it sweep a tournament at Hatton, North Dakota, and claim "the championship of this section." The *Fargo Forum* reported that for the series "Hurley, who came to Cooperstown from the Grace City team, played a wonderful game of first base and hit the ball hard."[5]

Hurley returned to Fargo on August 6 and organized "an All-Star team" of local players to challenge the Moorhead Athletics for the intercity

---

[3] Kemp, David, "Northern League: Proud Tradition," northernleague.com (official website of the Northern League).

[4] *Grace City Gazette*, Foster County, North Dakota, compiled from weekly editions beginning May 28, 1919 through July 2, 1919. "Local Nine Victories in Two Big Games," *Grace City Gazette*, June 11, 1919, sports section. The following is a general note applicable to all the North Dakota small city newspapers discussed in this book. Baseball coverage of the hometown team in small weekly newspapers was sporadic and incomplete at best. Some games, especially out-of-town games, are not covered at all. Other games are covered with a story that may vary in length from a full column to only a sentence or two. Still others may have a relatively detailed play-by-play and a full box score. The completeness of coverage varies dramatically not only from newspaper to newspaper, but also from issue to issue of the same newspaper. Thus, any references in this book to a team's season record or to a player's reported individual statistics are of necessity incomplete. The author nevertheless hopes that reference to whatever local documentation provided will at least give the reader a flavor as to Hurley's abilities and shortcomings as a baseball player.

[5] *Griggs County Sentinel-Courier*, Cooperstown, Griggs County, North Dakota, information compiled from weekly editions beginning May 29, 1919 through August 7, 1919. "Cooperstown Closes Season," *Fargo Forum,* August 6, 1919, sports section.

championship. The All-Stars were "made up largely of semi-professional players who have been playing ball with teams over the state this summer." On Fargo's squad was infielder Johnny Knauf, "a natural hitter," who would later become one of the first boxers in Jack's boxing stable.[6]

Publicity for the game received a boost when the Tower City team wrote to the *Forum* claiming that the Moorhead Athletics had reneged on a prior agreement to play Tower City on the same day as the game with the All-Stars. The letter concluded "it is hoped that next year the Moorhead aggregation will see its way clear to keep a scheduled game" rather than "automatically cancel to the preference of a bunch of Fargo pickups."[7]

The reply from Fargo's 21-year-old manager was swift and to the point. Clearly, Hurley's army service had not damaged his self-esteem. "If the managers of Tower City think the Fargo team that will play Moorhead next Sunday is 'a bunch of Fargo pickups,'" he told the *Forum*, "let them tackle us. We will play them for money, marbles or chalk any time and place they name. Tower City, I heard, had a good team, and probably could have won from Moorhead, but I resent having my team called 'a bunch of pickups.'"[8]

The game was noteworthy for the fine pitching of Moorhead's Lefty Carlander, a former star with North Dakota University, who, though he was "forced to extend himself in five of the nine innings through errors of his teammates, ... pulled out of several tight places with strike-outs. He fanned 12 of the All-Stars." Carlander yielded only four hits but, unfortunately, Moorhead's 11 errors were too much for even his stalwart effort.

Fargo's All-Stars took the lead in the fourth inning when Hurley's "timely two-bagger broke up Moorhead's lead." On the downside, Jack also led the way at second base in contributing three of his team's eight errors. The one bright spot in the field was "Johnny Knauf, the youngster third baseman for Fargo, (who) was easily the fielding sensation, making five putouts and seven assists without a miss." Despite manager Hurley's sloppy field play, the All-Stars managed to win, 5 to 2.[9]

North Dakota's 1919-20 boxing season was enlivened by the decision of Labe Safro to make his home in Fargo. Safro, one of the early "sports personalities" in the region, came to the attention of Fargo fans in 1912

---

[6] "Moorhead Team to Meet Fargo Today," *Fargo Courier-News*, August 24, 1919, sports section. "Fargo to Play Moorhead for Intercity Title," *Fargo Forum*, August 19, 1919, sports section.

[7] "Tower City Claims Moral Victory over Moorhead Semi-Pros," *Fargo Forum*, August 21, 1919, sports section.

[8] "Hurley Hurls Defy to Tower City Team," *Fargo Forum*, August 22, 1919, sports section. These articles are early examples of Hurley's ability, in any context, to manipulate the press and create reasons for fans to buy tickets.

[9] "Fargo All-Stars Win First Game for Title from Moorhead, 5 to 2," *Fargo Forum*, August 25, 1919, sports section. "Boardman Is Hope of Fargo Fandom Sunday," *Fargo Forum*, August 27, 1920, sports section.

through his rivalry with Leo Kossick. However, even then, Labe was well known in the Upper Midwest as an exceptional all-around athlete.

Safro, known as "the Jewish Lion," had made a name for himself as the starting halfback for the highly regarded semi-pro football team, the Minneapolis Marines. The Marines, comprised mostly of blue-collar athletes who had never gone to secondary school, dominated football in the region from 1910 through 1917.

From 1913 to 1917, the Marines won 34 regular season games without a loss or tie. During these years, the main attraction of each Minnesota football season was the annual Thanksgiving Day game between the Marines and a team of college all-stars. Prior to World War I, the two teams had split the series, each winning two games with one tie. After the war, the Marines re-organized and were a founding member of the National Football League (NFL) when the league was established in 1922. Unfortunately, financial woes required the team to drop out the end of 1924.[10]

Safro made his mark in sports other than football as well. He started boxing as a pro in December 1909, and within a few years tough bouts against Mike Gibbons, Kid Graves, and Mike O'Dowd led Minneapolis sports editor and referee George Barton to recognize him as one of the best welterweights in the Midwest. Safro also excelled in baseball and was a Twin Cities' handball champion. In between these activities, he toured in vaudeville with his bag-punching and rope-skipping routine. The climax of each stage show featured his specialty of working ten speed bags at once.[11]

Safro continued to box, entertain, and play football until the outbreak of World War I. After enlisting at Camp Dodge in August 1917, he won the camp middleweight boxing championship and so impressed his officers with his all-around ability that he was sent to Officers' Training School at Camp Pike, Arkansas. After graduating, Labe was made a lieutenant, one of only two such commissions received by pro boxers during the war. By the time the Armistice was signed, he had advanced to company commander.[12]

---

[10] Quirk, Jim, "The Minneapolis Marines: Minnesota's Forgotten NFL Team," *The Coffin Corner*, Volume 20 (1998).

[11] L'Amour, Louis, *Education of a Wandering Man*, (Bantam Books, 1989), p. 15. L'Amour grew up in Jamestown, ND when Safro and later Billy Petrolle were around the gyms and auditorium there. L'Amour took to boxing as a youth and boxed extensively in the gym with Billy Petrolle and his brother, Pete Petrolle. About Safro, L'Amour remembers:

"In the YMCA gym I worked out a few times with Labe Safro, who had been a crack welterweight and middleweight fighter during the days of Mike Gibbons, Mike O'Dowd, and Kid Graves. Labe was umpiring baseball in Jamestown and worked out every day. He was a phenomenal bag puncher and had punched bags in vaudeville, keeping ten bags going at once."

[12] "Boxer-Officer," *Fargo Courier-News*, c. November 23, 1919, sports section. "The Man Who Boxed Ring Celebrities Will Appear in Labor Day Ring Card," *Fargo Forum*, August 23, 1919, sports section.

Labe moved to Fargo in April 1919 after his discharge and opened a branch office at 612 Second Avenue North for the Northwest Tire Company, a distributor for Lee Tires. In May, he began offering boxing classes at the YMCA and also engaged in his first post-war bout, scoring an eight-round win against Mark Moore at the Elks club. Before long he was refereeing and serving as matchmaker for amateur bouts at the club too.[13]

During his time in Fargo, from April to December 1919, Safro won six straight bouts, including four which took place in the Fargo-Moorhead area. Wherever he fought, his talent and speed impressed not only spectators, but his foes as well, one of whom told a *Fargo Courier-News* reporter afterward that Labe showed him "more gloves in the time they boxed than (he) thought there were in the state."[14]

The most highly publicized of Safro's Fargo bouts was his Labor Day contest against Frank Mantell of Canada on September 1. Prior to the fight, Labe held outdoor workouts at the Riverside boat house which were open to the public. Safro's skill with the jump rope and punching bag were big hits with the family-oriented resort crowd, consisting mostly of people who never had seen a boxer up close before. A *Fargo Forum* writer described his Sunday workout eight days before the fight:

> "Interest in the coming attraction has exceeded expectations. Not only is this indicative from the sale of seats, but is shown in the large number that turn out each afternoon to watch Safro go through his training at the Riverside boathouse.
>
> "'Here he comes,' shouted a bunch of kids in their swimming tights when Safro made his appearance at his training quarters yesterday afternoon. Within five minutes, the territory in the vicinity of the boathouse looked as though there was a great child's festival. "'We are with you, Labe,' said one little fellow, who went up to the Fargo pride and shook the hand of the boxer.
>
> "One little fellow went up and tried to pinch the muscle on Safro's arm. The muscular founder didn't move. "'Gol, Labe, but you sure got a lot of muscle,' said the boy. "Labe smiled his characteristic smile.

---

[13] "Safro to Manage Fargo Tire Firm," *Fargo Courier-News*, c. May 7, 1919, p. 7. "Fargo Fighter Starts Training," *Fargo Courier-News*, November 16, 1919, sports section. "Elks Are to Stage Good Boxing Card," *Fargo Courier*-News, October 23, 1919, sports section. Safro fought Mark Moore twice in Fargo, once in May 1919 as set forth in the text and again on November 27, 1919. Their second fight is worthy of mention as a rare instance of a fighter being kayoed twice in one fight. Referee Jimmy Potts counted Moore out in one minute 20 seconds of round nine, but due to protests from the crowd, the fighters and the referee agreed to resume the fight as entertainment, and Safro knocked Moore through the ropes in the 10th round.

[14] "Speed Is Promised Fargo Boxing Fans at Labor Day Meet," *Fargo Courier-News*, August 29, 1919, sports section.

Labe Safro the fighter, c. 1920.

Labe in Fargo, 1920-'21.

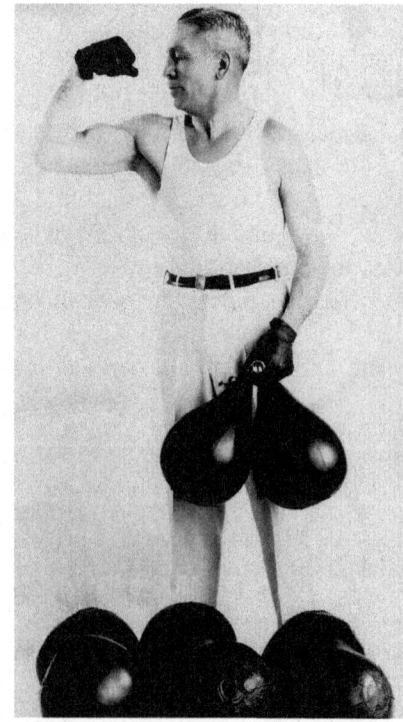

Safro, the bag puncher, 1945.

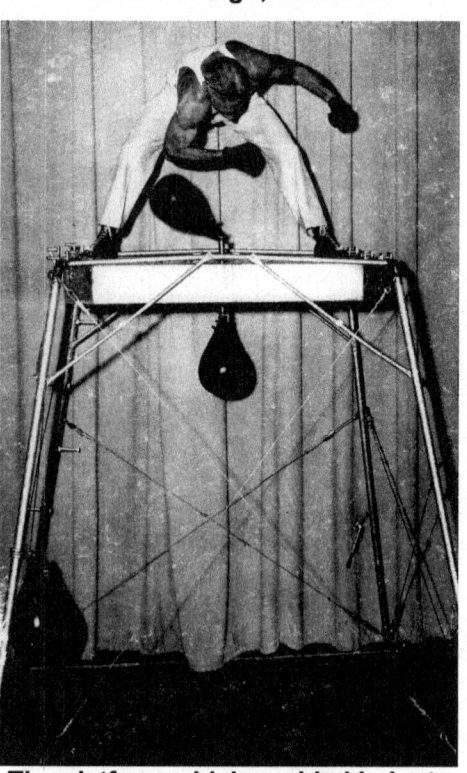

The platform which enabled Labe to punch 10 bags at once.

Safro and his punching bags. Labe billed himself "World Champion Bag Puncher," and he performed professionally well into the 1950s.

"Women were seen with the spectators gathered at the boathouse to watch the Fargo boxer perform. One of them made a remark that she never knew a boxer could skip rope. Then Safro boxed 'Submarine' Smith, of Moorhead, for three rounds, giving one of the prettiest exhibitions since the two began their workouts for the best card ever booked in Fargo. All indications now are that there will be a number of women among the spectators at the Labor Day card, as there were in Moorhead a month ago when Safro met Ray Johnson."[15]

The Safro-Mantell match was important enough for George Barton to make the trip from the Twin Cities to referee. Mantell started strong and put up a good battle for two rounds, but faded soon after, and was counted out in the fifth round. In his syndicated column written years later, Hurley recalled seeing the fight at the Fargo Auditorium that Labor Day evening.[16]

On September 18, Safro announced he was organizing a Fargo-Moorhead pro football team. He already had secured the services of Dewey Lyle, his teammate on the Marines before the war. Tryouts were set for September 21, 1919. Unfortunately, interest in Labe's ambitious endeavor was lacking. Had his effort been successful, Fargo might have landed an NFL franchise when the league began operations two years later.[17]

Throughout the fall of 1919, Safro toured eastern North Dakota and northern Minnesota, giving bag-punching and rope-skipping exhibitions. Included among his stopovers were shows in the North Dakota towns of Lisbon, Valley City, Jamestown, and Grand Forks; as well as in the Minnesota communities of Duluth, Virginia, and Hibbing.[18]

Safro left Fargo in December 1919 when a brother living in San Jose, California convinced him to move west for lucrative boxing engagements. Things did not pan out in the Golden State, however, and Labe soon returned to the Midwest where he opened a training camp on Lake Calhoun near Minneapolis catering to an upscale clientele.[19]

Although Safro lived in Fargo only nine months, future boxing men like Hurley owed a debt of thanks to the dark-haired adonis, whose jaunty showmanship revived the sport's fragile pre-war popularity and introduced boxing to a whole new audience. Labe was the first to attract women to the

---

[15] "Kids Wild over Safro as Fargo Boxer Works Our Each Afternoon," *Fargo Forum*, August 26, 1919, sports section.
[16] "Bantams Bout Features Card," *Fargo* Forum, September 2, 1919, sports section. Hurley, Jack, "Ring Rations," *Fargo Forum*, February 18, 1934, sports section.
[17] "Safro to Start Professional Football Team," *Fargo Courier-News*, September 18, 1919, sports section.
[18] "Safro Returns from Trip thru Minnesota," *Fargo Courier-News*, December 9, 1919, sports section.
[19] "Benson Here to Train for Bout," *Fargo Courier-News,* May 18, 1920, sports section.

sport, paving the way for the "Ladies Night" shows which later would become so popular. In addition, his engaging personality was a source of inspiration to the young people who were the region's upcoming generation of boxing fans and participants.

The 1919-'20 fistic season also was noteworthy for the debut of Russie LeRoy, a boxer whose importance to Fargo eventually would surpass that of Safro. LeRoy, whose birth name was Russell Miladore Backer, was born in Motley, Minnesota March 31, 1902, to parents of German heritage. In 1904, the family moved to Fargo, where he attended Lincoln grade school at Fourth Street and Sixth Avenue North. He soon took a shine to sports and paired with brother Lester to form a battery on the school baseball team.

According to the *Fargo Tribune,* Russie, "had his quota of fights with members of his gang, but he was never regarded as an exceptional fighter until Jack Hurley saw him in a fight with a newsboy. LeRoy was selling papers at the time and he impressed Hurley."[20]

LeRoy started taking lessons from Hurley in the fall of 1919. With just three months' instruction under his belt, Russie made his pro debut in the bantamweight division on February 6, 1920, winning a ten-round newspaper decision over the veteran Submarine Smith. The relationship between LeRoy and manager Hurley would last, except for a one-year period of dissension, until Russie retired from the ring ten years later.[21]

Russie adopted the ring surname of "LeRoy" shortly before his first bout to honor an elder brother who died in infancy. Sensing Russie might have special talent, local reporters took an immediate liking to the friendly, blond-haired youngster. The *Courier-News* was especially effusive in its praise of "the Kid's" first fight and gave the bout lead coverage even though it was only a preliminary attraction:

> "The real bout of the evening was the go between Submarine Smith of Moorhead and Kid LeRoy of Fargo, who made his first professional appearance last night. The fight was LeRoy's all the way...
>
> "Had in-fighting been allowed in this bout it is the opinion of the fans present that LeRoy would have stowed Smith away early in the game. The Fargo boy shows a wonderful confidence in himself for one so young in the game and with more experience will

---

[20] "Russie LeRoy Lauded by Boxing Fraternity," *Fargo Forum*, March 10, 1934, sports section. Hurley, *op. cit., Fargo Forum*, August 24, 1930, sports section. Dunn, Ed, "Russie Confident of Defeating Van," *Fargo Daily Tribune,* January 29, 1924, sports section.

[21] The bantamweight limit is 118 pounds. Russie would later outgrow the featherweight (126 lbs.), junior lightweight (130 lbs.) and lightweight divisions (135 lbs.), and would finish his career in the junior welterweight division (140 lbs.).

probably be a comer in the squared circle. The crowd was with him all the way."[22]

Russie was undefeated in all four of his fights during the 1919-1920 boxing season. In addition to the fight with Smith, he came out slightly ahead in a three-bout series against Jimmy Woodhall of Fergus Falls, Minnesota, winning one newspaper decision and drawing twice. His only other ring appearances were in two exhibition bouts with Johnny Knauf, who began his pro boxing career two months earlier than LeRoy.

Hurley started out his 1920 baseball season with the Gwinner Swedes in Sargent County, North Dakota. He played first base in each of Gwinner's 13 games, beginning with the season opener on May 17 and continuing until the team disbanded in mid-June. During this stretch, Jack also played at least one game for the Milnor town team, helping out with some of his Gwinner teammates when Milnor was short of players.[23]

After his stint in Gwinner, Hurley moved on to play third base for Lisbon's baseball team in Ransom County, North Dakota, for no fewer than four games from June 29 through July 5. The *Lisbon Free Press* published his batting average on July 8 as a team leading .389. The average probably combined his Gwinner and Lisbon experiences since the two teams were playing against the same opposition.[24]

On July 9, Manager Dolly Elder of Bismarck, North Dakota's town team sent for Hurley where he filled in for six games at third base, shortstop, and right field. Although the *Bismarck Tribune* mentioned a few smart sacrifice bunts and some alert base running, Jack's two singles in 16 at-bats apparently failed to impress Elder. On July 29, Hurley was released in favor of Harper who, as "one of the best infielders in the Northwest," became available when the "fast Brinsmade team ... disbanded."[25]

Hurley was back in Fargo on August 8 wearing a Fargo Athletics uniform for the final game of the intercity series with Moorhead, the same rivalry Jack himself inaugurated a year earlier. He played right field in the Athletics' 4-1 win, going hitless in three trips to the plate, but contributing a sacrifice bunt which helped set the table for two runs.

---

[22] "Russie LeRoy Lauded by Boxing Fraternity" (surname of Leroy). "Prelims Stage Exciting Bout," *Fargo Courier-News*, February 7, 1920, sports section (quotation).

[23] *The Prairie Press*, Gwinner, Sargent County, ND, weekly editions of May 20 and 27, June 3, 10, and 17, 1921.

[24] *The Lisbon Free Press*, Lisbon, Ransom County, ND, weekly editions of May 27, June 17, July 1 and 8, 1921.

[25] "Baseball Club Gets New Stars for Season," *Bismarck Tribune*, July 9, 1920, sports section. "Several Games Scheduled for Baseball Club ... Brown and Hurley Gone," *Bismarck Tribune*, July 29, 1920, sports section.

Jack played third base for the Athletics in the season's final game August 30, a 5-1 win over Grand Forks. Again, he was hitless in three times up. He also committed Fargo's only error in five chances in the field.[26]

As in the case when Hurley and his Gwinner teammates helped out at Milnor, small-town baseball teams in the 1920s frequently would enlist the aid of non-roster players to bolster their chances in a big game against a major rival. It was likely around this time that Jack held himself out as a "hired gun" to the town of Colfax, North Dakota. Hurley recalled the incident in his syndicated column a few years later:

> "Several years ago the conductor of this column was selected to pitch a baseball game for a small North Dakota city. Although I was not supposed to be a pitcher by trade, I thought I could go out and fool the small town batters with my experience and knowledge of the national pastime.
>
> "However, as in all small towns, the management hires a pitcher and expects him to win the game single handed ... As the game started, I looked around to see the club I was pitching for, and I must say that I did not gain much confidence watching them handle the ball in practice. However, the ballgame started, and without any exaggeration, I had a terrible time trying to retire the other team.
>
> "It wouldn't rain, and there weren't any trains leaving town, so I just had to make the best of it. I just forgot what the final score was, but it was quite large, and as I remember, it sounded like the score of a track meet. Our team, on the other hand, failed to make a single run, which was quite bad.
>
> "In collecting my money after the ball game, I informed the home town manager that I never had a chance to win the ball game at any time, inasmuch as his team failed to get me any runs, and that ball games cannot be won without runs.
>
> "... There is an old saying to the effect, 'that it is an ill wind that blows no good,' and such was the case in this instance for me, I received two telegrams from Mike Kelly, who was at that time manager of the St. Paul baseball club. One of the wires said, 'Don't come,' and the other said, 'Be sure and don't come.'
>
> "That one experience was enough to convince me that I was not cut out to be a baseball pitcher. It's bad enough pitching and having those heavy hitters hit them back at you like bullets, but supposing some of those fans should take a notion to get out the tar and feathers?"[27]

---

[26] "Boardman Unbeatable in Sunday Game," *Fargo Forum*, August 31, 1920, sports section.
[27] Hurley, "Broadway Breezes," *Fargo Forum*, February 12, 1928, sports section. Brougham, Royal, "Chitter-Chatter," *Seattle Post-Intelligencer*, November 11, 1953, sports section. Whether the game at Colfax occurred in 1919, 1920 or 1921 is a toss-up.

Hurley ended the 1920 season umpiring a YMCA championship game between the Fargo Allisons and the Moorhead Kossicks, a team sponsored by Leo Kossick, Jack's first boxing hero. At a critical stage in the game, Hurley failed to call an obvious balk on the Allisons' pitcher, resulting in a Kossicks' runner being called out trying to steal second base. As a result, the Kossicks were deprived of a scoring opportunity which might have changed the outcome of the game. The Allisons ended up winning 2-1.[28]

Early in the 1920-'21 boxing season Hurley added two fighters to his stable. The first addition was Moorhead's Johnny Knauf, who had played so well in the 1919 Fargo-Moorhead All-Star baseball game. Knauf began boxing on his own as a lightweight the prior year, winning four of his six bouts in Fargo while losing once and drawing once. Jack was impressed with Johnny's potential and was able to convince him he needed a manager and trainer to have a real chance at a successful boxing career.[29]

Hurley's other recruit was welterweight Jack Bailey, who studied boxing during the war under Mike Gibbons at Camp Dodge. Like Hurley, Bailey served in the trenches and was hospitalized, but for exposure to poison gas rather than frozen feet. Before going abroad, he served as a sparring partner to prepare leading middleweight Eddie McGoorty for the Allied boxing tournament in England. After the war, McGoorty returned the favor by working with Bailey in Chicago and helping him launch a pro career.[30]

The American Association's St. Paul Saints baseball team of 1920 has been rated as the sixth-best baseball team in all of minor league baseball history. Likewise, the Saints' manager, Michael Joseph Kelly, is recognized as one of the greatest managers in minor league history. Kelly managed teams in the American Association for 28 years and is third place on the list for most minor league victories with 2,390 lifetime wins. Weiss, Bill and Wright, Marshall. "Team #6 1920 St. Paul Saints (115-49)." MILB.com (the official website of minor league baseball). Hurley's reference to Kelly is at least partially apocryphal. However, it seems reasonable that, as Jack intimates, he might have solicited an opportunity to try out with the Saints. If so, the real reason his request was ignored probably had nothing to do with the Colfax game, but was more likely because St. Paul had such a good team, and no positions were available. As will be discussed later in this chapter, Jack did try out for another American Association team, the Louisville Colonels, most likely in 1921.

[28] "Nemzek in Demonstration" (subtitle), *Fargo Forum*, September 7, 1920, sports section. Interestingly, Joe Nemzek, the runner called out trying to steal a base when Hurley failed to call a balk, protested the call by refusing to leave the field after he was called out. Instead, he "riveted himself on third base until Leo Kossick, manager of the Kossicks asked him to go to the dugout, after play had been delayed 20 minutes."

[29] "Three Popular Local Boxers," *Fargo Forum*, January 13, 1921, sports section.

[30] "Plans Complete for Boxing Show," *Fargo Forum*, November 17, 1921, sports section. McGoorty, from Oshkosh, Wisconsin, still was rated among the best fighters in the world. He had the reputation as possessing boxing's hardest left hook for a man his size and was good enough to win a newspaper decision over Mike Gibbons in New York when Gibbons was at his best. Eddie moved to Australia in December 1913 where he lived off and on until June 1917. At the time, many of the world's top middleweights traveled to Australia to participate in an elimination series to establish a world middleweight champion. McGoorty won Australia's version of the world title on January 1, 1914, by stopping Dave Smith in the first round, only to lose it in a disputed 20-round decision to Jeff Smith on March 14.

Welterweight Jack Bailey, who was with Hurley from 1920 to 1924.

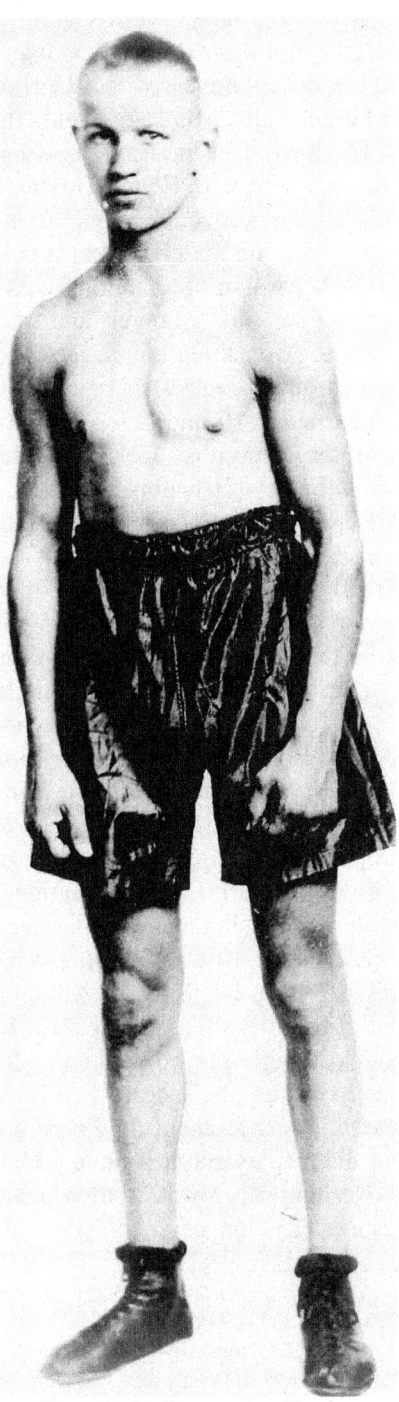

Russie LeRoy, who Hurley managed from 1921 to '30.

With three boxers to keep busy, Hurley expanded his horizons beyond Fargo-Moorhead to neighboring communities. In the 1920-'21 season, Jack's boxers appeared in five shows each at Fargo and Grand Forks; two in Fergus Falls, Minnesota; and one at Valley City, North Dakota.

The busiest of the trio was Knauf, who won eight of ten bouts, drawing once in Fargo with Chuck Traynor and losing a close decision in a rematch. Johnny was especially popular in Grand Forks where he headlined four shows, scoring three knockouts before the loss to Traynor.

Hurley was more cautious with LeRoy. Though he had been with Jack longer, he was younger and more inexperienced than Hurley's other charges. After three bouts, Jack took Russie aside in early January and put him through a refresher course. Hurley had seen some flaws in his style which needed fixing before they became too ingrained to change. For the next three months, Jack could be seen in ring togs at the Knights of Columbus gym teaching his young hopeful proper footwork and balance.

LeRoy returned to record an eight-round draw against Jimmy Woodhall at Fargo on April 8 and an eight-round newspaper win over Kid Goodrie at Grand Forks on May 6. For the season overall, Russie garnered three newspaper wins and two draws with Woodhall. The LeRoy-Woodall bouts were the last in the duo's two-year rivalry, since Russie had outgrown the bantamweight limit of 118 pounds. The final tally in their spirited series totaled one newspaper decision for LeRoy and four draws.

Jack Bailey's first fight for Hurley did not take place until January 1, 1921. The *Forum* reported he had been slow to recover from the gassing received in the war and this "bothered him considerably in getting into proper condition for his fights." Bailey regained much of his strength by season's end, however, winning bouts against Young Denny and Kid Miller, and losing a newspaper decision to Charles Fuhrman, all at Fargo.[31]

For the first time since the war ended, Fargo fielded a strong semi-pro baseball team in 1921. The Athletics began the season May 14 and won two out of their first three games. Hurley started at first base in all three games and seemingly played well enough to hold onto his job by registering three hits in 11 at-bats, scoring two runs, and stealing two bases. Even so, Jack was not in the lineup for Fargo's next game against Valley City May 22, nor did he play another game with the team for the rest of the season.[32]

Nothing more was written again about Hurley until June 12, when he resurfaced, not as a player but as a base umpire. Although Fargo

---

[31] "Three Fargoans Will Be Seen in Boxing Bouts to Be Staged Here," *Fargo Forum*, February 9, 1921, sports section.

[32] "Locals Take Opener 7 to 2 Yesterday," *Fargo Courier-News*, May 15, 1921, sports section. "Fargo Takes Sunday Game; Score 5 to 4," *Fargo Courier-News*, May 17, 1921, sports section. "Athletics Lose to Blacks; Ready for Valley City," *Fargo Courier-News*, May 22, 1921, sports section. "Needham Blows Up in Seventh and Fargo Loses by 6 to 4 Count," *Fargo Forum*, May 23, 1921, sports section.

newspapers make no mention of his whereabouts during this three-week hiatus, circumstances suggest he likely spent at least part of the time trying out for the American Association's Louisville Colonels baseball team.[33]

Years later, Hurley would tell Robert Houston of the *Omaha World-Herald* that a friend recommended him to the American Association but a tryout convinced him "he'd never make it to the major leagues, so [baseball] was out." On another occasion, Jack told *Seattle Times* reporter Vince O'Keefe he signed with Louisville as an infielder, but the experience left him homesick and happy to return to Fargo. In neither article, however, did Jack say when his date with the Louisville club occurred.[34]

Certainly, an emergency call from Louisville is consistent with Jack's abrupt and otherwise unexplained disappearance in May of 1921, as is the absence of other unaccounted-for blocks of time in his life when such a trial might have occurred. So too, his decision to give up his role as a player when he returned in favor of umpiring suggests whatever happened while he was gone must have caused him to reevaluate his career.[35]

A tryout for Hurley during this period fits what was happening in Louisville, as well. The team began the season with six sraight wins, but by May 20 its record had fallen to 13-14, and the club was experiencing serious lapses in fielding. Its infielders were battling injuries, and its 34-year-old manager Joe McCarthy, previously retired as a player, had inserted himself in lineup as an emergency measure. The club's need for an infielder was acute; and since the Colonels were starting a series in Milwaukee May 23, it was an easy matter for Jack to meet the team there for a tryout.[36]

---

[33] "Valley City Is Defeated 6 to 4 in Fourth Game with Athletics," *Fargo Forum*, June 13, 1921, sports section.

[34] O'Keefe, Vince, "A Long Night with the Pals of Deacon Jack," *Seattle Times*, November 21, 1972, sports section. Houston, Robert, "Hurley: One of Boxing's Great Figures," *Sunday New York World-Herald Magazine*, January 13, 1952, p. 10-G.

[35] The fact that the Fargo ball club was forced to hold its own emergency tryouts to replace Hurley makes it clear Jack's departure was sudden and unexpected. "Hillsboro and Fargo Playing Two-Game Series Starting Today," *Fargo Forum*, May 28, 1921, sports section.

[36] After winning its first six games, the Louisville club went into a tailspin, losing five straight and playing less than .500 ball through May 20. On April 29 and May 2, the *Louisville Times* characterized the team's fielding as "ragged" and "miserable." On May 10, manager Joe McCarthy was said to be looking to add "some additional talent soon." On May 14, shortstop Pelham Ballenger was reported as having injured a shoulder, causing McCarthy to insert himself at that position. On May 20, the *Louisville Times* again noted that "the fielding of the Colonels was bad." "Colonels Will Tackle Indians in Next Series," *Louisville Times*, April 29, 1921. "Colonels Meet Hoosiers Again at Indianapolis," *Louisville Times*, May 2, 1921. "Colonels Begin Western Series at Minneapolis," *Louisville Times*, May 10, 1921. "Saints Series Starts," *Louisville Times*, May 14, 1921. "Colonels Play Knabe's Blues in Second Tilt," *Louisville Times*, May 20, 1921.

At the end of May, the Colonels made an abrupt turnaround, and by mid-June the club took over the league lead. The team would finish 4-1/2 games ahead of the second-place Minneapolis Millers to win the American Association pennant race with a 98-70 win-loss record. At the end of the regular season, the Colonels would go defeat the Baltimore Orioles

One player who would have welcomed Hurley when he arrived was the Colonels' right-fielder Alfred (Al) Ellis, who began his baseball career in 1915 as a pitcher for the Fargo-Moorhead Graingrowers of the Northern League. Jack had been the Fargo-Moorhead batboy the prior year, and he and Ellis undoubtedly knew each other through this connection. Al was a native of Harmony, Minnesota, and he may have heard of Jack's .389 batting average at Lisbon in 1920 and recommended him to McCarthy.[37]

Returning to Fargo, Jack umpired no less than 13 Athletics' home games between June 12 and September 18. He also made a cameo appearance at first base when he took the field August 29 for a shorthanded Moorhead squad at the annual intercity game against his ex-Fargo teammates. In what may have been his last game as a semi-pro player, Jack registered one hit in four at-bats, while committing one error in 17 chances at first base.[38]

The highlight of the 1921 season was an exhibition game on September 2 between the Athletics and the vaunted Minneapolis Millers of the American Association. A record crowd of 2,394 paid $2,268 to watch the Millers defeat the hometown team 5-4 in a surprisingly close game. The Millers left town in a happy frame of mind since their $1,020 option for a gate percentage more than doubled their minimum guarantee of $500.

The Millers were also happy with the local umpires. "Slingsby umpired on balls and strikes and Jack Hurley on bases," noted a *Forum* scribe. "One of the Millers said after the game that (they) have played several exhibition games this season where the umpiring has favored the home club. 'I don't know when I have played in an exhibition game where the umpiring on balls and strikes was decided with such good judgment as in your Fargo game. Hurley also gave us satisfaction in his decision on the bases.'"[39]

Any lingering doubts about the date of Hurley's ill-fated attempt to land a spot on the Louisville roster would seem to be resolved by a September 20th, 1921 *Courier-News* article summarizing the plans of Fargo's ballplayers as they returned to their homes for the winter. After running

---

of the International League in the minor leagues' "Junior World Series," five games to three.

McCarthy remained Louisville manager until 1925 when his team won another pennant with a record of 106 wins and 61 losses. His success in the minor leagues landed him the job with the Chicago Cubs in 1926 where his team won a National League pennant in 1929. In 1931, McCarthy moved on to manage the New York Yankees, a job he would hold through the 1946 season. During that time, his teams would win eight American League pennants and seven World Series. He would finish with a winning percentage of .615, the all-time highest for a major-league manager. Despite never playing in the major leagues, he would be elected to baseball's Hall of Fame in 1957. Remarkably, in his 34 years as a manager at all levels, only one of his teams would have a losing season or finish lower than fourth place.

It is not surprising there is no mention of Hurley's tryout in the Louisville papers since it would have been a private workout, and he never officially landed a place on the roster.

[37] Cook, Tom W., "Once School Teacher," *Louisville Times*, April 2, 1921, sports section.
[38] "Athletics Win from Neighbors," *Fargo Courier-News,* August 30, 1921, sports section.
[39] "Crowd of 2,394 People Watched Millers Defeat Fargo Athletics," *Fargo Forum*, September 3, 1921, sports section.

LOUISVILLE, AMERICAN ASSOCIATION, BASE BALL CLUB, 1921, LOUISVILLE, KY.

1, Massey; 2, Miller; 3, Ellis; 4, Koob; 5, Gaffney; 6, Cullop; 7, Wright; 8, Tincup; 9, Kirke; 10, Saunders; 11, Kocher; 12, Ballinger; 13, Estell; 14, Acosto; 15, Long; 16, Herzog; 17, McCarty; 18, Meyers; 19, Schepner.

Future Hall of Fame manager Joe McCarthy gave Hurley a tryout with the Louisville Colonels.

Ex-Graingrower Al Ellis may have told McCarthy about Hurley.

through the list of players, the article ended with a note about Jack: "'Colonel' Hurley, base umpire, will give his time to looking after his string of boxers who are scheduled to appear in many ring contests this season."[40]

Hurley's christening as the "Colonel" was obviously a dual reference to his tryout with the Louisville Colonels and his status as "colonel" in charge of his boxing stable. It was the first use of the title in connection with Jack; and the moniker would stick, as it continued to be used by Midwestern scribes even after he moved from Fargo to Duluth in 1927. In any event, the article provides additional confirmation that the trial occurred in 1921.

It may have been after reading about Hurley's boxing plans that his brother-in-law, Bill Comrie, just married to Jack's older sister, Margaret, suggested that Hurley should find a steady job. Traveling around the countryside with fighters was well and good for someone who had no responsibilities, but not for the oldest adult male still living at home in a family without a wage-earning husband or father. Jack had been out of the army 2-1/2 years, and it was high time to get to work.

According to family lore, Hurley told Bill he was "going to get a job" – maybe someday. Jack could see his brother-in-law's point. He felt an obligation to the family, but he still was not interested in pursuing a traditional occupation. What he meant when he said he was "going to get a job," was that he had a plan, the course of which was clarified by his failure to make it as a baseball player. He suspected all along he was not good enough, but old dreams die hard. He had, at least, given it his best effort.[41]

Even if his family did not realize it, Hurley already had assembled the ingredients for his future career. He had developed three fighters who he hoped would be popular in the coming year. He had proven his ability as an organizer of baseball teams and promoter of all-star games and had developed good relationships with the local press and most of the city's important sportsmen. All he needed was to blend his talent for handling boxers with his skill at publicizing and promoting baseball games.

Hurley had learned there was only small change to be made if he limited himself to managing boxers. To make real money, he had to run the whole show. In the future, he would take a manager's share of his fighters' purses, pay expenses, compensate the other boxers, handle publicity, rent the auditorium, and bring what was left home to his mother. Jack and his family couldn't have known it at the time, but within 1-1/2 years, he would be well on his way to becoming North Dakota's premier boxing promoter.

---

[40] "Fargo Players Tell of Plans," *Fargo Courier-News,* September 20, 1921, sports section.
[41] The story of Bill Comrie's conversation with Hurley was related to the author in May 2006 by Carol Olson, the daughter of Margaret and Bill Comrie.

CHAPTER 7

"WE'LL BE ROBBED!!"

Fight dollars were scarce and one of my boys, Russie Leroy was to box Johnny Knauf in Jamestown, North Dakota. But Knauf came down with tonsillitis, and the promoter said if I couldn't dig up a substitute he'd call off the show. I couldn't think of anyone to get on short notice, but I couldn't bear the idea of missing out on a $200 shot, so I told him a good New York lightweight, Jack Doyle, had stopped off in Fargo on his way to California, and I could get him for $250. The figure was a little stiff, but the promoter gave me the okay. Of course, Jack Doyle was just an alias for Jack Hurley.

I thought I detected a gleam of satisfaction in LeRoy's eyes when I told him about it. He didn't think much of me getting $250 for my end and also for cutting in for my piece of his $200. I knew what LeRoy had in mind. I had been in the habit of cuffing him around plenty in the gym, and he figured he would square up with me. I could do all right in the gym for a round or two, especially when I could call a halt as soon as I began to tire, but LeRoy knew this would be different – a real fight with small gloves.

We pulled into Jamestown, and all day we didn't meet a soul who knew me. That is, not until we climbed into the ring. Who should be the referee but a tough railroad cop named Bill Duffy, who knew me all too well. "What are you two thieves trying to get away with?" growled Duffy as we came to ring center. "Not a thing, Bill," I said. "This is going to be a real fight." "It better be," he rasped. "The first sign I see of you boys doing any funny business, out you both go and I'll see you get no dough."

Well, that did it. We couldn't afford to blow the dough. We went at it from the first gong. The customers yelled for LeRoy to flatten the New York dude and don't think Russie didn't try. It was awful tough going for me, in no shape and with six rounds to go. In the fourth though, I got LeRoy in a corner, wide open for a right, and I let him have it with all the power in my skinny frame. Trying to knock out my own fighter! Just imagine that! I shook him but he didn't fall, and from then on I had it tougher than ever.

How I stuck the six rounds I don't know. But I was still there at the finish. LeRoy got the newspaper decision, but I got the $250. It was a humdinger of a fight and the promoter wanted to sign us on the spot for a return match, but I told him I had to get along to California. After that one fight, Doyle vanished from the face of the earth.

It makes me laugh to hear fighters say how tired they are in a fight. They don't know what tired is. I was tired for weeks. [1]   – Jack Hurley

---

[1] Wood, Wilbur, "Jack Hurley Is a Rare Bird," *New York Sun*, January 11-13, 1949, sports section. The quote has been edited slightly to fit the context. Hurley's tale is based on an

****

Jack Hurley started the fall season September 28, 1921, by taking his three men to the American Legion's state convention at Jamestown, North Dakota. Hurley's two aces, Johnny Knauf and Russie LeRoy, won their fights, but Jack Bailey lost a newspaper decision to Leo Stokes. The show was so well received that the Legion's local Jamestown post reserved a date for another evening of bouts at its initiation ceremony December 2, 1921.[2]

Hurley left with Bailey and LeRoy October 3 to hunt for fights in St. Paul, but to no avail. Matchmaker Jack Reddy was happy to employ Jack's

---

event that occurred the evening of December 2, 1921. There is no reference to the bout in the *Jamestown Daily Alert*, presumably because the event was merely an evening of private entertainment for the local Jamestown post of the American Legion. The evidence comes from a *Fargo Forum* article published the morning of the bout:

"Hurley and his boxers left this morning for Jamestown, where they will present a series of exhibitions tonight for the Jamestown post of the American Legion. Hurley will mix a few rounds with Russie LeRoy while Snowball Draxton and Kid Sparks are scheduled to stage a little entertainment. If these boys do as well as they did for the Elks last Saturday, Jamestown legionnaires are due for a real treat. Gyp Ferris and Kid Franklin, both of Fargo are scheduled to box a four-round curtain raiser. Johnny Knauf, Hurley's promising welterweight, was scheduled to box with LeRoy but a bad attack of tonsillitis forced him to abandon the trip."

In Hurley's version as related to Wilbur Wood, Jack presents the event as a bonafide bout rather than an exhibition and glosses over the fact that Johnny Knauf was then a member of his boxing stable, as well. In fact, Jack was probably providing the entire night's entertainment for the Jamestown legionnaires by bringing six boxers with him from Fargo to fight three separate exhibition bouts. It is likely Hurley was given a fixed budget to provide a package of entertainment and that he paid each boxer a separately negotiated amount. He then probably paid himself what was left over. It is therefore doubtful that Jack really had to answer to anyone about who LeRoy would be boxing as long as the result was pleasing.

In substituting himself for one of his own boxers, Hurley was not really engaging in the subterfuge which he portrays in his story. In fact, it is almost certain that the main legionnaire operatives, including the referee and the legion's business manager, would have recognized Jack and not have fallen for such a ruse. Jamestown had been the site of a three-day state American Legion convention on September 28, 1921, just two months earlier. As part of the convention's entertainment each of Jack's three fighters (LeRoy, Knauf, and Bailey) had appeared in extensively advertised and well-reported bouts against arm's length opposition. While a typical rank and file legionnaire might not have recognized Hurley two months later, the hard-core sporting gentry among them would certainly have known him.

Furthermore, since Hurley's participation in the event had been published in the *Forum* on the morning of the event, it is unlikely that it could have remained a secret in Jamestown, only 90 miles away. If Jack and his stable could leave in the morning in time to arrive for the evening's show, so could the morning edition of the *Forum*, probably on the same train. If Hurley told a *Forum* reporter in advance that he was fighting in the exhibition, he would have been forced to tell the legion's management, as well.

Nevertheless, it is probably true that if Hurley had not stepped into the breach, LeRoy's purse would have been lost and possibly even the whole show canceled. Obviously, there was more going on than meets the eye. Jack still was trying to establish himself as a reputable supplier of boxing merchandise. This was very likely one of Hurley's early ventures into matchmaking outside the city limits of Fargo. At the time, the American

men as sparring partners, but he was hesitant to use them on shows because they were unknown in the Twin Cities. The only consolation for Hurley's battlers was a chance to work out with Mike Gibbons at the Rose Room gym. The sessions were particularly helpful to Jack Bailey, whose improvement came in for special mention after he returned to Fargo.[3]

Frustrated, Hurley returned to Fargo two weeks later and attempted to place his trio on a November 3rd card promoted by the Fargo Boxing Club, owned and operated by Frank J. Sullivan and Jack Clemmer. Jack believed LeRoy and Knauf had proven themselves as Fargo's best fighters the prior year and were entitled to main-event pay. It did not take long for Hurley and the new club to lock horns over what Russie and Johnny were worth.

Sullivan and Clemmer had entered the promoting business as a sideline to their main occupations. Sullivan worked as a manager at Berger's Billiards and Pool Hall on Third Street North, while Clemmer held down a job as a *Courier-News* pressman. Prior to the November 3rd show, they announced their club was reducing its admission prices, which had been a standard $1.50, $2, and $3; to $1, $1.50, and $2. They also said all ladies, whether accompanied by a male escort or not, would be admitted for free.[4]

Sullivan explained his reason for reducing prices to the *Courier-News:* "I want to see the fight game gain a foothold in Fargo. In the last card I put

---

Legion was one of the most important sponsors of boxing in North Dakota. If the show failed, Jack would have had all of Jamestown and five disappointed fighters on his hands, as well as a newly acquired reputation as a would-be matchmaker/manager who could not deliver the goods. As the text of this chapter explains, Hurley was feuding with a local Fargo promoter and was having trouble landing fights for his men at this time. He was literally scrambling just to keep his fighters happy and his own dream alive. Desperate circumstances required desperate measures.

Even though Hurley could not have passed himself off as "Jack Doyle" to those in the know, it is likely he still may have used a pseudonym. It was common practice at the time to use aliases and "fighting names" to introduce boxers. A little bit of showmanship might have entertained those who did not know him and who might have been impressed by a boxer coming all the way from New York. At worst, those who knew him would at least have been amused.

Finally, there is other evidence that Hurley's charge, Russie LeRoy, did in fact use the opportunity to "square up" things with his manager. Nine years later, Jack's mother told a *Fargo Forum* reporter that she had been "horror-stricken" when her son came home from the Jamestown exhibition "bruised and bleeding." Mother Aids Jack Hurley," *Fargo Forum,* December 28, 1930, sports section).

It is not surprising, then, given the beating he took at the hands of LeRoy, that Hurley felt entitled to make the most of the occasion by embellishing it for future audiences. The story became one of his early-career favorites and its entertainment content improved with each telling.

[2] See opening vignette and first footnote to this chapter.

[3] "Jack Hurley to Take Boxers to Twin Cities," *Fargo Courier-News*, October 2, 1921, sports section. "Boxers Start on Final Lap," *Fargo Forum*, October 26, 1921, sports section. "Boxers Have Last Workout," November 1, 1921, sports section.

[4] "Boxing Show Prices Attracting Crowds," *Fargo Daily Courier-News,* October 22, 1921, sports section.

on my profit amounted to $36.40, but I was glad to break even. The fight game holds me. I like to get before the crowd in the ring to announce the battlers, and the cheers are music in my ears. It's not the amount of the gate receipts that bothers me but, the amount of interest I can create for the greatest sport on earth, that tempts me to stage fights in Fargo."[5]

Hurley was able to negotiate a fair price for Bailey on the undercard, but the promoters were not prepared to pay what Jack thought LeRoy and Knauf were worth. "I tried to get Johnny," Sullivan told the reporter, but "Knauf refused to meet all the men I named for one reason and another, and besides, I am arranging a popular-priced entertainment and am not prepared to pay a Tex Rickard rate for a boxer of any kind. Knauf made his price prohibitive, that's all there was to it."[6]

Hurley's experience with Sullivan was an early example of what would become his pet peeve – the infiltration of "amateurs" into the boxing business. For the rest of his life, he would wage a one-man war against what "the shoemakers and ribbon-counter clerks" who let their enthusiasm overrule their judgment. Sullivan's notion that he was happy to break even because he enjoyed announcing the fighters and hearing the crowd's cheers marked him as just the kind of "amateur enthusiast" Jack abhorred.

Sullivan's excuse that "Knauf refused to meet all the men named" represented to Hurley an unacceptable infringement on his own prerogative as manager to choose his fighter's opponent, especially when the money offered was not commensurate with the risk presented. The reasons Sullivan gave for not being able to pay what Jack thought Knauf was worth was especially galling to Jack. Reducing admission prices for men and giving tickets away to women was not his idea of how to run a business.

Sullivan's commitment to "popular-priced entertainment" and his vow against paying a market rate "for a boxer of any kind," meant he was not the kind of promoter Hurley was interested in supporting. In Jack's mind, Leroy and Knauf's popularity merited an increase rather than a reduction in ticket prices. What Fargo needed was a man like Rickard who could recognize an attraction and then educate, cajole, and challenge the public to support the event.

His disagreement with Sullivan and Clemmer notwithstanding, Hurley was able to land spots in Fargo for Le Roy and Knauf on special holiday Thanksgiving and New Year's shows promoted by the Fargo Elks club. The Elks had imported Jack Reddy to serve as matchmaker for both events. The St. Paul man understood the value of both fighters as local attractions, and Hurley was able to negotiate terms for each of his charges.

---

[5] "Sullivan Plans Big Fight Card," *Fargo Courier-News*, c. September 17, 1921, sports section.
[6] Callaghan, M. J., "Dilworth Fans Back Mullen", *Fargo Courier-News*, October 11, 1921, sports section.

The Thanksgiving show was held Saturday, November 26, two days after the holiday. Both Fargo papers agreed LeRoy's eight-round contest with Len Schwabel of St. Paul was the best fight on card. Both had Leroy winning handily, scoring five rounds for Russie and three even. Even so, Len landed some telling blows and was credited with a game performance.

Johnny Knauf won an eight-round newspaper decision over Perry Bliven of Grand Forks on the New Year's card presented Monday, January 2, 1922. Knauf's speed and skill had improved noticeably over his past local fights. Hopelessly outclassed, Bliven was forced to clinch to avoid a kayo, and fans intermittently booed the action. Reddy billed the fight as a battle for the "welterweight championship of North Dakota," and the newspapers agreed Knauf fought well enough to deserve the designation.

Jack Bailey, the "hard luck kid," was scheduled to appear on the New Year's card, but an infected toe suffered in training turned into blood poisoning, and his foot swelled to twice its normal size. The illness was especially unfortunate since he had won his two most recent fights and was showing signs of returning to full strength after the relapse he suffered the prior year from his World War I gassing. As a result of this latest illness, he was hospitalized and would not return until July 1922.[7]

In addition to the Fargo and Jamestown shows, Hurley and his troupe spent a good deal of time during the season seeking fights in the North Dakota communities of Grand Forks, Bismarck, and Lakota, as well as traveling to more remote out-of-state locales like Thermopolis, Wyoming; Aberdeen, South Dakota; and Detroit Lakes, Minnesota.

LeRoy's toughest contests during the season's first half were two 10-round draw decision bouts at Grand Forks. On December 9, 1921, the *Grand Forks Herald* voted his fight with George Bowers a draw after awarding each boxer two rounds and scoring six rounds even. On January 27, 1922, the *Herald* gave LeRoy an edge in rounds won against Len Schwabel, four rounds to three, with three even, but ruled the fight a draw after giving Schwabel "credit for doing practically all of the leading."[8]

---

[7] "Jack Bailey Is Unable to Box, *Fargo Forum*, November 25, 1921, sports section. In the days before penicillin, blood poisoning was a primary cause of death among athletes. Any injury involving bone or teeth had to be monitored very carefully so that it would not develop into a case of blood poisoning. Les Darcy, Jimmy Delaney, and Young Stribling were some of the famous pugilists who died from the illness, which occurred as a secondary consequence of bone or tooth injury. (Note: Stribling's death from blood poisoning was a result of broken bones suffered in a motorcycle accident, not in the ring.) Bailey's prognosis for recovery was enough in doubt at the time for the Fargo boxing community to stage a card for his benefit on January 20, 1922. LeRoy won a newspaper decision over Freddie Lambert in the main event, and the proceeds were donated to Bailey. Luckily, he recovered from the disease and was able to resume his boxing career in July 1922. "Russie LeRoy Outpoints Lambert in Eight-Round Go," *Fargo Forum, January 21, 1922, sports section*.

[8] "Leroy and Bowers Fight Ten-Round Draw," *Grand Forks Daily Herald*, December 10, 1921, p. 10. "Leroy and Schwabel Fight Ten-Round Draw," *Grand Forks Daily Herald*,

An interesting example of Hurley's methods took place in Bismarck on February 17, when Knauf fought Jacob (Battling) Krause of Hazen, North Dakota. Although Krause was outweighed by 14-1/2 pounds, the *Bismarck Tribune* declared him winner by newspaper decision. Afterward, Jack apparently ran to the telegraph office and wired his own version of the fight to Fargo, since both the *Forum* and the *Courier-News* described the bout as a win for Knauf even though neither sent a reporter to Bismarck.[9]

On February 22, the Fargo newspapers announced the signing of Krause to a March 2nd main event against Buddy McDonald of St. Paul. In addition to their first look at the Hazen Stoneman, Fargo fans would be treated to a 10-round semifinal between LeRoy and Bowers. The latter bout was billed as a grudge-match follow-up to the draw the two men had fought previously at Grand Forks. The contest was especially important to Russie as an opportunity to erase one of the few blemishes on his record.

These first announcements neglected to mention the show would be Hurley's first as a boxing promoter in Fargo. Jack had been waiting for a lull between cards presented by the Elks club and Sullivan and Clemmer's Fargo Boxing Club. Fargo had been without a fight card for over a month, and the time was ripe for another. For his first venture, Jack enlisted the financial backing of Fargo businessman Ralph "Slim" Barkley.

Afterward, the *Forum*'s J. A. (Pat) Purcell praised Hurley's debut lavishly. "The show was a complete success from a spectators' standpoint," the reporter observed, "and the promoters reported they lost no money on the affair. The bout between LeRoy and Bowers was the only match of the evening that furnished any scientific work, but the crowd apparently wanted blood and thunder and they certainly got it."

Purcell reported Krause received a "terrible beating" from MacDonald, but somehow managed to last the ten-round distance and maintain his record of having never been knocked out. The action in the LeRoy-Bowers semifinal was close for four rounds until Russie took charge and scored a knockdown at the end of the fifth. Bowers reached his corner on wobbly legs, but he was unable to come out for the next round, and LeRoy's hand was raised as winner on a six-round knockout.[10]

The next day, LeRoy traveled to Aberdeen, South Dakota, where he won a ten-round decision over his other nemesis, Len Schwabel. Incredibly, he had defeated on successive days Schwabel and Bowers, who both held him to draws earlier in the season. The victories meant LeRoy could now boast

---

January 28, 1922, p. 8.

[9] "Knauf Shades 'Bat' Krause," *Fargo Forum*, February 18, 1922, sports section. For one of the best discussions about the practice of racing to the telegraph office, the reader is referred to Griffin, Marcus, *Wise Guy – James J. Johnston: A Rhapsody in Fistics*, (Vanguard Press, New York, 1933).

[10] Purcell, J. A., "Bismarck Man Gets Terrible Beating from Bud McDonald," *Fargo Forum*, March 3, 1922, sports section.

a win over every fighter he had fought and an overall record of 12 wins and six draws. In the past year, he had improved dramatically and had reached the point where he was a regional attraction.

Though LeRoy and Schwabel were ferocious competitors inside the ring, they were friends outside. Years later, Hurley recalled the match in an article for the *Forum*. "I remember an incident that happened ten years ago in Aberdeen," wrote Jack. "Russie LeRoy was boxing Len Schwabel. The bout was to go on after an Elks' initiation ceremony, real late at night. It was freezing cold, and poor Schwabel was uncomfortable in his room in a cheap hotel, where he was resting before being called to the arena.

"LeRoy had a nice warm room, so I took Schwabel over and put them in the same bed. They slept together for three hours and were awakened and taken to the arena. And how they fought. Schwabel was on the floor three times during the early part of the bout, but at the end was giving as good as he received. It was a real fight and after it was over, they shook hands and went back to LeRoy's room and slept in the same bed again."[11]

On March 4, Sullivan and Clemmer announced their intention to stage a March 17th St. Patrick's Day show. However, the Fargo Elks announced on the same day that the organization had scheduled a show for March 25 with all profits going to the Elks welfare association. As a courtesy, Sullivan and Clemmer agreed to postpone their promotion until April.[12]

The Elks' show was a sell-out. A crowd of 2,500 filled the Fargo Auditorium to watch LeRoy win a ten-round newspaper decision over Eddie DeBeau. A large sum was earned for the Elks welfare association.

Prior to the main event, the Elks allowed Sullivan to announce that his Fargo Boxing Club was attempting to sign Leo Stokes as a featured performer for its next program on April 7. Apparently, Sullivan thought since his club had stepped aside for the Elks charity promotion, it should be first in line to present the next Fargo show.[13]

On March 31, Hurley announced that for his second venture he had signed Johnny Noye, a Minneapolis lightweight, to fight LeRoy April 17. Jack followed up with a press release a few days later stating he had signed Leo Stokes to fight Jack's newest protégé, Tommy Ray, in a semifinal.[14]

---

[11] Hurley, Jack, "Ring Rations, *Fargo Forum*, November 1, 1931, sports section. This was the third and final fight between Schwabel and LeRoy. Schwabel later gave good accounts of himself in fights with two other Hurley protégés, Billy Petrolle (twice) and Spud Murphy.
[12] "Another Boxing Bout Promised," *Fargo Courier-News*, March 5, 1922, sports section. "Fargo Elks Plan Athletic Show," *Fargo Forum*, March 4, 1922, sports section.
[13] Purcell, "Fargo Battler Sends St. Paul Man to Carpet in First Round," *Fargo Forum*, March 27, 1922, sports section.
[14] Purcell, "Fargo Battler to Meet Tough St. Paul Boxer on 10 Round Go," *Fargo Forum*, April 1, 1922, sports section. "Tommy Ray to Fight Stokes," *Fargo Forum*, April 6, 1922, sports section.

As a matter of courtesy, competing promoters in the same city generally observed an informal agreement against publicizing the details of a future show until after their rival's pending event had taken place. The reasoning behind this custom was that if a fan was offered one event at a time, he would buy a ticket for each show as it came along. If two shows were advertised simultaneously, then he might become choosy and buy only one.

Hurley's announcement, made while his rival's show was pending, constituted a breach of etiquette and was tantamount to a declaration of war against Sullivan and Clemmer's Fargo Boxing Club. Jack's promotion would feature not only LeRoy, but also also Leo Stokes, the Fargo club's main attraction, all for the price of a single show. By signing Stokes away from his competitors, Jack had upstaged their efforts by proving he could bring a more entertaining brand of boxing to the city than they could.

Unable to secure the services of its own headliner, the Fargo Boxing Club bowed to the inevitable and suspended its plans for the April 7th show.

The *Courier-News*' lead sentence April 18 stated that "Hurley's [second] fight card, staged at the Fargo Auditorium last night, was a grand success." The main event, however, was memorable more for what happened afterward than for the ring action. Writing in the *Forum* 12 years later, Jack recalled that the fight itself was a dull affair, but the end "a near riot."

"Outside of LeRoy sticking a long left hand in Noye's face," wrote Hurley, "there wasn't a punch landed in ten rounds. Noye's legs were a little unsteady and he could never get quite close enough to nail Russie. As the bell rang ending the fight, LeRoy put out his hands to shake hands. This was the closest Noye had gotten for 30 minutes and he took advantage of the situation, belting LeRoy with his famous left hook. Then the fun began.

"LeRoy threw more punches the next 10 seconds, than he did the whole 10 rounds. It was the best exchange of the evening. Seconds and fans jumped in the ring and before order was restored, Johnny Nichols, St. Paul welterweight, who was handling Noye, got hit in the eye and received the only mark of the fight. With that, LeRoy's father slapped Noye on the back – and not gently – telling him he was a very poor sport. Noye turned around as though to hit Russie's dad, and the riot was on again. But cooler heads prevailed."[15]

In the semi-final, Leo Stokes won a ten-round newspaper decision over the newest member of Hurley's stable, Tommy Ray.[16]

Sullivan's partner, Jack Clemmer, announced at ringside prior to the LeRoy-Noye match that the Fargo Boxing Club was presenting its "next big fight card for Fargo" May 2. Clemmer told the audience that Chuck

---

[15] Ostman, Art, "... Fans Pleased with Card – Johnny Noye Badly Outclassed. Tries to Start Rough-House," *Fargo Courier-News*, April 18, 1922, sports section. Hurley, "Shadow Boxing," *Fargo Forum*, March 4, 1934, sports section. "Purcell,, "Fargo Battler Makes Old Ring Head Look Bad in Every Round," *Fargo Forum*, April 18, 1922, sports section.

[16] Tommy Ray would have a few more fights in 1922 and fade out of the Hurley picture.

Lambert of St. Paul and Silver Perry of Miles City, Montana, already had signed contracts with his club to appear in the main event. Three days later, Hurley countered Clemmer by telling a *Forum* reporter he had signed crack St. Paul lightweight, Bobby Ward, to box Russie LeRoy "early in May."[17]

Hurley had decided again to ignore established custom. He was not going to wait in line. He was operating from a position of strength. He had in LeRoy the attraction people wanted to see. Now was the time to confront the competition and determine who the best promoter in North Dakota was.

This time Sullivan and Clemmer did not back down. The two boxing clubs were going up against each other head-to-head in open warfare. There were going to be two boxing shows in "the Gate City" within ten days of each other. The date of the Fargo Boxing Club's card was moved back a day to May 3. Hurley's show was set for May 12.

The danger to the boxing public of a full-scale promoters' war is that the consumer's dollar might be split so that no one is able to succeed. If anything, Hurley had more at stake than his competitors, who possessed income sources independent from boxing.

If Hurley was acting ruthlessly, it was out of necessity. For him, it was a make-or-break moment. Immediate results were critical because of resistance he was encountering on the homefront from his mother and her brother, Dan Healy. Almost 40 years later, Jack recalled the situation for *Sports Illustrated* columnist Jack Olsen.

"Uncle Dan told Ma that boxing wasn't a nice business, and I was disgracing the family name," Hurley said. "I said, 'Ma, I am not going to disgrace the family name. I have an ability to teach fighters, and I'm going to develop a fighter from this town that will make the town proud of the town, not of me.' I said, 'Ma, as long as I don't get in any trouble, and don't steal any money, why don't you let me have a shot at it?' So, reluctantly, she let me go ahead."[18]

Sullivan and Clemmer's show on May 3 was a feast for fans but a fizzle at the box office. The *Forum*'s headline read in part: "Small Gathering of Fans See Interesting Program." In the main event, Lambert won 10-round newspaper decision over Stokes, who was substituting for Silver Perry.[19]

Hurley's show nine days later, on the other hand, was an unqualified success, both artistically and financially. LeRoy scored the most important victory of his career to date by winning the ten-round newspaper decision over a far more experienced Bobby Ward. The *Forum* reported that from "start to finish it was a well balanced card that would stack up well beside

---

[17] "Big Fight Card Is Billed for May 2," *Fargo Courier-News*, April 18, 1922, sports section. Purcell, "Bobby Ward of St. Paul to Meet Russie LeRoy," *Fargo Forum*, April 21, 1922, p. 14.

[18] Olsen, Jack, "Don't Call Me Honest—Part I," *Sports Illustrated*, May 15, 1961, p. 86.

[19] Purcell, "Heavyweights Put Up Fight," *Fargo Forum*, May 4, 1922, sports section.

previous cards here this winter." The *Courier-News* added that a "large crowd attended the show, which was put on by Jack Hurley."[20]

The success of his third show was a vindication of all the work Hurley was putting into his new business. He had proven himself to be the best promoter in the city. More importantly, he showed he could make a living from boxing to his mother, his Uncle Dan, his brother-in-law Bill Comrie, and to everyone else who had questioned his career choice.

"So, now I run a couple of shows," Hurley told Olsen, "and I come home, and I drop 100 $1 bills on the table loosely, and Ma ran and pulled down all the blinds. She said: 'We'll be robbed.' I said: 'That's for you.' She said: 'I don't need anything.' She already had one dress. So she hid the money in dishes and closets and other places. If anybody would've have robbed us it would've taken him three weeks to find all the money.

"Now, Uncle Dan tells Ma he wants a free ticket to the next fight. I say 'Ma, Uncle Dan can never get a free ticket; nobody gets free tickets except the press.' She looked like she was going to cry, so I put $3 on the table and say, 'He can buy a ticket with that, but he can't have a free ticket.'"

While proving himself, Hurley overcame another obstacle. Unhappy with the press coverage for his first show, he started his own newsletter which he delivered to billiard parlors, tobacco shops, barbershops, fraternal organizations, and other spots where people were "sitting around doing nothing." To his amazement, Jack sold $300 worth of advertising to local retailers. After his first issue, an envoy from one of the established papers came by and promised plenty of publicity if he discontinued his newsheet.

"So I said O.K.," Hurley told Olsen, and "this guy gave me so much space it was embarrassing. My first show drew $700, and my second show – with the aid of the free newspaper – sold $1,600. Then the daily began giving full coverage, and the third show drew $3,200. I was so embarrassed at all the publicity he gave us I asked him to cut it down a little."[21]

Fargo's American Legion post promoted the season's last show on June 6, 1922, in connection with an initiation ceremony held earlier in the day. Hurley had first refused the legion's offer to LeRoy, but he relented after the legion threatened to sign another fighter. As it turned out, Russie was lucky to salvage a ten-round newspaper draw with Milwaukee lightweight Eddie Boehme. In the semifinal, Jack's new charge, Al Biddle, also fought a crowd-pleasing draw with Freddie Lambert of St. Paul.[22]

Hurley ended the 1921-'22 season as it began – once again selling the services of his stable to the American Legion – this time to a post at Detroit Lakes, Minnesota in connection with its annual July 4th celebration.

---

[20] Purcell, "LeRoy Outpoints, Bobby Ward," *Fargo Forum*, May 13, 1922, sports section. "Russie LeRoy Shades Ward," *Fargo Courier News*, May 13, 1922, sports section.

[21] Olsen, pp. 85-8.

[22] Purcell, "LeRoy and Boehme Stage Furious Fight. Biddle Holds Lambert Even," *Fargo Forum*, June 7, 1922, sports section.

"WE'LL BE ROBBED!!" 127

Hurley's 3rd boxing show, Fargo Auditorium, May 12, 1922, Russie LeRoy-Bobby Ward. In the ring (left to right): unknown, Bobby Ward, his manager Jack Reddy, referee Leo Kossick, Russie LeRoy, and Hurley.

Close-up of the Russie LeRoy-Bobby Ward square-off, May 12, 1922.

Johnny Schauer    Len Schwabel    Johnny Noye

Unfortunately, LeRoy suffered his first defeat, losing an unexpected ten-rounder to St. Paul lightweight Johnny Schauer. In the semifinal, Bailey, finally over his protracted siege with blood poisoning, returned to action and defeated Chuck Lambert in eight rounds. In a preliminary, newcomer Biddle drew with Lambert's brother, Freddie, also in eight rounds.[23]

After the Detroit Lakes card, Hurley announced LeRoy was taking a rest. Russie had come a long way in a short time, but the season ended on a slightly down note with the Boehme and Schauer fights. *Forum* reporter Purcell offered this assessment of LeRoy's progress:

> "Six weeks rest no doubt will tend to put LeRoy back in the condition he was when he met and defeated Bobby Ward of St. Paul. Since that bout LeRoy has been far from right. He was decisively outpointed by Johnny Schauer of St. Paul and had a hard time earning a draw with Eddie Boehme of Milwaukee, his only two bouts since meeting with Ward.
>
> "Fargo fans have censured LeRoy severely since his July 4 bout with Schauer at Detroit. For the first time in his short career did the fans boo him and demand action. It was clearly evident that LeRoy was not himself in the Detroit Lakes ring or otherwise he would have given Schauer the fight of his life.
>
> "Fans have stated that LeRoy has not a fighting heart. He proved this beyond a doubt when he stood and exchanged punches with the hard-hitting Eddie Boehme.
>
> "What LeRoy needs most of all is a good rest ... He has met the toughest and cleverest lightweights in the Northwest, and Boehme and Schauer are the only two who might claim decisions over him. Bobby Ward, Johnny Noye, Eddie DeBeau, Johnny O'Donnell, Len Schwabel and George Bowers all have felt his lightening left and snappy right. LeRoy decisively outpointed each of them.
>
> "A reversal of form, natural to every fighter who engages in too many battles, and the fans claim he is slipping. LeRoy is nothing more or less than a beginner, and fans should remember he is but a youngster, being just past the 20 year mark. LeRoy still has two years to develop before choosing the tough ones. He has plenty to

---

[23] Purcell, "Bailey and Schauer Win Independence Day Bouts, *Fargo Forum*, July 5, 1922, sports section. The July 4th fight was Al Biddle's last under the Hurley banner. Biddle was apparently something of a vagabond, an experienced battler who migrated to Fargo from the West Coast, having had quite a few fights in Washington and California in the years before 1922. He seems to have latched onto Hurley mainly for the purpose of landing a few fights while checking out the scene in the Midwest. Biddle turned up in New York in 1924 and finally returned to the West Coast where he finished his boxing career at Vallejo, California in 1928. He may have been the father of Jack Biddle who hailed from Vallejo and who campaigned as a light heavyweight up and down the West Coast with mediocre success from 1941 to 1949.

learn of the art of infighting and as he learns his speed will increase.

"While he is but a beginner, he is no novice. He has a keen pair of eyes and is extraordinarily fast with his hands and feet. His clever footwork brought more than merely favorable mention from the Twin City fight critics. He has been hailed as a comer, and, some day if properly handled and trained, will be among the leading lightweights of the country."[24]

During the 1921-'22 season, LeRoy surpassed Johnny Knauf as Hurley's main meal ticket. From September 28, 1921 through July 1922, Russie recorded 11 wins, one loss and three draws. He fought at a killing pace the entire season, and only at the end did he show signs of fatigue.

Knauf, though hampered at first by tonsillitis, started the season well enough, scoring three wins and two draws in his five bouts. His year ended in February, however, when he not only lost by decision to Battling Krause at Bismarck, but also suffered a broken hand. At first, it was thought Johnny would be away from the ring just a few months, but the injury proved serious enough to keep him out of action until January 1923.[25]

Bailey's victory over Lambert on the July 4th card at Detroit Lakes improved his record for the 1921-'22 season to a respectable three wins, one loss, and one draw. Shortly afterward, however, Bailey journeyed to Wyoming where Hurley had arranged a series of bouts for him. While in training for the bout there, he suffered two broken ribs which would keep him out of action until December. In the meantime, Bailey returned to his home in Chicago to wait for the injury to mend.[26]

For the first time since he had started to play baseball, Hurley sat out the 1922 season. Although he would in the future play in a local amateur league, he would never play professional ball again. Undoubtedly Jack was looking forward to a little rest himself. He had either been playing baseball or hustling for his fighters non-stop for three years.

****

After a three-month lull in boxing, *Forum* reported on October 7, 1922:

> "Fight fans of Fargo and Moorhead will get their first action of the season on Friday, Oct. 27, when the first of a series of seven shows will be presented in the Fargo Auditorium under the direction of the Elks welfare association.

---

[24] Purcell, "LeRoy Will Take Complete Rest," *Fargo Forum*, July 8, 1922, sports section.
[25] "Bowers and McDonald to Fight Here March 2," *Fargo Courier-News*, February 22, 1922, sports section.
[26] Purcell, "Bailey, LeRoy Signed to Feature Elks Welfare New Year's Fight Card," *Fargo Forum*, December 18, 1922, sports section.

"According to an arrangement made by the heads of the welfare association all of the fights to be presented in Fargo this winter will be staged under their direction. All of the proceeds will be used for charitable purposes."

Hurley was stunned by this turn of events. The previous season he had proven for the first time in Fargo's history that boxing could be operated profitably on consistent basis. Now as a reward for his efforts, the local Elks club was cutting him out and moving in on the business that he had developed from next to nothing.

Although Hurley had been Fargo's most successful promoter, he was at a disadvantage when it came to competing with fraternal organizations which held themselves out as promoters. Groups like the Elks and the American Legion were firmly entrenched in the city, and their members formed a good portion of the city's fan base. These clubs advertised their shows as charitable ventures. Jack realized it would take some time to win a promotional war against such well-intentioned organizations.

As a result, Hurley decided to suspend his activities in Fargo for the time being. Sooner or later, boxing fans would tire of the mediocre fare these amateur promoters would inevitably provide. Jack could then return to Fargo and resume operations as before.

In October 1922, Hurley closed up shop in Fargo, rented a room at the Spalding Hotel in St. Paul, Minnesota, and established a new headquarters at the Rose Room gym in the city's downtown district. His plan was to book fighters from his hotel room, scout around for new fistic prospects at the gym, and see what might develop for him in the Twin Cities.

In a bit of tit-for-tat, Hurley told the *Forum* that "Russie LeRoy, Fargo's best lightweight tosser, will not make his fall debut in Fargo this season." It was his parting shot as he left Fargo for St. Paul. Obviously, he was not in a mood to assist the opposition, no matter how "charitable" their motives. If Jack was being forced out of town, he was taking the rights to Fargo's No. 1 boxing attraction with him. Jack may have lost the battle, but the war was not over. He would be back to fight another day.[27]

---

[27] Purcell, "Fight Season to Open Oct. 27," *Fargo Forum,* October 7, 1922, sports section.

CHAPTER 8

EXILE AND REDEMPTION

A little Italian fellow entered the Elks clubrooms, then over the Nestor billiards parlors, and asked for the matchmaker. "I'd like to fight on your next show," the bashful little fellow managed to roll off his tongue. On being questioned it was revealed the youngster was Billy Petrolle, age 17 and weight 126 pounds. Yes, he had some amateur experience in New York, but very little.

At that time Kid Fogarty of Bismarck was a student at the Agricultural College and matchmaker Hughes was anxious to build him up for future shows. So, Billy Petrolle was signed to meet Fogarty in the opening preliminary as a means of introducing the Bismarck fighter. During a public workout before the contest, Petrolle's gesture at shadow boxing was laughable. He resembled a bicycle rider attempting to brush horse flies off his forehead. In fact, it seemed that he was attempting to knock himself out.

Billy had a fine personality, and his ever ready grin made him something of a favorite with the railbirds before he stepped into the ring, but it did not seem possible that he could cope with the experienced Bismarck lad. George A. Barton, veteran Minneapolis referee, handled Petrolle's first fight, and we took it upon ourself to ask Barton to "see that the little Dago doesn't get punched up too much as he's a likable kid."

Fogarty had an edge, as we expected, in the first round by boxing cleverly until Petrolle sent Fogarty to the canvas for a count of four before the bell sounded. Fogarty was not seriously injured by the blow and walked unassisted to his own corner.

After a lively mix in the second round, Petrolle landed two hard rights in the body and then shot over a left uppercut that ended the bout. Fogarty went down like he had been slugged with a sledge and he never wiggled after landing on his back. Barton dismissed the formality of counting, dropped to his knees and started the work of reviving the fallen Bismarck fighter.

Quite damp with perspiration by the time he had brought Fogarty to his senses, Barton came over to where the writer was seated at the ringside, leaned over the ropes and asked, "Say, which one of those birds was I supposed to take care of?"[1]

— Pat Purcell

---

[1] Purcell, J. A., "Rambling Through Sportville," *Fargo Forum*, September 15, 1929, sports section. Purcell, "Homer Sheridan Defeats Silver Perry in Feature Event of Elks Show – Mullen Battles Gamely but Loses to Earl Blue," *Fargo Forum*, October 28, 1922, sports section. Most of the quotation is from Purcell's September 15, 1929 article. However, his later recollection of the first round and the kayo punch was at variance with his prior eyewitness account. The description of blows land from the earlier version has been inserted

****

Jack Hurley's migration from Fargo to St. Paul at the beginning of the 1922-'23 boxing season was as natural as the flow of spring water from one of Minnesota's 10,000 lakes to the Mississippi River. In addition to being close to Fargo, the Twin Cities' region of St. Paul and Minneapolis was the accepted center of boxing for the entire Midwest, more important even than Chicago, where the sport would continue to be illegal until 1925.

Inspired by Mike Gibbons' popularity, Minnesota passed a bill in 1915 legalizing ten-round no-decision boxing contests. To assure passage, the bill's supporters agreed to limit the number of franchises to a single qualified bidder from each of the state's three largest cities: Minneapolis, St. Paul, and Duluth. Each franchise was allowed to present a maximum of 12 amateur or pro shows per year. Another concession required promoters to pay a ten percent tax on gross receipts to the state's tuberculosis fund.[2]

Even with the restrictions imposed by the compromise legislation, boxing flourished in the Twin Cities. From 1915 to 1925, no pugilistic center in the world boasted more quality boxers than Minneapolis and St. Paul. In the early 1920s, over 500 boxers billed as "from St. Paul" plied their trade in arenas across the country. At Johnny Salvator's Rose Room Gym in St. Paul alone, a reported 149 practitioners worked out daily.[3]

Unfortunately, by 1922, the region's boxing prosperity was nearing an end. Within a few years, passage of favorable legislation by states more populous than Minnesota would shift the sport's center away from the Twin Cities. Legislative inertia by lawmakers would prevent enactment of a new law to keep up with the competition from other states. In addition, Mike Gibbons' decision to retire in June 1922 and the looming retirements of other St. Paul idols presaged an end to the sport's balmy days in the region.

At the beginning of the 1922-'23 season, however, local fans, as yet unmindful of the sport's fragile status, were preparing to enjoy the last hurrah of boxing's glory years in the Twin Cities. Entering the twilight of their careers, heavyweight contender Billy Miske and former middleweight champion Mike O'Dowd would both be seen for the last time in a St. Paul boxing ring. Former bantamweight champion Johnny Kewpie Ertle would also return for his farewell appearance before a local audience.

On happier notes, Tommy Gibbons, Mike's younger brother, would earn a shot at Jack Dempsey's heavyweight crown by defeating Miske in St. Paul; middleweight Jock Malone would continue to be a source of local pride by defeating Bryan Downey, Johnny Klesch, and Mike O'Dowd; and

---

for the sake of accuracy.
[2] Barton, George A., *My Lifetime in Sports,* (Lund Press, Minneapolis, MN, 1957) p. 55.
[3] Gold, Paul R., "Growing Up in St. Paul: Manager, Fight Promoter, Minnesota Game Warden – Johnny Salvator and His Impact on Boxing in St. Paul," *Ramsey County History, Volume 37, No. 2,* Summer, 2002, p. 21. Reddy, Jack, "Heard in St. Paul," *Ring Magazine,* February 1923, p. 34.

Jimmy Delaney would gain respect as a leading light-heavyweight contender with wins over Hughie Walker, Ted Jamieson, and Billy Shade.[4]

Hurley barely had settled into St. Paul's Spaulding Hotel in September 1922 when the *St. Paul Pioneer Press* announced Mike Gibbons and his former manager Mike Collins were forming a partnership to manage a stable of 25 boxers who Gibbons would train while Collins would handle booking arrangements. In addition to the St. Paul office, they planned to set up branch offices in the East, the Pacific Coast, Milwaukee, and Chicago.[5]

The new partnership united the two most important figures in Minnesota boxing history: Gibbons, the master boxer and theorist of the pugilistic art; and Collins, the wily manager and purveyor of fistic ballyhoo. The two Mikes had joined forces a first time 1-1/2 years earlier when Gibbons asked Collins to manage his return to the ring in a final attempt to achieve his lifetime dream of winning the middleweight title

Gibbons had been unsuccessful in a title bid November 21, 1919, when he lost a ten-round newspaper decision to fellow townsman Mike O'Dowd. Though experts suggested O'Dowd, who was ten years younger than Gibbons, could not have held a candle to him five years earlier, Gibbons was not consoled. Discouraged, he retired as a boxer and accepted posts as a boxing instructor at Illinois University and the St. Paul Athletic Club. He also started a correspondence school which taught boxing through the mail.

In early 1921, Johnny Wilson defeated O'Dowd in a 15-round decision to win the middleweight title. Once again, Gibbons felt "that old and unquenchable desire to get that middleweight crown making its presence known." Despite his 34 years, he believed he had the style to beat the new champion, and he decided to make one last run at the title. It was at this time that he enlisted Collins to handle his affairs.[6]

Although an eye injury ended his career before he could arrange a match with Wilson, Gibbons' return to boxing was otherwise successful. From April 1921 until his final retirement in June 1922, Mike won 26 of 29 bouts, netting the boxer and his manager a total of $131,000 and making his last year as a fighter the most profitable of his career.[7]

Gibbons gave Collins "full credit for my success in the business end of my campaign," and glowingly described him "as a man of sound business acumen, possessing a wide knowledge of the boxing game, and much sagacity, especially in the management and promoting ends, an expert on

---

[4] Based on a myriad of articles appearing in the *St. Paul Pioneer Press* from August through March 1923.
[5] "Fight Headquarters Here," *St. Paul Pioneer Press,* September 3, 1922, sports pages.
[6] Gibbons, Mike, "Mike Gibbons Tells How He Made Most Successful Comeback in Ring History," *Boxing Blade, 1922 Annual Review*, p. 16.
[7] Collins, Mike, "The Editor's Corner," *Boxing Blade,* December 6, 1924, p. 4.

Billy Miske who fought Jack Dempsey three times.

Middleweight champion Mike O'Dowd.

Bantam champ Johnny Ertle.

Light heavy Tommy Gibbons.

Middleweight Jock Malone.

Light heavy Jimmy Delaney.

Mike Gibbons retired as a boxer and partnered with Mike Coilins (right) in managing boxers when Hurley moved to St. Paul in 1922.

publicity, and an all together 'go-getter.'" Given their high regard for each other, the decision to form a new management team was an easy one.[8]

Despite his unconventional profession, Collins exuded a conservative aura and preferred to address new associates formally by surname. In surviving photos, he favors three-piece suits with a subdued tie and a gold watch chain. He displays neither tilted derby nor chomped cigar to detract from the sharp features of an intelligent-looking face. Alhough short in stature, his piercing gaze and firmly set jaw display a presence which must have commanded respect and instilled confidence in those with whom he dealt.

Collins was born near Hudson, Wisconsin in May, 1879. As a young man he worked on the family farm, rode logs on the turbulent Minnesota and Wisconsin rivers, operated threshing equipment for hire, and clerked in hotels. Sometime after 1900, he opened a saloon in Hudson and began promoting bouts on a bootleg basis. A surviving handbill dates him as staging a six-round exhibition between Mike Gibbons and George Barton in 1908. Census records show he was still running the saloon in 1910.[9]

Hudson was a town of 2,800 people located across the Mississippi River from Minnesota just 20 miles east of St. Paul. After the Wisconsin legislature legalized boxing in 1913, Collins, with admirable foresight and derring-do, built a large boxing arena in Hudson. There, he successfully promoted boxing on a regular basis for two years.

It was at Hudson that such St. Paul boxing greats as Mike and Tommy Gibbons, Billy Miske, Mike O'Dowd, and Johnny Ertle came to prominence. Twin City boxing fans, unable to see their heroes in their own cities, streamed across the river to see them at Collins' arena. Attendance of more than 5,000 people and gates of over $10,000 were commonplace. Collins' largest house was the Mike Gibbons-Eddie McGoorty show in March 1915 which drew 8,000 fans and a gate of over $19,000.

After boxing in Minnesota was legalized in 1915, Collins abandoned the Hudson enterprise, knowing he could no longer make a profit without the support of Minnesota fans. His plan was to forget boxing and provide for his family with a cushy $7,500 per year sales position offered him by a champagne distributor, but the lure of the ring was too strong.

Instead, Collins undertook to manage Fred Fulton, the Rochester Plasterer, a heavyweight boxer so named more for his skill as a legitimate plaster craftsman than for his fighting prowess. Fulton, a handsome blonde specimen standing 6-feet 6-inches tall, struck an impressive pose and could fight as long as the going did not get too rough. If it did, he had the tendency to take "the easy way out" and lie down.

---

[8] Gibbons, "My Eighteen Years in the Ring," *Boxing Blade,* May 30, 1925, p. 8.
[9] 1900 and 1910 U. S. Census. Collins, *Ring Battles of the Ages* (Boxing Book Publishing Co., 1932), p. 2.

Mike Collins' arena at Hudson, Wisconsin, located just across the Minnesota border. The upper photo shows construction during the winter of 1912-'13. The lower photo depicts the interior at the arena's opening in 1913. Boxing thrived at Hudson until the Minnesota legislature legalized the sport in 1915. The facility reportedly accommodated 8,000 fans and remains to this day one of the largest arenas ever built for the exclusive purpose of housing regular boxing cards. Photos courtesy of Jake Wegner and the late Willis Miller.

Collins purchased a small boxing club in Eau Claire, Wisconsin to build up Fulton as a national attraction. After a few wins in the Midwest against carefully chosen opposition, Collins began to tout Fred as the leading challenger for Jess Willard's heavyweight title.

Collins' efforts had the desired effect. On December 16, 1915, articles were signed for Fulton to box Willard in New Orleans during Mardi Gras week. Mike was guaranteed $20,000 for the match. Soon afterward, however, Fulton decided he did not need Collins anymore because he could find others to represent him for less money.

Needless to say, Collins was beside himself with indignation. He had turned down a good paying job, invested his entire $5,000 nest egg, and jeopardized the well-being of his family to obtain the Willard match. And now, just as they were about to cash in, Fulton had dropped Mike like a dead fish. In what might be considered poetic justice, however, Fred's bout with Willard fell through a few weeks after he left Collins.[10]

To make ends meet, Collins returned to his threshing business in the winter and managed A. G. Barnes' traveling circus in the summer. After a year with Barnes in 1915, Mike formed his own carnival and tent show in 1916 and 1917, enlisting the help of "champion open air announcer" Al (Big Hat) Fisher. Together, they toured small towns in the Midwest and the South with a motley troupe of "all-star" wrestlers and boxers.

By comparison, day-to-day carnival life made boxing seem like an innocent parlor game. Collins' performers challenged local toughs while masquerading as sports heroes. If no local talent was forthcoming to accept their challenges, suitable "ringers" were provided by carnival management.

Collins' main attraction was a dark-haired roustabout who dyed his hair blonde and impersonated leading heavyweight contender Frank Moran. Also popular was "Lady Kelly," who was billed as a world champion woman wrestler until she was picked up and thrown out of the ring by a local 200-pound Irish girl who claimed the $25 prize money. If ticket sales fell, a look-alike of movie queen Theda Bara could be passed off as the real thing and be relied upon to make a special appearance as guest referee.

Three seasons with the carnival led Collins to yearn for a return to the more serene and secure life of the prize ring. In January 1918, he acquired the Minneapolis boxing franchise, where he successfully promoted fights until 1922. At the same time he continued to manage the fistic fortunes of Johnny Ertle, Johnny Noye, Jock Malone, and, finally, Mike Gibbons.[11]

Collins was also involved in the publishing business. In 1920, he purchased the *Boxing Blade*, the first weekly boxing periodical to enjoy

---

[10] Collins, "The Editor's Corner," *Boxing Blade*, December 6, 1924, pp. 2-3.

[11] Collins, Collins' series on his carnival experiences from the following issues of the *Boxing Blade*: April 26, 1924, pp. 2, 12; May 10, p. 2; May 31, 1924, pp. 2-3; and June 7, 1924, p. 3. Collins, Mike, "Editor's Corner," *Boxing Blade*, December 6, 1924 and August 8, 1925, p. 2 (same page both issues).

nationwide distribution in the United States. The publication served the multiple purposes of supplying legitimate historical and up-to-date boxing information to its readers as well as providing its owner a soapbox for touting his boxing stable and presenting his opinions about the sport.[12]

In 1922, Collins liquidated his Minneapolis franchise and formed the partnership with Mike Gibbons to manage boxers. Their association would last until April 1925 when Gibbons retired from boxing to sell insurance. Within a few years, Collins would re-purchase the Minneapolis franchise and continue to promote boxing well past 1930.[13]

Collins would play an important role in the careers of both Hurley and his protégé, Billy Petrolle, by going out on a financial limb to stage Petrolle's non-title fight against world lightweight champion Sammy Mandell January 13, 1928. Later that year, Mike would promote the third of Billy's six fights against arch-rival King Tut (Henry Tuttle). Both fights were well received, producing receipts of $17,000 and $12,000, respectively.

The nerve center in St. Paul for all boxers, including those managed and trained by Collins and Gibbons, was the Rose Room gym, located downtown on St. Peter Street in the basement of the Hamm Building, then the headquarters for Hamm's Brewery. Boxing promoter Jack Reddy described the Rose Room as "one of the finest gyms in the country." One St. Paul reporter called the location "an ideal spot for a gymnasium" and commented that it had "all the modern conveniences that fighters want."[14]

The Rose Room was Hurley's hangout during his time in St. Paul. There, Jack bantered with reporters, managers, and railbirds; trained his fighters; and immersed himself in learning more about the boxing business.

The gym was also where Hurley solidified his friendship with the facility's owner, Johnny Salvator. Jack first met Salvator in October 1921 when he arranged two weeks of sparring sessions at the gym for LeRoy and Bailey. The two men crossed paths again July 4, 1922, in Detroit Lakes when Bailey won a decision over Salvator's fighter Chuck Lambert.[15]

---

[12] One of the best endorsements of the *Boxing Blade*'s impact appears in the memoirs of Louis L'Amour, *Education of a Wandering Man*, (Bantam Books, 1989), p. 18:

"At the time a boxing magazine was published in St. Paul, Minnesota (one of the great fight towns in its day). It was printed on pink paper like the more famous *Police Gazette* and was called the *Boxing Blade*. Aside from articles on boxers and boxing, old and new, it also published the decisions in fights all over the world. These decisions usually covered two or three pages in relatively fine print, and I was an avid reader of this weekly, with a good memory for who had fought whom and the result. I also learned how certain fighters reacted to southpaws, fancy-dan boxers and the like."

[13] "Mike Gibbons to Retire from the Fistic Business," *Fargo Daily Tribune*, April 19, 1925, sports section.

[14] Reddy, *op. cit.* "Minnesota Boxing News," *Boxing Blade*, May 14, 1921, p. 5.

[15] "Sully Changes Boxing Show," *Fargo Forum*, October 12, 1921, sports section. "Bailey Set for Chuck Lambert," *Fargo Forum*, July 3, 1922, sports section.

Mike Collins and Fred Fulton.

Collins and Jimmy Delaney.

Rose Room gym operator Johnny Salvator, Hurley's closest friend.

JACK HURLEY
Boxing Manager
Spaulding Hotel, St. Paul, Minn.
Telephone, Garfield 5861

Jack Hurley

Managing the following boxers:
Jack Bailey—158.
Mark Foley—158.
Al Biddle—138 to 145.
Russie LeRoy—135 to 138.
Jackie Nichols—120 to 126.

Jack's ad in 1923 Boxing Blade.

Salvator later told his son that Hurley was "his closest friend in the boxing business." There is no reason to believe Jack felt anything but the same toward Salvator. Indeed, since Hurley's entire life was boxing, it is probably safe to conclude that, after the death of Billy McCarney in 1948, Johnny became Jack's most enduring close friend.

The two men remained in contact the rest of their lives. When Hurley moved to Duluth and then to Chicago, the Salvators would visit Jack and his wife regularly to play bridge. When Salvator purchased the St. Paul franchise in 1931, Hurley helped out with the money to buy it. When Harry Matthews fought Rocky Marciano in 1952, Johnny and his wife cooked meals for Matthews in New York. When Jack took Boone Kirkman to St. Paul for a fight in 1970, he visited the Salvators at their home near St. Paul.

Salvator was born Johann Salwetter in 1891 on a farm in Serbia, the youngest son of seven children raised by German parents. After he started boxing, writers dubbed him "Salvator," the name of a famous racehorse of the era. He later adopted the name legally.

Under Serbian law, the eldest brother inherited the family's property when the patriarch died. As the youngest male child, he had no prospects for success in Serbia. His mother was afraid he would be drafted into the army and never be heard from again. She encouraged Johann to immigrate to America and so he did, docking alone at Ellis Island in 1907.

Arriving at St. Paul, Salvator tried a variety of menial jobs. He was working as a grocery store clerk when he met Billy Miske and the Gibbons brothers who were training nearby at Big Marine Lake. To the ambitious but impoverished young immigrant, the life of a boxer seemed to hold more promise than any other job within his reach.

Since boxing in Minnesota was illegal at the time, Salvator fought mostly outside the state, achieving his greatest popularity in Missouri. He had mixed success record-wise, but he earned a respectable living. One sportswriter wrote that Salvator was not a clever boxer, but was rather, "a bloody battler." His wife remembered that after several of his fights Johnny was so sore she was not able to even touch him on their way home.

During World War I, Salvator, not yet an American citizen, volunteered as a "dollar-a year" civilian sports instructor. In addition to boxing, he taught calisthenics and tennis to newly enlisted recruits. Afterward, he went into the movie theater business with his wife's family, but soon began managing boxers. The fighters he handled between World War I and the Depression included Al Van Ryan, Carl Augustine, Dago Joe Gans, Chuck Lambert, Rusty Jones, Johnny O'Donnell, Billy Light, and My Sullivan.[16]

Salvator purchased the Rose Room in May 1921. Aided by the post-war boom, the gym was a huge success. Soon, he was staging weekly amateur cards and charging $1 to each of the 1,000 fans which the gym could seat.

---

[16] Gold, pp. 21-23.

The bouts, though technically illegal, were running full tilt when Hurley hit town in 1922. Johnny's success encouraged the creation of other amateur clubs, but eventually the legitimate franchise holders objected, leading to a commission shut-down of all the sub-rosa shows including those at the Rose Room.[17]

At the Rose Room, Hurley was able to study Mike Gibbons' methods in much greater depth than on any of his prior visits to the "saintly city." Earlier, Jack only had time to watch the Gibbons brothers go through their training paces and, if he was lucky, ask a few questions afterward.

In the fall and winter of 1922-'23, however, Gibbons, now retired as a boxer, was spending all his time conditioning, training, and teaching boxers. Hurley had the unique opportunity to observe on a daily basis every phase of "the Gibbons method" while Mike instructed a wide range of pupils who were working on different aspects of their craft along whatever stage of the learning spectrum the master had mapped out for them.

Not only did Hurley watch, he became associate of the Collins-Gibbons combine, helping out whenever he was called upon. On several occasions, Jack was enlisted to travel out of town and work in a corner when the two partners had booked multiple fighters in different cities on the same night.[18]

Hurley added several fighters to his stable during his time in St. Paul. His prize catch was bantamweight Jackie Nichols who engaged in six fights for Jack over a three-month period. It was while working as a second for Nichols at a bout in Jamestown that Hurley first realized Billy Petrolle's potential. Other boxers Jack met during this time who later came under his management were Andy Bollin, Billy Ehmke, and Earl Blue. Hurley's teaming with Blue from 1925 through 1927 was especially fruitful.

Just as important to Hurley's future, was the opportunity the St. Paul stay afforded him to scout talent. In the era before film, TV, and digital copying, seeing boxers in action, or relying on the account of someone who had seen them, was the only way to evaluate ability. The experience of actually seeing the boxers meant Jack could use them in his Fargo shows without having to depend on the often unreliable or self-serving opinions of others.

While the presence of so many capable boxing men in the Twin Cities was exhilarating and stimulating, the sheer number of boxers, managers, and promoters who were already firmly entrenched in the boxing fabric of the Twin Cities made it difficult for an outsider like Hurley to become a success. Fans and promoters had their favorites among the local fighters, and with state law limiting Twin Cities' promoters to 12 shows per year, it was difficult for Jack and his fighters to break into this select circle.

---

[17] "Minnesota Boxing News," *op. cit.* Gold, p. 21. The Rose Room Gym had operated prior to Salvator's ownership, but Johnny remodeled it and staged his own "grand opening."

[18] "Earl Blue to Fight Mullen," *Fargo Forum*, October 27, 1922, sports section.

Additionally, Jack must have sensed, even as St. Paul boxing was enjoying its last bloom, that its salad days were numbered. The extended run of success by local heroes had made promoters complacent. Smug in the belief they possessed the world's best boxers, they failed to develop new talent to capture the public's imagination. Big-time boxing in the Twin Cities was dying a slow death, a victim of its own inbreeding.

Changing times were passing Minnesota by. The no-decision law enacted by lawmakers, so advanced for its time, was out of date. More progressive post-war legislatures in other states were in the process of changing their laws to allow decision bouts so their cities could obtain championship matches. In addition, these laws placed no limits on the number of promoters or the number of shows a promoter could stage.

In the coming years, although boxing in the Twin Cities would manage to survive, the sport would cease to grow and prosper as it did elsewhere.

****

If doors were not opening for Hurley in St. Paul, neither were things going as expected for the Elks in Fargo. The plan to earn profits for the club's welfare fund was not working out. Even so, the shows were not without their bright spots. Boxing addicts were abuzz about a fighter who had just moved to the area from New York state.

The Elks' first show of the 1922-'23 season, staged on October 27, featured victories for two St. Paul fighters managed by Mike Gibbons. In the main event, Homer Sheridan of Sioux City, Iowa, won a ten-round newspaper decision over Silver Perry of Miles City, Montana. In the semi-windup, Earl Blue of St. Paul, engaging in his third professional bout, defeated "Smiling" Jack Mullen of Fargo in eight rounds.

Gibbons was unable to make the trip to Fargo because Jimmy Delaney was boxing in Des Moines the same evening. In his stead, Mike sent Hurley to work as chief second in the corners of Sheridan and Blue.

The evening's most exciting event, however, was the debut of Billy Petrolle, later to become Hurley's marquis performer and the most famous boxer in North Dakota history. In the opening bout, Petrolle, 127 pounds, stopped Kid Fogarty, also 127, at 1:30 of the second round. According to the *Courier-News*, "Fogarty was not revived for about two minutes."[19]

---

[19] "Sheridan Is Too Much for Silver Perry," *Fargo Courier-News*, October 28, 1922, sports section. BoxRec has uncovered a four-round Petrolle match against Sammy Dorkins May 8, 1922, two days after Billy won the featherweight title in an Adirondack Association AAU tournament, and concluded that this bout was Billy's first pro venture. Amateur bouts of both four and six round distances were customary in the region during this time period. Billy's foe on the May 8th show, Sammy Dorkins, had never fought professionally before. By way of contrast, Kid Fogarty had engaged in at least five pro bouts when he fought Petrolle in Fargo. In interviews, Petrolle referred to the Fogarty fight as his pro debut. The evidence is equivocal, and the author has elected to stick with Petrolle's version.

Petrolle was born January 10, 1905, in Berwick, Pennsylvania. While he was still a child, the Petrolles moved to Schenectady, New York. His father was a railroad laborer, and the family was a large one, so they were always poor. To help out, Billy quit school in the seventh grade to work alongside his father in the Northern Pacific freight yards.

From the beginning, the Petrolles were a fighting family. Billy's oldest brother, Mike, boxed as an amateur as a 14-year old after the family moved to New York. Another older brother, Pete, began as an amateur in Schenectady the same time as Billy. Pete fought as a welterweight, and was a runner-up in the annual Adirondack A.A.U. tournament at Schenectady in 1922. Billy entered the same tourney and upstaged his brother by scoring a kayo to win the featherweight title. A few years later, younger brother Frankie would follow his elders and pursue a boxing career.

Billy moved to Dilworth, Minnesota, six miles east of Fargo, the fall of 1922 when the Northern Pacific transferred his father to its maintenance facility there. At the time of his Fargo boxing debut, he was working as a car checker in the railroad's freight yard. He continued to live with his parents in Dilworth throughout his time in the Red River region, commuting daily to Fargo by rail for his workouts until he married and moved to Duluth in 1926.

Petrolle's success in the Fogarty fight, and the easy money which went with it, convinced him he wanted to be a full-time fighter. He later recalled, "I got $60 for my first fight and I quit the railroad. I was making only $120 a month." After the Fogarty fight, he decided that as long as Fargo was having regular shows, he had no need for a manager.[20]

The Elks club held its second boxing card of the season December 1, 1922. In the main event Chuck Lambert of St. Paul, managed by Johnny Salvator, won a ten-round newspaper decision over Sailor Roy Benson. Another Salvator protégé, Vern Morris, was also successful in the semifinal, winning the eight-round decision over Joe Young.

---

[20] Thornton, Robert J., "Billy Petrolle's Magic Blanket," *Boxing Illustrated*, pp. 15-16. Schaefer, E. E., "Petrolle's Parents Root for Billy by Radio's Side," *Fargo Forum*, November 23, 1930, p. 3. "Seven Boxing Champs Made," *Schenectady Gazette*, May 6, 1922, sports section. "Petrolle Learns to Use His Left," *Fargo Daily Tribune*, December 22, 1923, sports section. Kolpack, Ed, "Petrolle, Jack Hurley Worked Without Contract," *Fargo Forum*, November 21, 1972, sports section. Information about Petrolle's early life is full of inconsistencies. The information presented here that Billy was raised in Schenectady is based on the Schaefer interview with his parents cited above. Other sources indicating he moved to Dilworth as a baby, or he grew up and worked in the coal mines near his birthplace of Berwick, Pennsylvania, or he moved to Fargo when he was a year old and then moved back east and then came west again are likely inaccurate. One source claims Billy had been in and out of the U. S. Navy by the time he was 16 years old. This may have been true if the tattoos on the inside of both his forearms shown in his ring photographs are any indication, but the author has not tried to prove or disapprove the assertion.

Mary and Frank Petrolle, whose move from Schenectady to Dilworth led to their son Billy's introduction to Hurley.

Billy Petrolle before he became known as "the Fargo Express."

Billy's older brother, Pete.

Billy's younger brother, Frankie.

Once again, it was Petrolle who sent fans home buzzing. According to the *Forum*, Billy "opened the show in a sensational manner when he sent Jackie Rose of St. Paul to the 'Land of Nod' in the second round. But one minute and 13 seconds of milling had been completed ... when Petrolle landed flush on Rose's chin with a hard right, and referee Billy Hoke could have counted 15 before the St. Paul man was able to get on his feet."[21]

Despite Petrolle's heroics, however, the Fargo Elks club's plan to raise money for its charity fund was not faring well. The *Forum*'s Pat Purcell reported that the Elks lost "more than $200" on its first show in October, and while "no money was lost in promoting the (December) affair ... the crowd did not reach expectations."[22]

After the October show, Purcell had put forward an explanation for the poor turnout: "The lack of attendance at the opening card probably was due to the fact that so many boxers unknown to Fargo fans were on the program ... When the next card is arranged ... several of the boxers who made good impressions at the first show will be given another chance. Several other boys who are well known to the local fans will also be considered, promoters have announced."

In response to this call for more local attractions, the Elks' promoters had opened negotiations with Hurley for LeRoy to appear on their next show December 1. While the parties were haggling over terms, LeRoy injured his shoulder in training and his appearance had to be put on hold.

A week after the December show, Purcell, in an article titled "Fans Want LeRoy," noted: "LeRoy's popularity in Fargo was demonstrated at the time of the last show when he was forced to withdraw from his scheduled bout ... When it was announced on the day of the show LeRoy would be unable to box, there was a big slump in the sale of seats and many tickets that had been reserved were not called for. This indicates that LeRoy has some friends, and the general dissatisfaction expressed by the fans over the semi-windup event strengthens the belief that they want LeRoy."[23]

The October promotion demonstrated beyond any doubt that Fargo fans wanted local attractions. The December show clarified matters further by proving the fighter they most wanted to see was LeRoy. The situation led to only one possible conclusion. If the Elks club wanted to be successful, its representatives would have to come to terms with the man they had run out of town three months earlier – LeRoy's manager, Jack Hurley.

The Elks club scheduled its third show of the season for January 1, 1923. According to the *Forum*, the event would feature "what promises to be the best fistic program ever offered by the Fargo Elks welfare association." Not

---

[21] Purcell, "Benson Loses Game Fight ..." *Fargo Forum,* December 2, 1922, sports section.

[22] Purcell, "Prelims Booked for Friday Card," *Fargo Forum*, November 28, 1922, sports section. Purcell, , "Benson Loses Game Fight During Closing Sessions," *op. cit.*

[23] Purcell, "Eddie DeBeau and Russie Would Draw Large Crowd," *Fargo Forum*, December 9, 1922, sports section.

only had the Elks signed LeRoy, but also the city's other two star attractions, Jack Bailey and Johnny Knauf as well. In addition, the club was seeking a suitable opponent for Billy Petrolle to open the show.

LeRoy had been out of action since July 4. In the interim, he had taken a job at the U. S. Post Office. According to reports, the job served to "develop LeRoy's shoulders and chest and ... make him strong and rugged." Gym workouts revealed that Russie "has lost none of his speed" and "is punching much harder and is able to assimilate punishment in the midsection." In the interim, he had outgrown the 135-pound lightweight limit and had advanced to the 140-pound junior welterweight division.[24]

Bailey and Knauf were returning after layoffs due to injuries. Although Hurley still managed Bailey, Knauf had left and was managing himself.[25]

The Elks club had taken Purcell's advice to heart and secured the best local talent available. The effort did not come without cost, however. In pre-fight publicity, the club disclosed the expenses it had incurred for the New Year's program were unprecedented. The *Courier-News* reported that "the fight will cost close to $3,000 to stage, but if the present demand for tickets continues a record gate in Fargo fistic annals should result."[26]

Hurley was exacting sweet revenge. If LeRoy and Bailey were going to fight for the club which put Jack out of business, he would make sure he received full value for their efforts.

The next morning, the *Forum* reported that "30 rounds of milling, practically every one featured by superb mixing, were witnessed by more than 1,000 fight fans."

In the headliner, LeRoy eked out a newspaper decision over Al Van Ryan. Russie, outweighed by 8-1/2 pounds, boxed carefully for nine rounds, but earned the verdict when "he out-slugged Van Ryan in the one glorious epoch in the fracas. Science was abandoned in favor healthy punching and Russie worked Van Ryan to the ropes. These two minutes of fighting regained a part of the popularity LeRoy lost in the early rounds."

In the semifinal, Chuck Lambert avenged his loss six months earlier by defeating Bailey in a ten-rounder which kept "fans on the edge of their seat throughout." In an earlier event, Knauf showed the effects of his long layoff, but won easily over Bennie Farness in six rounds.

In a preliminary, Petrolle "hit Submarine Smith of Moorhead with everything but the water bucket" to win a four-round decision. "Smith's

---

[24] Purcell, "Moorhead Boy after Farness," *Fargo Forum*, December 11, 1922, sports section. "Bailey Will Arrive in City Saturday Morning," *Fargo Courier-News,* December 29, 1922, sports section. "Bailey Here, Others Coming This Morning," *Fargo Forum*, December 31, 1922, sports section.

[25] Purcell, "Fans Believe Bailey Can Win from Chuck Lambert," *Fargo Forum*, December 30, 1922, sports section.

[26] "LeRoy, Knauf to Appear in Local Ring on Elks Card after Long Rests," *Fargo Courier-News,* December, 28, 1922, sports section.

cleverness was the only implement he had against Petrolle. The Dilworth lad fought as though his very existence depended on it, but in his eagerness to finish Smith, overlooked many chances and made wide swaths through the ozone."

The *Courier-News* reported a "record gate of $3,000 was taken in" at the New Year's show. Even with a record, however, receipts from the promotion barely covered expenses. After three programs, the welfare fund was still operating at a deficit. Although no announcement was forthcoming, the club abandoned its much heralded plan to stage seven cards during the season and quietly bowed out of the boxing business. [27]

Meanwhile, LeRoy was becoming frustrated with what he perceived to be Hurley's neglect. Prior to the new year, Russie had gone six months without a fight. LeRoy felt he was being used as a pawn in the feud between Hurley and the Elks club and that his career was suffering as a result. Now, after the Elks' last show, Jack had returned to St. Paul and was again showing no apparent interest in Russie's career.

On January 3, 1923, LeRoy told the *Courier-News* he was moving to the Twin Cities to place himself under the wing of Johnny Salvator. Russie indicated Salvator already had closed a match for him in Milwaukee. LeRoy first had met Johnny during his two weeks at the Rose Room gym in October 1921. Salvator attended the Fargo New Year's show as manager for Van Ryan and Lambert, and Russie spoke with Johnny then.[28]

Five days later, Hurley, in a letter to the *Courier-News,* took "exception to the article, which was written on information furnished by LeRoy, and denie[d] it." Jack obviously had spoken with Salvator and received assurance that he would not interfere with Hurley's contract with LeRoy.[29]

Foiled in his effort to change managers, LeRoy remained openly hostile to Hurley. When it became apparent the Elks club was not planning a show for February, Russie entered into an agreement to meet Eddie DeBeau of St. Paul in a show to be promoted by Hurley's arch-rival, Frank Sullivan. The *Forum* reported the incident on February 10:

---

[27] Purcell, "Sensational Finish Saves LeRoy, Van Ryan Contest," *Fargo Forum,* January 2, 1923, sports section. "Elks' Box Card Attracts Record Crowd, Gate Money Totaling $3.000 Received," *Fargo Courier-News,* January 3, 1923, sports section. The *Forum's* attendance figure of more than 1,000 was less optimistic than the *Courier-News'* $3,000 estimate for receipts. With tickets reportedly scaled at $3, 2.50, and $1.50, most of the seats sold would had to have been $3 tickets for receipts to have reached the $3,000 mark if the *Forum's* attendance figure was accurate. Given the seating arrangements in the Fargo Auditorium, this would have been unlikely.

[28] "Lambert's Manager Will Handle LeRoy," *Fargo Courier-News,* January 3, 1923, sports section. In fairness to Hurley, he had been negotiating bouts for LeRoy with promoters in Milwaukee, Minneapolis, and Devil's Lake during October and November, but the proposed fights had all fallen through.

[29] "Salvator Will Not Have LeRoy, Hurley," *Fargo Courier-News,* January 9, 1923, sports section.

"The situation is rather complicated. Sullivan says that both LeRoy and De Beau consented to fight for him. LeRoy acted without knowledge of his manager, Hurley. The youngster's pilot still has something to say about his fighter's activities, so in all probabilities Hurley will not let LeRoy fight for Sullivan."[30]

If nothing else, LeRoy's rebellion got Hurley's attention, and Jack returned to Fargo immediately. Within three days, he announced that he, not Sullivan, would be presenting the bout between Russie and DeBeau March 1. Efforts were also under way "to secure a worthy opponent for Jack Bailey for the semi-windup and somebody tough to meet Billy Petrolle of Dilworth in one of the preliminary events."[31]

Although LeRoy was unsuccessful in breaking free from Hurley, he achieved the larger objective of re-focusing Jack's attention on his career. Russie's action also motivated Hurley to capitalize on the opportunity presented by the Elks' decision to suspend its boxing operations. Unfortunately, however, the DeBeau fight was canceled when LeRoy suffered a training injury which put him out of action for two months.[32]

In a show of good faith, Hurley went ahead with the March 1st card, substituting a fight between Jimmy Delaney and Bailey for the LeRoy-DeBeau bout. Delaney, a Gibbons/Collins' protégé, was regarded as one of the world's premier light heavyweights. The Fargo papers lauded Jack for presenting fans "a much better event than the original plans called for."[33]

The next day the *Forum* reported that although Delaney deserved the decision, "Fargo fans went home singing the praises of Jack Bailey [who] had succeeded in putting up a good fight ... against the famous James J. Delaney of St. Paul." In the semi-windup, Johnny Knauf scored a one-round knockout over Jack Walker of Milwaukee.

In another tilt, Petrolle won his fourth straight fight in Fargo when, after "one minute and 56 seconds of chasing, he caught Lou Boomer and landed a right hand to the chin that terminated the bout. It was a clean knockout, Boomer's head hitting the floor before the remainder of his body settled."[34]

With the Elks' club out of the picture, Hurley decided to finish the boxing season by promoting a few more shows in Fargo. Immediately after the March 1st card, he returned to St. Paul to close out his affairs. By the

---

[30] Purcell, "Sporting Spotlight," *Fargo Forum*, February 9, 1923, sports section.
[31] Purcell, "LeRoy, DeBeau Argument to Be Settled Here on March 1," *Fargo Forum*, February 12, 1923, sports section.
[32] Purcell, "Clever Mauler to Meet Bailey," *Fargo Forum*, February 20, 1923, sports section.
[33] "Russie LeRoy Hurt; Plan New Headline Event for March 1," *Fargo Courier-News*, February 20, 1923, sports section.
[34] Purcell, "Fargo Battler Unable to Avoid Pretty Left Hand," *Fargo Forum*, March 2, 1923, sports section.

end of the month, he was back in Fargo living at home with his mother and sleeping in the upstairs bedroom she set aside for him.

In Jack's next show at Fargo April 6, hard-luck Jack Bailey suffered yet another setback in his fight against Mark Moore, this time in the form of a compound fracture on the left side of his jaw. Both newspapers had Bailey ahead on points when the bout was stopped at the end of the seventh round. On the undercard, Submarine Smith won a six-round newspaper decision over Len Schwabel of St. Paul. In the semifinal, Battling Krause made a hit when he knocked out Snowball Draxton in the third round.

Petrolle met the toughest foe he had faced at Fargo in a semi-windup with Jimmy Woodhall of Fergus Falls. Behind after five rounds, Billy came back to even the score. The *Forum* reporter described the action:

> "In the sixth round, Petrolle came out of his corner like a tiger, shooting haymakers at Woodhall from all directions. Near the close of the session Petrolle landed a right cross on Woodhall's ear and scored a clean knockdown. Woodhall took a count of nine and then succeeded in staying throughout the remainder of the session ... The knockdown scored in the final round was enough to more than even up the lead gained by Woodhall in the earlier rounds."[35]

For his last show of the indoor season May 11, 1923, Hurley matched LeRoy with Buddy McDonald of St. Paul. In an article which included Russie's own assessment of his progress to date, the *Forum* reporter wrote:

> "'I have just begun to realize how bad I must have looked during my fight with Van Ryan. I know that I danced too much, but in the future things are going to be different. From now on I'm going to fight. I can hit fast enough to beat any fighter to the punch I have met yet and I plan to make the most of my ability and quit dancing.'
>
> "LeRoy appeared to be in earnest when he declared he's through dancing. During his daily workouts he has shown an inclination to work with his gloves than his feet, and has been training faithfully.
>
> "When LeRoy started in fighting as a featherweight, all he knew was fight. He tore in and exchanged punches with all his opponents as he didn't know what a straight left was or that his feet were to be used for any purpose, other than to carry him towards his opponent. With his ability to use his left, either to hook or jab, and a little more aggressiveness, Russie should be a real pleasing fighter. And,

---

[35] Purcell, "Moore Is Awarded Bout on Technical Knockout in 8th," *Fargo Forum*, April 7, 1923, sports section. The *Fargo Courier-News* disagreed with the *Forum* and scored the fight for Woodhall on the basis of points accumulated in rounds before the knockdown.

any of the boys who lick him are certain to know they have been in been in a fight."[36]

Unfortunately, LeRoy's opportunity to show off his new aggressiveness had to wait until the next season. Eight days before the show, he re-injured his shoulder and Hurley was again forced to cancel his appearance.

Unable to find a replacement, Jack reduced ticket prices and went ahead with the card absent a star attraction. In the first of two eight-round bouts, Submarine Smith was matched against Red Blanchard of Battle Creek, Michigan. In a co-feature, Billy Petrolle was set to meet George Bowers.[37]

By this time, as evidenced by the following *Courier-News* account, Petrolle had acquired a considerable following:

> "Dilworth will attend the fight almost in a body because of the presence of popular Billy Petrolle on the card. Petrolle is strongly backed by the railroad men at Dilworth and they are confident that he will defeat Georgie Bowers of St. Paul in the eight round windup bout."
>
> "Petrolle has shown big improvement since his first appearance in Fargo less than a year ago ... In his first appearance Petrolle was wild and willing. He is still willing but has lost much of his wildness and has now reached a point where he can gauge his punches and economize on energy. He has learned a few of the finer points of boxing and can spar effectively.
>
> "Billy's forte is his punching power. He can hand out punishment with either hand and will make Bowers step along. Bowers is the same type of fighter as Petrolle, and the meeting of the two will be interesting."[38]

Submarine Smith continued his comeback on the May 11th show by winning a newspaper decision over Red Blanchard by a "slight margin." Much to the disappointment of his fans, Petrolle's fight with Bowers was canceled at the last minute due to George's failure to appear. Apparently, word had reached Bowers that Billy was no ordinary opponent. In any event, a Petrolle-Bowers contest was never rescheduled.[39]

The no-show led to a rift between Hurley and Petrolle. "I was promoting at Fargo," Jack recalled, "and doing fairly well. Nothing great, but making

---

[36] Purcell, "Russie Anxious to Prove He Can Lick St. Paul Man," *Fargo Forum*, April 21, 1923, sports section.
[37] Purcell, "Two Eight-Round Bouts to Feature Revised Mitt Card," *Fargo Forum*, May 3, 1923, sports section.
[38] "Seat Sale for Fight Opened," *Fargo Courier-News,* May 8, 1923, sports section.
[39] "Smith Shades Blanchard by Slight Margin," *Fargo Courier-News*, May 12, 1923, sports section.

a living. Well, anyway, one night when I was putting on a show one of the fighters didn't appear. His opponent was supposed to get $80 and insisted on being paid. I told him I wasn't going to pay because he had not boxed. But he wouldn't take no for an answer, so I gave him ten bucks. The fighter, Billy Petrolle, left saying, 'You still owe me 70 dollars.'"[40]

Petrolle's recollection was similar: "I'd had a couple fights and thought I was a pro. To me, Hurley was a skinny guy in a vest. But my ears perked up when he offered me $80 for a bout. For that kind of money, I'd have taken on Jack Dempsey. It was more than I made at the freight yard in weeks. On the night of the fight, the other fellow didn't show up, but I asked Hurley for my $80. He gave me $10. We didn't speak to each other for a year."

Ironically, Petrolle had been on the verge of asking Hurley to manage him. Billy realized if he was to advance he needed a manager to expand his horizons beyond Fargo and the surrounding area. Now that he had been cheated out of a purse, however, going with Jack was out of the question.[41]

Petrolle's options were limited. There were only a few nearby towns other than Fargo staging boxing shows. He was familiar with Jamestown, having fought on a couple of shows there, and had met local manager Lee Schrankel through his brother Pete who had just moved to Jamestown to be near the family. Apparently, Pete convinced Billy of Schrankel's honesty because the *Forum* reported on May 24 that Billy was joining his brother as a member of Lee's stable.[42]

With injuries keeping LeRoy out of action until August, Hurley took a break to serve as a playing manager for the Grand Recreation baseball team during the summer's early months. The Grands were one of seven amateur teams which competed in Fargo's new Commercial League organized by a variety of businesses and fraternal organizations. In addition to his duties as manager, Jack played first base, registering a .240 batting average. The Grands finished the season in third place with seven wins and five losses.

Hurley finished with baseball August 7, playing on a team of all-star pick-up players representing Fargo in the annual face-off against intercity rival Moorhead Athletics. Jack scored his team's only run in a 9 to 1 losing effort when he walked, advanced on a sacrifice, and scored on an error.

The next day, Hurley, with LeRoy and Battling Krause, who had joined Jack's stable in July, hopped a freight train to Des Moines, Iowa for a show on August 10. Years later, he recalled the incident in his syndicated column:

---

[40] Hopkins, Jack D., "Petrolle-Hurley Combination: An All-Time Duet," *Ring Magazine*, February, 1969, p. 31. The recollections of Hurley and Petrolle differ slightly. Jack recalled agreeing to pay Billy $90 for the bout and expenses of $20. Billy recalled the amounts as $80 and $10. Both remembered the disputed amount to be $70. For textual consistency, Hurley's quotation has been changed to reflect the amount recalled by Petrolle.

[41] Thornton, pp. 41, 54. Hopkins, *op. cit.*

[42] "Billy Petrolle to Live at Jamestown," *Fargo Forum*, May 24, 1923, sports section.

"When we'd get a fight out of town the promoter would always send round-trip tickets for me and my fighters, and we would always turn in the tickets for cash and ride the rods to the fight. I can remember many a night, sleeping with my head on a hunk of coal on the tender. But that little extra money was important.

"We thought nothing of beating our way on the rods all the way to Des Moines, 500 miles away, and back again. I remember going to sleep in the engine tool box to awake and find the train moving and the fighters gone. Railroad detectives chased them off but missed me. I had to wait at the next division point for the fighters to arrive on the next train as I couldn't do much without them."[43]

Luckily, the three knights-of-the-road made it to the show on time. LeRoy lost a close ten-round referee's decision to Roscoe Hall while Krause decisioned Bobby Jubbs in six rounds. Hall was a Des Moines favorite who had lost only once in 27 bouts. Russie would eventually box Hall four times with no clear advantage being demonstrated by either.[44]

A few days later, Hurley was in Wahpeton, North Dakota, where his fighters were headling a show for the American Legion state convention August 15. It was the third straight year Jack had put together an evening of entertainment for the state convention, each time at a different city.

The next day's *Fargo Forum* reported that LeRoy proved to legionnaires that "he is again Fargo's lightweight pride" and "is a fighter and not a dancer." LeRoy "stood toe to toe with Billy Carter of St. Paul and slugged until a crashing right to the jaw, followed by a hard left hook to the same spot sent the St. Paul fighter to the canvas" in the second round.

In a grudge re-match on the same card, Moorhead's Johnny Knauf "leaped into the air in an effort to send his right across" just as Battling Krause "started a low uppercut" "and Krause's blow landed foul." Knauf was declared the winner on a foul. The *Forum* reported that up until the end, "the 2,000 spectators that packed the opera house to its capacity were in a frenzy" for the entire time the two battlers "were exchanging thuds."[45]

The trio was back in Fargo September 3 for the annual American Legion Labor Day show at the fairgrounds. In the main event, LeRoy scored his

---

[43] Olsen, Jack, "Don't Call Me Honest, Part I," *Sports Illustrated*, May 15, 1961, p. 90. Hurley, Jack, "Shadow Boxing," *Fargo Forum*, July 22, 1934, sports section. The author has merged quotes from the two sources dealing with different aspects of the same incident. The ICC authorized a charge of $.036 per mile for train travel, making the price for a Fargo–Des Moines ticket $18. Thompson, Gregory Lee, *The Passenger Train in the Motor Age: California Rail and Bus Industries, 1910-1941* (Ohio State University Press, 1993).

[44] "Roscoe Hall Earns Newspaper Verdict over Fargo Man. LeRoy Unable to Avoid Stream of Lefts," *Fargo Forum*, August 11, 1923, sports section.

[45] Purcell, "Russie LeRoy Knocks Out Billy Carter in Second Round; Johnny Knauf Wins from Bat Krause on Foul in 3rd," *Fargo Forum*, August 16, 1923, sports section.

EXILE AND REDEMPTION

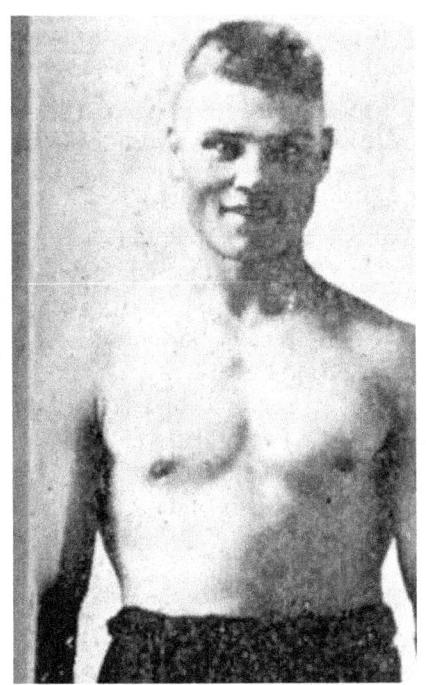

Light heavyweight Jack Bailey had a hard time in 1923. In addition to injuries, he lost decisions to Chuck Lambert (left) and Mark Moore.

LeRoy's big win in 1923 was by decision over Otto Wallace.

Venerable Submarine Smith won several comeback bouts in 1923.

biggest victory to date by winning a ten-round newspaper verdict over veteran lightweight Otto Wallace of Milwaukee. Krause was also victorious in a ten-round battle with Bennie Farness.

In a preliminary bout, Pete Petrolle, Billy's brother, won in six-rounds over Submarine Smith. It was Pete's first appearance in Fargo since his move west from Schenectady, where he had been a pro for several years.[46]

The back-to-back successes of the American Legion's two summer shows demonstrated boxing was increasing in popularity throughout North Dakota. As the indoor season approached, Fargo's rival "for-profit" promoters, Frank Sullivan and Jack Hurley, both announced their intent to capitalize on the upsurge by presenting bouts during the fall.

On September 17, 1923, the *Forum*'s Purcell reported that "two fight programs are scheduled for the entertainment of Fargo fistic enthusiasts, but both programs are booked" on the same date. Sullivan and his new partner, Frank McGoon, told Purcell that Johnny Knauf and Abe Wallace would meet in the main event on October 5, with Web Oakland of Fargo and Kid Wylie of Valley City going at it in the semi-windup.

The same article reported Hurley was planning a show the same evening featuring LeRoy and Battling Krause. Both programs were said to be scheduled for the Fargo Auditorium.[47]

The next day, Purcell tried to act as mediator between the two parties:

> "There is no reason why there should be any arguments between the local promoters. Hurley's boxers are in big demand throughout the Northwest at the present time and he will be too busy to promote shows regularly, so there will be plenty of room for Sullivan and Mc Goon.
>
> "However, unless the two factions can cover their tempers for a while and reach a mutual agreement there will be plenty of arguments and much dissatisfaction. Both Sullivan and Hurley have done considerable towards building up the fight game in Fargo and both deserve chances to promote cards. But, as long as they stay on different sides of the fence, neither will be satisfied and the fans will be the ones to suffer."[48]

As a result of the conflict, both promoters canceled their October 5th shows. Two weeks later, on October 4, the *Fargo Daily Tribune* reported:

---

[46] Dunn, Edward L., "Fargo Lightweight Hooks Way to Win," *Fargo Daily-Tribune*, September 4, 1923, sports section.
[47] Purcell, "Two Fight Cards on Oct. 5," *Fargo Forum*, September 17, 1923, sports section.
[48] Purcell, "Sioux Falls May Get L'Roy-Hall," *Fargo Forum,* September 18, 1923, sports section.

> "Jack Hurley has been granted the exclusive use of the Fargo Auditorium for fight promotions this season by W. P. Chestnut, secretary of the Fargo Commercial Club, it was announced yesterday. The action puts an end to the boxing war that has threatened to irreparably injure the boxing game in the city. Hurley has announced that he will stage at least one show a month during the season and possibly two some months. His first card has been announced for October 26."[49]

Obviously, Hurley had appealed to the club's board members as businessmen and trustees charged with using the Fargo Auditorium for the public good. The auditorium was a substantial asset, and the community had a right to receive a fair return on its investment and see the facility put to its full and best use. Other promoters not only had failed to draw enough at the gate to pay a decent rent, they had reneged on their pledges to present monthly shows and let the building remain idle for prolonged periods.

Hurley was the only promoter who had made a steady profit. The Elks promised the Commercial Club seven shows and staged only three. Frank Sullivan was a dreamer who consistently lost money and was unable to sustain a full season of business. Jack likely asked for the exclusive right to promote boxing on a trial basis for a year. If he met his commitment, then the contract could be renewed for longer periods later on.

The new arrangement came almost a year to the day after the Elks club had declared itself the sole boxing promoter in Fargo and forced Hurley to move to St. Paul. With a stroke of a pen, Jack had outmaneuvered his competition and secured the rights to the town's largest auditorium. Like his hero, Tex Rickard, he was in sole control of both the site and the attractions necessary to make boxing in Fargo a profitable venture.

The battle for control of boxing in Fargo was an early instance of what would be a continuing source of frustration for Hurley – his lifelong war against "amateurs" who repeatedly would get in his way and, as he would say, "louse up my payday." Jack would deal with the problem of rival promoters in many ways over the years, but his two favorite strategies were the ones he used against Frank Sullivan and the Elks club.

Against Sullivan, Hurley went head-to-head and forced the issue with competing shows that gave fans a clear opportunity to select which promoter furnished the best entertainment. Against the Elks, which enjoyed an advantage by virtue of its broad-based community involvement, Jack chose a less confrontational route by simply stepping aside for a few months and allowing the club's matchmakers to flail away and fail by the sheer weight of their own incompetence.

---

[49] "Hurley Secure Lease on Armory," *Fargo Daily-Tribune*, October 4, 1923, sports section.

More importantly, the episode illustrated that Hurley, at age 25, possessed all the attributes of a first-class promoter. In his first full season, he had demonstrated an innate talent for evaluating and exploiting his merchandise, as well as an uncanny ability to overcome problems and plan ahead – to sense when to move in and take advantage of a situation, and when to hold back or retreat. This knack of always knowing what to do, and when, would serve Jack well for the rest of his life.

CHAPTER 9

THE BEST $35 HURLEY EVER SPENT

I would like to know what Rickard could have done promoting in a small town. For instance, he should have had my task promoting in Fargo. That is a job. Before I can figure on any kind of a match I have to go around and feel the pulse of the 500 or 600 fight fans, to see what they want. Once I find out, I then am faced with the task of getting the fighters. But once the match is signed, I am just beginning to run into trouble.

I have my window cards printed and then I have to put 'em up myself to save money. And that is a tough job, as I have to 'sell' my fight in every barber shop I visit. I have to show the barbers how this or that guy is going to win. I shadow-box all over the joint. Say, when I get through putting up the window cards, I am punch drunk from hitting myself on the lug. But that is part of the game promoting in Fargo.

But that isn't all. I sell the ducats myself because I want to be sure I get all of the dough. I take the fighters to the gymnasium; introduce 'em and keep time while they box. Then I rush back and open up the ticket sale.

The day of the fight usually finds me goofy. Say the bout is on New Year's Day at 2:00 in the afternoon. They dance in the hall until 2 a.m. New Year's Eve, and then I have to go in there to arrange the ring and chairs. I usually have a mob of guys to help me, but they get soused while waiting for the dance to end. Then it is up to me to put up the ring by myself. If you've never put up a fight ring, you don't know what you've missed.

Well, I finish the building by 9 a.m., wash my face, and start the ticket sales again. Then I open up the doors of the fight arena, count the change and tickets, place the coppers in their positions and start the show. Again, I do all of the announcing, keep my eye on the gate and end up by seconding two or three fighters. And after everybody is paid off, I usually find I have only enough money left to buy me a good dinner, which I can't eat.

Yes, I guess Rickard was a great promoter, but I can't say he was the best, as he wasn't a small-town promoter. That is a test for a Rickard, a Barnum, and even a Hurley."[1]

— Jack Hurley

---

[1] McKenna, Lou, *St. Paul Pioneer Press*, January 26, 1931, sports section. Hurley's reference to dances at the Fargo Auditorium is correct. The second floor was known as the "Crystal Ballroom" in the 1930s and '40s. It was the site of one of the most famous early "live" recordings in jazz history. South Dakota State College student Jack Towers recorded the Duke Ellington band there at a dance November 7, 1940. The recordings, called by one music critic "the jazz equivalent of the Holy Grail," were not issued until 1978 when the session won a Grammy Award as the Best Jazz Instrumental Performance, Big Band. The second floor floor also was used for other events, including boxing, since the main floor was used exclusively as an armory by the North Dakota National Guard which donated the land.

****

Jack Hurley was present at Billy Petrolle's professional debut against Kid Fogarty at the Fargo Elks' club show October 27, 1922, but he did not realize Petrolle's full potential until six months later. By that time, Jack was living in St. Paul and was managing featherweight Jackie Nichols. The Jamestown Athletic Club contacted Hurley in St. Paul and offered him a bout for Nichols against Petrolle on the club's March 6, 1923 show.

The *Jamestown Daily Alert* reported the Nichols go "was Petrolle's third bout in six days and he had some bad bruises on his face" remaining from a match three days earlier. The fight was Petrolle's first ten-round contest:

> "In the first round, Nichols found his (Petrolle's) badly swollen eye and opened the partly healed wound under it so that blood flowed freely and for the whole ten rounds it was very bloody in appearance, though in reality neither one of the boxers was hurt very much.
>
> "Nichols forced the fighting much of the way and had the lead in the first, fourth, fifth, seventh, eighth and ninth rounds. The second was Petrolle's and the third a draw. Petrolle had a little the best of it in the sixth, and most every one gave him the tenth, which was a whirlwind of a fight. Petrolle's face was a sorry sight on account of being puffed out to nearly close his right eye and his face continued bleeding freely from the eye and a cut lip, which Nichols kept priming.
>
> "To judge from the appearance of the two men, the pace was telling more on Nichols than on Petrolle, and the fans generally were of the opinion that, had there been another round, Nichols would have hit the mat, while Petrolle looked as strong as ever, except for his bloody face."[2]

Years later, Hurley still marveled at Billy's showing that night. "Nichols was one of the ten best feathers in the world," recalled Jack, "and what an awful shellacking he gave Petrolle. Even so, Petrolle almost knocked him out in the last round, and I said to myself: 'Is this raw material here?'

"He looked like any other fighter to me that night except for three things which caught my eye. He was strong, tough, and game. The fellow he was fighting was a tough cookie who was winging them from left field. Most young fighters would cower in the same situation, but not Petrolle. He just kept boring in, throwing bombs right back."[3]

---

[2] "Well Balanced All-Fight Card and No Knockout," *Jamestown Daily Alert*, March 7, 1923, sports section.
[3] Heinz, W. C., "The Man Who Makes Fighters," *Esquire Magazine,* May, 1952, p. 103 (first paragraph). Hopkins, Jack, "Petrolle-Hurley Combination: An All-Time Duet," *Ring Magazine*, February, 1969, p. 30 (second paragraph).

As fate would have it, Hurley and Petrolle did not get together at that time. Instead, Jack was busy closing his St. Paul operation and resurrecting his business in Fargo. Hurley used Billy as a preliminary fighter on his Fargo shows in March and April, after which they had the disagreement over Petrolle's purse for the canceled fight with George Bowers on May 11. It was then Billy decided to leave the Fargo area to live with his brother Pete in Jamestown, and to box under the management of Lee Schrankel.

In Jamestown, the Petrolles crossed paths with a rangy, young native named Louis LaMoore, who would later earn fame as Louis L'Amour, writer of western fiction. LaMoore had learned the rudiments of boxing from his father and two older brothers. He first started working out at the local YMCA gym with Labe Safro, who visited Jamestown in 1921.

In his memoirs, published in 1989, L'Amour reminisced about the life of a boxer in the 1920s in general and about the Petrolle brothers in particular:

> "And then the Petrolle boys came to town. ... Pete Petrolle was a lightweight fighter out of Schenectady, New York. His manager at the time was a former boxer who owned and operated a café in Jamestown. His name was Lee Schrankel; he was also temporarily manager of Pete's younger brother, Billy.
>
> "Pete was a good, tough, knowing fighter who had already become as good as he was ever to get. Billy, on the other hand, was just beginning a career that would take him to the top, where he would defeat several champions in overweight matches (so the title was not at stake) but was never to win a championship himself. From featherweight to welterweight he fought all the good ones, and many of them were very, very good.
>
> "At the time there were at least 20 good fighters for every one there is now, and it was about the only way a young man could come off the streets and become somebody. Now, with basketball and football paying enormous sums, there are many other ways to reach the top, and even common labor pays more in a day than one received in a week in the 1920s.
>
> "Competition in the ring was very tough and a boy had to be good to get anywhere at all. Usually that meant a year or two fighting four- or six-round bouts before a fighter got a shot at anything longer. During those years he was learning, discovering how to cope with the different styles of fighting, and refining his own ...
>
> "How I met Pete Petrolle I do not recall, but evidently I heard he was looking for somebody to spar with. I was 14, but tall, with a good reach, and I knew enough about boxing to take care of myself. In the next few weeks I learned a lot more. I would guess I worked at least 50 rounds with Pete on various days before I met

Billy, and then I worked with them both. They took it easy with me, but I enjoyed the workouts and was learning rapidly."[4]

L'Amour's experience with the Petrolles was not wasted. Born with a taste for adventure, Louis left Jamestown at 15. While working at many manual jobs all over the country in the 1920s and '30s, he supplemented his income with boxing to earn money to live on and purchase books to read. As he recalled later, "There was not much money to be made fighting in small towns, but any money was good money to me in those rough years."[5]

L'Amour also worked for a time as a second and trainer of boxers. His final involvement in boxing was as coach of Golden Glove teams from Oklahoma and for the army which competed at Chicago's "Tournament of Champions." Later on, he drew extensively from his pugilistic knowledge during his writing career. Boxing anecdotes were prominently featured in many of his works, including such collections as *Hills of Homicide, Beyond the Great Snow Mountain,* and *Off the Mangrove Coast.*[6]

According to the *Forum*'s Pat Purcell, "Schrankel was a better café manager than a matchmaker." During his six months with Petrolle, Lee did not hesitate to match Billy against the toughest opposition in the Midwest. The game youngster held his own, but was absorbing a lot of punishment.

One of Petrolle's toughest fights was a rematch against Eddie DeBeau at Sioux Falls, South Dakota on October 23, 1923. Billy won a newspaper decision in their first bout at Jamestown a month earlier, but DeBeau had taken the fight on short notice. Eddie was eager for a return match since he was certain with proper training he could beat the less experienced Petrolle.

LeRoy fought a draw with Roscoe Hall on the same show. Russie was accompanied by Battling Krause, who worked LeRoy's corner because Hurley was unable to make the trip. When the two returned to Fargo, they told Jack "DeBeau gave Petrolle such a bad beating that the young fellow, then just 18, was unable to get out of bed the next morning."[7]

Not long afterward, while Petrolle was still in Jamestown, Hurley took a train to Dilworth and met with Billy's parents. "Your son could be a good fighter," Jack said."He's had a murderous time up to now because he doesn't know how to fight. If he goes on the way he is he won't amount to anything, and he'll get hurt. If he'd come to me, I could make a fighter out of him, teach him how to take care of himself, and he'd end up rich."[8]

---

[4] L'Amour, Louis, *"Education of a Wandering Man,"* (Bantam Books, 1989), pp. 15-18.

[5] L'Amour, pp.162-63. Interestingly, L'Amour's fistic debut as "Billy LaMoore" was on the American Legion card at Jamestown on September 28, 1921, against Johnny Knauf, at the time managed by Hurley.

[6] L'Amour, Beau and O'Dell, Paul J., "Biography," p. 2, *Official Louis L'Amour Website.*

[7] Purcell, J. A., "Rambling Through Sportville," *Fargo Forum,* September 15, 1929, sports section.

[8] Heinz, *op. cit.*

Early headshot of Billy Petrolle.

Louis L'Amour, famous author, more than 30 years after serving as Petrolle's sparring partner in Jamestown, ND.

Jackie Nichols, who Hurley was handling when he saw Petrolle would make a good fighter.

Eddie DeBeau, whose savage fight with Petrolle in Sioux Falls helped convince Billy to give Hurley a try as manager.

Jack's meeting with Petrolle's folks convinced them, but Billy was a harder case. He was unhappy with Schrankel, but he was not about to approach Hurley. In his view, Jack still owed him money and was not to be trusted. Instead, Billy decided to go to Minneapolis, look for some fights, and find a manager there. But before he left, he needed a haircut.

Waiting in Fargo for the train to Minneapolis, Petrolle stopped off at a barbershop for a trim and a shave. After the haircut and some friendly conversation about Billy's plans, the barber hurried out of his shop and left Petrolle alone in the chair with a steaming towel over his face to soften his stubby beard. The barber was a boxing fan and a friend of Hurley. A few minutes later, he returned to the shop with Jack in tow.

Hurley later described the incident for *Ring Magazine*. "When I saw this guy in a white coat running toward me," related Jack, "I thought my time had come. When he told me Petrolle was in his chair and that I should go over and talk to him, I immediately became interested. When I saw Petrolle again the first thing he said was, 'You owe me $70.'"[9]

"'Forget the 70,' I said. 'You'll get your chance to make that 10,000 times over.' 'Give me 35,' Petrolle said, 'and I'll stay with you.' 'If I give you the 35, what insurance have I got?' 'My word is good. What time do you want me at the gym?' 'Two o'clock.'" Hurley handed over the $35 and, as promised, the next day Billy showed up at the gym right on time.[10]

The *Fargo Daily Tribune* announced the partnership December 13, 1923:

> "Billy Petrolle ... has signed a contract with Jack Hurley, local fistic mogul, and henceforth will do all his boxing wearing the colors of the Colonel. Agreement was reached last evening after about three months of seeking by Hurley and evasion of the issue by Petrolle. Billy has felt right along he has not been capitalizing on his fistic ability to the extent he might. Petrolle is confident he is headed toward big things in the fistic world.
>
> "With Hurley as his pilot, Petrolle should step a long way to fame. Hurley knows boxing – witness Bat Krause who six months ago was nothing but a catcher – and should be able to teach the Dilworth Italian many things about the game. Hurley is a recognized manager in the Northwest and can secure fights for Petrolle where otherwise he could not get them."[11]

Purcell later recalled Petrolle's early days of gym work under Hurley's watchful eye:

---

[9] Hopkins, *op. cit.*
[10] Heinz, *op. cit.*
[11] Dunn, Edward L., "Petrolle Is Added to Hurley Stable," *Fargo Daily Tribune*, December 13, 1923, sports section.

"Hurley was operating a gymnasium in the basement of the Tweeden Hotel and he personally supervised the building of one of the greatest lightweights of the present day. Hurley started by teaching Petrolle his feet were made for something other than to brace himself on. For two months, Billy danced on chalk lines Jack drew on the canvas, learning balance and speeding up his movements. After the youngster could move around to the satisfaction of his teacher, the gloves were then tied on and another long, arduous period of fundamental drill was in order."[12]

Purcell's description of Hurley's routine with Petrolle is an early account of the regimen Jack employed in developing all his boxers, starting with LeRoy in 1919 and ending with Boone Kirkman in 1970. The Hurley method was his own version of the classic curriculum he learned spending countless hours watching Mike Gibbons train his boxers in St. Paul. The system called for boxing to be taught in discrete stages, each of which the student had to master before he was allowed to advance to the next stage.

In the first stage, the would-be boxer was taught the footwork he needed to smoothly maneuver around a canvas-covered ring floor. An area about five feet wide by 20 feet long was chalk-marked on the floor. There followed weeks of practice until the steps could be executed without thinking. Forward, backward, side to side, until each move was made effortlessly. Even after mastering the drill, the fighter would open each workout with these exercises for the rest of his career.

The footwork phase would last weeks or months before the next stage began. After a student showed enough progress, he would learn the basics of throwing the various types of blows. This stage taught the placement and movement of feet, thrust of calves and thighs, twisting of torso, and proper motion of shoulders, arms, wrists, and fists.

At first, the student would throw punches without any resistance. After mastering the correct movements for each part of the body, he would begin to practice each blow by "working" the heavy bag. Emphasis was placed on learning balance and leverage, and developing a rhythm or cadence to punching. Gradually, he would begin to throw punches in sequence with each other. Speed would come much later, only after the proper execution of footwork and punching had been completely mastered.

Punching and footwork would be practiced independently for hours and hours. After each became automatic, the student would begin a stage where the footwork was combined with punches, and the two practiced together over and over. The alliance of footwork and punching would result in the boxer developing "moves" and a style of his own. As in the prior stages,

---

[12] Purcell, *op. cit.*

thousands of repetitions were required to perfect every move until each was executed flawlessly without thinking.

During this time, the boxer would begin shadow-boxing against an imaginary opponent, practicing his own moves and countering those of an illusory adversary. Also about this time, the student might begin boxing in the gym. Facing a real opponent, he would gradually transform the punches, footwork, and moves he had been learning into actual practice.

After gaining a feel for the ring, he might practice more sophisticated moves with a trainer or sympathetic partner. The partner might throw light punches at him while the fighter learned moves to counter these punches.

Once all of these techniques were mastered and the fighter had some ring experience, he then could work on advanced strategies like feinting, drawing leads, slipping, pulling back, and laying traps. These techniques could only work properly if each building block along the way had been correctly put in place; only if proper footwork, punching technique, and balance had each been mastered in their precise order. These drills would be continued and improved upon throughout the fighter's career.

The footwork Hurley taught was the same shuffling style he had studied in the French forest near Heudicourt during World War I. With Jack's guidance, Petrolle combined the shuffle with a bob and weave patterned after Jack Dempsey's style. This method allowed Billy to duck, sidestep, or slip a foe's punches while at the same time staying in range to counterpunch. Hurley also taught Billy to concentrate primarily on body punching.

The slow-moving shuffle served as an invitation for opposing fighters to slow down and trade punches. Petrolle meanwhile would be ready to quickly shift his feet in alternative ways depending on the method and direction of his opponent's attack. At the same time, Billy would be setting himself for well-leveraged counterblows to either body or head, just as a bayonet fighter would counter an opponent's forward thrust.

In these early years, Hurley even donned the gloves with Petrolle, just as he had done with Russie LeRoy. Years later, in 1931, Billy recalled these sessions to a skeptical audience while training for a fight in St. Louis:

> "As he left the ring, someone asked Petrolle where he learned to use his left hand so effectively. 'From the old master, Jack Hurley, my manager,' Petrolle replied. 'Hurley!' exclaimed the questioner, 'what does he know about boxing?' It seemed ridiculous the long, lean, angular Hurley could ever show anybody how to box.
>
> "'He knows all the tricks in this racket,' Petrolle declared, 'he can't punch very hard, and he was never a pro fighter, but he boxed around the gym, and he is an accurate hitter. Why, he strapped my right hand down to my side for two weeks, and we worked with my left alone until I knew just how to use it, then he let me work with

the right hand.' Apparently, Hurley did a good job of instructing, for Petrolle surely appears to know how to use his left."[13]

The addition of Petrolle to his stable was only one of several important events in the busy life of promoter Hurley in the fall of 1923.

After securing the exclusive use of the Fargo Auditorium in October, Hurley decided his operation needed a better training facility than the Knights of Columbus gym. To accommodate both his fighters and visiting opponents, Jack leased the basement under the Tweeden Hotel at 415 Northern Pacific Avenue and outfitted it as a boxing gym, patterned after the layout of Johnny Salvator's Rose Room gym in St. Paul.

To help pay his rent, Hurley opened up the gym to amateur and novice boxers as well as professionals. He charged those who could afford it $2 per month and included free boxing lessons. Before long, the facility attracted enough talent to stage amateur boxing cards every week. Relying on his Rose Room experience, Jack launched his first amateur show December 18, 1923. He would continue to offer the cards on a weekly basis during the indoor season for as long as he operated a gym in Fargo.

The cards were not strictly "amateur" in the modern sense. A more accurate term might have been "semi-pro." Winners were offered spots in the preliminary bouts of Hurley's next pro card at the Fargo Auditorium. If the aspirant was unsuccessful in his "pro" debut, he could return to his amateur status the next week at the gym.

Likewise, an old pro, no longer possessing the stamina necessary for the pro ranks, would be welcome to display his waning wares over the four-round distance of an amateur bout. Submarine Smith, a 15-year veteran as a professional, finished his career in this fashion.

In essence, the bouts were analogous to baseball's minor leagues. Hurley's gym served as a farm system in which young hopefuls could develop their skills and test the waters before committing themselves full time to the boxing game. Among those who started at Hurley's gym in Fargo and later graduated to the pro ranks were Spud Murphy, Frankie Petrolle, Bud Welling, Willie Ascher, Ray Cossette, Billy Norton, Sherard Kennard, Tommy McGough, Babe Herman, and Earl Orton.[14]

The amateur shows were a boon to Hurley financially and otherwise. Every week hundreds of patrons paid 50 cents each for the privilege of admittance. More importantly, the cards served as a mecca for novice boxers who came to Fargo from all over North Dakota, South Dakota, and western Minnesota. Without having to travel or commit himself to managing a prospect, Jack could preview talent and exercise, in effect, a

---

[13] McGoogan, W. J., "Petrolle Shows Good Form in Workout for Tenorio Bout," *St. Louis Post-Dispatch,* April 8, 1931, sports section.
[14] Fitzgerald, Eugene, "The Sport Whirligig," *Fargo Forum,* March 13, 1933, sports section.

Fargo Auditorium as it appeared shortly after it was built, c. 1915.

The interior of the Fargo Auditorium which was re-christened the "Crystal Ballroom" whenever a dance was held. This photo, showing the stage, was taken about 1926 from a position opposite from where the photo of the 1922 LeRoy-Ward fight was taken (See Chapter 7 photo). The balcony railing has been enclosed for safety reasons. Bottom photo courtesy of the North Dakota State University Library.

first pick over the best prospects, not only in Fargo, but the entire region.[15]

After six weeks, the *Daily Tribune* reported the cards were a distinct success: "Interest in the amateur fights increases with every show. Hurley's present gym seems too inadequate to hold the crowd that throngs to the show and it is the wise fan who gets there early to get a seat."[16]

A key to Hurley's success was his close rapport with city officials and business people. This was critical in North Dakota, where "prize fighting" was still illegal under common law, and its almost indistinguishable sister, "boxing," was tolerated only at the whim of local authorities. While Wisconsin and Minnesota had boxing laws, North Dakota did not pass legislation clarifying the sport's status until 1935. Until then, boxing still inhabited a murky area between illegal and barely legal activity.

To combat this uncertainty, Hurley developed a working relationship with city attorney W. H. Shure, who supervised most of Jack's shows throughout his promoting career in Fargo. By keeping in close touch, Hurley and Shure were able to work out potential legal issues prior to each show before they became a problem. Jack later named Shure as the person "best qualified" to serve as the state's first boxing commissioner and gave credit to Shure's "kindly advice" for "whatever success I had."[17]

Although not immediately obvious, the legislative limbo in which North Dakota boxing resided actually worked to Hurley's advantage. The absence of a law meant that the state had no boxing commission, no license fees, no taxes, and no limits on number of shows per year. As a result, Jack, as promoter, was at liberty to appoint his own referees, act as his own inspector, and feature boxers under his own management on shows which he promoted, all activities normally regulated by a boxing commission.

The freedom from legislative interference, taxes, and fees which Hurley enjoyed in Fargo spoiled him for life. He would spend the balance of his career denouncing boxing commissions, all of which he claimed indiscriminately licensed "the shoe string peddlers, informers, newsboys, gangsters, racketeers and other Johnny-come-latelies who are promoting shows, managing and handling fighters ... simply because they paid the commission a small fee for a license ..."[18]

Hurley fondly recalled "the good old days" of promoting in Fargo to *Seattle Post-Intelligencer* columnist John Owen many years later:

---

[15] Purcell, "Schauer Feels Sure He Can Win," *Fargo Forum*, December 26, 1923, sports section.

[16] "LeRoy Leaves for Fight at Duluth," *Fargo Daily Tribune*, February 6, 1924, sports section.

[17] Hurley, Jack, "Shadow Boxing," *Fargo Forum*, April 7, 1935, sports section.

[18] Hurley, *op. cit.*, May 13, 1934 and April 7, 1935, sports sections.

"I was the manager, the promoter and the commission, for that matter. Do you know how we ran our preliminary bouts? The referee would give the fighters their instructions in the dressing room. When they got in the ring we introduced them and, BANG, they came out fighting. When the bout was over, the referee walked over and raised the hand of the winner. The fans loved it You know, you don't need anybody walking around collecting slips from judges who don't know what they're seeing anyway.

"I trained the referee myself. Before the bout, this is what he'd tell the fighters: 'Listen, I want both of you to put on a good fight. If you don't fight, I'm gonna toss you both out of the ring and you won't get no purse, no bus fare home, no nothing. Another thing. If your opponent hits you low, hit him back. There's no such thing as a foul here.'"[19]

Another important relationship Hurley nurtured was with the Dakota National Bank, the city's most important financial institution. On July 17, 1926, Hurley applied to the newly formed Illinois Athletic Commission requesting a license to manage boxers. In his letter of application, he listed five people as personal references. The name he placed at the top of the list was that of his personal banker, William (Bill) Stern, at the time the vice president of the Dakota National Bank.[20]

Because he was an aggressive young man brimful of ideas consistently exceeding his bankroll, Hurley's association with Bill Stern was almost inevitable. A cynical observer might point out that a banker's business was to make money by loaning money, but Stern's reputation transcended the ordinary stereotype. As one admirer put it, "Bill liked to help everybody."

Stern was the oldest of three sons of Alex Stern, a Jewish immigrant who founded a clothing store and later a downtown bank. Bill was born in 1886, attended Harvard, joined his father in business, and served as a commissioned lieutenant in World I. As a result of his service in France, he developed lifelong interests in aviation and veteran's affairs.[21]

After the war, Stern returned to work at his father's bank, serve on the national committee which founded the American Legion, and become an influential Republican committeeman. By the early 1920s, he counted Calvin Coolidge and Herbert Hoover among his many prominent friends. For the rest of his life, Stern would continue to exercise considerable behind-the-scenes influence in the party's national politics.[22]

---

[19] Owen, John, "The Tiger Is Coming," *Seattle Post-Intelligencer*, p. 36.
[20] Hurley, letter to Illinois Athletic Commission dated July 17, 1926, author's collection.
[21] Scates, Shelby, *Warren Magnuson and the Shaping of Twentieth-Century America*, (University of Washington Press, 1997), pp. 15-16.
[22] Knutson, Jonathan, "Stern Had Knack for Seeing Big Projects Through," *Fargo Forum*, feature section (undated clip).

Bill Stern, courtesy of North Dakota State University Library.

Moorhead native Warren G. Magnuson, 1936, then U. S. representative and later senator from Washington state.

Des Moines' Roscoe Hall, who gave Russie LeRoy four tough outings in the last half of 1923.

Clever Al Van Ryan waged multiple battles against both LeRoy and Battling Krause during the 1923-24 indoor season.

One young man Stern assisted along the way was Warren G. Magnuson, a Moorhead native born in 1905 who first came into local prominence as quarterback on Moorhead's high school football team in 1922. When Magnuson graduated in 1923, Stern provided Warren the financial help which enabled him to enroll at North Dakota University before transferring to the University of Washington in Seattle in 1925.

After graduating from college and law school, Magnuson became a prosecuting attorney in Seattle and then entered politics. He was elected as a Democrat to the U. S. House of Representatives in 1936, served in the U. S. Navy during World War II, and was voted into the U. S. Senate in 1944. Through his long service on the Senate's Commerce and Appropriations committees, he emerged as one of the most powerful figures in the Senate and became a close confidante to four Democratic presidents.

Bill Stern, who was "never one to argue about party principles or platforms" if they interfered with his "dedication ... to practical politics," continued to support Magnuson throughout his career even though they were members of different political parties.[23]

In the early 1930s, Stern became involved with the fledgling Northwest Airlines. Enlisting the support of a young, but even then politically well-connected Magnuson as lobbyist, Stern was able to secure the air-mail contract between Minneapolis and Seattle for the airline. Magnuson later went on to acquire an ownership interest in the enterprise while continuing to quietly protect the company's interests in Washington, D. C.[24]

Ironically, Magnuson took boxing lessons from Hurley during the senator's Fargo-Moorhead days. This connection would be useful to Jack in the 1950s when he claimed the International Boxing Club (IBC) was unfairly shutting his boxer, Harry Matthews, out of big matches. In response to these charges, the senator co-sponsored a federal investigation which exposed monopolistic practices and started the IBC's downfall.[25]

In the early 1960s, Hurley returned to Fargo to visit his younger brother Hank. During the visit Hank commented he wished he had kept all the newspaper clippings Jack had sent him over the years. Hurley, dismissing Hank's apologetic remark, replied, "Why don't you try taking those clippings over to Bill Stern at the Dakota National Bank and see how much you can get for them?" Apparently, Jack's recollection of his earlier business dealings in Fargo had not dimmed with the passage of time.[26]

---

[23] Knutson, *op. cit.* Magnuson was actually the prosecuting attorney for King County, the county in Washington State where Seattle is located.

[24] Scates, pp. 15-123.

[25] Brougham, Royal, "The Morning After," *Seattle Post-Intelligencer,* November 15, 1961, sports section. Brougham, "The Morning After," *Seattle Post-Intelligencer*, May 22, 1952, sports section. Meyers, Georg N., "Tunney Raps Solons for Ring-Probe Proposal," *Seattle Times*, August 12, 1951, sports section.

Possessing a line of credit in Fargo proved helpful to Hurley more than once. As LeRoy and Petrolle improved, Jack found it difficult to entice the more costly well-known fighters to Fargo because they feared the shows would not draw enough to pay their guarantees. Their reluctance placed Hurley in a dilemma. He wanted to take Russie and Billy east where the big money was, but unless they could garner some important wins first, New York promoters were not willing to take a chance on the newcomers.

In early 1926, Hurley was finally able to convince top contender Eddie (Kid) Wagner and former world lightweight champion Jimmy Goodrich to travel to Fargo to box his two tigers. Petrolle scored a sensational knockout over Wagner and LeRoy won impressively over Goodrich, but both shows lost money. Jack had to borrow the funds to cover his expenses even though both LeRoy and Petrolle chipped in by lowering their purses.[27]

When they returned to the East Coast, Wagner and Goodrich spread the word Hurley's name on a contract was a guarantee of getting paid. After their endorsements, Jack had no trouble convincing other fighters from the East to fight in Fargo. As a result of these wins, both Russie and Billy were able to make the trip east and further their careers.[28]

Later in the fall of 1926, when Hurley signed for Petrolle to fight Alf Simmons, who claimed to be champion of Great Britain, in Fargo, Hurley was required to place Alf's $5,000 guarantee in an escrow account. The amount of the guarantee reportedly was almost twice as much as Jack had ever paid a boxer previously. Again, a trip to Stern's bank was required to meet the commitment to post the money in advance of the fight.[29]

Even as he was fully engaged in courting Petrolle, outfitting a gym, and launching a new series of amateur shows, Hurley was busy fulfilling his commitment to present one professional boxing card each month at the Fargo Auditorium during the indoor season. For his first program October 26, 1923, Jack arranged a ten-round main event between Battling Krause and Johnny Knauf. In the semi-windup, LeRoy was pitted against Bill Hainrich of St. Paul, also over a scheduled ten-round distance.

The Krause-Knauf bout was the fourth match between the two warriors. They split their first two fights, with Krause winning a newspaper decision at Bismarck in February 1922 and Knauf on a foul at Wahpeton in August 1923. A third contest at Grand Forks on September 28 ended in a riot, with both men fighting on after the final bell. Afterward, fans piled into the ring to join the fracas until the police restored order. Newsmen called the bout a draw, so the issue of who was a better fighter remained unresolved.

---

[26] Author's conversation with Carol and Dick Olson, niece of Hurley and her husband, in May 2006.

[27] Purcell, "The Sportville Spotlight," *Fargo Forum*, March 24, 1926, sports section.

[28] Fitzgerald, Eugene, "Keeping in Line," *Fargo Forum*, September 20, 1936, sports section.

[29] Purcell, "$5,000 Must Be in Today," *Fargo Forum*, September 1, 1926, sports section.

Action at first was relatively tame, as Knauf's clever boxing built up a slight lead over the first four rounds. In the fifth, however, the fighters shook off their inhibitions and tore into each other like alley cats. Krause scored the bout's first knockdown in the sixth round with a right uppercut which landed flush on the chin. Johnny was up at the count of three, but another wallop by the Battler sent him down again for a one-count.

A combination of rights to the body and head by Krause sent Knauf down two more times for short counts in the eighth round, but by the round's end Johnny was battling back fiercely. Knauf opened the ninth with a strong attack and landed a left to the head which dropped Krause for a count of five, a punch which the Battler said later was one of the hardest he ever received. Krause arose and took the fight to Knauf, but Johnny was able to maintain his edge for the round with an effective long-range attack.

Despite Krause's advantage in the number of knockdowns, both Fargo newspapers had Knauf slightly ahead going into the last round based on the fact he "scored at least 10 points to Krause's one while they were on their feet." Unfortunately for Knauf, his lead was extinguished early in the round when Krause landed a terrific right that sent Johnny down for his fifth trip to the canvas. Knauf lasted the round, but the final knockdown evened the scoring, and both papers ruled the fight a draw in their post-fight articles.

Despite the bitter rivalry of the contestants, attendance was less than expected, and Hurley failed to meet expenses. Both Fargo papers were at a loss to explain why fans had not supported the card. The *Forum*'s Purcell wrote that the "show was certainly a corker and deserved much better support." Ed Dunn of the *Daily Tribune* echoed the sentiment and wrote that those who did attend "were pleased with every bout."[30]

Hurley's next show November 23 featured the fourth fight in another rivalry, this time between LeRoy and his nemesis, Roscoe Hall, of Des Moines, Iowa. So far, Hall held an edge, with close wins over LeRoy at Des Moines and Sioux Falls, South Dakota, and a draw, also at Sioux Falls. This bout was their first in Fargo, and Russie hoped the change would work to his advantage. Jack's other mainstay, Battling Krause, was not on the card since he was headlining a show that evening at Ellendale, North Dakota.

---

[30] Purcell, "LeRoy Scores Knockout Win over Bill Hainrick," *Fargo Forum*, October 27, 1923, sports section. Dunn, Edw. L., "Knauf and Krause Draw; Leroy Kayoes Hainrich," *Fargo Daily Tribune*, October 27, 1923, sports section. The *Forum* reports a total of four knockdowns by Krause in a subtitle to its headline, but seems to recite five in the text of its report, as did the *Daily Tribune* in its account. The discrepancy may result from differing interpretations of the second knockdown in the sixth-round action. The *Forum* reporter wrote "Knauf slipped to the floor and the referee counted one before he could arise." The *Daily Tribune* seems to call it a clean knockdown ("a similar blow a moment later sent the Moorhead lad down for the count of one"). In the absence of other information, the fact that the referee counted over Knauf seems to tip the scales in favor of calling Johnny's second trip to the canvas in the round a legitimate knockdown, bringing the total number of knockdowns he suffered to five as compared to Krause's one.

Once more, the two combatants waged a close fight, with LeRoy landing harder, and Hall boxing smartly and landing more frequently. Hall was hurt on several occasions, but each time rallied with clever jabs and hooks. The *Forum* favored Russie six rounds to three with one even, while the *Daily Tribune* – after taking points from LeRoy due to some roughhouse butting episodes – called the fight a draw. Attendance again was a disappointment, with the *Daily Tribune* describing the crowd as "small but appreciative."

Hurley's last show in 1923 featured a rematch December 14 between Hazen, North Dakota's Battling Krause and Johnny Salvator's stable ace, Al Van Ryan. The St. Paul boxer had given Krause a bad beating two months earlier at Mitchell, South Dakota while knocking him down seven times to earn a ten-round decision. Krause argued he was not in shape for the fight and begged Jack for a chance to even the score against Van Ryan.

Krause was proving a valuable addition to Hurley's stable. With Jack's local programs showing less profit than expected, the Battler's compulsive need to keep busy provided Hurley a major source of extra income for the season. During Krause's association with Jack – from July 1923 until May 1924 – he toed the mark 26 times, registering 15 wins, eight losses, and three draws, more bouts by far than any of Hurley's other fighters.

Claiming he already had engaged in over 400 bouts, Battling Jake Krause was a 24-year-old veteran with more than seven years' experience when he and Hurley joined forces. Although most of these contests remain undocumented, if Krause fought at same pace earlier as he did during his time with Jack, then his guess might not have been that far off.

Scribes in the Dakotas already had dubbed Krause "the Hazen Caveman" and "the Stone Man from Hazen" to honor his crude style and ability to absorb punishment. Fargo writers took a liking to the rugged Dutchman with the curly, dark locks and flattened features because his zany behavior furnished a steady stream of good copy. After Jack taught Bat a crouching defense, the local reporters could not resist re-branding him with their own tongue-in cheek pet names of "Duck" and "the Hazen Phantom."

Even if the frequency of Krause's bouts did not increase after joining with Hurley, the caliber of his opposition did. Ready to travel at the drop of a hat, many of his most important bouts were fought outside Fargo against some of the Midwest's best welterweights. Included among the boxers he faced and the places he visited were Bud Logan in Watertown, South Dakota; Joe Simonich and Al Webster in Helena, Montana; Roy Conley in Sheridan, Wyoming; and Gunner Joe Quinn in Duluth, Minnesota.

Years later in his syndicated column, Hurley paid tribute to Krause, while at the same time lamenting the fact the Battler never learned the rudiments of the trade which he seemed to enjoy so much:

The rough-and-ready nature of small-town boxing in 1922 is evident in this match between Battling Krause (left) and an unknown foe in North Dakota. Note the bare wood floor, the two unconnected ropes, & the ring's folding chairs. This bout predates Hurley's handling of Krause by at least a year. Courtesy Mercer County Historical Society.

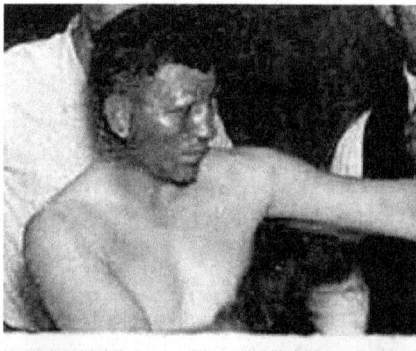

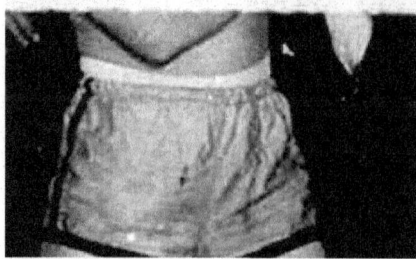

Close-up of Krause from top photo. Note the swelling on his face even before the bout begins.

Bud Logan gave the Battler a pasting at Watertown, South Dakota but didn't knock him out.

"I once had a fighter who seemed to thrive on punishment. I refer to Battling Krause who was looked upon as an iron man. But most of the beatings Krause took were before he learned to protect himself. Krause was really a remarkable fellow and if someone had taken him in tow before he learned a lot of bad habits, he could have developed into one of the greatest fighters of all time. The man had remarkable stamina and could take punches better than anyone I ever knew ... He was as chesty as Stanley Ketchel ever was and had the courage of a lion. It's too bad the fellow didn't have the proper opportunity to develop his talent.

"And what color this same Krause had. He did some funny things that furnished newspapermen with material for stories. I remember one time when Krause was supposed to catch an early morning train for a certain match. I stayed up all night to get him up at 6 a.m. After I sent him to the station, I took his place in bed.

"Imagine my surprise upon arising at noon to find Krause in bed with me. He had arrived at the station 20 minutes before train time and, falling asleep in the waiting room, had missed his train. What a story Westbrook Pegler or Damon Runyon could have written on that incident ...

"I have only enough space left to tell you of one incident where Krause proved his toughness. That was in his bout with Bud Logan at Watertown, South Dakota. In this bout, Krause had both eyes out and two ribs broken as early as the fourth round. Yet, he fought back all the way and was never in danger of being knocked out. And Logan had the kick of a mule wrapped up in each hand.

"Battalino was tough and so were a lot of others. But Krause, who fought all comers from 145 to 200 pounds, gets my vote. It's too bad he didn't take fighting more seriously and have an opportunity to show his wares in New York."[31]

When Krause entered the Fargo ring December 14, 1923, it was to settle his second vendetta in four days. The Battler had scored an eighth-round kayo over Johnny Knauf at Grand Forks on December 11 in the fifth bout of their series. Now, almost unbelievably, Krause was facing his other arch-rival, Al Van Ryan, on just three days' rest. Fortunately, Jake emerged from the Grand Forks match unscathed and ready to give his best effort.

In a reversal of their first bout, Krause was awarded a narrow decision over Van Ryan by both Fargo papers. Scoring the bout four rounds for Bat, three for Van Ryan and two even, Purcell wrote in the *Forum* that "Krause

---

[31] Hurley, "Ring Rations," *Fargo Forum*, August 9, 1931, sports section. Hurley, "Shadow Boxing," November 11, 1934, sports section. Quotation includes excerpts from both of Hurley's columns.

fought the best fight of his career, landing many hefty punches on Van Ryan's face and body and, contrary to his general practice, made Van Ryan miss innumerable times while fighting at long range, and kept the St. Paul man fairly well tied up when at close quarters."

Afterward, Purcell noted that "the ringside sections were scarcely populated while the cheaper seats in the gallery were well filled, the boys evidently saving their money for Christmas." [32]

Hurley spent 1923's last two weeks preparing for the first of what would become for him an annual event. All three of his promotions during the indoor season had drawn modest crowds, and he was hoping a special New Year's Day show would put him solidly on the positive side of the ledger.

LeRoy had won both of his two fights since his last local bout November 23. Apart from his hotly contested series with Roscoe Hall, his only setback of the indoor season was a close decision loss in September at St. Paul to Salvator's Van Ryan, whom Russie had previously beaten. Since Labor Day, he had compiled a record of six wins, two losses, and one draw.[33]

As LeRoy looked ahead to 1924, he was three months shy of his 22nd birthday and had been fighting as a pro for four years. Russie had engaged in 40 fights, posting 28 wins, seven draws, four losses and one no-contest. Of the three men who had beaten him, only Johnny Schauer had demonstrated a clear superiority over the Fargo man.

Hurley knew LeRoy had improved since his match with Schauer 1-1/2 years earlier, but Fargo fans still remembered Russie's listless performance. To redeem himself and advance his career beyond the Dakota borders, LeRoy needed to square his account with Johnny Schauer.

On December 19, 1923, Hurley announced he had completed arrangements with Mike Gibbons and Mike Collins, Schauer's managers, for their charge to meet LeRoy in the main event of the January 1, 1924 show. Purcell commented in the *Forum*:

> "Fargo fans no doubt will be delighted to hear that Schauer is confident, for this means that they will see a real fight New Year's Day. LeRoy is bubbling over with confidence, and yet, he is not over-confident. Hurley has brought his protégé along to the point where he realizes that a bad showing at this time will spoil the pretty record he has made in recent bouts, and would knock him back to the beginning point again.

---

[32] Purcell, "Battler Carries Early Rounds; Al Finishes Good," *Fargo Forum*, December 15, 1923, sports section.

[33] A point of dispute in LeRoy's record arises as a result of LeRoy's November 23rd fight with Hall when the *Fargo Forum* voted in favor of Russie as winner and the *Daily Tribune* called the fight a draw. Interestingly, Hall reportedly admitted to the *Forum* after the fight that LeRoy had bested him. If the *Daily Tribune's* view of that fight is accepted, then Russie's overall record during the period would be 5-2-2.

"Russie admits that he took a licking for a few rounds from Schauer at Detroit and then proceeded to hike out of danger. But, according to Russie that fight is history ... LeRoy is punching harder and faster than he ever has in his career. He can punch hard and fast enough to take the lead in the first round, and if he is willing to catch one now and then, he can score a decisive win. And it should be a good fight while it lasts."[34]

The *Daily* Tribune's Ed Dunn had this to say before the fight:

"Schauer is a rugged fighter. He hits hard with either hand and is dangerous at infighting. LeRoy's improvement in the past year should make him on a par with Schauer and the fight would be a good one. Schauer's most recent bid for fame was his kayo victory over Eddie Boehme of Milwaukee, who fought a draw with LeRoy here in 1921."[35]

The *Daily Tribune*'s title headline in its January 2nd fight report opened with the happy news, "Local Boy Wins All Ten Rounds." Purcell, in the *Forum,* elaborated with a detailed account of the action:

"The first round nearly cost the Auditorium association the price of a new roof. LeRoy tore loose from his corner with the sounding of the first gong and brought all his heavy artillery into play. The Fargo youngster saved none of his big guns, and Schauer was in front of such a vicious attack that he was completely bewildered.

"A terrific left to the body shortly after the sounding of the first gong staggered Schauer and a right swing to the jaw sent him down for the count of two. Russie ripped in as soon as the soles of Schauer's shoes touched the deck and another vicious right sent him reeling across the ring. LeRoy forced Schauer into the ropes in a neutral corner and battered him with both hands, but the St. Paul man was in excellent condition and managed to wobble to his corner for a short rest.

"The fans were astounded and could hardly believe their eyes when they saw Russie pounding the St. Paul man unmercifully with both hands and by the end of the round they were all but standing on the seats, shouting themselves hoarse.

---

[34] Purcell, "Schauer Feels Sure He Can Win," *Fargo Forum*, December 26, 1923. sports section. During Schauer's career his name was variously spelled as Schauer, Schauers, Shauer, Shauers, and Showers. For consistency, the author has opted to use BoxRec's spelling of "Schauer" throughout this volume.

[35] Dunn, "Amateur Card Is Offered Tonight," *Fargo Daily Tribune*, December 19, 1923, sports section.

"Russie continued his aggressive tactics in the second round and managed to blacken Schauer's left eye and to open a cut on his nose. At the close of this stanza LeRoy's hair was still slick as when he entered the ring while Schauer looked as though he had been fighting a tornado. ...

"In the fifth frame ... Russie had Schauer backed against the ropes and he landed three times with his left, body-jaw-body, without a return. The flashy piece of work brought a tremendous cheer from the crowd, for it was the neatest bit of fighting that has been seen in the Fargo ring for some time ...

"In the final frame, Schauer came tearing out of his corner and made a determined effort to win by a knockout. LeRoy kept out of danger by clever ducking and blocking until the round was about half spent, and then he fought furiously in an effort to beat his man down for a final count. Schauer was kept busy for a full minute trying to avoid that punishing left hand to the body, but the target was there and LeRoy found it often enough to win the final round. Russie was comparatively fresh when he stepped from the ring while Schauer's body was scarlet, LeRoy's hard body blows leaving their mark." [36]

In the semi-windup, Billy Petrolle, in his first effort under the Hurley banner, had his hands full in winning an eight-round newspaper decision over classy but out-gunned Irish Kennedy. Petrolle's "willingness to mix, his ability to absorb anything that Kennedy had to offer and still send over powerful blows won him the fight."[37]

Hurley imported Billy Hoke, matchmaker for the Minneapolis Boxing Club, to referee the card. Hoke said after the fight he was impressed with LeRoy and would find him a spot on a Minneapolis show in the near future.

Although the New Year's show advanced LeRoy's career, it failed to achieve its promoter's goal of financial success. According to the *Daily Tribune*, an unanticipated conflict with an Elks club festivity was likely the reason for a poor turnout of only "about 800 fans."[38]

The day after the show, "Promoter Jack Hurley announced ... that, while he didn't lose money, 'he didn't make a dime.'"[39]

---

[36] Dunn, "Local Boy Wins All Ten Rounds," *Fargo Daily Tribune*, January 2, 1924, sports section (title caption). Purcell, "Russie Drops Schauer in Fast First Round," *Fargo Forum*, January 2, 1924, sports section (textual quotation).
[37] Purcell, *op. cit.*
[38] Dunn, "All Boxers Ready for Starting Gong," *Fargo Daily Tribune*, sports section.
[39] Purcell, *op. cit.*

CHAPTER 10

FIGHT FANS, NOW HEAR THIS!

I can't forget taking Billy Petrolle, Russie LeRoy, and Battling Krause to Moose Jaw, Saskatchewan in January 1924, where they boxed Young Runcorn, Norman Wilson and Battling Moran, respectively. The show was held in an armory on the outskirts of the city and on this night in particular, they experienced the worst snowstorm in 20 years. We didn't draw a corporal's guard as it was 46 degrees below zero.

We wired home for money and waited all the next day for it to arrive. We finally bailed out of the hotel and got on the train back home to Fargo. If I ever get stranded again, I hope it is some place where the climate is warmer than it is in Moose Jaw in the winter.

Later in the spring of that same year, we almost did get stuck again when I was promoting the Billy Petrolle-Len Schwabel match at Jamestown. I thought the show was going to make a nice little profit as boxing shows there always drew a good crowd. I was charging $1.50 and $2.00 for my tickets. The evening of the show, I found out that across the street the high school was offering a school play for 35 cents a copy. Did they pack them in? Did they ever. I mean the high school players!

After the fight, Billy and I had to hop a freight train home.[1]

– Jack Hurley

****

The end of 1923 and the beginning of 1924 brought a multitude of changes to Hurley's stable in addition to the arrival of Billy Petrolle. On November 1, 1923, the *Fargo Forum* reported that Moorhead featherweight Roy (Submarine) Smith "signed a contract with Jack Hurley and has promised to make every effort to get himself in proper condition."

Smith had been fighting around Fargo even before Hurley frequented Kossick's gym in the basement of Saumweber's barbershop. Known as a playboy who spent his earnings before receiving them, Sub had served as a stepping stone for many ringsters, including LeRoy and Petrolle. The *Forum* reported the "Moorhead boxer has saved himself from many terrible beatings by his clever generalship when he was not in condition," but that "if Smith gets in shape, there are still plenty of fighters that he can lick."[2]

---

[1] Hurley, Jack, "Shadow Boxing," *Fargo Forum*, July 22 and August 5, 1934, sports sections. Hurley told the stories as two separate anecdotes in his syndicated column. The author added the last sentence based on an interview of Hurley's brother Hank who recalled that in "the early days Jack and his three fighters would hop a freight to Jamestown for the card and take another freight back to Fargo." Kolpack, Ed, *Forum*, May 18, 1983, p. C-2.

Hurley agreed to take control of Smith's affairs on a trial basis, but only if Smith "promised to take good care of himself and work hard." The *Daily Tribune* noted that Jack "will not monkey with him unless he has the goods to go out and make some money for the Colonel. To get the money a fighter must fight, Hurley declares, and Smith has got to be able to stand in there and show the boys that he is not through."[3]

Smith did reasonably well under Hurley's management, winning three of four fights with one draw between November 30, 1923 and February 29, 1924. However, it was apparent Sub was fit only to fight in preliminary bouts, and the two agreed to terminate their relationship. For the next few years, however, Hurley the promoter would continue to use Smith as a trial horse on his pro cards and against young boxers on his amateur shows.

Johnny Knauf was another fighter Hurley took on during the winter of 1924. Jack had managed him during the 1920-'22 seasons when a dispute over monetary matters led to a parting of the ways.

On February 26, 1924, the *Daily Tribune* related Hurley had settled "differences of long standing" with Knauf. During the time Johnny had been handling his own affairs, he "made little progress in the fistic game and now realizes that it is vital ... to have an influential manager. Hurley has the reputation among promoters in the Northwest as a square-shooter and any boy recommended by him is accepted on his word."[4]

Knauf had been inactive since suffering a broken thumb in his bout against Battling Krause at Grand Forks in December 1923. Unfortunately, his comeback with Hurley would last for only two bouts. On March 8, he earned an eight-round newspaper draw with Al Conway in Duluth. Later in the month on March 25, he made a disappointing showing in Fargo against Al Van Ryan of the Salvator stable, losing a ten-round decision.

After the Van Ryan bout, Knauf left Hurley again and took a six-month rest. In October 1924, Johnny moved to Grand Forks, North Dakota, where he resumed his boxing career under his own management. He later would figure again in the Hurley saga as a foe of LeRoy and Petrolle in 1925.

On March 4, middleweight Billy Ehmke of St. Paul also signed a contract with Hurley. The *Fargo Forum* described Ehmke as "not a world beater ... but well known to Fargo fans" as "a good tough fellow who fights all the way and his willingness to mix and ability to punch has made

---

[2] Purcell, J. A., "Sub Smith Will Box for Hurley," *Fargo Forum,* November 1, 1923, sports section.
[3] Dunn, Edward. L, "Hall Wants Too Much for Fracas," *Fargo Daily Tribune,* November 2, 1923, sports section. Dunn, "Kane signed to Meet Sub Smith,"*Fargo Daily Tribune,* November 15, 1923, sports section.
[4] "Johnny Knauf to Fight for Hurley," *Fargo Daily Tribune*, February 26, 1924, sports section.

him a big favorite in northwest circles." Local enthusiasts particularly remembered Ehmke's great fight against Leo Stokes in November 1921.[5]

Ehmke was with Hurley for almost a year. During that time, he performed well, winning four of eight bouts, drawing in three, and losing once by disqualification. They ended their relationship amicably in January 1925, when Hurley took Petrolle and LeRoy on their first eastern tour.

On a sadder note, Jack Bailey informed Hurley in a letter from Chicago that he was retiring from the ring. The announcement was a disappointment to both his manager and to Fargo boxing fans because Bailey's willing style had made him "popular over the Northwest for several years."[6]

In three years with Hurley, Bailey engaged in only 15 bouts. During that time "Jay Bee's" career was interrupted four times for health reasons. Most recently, on April 6, 1923, Bailey had suffered a broken jaw when he was hit by a right uppercut against Mark Moore at the Fargo Auditorium.

After an eight-month respite, Bailey returned to Fargo for a bout with Freddie Mayer on the December 1923 Krause-Van Ryan card. Just before leaving his Chicago for Fargo, he wrote the *Forum* explaining his upper teeth had been extracted during World War I as a result of gas burns. While treating him for the jaw fracture, his doctors concluded his war experience made him especially disposed, not only to injury, but also to the episodes of weakness and blood poisoning he had endured the past few years.

The *Fargo Forum* had reported a few days before the Mayer match that Bailey's problems were solved:

> "Bailey wrote a short time ago that he has succeeded in securing a rubber mouthpiece that will serve the purpose in place of his upper section of teeth …
>
> "Bailey declares that the mouthpiece takes the strain of a hard punch on the chin off his lower jaw, and that he has taken many hard wallops while training without any great pain. Bailey declared in his letter that the new mouthpiece has given the confidence that he lacked when he appeared in Fargo in the past and is now ready to undertake the hardest campaign Hurley can arrange."[7]

Unfortunately, even with a mouthpiece, Bailey could not overcome the demons which followed him home from France. Although he kayoed Mayer in three rounds, he himself was kayoed by Al Webster February 1, 1924, at Sheridan, Wyoming. Afterward, Bailey again complained of weakness, this time from a flu. When he failed to regain his strength after two months he

---

[5] "Ehmke Joins Hurley Stable," *Fargo Forum,* March 4, 1924, sports section.
[6] "Jack Bailey to Quit Mitt Game," *Fargo Forum,* March 25, 1924, sports section.
[7] Purcell, "Fargo Men Will Fight at Forks," *Fargo Forum,* December 11, 1923, sports section.

decided to "quit the mitt game." On March 25, Bailey finally wrote "that he had landed a good job" and was "through with the ring game for a long time, and probably forever" unless "his health is ever normal again."[8]

The signings of Knauf and Ehmke re-affirmed Hurley's position as the pre-eminent boxing impresario in the Dakotas. The *Daily Tribune* reported that "with the return of Knauf to the fold, Hurley now has every drawing card in North Dakota and western Minnesota under his direction."[9]

Early 1924 found the Hurley corps barnstorming not only in the Dakotas but also in various other Midwestern states and provinces: from Helena, Montana in the West, to Duluth, Minnesota in the East; and from Moose Jaw, Saskatchewan in the North, to Des Moines, Iowa in the South.

Billy Ehmke was a hit in Casper, Wyoming and in Butte, Miller City, and Miles City, Montana. Battling Krause caught on in Des Moines, Iowa; Sheridan, Wyoming; and Helena, Billings, Butte, and Miles City, Montana. LeRoy was popular in Helena; Redfield, South Dakota; and Duluth, Minnesota. Petrolle won the hearts of fans in Helena and Duluth.

Meanwhile, Hurley expanded his promoting business to include shows not only in Fargo but also in other North Dakota communities as well. Between February 1 and July 1, Jack staged a total of nine shows at four different cities: five in Fargo; two in Jamestown; one in Minot; and one in Mandan. In addition, he still found time to arrange the weekly amateur cards at his basement gym in the Tweeden Hotel.

Although Hurley preferred to travel with his fighters, his itinerary often forced him to make other arrangements. Occasionally, he was able to schedule two of his boxers on the same card. For example, Jack sent Leroy and Petrolle to both box and second each other on a card in Helena. Russie worked in Billy's corner for the semifinal, and Petrolle returned the favor for LeRoy in the main event.[10]

For a show in Des Moines, Hurley sent Petrolle along to second Krause even though Billy was not on the card at all. On other occasions, Jack would send his fighter to a location a few days in advance and join him the day of the bout. Sometimes, if a local handler could be found, the fighter would travel to an engagement by himself.[11]

Hurley likewise used his pro fighters to teach the novice boxers who trained at his gym. As a publicity stunt for his weekly amateur shows, he typically featured contestants allegedly from the stable of Krause in

---

[8] "Jack Bailey to Quit Mitt Game," *op. cit.*
[9] "Johnny Knauf to Fight for Hurley," *Fargo Daily Tribune*, February 26, 1924, sports section.
[10] "Russie Wins Honors in Nine Rounds with Slashing Left," *Fargo Forum*, June 26, 1924, sports section.
[11] "Hurley Fighters Off to Moose Jaw," *Fargo Daily Tribune*, January 13, 1924, sports section.

FIGHT FANS NOW HEAR THIS! 185

Middleweight Billy Ehmke, who Hurley handled in 1924.

Dago Joe Gans, Johnny Salvator's welterweight who appeared on several of Hurley's Fargo cards.

Hurley's ace, Billy Petrolle.

Music of Les Backer, LeRoy's brother, who did office work for Hurley.

matches against boxers trained by Petrolle or LeRoy. Often, Russie and Billy would referee when a member of the other's stable was boxing.

Alternatively, Jack might hire the out-of-town main-eventer featured on a pending pro card to act as a "guest referee" for an amateur show.[12]

Hurley also used Fargo resident W. Oscar (Swede) Hammergren to run errands, oversee the gym, and stage amateur shows in his absence. On one occasion, Hammergren accompanied LeRoy and Petrolle to Duluth where they were required to report with a handler three days before a fight. Jack later arrived in time to second his boxers in their respective bouts.[13]

Hurley recruited LeRoy's brother, Les Backer, to serve as part-time office manager and ring announcer. Among other duties, Les handled ticket sales and acted as press spokesman when Jack was on the road.[14]

Backer's outgoing personality was of real benefit during the two seasons he was with Hurley. Les had already made a name for himself in local supper clubs as an entertainer and banjoist with his own vocal quartet. Within a few years, he would enjoy modest success as a recording artist and vocalist with a variety of orchestras in the Midwest.[15]

Hurley's friendship with Johnny Salvator was another asset on which Jack relied. Of the nine main events he staged in Fargo during the 1923-'24 indoor season, Salvator's fighters provided opposition for Jack's headliners five times. When he was struggling to break even, Hurley appealed to Johnny. Jack had lost money on three straight cards and was trying to finance his show on February 29, 1924. Would Johnny accept a percentage rather than a flat gurantee for Dago Joe Gans to meet Battling Krause?

Salvator agreed to the percentage, but only if Hurley would increase his ticket prices. Prices for tickets on the first floor of the auditorium were to be raised from $2.50 to $2.75, the lower gallery rows from $1.50 to $2.20, and general admission from $1.00 to $1.65.

Salvator also agreed to arrive in Fargo with Gans earlier than usual to help generate interest in the bout. In essence, Johnny was sharing the risk with Hurley as well as giving him free advice on how to improve his business. In addition, he was affording Jack much needed cover so he could raise his ticket prices without upsetting frugal Fargo ticket-buyers.[16]

---

[12] "Krause's Fighter Flops," *Fargo Forum*, February 28, 1924, sports section.

[13] "Salvator Has Not Okehed Le Roy Go," *Fargo Daily Tribune*, January 15, 1924, sports section. "L'Roy in Duluth Tonight for Go," *Fargo Forum*, April 8, 1924, sports section.

[14] Dunn, "Petrolle Breaks Jaw of Kennedy, Wins," *Fargo Daily Tribune*, March 1, 1924, sports section. Purcell, "Rugged Mixers Will Clash in Semifinal Go," *Fargo Daily Tribune*, December 21, 1924, sports section.

[15] Purcell, "Dave Barry Will Referee Fistic Card Here Jan. 2," *Fargo Forum*, December 27, 1927, sports section. Backer recorded over a dozen songs with the Walt Anderson Orchestra for the Gennett record label at St. Paul in 1927. His success as a recording artist eventually led to radio contracts in 1928 with three different Chicago-based broadcasting stations.

[16] Purcell, "Tough Welterweights to Mix in Gate City Arena," *Fargo Forum*, February 16, 1924, sports section.

Although Gans defeated Krause, the show was Jack's most financially successful card of the season. The *Forum* reported "the program was well attended, and Hurley must have at least broken even."[17]

****

The 1924-'25 indoor season found Hurley facing a number of quandaries. The prior February, LeRoy followed up his New Year's win over Johnny Schauer by defeating Al Van Ryan. Although these victories established Russie as the best lightweight in the Upper Midwest, Jack was unable to land a match for Russie with a nationally ranked challenger.

Leroy was now a 22-year-old veteran of 56 pro fights. His record showed 42 wins, four decision losses, 7 draws, two disqualification losses, and one no-contest. Clearly, he needed a "breakthrough" win to elevate him above his status as a local attraction to one who could command bigger purses. Efforts to attract former featherweight titleholder Johnny Dundee and junior welterweight champion Pinkey Mitchell to Fargo had failed the previous season because the guarantees they sought were too high.

Nineteen-year-old Billy Petrolle was in a similar position, having won 15 of 17 bouts the prior season. He had avenged his one loss against Rusty Jones with two subsequent victories over Jones. Billy's other blemish was a ten-round draw suffered at the hands of Jimmy Lundy in the latter's hometown of Helena. His biggest wins were newspaper verdicts over Sammy Leonard on March 13 and Otto Wallace on March 24, 1924. Overall, his record was 25 wins, three decision losses, and three draws.

Leonard, a University of Minnesota dental student, had been regarded as Minneapolis' best lightweight prospect at the time. Petrolle, still a featherweight, figured to be just another victim for Sammy. *Minneapolis Tribune* sports editor George Barton refereed the bout at the National Armory in Minneapolis. The next day, he awarded Billy the newspaper decision and came away convinced the young Italian was a boy to watch.

The Wallace fight was important both because Otto was a veteran of 200 fights and because he had fought LeRoy only six months earlier. The Petrolle-Wallace bout therefore represented a chance to judge the relative progress of Hurley's two stars. At the end of the bout, both Fargo newspapers agreed Petrolle had won almost every round.

Though neither Fargo newspaper ventured a direct comparison between the two, it was apparent Petrolle would soon be challenging LeRoy as Hurley's leading breadwinner. Both boxers dominated the action in their bouts against Wallace, and there was no longer any basis to favor either Russie or Billy as the most worthy standard bearer of Fargo's fistic honor.

---

[17] Purcell, "Battler Unable to Keep Lead after Pretty Start," *Fargo Forum*, March 1, 1924, sports section.

Hurley was frustrated with Fargo's lack of support. In August 1924, he confided to the *Forum*'s Purcell he was in no hurry to promote any more shows in Fargo "unless the fans are willing to turn out."[18]

In Hurley's mind, his two star performers were outgrowing Fargo and Moorhead. The area's populace was just too small to provide the purses LeRoy, Petrolle, and their opponents could command elsewhere. According to the 1920 census, the total number of residents within the city limits of Fargo and Moorhead was just 30,000. In contrast, the populations of other Midwest cities like Sioux City, Duluth, Des Moines, and Omaha numbered 71,000, 99,000, 126,000, and 192,000 people, respectively.

Hurley spent a couple of weeks in July scouting these other cities and found promoters receptive to developing LeRoy and Petrolle as attractions. Headliners who "caught on" in those locales were regularly commanding purses as high as $750 and even $1,250, while in Fargo Jack could barely afford to pay $500. If LeRoy and Petrolle could establish themselves as idols in one of those cities, then they could earn larger purses, and maybe even secure matches against nationally recognized competition.[19]

And so, in the last half of 1924, Hurley decided to change his previous years' strategy of campaigning in the small towns in Montana, Wyoming, and Canada, and instead dedicate his out-of-town ventures to developing a following for his boxers in the larger pugilistic centers of the Midwest.

Hurley's fisticuffers invaded Sioux City July 26, 1924. In a main event, LeRoy scored a convincing one-round knockout over Jack Currie. In the semi-windup, Petrolle won an easy ten-round decision over Kid Worley.

The reception accorded the Fargo duo was exactly what Jack hoped for. The *Sioux City Journal* was especially enthusiastic about LeRoy's showing:

> "LeRoy lashed out with lightning lefts when they squared off, landing on Currie's body. Shifting his attack, he scored to the jaw with rights and lefts. LeRoy's punches had the stuff, and Currie's jaw and body didn't. That tells the story. LeRoy is the kind of fighter the fans of Sioux City would like to see again, but matched the next time with a worthy opponent ...
>
> "The fans were impressed with LeRoy and Petrolle, especially the former. LeRoy and Ace Hudkins would put up a slashing battle, one worth going miles to see. Some enterprising promoter probably will grab these two boys for a main go here in the near future. LeRoy said he could make 135 pounds for Hudkins who introduced from the ring last night, challenged any 135-pound man in the country.'[20]

---

[18] Purcell, "Sporting Spotlight," *Fargo Forum*, August 5, 1924, sports section.
[19] *Ibid.*
[20] "Bout Ends in Initial Round," *Sioux City Sunday Journal*, July 27, 1924, sports section.

The *Sioux City Daily Tribune*, on the other hand, was more impressed with Petrolle:

> "Billy Petrolle, a stablemate of LeRoy's out-pointed Kid Worley of Shelton, Nebraska, in probably the most sensational bout ever staged in Sioux City. The first three rounds saw the two slugging toe to toe.
> "Petrolle then assumed the defensive for two rounds and then with the advantage of the rest commenced to batter Worley about. However, Worley was too 'tough' to knock out but he was so punch drunk in the last three frames that he was unable to do much with Petrolle. The two boys enjoyed the mill and Petrolle, once fouled, took a few seconds rest and continued the bout with a grin."[21]

The *Journal*'s request for a contest between LeRoy and Hudkins of Lincoln, Nebraska, was granted. Promoter Tom Brisbane signed the two gladiators in a main event scheduled for August 29, 1924.

Nineteen-year-old Ace Hudkins was a rough, tough, slashing, ask-no-quarter type of fighter, who hit hard and was not particular about where his blows landed. When he fought LeRoy, Ace was at the beginning of a career which would see him become one of the 1920s' most popular fighters, the toast of both coasts – especially in Los Angeles and New York City.

Later that same year, Hudkins would campaign in Los Angeles where he immediately became one of California's best drawing cards. In 1926, a sensational four-round kayo over then undefeated Ruby Goldstein, the Jewel of the Ghetto, would establish him as a favorite in New York City. By the end of the decade, Damon Runyon, the country's most widely read sports columnist, would name Hudkins as his favorite action fighter.

Sioux City fans had seen Hudkins twice before. On May 24, he had stopped a local man, Si Sandage, in 6 rounds. He returned July 21 to outpoint Eddie DeBeau of St. Paul in ten rounds. In that bout, Ace incurred the crowd's wrath for repeatedly fouling his foe. The next day, the *Daily Tribune* offered a vivid description of Hudkins' foul tactics:

> "The victory of the Lincoln boxer was gained at the cost of considerable prestige, as his foul tactics were unpleasant to the crowd. He hit DeBeau four times after the bell, hit after the break, struck low, wrestled in the clinches and in the ninth round when DeBeau slipped to the mat and arose offering to have his gloves wiped free of the resin, Hudkins struck him, the St. Paul boxer being off guard."[22]

---

[21] "LeRoy Kayos Currie in First Round," *Sioux City Tribune*, July 28, 1924, sports section.

The LeRoy-Hudkins affair on August 29 was the semi-windup on a card featuring Sioux City's Earl McArthur in a ten-round tilt with Phil O'Dowd of Columbus, Ohio. McArthur topped the bill because he had fought virtually every bantamweight in the business, including champ Joe Lynch.

Although McArthur pleased his fans by winning a newspaper decision over O'Dowd, it was the LeRoy-Hudkins semi-windup which had them buzzing as they left the outdoor arena at Mizzou Park. The next day, Whitey Larsen described LeRoy's victory in the *Sioux City Daily Tribune* :

> "If there ever was a greater battle in this neck of the woods than Russie Leroy and Ace Hudkins put up, somebody out with it. There have been individual rounds of as hard fighting, but probably never such sustained action.
>
> "From the first bell to the last, these lightweights tore at each other like demons. It was one time that advance 'dope' ran true. The bout had been smoked up as a terrific battle and the best number on the card. It was.
>
> "In the estimation of the writer, LeRoy won the fight. Not by a city block or any such margin, but he certainly deserves the edge, not only on boxing, but on 'socking.' True, Ace swung some mean punches, but where did most of them, land? On the Fargo, North Dakota boy's hips, shoulders and top of his head!
>
> "On the other hand, LeRoy, an orthodox fighter, was wasting mighty little. He caught Hudkins time and again on the chin with short and sure punches. But Ace is tough. He doesn't go down like the average human. If he wasn't dizzy in the second round, he probably never will be. The fans marveled at the way he soaked up legitimate kayos and still kept going, battling like a tiger."[23]

During preparations for the bout, Hurley was introduced to Earl McArthur's manager, Sam Slotsky. The friendship would prove important because in 1931 the two men would form a short-lived but eventful partnership to promote boxing in St. Louis, Missouri.

Hurley took his two aces to Duluth on October 24 where Johnny Salvator was working as a matchmaker. The prior season, Salvator had saved many a show for Jack by providing boxers at reasonable prices. Now Johnny needed help putting boxing over at his new gig. Both LeRoy and Petrolle were given spots on the card, which featured a bout between

---

[22] "Ace Hudkins Wins Exciting Battle with Eddie DeBeau," *Sioux City Tribune*, July 22, 1924, sports section.

[23] Larsen, Whitey, "Ace Hudkins and Fargo Boy Stage Terrific Battle," August 30, 1924, sports section.

Stewart McLean of St. Paul and Lew Snyder of Bayonne, New Jersey.[24]

LeRoy's contest with Snapper Bill Garrison of Columbus, Ohio was the show's best match. Hurley told a Fargo writer that Garrison, who had won "16 of his last 18 fights" by kayo, "threw punches from every direction and any one of them looked like a sleep producer." Garrison was "anything but a setup," and "Russie did a nice piece of work in knocking that fellow out" in the fourth round. In his go, Petrolle met stiff resistance before kayoing Tom Tibbetts of Bemidji, Minnesota, also in the fourth round.

Salvator's venture was not without controversy, however. In the main event, McLean knocked down Snyder twice in the first round before Lew arose to drive "a deliberate left hand blow to McLean's groin ... the dirtiest blow ever struck in a Duluth ring." McLean was awarded the bout on a foul at the end of the first round. Afterward, police escorted Snyder "to his dressing room and later to his hotel to save him from mob violence."

Hurley agreed with news accounts, and said that Snyder's blow "was the foulest punch he ever saw struck" and that "only prompt action by the police department averted a riot." Luckily for Salvator, the workmanlike performances of LeRoy and Petrolle saved the show from being a bust, and fans left the auditorium in a happy frame of mind.[25]

Salvator returned the favor on October 31, by making his light heavyweight, Chuck Lambert, available to fight Hurley's newest charge, Al Webster, on Hurley's first Fargo show of the 1924-'25 indoor season.

Lambert spoiled Webster's debut with Hurley by winning a ten-round newspaper decision. In the semi-windup, Johnny Schauer, LeRoy's old rival from the Gibbons-Collins stable, used a ten-pound weight advantage to hold Petrolle to an eight-round draw.

The *Forum* reported that although the "fight program was a dandy" and "every bout was filled with action," the "promoter suffered a loss."

The day after the show, a disgruntled Hurley issued an ultimatum to Fargo's boxing fans in an interview with the *Forum* sports editor:

> "'Unless the attendance improves considerably on my next venture, there will be no more fights in Fargo,' Hurley declared today, in discussing prospects or another fistic program here. Hurley said he probably will make one more match, and if fans fail to turn out, he will take his stable and move to other fields."[26]

---

[24] "Chuck Lambert to Box Webster Here," *Fargo Daily Tribune*, October 22, 1924, sports section.
[25] "Russie LeRoy and Petrolle Score Kayos," *Fargo Daily Tribune*, October 25, 1924, sports section. Purcell, "Lambert Expects to Score Victory over Al Webster," *Fargo Daily Tribune*, October 26, 1924, sports section.
[26] Purcell, "Attendance Must Be Better or No Fights, Says Hurley," *Fargo Forum*, November 1, 1924, sports section.

Two weeks later on November 12, Petrolle was set to box another LeRoy nemesis, Roscoe Hall, in the latter's hometown of Des Moines, Iowa. Before the fight, Hurley told writers from both the Fargo and Sioux City newspapers that within the next few weeks he and his stable would likely be making Sioux City their new home. The *Forum*'s Purcell commented:

> "Petrolle's bout with Hall may be the first of a series of steps that may lead Hurley to pack his bags and take his fighters from Fargo for keeps. Hurley has received several tempting offers to change his abode to Sioux City, and if Petrolle succeeds in pleasing the Des Moines fans, Hurley will make his move accordingly."[27]

To the surprise of most fans, Petrolle won an easy decision over the clever Hall. Even Sec Taylor, sports editor of Hall's hometown newspaper, the *Des Moines Register*, admitted Roscoe "was decisively out-pointed." Noting LeRoy had experienced considerable difficulty in each of his three bouts with Hall, the *Forum*'s Purcell added that "this victory places Petrolle in position to demand a rating even with LeRoy and should mean that more important matches will be coming his way this winter."[28]

On November 21, LeRoy scored a three-round knockout over Joe McCabe in Omaha. Petrolle accompanied Russie to act as his second for the fight. Afterward, they hustled back to Sioux City where LeRoy was set to meet Ace Hudkins on November 24 in the long-awaited return bout. On the same card, Billy was fighting Bat Strayer in a ten-round semi-final.

Hurley stayed behind to organize a November 28th show in Fargo. Jack was keeping his promise to give boxing there one more try. Hurley would, of course, make the trip to Sioux City for LeRoy's bout against Hudkins.

On November 24, "a well-filled house" saw LeRoy win the newspaper decision over Hudkins. The *Sioux City Journal* reported Russie "pil[ed] up an early lead in the first six rounds and [had] such a wonderful boxing eye that he was able to keep out of danger" in the later rounds. The *Daily Tribune* observed that LeRoy had Ace "on the floor twice in the fourth round ... and that's all in the world that gave the former a slight shade."[29]

LeRoy's victories over Hudkins were the most important of his career. Immediately after his second loss to LeRoy, Hudkins left the Midwest in favor of California where the state legislature had just passed a law making

---

[27] Purcell, "Hurley Planning to Move Fighters to Sioux City," *Fargo Forum*, November 11, 1924, sports section.
[28] Purcell, "Petrolle Surprises Fans with Victory over Hall," *Fargo Forum*, November 12, 1924, sports section.
[29] Ryan, Joe, "Lightweights in Great Battle," *Sioux City Journal*, November 25, 1924, sports section. Larsen, "Omaha Battler Close to Kayo in Fourth Round," *Sioux City Daily Tribune*, November 25, 1924, sports section.

ten-round bouts legal. Ace would win six straight bouts within four months and lay claim to the California version of the world's lightweight title. In the next few years, Hurley would rely upon the Hudkins' conquests many times to convince promoters to use LeRoy.

In his supporting bout, Petrolle stopped Bat Strayer in the fifth round. The *Journal*'s Joe Ryan was enthused over Billy's work and wrote that his skills compared favorably with those of his more celebrated stable mate:

> "Billy Petrolle is a youngster who has all kinds of promise. A great similarity between his style and that of Russie can be noticed. Neither of them throws a punch unless he is almost certain it will land. Both have great left hands and both are great judges of distance."
>
> "The noticeable feature of this boy's work – and that of LeRoy – is that there is practically no waste of motion. They seem to be able to miss punches by a fraction of an inch and neither of them lets go unless he is fairly certain of hitting what he punches at … Keep your eyes on Petrolle because he's a real prospect."[30]

The stylistic similarities of the two fighters, as noted by Ryan, and the precision each displayed in evading punches and delivering their counter-blows, is testament to the effectiveness of Hurley's skill as a teacher. Ryan's report is an eyewitness account of the Hurley method in action – that a fighter's proper place is, as Jack would explain many times, at "the edge of the blaze, where he could go to work, but not in the flame itself."[31]

It would take Hurley and Petrolle six more years and a half-dozen trips to convince "ring experts" in New York what Ryan realized after seeing a few fights in Sioux City – namely, that Billy was not just a free-swinging club fighter, but a skilled strategist whose every move was calculated to make his foe do exactly what Petrolle wanted him to do.

The turning point finally would come in 1930 when, after an upset win over Jimmy McLarnin, the New York press embraced Petrolle as the most exciting boxer seen in Madison Square Garden that year. In succeeding years, he would become the most popular drawing card in New York and the toast of the city's boxing circles. For the time being, however, Jack and Billy would have to be satisfied with the plaudits of knowledgeable fans and sportswriters from the backwater towns of the nation's heartland.

Meanwhile, things were looking up in Fargo.

Hurley convinced veteran manager George W. (Biddy) Bishop to stop off in Fargo and make his two stable aces, K. O. Mars and Alex Novecky,

---

[30] Ryan, "Here and There in Sports," *Sioux City Journal*, November 25, 1924, sports section (first paragraph). Ryan, "Lightweights in Great Battle," *op. cit.* (second paragraph).

[31] Gregory, L. H., "Greg's Gossip," *Oregonian*, April 30, 1951, p. 3-1.

Gymnasium square-off between LeRoy (left) and Hudkins (right). Hurley can be seen in background, second from left.

Nebraska Wildcat Ace Hudkins.

LeRoy's Hudkins' wins led to a cover spot on the *Boxing Blade*.

available to fight LeRoy and Petrolle on the November 28th show. Bishop, a wily boxing man with over 30 years in the business, had handled numerous famous battlers in the early part of the century, including Young Peter Jackson, Kid Lavigne, and Aurelio Herrera.

Bishop and his charges were heading west for a series of engagements and were eager to secure a few fights along the way to defray expenses. Biddy even agreed to take a percentage of receipts in lieu of a guarantee.[32]

At first, Fargo fans suspected that Mars, who had been fighting as a pro since 1912, was "all through and will be a setup for LeRoy." The reaction of Bishop, a former newspaper sports editor, to these charges is a classic example of how a sage and cooperative manager, given the right circumstances, could help save a promotion.

In the days leading up to the show, Bishop flooded Fargo's sports desks with letters, testimonials, and news articles touting Mars' and Novecky's recent achievements. He wrote that within the past year Mars had defeated lightweight contenders Jack Zivic and Tommy Herman and earned a draw with new sensation and future lightweight champion Sammy Mandell.

Most notably, Bishop sent news reports that in his most recent fight Mars deserved a draw against Lew Tendler, who, until recently, had rated just behind champion Benny Leonard as the best lightweight in the world.

Bishop provided evidence that Novecky had "scored five successive kayoes last month" and had participated in 150 ring battles without being stopped. Biddy also furnished an article from a Cleveland paper describing Alex as "a second Battling Nelson ... because of his bulldog spirit." [33]

The *Daily Tribune* reported that "interest in the program took on a new complexion when it was announced that Mars and Novecky will arrive in Fargo four days before the bout ... Bishop must be convinced that Mars and Novecky will make a favorable impression or otherwise he would not show them in public until the day of the program."[34]

True to his word, Bishop and his boxers arrived in Fargo four days early. Free workouts were scheduled for 7:30 p.m. so that the largest number of fans possible would have an opportunity to check out the visitors.

After seeing Mars, sports editor Purcell noted that "a look at his face is enough to convince the most skeptical that Mars is a boxer of the first water. The Cincinnati fighter carries only one mark, a slightly damaged ear, which means that even the best of them have had a hard time planting

---

[32] "Bishop Taking Fighters West," *Fargo Forum*, November 4, 1924, sports section. Purcell, "Hurley Planning to Move Fighters to Sioux City," *op. cit.*

[33] Purcell, "Fargo Lad Meets Tough Foe on Nov. 28 Program," *Fargo Forum*, November 15, 1924, sports section. Purcell, "Hudkins Agrees to Fight at Sioux City on Nov. 24," *Fargo Forum*, November 18, 1924, sports section. Purcell, "Hurley Signs Alex Novecky for Semifinal," *Fargo Daily Tribune*, November 18, 1924, sports section.

[34] Purcell, "Russie LeRoy Leaves for Go in Omaha Ring," *Fargo Daily Tribune*, November 19, 1924, sports section.

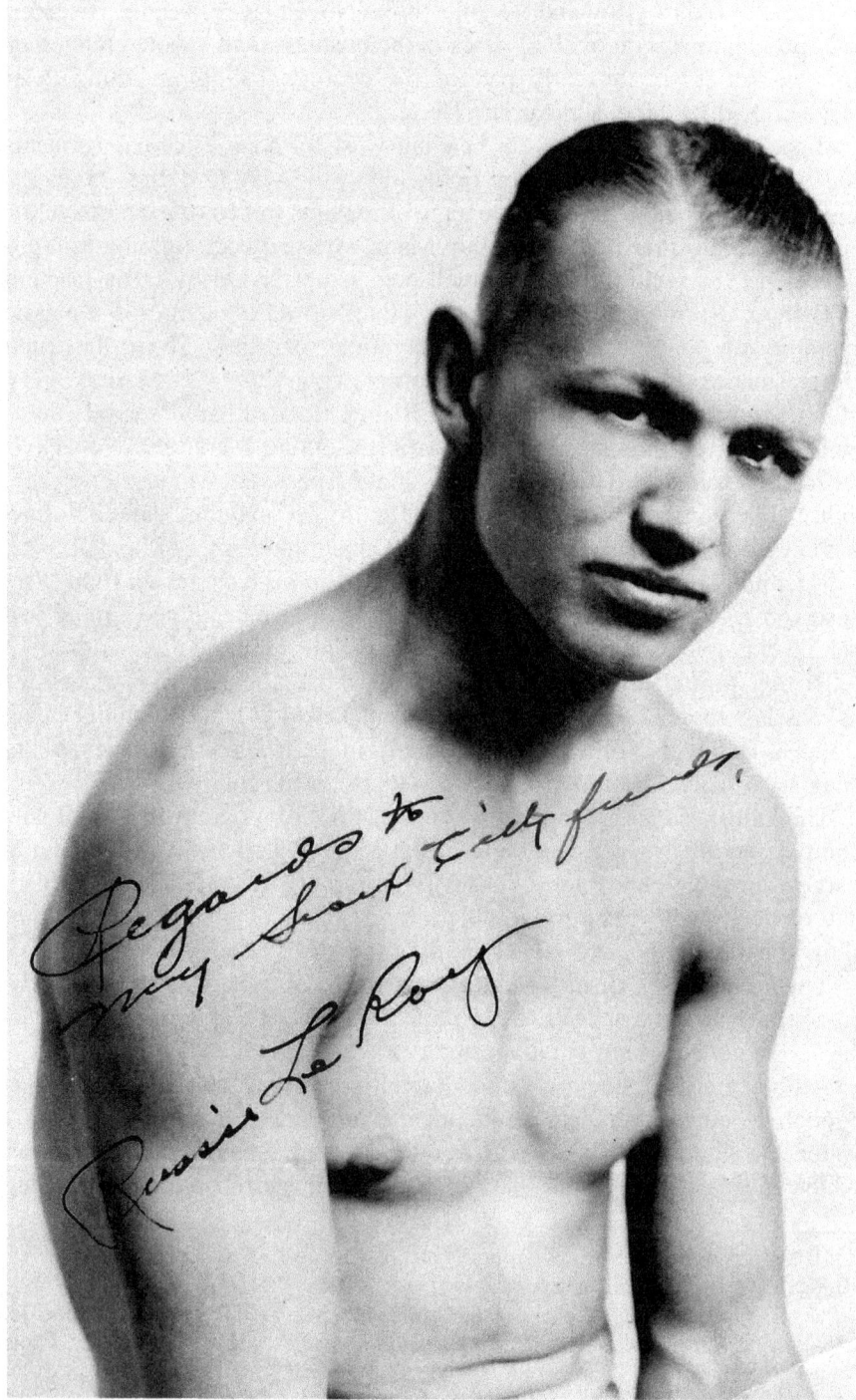

Russie LeRoy with an inscription to Sioux City fans when he was an attraction there.

punches on his chin ... He moves around the ring like the high-classed performer that he is advertised to be. He can move in every direction with equal agility and 11 fast rounds yesterday just gave him a light workout."[35]

Bishop's persistence and the favorable publicity from LeRoy's and Petrolle's out-of-town triumphs paid off. In front of a crowd "almost as good as the record-breaker for the LeRoy-Bobby Ward fight three years ago," LeRoy "decisively defeated K. O. Mars" in a "beautiful fight from start to finish." The *Forum* editor went on to write:

> "LeRoy, entering the fight with a broken knuckle on his left hand, completely outmaneuvered, out-punched and outfought the veteran warrior who on last August 11 succeeded in holding Lew Tendler of Philadelphia to a draw.
>
> "LeRoy entered the fight under a great handicap. Unknown to 90 percent of the fans here, Russie broke the knuckle of his index finger on the left hand in his fight with Ace Hudkins of Omaha at Sioux City last Monday ...
>
> "LeRoy's showing last night was the best he has ever made in a Fargo ring. He worked coolly at long range and threw but few punches that did not land. Mars blocked many blows and slipped a few, but LeRoy landed enough with that right to give him every round but the eighth, which was even, and there was a decided shortage of fighting in this round. At close quarters, LeRoy surprised even his closest followers. His right hand worked like a piston during the in-fighting, and his left was effective in stopping Mars' counters."

In the semifinal, Petrolle won a decisive but hard-earned decision over "cast-iron" jawed Novecky who "seemed to thrive on punishment (and who) every time he was hit ... came tearing back in for more."[36]

After a short rest, Hurley returned to Sioux City with his battlers for an American Legion show December 19, 1924. In co-featured main events,

---

[35] Purcell, "Dakota Pride Must Try Skill Against Southpaw," *Fargo Forum*, November 28, 1924, sports section. Purcell, "Mars Exhibits Real Ability in Work Here," *Fargo Daily Tribune*, November 25, 1924, sports section. At this time the *Fargo Forum* purchased the *Fargo Daily Tribune*. The latter paper lost its sports editor, and Purcell was writing for both papers at the same time, the *Tribune* in the morning and the *Forum* in the evening. This quotation combines Pat's comment from his columns in both papers. The *Tribune* later hired Jack Stewart to write about boxing for a few weeks until the paper was disbanded and the two papers combined to become, at least for a while, the "*Fargo Forum and Daily Tribune.*" For simplicity, the author has elected throughout this book to use the name "*Fargo Forum*" or more simply, the "*Forum*," for all of the paper's various configurations.

[36] Purcell, "Fargoan Whips Veteran with Broken Left Hand," *Fargo Forum*, November 29, 1924, sports section.

LeRoy and Petrolle were matched against Frankie Schaeffer and Charley Raymond, who were both handled by Chicago-based manager Ray Alvis.

On a night the weather limited attendance to the "smallest crowd that has seen a fight here in years," Hurley's men won lopsided decisions. Of more important to Jack's future, however, was his introduction to Ray Alvis.[37]

Like Hurley, Alvis was young, ambitious, and capable. At the time of the December 19th show, he had been a manager only two years and had already assembled a stable of 13 fighters. Although their trails would cross rarely over the next few years, the two men would keep abreast of each other's progress. In 1930, they would pool their resources and, for six months, form one of the largest booking agencies for boxers in the country.

The success of the LeRoy-Mars show in Fargo, and the poor attendance at the American Legion card in Sioux City, changed Hurley's mind about moving to Iowa. For the Fargo show, he had raised his ticket prices to $3 for reserved tickets and $1.50 for the gallery, and still attracted a large crowd. This experience convinced him Fargo fans were willing to pay more if they could be sold on the idea a program was worth the price.

For his 1925 New Year's Day show, Hurley raised ticket prices even higher to $3.30 and $1.65. Jack explained he was not actually increasing the price but merely asking the fans to pay the war tax. To further justify the "price adjustment," he announced he was importing veteran lightweight Mel Coogan from Brooklyn to meet LeRoy in the ten-round main event.[38]

Coogan's manager was the famed Joe Woodman, former pilot of the legendary Sam Langford. Mel had faced the world's best lightweights in the course of his 175-fight career, and was reputed to possess a fine defense and a right with "the kick of a mule." The signing of Coogan further showcased Jack's new confidence that Fargo fans were willing to fund the higher-priced talent needed to advance the careers of LeRoy and Petrolle.

A week before the New Year's show, Jack completed arrangements to take his two battlers east in early 1925. The trip was "an absolute necessity as Russie has licked every Midwestern lightweight in the game and now Hurley has to go to Brooklyn or New York for opponents, or match LeRoy with welterweights." Philadelphia was already scheduled as the first stop.[39]

The tour made LeRoy's bout with Coogan particularly crucial. A decisive win would be a springboard for well-paid engagements in the East.

Hurley's efforts were rewarded when LeRoy "firmly established a position among the leading lightweights of the world" by stopping Coogan in the first round. Especially gratifying to Jack was Russie's devastating

---

[37] Ryan, "Russie Wins as He Likes from Frankie Schaeffer," *Fargo Forum*, December 20, 1924, sports section.
[38] "Mel Coogan to Fight Russie in Fargo Ring," *Fargo Daily Tribune*, December 18, 1924, sports section.
[39] "LeRoy to Work at Forks Today," *Fargo Forum*, December 24, 1924, sports section.

use of the classic "pull-back" boxing move which Jack taught all his fighters to use against aggressive right-hand punchers.

In the next day's morning edition of the *Daily Tribune*, Pat Purcell described LeRoy's perfect delivery of the knockout punch:

> "More than 2,000 enthusiastic Fargo fight fans ... had just settled down in their chairs ... when LeRoy landed the finishing blow ... They were mixing near the center of the ring and Coogan started a right from a crouching position. LeRoy pulled back slightly, making Coogan miss and then let drive with a right hook that landed flush on Coogan's jawbone, just in front of the ear.
>
> "LeRoy put all he had in that blow, and that was sufficient. He fairly leaped with the punch and Coogan was raised completely off the floor. He dropped – as a police reporter might phrase it – with a dull, sickening thud. Coogan made an effort to rise but it was the instinct of the ring that prompted the effort more than any thought of his own, for he was completely out."

In the semifinal, Petrolle kayoed Eddie Root of Rochester, Minnesota in three rounds.[40]

The success of the LeRoy-Coogan show motivated Hurley to arrange another card before heading east. He quickly planned a gala promotion for January 30, featuring Russie against Eddie (Kid) Wagner from Max (Boo Boo) Hoff's stable in Philadelphia. Sadly, Wagner broke a hand five days before the show, and the bout was canceled.

On short notice, Jack cobbled together a feature bout between LeRoy and Johnny Tillman. Russie had won decisions over Tillman twice previously, but never had come close to kayoing the Minneapolis veteran.

The next day's edition of the *Daily Tribune* reported that after "unleashing a vicious two-fisted attack with the sounding of the first gong, Russie LeRoy of Fargo knocked out Johnny Tillman of Minneapolis here

---

[40] Purcell, "Right Hook to the Jaw Brings Sudden Finish," *Fargo Daily Tribune*, January 2, 1925, sports section. Purcell's account of the kayo punch LeRoy delivered to Coogan is an early description of the "pullback" move which was one of the weapons Hurley picked up from Mike Gibbons in St. Paul. Learning the "pullback" was an essential requirement for a Hurley fighter. Over 40 years later, in a moment of frustration, Jack's last fighter, Boone Kirkman, told Hurley he would never be able to learn the move. Jack's heated response was, "You have to because you can't be a fighter without it." Another of Jack's heavyweights, Harry (Kid) Matthews, mastered the pullback and employed it frequently. A young Zora Folley, stationed in the army at Fort Lewis, Washington in 1951, incorporated the move into his fistic repertoire after seeing Harry use it at a gym in Seattle. Folley can be seen executing the move successfully several times in his fight against Doug Jones December 15, 1962. The bout was televised, and a 16mm kinescope survives, VHS and digital copies of which are now in circulation among collectors. Zora, long a top-rated heavyweight in the 1950s and '60s, was well respected for his thorough knowledge of boxing.

last night in the second round of a scheduled ten-round affair." For the first time, Tillman "watched that extended arm fall" and toll the fatal ten count over him after "12 long, hard years of ring campaigning."

In the semi-windup, Petrolle packed too many guns for St. Paul's Reddy Blanchard. Even so, Blanchard put up a stiff battle and made Billy look awkward. The *Daily Tribune* reported "Petrolle's judgment of distance was terrible" and "he missed a hundred or more swings ... Were this fight to be scored by an English critic who believes that every punch ducked is as good as a punch landed – Blanchard would have at least earned a draw."[41]

On Monday, February 2, 1925, LeRoy, Petrolle, and Hurley boarded an eastbound train. They planned to make a short stopover in Milwaukee, spend a day in Chicago, and then on head to Philadelphia.

Before leaving, Hurley thanked fans for their support of LeRoy and Petrolle and promised that both would be identified as representatives of Fargo every time they stepped into a ring. "Russie and Billy will never be too good to fight in Fargo," Jack told a *Daily Tribune* reporter. "I only hope that someday I can bring them home as champions, run the show myself, sell the tickets at Steve Gorman's, have Leo Kossick referee, and have all the old familiar faces back in the first row of the gallery."[42]

Hurley likely recalled stories about a similar trip taken in 1912 by Luther McCarty, who left Fargo at age 20 and headed east to seek his fortune. Less than a year later, Lute returned as a hero after winning the white hope heavyweight title. In addition, Jack undoubtedly remembered telling his mother at the beginning of his career that he would uphold the family honor and develop a fighter who would "make the town proud of the town."

As the train pulled out, Hurley knew he was taking the two best fighters Fargo had to offer. Jack did not know whether they were good enough to become champions like McCarty. He was confident, however, they were ready to be tested, would fight hard, and would make Fargo proud.

---

[41] Purcell, "Fargo Mauler First to Stop Mill City Vet," *Fargo Daily Tribune*, January 31, 1925, sports section.
[42] "LeRoy, Petrolle, and Hurley Leave Monday on Eastern Campaign," *Fargo Daily Tribune*, February 1, 1925, sports section.

CHAPTER 11

GO EAST (AND WEST), YOUNG MEN

I can't forget arriving in Chicago on my first trip east with LeRoy and Petrolle hanging on to my coat tail, and me just following the crowd out of the station. If there had been a circus in town, we would have wound up at the circus. We had nine grips between us. Two were tied together with rope, and the redcaps in the different stations wouldn't give us a tumble. One look at our luggage convinced them we were not ready money.

The suit we bought Petrolle. We thought it was gray, but outside it was the same color as a mailman's. All Billy needed was the cap and he could have had a job. After a few days, the suit faded to a sickly purple and the pants became baggy at the knees. A fellow looked at Bill so long one time Bill finally asked him what he was looking at. The man asked him when he was going to jump. Bill had gotten caught in the rain and the suit shrunk. But Will got a pair of golf knickers out of the deal, which he still wears. Your correspondent, trying to be a big city slicker, rode the street car from downtown to where we were staying on the North side. I got lost, and on each car I boarded the conductor took my fare and gave me a transfer. I finally arrived home, tired and hungry, with a hand full of transfers. I must have ridden every car in Chicago.

Then on to Philadelphia, where we didn't know a soul or one street from another. Russie was all duded up in a short corduroy topcoat, which was all the rage out our way that year, but in the East he looked like an organ grinder who had lost his monkey. Bill wore a leather vest and looked for all the world like a second-story worker. I wasn't wearing a corduroy coat or leather vest, but I was far from being a walking fashion plate.

LeRoy, trying to be a big-towner, attended a stage show. During intermission, the crowd went out to smoke. Russie didn't smoke, but thought he would walk out with the others just for effect. When the break was over, he couldn't find his seat. He had left his ticket stub in his corduroy coat. LeRoy sat in several seats, but had to get up with the arrival of the rightful owners. The windup was, he viewed the remainder of the show from the rear of the house and waited until everyone left the theatre to find his coat and hat.

The three of us living in one room in Philadelphia. Petrolle was having trouble with his feet and had what might be called "halitosis of the foot." I came in early one morning, and the smell was terrific. I didn't want to wake the boys, so I got ready for bed in the dark. The odor was so bad it was impossible for me to sleep. After twisting and turning for half an hour, I got up and hung Petrolle's socks out the window.

Even that did not help, so I decided the breeze through the window was blowing the smell back into the room. I got up and wrapped the socks in a newspaper and placed them in a corner. The odor persisted, so I put the socks in the bathroom and closed the door. While adjusting my pillow, I discovered it was heavy and upon examining it, found a package of limburger cheese secreted there. We all had a good laugh, but between you and me, there wasn't much difference between the cheese and the socks.[1]

– Jack Hurley

****

On their way east, Hurley, LeRoy, and Petrolle stopped to visit with promoter Tom Andrews in Milwaukee while changing trains. California had just enacted a new ten-round boxing law, and Andrews offered to represent Hurley's boxers there. Jack listened intently, but was not interested in taking his fighters to the Golden State at that time.

The contingent continued on to Chicago where they laid over for a day and two nights at a downtown hotel. LeRoy and Petrolle trained at Kid Howard's gym to stay in shape and give "Windy City" railbirds a brief look at the two Dakotans they had heard so much about. The rest of the day was spent sightseeing and shopping for clothes and souvenirs.

The trio arrived in Philadelphia Thursday, February 5, 1925, and checked into the hotel which would serve as their base of operations throughout their stay in the East. After a workout at Philadelphia Jack O'Brien's gym in the early afternoon, they caught a train to New York City where they had tickets to watch Sammy Mandell, of Rockford, Illinois, fight Sid Terris of New York at Madison Square Garden that same evening.

The match was the first in a series of elimination contests to decide the successor to lightweight champion Benny Leonard, who retired January 15. Leonard had won the lightweight crown May 28, 1917, from Freddie Welsh and held it for over 7-1/2 years, longer than any man in modern boxing history. Born Benny Leiner in the ghetto of New York's East Side, Leonard was the idol of almost every Jewish male, young and old alike.

A near riot ensued after the decision in favor of Mandell was announced. Jewish fight fans had favored Terris, "the East Side Phantom," as the heir apparent to Leonard and were not shy in expressing their displeasure about the bout's unexpected outcome.

Although Mandell would lose his next elimination bout to the tournament's eventual winner, Jimmy Goodrich, he would go on to win the lightweight title from Goodrich's conqueror, Rocky Kansas, two years later on July 3, 1926. Within a few years. Petrolle's career would advance to the point where instead of buying a ticket to see Mandell and Goodrich fight, he would be facing each of them in the center of a boxing ring.

---

[1] Hurley, Jack, "Ring Rations," *Fargo Forum*, April 16, 1933 and August 5, 1934, sports sections.

The next few weeks saw Hurley making rounds to the boxing clubs most likely to offer his boys a spot on one of their fight cards. On February 15, the *Fargo Daily Tribune* reported that "the Kernel is evidently taking Quakertown by the ears." Included in the article were portions of Jack's first letter from Philadelphia:

> "Promoters in Springfield, Boston and Philadelphia want my lads, and we're going to take all the bouts they can offer as soon as they line up the opponents, no matter who they are ... Mike Schultz, 'the toughest boy in town,' had a couple of fights on and couldn't get any sparring partners. So I bounced up and offered to let him work with LeRoy and Petrolle. The other boys said he hit too hard for them so my act made quite a hit with these fight-crazy Quakers.
>
> "Records don't mean a thing down here, just like my batting average in the Commercial League. The fighters in this town have to show the fans a good healthy wallop or all they glean for their efforts is the festive raspberry. We're popular down here. Wherever we go they say 'that's them. Those are the cow-puncher fighters from North Dakota.'
>
> "These boys here believe that North Dakota is only a few miles from Alaska, a cold wilderness inhabited by cow herders, Eskimos, and socialists. In fact one writer here in his story spelled Fargo, 'Farley,' and all the scribes have admitted that they hardly ever heard of the place before. It won't be long though until Fargo will be as well known here as the Kaiser was in Berlin before the war."[2]

Hurley arranged for Petrolle's first bout in the east to be in Holyoke, Massachusetts with help from Joe Kossick, Leo's brother, who had moved there from Fargo to set up a Ford dealership. Joe visited the offices of the area's leading newspaper and drew the wrath of all Holyoke by claiming that Petrolle and LeRoy were "too fast for Holyoke."

The local promoter, Art Greaney, was eager to defend his city's honor and told Kossick to "bring on your North Dakota champions." Greaney matched Petrolle in a main event against Sylvio Mireault on February 27. The contract called for the boxers to enter the ring at 128 pounds.[3]

Although Mireault was a promising prospect, the bout was expected to be a warm-up for the stiffer competition Petrolle could expect to face in Philadelphia. A week prior to the fight, Billy weighed 130 pounds and

---
[2] "Eastern Men Offer Hurley Future Mixes," *Fargo Daily Tribune*, February 15, 1925, sports section.
[3] "Gate City Boxer to Fight Sylvio Mireault at 128," *Fargo Daily Tribune,* February 17, 1925, sports section.

thought it would be safe to visit his brother Pete who had moved back to Schenectady. The day of the bout, Billy returned to Holyoke, stepped on the scales, and registered 8-1/2 pounds above the required weight.

The *Daily Tribune*'s February 28th headline proclaiming "PETROLLE FLATTENS MIREAULT IN FIRST ROUND," told only part of the story. Years later, Hurley would recall that "Billy reduced eight pounds by weighing-in time. He knocked his opponent out in the first round which was a break for him because he weakened himself plenty making the weight and didn't really get over the ordeal for six months."[4]

Hurley's vow in the *Daily Tribune* to accept anyone as a foe for LeRoy and Petrolle "no matter who they are" was as much a recognition of reality as it was a bold declaration of bravado. Far removed from his home base of Fargo, Jack no longer had the luxury of being able to handpick the opposition for his cubs. Russie and Billy would have to accept whatever the promoters threw at them and make the best of the opportunity.

For their first starts in Philadelphia, Hurley lined up spots for LeRoy and Petrolle on a March 2nd card promoted by Jules Aaronson at the Arena Athletic Club. Russie, at 138 pounds, was matched against 21-year-old Danny Cooney, also 138, of Trenton, New Jersey. In his most recent bout, Cooney had scored his first big win against welterweight contender Clonie Tait. Billy, 130 pounds, was facing undefeated Babe Ruth (no relation to the baseball Bambino), 128-1/2, from Louisville, who had just attracted attention with a victory over junior lightweight contender Red Chapman.

Boxing writer Perry Lewis of the *Philadelphia Inquirer* vividly described the importance of the March 2nd bouts to each of the contestants:

> "Leroy and Petrolle achieved many dazzling successes in the Midwest, and because of their repeated triumphs, finally decided to invade the East. It was an important step in their young lives. A failure here will send them back home ragged in defeat with much of their prestige stripped from them. On the other hand, a string of victories here in the effete East, and their fortunes are made.
>
> "They make their eastern debut here tonight, and both have been bracketed with very formidable opponents. Billy and Russie realize that they must win to get away in this section of the country on the right foot. They have plenty at stake.
>
> "So has Babe Ruth. The bambino is a youngster in point of years, but is somewhat older in ring experience. He has met and defeated more than a score of opponents, and has yet to suffer a reverse. The Babe is ambitious. He has his eye on a title, and even though he is meeting a man who is regarded as more formidable

---

[4] Hurley, *op. cit.*, April 16, 1933, sports section.

than any other opponent he ever faced, he does not propose to accept a setback. He has, too, much at stake.

"What is true of Ruth is true of Cooney. Danny is young, ambitious and smart. He will not brook failure. Fur should fly as well as fists when these ... men go into action, for all have progressed to that point in their pugilistic careers where they cannot AFFORD to be beaten."[5]

If LeRoy and Petrolle were keyed up for their first bouts in a major boxing center, then the same was true for Hurley as well. Russie and Billy were Jack's pugilistic "firstborns," who he had personally nurtured from their fistic cradles. He served not only as their promoter, trainer, and manager, but as a colleague and mentor as well. Their debut in Philadelphia was at least as big a moment for him as it was for them.

Writer W. C. Heinz, Hurley's friend and admirer, later observed that "to Jack a fighter was a tool, and he was always looking for the tool that, when he finished shaping it and honing it over the years, would be the perfect tool to do the perfect work. He put all of himself into it, and when a Hurley fighter went into the ring Jack took every step with him. That fighter was what Jack would have been if he had the body for it, and that is why it took so much out of Jack when, under pressure, the tool broke."[6]

Hurley explained to Heinz how he felt about each one of his fighters: "You raise him like a baby. That ring is a terrible place to be in if you don't know what you're doing in there, but you teach him to survive. You teach him how to make his first steps, and you bring him along until he becomes a good fighter and starts to make money."[7]

Although Hurley maintained a calm exterior, years of stress brought on by his vigilant oversight of so many shoestring promotions was taking its toll. Before each card, Jack busily negotiated terms with promoters and managers, sold the show to reporters and the public, and directed the smallest particulars attendant to each event. Once a bout started, the best he could do was to sit helplessly in the corner until the round ended and observe his fighter's mistakes and missed opportunities.

Although the passage of time eventually would shelter Hurley in a protective cloak of cynicism, his constitution in 1925 remained vulnerable to the vicissitudes of fistic fortune. At 27 years old, Jack already suffered from intermittent stomach pain, the first of several afflictions which would eventually make him look at least ten years older than his actual age.[8]

---

[5] Lewis, Perry, "Boxers Here Tonight Have Much at Stake," *Philadelphia Inquirer*, March 2, 1925, sports section.
[6] Heinz, W. C., "Once They Heard the Cheers," (Doubleday & Co., 1979), p. 131.
[7] Heinz, p. 139.
[8] Watson, Emmett, "The Needle," *Seattle Post Intelligencer*, August 19, 1951, sports section.

"Everyone says, 'How calm he is,' Hurley once explained. "I'm not calm. I'm eating my insides out. Do you know what I got from Petrolle? I got ulcers. Two-thirds of my stomach is gone. I have to eat every three hours. I've had 21 operations on my sinuses. I've had my appendix out. Boxing has made me a wreck. I sometimes think that I should have gone into the insurance business."[9]

The evening of March 2 afforded little relief to Hurley's tender tummy. The next morning, the *Fargo Daily Tribune* informed its readers that the "Fargo team of boxers ... both finished second to a pair of hard-hitting native sons" from the Philadelphia area. "Babe Ruth, Philadelphia featherweight, received the verdict of the judges over Petrolle, after ten sensational rounds of fighting ... Danny Cooney, of Trenton, also fought his way to the judge's decision in ten rounds over LeRoy."[10]

The *Inquirer* reported that "for fast and reckless action, the battle between Babe Ruth and Bill Petrolle ... left nothing to the imagination" and was "the most furious local devotees of the ring have seen this year." "Ruth was awarded the verdict ... (but) this Petrolle person can come right back anywhere and pack them in. He took enough punishment to stop half-a dozen men, was knocked down for a count of nine with a smashing right in the fourth round, but came back to fight his clever foe fearlessly toe to toe."[11]

The *Evening Bulletin* offered the opinion that "if it hadn't been for the fact Ruth almost hit a home run on Petrolle's chin in the fourth round, the decision might have gone to the Fargo ringman ... The decision against Petrolle wasn't to the liking of the fans, for he forced the milling and went to Ruth, and he was willing to take any of Ruth's smacks to score."[12]

Unfortunately, LeRoy's performance failed to impress the fans. The *Fargo Daily Tribune* reported "the bout was fairly fast but the spectators didn't get much of a 'kick' out of it. Cooney kept his left hand extended throughout the contest and LeRoy was unable to break through Danny's guard and put over a knockout punch. Cooney out-boxed LeRoy, winning about six of the ten rounds."

After the show, Hurley wired home this message to the *Daily Tribune* :

> "We lost both decisions. Neither Cooney nor Ruth would fight and both are hard to make showings against. They did nothing but run and slap, although Ruth is a good puncher. He knocked Petrolle

---

[9] Heinz, "The Man Who Makes Fighters," *Esquire Magazine,* May, 1952, p. 104.
[10] "Billy Makes Hit in Flashy Bout with Babe Ruth," *Fargo Daily Tribune,* March 3, 1925, sports section.
[11] Lewis, "Lee Anderson Proves Tartar for Marine," *Philadelphia Inquirer,* March 3, 1925, sports section.
[12] Title unavailable, *Philadelphia Evening Bulletin,* March 3, 1925, sports section.

down in the fourth round for a nine-count, but Billy got up and chased him for the remainder of the fight.

"Fans hooted the Petrolle-Ruth decision for 15 minutes. Both boys are pleased, though they lost. All the fighting was done by LeRoy and Petrolle, Cooney and Ruth fighting defensive fights. They ran all the time and wouldn't take a chance with my boys. Billy fights Al Shubert at Holyoke March 13 for ten rounds. Neither of the boys is hurt nor shows a mark. We're not downhearted."[13]

Al Shubert was a veteran with over 12 years of ring experience. The New Bedford native had faced seven champions and defeated four of them: Johnny Dundee, Pete Herman, Kid Kaplan, and Jimmy Goodrich. Shubert was past his peak, but was still able to give a good account of himself.[14]

The next morning, the *Daily Tribune* reported "a decisive win" for Petrolle, who won "eight of the ten rounds, all of which were packed with features." Billy "knock(ed) the veteran down ... for the fourth time in his career in the seventh round for a count of nine." The Fargoan tired in the last round and "was out on his feet, but survived because of stamina." Afterward, Art Greaney was so pleased with the show he announced both boxers would return to headline separate cards as soon as possible.

Immediately after the fight, Hurley sent a wire to both Fargo papers: "Sensational fight – decision is popular – Shubert tough and smart."[15]

Sensing Petrolle would pack the house in Philadelphia, promoter Jules Aaronson matched Billy against Bobby Garcia, then rated as one of the world's top five featherweights. Remarkably, Aaronson was elevating Petrolle to main-event status on the March 23rd show even though Billy had lost to in a semifinal bout on the previous card.

Garcia, known alternatively as "the Army Assassin" and "the Mexican Wildcat," had just defeated top contenders Joe Glick and Babe Herman and was at the height of his career. He had also previously held his own in three fights with new featherweight champ Louis (Kid) Kaplan, earning a draw in one bout and losing close decisions in the other two.

The Petrolle-Garcia bout was scheduled for ten rounds. Billy weighed 126 pounds and to Bobby's 127-1/2. On the same card, LeRoy, 137-1/2, was fighting Sammy Fulton, 140, of Trenton, New Jersey in a six-round preliminary bout.

On the eve of the card, Hurley wrote to the *Fargo Forum* sports editor:

---

[13] "Billy Makes Hit in Flashy Bout with Babe Ruth," *op. cit.*
[14] "Billy Will Box Man Who Fought Five Champions," *Fargo Daily Tribune*, March 10, 1925, sports section.
[15] "Fargo's Flashy Boxer Gets 8 of 10 Fast Rounds," *Fargo Daily Tribune*, March 14, 1925, sports section.

"My boys will surprise the Philadelphia fans tomorrow night. Folks here are judging them by their first appearance when they were over-anxious to make good and were against two boys they couldn't make a showing with. They will change their opinion after the fights. Both LeRoy and Petrolle are in wonderful shape. They have been working hard and are now used to conditions here.

"Shubert cannot get Bobby Garcia, Babe Herman or Kid Kaplan to fight him. He holds two decisions over Kaplan. Then Babe Ruth, another of Billy's opponents is the best featherweight in the world according to Leo P. Flynn. Recently, Kid Sullivan (world junior lightweight champion) turned down $10,000 to face Ruth.

"'If Ruth ever meets Kaplan there will be a new featherweight champ,' says Flynn. Yet the Philadelphia fans booed the decision for ten minutes when Ruth was given the palm over Petrolle, after the two staged what was called 'the most sensational fight seen in Philadelphia this season.'

"Russie will be boxing main events in three weeks if he takes decisions in his next three fights.

"It keeps you on the jump here seeing promoters, but we are getting results, and the Eastern managers can't figure how we get all these fights. However, we aren't losing any sleep over them and are going along tending to business which I hope will land the biggest boxing plums obtainable for the boys before summer is underway."[16]

The next day's *Fargo Daily Tribune* reported "LeRoy and Billy Petrolle put up a duet of sensational fights ... Petrolle lost a slashing headliner to Bobby Garcia ... (and) LeRoy took all six rounds from Sammy Fulton."[17]

The *Philadelphia* Inquirer's Perry Lewis could barely contain his excitement:

"The bout between these two fast-stepping featherweights was one of the most sensational witnessed at the West Philadelphia palace of punch in many seasons. Petrolle, making his second appearance here in six weeks, gave Garcia what the latter's handlers conceded to be one of the Baltimore boy's hardest tasks of the year.

"From the opening bell until the final gong the contest bristled with action and, when the two battlers crawled under the ropes to go to their dressing rooms, the crowd, which numbered in the

---

[16] "Garcia Will Be Tough Foe for Fargo Scrapper," *Fargo Forum*, March 22, 1925, sports section.
[17] "Fargo Battlers Given Big Hand by Philly Fans," *Fargo Daily Tribune*, March 24, 1925, sports section.

neighborhood of 5,500, gave them a reception such as no two gladiators have received in this man's town in many moons.

"It was just a question of Garcia knowing a trifle too much for his foe. The Southerner started off in sensational style and carried the first six rounds, but commencing with the seventh Petrolle seemed to take on a new lease of life and gave Garcia the battle of his career ... Petrolle came out for the seventh round with renewed courage and from this point on fought such as he never has here before ...

"Russie LeRoy of Fargo, North Dakota won the judges' decision over Sammy Fulton, of Trenton, in the third bout ... The fans got a thrill out of this set-to, for it was hammer and tongs all the way. Fulton gave a great exhibition of how to take it. LeRoy, a tough scrapper from the West, hit Fulton with everything he had, but the Trenton lad remained on his feet."[18]

Unfortunately, Billy suffered a fractured right hand. Although the injury ended his tour, Hurley remained in Philadelphia with LeRoy. Meanwhile, Jack summarized Petrolle's progress in a letter to the *Daily Tribune*:

"Petrolle is the biggest card in Philadelphia. This seems strange when you remember Lew Tendler, Nate Goldman, Bobby Barrett, Danny Kramer, Ad Stone and Bobby Wolgast are located here.

"Billy's toughness, gameness, and quiet, pleasing personality have won the Philadelphia fans over and I have received some wonderful offers for him since the Garcia fight. However, I am going to hold him over as much as possible until the outdoor season when he can make some real money for his fights."

"If the people of North Dakota could have seen what a great boy Garcia is, they would be proud Petrolle stayed the limit with him. Even at that, I think Bill can lick him, if he is up to 130 pounds. He was too weak at 126. Garcia said after the fight that Billy was one of the toughest, gamest and best boys he had ever met. Garcia and Petrolle are sure to meet again.

"Did you ever hear of a lad coming to a city like Philadelphia, losing his first two fights and still being the biggest drawing card in town? That is just what Petrolle has done."[19]

On March 27, LeRoy, 136 pounds, now referred to in the East as "stablemate of the sensational Billy Petrolle," made his first start for

---
[18] Lewis, "Judges Award Garcia Decision over Petrolle," *Philadelphia Inquirer*," March 24, 1925, sports section.
[19] "Iowa Promoter Wants Russ for Hudkins Bout," *Fargo Daily Tribune*, March 29, 1925, sports section.

Babe Ruth decisioned Petrolle in Billy's Philadelphia debut.

Bobby Garcia also eked out a win over Petrolle in Philadelphia

LeRoy failed to excite Philly fans like Petrolle. He lost a 10-round verdict to Danny Cooney (left) & beat Battling Willard (right) in 6.

Greaney in Holyoke against Francis Rossi, 137-3/4, and won an easy ten-round decision as the injured Petrolle watched the bout from a ringside seat. After the bout, Billy returned to Fargo.[20]

LeRoy finished out the eastern campaign with decision wins over Dick Conlin in a ten-round main event April 9 at Williamsport, Pennsylvania and over Battling Willard in a six-round preliminary bout April 14 at West Philadelphia. The next day, LeRoy and Hurley boarded a train and headed for Fargo. They arrived two days later on April 17.[21]

"A large crowd cheered," wrote a *Daily Tribune* scribe, as "Hurley and LeRoy briskly stepped from Great Northern rattler No. 1 at 6 p.m. yesterday. There was no band, but the occasion demanded none. There was plenty of pep without it." The writer continued:

> "Mr. Hurley is not the 'Kernel' of old, who in the olden days was wont to appear occasionally in a flannel shirt. No indeed. The modern Hurley is trapped out like a plush horse, gaily sporting the latest eastern adornment ...
>
> "Arriving in town at 6, Hurley was in the stirrups and ready for business at 7:45 when he breezily entered the *Tribune* office to disclose his 'plans for the future.'
>
> "'You can tell the boys over the state,' jerked Jack in his usual forceful style, 'that the May 1 card here featuring LeRoy and Petrolle will be some fistic shindig.
>
> "'I have lined up Cooney of Trenton, New Jersey, the lad who beat LeRoy in the East and we expect a different story in this meeting. Russie has a new style now of weaving and bobbing in and out to evade a good left hand,' and Jack jumped off his chair and went through some Australian crawl antics, to show us just how LeRoy fights now ...
>
> "'We won't be here much longer than three weeks ... there is a possibility of our going to the West Coast. Harry Hochstadter of Chicago has offered me $5,000 for a LeRoy-Hudkins match, but I think the battle is worth $10,000, and we may go out to Los Angeles and get it.
>
> "'Do you know,' shot Jack, 'that Russie is the only boy in the world who has ever beaten Ace Hudkins? That will be some recommendation if we go west.'"[22]

---

[20] "Fargo Fighter Takes 9 of 10 Flashy Rounds," *Fargo Daily Tribune*, March 28, 1925, sports section.

[21] "Russ Laces Dick Conlin in Williamsport Contest," *Fargo Daily Tribune*, April 10, 1925, sports section. "Russie Takes Every Round from Battler," *Fargo Daily Tribune*, April 14, 1925, sports section.

[22] "Fargo Show on May 1 Will Be Sporty Affair," *Fargo Daily Tribune*, April 18, 1925, sports section.

The announcement of the May 1st fight card was received with enthusiasm. The Biblical adage "a prophet is not without honor except in his own hometown" was proving true. The success of the tour had whetted the appetites of Fargo/Moorhead fans and made them appreciate LeRoy and Petrolle more than before.

During their absence, virtually the entire male population in both cities had been following the duo's exploits every day in local newspapers. Indeed, their fans did not need to wait and read the *Daily Tribune* over coffee the next morning to learn how the two boys had fared in their bouts the previous evening.

Boxing aficionados instead gathered at the Grand Recreation billiard parlor on fight night and listened as an announcer read the 50-word summaries which were being teletyped to the parlor at the end of each round directly from ringside in Philadelphia and Holyoke.[23]

"The Grand Rec," as the establishment was commonly known, had been Fargo's sports nerve center ever since Steve Gorman bought Mac's Smokeshop in 1917 and changed its name to "Grand Billiards." In 1922, the business was incorporated as "Grand Recreations Parlors" after Gorman brought John McCormack in as a partner. A year later, the building was remodeled and bowling alleys were added on the second floor.

Gorman was born in 1890 at Moorhead, attended school there, and worked summers on a farm near Baker, Minnesota before moving across the Red River to Fargo in 1910. Prior to buying the smoke shop, he worked for the Fargo Pantorium as a wagon delivery driver and as a shipping clerk for the Crane Co. He also served 18 months in World War I, including overseas duty with the 34th Engineers, before returning to the cigar store.

The Rec was located next door to the Grand Theater at 620 First Avenue North on the south side of the avenue and just west of Broadway. The storefront, which faced north, was 50 feet wide. The building extended back 200 feet to the alley.

As a customer entered the front door, directly to his right along the west wall was a beautifully varnished wooden lunch counter about 50 feet long. In front of the counter were approximately 20 round, backless swivel stools with padded cheesecloth seats. Behind the counter in open view was a grill and soda fountain. Food served included soups, salads, "rib steak with a huge serving of mashed potatoes and lots of gravy," and, for 25 cents, "the best hot beef sandwich in Fargo."

A cigar counter with a cash register was located directly opposite the lunch counter along the east wall. All kinds of tobacco, cigarettes, and cigars, as well as tickets to every sporting event in town, were sold at this counter. Every payday, a paid courier with an armed guard would hand-

---

[23] "Fargo's Flashy Boxer Gets 8 of 10 Fast Rounds," *Fargo Daily Tribune*, March 14, 1925, sports section.

carry cash from Bill Stern's Dakota National Bank to the Grand Rec where hundreds of paychecks were negotiated every week.

The space between the counters formed a pathway for customers to mingle and access the Grand Rec's 13 pool and billiard tables, two snooker tables, and huge, black, ceiling-high scoreboard located in the building's rear half. The billiard tables were arranged in front of the snooker tables, which ran lengthwise along the south wall.

A scoreboard was mounted on the wall above the snooker tables. A three-foot wide, full-length walking platform was situated beneath the scoreboard. Mounted on the platform was a tickertape machine, which received teletyped reports of sporting events as relayed directly by Western Union. An employee who accessed the scoreboard from the walking platform then posted the results received from the teletype.

During baseball season, major-league scores were posted each half-inning and those of the American Association minor-league games every inning. A specially designed auxiliary scoreboard, depicting a baseball diamond, was set up for the World Series. A person behind the scoreboard would re-enact every play by manipulating a lever which operated wire-controlled ping-pong balls meant to represent the ball, the batter, and each base runner.

The wagering needs of the Grand Rec's gentry were serviced by Sparky Ruble, an independent contractor who "wrote book" on sporting events from a desk near the pool tables. Sparky was granted space for his "office" in exchange for his sponsorship of the teletype machine and scoreboard.

To protect his customers from default, Gorman required Ruble's brother-in-law, Isadore Horowitz, owner of Crescent Jewelry, to guarantee payment on all winning bets. Sparky regularly presented a "daily special," offering odds up to 30 to 1 as a pay-off for correctly picking the winners of four specially featured baseball games.

A stairway behind the lunch-counter grill led upstairs to eight bowling alleys on the second floor. The Grand Rec furnished "well appointed quarters" and restrooms for women to facilitate their use of the bowling alleys. Food and refreshments were delivered to the second floor from the downstairs kitchen via a dumbwaiter.

Gorman maintained a business office in the basement of the Grand Rec which also doubled on occasion as a private card room for semi-high stake games. The balance of the basement was an unfinished open space with a dirt floor used primarily for storage.

The Grand Rec was a vital part of Fargo sporting life in general and of Hurley's support network in particular. Not only was the building a central meeting place where he conducted business with managers, fighters, and reporters, but the enterprise also acted as his ticket-broker, serving not only as an outlet, but also as his agent for mail order reservations and sales.

Steve Gorman, proprietor of the Grand Rec.

Photo presented to Gorman referencing the days when Petrolle trained in the Grand Rec cellar.

Street view of Steve Gorman's Grand Recreation billiard parlor.

Grand Rec interior, 1940s. Gorman with a pipe near the cash register.

Steve Gorman (2nd from left) flanked by Cleveland Indians' manager, Steve O'Neill (left), Bob Feller (center) and his dad, Will Feller (right).

At 3:00 on the afternoon of every promotion, all the fighters on the card would weigh in on a scale set up in the entryway of the Grand Rec. After the show, managers and fighters would meet there to be paid. On occasion, when Hurley was short of space or sought to hold secret workouts, he would even have his fighters train at a temporary gym set up in what he jokingly referred to as "the cool, clean basement of the Grand Rec."[24]

Steve Gorman would continue to be a sports booster long after Hurley left Fargo. In 1932, he would co-found and become president of the Fargo-Moorhead Twins baseball team of the Northern League, a position he would hold until 1942. In 1936, Gorman would find himself in the center of a nationally publicized controversy by signing 18-year-old pitching phenom Bob Feller to a Twins' contract and then immediately assigning it to the Cleveland Indians in contravention of major league rules.[25]

---

[24] This was an in-joke, for the dirt floor portion of the Grand Rec was neither "clean nor cool," but rather "dirty and cold."

[25] In 1936, the major and minor leagues had a long-standing agreement which restricted major-league teams from signing players directly from the sandlots. At the time, most minor-league teams were not yet farm clubs of the majors, but instead operated independently. The agreement was designed to maintain the financial viability of minor-leagues by allowing teams to sign sandlot players and then eventually sell them to major league teams, thereby keeping the minor leagues in business with direct infusions of cash. In the Bob Feller case, the Fargo-Moorhead Twins became an early farm club when it signed a "working agreement" with the Cleveland Indians in 1934.

In 1936, the Twins signed Feller to a minor-league contract and then, before the start of the baseball season, assigned the contract directly to Cleveland. When Feller reported to Cleveland in 1936, he not only had never played for the Twins, but he had never even worn a Twins' uniform. In fact, the entire sequence of events had been carefully orchestrated by Cleveland's head scout, Cy Slapnicka, to circumvent the major-league/minor-league agreement in a scheme which the Twins club, its president, Steve Gorman, Sr. and, as it turned out, Bob Feller's father were willing participants.

After it became clear that Feller was in fact not going to play for the Twins, the Des Moines Demons of the Western League complained to the baseball commissioner Kenesaw Mountain Landis. The Des Moines club argued forcefully that its efforts to sign Feller to a minor-league contract had been thwarted by Cleveland in contravention of the major-league/minor-league agreement.

On December 10, 1936, Judge Landis met with all the interested parties for two hours behind the closed doors of his Chicago hotel room. Prior to the meeting, experts thought that the provisions of the major-league/minor-league agreement would be fully enforced and that Bob Feller would be declared a free agent. It was anticipated that this ruling would free Feller from his Twins/Cleveland contract and make him available to accept a lucrative contract with another major-league team, which was reportedly prepared to pay Feller an unprecedented signing bonus of $100,000.

Instead, Judge Landis ruled Feller the property of the Cleveland Indians while at the same time implicitly acknowledging that the Cleveland club had violated the major-league/minor-league agreement by ordering the Indians to pay $7,500 to the Des Moines club. The ruling was, in effect, a compromise that was hammered out between the parties in that Chicago hotel room.

According to what Steve Gorman, Sr., who attended the meeting, later told his son, Steve, Jr., Judge Landis was persuaded by the fact that the Indians, the Twins, and the Fellers were all satisfied with the existing arrangement. The payment of $7,500 apparently was large

In the 1950s, Eugene Fitzgerald, then sports editor of the *Forum*, organized a testimonial dinner to honor Gorman for his contributions to the community. Hurley, then living in Seattle, and Petrolle, making his home in Duluth, both attended the dinner in Fargo to pay respects to the old friend who had befriended them time and again when they needed help the most.[26]

On the May 1st show at Fargo, LeRoy, 136 pounds, was unsuccessful in his bid to even the score with New Jersey's Danny Cooney, 134, who had beaten Russie in their first bout at Philadelphia. Russie fought aggressively, "going after a knockout" the entire ten rounds, but Cooney, who "was probably the fastest product ever seen in a North Dakota ring," exhibited a "long left that seemed to be everywhere every time LeRoy bored in." The *Fargo Forum* gave Cooney five rounds, Russie three, and called two even.

In the windup, Petrolle, 131 pounds, won a ten-round decision over Cooney's 129-pound stablemate, Al Holzman, in "one of those slugging bees that we read about and seldom are privileged to see." The *Forum* described the bout as "a great fight, each taking plenty of punishment," and gave Petrolle seven rounds, Holzman two, with one even. "In all, the card

---

enough to also appease the owners of the Des Moines team.

What has been most puzzling to baseball historians is why Bob Feller and his father, Will Feller, agreed to the arrangement when Bob would otherwise have certainly received the $100,000 signing bonus from another team instead of the mere $15,000 salary that he received from Cleveland? Steve Gorman, Sr., told his son that Feller's father was adamant that the Cleveland team had been good to the Feller family and that Bob would play for no one else. The elder Feller felt so strongly about this that he had previously threatened to sue Judge Landis in civil court if he ruled otherwise. Was Will Feller's reaction strictly out of loyalty to the Cleveland organization or was some other motivation involved?

Another possible reason for Landis' decision might be that it would have been in conflict with the purpose of the rule he was enforcing to reward the Fellers by making Bob a free agent, if Landis felt the Fellers had colluded with Cleveland to circumvent the rule. If Landis found this to be the case, then allowing Bob to sign for a bonus with a team other than Cleveland would in effect have been rewarding the Fellers for "bad" behavior.

In any event, Judge Landis' ruling had long-term consequences for the economic structure of organized baseball. As a result, the major-league/minor-league agreement was for all practical purposes discarded and major-league teams became free to sign all players. Minor-league teams thus lost a major source of revenue and, in order to survive, more and more of them were forced to become farm teams as time went on. The quality of play in the minor leagues was further dissipated as parent teams siphoned off the talent from their farm teams. As the minor-league teams lost their star players, attendance at their games dropped, and they became even more dependent on parent teams for financial support. And so it went.

There were undoubtedly many other factors far beyond the scope of this footnote and its author's knowledge that also contributed to the centralization of baseball's power structure.

The era of high quality independent minor-league baseball finally came to a complete end in the 1950s when all the teams in the maverick Pacific Coast League were forced by economic considerations to become farm clubs to major-league teams.

The author is indebted to sports historian J Michael Kenyon for most of the information in this footnote.

[26] Information about Grand Rec and Steve Gorman, Sr., from the author's interview of Steve Gorman, Jr. and from newspaper advertisements of the period.

was the best ever staged in North Dakota, barring none ... and the packed house was given an excellent two hours of entertainment."[27]

On May 23, Hurley announced he had arranged for LeRoy and Petrolle to make their debuts in Los Angeles, California, June 23, 1925, at Jack Doyle's famous Vernon Arena. Russie was to meet Mushy Callahan in the main event and Billy was up against Frankie Fink in a preliminary. Under the terms of the contract with Doyle's matchmaker, Hayden (Wad) Wadhams, the trio was to arrive in Los Angeles June 16 so that Russie and Billy could be introduced at ringside at the prior week's boxing show. [28]

Before heading west, Hurley signed light heavyweight Earl Blue, of St. Paul, to a contract. At the time, Blue was on his way to Atlantic City, New Jersey to work as a sparring partner for Tommy Gibbons. Tommy, younger brother of previously retired Mike Gibbons, was training to fight Gene Tunney June 5 with the winner slated to meet Jack Dempsey for the heavyweight championship. Unfortunately for Gibbons, he would lose by kayo to Tunney and would retire from the ring shortly thereafter.[29]

The *Forum* reported Blue was 20-years old and had scored 15 knockouts in 29 fights. As additional proof of his punching power, the *Forum* pointed to Blue's average of almost two knockdowns per fight. Earl would join his new stablemates in Los Angeles following the Gibbons-Tunney fight after a short rest at his home in St. Paul. His first California contest would be against Tom Kelly in a six-round preliminary June 30.[30]

Hurley's first order of business in Los Angeles was to call on the sports desks of the city's six daily newspapers to tout the fistic abilities of LeRoy and Petrolle. Jack's visit with the *Los Angeles Times'* reporter was particularly well received:

> "About the most interesting trio to invade California since the boxing law is the cargo from Fargo, North Dakota. They are Russie LeRoy, 22; Billy Petrolle, 19; and Jack Hurley, 27, their manager.
>
> "... LeRoy, with two newspaper decisions over Ace Hudkins, is to meet the most distinguished newsboy of Los Angeles, Mushy Callahan. Petrolle, a few pounds lighter than LeRoy, starts against Frankie Fink in the semifinal. Any boxer who can beat Hudkins has something on the cuff. Petrolle, so his manager claims, is just as good a fighter as LeRoy, but of a different style.

---

[27] Yocum, Ed, "Russie's Attempts for Knockout Cost Him Bout," *Fargo Forum*, May 2, 1925, sports section.

[28] "LeRoy, Petrolle Carded for Coast Bouts June 23," *Fargo Forum*, May 23, 1925, sports section. Sol Plex, "Ernie Owens Doc's Choice; Both Go East," *Los Angeles Examiner*, June 1, 1925, sports section.

[29] "Billy Petrolle's Jaw Cracked in Grand Forks Mix," *Fargo Forum*, May 17, 1925, sports section.

[30] "Lombardi to Meet Murphy," *Fargo Forum*, September 1, 1925, sports section.

Russie LeRoy, Jack Hurley, and Billy Petrolle in California.

Promoter Jack Doyle booked Hurley's fighters in Los Angeles.

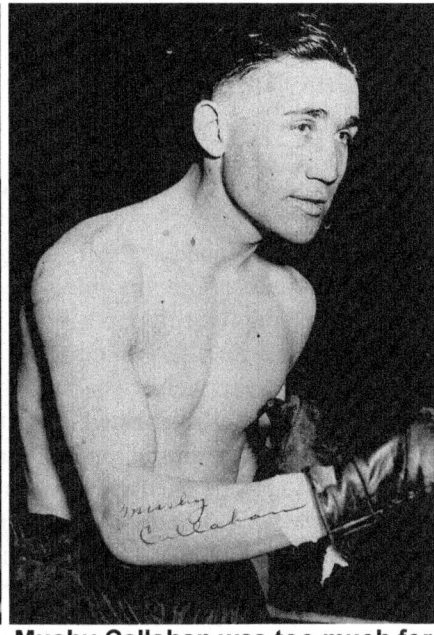

Mushy Callahan was too much for Russie LeRoy to handle.

"'LeRoy beat Hudkins twice,' says Hurley. 'That's pretty decisive for him. But I believe Petrolle would knock Hudkins out if they ever meet.'

"That is another interesting angle of the cargo from Fargo. This Hurley is one of the few managers who glistens with individuality. They say fighters of today are different from those of yesterday. This youthful manager is different, too.

"Hurley gave the sporting editors a surprise by calling on all of them the first few hours he landed. He is all business. He hustles, not only to get matches, but also to get his fighters on the map. It seems to be a peculiarity of this cargo from Fargo.

"Hurley has hustled ever since he can remember. His family moved to Rainy River, Ontario, when he was 13. The father, an employee on the Northern Pacific, was killed in an accident. This left the boy as the sole support of his mother and sisters. They went back to Fargo. Young Jack used to sell papers in the early mornings, work at a print shop during the day and usher at a theater at night.

"Then he decided to be a fighter. But a fighter's money is uncertain. After thinking it over, he ... figured he could make more money managing fighters than fighting fighters. For his bit as a manager this is what he did: went on the road with them; rubbed them down; taught them in the gym; got the matches, paid for telegrams and phone calls; and wrote all the letters.

"Among this lot of boys were Russie LeRoy and later on Billy Petrolle. That was the beginning of the present cargo from Fargo."[31]

Hurley hoped a LeRoy victory over Mushy Callahan would lead to a lucrative third match between LeRoy and Ace Hudkins. Unfortunately, Russie faced a Callahan at the height of his career. Mushy had graduated to the main-event class in his previous three bouts and had won them all against increasingly stiff opposition. Within 15 months, he would defeat Pinkey Mitchell in a ten-round decision at the Vernon Arena to win the world's junior welterweight championship.

At the gong, LeRoy rushed out of his corner "at top speed" to meet Callahan only to run straight into a crushing right that put him "back on his heels, and though he tried gamely, he never got back on his toes." Russie "hardly knew what (he) was doing from that time on." The end came in the third round when another "bone-crushing right landed squarely on the jaw sent the Dakota boy sprawling across the ring for a clean knockout."

---

[31] "Conqueror of Hudkins Here," *Los Angeles Times*, June 21, 1925, sports section.

In his six-rounder with Frankie Fink, "Petrolle made a great impression in defeating Fink, a pretty fair sort of lightweight. Petrolle took every round and never once backed up no matter how tough the going. On the other hand, he had Fink in constant retreat under stiff body punishment. Petrolle fought a clean, aggressive battle and established himself a drawing card at Doyle's. He's not yet a corking lightweight but he's a prospect ..."[32]

Afterward, Hurley sent a wire to the *Fargo Forum*: "Callahan is a coming champion. LeRoy stopped in third round. Three knockdowns before towel was tossed in. Petrolle won decision over Frankie Fink, taking every round. No knockdowns, but Billy made the same hit he made back east. Earl Blue fights Tom Kelley here next Tuesday."[33]

LeRoy's devastating loss ended his dream of a third bout with Hudkins. Three days later, LeRoy left for North Dakota after telling reporters he was planning to take a long rest from the ring. Hurley remained behind with Petrolle and Earl Blue to continue their western campaign.[34]

On June 30, Blue, weighing 165 pounds, made his California debut, knocking out Tom Kelly, also 165, in three rounds at the Vernon Arena. Earl impressed ringsiders as "the sort of fellow who should get a lot of work. He can sock and he's not hard to hit ... and he is sure to be a good card." In the main event, lightweight Phil Salvadore won a ten-round decision over Tommy O'Brien.[35]

Hurley created quite a stir by outfitting Blue in a powder blue cap and bathrobe, and having him introduced as "Earl (Little Boy) Blue." Los Angeles Herald reporter Fane Norris, obviously smitten by the contrast between Earl and the nursery rhyme, described the scene to his readers:

> "Young Jack Hurley, boxing manager ... from North Dakota ... introduced to the Vernon fans a rough, tough citizen of the prize ring who answers to the soft and pretty name of Earl Blue. Earl looks as it he would be at home hurling a battleaxe in the north woods, but Hurley dolled him up in a pale blue robe and a dinky baseball cap that would have been undersize for a kid of six. The big fellow was a sartorial scream, and due to the unusual makeup, he was the hit of the evening.
>
> "This little boy Blue can hit just as his manager said he could. He is a crude sort of performer so far as boxing goes, but he surely

---

[32] Kelly, Mark, "Left Hook to Body Brings Fight to End," *Los Angeles Examiner*, June 24, 1925, sports section. "Blue Wins in Coast Fight," *Fargo Forum*, July 1, 1925, sports section. "Dakota Idol Is Easy Prey," *Los Angeles Times*, June 24, 1925, sports section.

[33] "Russie LeRoy Suffers His First Kayo; Petrolle Wins," *Fargo Forum*, June 24, 1925, sports section.

[34] "LeRoy Departs for 'Far Away Fargo,'" *Los Angeles Examiner*, June 27, 1925, sports section.

[35] Norton, Fane, "Finishes Fast" (subtitle), *Los Angeles Herald*, July 1, 1925, sports section.

Light heavyweight Earl Blue.

Blue (right) with Tom Gibbons & Sammy Mandell helping Tom prepare for Tunney.

Earl Blue in his robe waiting for a turn to spar with Gibbons (right).

can sock, and he demonstrated his walloping proclivities to the satisfaction of the spectators and to the distress of Tom Kelly, who was on the receiving end of the punches.

"Last week, Hurley's boxers, Russie LeRoy and Billy Petrolle, entered the ring attired in blankets that would have made a Navajo Indian take to his teepee. Hurley believes in adding a bit of color to the game of fisticuffs, and the fans apparently like it."

Although Earl's blue bathrobe made a big impression at the time, it was Petrolle's blanket which would capture boxing fans' imagination over the long-term and acquire a mystique of its own. As time went on, the blanket would become spattered with the blood of over 100 fights, but Billy would never have it cleaned, allegedly because he feared a washing might offend the Navajo gods and bring him bad luck.

A week later on July 7, Mushy Callahan decisioned St. Paul's Johnny O'Donnell in 10 rounds at the Vernon Arena. In the semi-windup, Petrolle was awarded a win on a foul in the third round over Johnny LaMar when the latter struck a low blow "with his left, and Petrolle sank to the floor writhing." In his second Los Angeles start, Blue won a convincing four-round decision over Jack Lee in the opening preliminary bout.

Of the Los Angeles papers venturing an opinion after the Petrolle-LaMar bout, two had LaMar ahead at the time of the foul, and one had honors even. All accounts agreed Blue won every round of his contest. The *Los Angeles Examiner* noted that "Lee walked in with 17 teeth chattering. He walked out with 15 chattering – two were knocked out."[36]

Petrolle's last fight in Los Angeles was a six-rounder against Jimmy Hackley on July 28, once again at the Vernon Arena. Although the referee called the fight a draw, ringsiders disagreed. One scribe offered an opinion that "Petrolle had all the better of it ... (he) was robbed." Another commented, "Hackley was licked to a frazzle and was no more entitled to that consideration than the writer, who was merely a ringside spectator." In the main bout, Eddie Huffman won a decision over Bert Colima.[37]

A week later, on August 4, Earl Blue won the referee's decision over Lou Rollinger in a preliminary at Vernon. Blue had Rollinger on the canvas twice as he won every one of the six rounds. In the scheduled ten-round main event, the black nemesis of the heavyweight division, George Godfrey, scored a three-round kayo over Tiny Herman.

---

[36] Sol Plex, "Callahan Wins at Vernon," *Los Angeles Examiner*, July 8, 1925, sports section. "O'Donnell Bout Is Boost for Callahan," *Los Angeles Herald*, July 8, 1925, sports section. "St. Paul Fighter Drops Verdict to Local Star," *Los Angeles Times*, July 8, 1925, sports section.

[37] "Mexican Fades Before Gob in Closing Rounds," *Los Angeles Times*, July 29, 1925, sports section. "Fair Big Man Beats Fair Little Man as Colima Loses Again," *Los Angeles Evening Express*, July 29, 1925, sports section.

With summer's end at hand, Hurley boarded a Fargo-bound rattler on August 6 with Petrolle and Blue, hoping to cash in on the publicity generated by the tour. His plan was to stage a mammoth Labor Day card to showcase each of his traveling heroes in front of their hometown fans.[38]

Although the year's excursions had not seen any major breakthroughs, Hurley and his men could look back on their experiences with satisfaction. They had journeyed to the far ends of the nation, introduced themselves to a broader public, and earned the largest purses of their careers.

Most importantly, their prospects for even richer purses in the future were bright. The *Forum* reported that "according to the manager all three of his fighters are wanted both in the East and in the West for the fall winter season." Although nothing definite was decided, Hurley told the reporter that after a few shows in North Dakota, he would be ready to hit the road again with his troupe as soon as "the leaves start turning."[39]

---

[38] "Hurley Coming Back to Fargo; Blue in Easy Bout Tuesday," *Fargo Forum*, August 5, 1925, sports section.
[39] "Hurley Back from the Coast," *Fargo Forum*, August 13, 1925, sports section.

CHAPTER 12

PINKEY'S TALE OF A SORE TOE

The only time I ever cried over money in my life was in December 1925 when I was promoting fights in Fargo, North Dakota. I had been starving on $600 gates trying to figure out how to get the farmers, who used to come from miles around, to unbutton their coin purses. They used to have a double latch on those purses. My how they hated to part with that fin for a ticket. But they were loyal – come from 200 miles away, some of them.

I had my own boy, Russie LeRoy, going against Pinkey Mitchell, the junior welter champion out of Chicago. I got Mitchell for $5,000 and three train tickets. The show is an absolute sell-out. I promised the papers I wouldn't substitute. That's how sure I was Mitchell would go through with the fight.

I stand to take in more than $12,000, and being generous with everybody, the fight will cost me, maybe $7,500. That was close to $5,000 for me, and like I say, I'd been struggling in Fargo.

What do you think happened? Mitchell backed out. Four days before the fight, he backed out. I had to go down to the bank and get all that dough – thousands – and refund.

I stood there for two days and gave it back – in fives and tens. My ulcers were screaming. It was a most trying period of my life.[1]   – Jack Hurley

****

After returning to Fargo, Hurley announced his "big outdoor" Labor Day show would be held at the state fairgrounds on September 7, 1925. The card featured Petrolle against Carl Leonard and Earl Blue against an opponent "selected by the fans out of a group of five names submitted by Hurley." Jack also signed his former protege Johnny Knauf, now living in Grand Forks, for a third feature event against "an as yet unnamed opponent."[2]

---

[1] Watson, Emmett, "The Needle," *Seattle Post Intelligencer*, August 19, 1951, sports section. Watson's quote has been slightly modified to fit the context. Hurley's recollection of the dollar figures has been changed to conform to contemporary newspaper accounts of the amount of Mitchell's guarantee.

[2] "Carl Leonard Signed to Meet Petrolle Labor Day," *Fargo Forum*, August 25, 1925, sports section. "Fans Want LeRoy to Meet Knauf on Labor Day," *Fargo Forum*, August 26, 1925, sports section. This is Hurley's first use of a publicity ploy he would resurrect on many occasions over the years. Jack would provide a list of proposed opponents for one of his fighters and then tell sportswriters he was allowing "the fans" to select the opponent of their choice from the list. During the following days, Hurley would report to the sportswriters on the results of his informal "fan poll" and select the opponent based on these alleged results. Of course, this poll was entirely the product of Hurley's imagination. Jack always knew who his fighter's opponent would be in advance. The most notable of these "fan votes" resulted

Conspicuous by his absence from the card was Russie LeRoy. LeRoy previously had told the Fargo press that he would take two months' rest after his loss in June to Mushy Callahan. Now, Russie was threatening to postpone his return to the ring further by blaming his loss to Callahan on "climate change and hot weather" and by refusing "to consider any fights until the frost was in the air" and "colder weather sets in."

Hurley, realizing LeRoy was reluctant to resume boxing, signed Knauf as an enticement for Russie appear on the card. Although they had never met in an actual bout before, they had boxed hundreds of rounds as stablemates. Knauf was now claiming he was LeRoy's fistic superior. Jack knew if any opponent could motivate Russie to emerge from his self-imposed exile, it would be Johnny, a man whom LeRoy was certain he could beat.

Hurley had two reasons for wanting LeRoy back in the ring as soon as possible. The first was he suspected Russie was still upset over his loss to Callahan and that he might be questioning his own abilities. LeRoy had experienced a similar malaise following his uninspired fight with Johnny Schauer in July 1922. After that bout, Russie had gone without fighting for six months. At the time, Jack had been so preoccupied with his move to St. Paul that he had not paid sufficient attention to LeRoy's mental state.[3]

Hurley was determined not to make the same mistake again. He feared that unless LeRoy could be persuaded to return to the ring quickly, he might take another layoff. At 23 and with six years' experience, he was entering what normally would be a fighter's most lucrative period. A long absence at this juncture would be particularly detrimental to his ring career.

Secondly, even though Petrolle had impressed boxing fans on two coasts, LeRoy was still Hurley's most popular boxer in North Dakota. If Jack learned anything from the fans after returning home, it was that they were even more eager to see their old favorite than Petrolle or Blue. If Hurley wanted the show to be a success, he was better off with Russie on the card.

LeRoy had, in fact, begun holding secret workouts at the Knights of Columbus gym as soon as he heard that Knauf would be in the show. Russie, unbeknownst to Hurley, told his friends "that if he finds within a day or two he can get into shape, he'll accept the match."[4]

Hurley, however, had to plan for every eventuality. Having been refused by LeRoy, Jack signed Minneapolis welterweight Jack Josephs to oppose Knauf. A week before the event, however, Josephs backed out. "Up against

---

in selecting Pete Rademacher to challenge Floyd Patterson for the heavyweight championship in 1957. Hurley's last use of this stratagem was to select Eddie Machen as an opponent for Boone Kirkman in 1967.

[3] McGlynn, Stoney, "Hurley Closes Bout Thursday," *Fargo Forum* August 28, 1925, sports section.

[4] McGlynn, "Chuck Lambert Will Meet Blue in Labor Day Battle," *Fargo Forum*, August 27, 1925, sports section. McGlynn, *Fargo Forum*, "Local Fighters Preparing for Labor Day Encounters," August 29, 1925, sports section.

it," wrote the *Forum*'s Stoney McGlynn, "Hurley again sought out LeRoy." This time Jack's pleas were successful and Russie agreed to appear.[5]

As a publicity stunt prior to the show, Hurley arranged to have his three stablemates "flip coins at the all-star baseball game Sunday afternoon" to "win their places on the card, the winner being awarded by getting the windup position." The stunt had the very real benefit of relieving promoter/manager Hurley from the duty of choosing which of his temperamental warriors was to receive top billing on the program.[6]

Petrolle won the toss, and with it, the right to have his bout billed as the main event.

LeRoy's return was spectacular, if not triumphant. After battling Knauf on even terms for three rounds, Russie took command in the fourth and appeared to be on his way to victory. Working at the center of the ring, LeRoy drove a stiff left to Johnny's jaw and followed up with a right hook that knocked him down near the ropes. Knauf was badly hurt, but was able to get on his hands and knees, in preparation to rise before the ten-count.

Overeager, LeRoy broke past referee Leo Kossick and landed two blows to the head while Knauf was was still down. Kossick immediately stopped the fight and declared Johnny the winner on a foul.

In the main bout, Petrolle, weighing 135 pounds, dominated Carl Leonard of New Richmond, Wisconsin, also 135, in the first two rounds before finishing him off after only 13 seconds of the third round. The round had barely started when Billy "caught Leonard right on the point of the chin, knocking him back with such force that the Badger's feet left the floor and he landed on the back of his head. It was fully three minutes before Leonard came to sufficiently to realize that he was knocked out."

Blue was also an easy victor over Chuck Foster of Minneapolis. Foster was a last-minute substitute when "the people's choice," Chuck Lambert, was injured in training. Kossick stopped the bout in the fourth round "after Foster had been cut to ribbons and was practically out on his feet from the results of some Dempsey-like punches ripped into his midsection."

After seeing Hurley's newest protégé the first time, McGlynn observed:

> "The Foster-Blue match was all Blue. Foster started out fancy, stepping hither and yon like one of Irene Castle's pupils, but a few hooks to the wind, some left jabs to the face and some wicked kidney punches soon took all the fanciness out of his stride. When Hurley said that Blue could punch, he said a mouthful ... Blue is not a flashy man, but he knows how to slip punches and has an effective left hand that teases the other man into leaving an opening

---

[5] McGlynn, "Hurley Closes Bout Thursday," *op. cit.*
[6] McGlynn, "Hurley's Battlers to Flip Coins for Places on Card," September 4, 1925, sports section.

for a pile driving right that would put anybody, if landed on, in canary land for a few minutes."[7]

Although McGlynn described LeRoy's loss as "disastrous," Hurley did not see it that way. Even though Russie lost, he had demonstrated clear superiority over Knauf. The bout lifted LeRoy out of his lethargy and removed any thought of retirement from his mind. His efforts were now entirely directed to proving that the loss to Knauf was a fluke. In addition, the unsatisfactory outcome set the stage for a promoter's dream, a lucrative re-match which would likely fill any auditorium in North Dakota.

Grand Forks boxing promoter, Tex Trotter, envisioning a sellout for his town, offered Hurley 33-1/3 percent of the gross receipts as LeRoy's share if the rematch were held in Grand Forks. The *Forum* reported the guarantee "would mean between $750 and $1,000 – the largest purse ever offered the Fargo battler by a North Dakota promoter. It was turned down by Hurley and when the 'Kernel' turns down $1,000 the day of miracles is not over."

Hurley refused the offer because he had his own plans to sign the fight for an all-star show he was staging in Fargo October 16. To satisfy Trotter, Hurley told Tex "you can have LeRoy to fight anybody but Knauf."[8]

After a week of negotiations, Hurley and Trotter agreed to terms for a main event in Grand Forks on October 1 featuring LeRoy against another former stablemate, Battling Krause. In order to build the gate, Trotter proposed to cash in on the rivalry between Russie and Johnny Knauf by having Knauf referee the LeRoy-Krause bout. In the spirit of compromise, but against his better judgment, Hurley agreed to the arrangement.

It was a decision he would live to regret.

Before the Grand Forks show, however, Hurley had to honor a September 25th date in Bismarck, North Dakota with Bismarck promoter Herb Hester. Hester had scheduled both Petrolle and Earl Blue in bouts against two local favorites at the City Auditorium.

Petrolle easily won his semifinal bout by stopping lightweight Nick Lombardi in the seventh round. Billy then took a seat with Hurley in Blue's corner to watch Earl fight Billy Conley in the main event. Conley was a big 180-pound Russian immigrant who outweighed Blue by over ten pounds. About 300 of Conley's countrymen were there to cheer him on.

Not one for finesse, Conley from the start attempted to overwhelm Blue with mauling tactics, and before the second round ended he succeeded in pushing Earl through the ring ropes three times. On one of these occasions, the ring post gave way and Blue fell entirely out of the ring, causing his

---

[7] McGlynn, "Finish Comes in Round Four," *Fargo Forum*, September 8, 1925, sports section.
[8] "Tex Trotter Seeks Return Go Between LeRoy and Knauf," *Fargo Forum*, September 10, 1925, sports section.

head to hit heavily on the stage floor. Earl was dazed by the fall, and it was several minutes before the fight could be resumed.

In the third round, spectators heard Blue make some unspecified threats against his adversary while they were fighting along the ropes. When Conley ignored Earl's warnings and continued his roughhouse ways, Blue let go with an uppercut from the floor which struck the big Russian far below the belt line. Conley's older brother, who weighed about 220 pounds, immediately jumped into the ring and went after Earl.

Seeing what was happening, Petrolle grabbed a water bottle and threw it in the general direction of Conley's brother. Just as Billy let it fly, the brother ducked, and the bottle hit Hurley, who had jumped into the ring to help Blue, squarely in the back. Years later, Petrolle still had a clear recollection of what followed:

> "The bottle broke in a million bits and almost pitched Hurley out of the ring, but the funny side of it was lost entirely in the scuffle between fighters, fans and police, who were trying to preserve order. The next day, I asked Hurley if he was hurt any by the bottle and he turned a startled face toward me, "Great Scott, was that what hit me? I thought that big Russian kicked me. My back is nearly broke."
>
> "That trip and another almost like it nearly ruined our reputation as a gentlemanly troupe of fighters, but we finally lived it down."

The *Bismarck Tribune* reported that "level-headed spectators succeeded in quelling the disturbance after somebody turned on the fire hose. In addition to his sore back, "Hurley, Fargo, manager of Blue and Petrolle, was struck in the face during the melee."After the crowd settled down, the refereed disqualified Blue and awarded the bout to Conley on a foul.[9]

The other trip Petrolle recalled was the free-for-all which took place six days later at Tex Trotter's LeRoy-Krause show in Grand Forks. For three rounds, LeRoy hammered Battling Krause "from rope to rope, landing terrific rights and lefts almost at will." Krause obviously was in way over his head, and Russie was on his way to an almost certain kayo.

As described by the *Forum*'s Pat Purcell, the bout's final moments seemed to bear out the ending spectators were expecting:

> "The fourth and concluding round was easily the best of the affair. They met in mid-ring and started trading lusty wallops. Krause landed twice on LeRoy's head with a left, and Russie went

---

[9] Carmichael, John, "Eight Years in Ring Have Given Petrolle Many a Chuckle," *Chicago Daily News*, May 18, 1931, sports section. "Near Riot Breaks Out on Verdict," *Bismarck Tribune*, September 26, 1925, sports section.

under and drove a vicious right to the ribs that made the Battler wince. Russie, sensing his advantage, tore in like a madman, pitching hefty blows from every angle. The Battler's head bobbed and twisted and he was in semi-dazed condition when LeRoy cornered him. Krause crouched low in a half-sitting posture on the middle rope of the ring. LeRoy, also in a crouch, sprang in to finish his foe and sent the left uppercut over which ended the fray."

It appeared to everyone at ringside that LeRoy was the winner by a knockout. Seconds later, however, referee Knauf stunned the crowd by raising Krause's hand and ruling Russie's final punch had been a foul delivered below the belt. Purcell's account makes it clear no one was more shocked by the decision than Hurley:

"The blow left the Battler sprawled on the floor, and Knauf then lifted him in order to award him the decision. Jack Hurley, LeRoy's manager, believing LeRoy had scored a knockout, waved his charge to a neutral corner. When Hurley saw Knauf raise Krause's hand, he leaped into the ring in a rage and launched a vigorous attack in the general direction of Knauf. Spectators and seconds soon were busily engaged in hammering each other lustily and a squadron of police was called to restore order. None of the prominent participants in the brawl was injured to any extent."[10]

Purcell reported the riot "caused the president of the Grand Forks city commission to announce that no more fights would be allowed" in the city auditorium. The Forum reporter lamented that "another budding fight center has turned up its toes and died ... Boxing has just naturally passed away for the time being so far as Grand Forks is concerned."

The *Forum* reporter concluded that the "outcome of (the) fight certainly can be classed as an unfortunate affair. It was another case of over-anxiety, for it was only a matter of a few rounds before Krause would have been forced to take the count ... Had LeRoy chosen to be a bit more careful and continued a relentless attack on Krause's kidneys, it is more than likely that Krause would have been forced to quit."[11]

On his return to Fargo, Hurley announced he was outfitting a new gymnasium, and its grand opening would be held October 9, 1925, in conjunction with the season's first amateur show. The gym was located in the basement of the Equity Building at 626 Second Avenue North.

---

[10] Purcell, J. A., "Russie Held Wide Margin Until Finish," *Fargo Forum*, October 2, 1925, sports section.

[11] Purcell, "The Sportville Spotlight," *Fargo Forum*, October 2, 1925, sports section.

Guests at the opening were to include the members of the city commission and officials from the police department. Presumably, since boxing in Fargo was tolerated only at the sufferance of these specially invited dignitaries, Hurley was planning to be on his best behavior and thus avoid any sequel to the events which disrupted the boxing game in Bismarck and Grand Forks during the preceding two weeks.[12]

Hurley had shut down his prior gym at the Tweeden Hotel just before leaving on the California trip. After their return, LeRoy and Petrolle had been alternating workouts at various gyms around the area, including the Elks club, the Knights of Columbus, the YMCA, and the unfinished dirt basement of the Grand Rec. During the same period, Blue had elected to work out near his home in St. Paul until making the trip to his fights.

According to Hurley, the new gym was the most up-to-date training quarters in the Northwest. "Boxing and wrestling sections are featured along with one of the finest handball courts in the country," he told the *Forum* reporter. "Shower baths, weights, punching bags and various other articles of gymnasium equipment have been installed. A bleacher seating system has been arranged to accommodate 700 fans."[13]

To assist in the management of this rapidly expanding business, Hurley hired 23-year-old Phil Terk to organize the gym and serve as matchmaker for his weekly amateur shows, as well as to help with the promotional details for the professional shows at the Fargo Auditorium.

Within a year, Terk assumed the role as Jack's operations manager and became a full partner in all his Fargo promotions, both amateur and professional. The partnership would survive a move to Duluth in 1927 and would continue until 1934 when they disbanded the operation altogether.

Terk was born in 1902, the son of Russian Jews who immigrated to the United States in 1904. The family settled in Chicago, where his father worked first as a clothes presser and later as a newspaper dealer. When he first met Jack, Phil was working in the Fargo area as a sales representative for the *Chicago Herald-Examiner* of the Hearst news chain.[14]

Years later, Terk recalled that before Jack knew any better, he used to give Phil complimentary tickets to the fights in Fargo. "Hurley didn't know that a paper had any department other than sports," said Phil. "I was in circulation and until he found out, he gave me passes to his shows. Later he got even; he made me his partner."[15]

During his early days in Fargo, Terk lived in an upstairs room at the Hurley family home at 1328 Second Avenue South. While living in the

---

[12] Purcell, "Will Meet Petrolle in Windup," *Fargo Forum*. October 9, 1925, sports section.
[13] "Hurley Plans Card Oct. 16," *Fargo Forum*, October 6, 1925, sports section.
[14] U. S. Census, 1910 and 1920.
[15] Sherrod, Blackie, "Jack Re-called," *Dallas Times Herald,"* November 1972, sports section.

neighborhood, Phil met his future wife, Sadie Horwitz, then a stenographer for Western Union. At the time, Sadie resided with her parents in a house just down the street from the Hurleys.

Fortunately, Hurley's first amateur show at the gym went off without a hitch. The card featured an intercity rivalry between Fargo and Grand Forks. At evening's end, Fargo boxers had the edge, winning a majority of the bouts.

In early October, Hurley announced he had signed LeRoy and Knauf to a rematch in Fargo in a semi-final bout October 16, 1925. The *Forum* reporter predicted that "LeRoy should win by a country mile but if he loses his head ... then the Fargo lad is due for a bad evening and a hard fight."

The writer noted that the "rivalry between LeRoy and Knauf and the bad feeling between Knauf and Jack Hurley, as the result of a little set-to following the LeRoy-Krause bout in Grand Forks two weeks ago, is certain to make the meeting tonight a vicious one."

In the main event, Petrolle was slated to meet Red Cap Wilson, of New York, a veteran lightweight with nine years' experience. Wilson had recently defeated George (K. O.) Chaney, but had lost decisions to Rocky Kansas, Joe Dundee, Tony Vaccarelli, Tommy Farley, and Ruby Goldstein. Hurley negotiated Wilson's appearance with Scotty Montieth, who also managed world featherweight champion, Louis (Kid) Kaplan.

Wilson was "a past master of the delayed right," when he would feint "two or three times and still be in position to punch effectively." The blow was dangerous because there was "but little chance to see it coming."[16]

According to Purcell, Billy won seven of ten rounds from Wilson who, "despite the fact that he suffered a badly broken hand early in the bout ... proved to be a tough customer and a good counter-puncher, which made it interesting all the way."

In the seventh round, Petrolle "caught Wilson square on the chin with a straight right which would have dropped an ordinary fighter. Not so with Wilson, however, the Gotham battler merely shaking his head and grinning ... In the tenth, Wilson started away in true New York style, throwing punches from every direction, but Bill soon calmed him down with a pair of well directed rights to the face and then proceeded to win the stanza."

In the semi-windup, LeRoy had a narrow edge over Knauf in the first two rounds. Johnny came out strong for the third and landed four left hooks without a return. They continued to spar for about a half-minute until Russie feinted with his left and then, shifting quickly as Knauf ducked, landed a straight right to the chin which dropped Johnny on all fours.

Knauf was up at nine "and was greeted with a left which sent him sprawling" for a second knockdown. Johnny survived the round, but was

---

[16] Purcell, "Durability of Wilson's Chin Deciding Point," October 16, 1925, *Fargo Forum*, sports section.

unable to come out for the fourth, and Russie was awarded the fight on a technical knockout. Afterward, Benny Berger, Knauf's manager, stated Johnny had broken his left thumb in the third round.

Oddly enough, the card was not a money-maker. The *Forum* reported that while "it was a dandy program and deserved much better patronage ... Hurley was forced to clip a neat slice off his bankroll before the last fighter was paid off."[17]

Jack apparently had outsmarted himself by not accepting Trotter's offer of a big purse for LeRoy-Knauf bout in Grand Forks. The fight proved that although Fargo enthusiasts would pay to see LeRoy and Petrolle fight up-and-coming boxers like Danny Cooney and Mel Coogan, they were tired of seeing them matched against recycled local products like Knauf and used-up warhorses like Red Cap Wilson. Fans clearly believed Russie and Billy had moved up in class and rated tougher opposition.

The second amateur card at Hurley's gym, held the evening prior to the Petrolle-Wilson show, featured the one and only ring appearance of Hank (One-Punch) Hurley, Jack's 15-year-old brother. Hank was called into service when one of the scheduled boxers failed to appear. As Jack later recalled, the incident had serious repercussions in the Hurley household:

> "One night I got a show scheduled ... and one of the fighters don't show up. In comes my brother and he's just had supper. I said, 'Get your clothes on, Hank, you got a fight.' He says, 'I just had my supper.' I says, 'I don't care, you got a fight.' He says, 'I'll tell Ma.' I says, 'I can't help it. Get your clothes on.'
>
> "Well, he made it through this four-round no-decision fight, and then he got sick to his stomach. The next morning I come down to breakfast, and Ma doesn't say a word to me. I say, 'What's the matter?' She says, 'You're a nice fellow.' I says, 'What'd I do now? She says disgustedly, 'Making Henry fight!'
>
> "Then Hank comes in, and he says, 'OK, I fought, now give me the dollar you're supposed to give.' I says, 'What do you want me to do, jeopardize your amateur standing? So, a week later I took him down and bought him a suit and an overcoat."[18]

Although technically a no-decision affair, the *Forum* reported Tommy McGough earned a decision over One-Punch "by a comfortable margin."[19]

---

[17] Purcell, "Russ Gets Technical Kayo Win," *Fargo Forum*, October 17, 1925, sports section.
[18] Olsen, Jack, "Don't Call Me Honest – Part I," *Sports Illustrated*," May 15, 1961, p. 88.
[19] "Tommy McGough Too Much for Hurley in Amateur Feature Go," October 16, 1925, sports section. Tommy McGough would graduate from Hurley's gym to become a successful professional fighter.

On October 29, Hurley traveled with Petrolle to LaCrosse, Wisconsin where Billy fought the tough veteran Milwaukee lightweight, Joe Jawson, in a ten-rounder. As had become his habit, Petrolle started slowly and was able to salvage a draw only after a strong rally in the late rounds.[20]

At the time, Hurley sensed the potential for some good gates in Fargo with LeRoy. Petrolle, however, was a bigger attraction in the East than at home. To take advantage of both situations, Jack sent Billy east on his own and placed him under Joe Kossick's care in Springfield, Massachusetts. Since Kossick had arranged Petrolle's prior bouts at Holyoke, Jack and Billy felt comfortable with Joe as their East Coast mentor.

Between November 1925 and January 1926, Petrolle engaged in four fights under Kossick's direction. Billy won convincing decisions against Steve Smith and Ruby Stein, dropped a close but undisputed verdict to Johnny Drew, and lost a hotly disputed decision to Charles Manty. Each bout was well-received by the crowds, and at the end of the tour, Petrolle's reputation as a ready and willing drawing card was better than ever.

Unfortunately, the conclusion of 1925 was not as productive for Hurley's third stable ace, Earl Blue. On October 30, he traveled to Minot, North Dakota and suffered a broken hand in a losing effort against Mark Moore. Blue had defeated Moore in an earlier bout and was ahead in the Minot fight until the contest was stopped due to the injury. The hand was expected to keep Blue out of action for at least six weeks.[21]

Meanwhile, Hurley imported Pittsburgh lightweight Tony Ross to oppose LeRoy in Fargo November 6. Ross was billed as "a pocket edition" of middleweight champ Harry Greb, with whom Tony sparred regularly. Beforehand, it was advertised Greb would second his protégé in the bout, but a last-minute change in the titleholder's plans prevented his attendance.

The *Forum* described Ross' physique as "perfectly proportioned. His well-set shoulders are finely muscled, the cords of strength rolling easily under his glistening skin ... From shoulders to hips, he tapers down to such an extent that a rear view of his back offers a perfect V-shaped model. His legs are long and lean, indicating both strength and speed."

According to the *Forum*, Ross' record included a win over Phil McGraw, a draw with Cuddy DeMarco, and a close fight with ex-junior lightweight champ Jack Bernstein.[22]

Purcell's report the morning after the LeRoy-Ross fight was exultant:

---

[20] "Petrolle, Jawson Battle Ten Hard Stanzas on Even Terms," *Fargo Forum*, October 30, 1925, sports section.

[21] "Tony Ross Will Arrive in Fargo Today to Finish Training Work," *Fargo Forum*, November 2, 1925, sports section.

[22] "LeRoy to Top Mitt Program," *Fargo Forum*, October 27, 1925, sports section. Purcell, "Rugged Mauler to Box Cyclone Joe Gans Here," *Fargo Forum*, November 4, 1925, sports section.

"A short right hook, one which traveled less than six inches, landed square on Tony Ross' chin in the sixth of a scheduled ten-round fight at the Fargo Auditorium last night ... LeRoy's finishing punch came like a bolt from a clear sky, and sent down a warrior who never before had heard a referee toll the fatal "ten" over his prostrate form ...

"Last night Russie LeRoy rose to heights which this writer did not believe he ever would. Russie mixed boxing with fighting. He jabbed, hooked, blocked and even ducked. His left hooks were hard, usually well-timed drives to the stomach which hurt Ross and slowed him up. He crossed with his right in the chin on three different occasions, and all three of them hurt Ross.

"LeRoy was cool, boxed even cautiously at times. Then, again he launched two-fisted attacks which sent Ross flying to cover, but never once did Russie lose his head. It was the best fight this writer has ever seen LeRoy offer ...

"The sixth started at a furious pace ... They were in the center of the ring, fighting hard when ... LeRoy saw the opening and drove home that short right hook. Ross toppled over backwards, his head striking the floor with a resounding thud ... When Ross' head hit the floor, the fans rose to their feet in a wild frenzy for they realized they had seen LeRoy knock out truly a great little fighter. For more than five minutes they kept up an uproar, which surpassed by far any demonstration we have witnessed at a boxing show in Fargo.

"LeRoy, after assisting Ross to his corner, could hardly restrain himself. He beamed happily at the world in general, for he realized he is on the upward path once again after a short backward slide."

In a six-round preliminary bout on the LeRoy-Ross card, My Sullivan, a Johnny Salvator protégé from St. Paul, won a decision in his pro debut over Frankie Camden of Virginia, Minnesota.[23]

Afterward, Hurley told the *Forum* he would remain in Fargo for another show: "I had originally planned to leave for the East immediately after the LeRoy-Ross program, but as that venture was a financial success, and the fans seem to want another program ... I will stay until Nov 27 if I can get Frankie Bull, lightweight champion of Canada, to meet Russie here."

The match with Bull was doubly attractive to Fargo boxing fans. Not only was Bull a champion, but a year earlier LeRoy had been slighted by Canadian boxing authorities. Russie had signed to fight Bull in Winnipeg,

---

[23] Purcell, "Right Hook Is Curtain for Italian," *Fargo Forum*, November 7, 1925, sports section.

New York City's Red Cap Wilson.

Milwaukee veteran Joe Jawson.

Canadian lightweight, Frankie Bull, a LeRoy victim in 1925.

St. Paul welterweight My Sullivan made his debut at Fargo in 1925.

but the Manitoba Boxing Commission forbade the contest on the ground that LeRoy was not good enough to oppose Canada's champion.[24]

After ten days of negotiations, Hurley finally signed Bull, but for a sum "much higher than he has ever had to pay any fighter to appear here." Jack also agreed to let Bull enter the ring at a stipulated weight of 140 pounds instead of the normal 135-pound lightweight limit.

LeRoy squared accounts with the Manitoba commission November 27 by kayoing its champion in the second round of a scheduled ten-rounder.

The bell for the first round had barely sounded when "LeRoy met Bull in the middle of the ring and landed the first telling punch before the Canadian had a chance to get his arms moving." That "first punch dazed the champion so badly that he jumped up before he fairly realized that he had been knocked down ... Before Bull had time to cover LeRoy drove home another right that sent the Canadian down for the second time."

Bull lasted the first round "by poking a left to LeRoy's face while Russie, boxing in a crouch, fired many stinging lefts into the body of his foe." The kayo came in the second when Russie "feinted Bull into throwing a left hook. LeRoy stepped outside that hook and sent home a wide left swing which landed square on Bull's chin and ended the fray."

Afterward, Purcell exulted over LeRoy's recent improvement: "Again last night, LeRoy demonstrated he is stepping out of the give-and-take class into the division where good fighters land effectively without getting their heads punched off in their efforts to land."

In a preliminary bout, My Sullivan fought a six-round draw with Hurley's top young prospect, Spud Murphy of Moorhead.[25]

With LeRoy's confidence at an all-time high, and all of Fargo talking about his last two bouts, Hurley set out to arrange a New Year's Day card which would capture the imagination of the entire state, and surpass all previous North Dakota attendance records.

Hurley first contacted New York promoter Humbert Fugazy in an effort to secure LeRoy a bout with world lightweight champion Jimmy Goodrich. In July 1925, Goodrich had won the tournament staged to install a successor to retired champion Benny Leonard. Unfortunately, Jimmy had just agreed to put his title on the line against Rocky Kansas on December 7. Kansas, in fact, would defeat Goodrich to become the new titleholder.

Other efforts to sign Tommy (Kid) Murphy, who recently had defeated Eddie (Kid) Wagner, and Luis Vicentini, the only man to ever score a clean knockout over Rocky Kansas, proved fruitless due to prior commitments.[26]

---

[24] "Big Offer Forwarded to Monarch," *Fargo Forum*, November 10, 1925, sports section.
[25] Purcell, "Canadian Champ Says Russie Was Lucky to Land Deciding Punch," *Fargo Forum*, November 28, 1925, sports section.
[26] Purcell, "Russie May Get Bout In Twin Cities," *Fargo Forum*, December 1, 1925, sports section.

Hurley next approached Billy Mitchell, brother and manager of Pinkey Mitchell, world junior welterweight champion. Jack previously offered Pinkey a flat $5,000 to defend his title against LeRoy, but the Mitchells turned the offer down, demanding $7,500.

Now, Hurley upped his offer to $5,000 plus expenses and three round-trip train tickets. He also enlisted the aid of Doc Hoffman, a well known Milwaukee fight figure, to negotiate with the Mitchells on his behalf. This time they accepted and agreed to be in Fargo three days prior to the show.[27]

Terms called for the men to fight at catch-weights. In order to claim the title, LeRoy had to weigh at or below the junior welterweight limit of 140 pounds. Mitchell, on the other hand, did not have to make weight. Since North Dakota was a no-decision state, Russie's only chance to win the title would be by a knockout or if Mitchell committed a foul.[28]

On December 16, the *Forum* reported "more than 400 ringside seats" were sold the day after the fight was announced, and that "every mail" would bring "additional orders."

To accommodate a record-breaking crowd, Hurley intended to re-arrange seating on the Fargo Auditorium's main floor to add 500 seats to supplement the 750 usually used for boxing. He also planned to clear the stage and move 500 bleacher seats from his gym onto the stage. The sale of these 1,750 reserved seats together with 1,250 balcony seats would allow for "the biggest fight crowd ever assembled" in North Dakota.[29]

Tickets for reserved seats on the main floor and the lower part of the balcony were set at $5. Non-reserved balcony seats were priced at $3. This scale was the same as at the LeRoy-Eddie (Kid) Wagner card the previous January. Ticket sales for that show had been brisk up to the time Wagner

---

[27] "Will Offer $5,000 for Title Match," *Fargo Forum*, December 5, 1925, sports section. "Hurley Renews Offer for Mitchell Battle," *Fargo Forum*, December 11, 1925, sports section.

[28] Purcell, "Fargoan to Weight Less Than Limit," *Fargo Forum*, December 15. 1925, sports section. "Catch-weights" meant neither fighter had to make a particular weight. Typically, in cases when a championship was at stake, both fighters had to come in under the specified weight for the division. In such cases, if the challenger could not make the weight then he could not claim the championship if he won. If the champion could not make the weight then he risked forfeiture of his title even before he stepped into the ring to fight. In contrast, the LeRoy-Mitchell contract, being a catch-weight agreement, did not require either fighter to make any particular weight, but LeRoy was given the option to come under the junior welterweight limit of 140 pounds and, in the event of victory, claim the title. Mitchell, on the other hand, could come in over the limit without risking forfeiture.

This worked to Pinkey's advantage because at this point he was having trouble making the junior welter limit of 140 pounds. On the other hand, he was making a concession by allowing Russie an opportunity at the title and not requiring him to weigh more than 140 pounds. Promoter Hurley was therefore able to advertise the bout as a championship contest.

[29] Purcell, "Salvator Willing to Let Star Help Russie," *Fargo Forum*, December 16, 1925, sports section. "Fargo Preparing for Largest Fight Throng in N. D. History," *Fargo Forum*, January 6, 1925, sports section.

was injured and the bout canceled. Jack therefore had reason to believe fans would accept the increased prices for the special show without complaint.[30]

Immediately after the bout was arranged, Hurley asked Salvator to send his welterweight, Rusty Jones, to Fargo a few days in advance of the fight to serve as LeRoy's sparring partner. Jones featured a stand-up style with a fast left jab and a hard right cross similar to Mitchell. Johnny readily agreed to this arrangement as long as Jack agreed to pay Jones' expenses and furnish him a prime spot on the New Year's card.[31]

The *Forum* reported on Sunday, December 27, "that the advance seat sale has been as big as expected. The majority of the Fargo fans have purchased their tickets while many out-of-town fans have placed their orders. If Mitchell arrives on scheduled time the advance sale is certain to be boosted considerably and the out-of-town sale will depend largely on the weather and condition of the roads on the day of the fight."[32]

On December 29, with all arrangements completed, a promoter's worst nightmare happened. Mitchell's manager/brother, Billy, phoned Hurley and canceled Pinkey's appearance. Billy told Jack the champion was "suffering from an infected toe and will not be able to fight for at least two weeks."

The Forum reported "the news came as a distinct shock to Hurley and local fans who believed that Mitchell was in fine fettle and ready to defend his crown here Friday." Pinkey requested that the show be postponed for two weeks, but Jack declined. He had promised fans there would be no substitutions or postponements. Many patrons who had purchased tickets for the New Year's date might not be able to attend during a regular workweek. He did not rule out rescheduling the show later date, however.[33]

The next day, Hurley set out to reschedule the LeRoy-Mitchell bout. He phoned Billy Mitchell, who apologized for his brother's non-appearance and offered to reimburse Jack for his losses due to the cancellation from the champ's future purse in Fargo. Billy also said his brother's toe was responding to treatment, and he would be ready to fight in 10 days.

Hurley made it clear any new agreement would include a guarantee that Pinkey would be on hand at the agreed date. Jack told the Milwaukee manager he would require a certified forfeiture check of $500 before he would advertise the program or reserve the auditorium. "No more sack holding for me," Hurley told the *Forum* writer.

Taking no chances, Jack phoned Salvator in St. Paul and asked him to travel to Milwaukee and close the deal with the Mitchells, who Johnny

---

[30] Purcell, "Hurley Signs Leading Mitt Man of World," January, 18, 1925, p. 12. Watson, *op. cit.*

[31] Purcell, "Salvator Willing to Let Star Help Russie," *op.* cit.

[32] Purcell, "Champ Sure He Can Stop Fargo Entry," *Fargo Forum*, December 27, 1925, p. 15.

[33] Purcell, "Infected Toe Forces Star to Take Step," *Fargo Forum*, December 30, 1925, sports section.

LeRoy (left) with unidentified foe, possibly Tony Ross, at the Fargo Auditorium, c. 1925. Courtesy North Dakota State University Library.

The brothers Mitchell all attended the title fight in Fargo: Champion Pinkey; manager Billy; and Ritchie, a former top-rated lightweight.

had known for 15 years. Hurley felt "if anyone can make a suitable deal with the Milwaukee men, Salvator can."[34]

Salvator wired on January 3 he had completed negotiations for the fight to be held January 14, and had obtained a forfeiture. Furthermore, as added insurance, he had taken possession of Pinkey's championship belt, valued at $3,000, and forwarded both the check and the belt by registered mail.[35]

Two days later the belt and check arrived and were immediately put on exhibit in the Grand Rec's show window. Also displayed was Salvator's letter explaining the hard time he had talking the Mitchells out of the belt. It was reportedly the first time it left Milwaukee since Pinkey won the title.[36]

To further promote the event, Hurley invited ex-lightweight champ Battling Nelson to visit Fargo and help with pre-fight ballyhoo. Sports editor Pat Purcell furnished *Forum* readers the Battler's ghost-written impressions of LeRoy and Mitchell on a daily basis leading up to the tilt.[37]

As soon as the Mitchells arrived on January 11, reservations flocked in from out of town. The *Forum* reported orders were "received from large delegations from Grand Forks, Wahpeton, Valley City, Jamestown, Devil's Lake, and many smaller places in the state. Detroit Lakes, Barnesville and Breckinridge will contribute the largest Minnesota delegations." The day before the fight, numerous fans had already checked into local hotels.

A last-minute objection to Leo Kossick as referee by the Mitchell camp was resolved when the parties agreed to have Salvator referee the bout.

LeRoy stood 5-feet-7 inches tall and weighed less than 140 pounds when he stepped on the Grand Rec scales at 3 p.m. on January 14. In accordance with the championship rules then in effect, Russie weighed in six hours

---

[34] Purcell, "Mitchell Is Willing to Post Forfeit to Assure Appearance," *Fargo Forum*, January 3, 1926, sports section.

[35] Purcell, "Champion to Clash with Russie LeRoy," *Fargo Forum*, January 5, 1926, sports section.

[36] Purcell, "Champ's Belt, Forfeit Check Now in Fargo," *Fargo Forum*, January 7, 1926, sports section. Purcell, "Salvator Willing to Let Star Help Russie," *op. cit.* "Fargo Preparing for Largest Fight Throng in N. D. History," *Fargo Forum*, January 6, 1925, sports section. Purcell, "Hurley Signs Leading Mitt Man of World," January, 18, 1925, p. 12. Watson, *op. cit.* Purcell, "Salvator Willing to Let Star Help Russie," *op. cit.* Purcell, "Champ Sure He Can Stop Fargo Entry," *Fargo Forum*, December 27, 1925, p. 15. Purcell, "Infected Toe Forces Star to Take Step," *Fargo Forum*, December 30, 1925, sports section. Purcell, "Jack Dempsey May Exhibit Powers Here," *Fargo Forum*, December 31, 1925, sports section. Purcell, "Victor Comes from Behind to Win Tilt," *Fargo Forum*, January 2, 1926, sports section. Purcell, "Mitchell Is Willing to Post Forfeit to Assure Appearance," *Fargo Forum*, January 3, 1926, sports section. Purcell, "Champion to Clash with Russie LeRoy," *Fargo Forum*, January 5, 1926, sports section. Purcell, "Champ's Belt, Forfeit Check Now in Fargo," *Fargo Forum*, January 7, 1926, sports section.

[37] Purcell, "Former Champ Thinks Russie May Reach the Top," *Fargo Forum*, January 10, 1926, sports section. Nelson, Battling, "LeRoy in Good Shape for Battle, Bat Says," *Fargo Forum*, January 13, 1926, sports section. Nelson, Battling, "Mitchell a Finished Fighter, Nelson Says," *Fargo Forum*, January 14, 1926, sports section.

before the fight in the presence of a notary public and two official witnesses. Mitchell did not officially weigh in, but he was 5-feet-11-1/2-inches tall and scaled an estimated 149 pounds at the start of the fight.[38]

Purcell described the contest in the next day's *Forum*:

> "In a bout which fairly sizzled with action from start to finish, Pinkey Mitchell of Milwaukee won a hairline decision over Russie LeRoy of Fargo over the ten-round route in the Fargo Auditorium last night, before the largest fight crowd ever assembled in North Dakota. It was truly a great battle, the champion being forced to rally desperately in the last four rounds in order to pull through victorious.
>
> "LeRoy started away at a terrific clip in the opening stanza and won that round with a driving attack which sent the champion back on the defensive after an opening rally. ...(T)he Fargo fighter ... continued his driving attack through the second, third and fourth rounds ...
>
> "With the opening of the fifth round, Mitchell loosened up a bit and succeeded in holding the Fargoan even during this and the sixth rounds ... Near the end of the sixth round, it was evident that LeRoy was tiring. He was outweighed at least eight pounds ... and the champion's heft and strength asserted itself about this time.
>
> "Mitchell shocked the crowd early in the seventh round when he nailed LeRoy with a perfectly timed right cross to the jaw and the Fargo fighter went down for a count of nine. ... At the start of the eighth ... Mitchell opened a big cut over his opponent's right eye with a stinging left hook. The blood soon streamed into the eye, rendering the optic practically useless for the remainder of the session ...
>
> "Pinkey carried the eighth and ninth stanzas by jabbing effectively with his left and he drove his right home to the body

---

[38] Purcell, "Both Battlers Reported Fit for Struggle," *Fargo Forum*, January 14, 1926, sports section. This article was written before the weigh-in. It estimated Mitchell's weight at the weigh-in as 142 pounds and at ringside as 144, based on information from Mitchell's trainer. The article also predicted Russie's weight at the weigh-in as "under 140 pounds."

In Purcell's post-fight article (see citation in next note), Mitchell's weight was given as 149 pounds at fight time. Where this figure came from is not reported. It likely was obvious to everyone at ringside that Pinkey weighed more than his trainer claimed before the fight.

Russie's actual weight at the weigh-in is never directly reported, only that it was less than the 140-pound limit. Purcell estimated LeRoy's weight at fight time to be "at least eight pounds" less than the champ, that is, Russie was thought to weigh 141 pounds at fight time. This means he likely weighed in at 139 pounds since Purcell in his January 14 article (see above) equated Pinkey's estimated 142 pounds at weigh-in time with 144 pounds at ringside.

Actual weights at fight time are always considerably higher than at the weigh-in because of food and liquid consumed after the fighters weigh in.

several times ... Shortly after the start of the tenth round, Mitchell landed another perfectly timed right cross and LeRoy went down for a ... count of six ...

"Taken all in all, it was a great battle. ... LeRoy fought desperately all the way, but at the start of the contest his over-anxiety to land a knockout blow hampered his work, and as the contest progressed Mitchell's great strength and his weight advantage helped to aid in the undoing of the North Dakota fighter. Russie fought a great fighter last night and, in our opinion, he did a dandy job of it."

In the semi-windup, Salvator's Rusty Jones knocked out Jack Burns of Milwaukee in the third round. Ex-lightweight champ Battling Nelson refereed the bout "in bang-up style."[39]

When the money was counted, the fighters paid, and the Mitchells returned to their hotel room, Hurley and Salvator retreated to one of Fargo's few late-night restaurants, the "La Chateau," on Front Street for a low-key celebratory dinner. Although LeRoy had lost, it was a good fight, and the show had been a sell-out. Jack owed Johnny a dinner, anyway, for all the help he had provided in arranging the match.

After the meal, conversation turned to the cancellation of the original show four days before the New Year. Hurley said the ordeal of refunding the money and the uncertainty over whether he'd lost his big payday forever, made him a nervous wreck. Jack never had so much trouble over such a little thing as a sore toe before, and he hoped he never would again.

Listening to Hurley, Salvator was quiet, as if he wanted to say something but didn't quite know how. After a while, Johnny's face eased into a grin, and he cautiously leaned across the table. "Funny thing," he told Jack. "I was talking to Billy Mitchell about that toe. I don't know whether I should tell you or not, but it turns out the toe wasn't infected at all."

"Pinkey told his brother he couldn't go through with the January 1 fight because he had to go to a party. His wife gave him an ultimatum – he had to take her out for New Year's Eve, or else she'd divorce him. Pinkey told Billy to think of an excuse to tell you, and the sore toe story was all he could come up with."[40]

With that, Salvator reached over, picked up the check, and said, "Jack, how about if *I* buy *YOU* the dinner?"

---

[39] Purcell, "Two Knockdowns Give Champion Scant Edge," *Fargo Forum*, January 15, 1926, sports section.

[40] Houston, Robert, "Hurley, One of Boxing's Great Figures," *Sunday New York World-Herald Magazine*, January 13, 1952, p. 10-G.

CHAPTER 13

WHO WAS THAT MASKED MAN?

I was his manager. He was my Masked Marvel. And what a fighter. Twenty-one bouts he had, and 21 wins by knockouts. That was his lifetime record. But quick knockouts ... Gosh, how the years go. Lynn Nelson, my old Masked Marvel.

Lynn was a kid playing baseball around Fargo then. It isn't a big town, you know; you get to know everybody. Lynn was a good athlete and liked to hang around the gyms. Now and then he'd put on the gloves, and you could take one look at him and there it was. Just like that, you saw a fighter that couldn't miss. He could belt and he could move and he could learn. You never told him anything twice. Just a natural, if there ever was one.

More for fun than anything, I got him a couple of bouts, and just for fun he took 'em. He was a little worried if it got around that he was fighting, his ball club wouldn't like it. So I billed him simply as the Masked Marvel.

I took the top of a lady's silk stocking, pulled it over his head and down over his face, cut it off, tied it shut at the crown and cut a couple of holes for his eyes. He went in there wearing that mask and bing, bang, he stiffened his guys as fast as you could blink.

We never told anybody who the Masked Marvel was, but it wasn't exactly a secret. That black silk mask, when he caught a glancing punch the mask would slide and take the skin with it, leaving a red, abraded place like the floor-burns a basketball player gets.

The Masked Marvel would belt somebody out one night and the next day Lynn would show up at the ball park with a face like the Belair Stud silks – white with red polka dots. The other players would ride him, and Lynn would just grin and say nothing.

With every start he got better. It was pretty clear he'd have to make up his mind soon. Baseball or fighting. He asked me what he should do. I told him, "Lynn I can't answer that for you. You've got to make up your own mind. But I can tell you this: you can be a great fighter. I mean great."

Well, he went away and when he came back he said, "Jack, I like to fight and I guess maybe I could make a lot of money fighting. But all I've ever wanted to do is play ball. You won't be mad at me if I quit fighting?"

I said, "No, Lynn, I won't be mad at you." And he said, "I can't help it, Jack. I've just got to be a ball player." He was kind of apologetic about it, like a kid. So that was the end of the Masked Marvel. [1]   – Jack Hurley

---

[1] Smith, Red, "Views of Sport – The Saga of Line Drive Nelson," *New York Herald Tribune*, January 20, 1949, sports section. The article has been edited to fit the context.

The evidence supports the proposition Nelson had some bouts, won them all, wore a mask, and fought under the name "Masked Marvel," but exactly where and when he had 21

****

After Russie LeRoy's valiant stand against the much heavier Pinkey Mitchell, Jack Hurley turned his attention to advancing the prospects of his other mainstay, Billy Petrolle, who had been campaigning on the East Coast during the past two months. LeRoy's right eye, badly cut in the Mitchell fight, had required five stitches. Russie was expected to be out for at least a month before he could resume serious training.[2]

While boxing in the East under Joe Kossick's care, Petrolle had some exciting moments. In a bout at Hartford, Connecticut on December 17, 1925, Bridgeport's "Hungarian Bearcat" Steve Smith nailed Billy with a punch under the right eye. Within 10 seconds, the eye swelled to the size of a fist and closed up tight. Petrolle had made a mistake by blowing his nose, which caused the area around the eye to fill up with blood and air.

At the end of the round, the referee followed Petrolle to his corner and said he was going to stop the fight because he feared another punch might cause Billy to lose his sight. Petrolle's second was Jack Brady, trainer of light-heavyweight champ Tommy Loughran. Brady told the referee the eye would be open and as good as ever by the start of the next round. The referee said he would be back to examine the eye before the bell rang.

Brady took a safety razor out of his surgical kit and lanced the swollen area under Billy's eye. Then he put his mouth to the lanced area and sucked out the blood and air. The opening around the eye immediately returned to

---

matches remains a mystery. The author has been able to track down four Nelson/Masked Marvel bouts in amateur shows at Hurley's gym in March and April 1926. It is possible there were some bouts in other venues during this time, but the author finds it unlikely. It is doubtful that Nelson would have been allowed to wear his mask and remain anonymous if he was fighting for other promoters. Hurley himself would use the same ploy again in Duluth two years later, masquerading a different prospect as "the Masked Marvel."

It is possible for the sake of a good story Hurley combined the bouts of both "Masked Marvels" to arrive at 21 fights. By May 1, 1926, Nelson was pitching for Steve Gorman's Grand Recreation Parlors baseball team in the Fargo Commercial League and was never interested in boxing again. Whether the bouts should be considered "professional" or "amateur" is problematical as well (see discussion in Chapter 9).

If Nelson did have 21 bouts, whether amateur or pro, they likely occurred before he began working out at Hurley's gym in 1926. Lynn made a passing reference to some pre-1926 bouts in an interview given when he was pitching for Syracuse in the International League in 1941. "Pitcher Lynn Nelson of Chiefs Passed Up Chance to Star as Boxer to Continue His Baseball Career." *Syracuse NY Herald-Journal*, May 28, 1941, sports section.

The claim Nelson or Hurley never revealed the Masked Marvel's identity is incorrect. Lynn scored knockouts wearing his mask against Al Johns on March 12, 1926, and against Al's brother John Johns on March 26, 1926. Nelson took his mask off in his bout against Ted Citrowski on April 9, 1926 because he couldn't breathe and fought again without it on April 23, 1926 against Fritz Kowalski, although he retained billing in both bouts as "the Masked Marvel." The claim Nelson won all his bouts by knockout is sheer hyperbole. Nelson's wins over Citrowski and Kowalski were four-round decision wins, not knockouts.

[2] Purcell, J. A., "Rambling Through Sportsville," *Fargo Forum*, January 16, 1926, sports section.

normal. Brady then cleansed the wound and applied Monsel's solution to seal it up. The entire procedure took about 30 seconds.[3]

In his description of the fight, *Hartford Daily Courant* sports editor Johnny Greene fashioned a "nom de guerre" for Petrolle that still lives on, even though eyewitnesses to his ring exploits have long since passed away:

> "The 'Fargo Express' blew in on time, as usual.
> "Billy Petrolle, fighter from the wilds of North Dakota, last night scored a decision victory over Steve Smith, rugged battler of Bridgeport, in a 12-round bout that sent many a fan home with a whisper where once was a powerful pair of lungs.
> "While Petrolle's good right mitt was raised aloft at the end of a dozen stanzas of smashing glove tossing, it was with his other hand that he won the battle. Only the smart use of his southpaw glove overcame a slight Smith lead and brought him through to victory.
> "There were no knockdowns. Few fighters of today could stand up under the avalanche of terrific smashes each sent forth during the course of the evening's festivities and stand up under them. But Billy and Steve are of the oak variety – each stood solid smashes to

---

[3] Hurley, Jack, "Ring Rations," *Fargo Forum*, October 25, 1931, sports section.

This situation was a precursor to one involving trainer Frank Percoco and boxer Rocky Graziano during Graziano's second fight with Tony Zale in 1947 at the Chicago Stadium. In that fight, Rocky came back from almost certain defeat to knock Zale out in the sixth round and win the middleweight title. At the end of the fourth round, Rocky's right eye was in the same shape Billy's had been in the Petrolle-Smith fight more than 20 years earlier. Like Brady, Percoco lanced the area beneath the eye and relieved it of the blood and air that had been trapped there. Instead of a razor and human suction power, Frank used a coin to break the skin under the eye and applied pressure to it with the coin to expunge the blood and air.

Apparently, Petrolle's second, Jack Brady, left home that evening without any loose change in his pocket, a no-no for any boxing trainer, i. e., as a commercial used to say "don't leave home without it!" Either that or Frank Percoco had forgotten to pack his Gillette safety razor to take with him to the Graziano-Zale fight!

In a more serious vein, Monsel's solution, so-named because of Leon Monsel's discovery during the Crimean War in 1852 that a mixture of ferrous sulphate and water had a beneficial effect in reducing bleeding, is an effective anti-coagulant, but its use has been banned in most present day jurisdictions because the solution, in effect, burns skin tissue to close the wound. The solution has the potential of complicating the healing process by killing the tissue adjacent to the wound and is also potentially damaging to the cornea if it gets into the eye. Avatene, Thrombin, and Adrenaline are the only anti-coagulants allowed in a fighter's corner by most boxing commissions in the present era.

The procedure of lancing the tissue around the eye has also fallen out of favor, if it was ever in favor. The potential for cutting nerves and muscles as well as causing infection is now thought to be too great by reputable cut men. The present feeling is that the proper application of pressure to the affected area, if feasible, is the safest and most effective procedure to close a wound.

As a note to this note, it might be mentioned that Hurley, as matchmaker, co-promoted the second Graziano-Zale fight, along with his partners Jack Begun and Irving Schoenwald.

the body, head and jaw but neither even trembled before storm after storm.

"It was a great fight, just as advance indications pointed. Smith went away to a slight lead, clung tenaciously to it until the tenth round, and then fought furiously to offset a Petrolle rally. Smith's best wasn't quite good enough. Petrolle's left hand just beat Smith to the punch, and Referee Jim Keefe's decision satisfied the entire assemblage which cheered loud and long."[4]

Shortly after reading Greene's article, Hurley visited a Northern Pacific train station and obtained a head-on photograph of a steam locomotive whipping down the track, stack blowing, and leaving in its wake a billowing plume of thick, black smoke.

Hurley searched through his photo files, located a menacing headshot of Petrolle, and superimposed the photo over the center of the charging locomotive. Jack ordered some brochures which mated these images to a caption touting the fistic prowess of Billy as "the Fargo Express." Finally, he mailed these brochures to virtually every boxing writer in the country.

From that moment forward, the name "Billy Petrolle" and the moniker "Fargo Express" bcame inextricably linked. Sportswriters throughout the country found it easy to extol the fighting qualities of "Billy Petrolle, the Fargo Express," simply because the phrase fell so trippingly off their typewriters and connected so resoundingly with their readers.

****

Four days after the LeRoy-Mitchell battle, Hurley opened negotiations with Max (Boo Boo) Hoff for a contest between Petrolle and Hoff's boxer, Eddie (Kid) Wagner to be held at the Fargo Auditorium February 5, 1926.

Hurley met Hoff in 1925 when Jack and his fighters headquartered in Philadelphia for a couple of months. In addition to being a boxing manager, Max was at least as well known as Philadelphia's boss of the underworld.

During the Prohibition, Hoff grew wealthy selling alcoholic beverages illegally diverted from manufacturing plants ostensibly built to distill industrial alcohol and solvents. Max also controlled several nightclubs which provided additional income and multiple venues for launching a variety of illegal gambling, liquor, and weapons distribution ventures.

Although some of the money was used to bribe police and other public officials, most of it was laundered through investment and bank accounts opened in the names of fictitious depositors. The funds from these accounts

---

[4] Greene, Johnny, "Billy Petrolle Wins Thrilling Encounter," *Fargo Forum*, December 19, 1925, sports section. A longer version of this article appeared in the morning edition of the *Hartford Daily Coursnt*. This abbreviated version was published in the Forum.

BILLY PETROLLE
"THE FARGO EXPRESS"
JUNIOR LIGHTWEIGHT AND
LIGHTWEIGHT CONTENDER
DIRECTION
JACK HURLEY, FARGO, N. D

THE FARGO EXPRESS

The Hungarian Bearcat, Steve Smith, (upper left) whose fight with Petrolle led Johnny Greene to dub Billy "the Fargo Express." Billy is seen at right displaying his new moniker. At bottom left is a picture from Hurley's publicity file making use of Greene's invention.

were used to purchase an assortment of legal investments. Hoff's boxing stable was a legitimate use of this money which gave him great pleasure.[5]

At first, Hoff demanded that Hurley arrange two matches for Wagner in the Midwest to make the trip worthwhile, but Jack was unable to find another promoter able to meet Wagner's price for a second bout. Hurley countered by meeting Hoff's terms for a big guarantee and adding an option for a percentage of gross receipts should that amount exceed the guarantee.

Eddie (Kid) Wagner was a tough customer, never having been kayoed since achieving top-contender status four years earlier. Still only 25, he held victories over Red Cap Wilson, Cuddy DeMarco, Johnny Dundee, Phil McGraw, Danny Kramer, and reigning featherweight champ, Louis (Kid) Kaplan. His most impressive win had been a six-round kayo of the "Jewel of the Ghetto," Sid Terris, then already tabbed a potential champion.[6]

Just a year earlier, Wagner had lost a tough decision to Jimmy Goodrich in the elimination tournament which determined a successor to retired champion Benny Leonard. At the end of ten rounds, the judges ruled the fight a draw and ordered two extra rounds to decide the winner. Goodrich had an edge in the overtime sessions and went on to win the championship.

According to the *Forum*, Fargo fans, who had not seen Petrolle in action since he fought Red Cap Wilson four months earlier, were impressed with his gym work as he prepared for Wagner. Whereas against Wilson, Petrolle appeared to be "a mechanical fighter without color," he now was "a colorful Billy – a Billy who does not only think for himself and think fast, but a Billy who delights in pulling the unexpected. Throughout the sessions, Billy constantly shifted from one style of attack to another."

Petrolle's "weaving, bobbing style proved most bothersome" and he "looked shiftier on his feet and harder to hit." "He not only bewildered his opponents with his speed, but he surprised the fans who were expecting to see the old plodding machine-like Billy."

Ringsiders came away with the impression that "Billy's fighting away from Hurley gave him the needed something that will make him the same kind of favorite here as he is in other rings." Billy previously relied on "his manager to do most of the battle planning" but "away from Jack's guiding hand Billy was forced to do a lot thinking himself – the result is that now he thinks and acts for himself in the ring. And he acts quickly and wisely."[7]

On January 29, Hurley received the offer Petrolle had been working toward ever since his East Coast invasion a year earlier. Tex Rickard's

---

[5] Desmond Parry, "Remembering Max 'Boo Boo' Hoff," *American Mafia.com*, August 2006 (PLR International, 2006).

[6] Purcell, J. A., "Terrific Right to Jaw Ends Great Mix," *Fargo Forum*, February 6, 1926, sports section. Purcell, J. A., "Quaker City Star Shows Great Speed," *Fargo Forum*, February 4, 1926, sports section.

[7] McGlynn, Stoney, "Fans Will See New Petrolle When He Meets Wagner Here," *Fargo Forum*, January 31, 1926, sports section.

matchmaker Jess McMahon wired that if Billy scored a clean-cut win over Wagner, he would be given a spot at Madison Square Garden in February.[8]

The stage was set for Petrolle's most important battle to date.

The opening sentence of Purcell's report the morning after the fight told the whole story: "Billy Petrolle, the Fargo Express, knocked out Eddie (Kid) Wagner, of Philadelphia, in the last round of a scheduled ten-round contest here last night. One terrific right uppercut, which landed flush on the side of Wagner's jaw after exactly one minute of milling in the final stanza left the clever little battler from Philadelphia stiff on the canvas."

The first round opened as Wagner "stabbed Bill with a hard left and then grinned confidently, evidently believing that he had a setup. Bill bobbed and ducked for a few seconds and then launched the most vicious body attack this writer has ever been privileged to look at" as "Eddie made a vain effort to stem the attack while clinching. When he did succeed in getting hold of Bill's flying arms, he was a sick looking fellow."

Purcell gave "the sturdy little Italian every round except the fourth." Wagner was floored by a right uppercut in the sixth, but was up instantly.

The knockout came in the tenth round with Wagner's back to the ropes and his arm cocked to block an expected right to the body. Instead, "Petrolle's right met him square on the side of the jaw and Wagner fell backwards his head striking the floor just outside the ring while his body was stretched across the lower rope. Petrolle rushed straight for the farthest corner and Kossick started to count immediately." "Wagner was carried to his corner," and "it was fully 10 minutes before he regained his senses."

In preliminary bouts, My Sullivan won a six-round decision over Frankie Camden of Virginia, Minnesota, and Spud Murphy of Moorhead decisioned Vic Walters of St. Paul, also in six rounds.[9]

The one down note for the promotion was the turnout. The *Forum* reported that although "attendance would have been good for an ordinary program," it "fell decidedly short when it is considered that the main event was good enough to headline a program of any city in the country."

In a column written a few days later, Purcell analyzed Petrolle's progress since his last Fargo ring appearance:

> "He has developed so rapidly in the past four months that the night he knocked Eddie (Kid) Wagner out he did not even look like the same fellow who struggled through to a victory over Red Cap Wilson here last October.
>
> "Petrolle was the crudest sort of fighter when he started. He always could hit, but with Hurley's guiding hand, he has learned to move correctly and he bobs, ducks, and weaves around in such a

---

[8] McGlynn, Stoney, *Fargo Forum*, January 30, 1926, sports section.
[9] Purcell, "Terrific Right to Jaw Ends Great Mix," *op. cit.*

Philadelphia's Eddie (Kid) Wagner

Manager Max (Boo Boo) Hoff

Madison Square Garden matchmaker Jess McMahon

Sammy Vogel decisioned Petrolle in Billy's Garden debut.

manner that he rarely ever is still long enough for an opponent to 'take picks.' He looks as though he is comparatively easy to hit but by his continued bobbing he forces opponents to shoot at a moving target and catches the majority of the punches on top of his head."[10]

After Petrolle's win, Billy McCarney, acting as Hurley's New York agent, wired that, true to his word, McMahon had set February 19 as a date for Petrolle's Madison Square Garden debut. The fight would be the first on a card featuring European middleweight champion Tommy Milligan and Pittsburgh welterweight Jack Zivic. McCarney cautioned Hurley not to accept Jess' offer until talking with McCarney over the phone.[11]

McMahon's offer of $1,000 plus two train tickets came two days later. After consulting McCarney, Hurley turned it down and countered with a proposal for $3,000 plus two tickets. A few days later, he came to terms with Jess for an undisclosed amount. Petrolle was to fight lightweight Sammy Vogel at weights not to exceed 134 pounds.[12]

When Hurley arrived in New York, Hartford promoter George Mulligan contacted Jack and signed Petrolle for a guarantee of $2,500 to meet featherweight champion Louis (Kid) Kaplan at the Hartford Armory in an over-weight bout on March 1. Billy had made such a hit at his two prior bouts there in December and January that Mulligan did not even make the fight contingent on the outcome of Petrolle's bout with Vogel.[13]

Sammy Vogel was a 23-year-old veteran with 45 fights and almost six years' experience. Vogel had won 22 of his most recent 25 fights, his sole defeats during that run coming against former world lightweight champion Jimmy Goodrich and the sensational Argentine battler, Luis Vicentini, who was the only man to ever kayo reigning lightweight champ Rocky Kansas. Like Petrolle, Vogel was making his Garden debut.

Wilbur Wood, writing for the *New York Sun*, aptly summarized the challenge Petrolle faced on February 19:

> "The Westerner, in spite of his knockout of Eddie Wagner a couple of weeks ago, will have to beat Vogel to establish himself

---

[10] Purcell, J. A., "Rambling Through Sportsville," *Fargo Forum*, February 15, 1926, sports section.

[11] "Hurley Turns Down Bout in Gotham Arena," *Fargo Forum*, February 9, 1926, sports section.

[12] Purcell, J. A., "No Opponent for Express Named As Yet," *Fargo Forum*, February 11, 1926, sports section.

[13] "Feather King, Fargo Express Meet March 1," *Fargo Forum*, February 17, 1926, sports section. The featherweight limit was 126 pounds. Kaplan and Petrolle's contract called for weights not to exceed 133 pounds. Kaplan had decided he was outgrowing the featherweight division and it was just a matter of time until he could no longer continue as champion. He defended his title one more time against Bobby Garcia June 28, 1926, and then abdicated his championship July 6. Kaplan thereafter fought as a lightweight (135-pound limit).

here. New York fans take everything that happens outside of Father Knickerbocker's precincts with more than the proverbial grain of salt. But if Billy can take Sammy into camp there will be no question as to Petrolle's merits. Sammy is stepping along at a dizzy clip and expects to be in line for a shot at the lightweight title before the end of the summer."[14]

Wood's report of the Petrolle-Vogel affair is interesting because he was seated near Billy's corner and could hear every word Hurley said between rounds. Wood also conveyed the event's importance to its participants:

"The ten round semifinal ... was a good enough fight, but it did look rather drab following the 10-round shindig between Sammy Vogel of Harlem and Billy Petrolle, who came out of Fargo, N. D., to show the blasé New York fans how they fight out in the wide open spaces, where men are men and women are deputy sheriffs ...

"It was the first Garden showing for each and they were there to do or die. Vogel, a pale, seemingly frail, sharp-shooting boxer, master of almost all the tricks of the trade, is a cool, clever workman. Petrolle, shorter and more solidly built and with the ability to take punishment that marks most of the gladiators of Italian descent, matched an iron chin and a heavy right-hand punch against Vogel's tricks.

"Vogel, for all his smartness, made two bad mistakes. Rather, he made the same mistake twice. In the second round he stepped out of a clinch with his hands down and received a lightning right hook on the chin that put him down for a count of six. Sammy, though badly stung, made a splendid recovery and at the bell he once more was methodically altering Petrolle's features with his darting left.

"Round after round Vogel continued his assault. His snappy left beat a steady tattoo on Petrolle's face. Sometimes he cut loose with heavy rights. In the fifth Petrolle's right flashed to Vogel's chin again and Sammy went hurtling into the ropes. But he came back nobly and rocked the Westerner with a right to the head.

"'You're fighting like a farmer; get hep to yourself,' remarked Petrolle's manager as Billy came back to his corner. "But try as he might, Petrolle could not escape that punishing left in the sixth, seventh, eighth and ninth. The steady pounding was having its effect. He was staggered, sent back on his heels, more than once.

"Just before the tenth began, Petrolle's manager, boiling over with rage at the sight of his fighter being used as a chopping block

---

[14] Wood, Wilbur, "Will Sign Today for March 15 Unless Commission Forbids" (subtitle), *New York Evening Sun*, February 16, 1926, sports section.

in his New York debut, handed the following parting instructions to his protégé: "'Tin can for the first minute; then step on it and knock that guy stiff.'"

"Petrolle followed instructions almost literally. For 60 seconds he backed away as best he could from Vogel's left. Then he began to plunge in. Some of his vicious rights found their mark.

"With a little less than a minute to go Vogel made the same mistake of which he had been guilty in the second round. He stepped out of a clinch with his guard low. This time Petrolle loosed a prodigious left which connected squarely on Vogel's jaw.

"Sammy, in bad shape, managed to get up at eight. For the next 30 seconds he took a terrific beating. Somehow he managed to remain perpendicular. When the final bell clanged he was fighting back once more. That last desperate rally by a beaten fighter thrilled the crowd as a last stand always does.

"When Joe Humphreys announced the verdict in favor of Vogel a chorus of booing broke out and lasted for several minutes. However, if the boys will think it over in the calm of the morning they will realize it was the proper verdict. The judges, on a rounds won basis, or any other, could have given only that decision."[15]

The crowd's demonstration was "a verbal tirade which continued for five minutes and prevented the introduction of the principals in the semi-final." Only the start of action in the next bout eventually quieted the throng.[16]

Not all reporters were happy with the verdict. The *New York Evening Journal*'s Frank O'Neill wrote that all but three of the 15,000 in attendance disagreed with the verdict and those three "were the judges and Vogel."[17]

Hype Igoe, writing in the *New York World*, agreed with the verdict, but challenged New York's system of scoring bouts on a strictly rounds basis:

"The crowd set up a dreadful din over the decision. There was not any question as to which man was the stronger and master at

---

[15] Wood, Wilbur, "Milligan Outpoints Zivic," *New York Evening Sun*, February 2, 1926, sports section. Hurley's instruction to "tin can" recalls a similar situation September 13, 1950, when Jake LaMotta knocked out Laurent Dauthuille with just 13 seconds remaining in the 15th and final round of a world middleweight title bout. LaMotta was behind on points and about to lose his title. For the first half of the round, Jake also "tin-canned" or "played opossum," as had Petrolle against Vogel, and then plunged into a last-gasp attempt to knock out Dauthuille. In LaMotta's case the tactic proved successful. Jake was well known for pretending to be hurt or tired and then turning the tables on his foe with an offensive surge. He would employ the strategy at almost any time in the fight, not only in the last round.

[16] "Petrolle Twice Floors Vogel But Loses Bout," *Hartford Daily Times*, February 20, 1926, sports section.

[17] O'Neill, Frank F., "Vogel-Petrolle Bout Hits Solons on Eye," *New York Evening Journal*, February 20, 1926, sports section.

the finish, but Vogel had the greater number of rounds to his credit despite these knockdowns and close shaves.

"That's why the system will always be in disfavor. It places no premium on a real finish as Petrolle staged here last night."[18]

After the Vogel bout, Hurley wired these words to the *Forum*: "Petrolle made the biggest hit of any fighter who has shown here in ten years and is in demand by every club in New York City. My opinion is, he didn't do himself justice. He seemed astounded at the crowd and was slow to get started. However, critics here say it was better than a win and he will be back at the Garden immediately after the Kaplan bout at Hartford. Vogel is rated as a wonderful fighter."[19]

On February 23, Hurley wired from New York he had closed a fight for LeRoy against ex-lightweight champion Jimmy Goodrich in Fargo on March 5. Both fighters had agreed to weigh not more than 137 pounds. Phil Terk, now officially Jack's partner and operations manager in Fargo, told the *Forum* tickets would go on sale at the Grand Rec immediately.[20]

Word of Petrolle's thrilling go with Vogel reached Hartford long before Billy stepped through the ropes to fight the city's hometown hero, world featherweight champion Louis (Kid) Kaplan, at the armory March 1, 1926.

For a full week, the Hartford press featured lengthy articles about Petrolle and "the Kid." The day after the Petrolle-Vogel fight, the *Hartford Daily Times* ran descriptions of that bout written by boxing scribes from three New York newspapers. The day before the Petrolle-Kaplan bout, the *Times* presented a half-page double-column article featuring predictions of its outcome by 13 writers from New York and Brooklyn.[21]

On the night of the fight, a reported 12,000 fans "stormed the State Armory ... far in excess of expectations," and created "a jam that held up the opening of the show more than an hour and necessitated heroic methods to get the crowd within the arena. Even with the emergency measures ... there were many who did not get inside for the events of the evening."[22]

---

[18] Igoe, Hype, "Winner All But Out in Last Round," *Fargo Forum*, February 20, 1926, sports section. Igoe, as "Special Correspondent," wired the article he had written for the *New York World* for publication in the *Forum*.

[19] "Hurley Says Express Was Below Form," *Fargo Forum*, February 21, 1926, sports section.

[20] Purcell, J. A., "New York Star Accepts Match at 137 Pounds," *Fargo Forum*, February 24, 1926, sports section.

[21] "Petrolle Twice Floors Vogel But Loses Bout," *Hartford Daily Times*, February 20, 1926, sports section. Compilation of 13 Opinions, *Hartford Daily Times*, February 28, 1926, sports section.

[22] "Kid Kaplan-Petrolle Bout Brings Deluge of Fight Fans to Armory," *Hartford Daily Times*, March 2, 1926, sports section. "6235 Pay $22,703 to See Armory Bouts," *Hartford Daily Times*, March 2, 1926, sports section. Even though a record number of over 9,000 people out of the 12,000 outside the armory were finally admitted inside, paying customers

Caught in the maelstrom were Hurley, trainer Jack Brady, and Petrolle. Prevented from entering the armory by the record crowd, the trio was forced to stand outside for more than two hours. Finally, at about 10 p.m., Jack called the promoter from a pay phone and said the fight was off unless they were admitted into the armory immediately. Even after police cleared a rear entrance, they almost had to fight their way inside with their fists.[23]

The next day, the *Forum*'s special correspondent reported that except for "the first round, which was an even affair and the third, in which Petrolle did his best fighting, Kaplan won all the way."[24]

The *Hartford Daily Courant* recounted that while "Petrolle kept to his feet throughout the fight, there were a few times when he was in dire distress ... From ringside it appeared that Kaplan was wide open, but Billy had decided early in the bout that caution was the better part of valor ... Sometimes it seemed that Petrolle was about to let loose that right hand of his but he always thought better of it; also the Kid simply kept him backing away so fast that he could not get set to let it go."

Unfortunately for Petrolle, he caught Kaplan in his best fight. Afterward, the Kid told reporters, "I never felt as good as I did in there tonight."

In addition, although Hurley did not offer an excuse at the time, he later told the *Forum* that Billy broke a bone in his right hand in the second round and would need several weeks of rest before he could resume training.[25]

Before returning to Fargo for the LeRoy-Goodrich contest, Hurley conferred with Jess McMahon. The Garden matchmaker previously had offered Petrolle a preliminary spot on a card a week after the Vogel fight, but Jack declined, suggesting Billy deserved a shot at top contenders Phil McGraw, Stanislaus Loayza, or Jack Bernstein in a main event.

---

counted for only 6,235 of a crowd which paid total gross receipts of $22,703. Kaplan's 30 percent share was $5,951, while Petrolle earned a flat guarantee of $2,500. Taxes and other expenses approximated $8,000, leaving $6,000 profit to be split on a 25%-75% basis between the state armory and the promoters.

Unpaid admissions, resulting from the issuance of free passes to 1,200 national guardsman, several hundred militiamen, and "the usual quota" of 335 complimentary ticket holders, together with many others who just "crashed the gate," limited the amount of receipts considerably.

The *Hartford Daily Times* observed after the fight that "if the crowd had been handled efficiently at the entrances ... it is likely that the gate would have shown at least 10,000 paid admissions" and gross "receipts of about $35,000, a profit of $10,000 plus."

[23] Purcell, J. A., "Rambling Through Sportsville," *Fargo Forum*, March 7, 1926, sports section.

[24] "Champion Has Best of Battle," *Fargo Forum*, March 2, 1926, sports section.

[25] Fight report, *Hartford Daily Courant*, March 2, 1926, sports section."Feather Champion to Meet Boxer Petrolle Knocked Out," *Hartford Daily Time*, March 3, 1926, p. 22. Purcell, J. A., "The Sportville Spotlight," *Fargo Forum*, March 6, 1926, sports section.

WHO WAS THAT MASKED MAN? 257

Louis (Kid) Kaplan defeated Petrolle at Hartford March 1, 1926.

Jimmy Goodrich, ex-lightweight king, lost to LeRoy March 5, 1926.

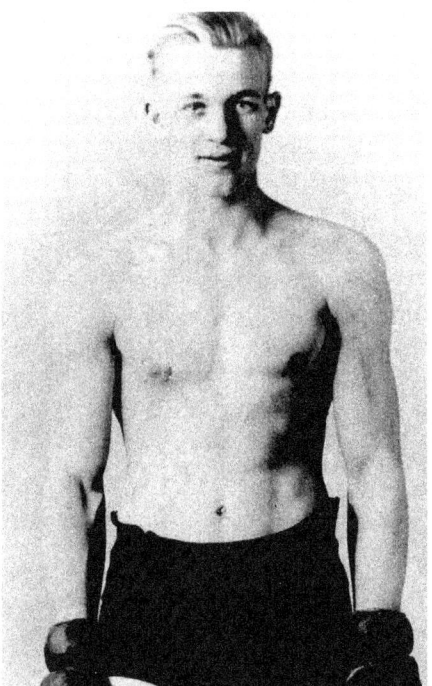

Earl Blue (left) lost to Johnny Salvator's Dago Joe Gans (right) in March 1926, but defeated Lou Hampton in a bout at Fargo on May 21.

This time Jess told Hurley "it is more than possible" he would "throw Billy in with one of the three in a main event" May 7, 1926, "immediately after Ringling Brothers circus leaves the Garden late in April."[26]

McMahon also said that if LeRoy could win as impressively over Goodrich on March 5 as Petrolle did over Wagner earlier, he also would be given a spot at the Garden. Jess told Jack, "Tell your boy to do his stuff and we'll take care of him as far as eastern ring engagements are concerned."[27]

Hurley arrived home the day before the LeRoy-Goodrich match, barely in time to handle final arrangements for the program and work as a second in LeRoy's corner. Just before the match, Jack told the *Forum* reporter a kayo win over former champion Goodrich would put Russie in line for a title bout against new lightweight champ Rocky Kansas.

On March 5, LeRoy defeated Goodrich, carrying seven of 10 rounds. Unfortunately, the bout, though hard-fought and thoroughly enjoyed by Fargo fans, failed to send any shock waves back to Eastern fight centers.

According to Purcell, the fight's most exciting moment came at the end when "Goodrich, realizing he was far behind, launched a vicious attack. LeRoy, whose temperament makes him fight when the going gets rough ... started pitching enough left hooks to give him a crooked arm for life."

Purcell continued, "One of these hard smashes landed square on Goodrich's stomach and the Buffalo fighter's hands dropped. Russie was quick to take advantage of the opening and he drove over a hard right to the face which sent Goodrich reeling across the ring."

The blow made Goodrich's "knees sag and he grabbed the ropes for support. Goodrich ducked a terrific left ... and then grabbed and wrestled like a madman to protect himself from another of those devastating wallops. Before Referee Kossick could pry them apart, the round and fight was ended ... It was a great finish and the fans were standing on their chairs pleading for a finishing wallop when the gong was tapped."[28]

The *Forum* reported attendance "was not as good as expected." LeRoy received nothing for his effort, and Hurley dropped about $1,000 on the card. The show was Jack's second consecutive unprofitable program in Fargo. Previously, he had barely broken even on the Petrolle-Wagner show after paying Billy less than one-fourth his normal purse.[29]

---

[26] "The Sportville Spotlight," March 6, 1926, *op. cit.* Madison Square Garden's relationship with the circus began in 1919 when the newly combined Ringling Brothers Barnum and Bailey Circus debuted at the second Garden building. When Tex Rickard took control of the Garden in 1920 he looked to the Ringlings for financial assistance and the family became a major investor in the Garden corporation. The circus has continued to have first call on the Garden's April dates from 1919 up to and including recent times.

[27] Report, *Fargo Forum*, February 25, 1926, sports section.

[28] Purcell, J. A., "Fargoan Carries 7 Rounds," *Fargo Forum*, March 6, 1926, sports section.

[29] Purcell, J. A., "The Sportville Spotlight," *Fargo Forum*, March 24, 1926, sports section.

After the Goodrich bout, Hurley attended to several matters which had been piling up during his trip to New York. Earl Blue's hand, broken in his October 1925 fight with Mark Moore, had completely healed, and now Blue was craving action. On March 17, 1926, Jack accompanied Earl to St. Paul where he lost a disputed six-round decision to Johnny Salvator's middleweight ace Dago Joe Gans. On March 26, they traveled to Green Bay, Wisconsin where Blue kayoed Glenn Clickner in one round.[30]

Jack also took time out to look over the latest crop of amateurs at his gym. Cecil (KO) Nelson, 15, and Eddie (Sach) Nelson, 18, had turned up shortly after their family moved to Fargo from Leonard, North Dakota. The brothers started working out in late December and were soon fully engaged as combatants on Phil Terk's weekly amateur shows.[31]

Sometime in February or March, a third brother showed up. Already well known locally as a star pitcher for Casselton, North Dakota's town baseball team, Lynn Nelson, age 21, had fought a few amateur bouts in 1924 and 1925 before moving to Fargo. Soon, his efforts caught Hurley's attention. Curious to see how good Lynn was, Jack showed him some moves, watched him box a few times, and was impressed.[32]

Hurley asked if Lynn was interested in becoming a fighter. The young athlete replied no, he had his heart set on playing baseball and was just staying in shape for the coming season. Besides, he didn't want to get the reputation as a roughneck because it might harm his career as a ballplayer.

Nelson's response brought to the surface an idea which had been brewing in Jack's mind for awhile. In 1921, a wrestler, covering his face with a silk mask and billing himself as "the Masked Marvel," had passed through Fargo. The wrestler challenged local grapplers and agreed to take off his mask and reveal his identity if defeated. The Masked Marvel hadn't been beaten in Fargo, but afterward he lost a match in Albert Lea, Minnesota.

The Marvel turned out to be Louis Pergantas of New Hampshire and he claimed to have been unbeaten in 42 matches before the Albert Lea affair. Although defeated, he had earned a tidy sum while the masquerade lasted.[33]

In addition, still fresh in the minds of Fargoans was an appearance a month earlier of "Masked Marvel X," a "former world's pocket-billiards champion" and contender "for the world's three-cushion billiards

---

[30] Purcell, J. A., "The Sportville Spotlight," *Fargo Forum*, March 20, 1926, sports section. Purcell. J. A. "Express May Get Contest with Morgan," *Fargo Forum*, sports section.

[31] U. S. Census, 1920. See various articles in *Fargo Forum* sports sections between January 1 and March 31, 1926.

[32] "Pitcher Lynn Nelson of Chiefs Passed Up Chance to Star as Boxer to Continue His Baseball Career," *Syracuse NY Herald-Journal*, May 28, 1941, sports section.

[33] "'Masked Marvel' Thrown by Mayre (sic)," *Fargo Forum*, January 11, 1921, sports section. The correct name of the wrestler who defeated Pergantas was actually Helmar Myre of Albert Lea, Minnesota.

Masked Marvel Lynn Nelson pitching for the Philadelphia A's, 1938.

championship." "X" had shown his wares to a full house in several exhibition matches against local champions at the Grand Rec in February.[34]

After listening to Nelson's reservations about appearing in public as a fighter, Hurley asked himself a question, "If 'the Masked Marvel' gimmick can work in wrestling and billiards, then why not boxing?" Jack ran his idea by Lynn who was amused and agreed to to give it at try.

Hurley's "Masked Marvel" debuted March 12, 1926. During the next six weeks, he had four fights. He won his first two bouts by knockouts in the second round. The masquerade ended in his third bout when Lynn removed his mask because it interfered with his breathing while still managing to win a four-round decision. Billed as "Lynn Nelson, 'Masked Marvel,'" but without a mask, he won his last bout in Fargo April 23, also by decision.[35]

Sometime around the beginning of Fargo's baseball season in early May, Lynn Nelson concluded his final workout at Hurley's gym, returned to his post as a pitcher in Fargo's Commercial League, and never boxed again.[36]

Nelson played pro baseball for 18 years, including seven years in the major leagues with the Chicago Cubs (1930, 1933-'34), the Philadelphia Athletics (1937-'39), and the Detroit Tigers (1940). In 1937, he hit .354 in 113 at-bats with four home runs, not only pitching, but also playing outfield and pinch-hitting. In 1938 and 1939, he was the Athletics' best pitcher, winning 20 games and losing 24 for a .456 winning percentage. Over the same period, the Athletics' winning percentage as a team was only .356.

Columnist Red Smith learned from Hurley that Nelson had been a boxer. Smith covered baseball for the *St. Louis Star* in 1930 and saw Lynn then. "When he joined the Cubs," Smith recalled, "he signed his name L. D. Nelson, so of course the baseball writers out there soon tagged him 'Line Drive' Nelson. You could say they called him that because of the way he hit, for he was a pinch-hitter who could really mangle a curve. But the painful truth probably is it was his pitching which inspired the nickname.

"... He was a gentle, quiet guy," Smith continued, "rather stockily built and a bit below average height. Not big, say a full-grown middleweight. He almost never had any trouble with anybody, and never did he talk about himself. He wasn't a guy to walk away from a fight; he just wasn't a guy to

---

[34] "Masked Marvel X Is Victor in Two Tests," *Fargo Forum*, February 19, 1926, sport section.

[35] "Masked Marvel KOs Al Johns in First," *Fargo Forum*, March 13, 1926, sports section. "Kowalski to Meet Masked Marvel," *Fargo Forum*, April 6, 1926, sports section. "Marvel Unmasks But Wins Battle Easily," *Fargo Forum*, April 10, 1926, sports section. "Nelson Earns Decision over Ted Citrowski," *Fargo Forum*, April 24, 1926, sports section.

[36] "Rookies, Veterans to Carry the Grand Pennant Burden," *Fargo Forum*, May 1, 1926, sports section. Baseball turnouts for Fargo's Commercial League teams were May 1. Nelson started 1926 with Steve Gorman's Grand Recreation "Grands." Before the season ended he would make a big jump by pitching one game for Kansas City in the American Association.

get involved. You could have been his friend for 20 years and never know he'd ever been a professional fighter."[37]

Nelson completed his major-league career with a lifetime batting average of .281 and a pitching record of 33 wins and 46 losses. His last season was in 1943 with Syracuse of the International League. He retired to Kansas City where he owned and operated a bar until his death on February 15, 1955, 9 days short of his 50th birthday.[38]

With boxing shut down at Madison Square Garden until May 1926, Hurley cast a hopeful eye toward the closer fight centers of St. Paul, Omaha, and Milwaukee. Over the next few months, Jack hoped to show his boxers in cities where he could receive straight guarantees and not have to worry about meager gate receipts in Fargo. Unhappily, the stars in the March skies of the Midwest were not in alignment with Hurley's agenda.

In St. Paul, matchmaker Jack Reddy's attempts to land Petrolle a bout with either Sammy Mandell or junior lightweight titleholder Tod Morgan fell through. Similarly, Reddy's efforts to secure LeRoy a fight with Johnny O'Donnell also were to no avail. A proposed match in Omaha for Billy against Morgan, Mike Ballerino, or Babe Ruth was never closed. Finally, Russie's match against Billy Bortfield in Milwaukee, scheduled for March 23, was canceled at the last minute due to a case of influenza.[39]

A disgruntled Hurley returned from St. Paul at the end of March and plopped into a cozy chair at the office of *Forum* sports editor Pat Purcell:

> "'Waddya' been doin','Hurley was asked.
> "'Waddya'think,' he replied venomously. 'I'm not a washing

---

[37] Smith, *op. cit.*

[38] Based on official statistics, Nelson's connection with Kansas City was strong and enduring. He pitched for the team from the end of 1926 through the 1929 season. In the 1929 season he was the starting pitcher for Kansas City in the final game of the "Little World Series," throwing a complete game in a winning 1-0 effort against the Rochester Red Wings. Future Hall-of-Famer Paul Derringer was the opposing pitcher in the championship game.

At Kansas City, he attracted Chicago Cubs' manager Joe McCarthy's attention with two stellar outings against the Cubs in exhibition games. McCarthy signed Nelson to his first major league contract, explaining, "Our fellows couldn't do a thing with him. He had the most 'swift' you ever saw and plenty else to round it out – change of pace and best of all, plenty nerve. He pitched right up to Hornsby and Hack and had 'em swinging like a blind heavyweight fighter."

During his long career, Nelson also had successful stints in the Pacific Coast League, the Southern Association, and the International League. Lynn won an additional 122 games as a minor-league pitcher, almost all of them for teams in the "high" minor-leagues.

[39] All articles in this note are by Purcell, J. A. and are from the *Fargo Forum*: "Victory Gives over Goodrich Gives Russie Battle," March 10, 1926, sports section; "Bortfield Is Ill; Go with LeRoy is Off," March 14, 1926, sports section; "Duluth Legion Makes Bid for Bout Between Petrolle-Kansas," March 17, 1926, sports section; "The Sportville Spotlight," March 20, 1926, sports section.

machine salesman. I sell fighters and right now business is rotten ... Every promoter in the country wants to use Billy Petrolle and all those who have heard of Russie LeRoy want him, but right now most of 'em refuse to show enough currency, and our days of boxing for our health are over.

"'Then, there's a mob of lightweight fighters who like to make people believe they can fight, but none of 'em want any of Billy's stuff. Jack Reddy tried hard to get someone to fight Bill in St. Paul ... but he couldn't even get a rise out of 'em. Then down in Omaha Jack Isaacson has burned up a small fortune in telephone calls trying to get someone to fight Billy and he got the same run-around those bums handed Reddy.

"'I spent enough to pay for the winter's coal trying to help both promoters make a suitable match and was on the way to the poorhouse when I got word that the LeRoy-Bortfield fight was called off. I hopped a rattler and made a quick getaway for home before something really did happen.

"'Don't ask what I intend to do. I'm going to stay put right here until Madison Square Garden reopens after the circus leaves in late April and then we're off for the East. If there's any Midwest promoters who can make a real match, I'm willing to talk business, but I'm going to spend the majority of my time getting Russie ready to go east, and will send a couple of bales of advertising on ahead to let them know we'll be there soon to get that crown worn by Rocky Kansas.'

"Here the interview ended, it being evident that the week spent in a telephone booth has not improved the genial kern's temper to any noticeable extent."[40]

In April, neither Hurley's luck nor his disposition would get any better. Proposed bouts for Petrolle in Duluth against lightweight champ Rocky Kansas and Sammy Vogel fell through. A match for LeRoy in St. Paul against Billy Shauers failed to materialize.[41]

On April 21, McMahon delivered the biggest blow of all. After a wire confirming Petrolle's May 7th engagement at the Garden, Jess changed his mind and wired again that he was unable to use Billy on that date after all.

McMahon's telegram left Hurley's carefully planned timetable in a shambles. Jack had been eager to send both Petrolle and LeRoy into action as often as possible before June 1 to get them ready for the important outdoor season. He had planned both of their itineraries around the Madison

---

[40] "Hurley Should Be Sick," *Fargo Forum*, March 16, 1926, sports section.
[41] Purcell, J. A., "Reddy Wants Russie to Mix with Shauers," *Fargo Forum*, March 31, 1926, sports section.

Square Garden May 7th date. Now he was being forced to consider less lucrative engagements just to keep his duo in fighting trim.[42]

Petrolle was in Sioux City on May 3 winning a hard-earned decision over tough veteran Joe Jawson. The next day, LeRoy, turned up in Minot, North Dakota, where he kayoed Perry Bliven in six rounds.

After evaluating requests for from several small clubs in Iowa, Hurley decided "he would rather show them in Fargo" before summer ended "than work at other places for short money." Unfortunately, bad luck continued to dog him even after lowering his sights and returning to Fargo.[43]

Hurley's first choice for Fargo was to match Billy in a return bout with Sammy Vogel on May 7. Just a few days after Jack's return from New York after signing Vogel on April 27, his manager, Pete Reilly, cancelled because Sammy contracted a cold. Jack then signed Tommy (Kid) Murphy for May 21, only to have him back out with a case of the grippe.[44]

A disheartened Hurley vowed to find Petrolle a foe for the May 21 show no matter what:

> "This is the worst break I've had in the boxing game. Murphy is sick. I know that, for I spent a pretty fair bankroll on long distance telephone checking ... I know fans will be disappointed, for they want to see Billy work. And, they are not half as disappointed as I am, for now I stand to lose more than $800. In fact, I cannot afford to call off the show and will get someone if I have to pay $1,000 more than any boxer has ever received for a fight in this state."[45]

Luckily, Hurley found Danny Cooney of Philadelphia available on short notice. Cooney was the perfect fighter to fill the auditorium. A year earlier he had won a convincing ten-round decision over LeRoy in Fargo. Fans knew without any doubt Danny would put Petrolle's skills to a stiff test.

The May 21st program also saw the return of Earl (Little Boy) Blue to Fargo after an absence eight months. After losing the decision to Dago Joe Gans in March, Blue had turned things around with two straight knockouts. Earl's opponent in the show's ten-round semifinal was Lou Hampton, of Trenton, New Jersey, who accompanied Cooney from Philadelphia.

In a bout Purcell described as "the greatest exhibition of fisticuffing Fargo has seen this season, or in any recent season ... up to the time of the untimely finish," Petrolle was declared the winner in the fourth round over

---

[42] "Petrolle Fails to Land Garden Bout," *Fargo Forum*, April 21, 1926, sports section.
[43] "Petrolle Fails to Land Gardens Bout," *op. cit.*
[44] "Vogel Cancels Bout with Petrolle Here," *Fargo Forum*, May 4, 1926, sports section. Purcell, J. A., "Card Will Be Staged on Friday," *Fargo Forum*, May 15, 1926, sports section.
[45] Purcell, *op. cit.*

Cooney when Danny landed two low punches which caused Billy to slip "to the floor, writhing in agony."

As the referee waved Cooney to his corner "Hurley leaped into the ring and announced that Petrolle did not want to win the fight on a foul if it were possible for him to recuperate enough in a few minutes to continue. After three minutes of rest, Petrolle was unable to leave the ring unassisted, and he was awarded the contest on a foul."

Prior to the foul, the fighters tore "at each other like ravenous lions and traded blow for blow until Cooney was forced to give ground." The action "brought out the wildest cheering the old auditorium has experienced in many a day. The gallery gods were hanging on the rails, while the $5 customers were barely able to keep in their seats. It was a very unsatisfactory ending ... but fans seemed to realize it was impossible for Petrolle to continue and they accepted the referee's decision without a dissenting murmur."[46]

In Purcell's opinion, "Petrolle's terrific smashes to the body had given him a decided advantage in the milling up to the time of the low blows." Some fans believed Cooney's low blows were intentional, but most thought Petrolle's left hook at the beginning of the fourth round hurt Danny and left him fighting more on instinct than anything else. Physicians explained the next day that the blows, which were very painful, had cramped Billy's groin muscles, making it temporarily impossible for him to use his legs.

In the ten-round semifinal bout Blue kayoed Hampton after 30 seconds of the third round "with one well directed right to the chin."

Two days later, Hurley and Petrolle boarded a Northern Pacific "rattler" and headed east. They would stop off in Milwaukee on May 24 to second LeRoy in a main event against Billy Bortfield. Then, after a short layover in Chicago, the trio would continue on to New York where Billy was scheduled to fight Sid Terris, the "East Side Phantom," on June 4 in a main event on the opening card of the outdoor season at Coney Island Stadium.[47]

Earl Blue would remain behind to fulfill a June 3rd commitment in Green Bay and then join them on the East Coast later in the month.

As a summer strategy, Hurley planned to concentrate on showing his fighters in the large fight centers around New York and Chicago. Jack would do his best to help them collect their fair shares of the bountiful harvest the boxing game was sure to yield during the outdoor season.

****

Only 2-1/2 months earlier, Hurley had returned to Fargo from his first eastern trip, optimistic about the prospect of enjoying a lucrative spring

---

[46] Purcell, J. A. "Low Blows End Great Mitt Bout," *Fargo Forum*, May 22, 1926, sports section.

[47] "Bill Petrolle Set to Leave for New York," *Fargo Forum*, May 23, 1926, sports section.

with his fighters in the Midwest. Events conspired to defeat these plans and the expected monetary haul never happened. Instead, His efforts devolved into an endless series of futile exercises, almost like a cat chasing its own tail.

Now, Hurley was anticipating his return to the East, not only because of its appeal as an exotic new place, but also as a refuge away from a home that was rapidly becoming too small to accommodate his growing ambition.

For Jack Hurley, the ties binding him to Fargo were slowly being loosened by the gradual but persistent pull of New York and its lure as a city of almost unlimited opportunity.

CHAPTER 14

FINDING THE GREAT WHITE WAY

You're a young guy visiting your first training camp outside New York City. You play a little bridge and the boys ask you to sit down and fill out a foursome. You're flattered to be asked. You take a seat and are introduced to Mr. Pete Reilly who you have heard is a shrewd operator and the manager of light heavyweight champion, Jack Delaney. Reilly is standing by watching the game.

What you don't know are things that the boys at the table do know. That Reilly is known, not only for his managerial ability, but also as the biggest practical joker in the business. And that he isn't at all particular who the fall guy happens to be. His specialty is kibitzing card games, and his reputation for being handy with implements other than just his fists, keeps most of his victims from getting very angry.

You sit down at the table and the phone rings. You answer it and there is no one there, but you wind up with a black ring around your ear from something planted in the receiver. Just about the time you are trying to concentrate on a hand, you receive a real call. On the other end of the line is a voice impersonating some well-known tough guy. He accuses you of doing something or other and threatens you with bodily harm if you are not out of the state within 24 hours. You explain there must be some mistake, but to no avail. The tough guy gives you a final warning and hangs up.

You're pretty upset by this time but decide to finish out the rubber. The boys are waiting. It's your deal. As you pick up the deck, a gadget explodes, and if you have a strong heart you only hit the ceiling. The boys notice your condition and ask if anything is wrong. You finally break down and tell the other members of your foursome about the threats and mention the man who made them. Being in on the play, they advise immediate action.

Nobody can agree on what to do. It would be suicide to defy the tough guy, and just as bad to call the police because you couldn't prove anything in court, and when the tough one was released, he'd get you sure. You are about to leave when Reilly comes to the rescue. He knows the underworld character well. In fact, they are just – like – that (holding two fingers close together). Reilly advises a trip to the city where he thinks he can square matters without bloodshed. His car is outside, and he will drive you.

That's okay by you. Anything to bring this incident to a peaceful settlement. So you are seated in the back seat, with a sympathizer on either side. Reilly steps on the starter and a bomb explodes, filling the car with smoke. Reilly moans and slumps over the wheel. Someone yells fire! You can't breathe, and try to get out, but every avenue of escape is blocked by the hysterical men on either side of you.

When they are sure you are a physical and mental wreck, they tell you it was all in fun.

I've been through this mill and have been waiting to see some new hands run the gauntlet, but by the looks of things I'll be waiting a long time.[1]

– Jack Hurley

****

Christened variously "the Roaring '20s," "the Jazz Age," "the Prohibition Era," "the Golden Age of Sports," and "the Lawless Decade," the years from 1920 to 1929 spawned the most dramatic series of social changes the United States had ever experienced.

Fueled by the recent war experience, a booming economy, increased urbanization, and such potent inventions as radio, the phonograph, talking pictures, and the automobile, the 1920s produced a revolution in social mores which caused young people to distrust the values of their parents and experiment with new lifestyles. Nowhere in the country were these changes more evident than on the streets of New York City.

With a rapidly increasing population already numbering more than six million, New York City in the first decade after World War I became a Hercules unchained, an aroused giant, newly awakened from the repressive Victorian Era and the burdens of war, with an appetite which fed on excitement produced by the novel, the unusual, and the controversial.

The puritanical hand of the past, which reached out in the form of Prohibition and attempted to reverse the tide of social change, only served to fuel the fires of rebellion even more. The passage of the 18th Amendment and the Volstead Act, enacted on the eve of the Great War, already seemed but a distant memory and an outdated legacy of an antiquated generation.[2]

No matter where a visitor might go, he or she could see, hear, and almost touch the electric energy which enveloped the city. New York's vibrancy seemed to operate as a huge magnetic field which summoned the country's most ambitious, creative, and energetic people and drew them to its center.

Even as the shoe leather of its natives was wearing thin on the pavement, the streets of New York took on altogether different meanings to millions of Americans who had never seen them. To these cousins from the country's

---

[1] Hurley, Jack, "Shadow Boxing," *Fargo Forum*, September 6, 1936, sports section. The anecdote has been edited and some connecting text has been added to fit the context of the present story. Hurley wrote the piece in September 1936 when he was in New York to cover the Braddock-Schmeling fight for his syndicated boxing column. Due to a combination of politics and economics, the bout had just been canceled. At the beginning of the column (not included here), Jack expresses regret about the cancellation because he was looking forward to catching up on his card-playing at the training camps. He also was sorry he would not be able to see any practical jokes played on new victims similar to the one (presumably) played on him at his first big-time camp.

[2] The 18th Amendment to the United States Constitution banned the manufacture, sale, transportation, and consumption of alcohol in the United States of America. The Volstead Act was the law passed by Congress to implement and enforce the 18th Amendment.

heartland, names like "Tin Pan Alley," "Lenox Avenue," and "Broadway" were not so much designations of places as descriptions of states of mind.[3]

These streets, and the opportunities they presented, served as beacons marking the spots where success was measured. During the 1920s, tens of thousands of people from all corners of the country flocked to New York to follow their dreams. It was Broadway more than any other thoroughfare which came to be regarded as the center of popular culture in the 1920s.

In the era just preceding World War I, Broadway was a street of elegant theaters, upscale restaurants, and luxurious hotels catering to an elite clientele. Many of these enterprises had been funded by revenue from the sale of vintage wines and other alcoholic beverages.

Prohibition put these sedate establishments out of business. The decade found Broadway's fancy hotels and fine cafes replaced by "a raucous jungle of chop-suey restaurants, hotdog and hamburger shops, garish nightclubs, radio stores equipped with blaring loudspeakers, cheap haberdasheries, fruit juice stands, dime museums, candy and drugstores, speakeasies, gaudy movie houses, flea circuses, penny arcades, and lunch counters."[4]

This Broadway, created in Prohibition's image, never shut down. Bright lights from nightclubs, theaters, movie palaces, restaurants, and various 24-hour joints shimmered like the summer sun all night long. At 42nd Street, a lighted sign on the Times Square Building flashed the news continuously.

The Paramount Theater, featuring first-run movies and floor shows, occupied almost a full block of space on Broadway from 43rd to 44th Street, with the city's first Walgreen's Drug Store on the corner and the Astor Hotel and Child's Restaurant across the street. Across from the Paramount was Loew's State Theater, which offered M-G-M movie debuts; around the corner the Rialto featured the latest Westerns; and up the street toward 43rd the Palais Royale boasted symphonic jazz by the Paul Whiteman Orchestra.

If one was not averse to a stroll up the famous "Great White Way" through a bevy of theaters, shops, and restaurants, he or she could walk to 49th and drop in at Lindy's, Broadway's most famous restaurant. Holding court in a far corner every night until the wee hours of the morning, after making his 7 p.m. deadline, would be Damon Runyon, star columnist for

---

[3] "Tin Pan Alley" was a nickname given West 28th Street between Broadway and 6th Avenue where many popular music publishers had their offices. As such, the name came to be a generic term describing the business of publishing American popular music. "Lenox Avenue" is a street in Harlem extending from Central Park North (110th Avenue) to 147th Avenue. The street was at or near the location of many famous jazz clubs where the greatest black jazz musicians of the era entertained primarily white audiences. As such, the term "Lenox Avenue" came to be associated with the place where the hottest of the hot jazz of the 1920s was played. "Broadway," as used in the popular culture, refers to that section of Broadway located on the west side of midtown Manhattan running from 42nd to 53rd Streets. "Broadway" was and still is famous as the theater and amusement center of New York City.

[4] Ashbury, Herbert, *The Great Illusion*, in Perrett, Geoffrey, "America in the Twenties: A History," (Simon and Schuster, New York, 1982), p. 177.

William Randolph Hearst's flagship newspaper, the *New York American*. Runyon would invariably be talking shop with other famous newsmen, like Walter Winchell, or else be researching his next day's column.[5]

Runyon's research consisted of observing patrons, listening in on conversations, and chatting with Lindy's regulars, comprised in large part of gamblers, politicians, fight managers, entertainers, lawyers, showgirls, and mob figures. One of the most fertile fields for his studies was the table of Arnold Rothstein, the most famous gambler and "fixer" of his day.

Rothstein used his table at Lindy's as his office. At any given moment, depending on who was looking to place a bet or influence an outcome, his guests might include such renowned mob figures as Owney Madden, Larry Fay, Dutch Schultz, and Lucky Luciano.

Runyon would later become wealthy recycling what he learned during these seemingly misspent hours into short stories and Hollywood movie scripts. The characters appearing in those works, all based on gamblers and mob members he met in Lindy's, became archetypes for virtually every gangster movie produced in the 1930s and 1940s.[6]

And so, in late spring of 1926, in the midst of New York's most tumultuous era, a couple of North Dakota dream-seekers stepped off the train at Grand Central Station, hailed a cab, and headed toward Broadway's Great White Way in search of fame and fortune.

Although Hurley and Petrolle had been to New York when Billy fought Sammy Vogel at the Garden in February, the present trip was more than just a visit. Jack did not tell the folks back in Fargo, but he had plans for an extended stay. To that end, he had arranged to share an office on Broadway and was expecting to make it a permanent headquarters.

Hurley's office was in Room 305 of the Publicity Building at 1576 Broadway. He was invited to share the space by his friend, Billy McCarney. The "old professor" and his new partner, Joe Jacobs, had begun renting the office earlier in the year and already were well established there.[7]

In-as-much as the office had room for another desk and a couple of extra chairs, the arrangement suited everybody. A phone had been installed previously and, as the three tenants did not have a secretary, an extra body to answer calls gave them more time to take care of matters outside the office. In any event, since fight managers tended to be on the road much of the time, it was rare they all would be there at the same time, anyway.

---

[5] Davis, Charlie, *That Band from Indiana*, (Mathom Publishing Co., Oswego, New York, 1982), pp. 113-118. "The Great White Way" is a nickname for "Broadway." The nickname first appeared in the 1880s when the street became one of the first in the United States to have electric light posts. Later in the early 1900s and thereafter, the name took on a new meaning which signified the illumination of the street from the millions of theater marquis and billboard lights in the area.

[6] Clark, Tom, *The World of Damon Runyon*, (Harper & Row, Publishers Inc., New York, New York, 1978), pp. 171-193.

[7] Advertisements, *The Ring*, January, 1927, p. 39, 53.

WE WISH EVERBODY A HAPPY AND BETTER NEW YEAR IN 1928

BILLY McCARNEY   **JOE JACOBS**

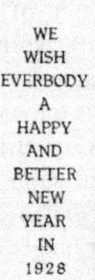

New York's busiest and most dependable fistic office herewith extends to all the promoters of the country, also foreign promoters, a hearty invitation to phone, wire or write. We are always on the job, day and night, ready to aid you. It is our pleasure to do everything in our power to help you put over your pet show.

We Are Booking the Following Boxers Out of This Office:—
Frankie Genaro, Flyweight; Joe Glick, Junior Lightweight; Jack McVey, Welter-Middleweight; Solly Seaman, Lightweight; Sammy Vogel, Junior Welterweight; Andre Routis, of France, Featherweight; Eddie "Kid" Wagner, Lightweight; Jack McFarland, Welterweight; Phil Krug, Middleweight.

We can help you in your negotiations for Jack Delaney and Mickey Walker, the ring's most Colorful Battlers

PHONE   WIRE   WRITE

McCARNEY & JACOBS

1576 Broadway   Phone Lackawanna 7905   New York City

Jack Hurley, circa 1926.   **The McCarney-Jacobs firm with whom Jack shared the office on Broadway.**

The Great White Way, Broadway above Times Square at night.

From Hurley's point of view, the opportunity to be located "where the action was" and to work alongside two of the most well-connected managers in the business was a stroke of good fortune. In addition, he was fortunate to make his move to New York when he did.

Professional boxing in the summer of 1926 was enjoying a popularity even its most ardent supporters could not have predicted when it became legal in 1921. The sport was in the middle of a Golden Age, flourishing at all levels as it never had before and never would again. Opportunities to see prize fights in New York City abounded both at neighborhood boxing clubs and at the huge outdoor championship shows presented periodically throughout the summer at the city's major-league baseball stadiums.

The center of activity was, of course, Madison Square Garden in downtown Manhattan, where promoter Tex Rickard and matchmaker Jess McMahon staged bouts each Thursday. The third structure to bear the name, the facility had opened just six months earlier in November 1925, at a new site located over a mile uptown from the prior Garden buildings and much closer to Broadway and the theatrical district.

Rickard was the moving force in organizing construction of the new building, which cost $5,650,000. Ticket-broker Mike Jacobs helped Tex raise $125,000 to get the project going, but once the land was secured a syndicate of six wealthy investors put up most of the balance. The structure took less than a year to build, and Rickard was installed as the corporation's first president with a 20-year contract calling for a $30,000 per year salary.[8]

Altogether, New Yorkers had a choice of at least 16 sites which featured boxing every night except Sunday. In Manhattan, five promoters in addition to the Garden held shows on a regular basis. Elsewhere, Long Island and Brooklyn boasted three venues apiece, the Bronx two, and Queens and Harlem one each. In addition, across the Hudson River, just a 20-minute subway ride from Manhattan, Laddy Kusy presented boxing on Mondays at his Laurel Garden Athletic Club in Newark, New Jersey. In Jersey City, George Mulligan presented semi-weekly shows at Boyle's 30 Acres.[9]

Despite all this competition, however, Rickard continued to set the pace at the Garden. The old Klondiker's two most profitable indoor shows during the summer of 1926 were the Joe Dundee-Mickey Walker fight, which drew a crowd of 10,507 paying $50,168, and the Tiger Flowers-

---

[8] Fleischer, Nat, *50 Years at Ringside* (Fleet Publishing Corp., New York, NY, 1958), p. 106. Samuels, Charles, *The Magnificent Rube* (McGraw-Hill Book Co., Inc., New York, NY, 1957), p. 270.

[9] Specifically, boxing was presented on a regular basis during portions of 1926 at the following venues: in Manhattan at the Lenox Sporting Club, the Pioneer Athletic Club, the 22nd Engineer's Regiment, the 9th Regiment, and the 102nd Medical Regiment; in Long Island at the Steeplechase Arena and the Long Beach and Dexter Park stadiums; in Brooklyn at the New Broadway Arena, the New Ridgewood Grove Sporting Club, and Coney Island Stadium; in the Bronx at the Columbia Sporting Club and the New York Velodrome; in Queens at the Queensboro Stadium; and in Harlem at the Commonwealth Athletic Club.

Harry Greb rematch for which 15,376 people contributed $75,176.

Even so, promoter Charlie Henderson and matchmaker Jack Epstein at Coney Island Stadium, and Si Flaherty and Tom McArdle at Queensboro Stadium, were giving Rickard a run for his money. In 1926, Henderson and Epstein established Coney Island as the lightweight division's leading venue. From May through September, the club featured a steady diet of such exciting ringmen as Sid Terris, Ace Hudkins, Stanislaus Loayza, Ruby Goldstein, Ray Miller, Eddie Anderson, Phil McGraw and Joe Glick.

It was at Coney Island that Billy Petrolle made his first New York appearance during the summer season. As luck would have it, the club had hired Billy McCarney to help with publicity. When Henderson wanted to feature Sid Terris in a main event, McCarney suggested Petrolle as an opponent. The Terris-Petrolle bout ended up as an artistic and financial success, with 13,327 paid admissions grossing $34,937.

Coney Island's most popular fighter in 1926, however, was Ace Hudkins. The Nebraska Wildcat's bout with Stanislaus Loayza August 6 drew 18,000 people, with a gate of $40,000. On August 27, Ace's fight against Phil McGraw pulled in 14,000 fans, with receipts tallying $37,500.

At Queensboro Stadium, Flaherty and McArdle concentrated most of their effort on the middleweight, featherweight, and bantamweight divisions. The club's stellar attractions for the season included Maxie Rosenbloom, Dave Shade, Tony Canzoneri, Louis (Kid) Kaplan, Bushy Graham, and Jack Bernstein. Queensboro's shows drew 7,000 to 10,000 fans and gates of $15,000 to $23,000 throughout the summer.[10]

Even as he successfully defended his supremacy as New York's leading purveyor of weekly fistic fun, Rickard's status as the city's preeminent promoter of huge outdoor shows was facing a serious challenge. These shows, presented in any one of the city's three big-league ballparks during the summer, represented a much greater potential for profit than the weekly shows. The man who stepped forward to challenge Rickard in this market was an unlikely 41-year-old banker named Humbert J. (Jack) Fugazy.

Fugazy was the son of Louis V. Fugazy, who emigrated to the United States as a youth from Genoa in 1865. During his working years, Louis amassed a fortune in his adopted country as a banker. In later years, the elder Fugazy became a philanthropist in the Italian community and served

---

[10] General information about boxing clubs was gleaned from the May through October 1926 sports pages of *The New York Sun* (Wilbur Wood, boxing writer), *The New York Evening Journal* (Sid Mercer, boxing writer), *The New York Telegram* (George Underwood, boxing writer), and *The New York Evening Post* (William Morris, boxing writer). The identities of the promoters and matchmakers were obtained from those same newspaper sources and from advertisements in *The Ring*, January, 1927. Information about attendance and gate receipts were obtained from those same newspaper sources and the *Ring Record Book.* Fleischer, Nat, *The Ring Record Book and Boxing Encyclopedia, 1955 Edition* (The Ring Book Shop, New York, New York, 1955), pp. 46-48, 53-54.

as president of the Italian Hospital, which he co-founded.[11]

As a young man, Humbert, even while working in his father's business, tried his hand at boxing. Fighting under the name of Jack Lee, he was good enough in his 11th pro bout to defeat the famous Kid Broad. When his father found out about this second career, he warmly congratulated his son, but nevertheless made him choose between boxing and banking. Humbert chose to return to the bank even though he still was undefeated as a boxer.

In 1925, the officials at the Italian Hospital decided to raise money for its charity fund by staging a boxing show. Humbert had remained interested in boxing and volunteered to serve as promoter for the hospital's big event.

The card turned out to be the most successful charitable promotion in boxing history as well as one of the most entertaining all-star fight cards ever seen in New York. On July 2, 1925, a Polo Grounds crowd of nearly 50,000 people, paying almost $400,000, saw middleweight champion Harry Greb win a savage 15-round brawl from welterweight king Mickey Walker.

In other bouts, welterweight Dave Shade kayoed light heavyweight Jimmy Slattery in three rounds, and Jack Dempsey's "black nemesis," Harry Wills halted Charlie Weinert in two. Weinert's manager was Billy McCarney. The card netted the hospital $100,000. It also reignited Humbert's interest in boxing and gave him instant credibility as a promoter.

Encouraged by the success of the prior year's show, Fugazy entered the boxing business in a big way in 1926. Although never destined to run a year-around club, he proved adept at promoting summer bouts in large open-air arenas. Before the end of the decade, he would present approximately 20 outdoor shows, almost all of them successful.[12]

Fugazy promoted four shows at Ebbets Field during the 1926 outdoor season. On June 3, 15,000 fans paid $45,000 to view Tod Morgan's successful defense of his junior lightweight title by a six-round kayo against Kid Sullivan. An estimated 18,000 people contributed $50,000 on August 20 to watch Andre Routis of France earn a 10-round decision over Cowboy Eddie Anderson. On October 12, 21,097 fans paid $133,514 to see Jack Sharkey win on a foul in the 13th round against Harry Wills.

It was Fugazy's promotion of the Paul Berlenbach-Jack Delaney light-heavyweight title fight on July 16, however, which alerted the public that Rickard had a true competitor in the presentation of major outdoor spectacles. For that bout, 49,146 fans jammed Ebbets Field and paid $461,789 to see Delaney win a 15-round decision and the title.

The card was the year's most successful boxing show in New York. By contrast, Tex's lone outdoor promotion on June 10, featuring Berlenbach's defense against Young Stribling, realized receipts of "only" $213,387.[13]

---

[11] "Louis V. Fugazy, Banker, Dies at 93," *New York Times*, August 7, 1930, p. 17.

[12] "Humbert Fugazy, Boxing Promoter," *New York Times*, April 8, 1964, p. 43.

[13] See note 9.

Ace Hudkins was a New York headliner in 1926.

Humbert Fugazy staged outdoor bouts for an Italian hospital charity.

Rickard signs Tunney to fight Dempsey. Tex's assistant, Richard Dunn is behind Tex. Tunney's manager, Billy Gibson, is right of Gene.

Although Rickard ran a distant second to Fugazy in New York, he was by no means losing his grip as the world's leading boxing promoter. The reason for his apparent "decline" was his quest for bigger game, which led him to a site outside New York. The game he sought was a heavyweight title bout which would yield him another million-dollar gate.

In the three years since his knockout of Luis Firpo in 1923, heavyweight titleholder Jack Dempsey had been living life as boxing's most celebrated champ to the fullest. Moving to California to work in movies, Dempsey bought a $100,000 hacienda where, in between European holidays, he spent his time wining, dining, and wooing Hollywood starlets.

In 1925, Dempsey married one of them, Estelle Taylor, and after a few months of wedded bliss started to think about returning to real life. He was getting restless and was starting to heed the calls of reporters urging him to either return to the ring or retire. He decided to return. He was not ready to give up his championship, at least not without a fight.

Dempsey agreed to defend his title in 1926. Rickard originally planned to stage the show at New York's Yankee Stadium. However, when Tex rejected logical contender Harry Wills in favor of Gene Tunney because Wills was a black man, New York's department of licensing refused to grant Dempsey a license. Rickard's response was quick and direct. The next day, August 18, he announced he was moving the bout to Philadelphia.[14]

Tex claimed he refused to make the Wills match because "tremendously powerful figures in Washington insist that only white men can fight for the heavyweight championship." Oddly enough, these powerful people, if they existed, forgot to tell the New York licensing authorities about this policy.[15]

True to his word, in little more than one month, Rickard successfully completed the monumental task of moving the promotion to Philadelphia. On September 23, 120,757 boxing fans saw Tunney win the heavyweight title from Dempsey at Sesquicentennial Stadium in the pouring rain. Gate receipts of $1,895,733 surpassed the prior record set by another Rickard-Dempsey promotion, the 1921 Dempsey-Carpentier fight, by $106,495.[16]

Though he lost the battle with Fugazy in New York, Rickard had moved the battlefield to Philadelphia and retained his position as the world's leading boxing promoter.

Meanwhile, even as he was adjusting to New York, Hurley was avoiding the pitfalls which confronted most newcomers to the local fistic scene.

McCarney's offer to share his office was by no means the only benefit Hurley received as a result of his friendship with the "old professor." Far more important to his pocketbook, and also to his future reputation and

---

[14] Roberts, Randy, *Jack Dempsey, The Manassa Mauler*, (Louisiana State University Press, Baton Rouge and London), pp. 193-219.

[15] Kahn, Roger, *A Flame of Pure Fire, Jack Dempsey and the Roaring -'20s*, (Harcourt Brace & Company, New York, San Diego, & London, 1999), p. 384.

[16] Fleischer, *The Ring Record Book and Boxing Encyclopedia, 1955 Edition*, p. 51.

well-being, was the shelter Billy provided him from a pernicious local practice which plagued almost every new arrival – the unofficial requirement that every new fighter must have an "Eastern representative."

An "Eastern representative" was a New York manager who had connections with local promoters, matchmakers, and gym owners. Boxers arriving without such a representative normally were shut out of big clubs like Madison Square Garden, Coney Island and the Queensboro Stadium. These fighters had to break in at the small neighborhood clubs. [17]

If, after a few bouts, the fighter became an attraction at a small club, his manager inevitably would be approached by one or more interested "Eastern representatives." If the newly arrived manager was lucky, these representatives might bid up the price against one another to buy the fighter's contract from the manager, either in whole or in part. Alternatively, the newcomer might be forced to surrender partial or full ownership of his fighter's contract in exchange for little or even no money at all.

In either circumstance, a part or all of the consideration received by the manager and the fighter would be a promise to appear at a major club like Madison Square Garden or the Coney Island Stadium. In each case, the boxer and manager had little choice but to work with one of these representatives, if they wanted to advance their prospects in New York.

Despite popular legend, these transfers of ownership, at least in the 1920s, usually occurred without bodily harm. Ordinarily, the prospect of being frozen out of lucrative bouts in the big clubs was sufficient to convince a manager and his boxer to cooperate.

---

[17] The term "Eastern representative" was used by Jimmy McLarnin when asked about mob influence in boxing during a video interview taped for airing on a television show in Italy. The author was provided a copy of the interview by boxing historian J. J. Johnston.

Oddly enough, McLarnin was one of the few boxers who did not have to enlist the aid of an "Eastern representative." The reason for this is due to a combination of circumstances. First, Jimmy was already an established attraction in Los Angeles and Chicago when he came to New York in 1928. His knockout of featherweight champ Kid Kaplan in Chicago had already made him a sensation before came to the city. As a result, he was able to bypass the usual protocol by signing directly with Rickard himself for his debut at Madison Square Garden against the Jewish idol of the era, Sid Terris. McLarnin knocked out Terris in sensational fashion in the first round and instantly became the Irish idol of the age. Due to Jimmy's immense popularity as a drawing card, Rickard, who was powerful in his own right, was not going to let local custom stand in the way of the large profits an attraction like McLarnin would realize. Secondly, Jimmy was managed by a middle-aged Englishman named Pop Foster. Foster had literally grown up fighting in his father's boxing booths in England in the 1890s, had managed fighters since the 1900s, and, as an older enlistee, had been wounded in World War I and hospitalized from a shrapnel injury for two years. Foster was not a man who was intimidated by the mob. Foster was, in fact, approached by "Eastern representatives" after the Terris fight, and he told them to "go to hell." Finally, Jimmy was a handsome (his nickname was "Babyface"), softspoken, personable young man who immediately captivated reporters. Due to McLarnin's popularity and also to the respect Foster commanded, any incident regarding the health of either would likely have attracted too much attention for anyone to take enforcement action against them.

Since it did not affect their bottom line, New York promoters went along with the system. The promoters had to rely on local managers to provide them with boxing talent on a day-to-day basis, sometimes on short notice. Doing business with men with whom they were familiar simplified their tasks. Local boxing writers viewed the managers as friends and relied upon them for information, so they likewise did not challenge the practice.

The New York boxing commission, busy regulating such innocuous practices as over-weight non-title matches and flat monetary guarantees for boxers in lieu of supposedly inflationary percentages, appeared oblivious to what was going on. In any event, even if the conduct came to its attention, it is understandable the commission would decline to interfere with an arrangement that was so favorable to managers from its own state.

Nevertheless, these unfair practices had an adverse effect on the newcomers in particular and on the sport in general. An out-of-town manager was harmed because the underlying element of coercion inherent in the arrangement made it certain he would not receive full compensation for the transfer of ownership to the local representative, if he received any at all. Additionally, the local man's share of the purse generally came out of the visiting manager's percentage rather than the fighter's.

The manager also lost control over decisions a manager normally made. In many cases, he no longer retained authority to negotiate the size of his fighter's purse or the selection of his foes, at least for bouts in New York.

Often, the out-of-town manager either became disgusted and left on his own or was pushed out of the picture altogether. On the other hand, some representatives liked working with the manager, who knew the fighter and continued to take care of his daily needs. The original manager usually accompanied the fighter to bouts outside New York, allowing the local man to remain in the city.

The boxers were harmed because they were deprived of the services of their manager of first choice. The original manager often had been with the fighter from the beginning and had charted the prior course of his career. It was rare that an "Eastern representative" looked after a fighter's interests with as much care or independence as his original manager.

The greatest harm resulting, however, was the damage done to boxing itself. By virtue of this system, a window was opened through which organized crime was first able to infiltrate boxing's organizational structure.

Although boxing prior to the 1920s produced its share of wheelers and dealers, it had been virtually devoid of criminal masterminds. By and large, the underworld operated on the sport's periphery, its presence limited to gamblers who sometimes influenced the outcome of specific bouts by fixing fights either with bribes, threats or, on occasion, even deeds of physical violence. These men were not boxing men per se, but instead were greedy opportunists who used the sport to illegally enrich themselves.[18]

Prohibition and its fusion with the "Eastern representative" scheme changed all this, however. Along with rotgut booze, lavish nightclubs, speakeasies, and hot jazz, another of the era's gifts to the Roaring '20s was mob racketeering. The rackets generated an abundance of cash from sales of bootleg liquor which, coupled with the freewheeling atmosphere of the times, made it natural for mobsters to seek out interesting forms of legitimate investments to launder money. Boxing was a perfect vehicle for a sports-minded racketeer to invest and enjoy his money at the same time.

Compared to activities like bootlegging, gambling, drug-dealing, prostitution, and extortion, money earned in boxing was as clean as yesterday's freshly washed table linen.

With the "Eastern representative" system already in place, it was easy for a nouveau-riche crime baron to become an owner of successful fighters. Instead of developing them from the ground up, a racketeer could move in on out-of-town managers and, working through local men, buy interests in fully developed prospects at bargain, coercion-deflated prices.

In the 1920s, New York boxing's most powerful mobster was Owney Madden. Born in Leeds, England in 1891, Madden emigrated to the U. S. as a ten-year old in steerage with his sister on the S. S. Teutonic. His widowed mother had made the trip earlier and then sent for her children when she could afford passage. Within a year, Owney joined a gang, called "the Gophers," and became known as a good man to have on your side in a street fight, and as being especially handy with a lead pipe and gun.

In 1914, Madden was arrested for killing one Patsy Doyle, a member of a rival gang called the "Hudson Dusters," and sentenced for 20 years to Sing Sing prison. He was released on parole in 1923. Known as "Owney the Killer," Madden soon set up an organization bootlegging beer on the west side of Manhattan in the "Hell's Kitchen" area. His staple was a product known on the streets as "Madden's No. 1 Beer."

Madden used his skills as enforcer and merciless muscleman to work his way into other organizations. In 1924, he partnered with Big Bill Dwyer, a former adversary who specialized in bootlegging hard liquor and who enlisted Owney's help to defend his turf and police some of the more recalcitrant members in his network.[19]

---

[18] The discussion about the "Eastern representative" is derived from the author's study of the following New York daily newspapers from 1926 through 1932: *New York Sun, New York Daily Mirror, New York Evening Journal, New York Evening Post, New York World, New York Evening Graphic, New York Daily News,* New *York Herald Tribune, New York World Telegram, New York American, New York Times, Brooklyn Citizen, Brooklyn Daily News,* and *Brooklyn Daily Eagle*.

[19] English, T. J., *Paddy Whacked: The Untold Story of the Irish Gangster,* (Harper Collins, 2005), pp. 117-122.

Owney also formed an alliance with another rival, Big Frenchy De Mange, with whom he established some of the most famous and glamorous nightspots of the era, including the Cotton Club, the Stork Club, the Club Abbey and the Silver Slipper.

Known by the more elegant title of "the Duke of the West Side," Madden brought a veneer of pretentious refinement to the otherwise sordid business of organized crime. Steadfastly maintaining sedate personal habits and a contrived old-world accent, he was the first mobster to wear expensive suits and require his associates to do likewise. His innate sense of style was displayed further by the lush decor gracing his nightclubs and "the strict decorum and studied elegance expected of both staff and customers."[20]

By 1929, Madden owned shares in at least 20 fighters. Managers fronting for Owney included such old boxing hands as Bill Duffy, Pete (the Goat) Stone, Joe Gould, Dave (Schnozzleheimer) Brown, Frank Bachman, and Walter (Good Time Charlie) Friedman.

Fighters who fell under Owney's mostly benevolent patronage included champions like Phil Rosenberg, Maxie Rosenbloom, Bob Olin, Jackie Fields, and Jimmy Braddock; and top contenders such as Ace Hudkins, Leo Lomski, Archie Bell, Phil KO Kaplan, Dave Shade, Kid Francis, Earl Mastro, Harry Smith, Billy Townsend, and Ray Miller.[21]

Madden was also said to hold an interest in Primo Carnera along with Bill Duffy. Carnera won the heavyweight title in 1933 under suspicious circumstances. According to Primo's biographer, Frederic Mullally, at least 16 of the giant Italian's first 23 bouts in the U. S. were fixed. Madden later denied owning any part of Carnera's contract, claiming all he ever did was lend Duffy funds to bring Primo over from Italy when Duffy was broke.[22]

Owney was a regular at Madison Square Garden fights, always sitting in the same first-row seat on the Eighth Avenue side of the ring between Frenchy De Mange and Big Bill Dwyer. He was the type of boxing fan who lived and died with each blow thrown. As one observer put it, he "faints, ducks and rides with the blows, just as if he were in the ring."

Madden's motive for owning fighters was more for fun than profit. Cronies claimed he was a sucker when it came to helping fighters, and that he lost a small fortune to them in unpaid loans. Even though he was highly visible at ringside, Owney tried to avoid publicity in connection with the fighters he owned. Apart from his skillful use of local representatives to acquire his fighters, he rarely, if ever, utilized ruthless tactics in boxing which he so readily employed in his other endeavors.[23]

---

[20] Jerving, Ryan, contributor; Wintz, Cary D. and Finkelman, Paul, editors, *Encyclopedia of the Harlem Renaissance*, (Routledge, 2004).

[21] Parker, Dan, "Madden Set-up for Pugs," *New York* Daily *Mirror*, sports pages.

[22] Mullally, Frederic, *Primo, the Story of 'Man Mountain' Carnera*, (Robson Books, 1991), pp. 54-63.

[23] Parker, *op. cit.*

If managing fighters was a hobby for Madden, it was a bread-and-butter business for other New York managers. The man who developed "the local representative" gambit to high art and really made it pay was Pete Reilly.

A Brooklyn native born in 1889, Reilly played pro baseball as a young man in the Georgia State and Eastern leagues. After his playing days were over, he continued to live the sporting life and purchased his first boxer in the summer of 1923 from Connecticut boxing promoter Al Jennings for $900. Jennings originally harbored great hopes for his protege, but lost interest because the youngster could not seem to win the big ones.

Reilly learned the ins-and-outs of boxing quickly and had good luck from the start. In three years, he made the boxer, whose name was Jack Delaney, a consistent winner and led him to the world's light heavyweight championship. Delaney won the title from Paul Berlenbach at Humbert Fugazy's big show staged at Ebbets field on July 16, 1926.[24]

A month later on August 20, Reilly showed up at Madison Square Garden to handle a preliminary fighter. On the day of the fight, his fighter became ill and was scratched from the card. With free time on his hands, Pete stayed to watch European featherweight champ Andre Routis of France make his American ring debut in a main event against a highly regarded Eddie (Cowboy) Anderson from Wyoming.

Routis won the fight in a walk and was an instant sensation. The *New York Sun*'s Wilbur Wood wrote he "battered Eddie Anderson, Wyoming cowboy, all over the ring for 10 rounds, smothering all of Eddie's attempts to rally. Routis virtually 'stole the show.' He was cheered for several minutes as he made his way to his dressing room ... What a fight! Routis proved that sometimes they come tough from the other side. Not often, but sometimes."[25]

Exercising his prerogative as an "Eastern representative," Reilly went to Routis' dressing room after the fight, explained the facts of a boxer's life in New York to him, and left with a smile on his face. A few days later, the *Sun* announced he was the new manager of European sensation Andre Routis. As it turned out, Pete again captured lightning in a bottle. Two years later, Routis defeated Tony Canzoneri to win the world featherweight title.[26]

After a while, Reilly came to be called the "Silver Fox" because of his prematurely silver-grey hair and his reputation as a shrewd strategist. His soft voice and unassuming manner belied a strong personality and lulled the uninitiated into underestimating him. He was known as a practical joker and as the alleged inventor of the "hot-foot," a gag in which a lighted match is

---

[24] Williams, Billy, "The Life of Reilly," *The Ring Magazine*, May 1951, p. 16.
[25] Wood, Wilbur, "Dundee Victory over Bretonnel," *The New York Sun*, August 21, 1926, sports section.
[26] Wood, "Persson, Mun Hansen and Others to Box Tomorrow – Hudkins in First 15-Rounder," *New York Sun*, August 25, 1926, sports section.

secretly inserted between the upper and lower souls of the victim's shoe.[27]

Reilly was rumored to be close to several mobsters, and he did little to dispel the notion. His anecdotes and practical jokes were laced with hints about racketeers he claimed to know, and he did not hesitate to use these rumors to his advantage in negotiations. Boxing people took them seriously and maintained a healthy respect for the dapper Irishman.

Reilly's new champion was not destined to be featherweight king for long. At the time he won his title, Routis had already been boxing more than 10 years and was nearing the end of his career. When it became clear to Reilly that Andre would likely lose the title in his next defense, Pete hit upon a scheme which would allow him to control the featherweight title indefinitely, even if Routis was no longer good enough to hold it.

Acting covertly, Reilly acquired an interest in Battling Battalino, a contender virtually unknown to the public outside of New England. Using the tactics he had mastered as an "Eastern representative," Pete promised Battalino a shot at Routis as an inducement for Bat to sign with him. Reilly scheduled the fight between his two boxers at Battalino's hometown of Hartford, Connecticut. On September 23, 1929, Bat defeated Routis to become featherweight champion and to preserve Pete's hold over the title.

After two years and five successful title defenses, Battalino grew to the point where he could no longer make the 126-pound weight limit without starving himself. As with Routis, it was obvious his days as titleholder were numbered. Once again, Reilly scouted around for a successor.

Reilly quietly acquired the contract of clever, light-punching featherweight Freddie Miller, whom Battalino had defeated in a non-title bout in 1931. Employing the same strategy used with Routis, Pete matched Bat against Miller in a title bout at Freddie's hometown of Cincinnati on January 27, 1932. Selling Battalino a part of Freddie's contract, Reilly convinced Bat to take a dive and lose the title to Miller.[28]

---

[27] Bromberg, Lester, "Colorful Managers Pilot Young Foes in Garden," *New York World-Telegram*, November 30, 1939, sports section. Williams, *op. cit.*

[28] Heller, Peter, *In This Corner*, (Simon and Schuster, New York, 1973), pp. 146-147. In this interview, Battalino says Reilly told him to take a dive, and that "I laid down, stretched out." Bat also commented: "He was one of the biggest racketeers, Pete Reilly, my manager."

Reilly was a complex man. Despite his mob connections, he was widely respected in the boxing business. Nat Fleischer described him as "one of the most fabulous characters of his era" and said that "they came no better than Pete Reilly in the fistic profession."

According to Fleischer, Reilly introduced a whole host of innovations which made boxing a safer sport. To Reilly, Fleischer attributed: the first use of a special salve to stop the flow of blood, sterilized pads, ice bags, and a trainer's kit bag with special tools, all for corner use; the demand that the New York Boxing Commission adopt an extended ring apron, cork floor covering, and additional padding under the ring canvas to produce a safer ring floor; the introduction of clean, white, unbleached shirts for each training session, special tightly fitting speed and heavy bag gloves, and the use of eye wash after each training period, all to prevent training injuries and infection. Fleischer, "Nat Fleischer Says," *Ring Magazine*, May, 1951, pp. 19-20.

Pete Reilly (left) with his light-heavy champ Jack Delaney.

Andre Routis, of France, Reilly's first featherweight titleholder.

Christopher (Battling) Battalino, Reilly's next featherweight king.

Frank Carbo's mugshot. His Police file no. was B-95838.

This time, Reilly went too far. Battalino tried to comply but, being unused to faking knockouts, he was entirely unconvincing. When Bat sank to the canvas without being hurt, the referee refused to count and instead ruled the bout "no contest." The decision upset Reilly's carefully conceived plan to maintain control of the championship. Sportswriters hailed the referee's courage in seeing through the scheme and declaring the bout no contest instead of falling for the ruse and declaring Miller the winner.

Battalino's title was declared vacant, and the National Boxing Association (NBA) announced a tournament to determine a new titleholder. With regard to Reilly, writers were of two minds. Some condemned his action and thought he should be indicted or barred from boxing. Others shrugged their shoulders and figured since the charges could not be proven in court, nothing could be done. All agreed that in losing control of the title, Reilly finally had received at least a part of what he deserved.[29]

In the end, however, Reilly was not to be denied.

A year later, Freddie Miller would rebound to defeat the NBA's new titleholder, Tommy Paul, and become Reilly's third featherweight champion. Miller would hold the title for more than three years and defend it successfully a record 12 times. After having suffered what appeared to be an irreversible setback, the wily Silver Fox would once again confound his critics and regain control of the featherweight title.[30]

Although the furor died down, Reilly's conniving ways had far greater negative consequences on boxing's future than anyone then imagined. The reason for this was that his predatory schemes had been duly noted by a man far more sinister than any ordinary boxing manager or promoter.

In the mid-1930s, a blue-collar hit-man for Murder Inc. named Frankie Carbo would look for a racket which posed less risk to his freedom than his prior vocations, which had involved accusations of grand larceny, assault, armed robbery, murder, and other forms of mayhem. Carbo was a fight fan and, while he had dabbled in managing a few small-time boxers, he had never applied his criminal mind to earning a livelihood from the fight game.

In 1935, Owney Madden was in the middle of a stretch at Sing Sing Prison for a parole violation. His incarceration created a vacuum in the mob's boxing business, which Carbo saw as an opportunity to fill and pick up a little extra spending money along the way.

In this endeavor, Carbo had the mob's support. Boxing always had been more of an amusement than a money-making enterprise, anyway. The sport's return on effort expended was hardly worth the trouble compared to other investment opportunities such as the liquor, gambling, blackmail, and

---

[29] Parker, "Cincinnati Not So Batty," *New York Daily Mirror,"* January 29, 1932, sports section. The basic scenario for the three title exchanges is set out in Parker's article. Dates of title changes come from Fleischer, *op. cit.*, p. 241.

[30] Fleischer, p. 244.

protection rackets. Frankie's 15 arrests, which included two murder charges and one manslaughter conviction, atttracted too much heat from the authorities. Maybe allowing him the boxing franchise would keep him out of trouble. A career change for Mr. Carbo might be good for all concerned.[31]

As a student of boxing and a convicted felon, Carbo had followed Reilly's career with interest and watched him become one of the most prosperous managers in boxing. He admired Pete's wily methods and knew him to be the right man for a special project he had in mind.

Carbo secretly acquired a part interest in Eddie (Babe) Risko, who had won the NBA's version of the world middleweight title from Teddy Yarosz in 1935. Risko's leading challenger was a youngster from Tacoma, Washington named Freddie Steele. Everyone who had seen Steele fight said he was a sure bet to defeat Risko when the two fought.

To determine whether or not this was really the case, Carbo allowed Risko to fight Steele in an over-weight non-title match at Seattle, Washington on March 24, 1936. To protect his interests, Frankie sent Pete Reilly to Seattle with the Risko party.[32]

As expected, Steele won a decision over Risko, scoring three knockdowns in the process. Afterward, Reilly returned to New York with a report for Carbo. He also returned, in accord with Frankie's instructions, with an agreement from Steele's manager that Carbo was to become a silent partner in the ownership of Freddie's contract in exchange for a title shot.

Less than four months later, on July 10, 1936, the arrangement was sealed when Steele won a 15-round decision and the middleweight title from Risko in Seattle. Once again in attendance at the match, this time as aide-de-camp to Freddie rather than Risko, was Pete Reilly. Although it was then thought Reilly had acquired a share in the new champ, it later came to light that Carbo, and not Pete, was cut in as an owner of Steele's contract.[33]

---

[31] Coughlan, Robert, "How the IBC Runs Boxing," *Sports Illustrated*, January 17, 1955, pp. 14, 48. Heinz, W. C., "Is Boxing Crooked – Or Isn't It?" *Sport Magazine*, July, 1957, pp. 19, 76-77.

[32] Sharp, Dick, "'We'll Find Out Whether Steele Can Fight' – Reilly," *Seattle Post-Intelligencer*, March 21, 1936, sports section.

[33] "Promoter Won't Sign Up Inferior Rivals for Fred," *Seattle Times*, September 24, 1936, sports section. Brougham, Royal, "The Morning After," *Seattle Post-Intelligencer*, July 26, 1938, sports section. It has always seemed curious to the author that in their three fights Freddie Steele was never able to knock out Babe Risko. Steele handled him easily in the first fight and had him down three times. He had a legitimate reason for holding back and refraining from a knockout in that fight, i. e., Freddie did not want to scare Babe away from a subsequent title fight. In the second fight, however, Steele had Risko down in the very first round and then, at least from the author's perspective after watching the film, never really tried to knock Babe out thereafter. Freddie's third bout with Risko was a title defense in New York. Once again, Steele won easily but never even came close to knocking Babe down. During his career Risko was knocked out eight times, mostly by lesser fighters than Freddie. In his own career, Steele had proven himself a murderous puncher and was the only man to knock out Vince Dundee and Ken Overlin, both of whom retired as former former

Reilly, like a good soldier, had followed orders perfectly. Just as he had done on his own behalf with the featherweight title, he helped Carbo to "muscle in" on Steele and installed Frankie as secret owner of the middleweight title and Freddie as its temporary custodian.

Carbo controlled the middleweight title through the reigns of four champions until Tony Zale broke the chain and defeated Frankie's then champ, Al Hostak, in 1940. By that time, Carbo had lost interest in chasing the title around the country and shifted his focus to his native New York where he formed a relationship with Mike Jacobs who, through his 20th Century Sporting Club, had become the sport's most powerful promoter.

In contrast to Madden, boxing for Carbo was not just a hobby, but rather his chief means of livelihood. Although he could be charming and solicitous if the situation required, he was not above resorting to physical coercion to get his way. Fortunately, implementation of such a tactic was rare because his reputation was usually all that was needed to act as the "convincer."

While Jacobs arranged big-ticket matches in the 1940s, Carbo eased his way into Mike's confidence by helping him put together many of the lower-profile contests in the lighter weight divisions. Using the promoter's office as his headquarters, Frankie held open sessions daily and acted as an informal intermediary on Mike's behalf to secure the services of many top-ranked fighters who did not have ready access to Jacobs.

Of course, Carbo did not work for free. Before long it became common knowledge that, in exchange for a chance to show a fighter in New York, an unconnected manager would have to give "a piece" of the boxer to one of Frankie's specially selected "co-managers."[34]

In 1949, Jacobs retired and sold his boxing monopoly to a new corporation, the International Boxing Club (IBC), controlled by Chicago industrialist Jim Norris. The new group was quick to expand its monopoly position by buying exclusive contracts for weekly boxing shows from each of the newly established TV networks. To fulfill these obligations, the IBC found it convenient and necessary to rely on boxers controlled by Carbo.

The reason for this was that by this time Carbo, through his now extensive network of managers, controlled most of the important boxers on the East Coast. The IBC worked with Frankie because, in the words of one of its officials, he "always comes through." In essence, the arrangement was a union of two monopolies, the IBC, which as promoter controlled all the major venues and TV rights, and Carbo, who as a kind of super-manager controlled the fighters appearing on the IBC's shows. Literally, if a manager did not do business with Frankie, he did not do business with the

---

middleweight champions. In the author's view, the only reasonable explanation is that Freddie was under orders from Carbo to go easy on Risko so as not to reduce his earning potential, i. e. Carbo still owned a piece of Babe and still was sharing in his purses.

[34] Borden, Eddie, "Does Mystery Man Carbo Control Boxing,?" 1953 *Boxing Annual*, (Boxing and Wrestling, 1953).

IBC.[35]

In joining with the IBC, Carbo took the "Eastern representative" device, as first exploited by Madden and then refined by Reilly, to its highest level of development. He assembled all the elements from a system which had been around for 30 years and adapted them to the modern era of home TV.

Hurley's career spanned the entire period in which this system thrived and developed. The reason he wasn't ensnared in its web was due solely to the help he received from Billy McCarney. When Jack worked in New York in 1926, it was only because of McCarney that he did not have to share his fighters with a local manager. Because of Billy's backing, doors opened that otherwise would have been closed, and Hurley's boxers were welcome to fight anywhere he could convince a promoter they would be attractions.

Hurley would eventually meet Owney Madden, Pete Reilly, Frankie Carbo, and many others involved in boxing's shady practices. McCarney would teach him Madden was pleasant enough as long as he did not control your business; that if you worked a deal with Reilly you better examine it with a fine tooth comb; and that although it was okay to greet operators like Carbo casually in the company of friends, never, ever, take favors or accept their invitations to share a private meal, or even just a cup of coffee.

It did not take long for Hurley to adopt McCarney's practices as his own. Although Jack eventually would be viewed as an irascible iconoclast with an acerbic wit capable of stretching the truth and responding in kind to any charge or criticism, his basic integrity was never questioned. In the early 1950s, as one of the few independent managers left plying his trade in New York, Jack would play a major role in taking down the Carbo-IBC alliance.

Arguing the IBC unfairly prevented his fighter, Harry (Kid) Matthews, from obtaining matches in New York because "he wouldn't give the IBC crowd a cut of his fighter," Hurley took his case to the sportswriters. These men, who by then included some of his closest friends, had long been critical of the IBC's methods and were only too glad to rally around Jack's cause and use him as a spokesman for their own points of view.

Buttressed by the support of the press, Hurley's complaints were duly noted in the halls of the U. S. Congress. In August 1951, Jack's former boxing pupil, Warren G. Magnuson, then a senator from Washington State, and two colleagues, Senators Harry Cain, also from Washington, and Herman Welker of Idaho, introduced a bill seeking a senate investigation. Shortly afterward, L. Gary Clemente of New York introduced a House resolution also calling for an inquiry into the IBC's monopoly practices.[36]

Although it would take years, a federal trial court would eventually rule that the IBC was a monopoly guilty of promoting championship bouts in

---

[35] Coughlan, pp. 49-50.

[36] Watson, Emmett, *My Life in Print*, (Lesser Seattle Publishing, Seattle, 1993), p. 283. It bears emphasis that not only were Harry Matthews and Hurley residents of Washington State, but also that Matthews was an Idaho native with ties still close to that state.

restraint of trade. In 1959, the Supreme Court would affirm the trial court's decision and order the IBC dissolved.[37]

As for Carbo, his penchant for secretly manipulating championships would prove his undoing. In October 1959, he would plead guilty to charges in California for acting as an unlicensed matchmaker and for managing boxers without a license. He would subsequently be sentenced to serve two years in prison at Riker's Island in New York.[38]

In May 1961, a federal court would convict Carbo for conspiracy to extort a share of welterweight champ Don Jordan's earnings and for using interstate communications to transmit threats of harm to Hollywood promoter Jackie Leonard. Leonard, who refused to assist in the division of Jordan's purses, was beaten by unidentified assailants after receiving the threats. As a result, Carbo was sentenced to 25 years in a federal prison.[39]

McCarney and Hurley's friendship continued until Billy's death in 1948. By then, Jack, a boxing man for over 30 years, had acquired the reputation as a particularly unsentimental practitioner in a business singularly conspicuous for its lack of sentimentality.[40]

In going over some papers shortly before his father died, McCarney's son came across IOUs evidencing money owed to Billy, as well as a couple of notes documenting debts his dad owed to others, the largest being one to Hurley. Showing the papers to his father, the son asked what he should do with them. "Don't try to collect any of that stuff," replied Billy. "But if you can, I'd like Jack to get his money."

After McCarney's funeral, the son approached Hurley and offered to repay the money his dad borrowed. Obviously offended, Jack replied tartly, "I'll punch you right in the mouth. After everything your father did for me." Seeing the son's reaction, Hurley's expression softened perceptibly. After the heat of the moment had passed, Jack looked at him and said, "Look, if you've got an extra buck, have some masses said for your old man."[41]

---

[37] "IBC Ruled Boxing Monopoly by Federal Court Judge," *Seattle Post-Intelligencer*, March 9, 1957, p. 10. "IBC Ordered to Break Up by Court," *Seattle Post-Intelligencer*, January 23, 1959, sports section.

[38] Sullivan, Russell, *Rocky Marciano: The Rock of His Times*, (University of Illinois Press, 2005), p. 207.

[39] "Carbo to Stay in McNeil," *Seattle Post-Intelligencer*, February 14, 1963, p. 14.

[40] "Billy McCarney, Managed Fighters (obit)," *New York Times*, September 25, 1948, p. 17.

[41] Smith, Red, "Views of Sport," *New York Herald-Tribune*, August 28, 1957, sports section.

CHAPTER 15

ARRIVING, VIA 'DELAYED KNOCKOUT'

Billy Petrolle got married in July and had just rolled into New York off his honeymoon. He hadn't been in a gym for weeks. A picture called "The Big Parade" was playing the Astor Theater on Broadway and Billy bought a ticket for a buck sixty-five. Ruby Goldstein was boxing Johnny Ceccoli in Newark that same night. Goldstein weighed in for the fight in the afternoon and then without telling anybody went down to the railroad station after the weigh-in and grabbed a train for California.

The Newark promoter's name was Laddy Kusy. He calls me up in New York at 8 p.m. and says he's ruined. He says he's got 10 Gs in the joint already and only one fighter, Ceccoli. He says Petrolle can take him out of the bag. I told Kusy that they could have Billy for $2,500 and not a cent less, if I could find him. Kusy had no choice, so I ran down Broadway and waited for Petrolle in front of the theater.

Pretty soon, along comes Petrolle with a cap on him. He just had a big Italian dinner and is full of spaghetti and wine. I ask him, "Do you want to fight a guy in Newark tonight?" "Sure," he says, "if you can get the money back for my ticket. I ain't gonna throw away a dollar sixty-five. You get my money back, I'll take the fight." He's talking about a buck sixty-five. I'm talking about 25 hundred slugs. I said I'd pay for it. Petrolle wouldn't stand for that. He said I'd have to get the money back. So I went in and got the money for the ticket while Billy ran back to the hotel to get his gym bag.

On the way to Newark in the Hudson tube, he says how sorry he is to miss the picture, but he's not asked me yet who he's fighting or what he's getting. So I tell him who he's going up against and it's all right with him. When we reach the arena, he opens his bag and finds he's brought two right shoes. We had to borrow a left shoe for him. All the guys on the card that night had feet like Abraham Lincoln. The closest one to his size is three sizes too big, but he put it on and stuffed paper in it so it wouldn't fall off.

Petrolle was belting the juice out of Ceccoli, but he comes back after the second round real tired. I told him to coast a few rounds, and he does. Around the seventh, Ceccoli gets fresh and Billy puts him in his place. You should have seen him with that big shoe flopping around, and him full of spaghetti and wine. He had enough in the last round and we get the duke. But the remarkable thing is how he finished up good and strong to win.

After we'd been paid and we're on our way back to New York, Billy asks me, "How did you get that one so quick?" I told him I just stumbled into it. Petrolle's only comment was, "See if you can't stumble into another one."

You see, for Billy it was all just in a day's work.   — Jack Hurley

****

When the Northern Pacific from Chicago pulled into New York's Grand Central Station May 28, 1926, only two, instead of three, of Fargo's favorite sons disembarked from the train. Missing from the entourage was Russie LeRoy, who had broken his right hand in winning an otherwise easy 10-round decision from Billy Bortfield four days earlier in Milwaukee.[1]

Unfortunately, as in his bouts with Johnny Knauf and Battling Krause a year earlier, LeRoy's over-eagerness proved costly. Flooring Bortfield "with a nasty left hook" in round two, Russie hovered over his fallen foe rather than retiring to a neutral corner as the rule required. Over 10 seconds elapsed between the knockdown and the time the referee started to count.

After Russie went to the corner and the referee began to toll, Bortfield barely beat the count. Had LeRoy kept his head and obeyed the rules immediately, he would have been credited with a knockout and been on the train to New York the next day. Instead, the round ended shortly after Bortfield regained his feet. As luck would have it, Russie broke his hand the next round and had to go the full 10 rounds to gain a decision win.[2]

LeRoy's doctor advised he would be out of action until August, an especially severe blow to the Hurley-LeRoy pocketbook because early summer represented the best portion of the outdoor season. By late August, the public's attention already would be focusing on Jack Dempsey's heavyweight title defense against Gene Tunney set for September.[3]

Immediately after Hurley and Petrolle arrived in New York, Coney Island Stadium promoters whisked them away to an outdoor training quarters at Pompton Lake, New Jersey, later made famous as Joe Louis' favorite training camp. The promoters' willingness to incur such an expense indicated just how important Billy's June 4th bout with Sid Terris was.[4]

In addition to being Petrolle's first main event in New York, the athletic commission had just named Terris its No. 1 contender for the lightweight title. Boxing experts believed Rocky Kansas was nearing the end of his

---

[1] "Ratner, Willie, "Goldstein Runs Out on Ceccoli But Petrolle Fills the Breach," *Newark Evening News*, August 3, 1926, sports section. Ratner, "Petrolle Was on Way to Movies When He Landed Ceccoli Match," *Newark Evening News*, August 4, 1926, sports section. Wood, Wilbur, "Fistic Futures Are Baffling – Billy Petrolle Is Phlegmatic Warrior," *New York Sun*, November 26, 1930, sports section. Cannon, Jimmy, "The Shoe Went Flop, But Hurley's Boxer Didn't," *Seattle Post-Intelligencer*, April 29, 1966, p. 30. The story in the opening vignette uses elements taken from each of the above sources. The primary source is Hurley's story as recounted by Jimmy Cannon in 1966. Some editing has been done to fit the context and to reconcile minor inconsistencies in the several accounts, re-told by three different writers over a 40-year span.

[2] Levy Sam, "Brewer Pug Floored in Second Stanza," *Fargo Forum*, May 25, 1926, sports section.

[3] Purcell, J. A., "The Sportville Spotlight," *Fargo Forum*, June 6, 1926, sports section.

[4] Special Correspondent, "Billy Will Train at Compton Lake, N. J.," *Fargo Forum*, May 30, 1926, sports section.

career, and it was "a foregone conclusion that Kansas will be defeated by the first good man he meets." Beating Terris and obtaining a title bout with the titleholder then, before he could be beaten by anyone else, was Billy's best chance to win a title in the foreseeable future.[5]

At the same time, boxing had just become legal in Illinois. Jim Mullen, Chicago's leading promoter, was trying to put together an all-star show for his first big venture under the new law. Since Rickard and Humbert Fugazy already had all the champions in the heavier divisions under contract, Mullen was working hard to entice Kansas to defend his title in Chicago. Jim's candidate to oppose Kansas was Sammy Mandell, a 23-year-old native of Rockford, Illinois, who had an impressive record of 77 wins, 6 losses, and 5 draws and who had defeated Terris 1-1/2 years earlier.

In essence, rival promoters were engaged in a race to buy the opportunity to win the lightweight title for their respective heroes. Whether New York or Chicago landed the bout depended entirely on who would pay Kansas the most to defend his title. The question of the hour was which promoter would bid the highest? Rickard or Fugazy in New York on behalf of the Terris-Petrolle winner, or Mullen in Chicago on behalf of Mandell?[6]

This question remained up in the air as Billy and Sid prepared for battle.

In 4-1/2 years as a pro, Sid Terris had compiled the best record of any lightweight in the game with 87 wins, 5 losses, and 3 draws. His only loss in his last 37 bouts was to Mandell, a decision so controversial it caused a riot at the Garden. During the same run, Sid defeated the division's two most recent titleholders, Kansas, and his predecessor, Jimmy Goodrich.

Terris, known variously as "the East Side Phantom" or "the Blue Streak," was a ring wizard, a dancing master who peppered his foes with rapier-like left jabs seasoned with a dazzling array of stinging right crosses, left hooks, and uppercuts. His cleverness and speed were legendary. His one weakness was a lack of punching power. In 95 fights, he had scored only 14 kayos, many resulting from cuts rather than by clean knockouts.

Writers touted the go between Terris and Petrolle as a classic match between a boxer and a slugger. They remembered Billy's fight against Sammy Vogel four months earlier as New York's best fight of the year and predicted the coming battle would be just as pleasing.[7]

Due to heavy rain, the bout was postponed from June 4 until June 11. Odds favoring Terris 4-1 narrowed to 2-1 as last-minute bets were placed by a delegation of 100 fans who arrived from Fargo a day before the fight.[8]

---

[5] "Terris-Petrolle Bout Tops C. I. Show," *Brooklyn Daily Times*," May 30, 1926, sports section. Mercer, Sid, "Sid Mercer's Close-ups," *New York Evening Journal*, June 5, 1926, sports section.

[6] Mercer, *op. cit.*

[7] Wood, Wilbur, "Terris Meets Fargo Slugger," *New York Sun*, June 4, 1926, sports section.

[8] Special Correspondent, "Bets Favor Terris Win over Billy," *Fargo Forum*, June 4, 1926, sports section. "100 Fans Here to See Petrolle in Bout with Terris," *Brooklyn Daily Times*,

The next night, an "immense crowd, a capacity house" of 13,327 customers, paying $34,937, saw Terris win "the decision ... over Billy Petrolle of Fargo, N. D., at the end of 10 rounds ... by the skin of his teeth." George Underwood, writing in the *New York Telegram*, described the battle:

> "Those of us who trekked to Coney last night saw Sid Terris come back in all his pristine glory to beat Billy Petrolle in a mill replete with lightning fast, scintillating, scientific boxing, mixed with just the right admixture of pure and unadulterated slugging ... After his long layoff Sid Terris came back to prove he is the fastest, most clever lightweight in the game today. It took all of Sid's boxing wizardry to return him winner over Petrolle, who fought one of the greatest battles of his career and more than lived up to his nom-de-guerre of the Fargo Express.
>
> "The Fargo Express – clear the track and give him room!
>
> "Believe it ... Terris had to step as never before to get out of the way. Half a dozen times Sid almost bowled off the track. From the first clang of the gong, that little dark skinned, flash-eyed Italian from North Dakota tore after the Blue Streak. Chin tucked behind left shoulder, eyes blazing venom, launching rush after rush and ripping, tearing, slashing away with both hands.
>
> "Most of the time, Petrolle had Terris on the run. Those nimble feet of the boy from the Ghetto never twinkled faster than they did last night. Sid was forced to back step a 100 in nine flat again and again to keep from being run over by the Fargo Express. On the retreat, Sid volleyed away with lightning left jabs, occasionally staying his retreat long enough to step in with snappy left hooks, right crosses, and left and right uppercuts.
>
> "Even though bringing all the boxing wizardry at his command to his aid, Terris could not at times keep Petrolle from crowding him to the ropes or cornering him and pasting him with cruel hooks to the midsection and slams to the jaw ... 'Ah, no! the battle wasn't all one-sided. Far from it. There were times when things looked precarious – exceedingly precarious – for the dashing Mr. Terris."[9]

On June 15, four days after his razor-thin win over Petrolle, the New York State Athletic Commission named Terris Kansas' leading contender and ordered Rocky to defend his title against Terris no later than July 30. On June 19, the champion announced he was ignoring the commission's

---

June 10, 1926, sports section.

[9] Igoe, Hype, "Terris Has a Hard Time Beating Billy Petrolle," *New York World*, June 12, 1926, sports section ("skin of his teeth"). Underwood, George B., "Terris Back in Pristine Glory," *New York Telegram*, June 12, 1926, sports section.

order and instead signing to meet Mandell in Chicago July 3, 1926.[10]

Kansas' announcement was good news for Petrolle. The loss to Terris had eliminated for the time being Billy's chance at a title bout in New York, but it did not affect his stature in Chicago. If he could establish himself there, he still might get the inside track for a match with Mandell, the man who likely was to become the next champion.

In fact, Hurley had foreseen this possibility. During his Chicago stopover on the way to New York, he had met with Jim Mullen and mapped a plan, which if successful, would launch Petrolle as a Windy City drawing card. As a first step, Hurley and Mullen had discussed an appearance for Billy against Frankie Schaeffer on June 21 at Jim's East Chicago arena.[11]

Jack wired his acceptance of Schaeffer immediately after the Terris fight.

Before leaving for Chicago, Hurley phoned the *Fargo Forum* to formally announce he was moving his headquarters from Fargo to New York. He explained it was easier to give "Petrolle, Russie LeRoy, and Earl Blue the opportunities they deserve ... The distance from Fargo to New York is too great ... and I can save plenty of money each year by living in New York."

Although the *Forum* reported Phil Terk would probably be closing the gym and moving east to join Hurley, those plans were put on hold for the time being. As it turned out, Terk would continue to operate the gym and present amateur shows in Fargo for another year. When the time finally came to make the move, their choice for a new location ended up as Duluth, Minnesota rather than New York.[12]

In Chicago, Petrolle made short work of Schaeffer. Billy stunned Frankie early in the first round and backed him into a corner, raining blow after blow upon the dazed fighter. A one-two combination sent him to the canvas, and the referee tolled 10 as the beaten fighter rested on one knee.[13]

The next day, Hurley and Petrolle were back on the train to New York where Billy was set to headline a show on July 2. Before they left, promoter Mullen, impressed with Petrolle's work against Schaeffer, promised to feature Billy in a big show at Comiskey Park near the end of July.

For the July 2nd event, Coney Island matchmaker Jack Epstein had selected 21-year-old Ray Miller, known as "the Chicago Knockout King," as Petrolle's opponent. Although he had lost to Terris a month earlier, the New York newspapers were reporting that Billy's stock had taken "quite a jump as a result of his showing." For the first time, he was installed as a betting favorite in New York with odds quoted at 6 to 5 to his advantage.[14]

Miller was one of the lightweight division's most dangerous punchers.

---

[10] "Kansas Will Defend Fistic Honors," *Fargo Forum*, June 20, 1926, sports section.

[11] Purcell, "Fargo Lad Must Take Long Rest," *Fargo Forum*, May 27, 1926, sports section.

[12] "Jack Hurley to Make Headquarters in East," *Fargo Forum*, June 17, 1926, sports section.

[13] Special Correspondent, "Chicagoan Lands Only One Punch," *Fargo Forum*, June 22, 1926, sports section.

[14] "Miller Will Try to Derail Fargo Exp," *Brooklyn Daily Eagle*, July 2, 1926, sports section.

Sid Terris, the Eastside Phantom.

Chicago's Ray Miller.

In 1925, Rocky Kansas won the lightweight title from Goodrich.

Sammy Mandell defeated Kansas to take over the title in July 1926.

Over a 14-year career, he would win 81 bouts and register 33 kayos in 128 fights. Famous as the only man to stop Jimmy McLarnin, he would score one-round knockouts over Sid Terris and future junior welter champ Johnny Jadick. Ray was courageous, tough, and respected. Though he would lose 28 bouts, he would never be kayoed. In a 1929 fight with Tommy Grogan, he would hit the canvas six times, only to recover and stop Grogan in the fourth round.

In many ways, the careers of Petrolle and Miller paralleled each other. Each was regarded as a fearless battler with a left hook capable of ending a bout with one blow. Both were perennial contenders in from 1926 to 1934. Both would achieve their greatest recognition with sensational wins over Jimmy McLarnin. Neither would win a world title. Their July 2nd bout would be their first of three over a three-year period. While each would be a brutal affair, neither fighter would establish superiority over the other.

An estimated 4,000 avid fans, paying $8,000, braved threatening weather and heavy fog to see Petrolle take "everything Ray Miller had to offer in a 10-round bout at the Coney Island Stadium last night, and then come on to get a draw." Wilbur Wood, in the *New York Sun*, described the action:

> "It was a savage fight. Miller, winging away with his smashing left uppercut to the body, the best left uppercut we have seen in many a moon, started out as if to make short work of Petrolle. But Petrolle, game and tough, kept walking in for more. Miller had each of the first four rounds, except the second, in which Petrolle dropped him to the canvas with a right to the neck. Ray did not seem to be hurt much.
>
> "After the fourth, the fast pace began to make itself felt on Miller, and Petrolle started to cut down the Chicagoan's early lead. Miller was wild with his uppercuts in the fifth, missing a dozen of them, and had to take a pounding in the body at close quarters.
>
> "Petrolle also took the sixth. The seventh was all in Billy's favor. Miller was tired and the snap had departed from his punches. Petrolle had a shade in the eighth. Miller began to wake up toward the close of this frame, and in the ninth he had Petrolle in bad shape for a time. A left to the stomach hurt the Fargo boy badly, and Miller followed with a series of lefts and rights to the head. Petrolle had a shade in the 10th on aggressiveness.
>
> "All in all it was a very nice fight, worthy of a much larger gathering."[15]

On July 3, 1926, as expected, Sammy Mandell won a ten-round decision over Rocky Kansas to become lightweight champion. Mandell's win served

---

[15] Wood, "Miller and Petrolle Box Draw," *New York Sun*, July 3, 1926, sports section.

to ease the pain Hurley and Petrolle felt for not getting the decision against Miller. Billy could now definitely look forward to a fresh opportunity to establish himself in the new champion's home territory of Chicago.

With this in mind, they headed west again, stopping off in St. Paul July 13, where Petrolle dispatched Johnny Rocco in eight rounds. The next day, they were greeted at the train station in Fargo as heroes by a marching band and paraded down Broadway to the Elks club for a banquet dinner. Later that evening, friend and banker Bill Stern, who was also vice president of the North Dakota State Fair Association, hosted the duo at the fair.[16]

Jack and Billy barely had caught their breaths before boarding a train for Chicago July 15. True to his earlier promise, Jim Mullen had arranged a fight for Petrolle at Comiskey Park nine days later against Johnny Adams, a past Pacific Coast lightweight champion and conqueror of Ace Hudkins. Still just 21, Adams was already a veteran of 90 pro fights. In addition to Hudkins, he had defeated Phil Salvadore, Mushy Callahan, Frankie Fink, Oakland Frankie Burns, and Jimmy Hackley.

A native of San Bernardino, California, Adams had never been outside his home state and was looking to use Petrolle as an entree to bigger bouts in the East. Unfortunately, Billy proved to have too many sharp edges to serve as a stepping stone. After seven rounds of hard but one-sided battling, Petrolle's right to the chin at the beginning of the eighth knocked Adams through the ropes. Although Johnny raised his head off the floor, he fell back unconscious and was counted out in 54 seconds of the round.[17]

Reaction at ringside to Petrolle's performance was enthusiastic. The *Chicago Post*'s Jimmy Cochran, dean of the city's boxing writers, called Billy "a four-base hitter and is going to Babe Ruth the lightweights here, I am confident." Walter Eckersall wrote in the *Chicago Tribune* that the battle was "one of the greatest fights seen around Chicago in years." Afterward, promoter Mullen said he would attempt to match Petrolle with newly crowned champ Sammy Mandell in the near future.[18]

The last week in July found Petrolle tending to personal business. On July 26, 1926, he married Antoinette Rich at Duluth, Minnesota. Afterward, he told Hurley he planned to move to Duluth with his wife and buy a home.

Petrolle returned to New York August 1, deciding to delay his honeymoon until the end of the outdoor season. The next evening, before he even had a chance to resume training, Jack intercepted him on his way to a movie, and they boarded the subway train for Newark.

Promoter Laddy Kusy of the Laurel Garden Athletic Club was frantic

---

[16] "Hurley and Petrolle Honored by Fargoans," *Fargo Forum*, July 15, 1926, sports section.

[17] Opp, Jack, "Western Mauler Is Good," *Fargo Forum*, July 18, 1926, sports section.

[18] Opp, "Adams Badly Beaten," *Fargo Forum*, July 25, 1926, sports section. Eckersall, Walter, "Petrolle K.O.'s Adams in 8th Cyclone Round," *Chicago Tribune*, July 25, 1926, sports section.

because his main attraction, Ruby Goldstein, had mysteriously disappeared after the noon weigh-in and taken a train to California. A capacity crowd already had assembled and was waiting to see Goldstein fight Johnny Ceccoli in the 10-round main event. Kusy agreed to pay the handsome sum of $2,500 for Petrolle to fill in on short notice as Ruby's substitute.

When Hurley and Petrolle arrived, Kusy already had arranged for another substitute. Lightweight Sollie Castellane was in the dressing room ready to go on for the main event. As a solution, Kusy put the issue to the crowd – the boy receiving the most applause would fight Ceccoli. According to the *Newark Evening News*, Petrolle was the choice "by two handclaps and one raspberry." Billy, who never had fought in Newark before, waged "one of the greatest fights seen here in years" and won the 10-round decision easily.

Newark Star-Eagle reporter Tip Rosen noted that the "great fight put up by these lads made the fans forget about Ruby Goldstein." He also commented that Petrolle "saved the show last night, saved the boxing game here, and also helped to continue the running of a popular fight club."[19]

Exactly three weeks later, Petrolle returned to Laurel Garden "before the biggest crowd promoter Laddy Kusy ever entertained" and won a 10-round decision over Ruby Stein of Brooklyn. Afterward, Kusy was so excited he promised Hurley he would do everything in his power to match Petrolle against champion Mandell in Newark.[20]

Meanwhile, Earl Blue joined Hurley on the East Coast in July and immediately caught on in the neighborhood fight clubs. When Jack went west with Billy for the Rocco and Adams fights, he left Blue in McCarney's care. In two months, Blue won seven bouts without a defeat at clubs in Brooklyn and Newark. Although the quality of his opposition was mixed, he impressed sportswriters both with his punching power and his wardrobe.

Blue still wore the blue bathrobe and cap Hurley had assembled the prior year in California. While no longer new to western fans, the outfit was a novelty in the East. Stitched in huge red letters on his robe's back were the words "Little Boy Blue." One tongue-in-cheek writer noted the ensemble was neatly coordinated to enhance the purity of Earl's color scheme by hiding his blonde hair and accentuating the brilliancy of his azure eyes.

The promoter for Blue's July 9th bout at Brooklyn's Long Beach Stadium furnished his foe Frankie Brown an attractive brown bathrobe and trunks. Treating the event as a style show, the announcer introduced the fight as "a battle of colors" and asked fans to vote for the most pleasing outfit with

---

[19] Ratner, "Goldstein Runs Out on Ceccoli, but Petrolle Fills the Breach," *Newark Evening News*, August 3, 1926, sports section. Rosen, Tip, "Petrolle Proves a Good 'Sub' for Ruby," *Newark Star-Eagle*," August 3, 1926, sports section. This fight is the same one as described by Hurley in the anecdote which opened this chapter. The events described here were not in the anecdote.

[20] Marenghi, Anthony, "Petrolle Cuts Stein to Ribbons in Fight," *Newark Star-Eagle,* August 24, 1926, sports section.

Johnny Adams was kayoed by Petrolle in eight rounds at Chicago.

Johnny Ceccoli, who Petrolle fought in place of Ruby Goldstein in Newark.

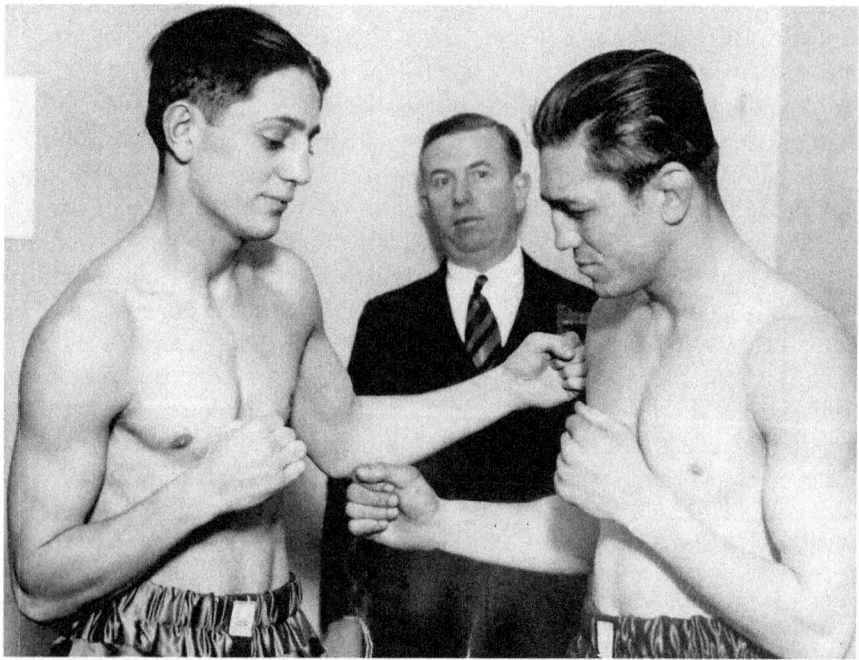

Ruby Goldstein (left) faces off December 19, 1926 with Ray Mitchell in his first fight since skipping out on Laddy Kusy 6 months earlier.

their applause. The results of the fight and the style show were the same – Blue was a knockout (winner) over Brown – in the second round.[21]

On July 26, Blue kayoed Gus Berger in one round at Laurel Garden in Newark. The next day, the *Evening News* reported that "(f)our times Blue had to bowl over Berger before he remained on the canvas. Every time Little Boy Blue blew Bergen's horn, Gus sat down."[22]

Blue was back at Laurel Garden on August 30 boxing Leroy (High Hat) McCullough of Washington, New Jersey, who contested Earl's claim as the evening's best-dressed boxer by wearing a "ludicrous brown derby and a screeching bathrobe." One reporter wrote the fighters "looked like members of a minstrel troupe as they climbed into the ring." The bout lasted only until Little Boy knocked off McCullough's high hat in the fifth round.[23]

Although these histrionics did not make Blue a better fighter, they set him apart from the run-of-the-mill pugilist and served to convince the public he was a colorful ring figure.

By early August, LeRoy's right hand had healed sufficiently for a return to action. His first fight of the summer was a ten-round semifinal against Spug Myers on Mullen's show at Comiskey Park on August 13, 1926. No set-up, Myers, at 23, was a year younger than Russie and boasted 56 wins, five losses, and 18 draws, a record roughly comparable to LeRoy's. Both fighters needed a win to advance into the big-money class.

In a fight the *Chicago Tribune*'s Walter Eckersall called "the best bout on the card," LeRoy and Myers fought a 10-round draw. After eight rounds, Spug piled up a seemingly insurmountable lead, but a ninth-round knockdown and a savage rally in the 10th pulled Russie even. Afterward, Mullen was so pleased he promised both a return match in September.[24]

The next day, LeRoy headed to New York, eager to make up for lost time due to his broken hand. Filling in as a last-minute replacement for Al Delmont on August 19, he kayoed Ritchie Roberts in two rounds in Perth Amboy, New Jersey. The next evening, substituting again on three hours notice for Sammy Vogel, Russie fought "a whale of a fight" against Jimmy Goodrich on an undercard at Ebbets Field, holding the ex-lightweight king even for six rounds before tiring in the last two and losing a close verdict.[25]

---

[21] "Mike Ballerino Gets Bad Break in Bout with Augie Pisano," *Brooklyn Citizen*, July 10, 1026, sports section.

[22] Ratner, "Ward Outboxes Krug at Laurel; Bain and Fagan in a Slugfest," *Newark Evening News*, July 27, 1926, sports section.

[23] Marenghi, "Ward Has Hard Time Winning over Cooper," *Newark Star-Eagle*, August 31, 1926, sports section.

[24] Eckersall, "14,000 Watch Sangor Wade into Champion," *Chicago Tribune*, August 14, 1926, sports section. Calkins, Charles E., "Idahoan on the Floor in Ninth," *Fargo Forum*, August 14, 1926, sports section.

[25] Albertanti, Francis, "Haley Stops It" (subtitle), *New York Telegram*, August, 21, 1926, sports section. Wood, James J., "Johnny Dundee Brilliant in Winning from Bretonnel; Routis Outfights Anderson," *Brooklyn Daily News*, August 21, 1926, sports section. "Verdict

In a last bout before heading home, LeRoy won a ten-round decision over Al Conway on August 30 for promoter Kusy at Laurel Garden.

LeRoy's arrival in New York provided Hurley another excuse for making the rounds to the newspapers and beating a drum for all three of his warriors at the same time. An article in *Self-Defense* magazine published in late 1926 provides a basis to judge both the performance of Jack's fighters in the ring and his own efforts at ballyhoo on their behalf:

> "Five months ago, from out of the West, came an unknown manager accompanied by a string of equally unknown battlers. The manager was one of those long lean fellows, with apparently no sense of humor. His name Jack Hurley, and his home stamping ground is Fargo, North Dakota. It is the wide open spaces, sure enough, that gave New York Hurley and his trio of scrappers. In the short space of time since he stepped off the rattler, Hurley has become one of the big figures in New York fight circles.
>
> "Hurley made his first big stab for publicity when he announced he was the engineer of the "Fargo Express," the name under which his great lightweight star, Billy Petrolle, travels. The next in line of his fighters, Russie LeRoy, also of Fargo, a junior welterweight, was labeled the "Second Section of the Fargo Express." This was another good bid for publicity. The big punch came a few days later when the story came out that Earl Blue, the light heavyweight, had tacked on to him the name of the "Caboose" of the Fargo Express.
>
> "All three names have proved to be great assets for the fighters and manager. All three of the men have done all that has been asked of them and are all gathering in big money ... It is the first time in the history of local fisticuffs, that an unknown manager has arrived, a la Hurley, with three unknown fighters to so quickly graduate the entire bunch into the main-event class."[26]

In an era where catchy phrases were keys to a journalist's heart, boxing writers quickly latched on to Hurley's metaphors and were soon spicing their articles with all manner of railroad phraseology. Their willingness to do so was not so much an appreciation of his literary work, as an expression of respect for the ardent young men from Fargo who succeeded, where others had failed, to crack the tough nut of New York boxing.

Hurley's arrival corresponded to the migration of a new generation of

---

Booed by Audience (AP), *Fargo Forum*, August 21, 1926, sports section. "LeRoy Knocks Out Roberts in Second" (Special), *Fargo Forum*, August 21, 1926, sports section.

[26] Gardner, Dale, editor, "Jack Hurley from the Wide Open Spaces – The Western Fight Manager Storms the Citadels of Eastern Fistiana," *Self-Defense*, (Ringside Publications, New York), January 1927, p. 7.

ambitious writers who were flocking to New York from all over to cover sports in the country's most exciting city. These men found in Jack a kindred spirit, and many became life-long friends. During the early period when his fighters were losing some heartbreaking decisions, the help of these writers was indispensable to his success. If they had not chosen to write favorably about his boxers, even in the face of multiple defeats, it is likely Jack and his charges might have returned to Fargo empty-handed.[27]

From the start, Hurley's appeal to journalists was undeniable. Having grown up with his nose in the sports pages every day, he knew instinctively that a carefully crafted anecdote was the best way to garner publicity. Newsmen were quick to realize that when Jack came to visit the next day's column, already fully formulated and edited, was strolling into the office. They also learned they did not have to worry that the same story would appear in a rival newspaper. Hurley prepared for each visit by taking time to devise a unique tale to fit the writing style of whoever he was visiting.

Hurley perfected an understated, casual delivery which came across to reporters as frank and convincing. Although he rarely smiled, his eyes would light up as he wove his smoothly plotted, low-keyed explanations with an apparent sincerity which belied their self-serving content. Invariably, his self-assured, at-ease way of speaking would leave the writer feeling as if he had had made a new friend who knew his topic and whose opinion was a valuable source for future information.

With New York's outdoor season winding down, Hurley headed west with LeRoy and Petrolle on August 31. Russie was scheduled to meet Spug Myers in a rematch at Cubs' Park in Chicago September 6. Billy was on his way to Fargo to headline a Labor Day show against Alf Simmons of Great Britain on September 10, the Friday after the holiday.

Although favored in the betting, LeRoy failed to match his prior effort against Myers and lost a ten-round decision. Evidently, Russie's surge of activity in August after his layoff, along with the train ride from New York to Chicago, tired him out. Myers forced the action, and fans booed because LeRoy seemed unwilling or unable to fight.[28]

Hurley left Chicago the next day to reach Fargo in time to work on final arrangements for the Labor Day show three days later. Petrolle had reached

---

[27] Many of the era's famous sportswriters migrated from other cities to New York at about the same time as Hurley. The *New York American*'s Ed Frayne started out in Los Angeles; the *Evening Post*'s Jack Kofoed came from Philadelphia; the *Sun*'s Wilbur Wood and the *Evening Journal*'s Bill Corum both hailed from St. Louis; and the *Telegram*'s Joe Williams and Harry Grayson had migrated from Cleveland and San Francisco, respectively. Veteran journalists who made the eastward trek to New York before World War I also saw something of themselves in the eager young man from Fargo. The *New York American*'s Damon Runyon had arrived from Denver in the early 1900s, while the *World*'s Hype Igoe and the *Evening Journal*'s Tad Dorgan both had come from San Francisco in 1906.

[28] Eckersall, "Rychell Boxes Sarmiento Ten Round to Draw," *Chicago Tribune*, September 7, 1926, sports section.

a stage where it was difficult to match him in Fargo. On one hand, the town was not large enough to generate revenue to pay Billy and a top opponent what they could earn in a bigger city. On the other hand, Fargoans would not turn out unless he was matched with a foe they believed competitive.

Hurley solved this dilemma by employing a few tricks he learned from the wise old birds he had been hanging out with in New York. Looking for a boxer who he could bring in at a reasonable cost and still market to the citizens of Fargo as a tough opponent, Jack found Alf Simmons, who advertised himself as the lightweight champion of Great Britain.[29]

Simmons had worn out his welcome in New York when it became obvious he could barely hold his own against ordinary competition let alone against top contenders. Of his four bouts in the U. S. before meeting Petrolle, Alf lost three. In addition, it was common knowledge among well-informed boxing people that his claim to a British title was false. Even so, Simmons continued to pass himself off as a champion and leading contender wherever he could find a gullible audience.[30]

After signing Alf to a Fargo fight, Hurley attended a New York commission meeting and presented for signature a resolution stating the commission would support a Petrolle-Sammy Mandell bout for the lightweight title if Billy defeated Simmons. Since Mandell had won the title from Kansas in contravention of the commission's ruling ordering him to

---

[29] Purcell, "Simmons May Be Another Fred Welsh," *Fargo Forum*, August 8, 1926, sports section.

[30] BoxRec, Record of Alf Simmons. Simmons told the New York press he had beaten Ernie Rice earlier in 1926 to win the British lightweight title. "Alf Simmons, English Champion, to Start Campaign at Coney Island," *Brooklyn Citizen*, July 20, 1926, sports section. "Frankie La Fay, Troy Lightweight," *Brooklyn Citizen*, July 24, 1926, sports section. Alf's claim was wrong on two counts. First, though he fought Rice three times, he failed to win any of them – their 15-round fight in March 1923 resulting in a decision loss, their second bout in March 1926 being recorded as a 20-round draw, and their last encounter the following June ending as a two-round disqualification against Alf. Secondly, the bouts were not for the title because they occurred after Ernie's title tenure. Rice won the title from Ben Callicott in April 1921 and lost it to Seaman James Hall in September 1922.

Simmons did score a four-round knockout over future British lightweight champion Harry Mason on April 24, 1922, but the bout occurred more than a year before Mason won the title from Seaman Hall on May 17, 1923. Thereafter, Mason evened the score with Alf by winning a 20-round decision in a title defense on December 15, 1924. Simmons therefore never had any legitimate claim to the championship on that account, either. The resume Alf presented to the newspapers was fraught with other inaccuracies, as well. Although he claimed to have beaten Eddie (Kid) Wagner, Phil McGraw, and Johnny Drew and to have fought draws with Sid Terris, Benny Bass, and Stanislaus Loayza there is no evidence to support his claims for any of those bouts. In fact, according to BoxRec he lost the bouts to Wagner and Loayza, and if he had any fights with McGraw, Drew, Terris, or Bass at all, researchers have not yet uncovered them. It is also interesting to note that although referee Kid McPartland ruled Petrolle won 9 of ten rounds against Simmons with one round even in their Fargo bout, by mid-November 1926 Alf was bragging to New York sportswriters he held Billy to a draw. Evidently, Simmons had quite an active imagination! Purcell, "Rambling Through Sportville," *Fargo Forum*, November 14, 1926, sports section.

Alf Simmons, British lightweight, who fought Billy Petrolle in Fargo.

Kid McPartland, the New York referee Hurley imported to put over the Petrolle-Simmons bout.

Hurley signing for the Petrolle-Alf Simmons fight as Petrolle and Alf watch. Standing are Alf's Eastern representatives Pete (the Goat) Stone (left) & Bill Duffy. Photo courtesy of the Hurley family.

fight Sid Terris, and since Petrolle was in good standing in New York, Jack had no trouble persuading the members to sign the document. [31]

Armed with the resolution, Jack told the *Forum* the Labor Day bout was "a sanctioned elimination contest ... between Billy Petrolle, the Fargo Express and Alf Simmons, the lightweight champion of Great Britain, the winner of which will meet Sammy Mandell ... late in September."

In addition, Hurley announced that, due to the extreme importance of the match, he had secured the services of respected New York referee Kid McPartland "to advise the commission as to the outcome of the bout." For a full month, the *Forum* published daily stories written by its own staff as well as by well-known New York publicists Alfred Lumley, Francis Albertanti, and even Billy McCarney, extolling the virtues of Simmons and referee McPartland. The newspaper called upon Fargo citizens to attend the bout as a matter of civic pride to assist its local hero in his title quest.[32]

On September 10, 1926, "the largest crowd of fight fans ever assembled in this state ... jammed every nook and corner of the auditorium" to see Billy Petrolle give "the lightweight champion of all Great Britain, a never-to-be-forgotten thumping." After the fight, McPartland told the *Forum* he would report to the New York commission "that Petrolle had won every round except the fifth which was even."[33]

Despite McPartland's promise, interest in the bout by the commission vanished overnight. Indeed, except for the sound of money jingling in the pockets of Jack and his fighters, nothing was heard about the matter again.

Based on experiences stemming from as far back as Billy Sunday's 1912 Fargo crusade, Hurley had developed a principle that would serve as a guiding light throughout all his years as a promoter. The principle, which might even be called "Hurley's Law," was "you gotta have a reason for a fight." What Jack meant by this statement was "you've gotta give the fans a reason to attend a fight." Indeed, to take it one step further, what Jack really meant was "if there isn't a reason for a fight you gotta invent one."

Hurley's move to New York, and his easy assimilation into the pre-existing network there, opened up a whole new set of possibilities for Jack, almost like a carpenter with a new set of tools. For the Simmons fight, his new tools were Alf himself, the New York commission, referee McPartland,

---

[31] "Commission Suggests Simmons-Express Bout," *Fargo Forum*, August 5, 1926, sports section.

[32] "Gotham Board Allows Hurley's Fargo Bout," *Fargo Forum*, August 12, 1926, sports section. Lumley, Arthur T., "Bout on Sept. 10 Program," *Fargo Forum*, August 15, 1926, sports section. Purcell, "Express Program Delayed," *Fargo Forum*, September 1, 1926, sports section. Albertanti, "McPartland Classes with Best Referees," *Fargo Forum*, September 2, 1926, sports section. McCarney, Billy, "McPartland Efficient Arbiter McCarney Says – Was Great Boxer," *Fargo Forum*, September 5, 1926, sports section.

[33] Purcell, "English Champ Knocked Down Twice During Contest Here," *Fargo Forum*, September 11, 1926, sports section.

and his new sportswriter friends. Applying Hurley's Law, Jack had used these tools to transform an otherwise meaningless fight into an attraction of seemingly international importance for the citizens of Fargo.

By the time Petrolle and his bride finally left on their honeymoon in mid-September, Hurley had returned to New York for the fall boxing season.

In Hurley's absence, Earl Blue had continued his winning ways. His most recent victory had been a three-round kayo over Frankie Carpenter, Jack Dempsey's chief sparring partner, on September 13 at Laurel Garden. Carpenter was a competent journeyman, well-regarded by reporters, with a respectable record of 27 wins, 13 losses, and six draws. The victory gave Blue his fifth knockout and his eighth straight win in an Eastern ring.

After Carpenter, Hurley campaigned to obtain a match for Blue with a leading contender. Claiming "Jimmy Slattery, Tiger Flowers, Johnny Risko, Jimmy Delaney, and Eddie Huffman [all] looked out the window at the mention of Blue," Jack finally landed Earl a ten-round semifinal against Yale Okun at Madison Square Garden on a November 1st show featuring heavyweights Bud Gorman and Harry Persson in a main event. [34]

Much to the dissatisfaction of 8,528 fans who made "a terrific outburst of hooting and jeering," Okun won the decision over Blue "after ten rounds of good and speedy fighting." The *New York Sun* described the action in detail:

> "The semifinal came just at the opportune moment. Prior to this point the card had been decidedly blah and the crowd was all ready to walk out ... So when Blue entered the ring in his baby blue robe and cap to match, the crowd was ready to continue the booing which filled the arena during the two previous bouts. Then Blue uncorked a streak of greased lightning from his long left and the crowd remained to cheer. He dumped Okun for the count of nine in the first and again sent the East Sider to his glove tips in the third.
>
> "For the first five rounds, the Westerner gave Okun quite the busiest 15 minutes he has encountered in many a day. Okun, usually a cool, calculating boxer, was completely at sea and he caught enough blows to last a year or more.
>
> "... Blue weakened in the last three rounds and blew the verdict right in this spot. Had he scored in one of these he could not have taken the decision away from him. As it was, it was close. Many thought that he should have received a draw while others deemed it Blue's fight by a safe margin. But win or lose, Blue caught on last night and he will be welcomed back any time."[35]

---

[34] Wood, "Three Newcomers" (subtitle), *New York Sun*, October 15, 1926, sports section.

[35] Igoe, Report to *Fargo* Forum, November 2, 1926, sports section ("good and speedy fighting"). Dayton, Alfred, *New York Sun*, November 2, 1926, sports section.

LeRoy was successful in two outings at Laurel Garden in Newark, kayoing Eddie Boyer in three rounds October 4 and copping a 10-round decision from Al Conway December 13. The latter bout was noteworthy since it marked Russie's first main-event on the East Coast. Conway had been a tough nut for LeRoy in a match 4-1/2 months earlier, and he surprised ringsiders by the ease in which he handled him in the rematch.[36]

Meanwhile, Petrolle returned from his honeymoon for his final 1926 appearance at Madison Square Garden October 29 against Hilario Martinez, lightweight champion of Spain. The contest was a semifinal on a card which featured Ace Hudkins against Phil McGraw of Detroit in the main event. To experts at the time, it appeared that Garden matchmaker Jess McMahon was doing neither Hurley nor Billy any favors.

Martinez had created a sensation by kayoing Henry Wallach in two rounds at his only prior Garden appearance, and there was talk he was being groomed to meet champion Mandell. Hilario also held a win over ex-featherweight king Johnny Dundee and would later add Jack Zivic, Sid Terris, Sammy Vogel, Andy Divodi, and ex-welterweight champ Jack Britton to his list of victims. Many ring experts at the time figured Billy was being served up as an opponent to showcase the Spaniard's talent.

A puzzled assemblage of 17,318 customers witnessed Petrolle's second-round kayo of Martinez. Everyone agreed he was rendered unconscious, but there were as many versions of what happened as there were spectators. Alfred Dayton's account in the *New York Sun* explained the confusion:

> "The spectators saw unfolded before their eyes one of the oddest incidents in local ring history. In this bout, Billy Petrolle, aptly termed the Fargo Express, won on a technical knockout over Hilario Martinez, the Spanish lightweight. The strange part of it all was that Petrolle won in such a manner without actually landing a knockout blow.
>
> "After a furious first round Petrolle came out winging. They went in close and Petrolle drove a left hook to the body. They came out of the clinch and Martinez straightened up, apparently uninjured. Then as Petrolle came at him again the Spaniard staggered back on his heels three-quarters of the way across the ring. He flopped into the ropes and fell out backwards, his head hitting on the corner of the platform as his body swayed on the lower strand ... balanced like a beam on a scale. At the end of the count he was carried to his corner, where he was revived shortly. He walked from the ring unaided, showing no sign of his tumble but in the dressing room a lump as big as an apple developed on

---

[36] "Russie Leroy Is Too Much for Al Conway at Laurel," *Newark Evening News*, December 14, 1926, sports section.

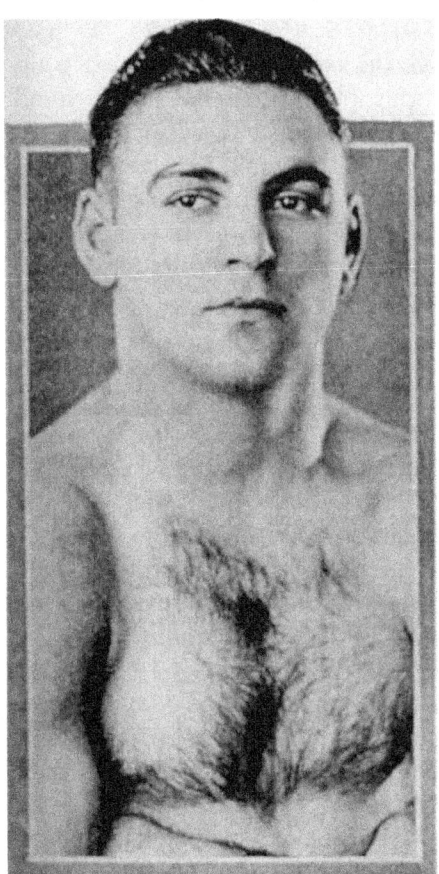

A loss to Yale Okun (above) in Earl Blue's Garden debut actually boosted Blue's reputation.

Hilario Martinez ran afoul of Petrolle's "delayed knockout punch" at the Garden.

Martinez counted out as he "balanced like a beam on a scale over the bottom rope," the victim of the "delayed knockout" punch.

the back of his head.

"All during the delay, before the principals in the [next bout] appeared on the scene, a curious buzz filled the arena. It all happened so quickly that they could not get the drift of events. Even the fighters themselves could not explain it. Martinez was at a loss to account for his actions, and Petrolle ... admitted that the left to the body was the last blow he landed. It was fully ten or 15 seconds later that Martinez hit the back trail, so Petrolle can't figure it out any more than the puzzled customers."[37]

The confusion continued the next day. One reporter thought Billy had pushed Martinez across the ring. Another wrote that "Petrolle half pushed, half hit" Martinez with his right." Others thought Hilario lost his balance trying to avoid a left hook, and then careened across the ring where he fell through the ropes and hit his head on the ring apron.

Hurley, however, had a different explanation. According to him, Martinez was the recipient of Petrolle's "delayed knockout" punch, a body blow so devastating it took a round or two to feel its full force. Jack explained the punch in detail to Tad Dorgan of the *New York Evening Journal*:

"This punch of Billy's is the hardest punch to the body you ever saw. It lands on the heart and induces slow, temporary paralysis ...

"Take the case of Johnny Adams. The punch landed in the sixth round. After that round, while Adams was sitting in his corner, he complained of numbness. 'I feel dead all over,' he told his manager. 'I can think but I can't move. I know what to do, but I can't do it,' and Adams collapsed in the next round without taking a solid blow. There's your delayed knockout.

"And what about Hilario Martinez? Petrolle landed his right to the heart in the first round. Martinez was counted out in the second, and he wasn't hit. Billy just pushed him out of a clinch and he went down. Both boys were conscious. Their eyes were clear and they tried hard to get up, but they were paralyzed.

"Then there was Joe Azzarella. Billy hit him early in the fight. Two rounds later Azzarella started a hard right. Billy sidestepped up, but he couldn't get to his feet. The old punch had begun to work."[38]

Hurley's "delayed knockout" theory caught the attention of almost every boxing writer in New York City. The bizarre ending of the fight combined

---

[37] Dayton, "Hudkins Wins over McGraw," *New York Sun*, October 30, 1926, sports section.
[38] Dorgan, Tad, ""Tad's Tidbits," *New York Evening Journal*, December 6, 1926, sports section.

Best Wishes for a Happy Yuletide and a Prosperous 1927
FROM

JACK HURLEY, ENGINEER OF THE "FARGO EXPRESS";

BILLY PETROLLE, "The FARGO EXPRESS," CARRYING 2 SLEEPERS;

RUSSIE LE ROY, "SECOND SECTION OF FARGO EXPRESS"

AND

EARL (LITTLE BOY) BLUE   "THE CABOOSE."

THE THREE GREATEST CLUB FIGHTERS IN THE WORLD

PETROLLE is the Lightweight generally regarded as the successor to Sammy Mandell, as Champion.

LE ROY is in Direct Line for the Junior Welterweight Championship.

"LITTLE BOY" BLUE is the Next Heavyweight Champion

Mr. Promoter: If you want to Show These Future Champions—Write! Wire! Phone!

JACK HURLEY, 1576 Broadway, N. Y. City.   Phone: Lackawanna 1905

Hurley's New York invasion proved a publicity boon for his warriors. All three appeared on the cover of the May 1927 edition of *Self Defense,* and Billy Petrolle received a solo spot *in The Ring*. At bottom is an ad which Jack placed in *The Ring*'s January 1927 issue.

Respect for Hurley's stable is shown in *The Ring*'s January 1927 issue picturing the top boxers in each division. Above are LeRoy (no. 1, top left), Earl Blue (no. 7, upper right), & Petrolle (no. 14, lower left). Jack was featured in *Self-Defense*'s December 1926 issue (lower right).

with Jack's compelling explanation made the writers want to believe the theory, even though it defied all reason. In any event, they all wrote about it and, as a result, gave Hurley his best publicity moment of the year.

At the end of November, Hurley and his fighters packed their bags and headed west. Jack had signed Petrolle and Blue to appear on a show in St. Paul November 26th. He had also secured an important third match for LeRoy against Spug Myers at Milwaukee on December 20, 1926.

Hurley's first year in New York was an eventful one. His fighters, virtually unknown outside the Midwest at the beginning of the year, now were being discussed throughout the country. Indeed, the January 1927 edition of *Self-Defense*, then the only U. S. magazine to publish monthly ratings, ranked all three of his boxers in the Top 10 of their divisions in separate sets of ratings compiled by two of the magazine's boxing experts.

Petrolle, still only 21 years old, was ranked No. 2 lightweight contender by one expert and No. 3 by the other. LeRoy, 24, was rated No. 2 among junior welterweights by one and No. 9 as a lightweight by the other. Blue, 22, held rankings as the No. 3 and No. 10 light heavyweight contender.[39]

Hurley would remember 1926 as the most exciting year of his life. In the future, he would manage many boxers, but never three leading contenders at once. He would encounter a variety of novel situations, but never so many people and events in such a short period of time. And, he would enjoy many triumphs, but never with the same satisfaction as when he strove to gain acceptance in the capitol city of his chosen profession.

New York City and the Big-Time, Jack Hurley had arrived!

---

[39] McCarney, "Boxers' Ratings," and Meade, Eddie, "Eddie Picks 'Em," *Self-Defense* (Ringside Publications New York), January 1927. In the text, McCarney's selection is listed first and Mead's second. Although McCarney arguably may have been biased because of his friendship with Hurley, there is no evidence that Mead was biased for or against Jack or his fighters one way or the other. The ratings in *Self-Defense* actually ranked all the best fighters in each division rather than just contenders. In other words, the champion of the division is included in the magazine's ratings. In the text, I have eliminated the champion from the ratings, as is the custom in present-day publications, so that just the contenders are rated. As an example, while Eddie Mead rates Earl Blue as the 11th best fighter in the light heavyweight division, I have shown him to be the 10th ranked contender.

It should be noted that while *Ring Magazine* featured Tex Rickard's annual ratings in the mid-1920s, the publication did not institute its monthly ratings until June, 1928.

CHAPTER 16

OUTDOORS, IN A BALLPARK

It was Padlock Day at Hurley's gymnasium Friday, and many ardent boxing fans wishing to see Billy Petrolle go through his paces were disappointed. The doors were locked and the curtains drawn, the building giving passersby the impression that the structure was deserted. However, on the inside it was entirely different. An unusual picture greeted the eyes of those lucky enough to talk their way past the watchful doorkeeper.

In the ring was none other than J. Cornelius Hurley, himself, togged out in ring clothes, his bony fists covered with six-ounce gloves. Backed against the ropes on one side was the Fargo Express, carefully watching every move by his lanky teacher. The scene recalled the days when Petrolle and LeRoy were novices, and Hurley used the gym under the Tweeden Hotel to teach his lads the difference between a left hook and a dropkick.

"Where's that heart punch you used to bowl 'em over with?" bellowed the Kernel at his protégé. "You haven't hit anyone below the whiskers since you dropped Tommy Murphy with that left hook to the face. You gotta' hit these birds where it hurts, and from now on I'm going to see that you do it. Suck in your left. Now duck this right uppercut and show me how you counter."

Bill did as instructed, and Hurley groaned. It was quite evident that the result of Bill's honest effort was not what Hurley desired. "Now listen, Bill, you've gotta' weave more when stepping in. You turn on that fan with your head still and a smart fighter will paste you five or six times before you can move."

After it was over, Hurley expressed his satisfaction with the result by saying, "Bill is just as anxious as ever to learn. We all get careless when not checked up from time to time. I believe that a few more days of private workouts will send out a new fighter, one capable of licking all the lightweights in the world as fast as they can be sent against him."

While we are on the subject of boxing, let it be said that the average layman has no business picking a quarrel with Mr. Jack Hurley. Tall and slender as he is, he packs a mighty wallop and steps around the ring with the ease and surety of a veteran ringman.

Hurley is a true observer. During that session with Petrolle he never missed a point – either right or wrong – his fighter did, and he also made it more interesting by showing Petrolle exactly how other fighters offer their wares. He demonstrated the effective points by which Billy's next opponent scores and showed him the defenses and counter punches, which should be effective.

It was a lesson for Petrolle. And the favored few, who were allowed to watch the workout, learned something about the "inside dope" of the manly art.[1]   – J. A. (Pat) Purcell

****

In December 1926, Laddy Kusy told Hurley that Sammy Mandell had agreed to fight Billy Petrolle in late January at Newark for a flat guarantee of $30,000. Kusy agreed to contribute $20,000 if Jack and Petrolle could raise the remaining $10,000. The proposal called for the fighters to weigh within the 135-pound lightweight limit. However, since New Jersey was a no-decision state, Billy would have to kayo Mandell to become champ.

After discussing the offer with Petrolle, Russie LeRoy, and Earl Blue, Hurley told Billy McCarney, who was handling his New York business to accept Kusy's offer if Jack could have until January 5 to raise the $10,000.

Hurley was promoting his annual boxing show January 1. In addition to Jack's plan to contribute his profits from the show, LeRoy and Blue agreed to waive their purses to raise the money to give Billy a chance at the title.[2]

Petrolle's opponent for the New Year's card was Tommy (Kid) Murphy of Trenton, New Jersey, who was managed by Leo P. Flynn. The bout originally had been scheduled for Newark on December 13, but at the last minute Hurley changed his mind and refused to sign the contract. He feared Petrolle would not be given a fair deal in Murphy's home state, and that Billy as a result might not get the match with Mandell.

Flynn took his case before the New Jersey Athletic Commission. In a meeting lasting four hours, Leo charged that Hurley and Petrolle had run out on a verbal agreement to fight Murphy in New Jersey, and that Tommy, not Billy, should be awarded the title fight against Mandell in Newark. Flynn urged the commission to reprimand Jack and enforce a 30-day suspension against Hurley and his fighters from working in New Jersey.

Hurley was ready for Flynn's argument. He produced the contract Leo had signed for Murphy to fight Petrolle at Fargo on May 21, 1926. At the time, Tommy pulled out five days before the match, claiming a case of "the grippe." At the commission meeting, Jack "jumped up and declared Petrolle was ready to sign contracts at that moment for a fight with Murphy, providing the latter would fulfill the agreement made ... to fight in Fargo."

The maneuver caught Flynn off guard and put him on the spot with the commission, which voiced its opinion that "Fargo is as good a place as any

---

[1] Purcell, J. A., "Jack Hurley Takes Active Part in Preparing Petrolle for Babe Ruth," *Fargo Forum*, April 16, 1927, sports section. Purcell's article has been edited to fit the context. Petrolle's rematch with Babe Ruth, originally scheduled for April 22, 1927, was canceled and never re-scheduled. References to Ruth have been deleted and replaced with a generic reference to Petrolle's "next opponent."

[2] Purcell, "Billy's Stable Mates Offer to Gamble Purses," *Fargo Forum*, December 5, 1926, sports section.

to settle the quarrel." Seeing the chance for a Murphy-Mandell bout slipping away unless he agreed to the Petrolle fight in Fargo, Leo told the commission, "'Produce the papers. I'll sign 'em.'" Before they "left the office of the commission, Flynn's name was on the dotted line."[3]

The *Fargo Forum* called the signing of the Petrolle-Murphy bout "the finest piece of matchmaking in North Dakota's boxing history." If nothing else, the episode proved Hurley was a force to be reckoned with when it came to vigorously representing the interests of his fighters. In matching wits with Leo P. Flynn, Hurley had out-foxed a man who managed the world's largest stable of important boxers and who, at Tex Rickard's suggestion, would become Jack Dempsey's manager in 1927.

Hurley's orchestrations in front of the New Jersey commission stirred the blood of boxing fans throughout the Dakotas, thus fulfilling the basic requirement of Hurley's Law – give people a reason to attend the fight. As in the case of the Petrolle-Simmons bout, Fargo fans were again convinced their support of the next show would have a direct bearing on whether their hometown boy would obtain a chance at the lightweight championship.

Petrolle's opponent, Tommy (Kid) Murphy, was the son of early bantamweight Kid Murphy (born Peter Frascella), who had claimed the world championship in 1907 by virtue of a 10-round decision win over Johnny Coulon. Although the elder Murphy was subsequently blinded in the ring, he raised his son to be a boxer almost from birth.

Just 21-years old, Tommy Murphy was at the height of a career which already had produced wins over Memphis Pal Moore, Panama Al Brown, Danny Cooney, Johnny Kochansky, Eddie Wagner, and Sammy Vogel. In the most recent year and a half, Murphy had been on a tear against the world's best lightweights and emerged undefeated. With a reputation as an exceptionally clever boxer with dazzling hand and foot speed, Tommy figured to have a style designed to give Petrolle plenty of trouble.

On the same card, LeRoy was slated to box Irish Danny Fagan of Newark, New Jersey in the semifinal. Although Fagan was an "in-and-outer" who tended to lose more often than he won, he was tough and had beaten Shuffles Callahan and Abie Bain, both well-respected fighters.

The Fagan match was important because LeRoy needed a win to get back on track after losing another decision to Spug Myers at Milwaukee December 20, 1926. That bout, their third encounter, was especially discouraging because the fight was even at the end of nine rounds. In the tenth, Myers nailed Russie with "an assortment of left hooks and right crosses" and had him groggy enough at the final bell to earn the verdict.[4]

---

[3] Purcell, "Trenton Flash Agrees to Fargo Date After Losing Newark Show," *Fargo Forum*, December 16, 1926, sports section.
[4] Levy, Sam, "LeRoy Is Loser in Semifinal," *Milwaukee Journal*, December 21, 1926, sports section.

Leo P. Flynn, famous New York manager who Hurley out-witted to land Petrolle's bout with Tommy (Kid) Murphy in Fargo.

Professor Billy McCarney as he looked at about the time he was handling Jack Hurley's business in New York.

Tommy (Kid) Murphy of Trenton, New Jersey.

Newark's Irish Danny Fagan fought Russie LeRoy in Fargo.

Unfortunately, a case of inflammatory rheumatism necessitated a last-minute cancellation of Blue's bout against Jack Denny on the New Year's show. Far more disastrous, however, was the effect the illness had on Earl's career in New York. Based on his strong showing against Yale Okun, Jess McMahon had promised Hurley a January slot for Blue in a Madison Square Garden main event against Pat McCarthy. The illness forced a cancellation of his Garden appearance and sidelined him for 2-1/2 months.[5]

Forum sports editor Pat Purcell reported that "after one minute of fighting in the third round" the end of the Petrolle-Murphy bout "came so suddenly that it electrified a near capacity crowd at the Fargo Auditorium." Billy ducked a right and "quick as lightning ... jumped in and landed a hard left swing flush on Murphy's jaw. The blow raised the Trenton fighter fully a foot off the floor and he fell heavily on his shoulders."

Up at the count of nine, Murphy ran into a "perfectly timed right hook ... fell backwards, and never moved a muscle until a few seconds after the completion of the count." Purcell concluded that "Murphy proved to be the fastest bit of boxing humanity that we have ever seen, but ... it is hard for us to picture a fighter fast enough to stay away from Billy's clutches."

In the semifinal, LeRoy, 144-1/2 lb., won a ten-round decision over Fagan, 149-1/2 lb. The *Forum* reported Russie waged "a heady fight against a cagey veteran ... which had the crowd in an uproar from start to finish."[6]

Four days after Petrolle's victory, Hurley announced he had concluded a deal with promoter Jim Mullen for Billy to fight Sammy Mandell for the lightweight title at Chicago. Mullen had outbid Laddie Kusy for the bout and had secured a verbal commitment from Mandell's manager, Eddie Kane, to defend the title against Petrolle.

The match tentatively was set for Comiskey Park in early May as the feature attraction in Mullen's first open-air show of 1927. The plan required Billy to engage in two fights at Chicago before the Mandell fight to build up his following in the Windy City. If Jim was going to take a chance on the bout he wanted to insure it made money. Although not mentioned at the time, the arrangement included an understanding that if Billy faltered in the first two contests, Mullen could opt out of the title match.[7]

Petrolle's first bout was against Spug Myers January 20 at the Coliseum. Myers' rapid rise was largely a result of his two wins over LeRoy. Most recently, Spug had defeated Sid Barbarian in a ten-round fight in New York.

Though Petrolle was favored in the betting 2 to 1, the contest itself proved anything but an easy affair. Floored by a left to the midriff in the

---

[5] "Earl Blue May Never Appear in Ring Again," *Fargo Forum*, January 9, 1927, sports section.

[6] Purcell, "Fargo Express Puts Trenton Boxer Out with 2 Hard Blows," *Fargo Forum*, January 2, 1927, sports section.

[7] Purcell, "Hurley, Mullen Come to Verbal Terms; Chicago Scene of Fight," *Fargo Forum*, sports section.

"*The Training Place of Champions*"

MULLEN'S LOOP GYM
180-184 W. RANDOLPH ST. - *Phone* FRANKLIN 4215
CHICAGO

July 17th 1926

Illinois Athletic Commission
210 East Ohio St.,
Chicago, Ill.

Gentlemen:

    I desire a license to manage boxers in Illinois. I have Billy Petrolle under my management and he is on the card at White Sox Park, July 24th.

    I have licenses to manage boxers in Massachusetts, Connecticut, New York, Pennsylvania, Wisconsin, Minnesota, South Dakota and California. I have been managing boxers for seven years.

    Am twenty-seven years of age, a citizen of the United States being born in Fargo, N.D. Am not married. Have never been disciplined or penalized by any State Athletic Commission.

References: Wm. Stern, Dakota National Bank, Fargo, N.D.
             Jess McMahon, Madison Square Garden, New York City.
             James C. Mullen, 180 W. Randolph St., Chicago.
             Steve Gorman, Fargo, North Dakota.
             Walter Eckersall, The Tribune, Chicago, Ill.

Very truly yours,

Jack Hurley

Jack Hurley
Fargo, North Dakota.
Manager of Billy Petrolle.

License # 15

A GYMNASIUM
FOR
BUSINESS MEN
AND ATHLETES
BOXING
WRESTLING
HAND BALL
BATHS
MASSAGE
GYMNASTICS
HEALTH BUILDING
PHYSICAL TRAINING

THE MULLEN-HOCHSTADTER ENTERPRISES, INC.

When in Chicago in the 1920s, Hurley made Jim Mullen's Loop Gym his headquarters. Above is Jack's original application for an Illinois manager's license, the 15th issued under the state's new boxing law. Of particular interest are the five people he chose as character references in support of the application.

fifth round and way behind in scoring at the end of the eighth, Billy waged a ferocious rally in the last two rounds to fend off certain defeat. Only a desperate, roundhouse right which knocked Myers to the canvas in the ninth and a whirlwind finish in the tenth salvaged a draw for Billy.[8]

Mullen was unfazed by Petrolle's narrow escape. Afterward, he gave Billy a beautiful ring inscribed with the words "To the next champ." As far as Jim was concerned, Petrolle was still in line for the lightweight-title shot.

Rather than re-matching Petrolle with Myers and eliminating one of them from the picture, Mullen continued to tout Billy as a lightweight contender while moving Spug up to the junior welterweight class.

Myers' next fight would be a non-title affair against junior welter champion Mushy Callahan on February 10. Spug would in fact defeat Callahan and earn another bout with the titleholder at Chicago on May 31. In this fight, with the championship at stake, Callahan would redeem himself and win a close ten-round decision over Myers to retain his title.

Although Hurley spent the first two months of 1927 in the Midwest, he still zealously maintained his status as a resident of New York City. Even while in Fargo, he continued to conduct much of his business through the office he shared with McCarney and Joe Jacobs in the Publicity Building.

Hurley also kept a room in New York at the Times Square Hotel on the corner of 43rd Street and Eighth Avenue during this time. The building, built in 1922 as a tourist hotel for men, provided over 1,000 inexpensive studio apartments which were ideal for part-time residents of the city. Jack would maintain a room at the hotel off and on into the 1930s.[9]

Since Hurley was one of few Fargoans with a New York address, Purcell asked Jack in the fall of 1926 to write him every week about what was happening in the Big Apple. By November, his letters had become a full-fledged Sunday column in the *Forum* entitled "Broadway Breezes." Except for a 1-1/2-year hiatus in 1928-30, he would continue to write a weekly column under a variety of titles, both in the *Forum* and on a syndicated basis for other papers, until just after the U. S. entered World War II.

Even though the primary focus of "Broadway Breezes" was boxing, Hurley's early days on the prowl in New York led him to a variety of other athletic events. Almost invariably, his promotional instinct caused him to seek out big spectacles which attracted huge crowds.

Jack's column about the six-day bicycle races at Madison Square Garden evinced a sense of awe at what people would pay good money to see:

---

[8] Opp, Jack, "Both Upset by Punches in Contest," *Fargo Forum*, January 21, 1927, sports section.

[9] Oser, Alan S., "Perspectives: Housing the Dependent; Times Square Hotel as the Biggest S. R. O.," *New York Times*, December 1, 1991, real estate section. As of April 2008, the hotel remained a thriving 652-room S. R. O. (supported single room occupancy) facility that was refurbished in the early 1990s in by New York City. Hurley's advertisement in a 1927 *Self Defense* magazine lists the hotel as his residence.

"Can you imagine 18,000 people standing up, yelling themselves hoarse at a bunch of guys riding bicycles around a track? When you stop to think that this takes place at 3 o'clock in the morning it makes it all the worse.

"A few years ago, people went to the Garden when the races opened and remained there for the entire week, living on hot dogs and soda pop, exclusively. However, the powers-that-be wised up to the fact that the folks were getting free lodging all week for the price of one admission ticket, so they simply passed a rule that the place must be cleared out at 6 o'clock morning and evening. This was good for the race promoters but it was a sad blow to the boys who are short of room rent and who formerly made the Garden their home for the week of the six-day grind."[10]

A bit of "the small-town boy comes to the big city" mentality is evident in Hurley's description of his first visit to a major-league hockey game:

"What a wonderful place this world is, and what wonderful things have been accomplished during the last century! On a Thursday night recently I witnessed a hockey game at Madison Square Garden. The temperature of the huge amphitheater was 57 degrees and it was just like being in a downtown theater.

"There was a 25-piece band to furnish music for fancy skaters between periods of the hockey game, and it was a wonderful spectacle to gaze at. The fancy skating troupe was good and the hockey game was better. The Montreal Maroons opposed the New York Americans and the Canadians won 2 to 1. These clubs are members of the National Hockey League which is made up of 10 teams. The games draw capacity 3 times a week and the venture is a success to all concerned.

"What I want to bring out is that the very next night I attended the Tod Morgan-Carl Duane junior lightweight championship bout in the same arena. The ice was gone and the Garden was once again the greatest boxing palace in the world. I am told that the ice can be taken out or put into the arena in 3 to 4 hours."[11]

Hurley was not a football fan, but curiosity "forced [him] to spend $10 to see the Army-Notre Dame football game in search of writing material." Jack wrote that two things about the game impressed him: "One was the 63-yard run for a touchdown by Christy Flanagan, and the other was the size of the crowd – 73,000 people. Can you imagine that? How I would like to

---

[10] Hurley, Jack, "Broadway Breezes," *Fargo Forum*, December 12, 1926, sports section.

[11] Hurley, *op. cit.*, November 28, 1926, sports section.

draw that kind of a house in Fargo for one of my fight cards."[12]

Hurley's bias against amateur sports and his skepticism about those who sponsored them were evident in his observations about the annual Army-Navy football game:

> "More than 110,000 people witnessed the Army-Navy game at Chicago. The gross receipts totaled $1,000,000. Each college received $100,000 as its share. It's none of my business, but I wonder who got the rest of the receipts?
>
> "When you consider two teams from the East can come to Chicago and draw that kind of money, then nothing seems impossible. The players were unknown to 90 percent of the people at the game, so what is it that attracted them to the contest?
>
> "Some years ago a wise man remarked that 'the man who invented interest was indeed a smart fellow.' I venture to say that the man who invented interest was not smart at all compared to the man who invented 'Amateur standings.' What a rule that turned out to be. The players draw those big gates and don't get a dime."
>
> "Every time I get near a stadium and watch the fans lay down on the mahogany I get sick. I simply can't stand to see those colleges get all that money."[13]

Hurley was back in New York on March 3, 1927, in time to see Jack Sharkey knock out Mike McTigue in 12 rounds at Madison Square Garden. Jack was impressed by Sharkey's showing, but convinced that, if the former sailor Dempsey were to meet in the ring, the Manassa Mauler would win.[14]

In New York, Hurley caught up with LeRoy and Blue, who had been training a couple of weeks under McCarney's tutelage at the Pioneer Gym. Jack was in Russie's corner for his first Eastern bout of the year March 7.

Over the following two months, LeRoy engaged in five fights in the East with mixed results. He split the verdicts in four newspaper decisions, and lost the other bout on a disputed low blow while leading in the scoring. After a May 9th match at Holyoke, Massachusetts, Russie ended his Eastern swing and spent the rest of his career headlining cards at smaller venues in the Midwest, never again to fight east of St. Louis.

Blue's first bout after regaining his health was on March 14 at Laurel Garden in Newark against Al Traynor. He won three fights on the East Coast before traveling to Waterloo, Iowa to fight a draw April 20 with George Bourland. Afterward, Blue returned to New York to prepare for the

---

[12] Hurley, *op. cit.*, November 21, 1926, sports section.
[13] Hurley, *op. cit.*, December 5, 1926, sports section. Purcell, "Sportville Spotlight," *Fargo Forum*, November 28, 1926, sports section.
[14] Hurley, *op. cit.*, March 13, 1927, sports section.

most important fight of his career, a ten-round semi-final against Jack DeMave May 9 at Madison Square Garden.[15]

Hurley and Petrolle were in Chicago on April 12 when Billy was set to battle King Tut of Minneapolis at the Chicago Coliseum. The fight was the next leg in Mullen's campaign to develop interest in the Mandell-Petrolle bout he hoped to promote later in the spring. As such, a good showing by Billy once again was crucial to his championship hopes.

Unfortunately, Tut reported with "a bad cold ... a subnormal temperature, and low vitality," and the commission doctor refused to pass him for the bout. In his place, Freddie Mueller, a little known lightweight from Buffalo, New York, was recruited as a last-minute substitute to fight Petrolle.

At the sound of the first bell, Mueller surprised everyone by taking the fight to Petrolle. He jarred Billy with a long swing and, when the Express slowed him down with a right flush on the jaw, Freddie went into a clinch.

Mueller controlled the first half of the bout with the same combination of rushing and clinching. It was not until the middle of the fight that Petrolle figured out Freddie's style and began to take charge. Billy knocked down Mueller in the sixth round and won the last three rounds easily.

Petrolle's late surge was not enough to overtake Mueller's early lead. At the end of ten rounds, the judges called the fight a draw. Most of those in the crowd had pulled for the underdog, and they did not hesitate to voice their opinion Freddie deserved the decision.[16]

Afterward, Hurley told the *Forum*'s Purcell that "Billy fought a dandy fight, but Mueller did the same so it was a draw. The woods are full of fighters who can fight and only need a chance to make a name for themselves. Petrolle was made overnight when he stopped Eddie (Kid) Wagner, and believe me Mueller is made too ... Right now we're going to forget about Mueller and start sawing wood for the [next] fight."[17]

Hurley never had been more serious when he said Petrolle would start "sawing wood" for his next fight. Despite his positive words about Billy's showing against Mueller, Jack feared Billy might lose the Mandell match unless he turned things around. Two straight draws in Chicago could not help but raise doubts in Mullen's mind about the bout's financial viability.

Hurley had noticed Petrolle was not throwing enough body punches and

---

[15] BoxRec.com, Russie LeRoy and Earl Blue. Note: BoxRec is a work-in-progress website. Records evolve over time as researchers discover more information.

[16] Eckersall, Walter, "$35,000 House Sees Shade Win Slow Bout over Krug," *Chicago Tribune*, April 13, 1927, sports section. Opp, Jack, "Billy Gets Late Start Against Sub," *Fargo Forum*, April 13, 1927, sports section.

[17] Purcell, "Express to Prepare for Ruth Today," *Fargo Forum*, April 15, 1927, sports section. Petrolle had a fight scheduled for April 22 against Babe Ruth in Fargo. However, that fight was canceled at the last minute at the request of Mullen who summoned Hurley and Billy to Chicago to discuss arrangements for possible upcoming fights. No mention of the Ruth fight has been made in the text to avoid confusion since its scheduling and subsequent cancellation have no real bearing on the narrative.

was getting hit too often in his last two fights. Two days after the Mueller bout, they returned to Fargo where, in sessions behind closed doors, Jack took Billy to the "woodshed" to correct these lapses before his next fight.[18]

Petrolle was set to face Cuddy DeMarco, of Pittsburgh, in a ten-rounder April 25, 1927, for Laddy Kusy at Laurel Garden. The Fargo duo planned to reach Newark early so Billy could train there a few days before the bout.

Just as Hurley and Petrolle were leaving, Mullen asked them to stop in Chicago for a few days to discuss future plans. The stopover disrupted Billy's training schedule. He spent five of the next seven days on trains, and was not able to do any boxing at all before the Newark fight.[19]

At the fight on April 25, while "dissatisfied fans sent up a volley of boos," referee Henry (Hen) Lewis stepped between Petrolle and DeMarco during the fourth round, declared "there was too much stalling," and ruled the bout "no contest." Lewis had been unhappy from the start and issued warnings to both battlers in their corners at the end of each round.[20]

In Lewis' opinion, the boxers were out to collect a payday without giving their best. Afterward, he said, "I have seen Petrolle fight before, and I think he should knock DeMarco out in a couple of rounds. True enough, Petrolle chased DeMarco and threw plenty of punches, but he missed too many and the fans were led to believe that he was missing them on purpose."[21]

Hurley explained that the reason Petrolle had missed so many punches was his timing was off due to his week of inactivity. As it was, he had done his best, but DeMarco's hugging and running tactics made it difficult for Billy to land solidly. Jack offered the fact that the promoter had paid Billy in full after the fight as proof that his effort had been an honest one.[22]

Lewis said the boxers had been paid without his recommendation. A few days later, New Jersey's chief boxing inspector, Platt Adams, ordered Petrolle to return "six-tenths" of his $1,500 purse, a sum amounting to a pro-rata share of scheduled rounds not actually fought.[23]

A call from the New Jersey commission to Hurley's New York office elicited an answer from "his secretary" that although Jack was not available to take the call, "he would positively never pay back one cent."[24]

---

[18] Purcell, "Jack Hurley Takes Active Part in Preparing Petrolle for Babe Ruth," *op. cit.* This article describes the scene depicted on this chapter's opening page.

[19] Purcell, "Sportville Spotlight," *Fargo Forum*, April 27, 1927, sports section.

[20] "Action Is Lacking in Newark Go," *Fargo Forum*, April 26, 1927, sports section.

[21] Hurley, *op. cit.*, May 1, 1927, sports section.

[22] "Petrolle and M'Graw Fight Is Called Off," *Fargo Forum*, April 27, 1927, sports section.

[23] Ratner, Willie, "Laurel Fighters Ordered to Return Part of Purse," *Newark Evening News*, April 27, 1927, sports section. "Hen Lewis Has a Say on Fiasco," *Newark Evening News*, May 2, 1927, sports section.

[24] "Sir Joe Glick and Anderson Fined Heavily," *Newark Evening News*, April 28, 1927, sports section. Ratner, "Amster to Box Castellane Under His Own Management," *Newark Evening News*, May 5, 1927, sports section. Ratner, "Solly Castellane a Hero with Boxing Fans of Hill," *Newark Evening News*, May 10, 1927, sports section.

Spug Meyers (left) and Freddie Mueller (right) sidetracked Petrolle's plan for a title fight by holding him to draws in bouts for Jim Mullen.

Petrolle lost another chance for a title shot when Hen Lewis (right) ruled his bout with Cuddy DeMarco (left) "No Contest."

The unsatisfactory outcome of the DeMarco fight effectively ended Petrolle's hope of a title bout with Mandell during the 1927 outdoor season. Instead, Mullen shifted his attention to the Myers-Callahan junior welter title contest. In addition, Detroit promoter Floyd Fitzsimmons canceled a match between Billy and Phil McGraw scheduled for May 6.[25]

When the cancellations began rolling in, Hurley fought back with both barrels blazing. Jack claimed the real reason Lewis had stopped the fight "was on account of a promoter's war in Newark." New Jersey referees were not hired by the promoter but were instead appointed by the commission. Hen Lewis was a close associate to "the Four Horsemen," a promotional firm in direct competition with Kusy's Laurel Garden Athletic Club.

Jack argued Lewis unjustifiably had halted bouts on four other Laurel Garden shows prior to the DeMarco fight and ruled all of them "no contest" to harm Kusy's business. Hurley called Hen "incompetent" and accused him of "playing to the gallery" and "encouraging the crowd to show its disapproval at every opportunity," instead of being "honest and capable enough not to be swayed by the angry mob" as he was "supposed to be."[26]

The "Four Horsemen" were actually Nick Kline, Babe Culnan, Harry Blaufuss, and Frank Black. These partners, who called their business the National Sportsmen's Club, had operated Newark's most successful boxing club before Kusy began to promote fights at Laurel Garden four years earlier. Since that time, the "Four Horsemen" had lost out to Kusy to the point where their club "seldom puts on a show."

When Hurley accused Lewis of undermining the interests of the Laurel Garden Athletic Club, he was by inference accusing the "Four Horsemen" of working behind the scenes to do the same thing. Indeed, Nick Kline, one of the "Horsemen," had attacked the quality of Kusy's shows in the Newark newspapers and publicly praised Newark referees for "throw[ing] boys out of the ring for stalling."[27]

In support of Hurley's denunciation of Lewis, Lou Rabin, who doubled as a boxing manager and as Kusy's press agent, announced that as far as he was concerned "all local referees were incompetent to referee matches in which [Rabin's] fighters figure." Rabin said he was not speaking for Kusy or the Laurel Garden club, but only for himself as manager of Bobbie Amster, who was scheduled to appear at the club's next show.

Unfortunately for Kusy and Hurley, the New Jersey commission put its full support behind referee Lewis and suspended the boxing licenses of Petrolle and DeMarco one year for not returning the purses they had received. The commission also fired its deputy inspector, Henry Schwinn,

---

[25] "Petrolle and M'Graw Fight Is Called Off," *Fargo Forum*, April 27, 1927, sports section.
[26] Hurley, *op. cit.*, May 1, 1927, sports section.
[27] Dodge, "Close-Ups on Latest in Sport," *Newark Star-Eagle*, May 11, 1927, sports section.

who had authorized Kusy to pay the two boxers after their bout. Finally, the commission suspended Rabin until such time as he would apologize for calling the commission's referees incompetent.[28]

As a result of the controversy, Kusy, who had started promoting for the fun of it, returned to his butcher business and retired from boxing, never to promote again. Within two weeks, the National Sportsmen's Club assumed the Laurel Garden lease and was promoting its boxing shows. For his part, Hurley took his fighters to more welcoming territories, never to return to Newark until 1944, more than 17 years later.

Hurley immediately set out to rehabilitate Petrolle's reputation. Realizing he would have to take whatever came their way for awhile, Jack accepted bouts on short notice against Johnny Hayes in Philadelphia on May 2 and against Jack Duffy in Akron, Ohio May 26. Billy came through in grand style in both fights, dispatching Hayes in five rounds and Duffy in one.

On May 29, Hurley announced he had secured a match for Petrolle against Billy Wallace as part of a mammoth lightweight elimination tournament at the Polo Grounds on June 15. The show was advertised as a charity benefit for the Catholic Boys' Clubs. Besides Petrolle-Wallace, the featured bouts included Sid Terris in a face-off against Ruby Goldstein, Ace Hudkins battling Sergeant Sammy Baker, and former featherweight king Louis (Kid) Kaplan meeting future welterweight titleholder Jackie Fields.

During this same time, Earl Blue had been training for his big chance on May 9 against Jack DeMave, the "Hoboken Adonis," at Madame Bey's deluxe outdoor training camp at Summit, New Jersey. DeMave had won six of his last seven bouts and was expected to enter the ring at even money against "Little Boy." The lone blemish on DeMave's otherwise perfect record during the string had been a draw with tough Johnny Risko.

Once again, the bugaboo of an unanticipated "last-minute substitute" derailed Hurley's carefully planned agenda. On the day of the fight, DeMave failed his pre-fight physical exam when he reported to the weigh-in with a large boil. George LaRocco, a journeyman heavyweight from nearby Westchester, was chosen to take DeMave's place.

On May 10, the *New York World*'s Hype Igoe reported the night's action:

> "Little Boy Blue lost a hard fought contest against George LaRocco in the second ten-round bout in Madison Square Garden ... It was a bitter struggle with Blue dangerously close to victory at times. By the same token he was often close to defeat via a knockout ... It was about as hard punching set-to as you'll see between 180-pounders ...

---

[28] Ratner, "Laurel A. C. Press Agent Must Make Public Apology," *Newark Evening News,* May 4, 1927, sports section. Ratner, "Amster to Box Castellane Under His Own Management," *Newark Evening News*, May 5, 1927, p. 16-X.

"First one and then the other rocked under punishment. They stood toe to toe and traded rights as if they had been love taps. LaRocco got the range of Blue after a time and he drubbed many a hard smack to Boy's chin.

"Blue would stand up in his corner each time the ten-second signal blew and would rush out fighting. Blue was floored for a count of nine in the sixth round. They traded rights and LaRocco's was the one to land hardest. The bell came to Blue's rescue."[29]

As usual, Jack put on his best face possible. "Blue, even though he was defeated, did not lose any of his former prestige," he argued. "Decisions don't mean anything in New York. The fans like to see the boys who can sock and Little Boy Blue can do that little thing to the queen's taste."[30]

The truth of the matter, however, was that Blue's best days were for all practical purposes over. Earl would win his next fight by a one-round kayo on July 19 at Fargo, but thereafter his career would take a nosedive.

Just two days later on July 21, Bearcat Wright would kayo Blue in two rounds at Minneapolis. Discouraged, Earl would leave Hurley and cast his lot with New York manager Bill Reedy. Under Reedy, Blue would never again win a fight. His record after leaving Hurley consisted of two draws, two decision losses, one disqualification, and seven knockout defeats.[31]

Whether Blue would have fared better with Hurley is a matter of conjecture, but his record afterward supports the view that Jack's careful management took him about as far as his abilities allowed. Reedy's efforts matching Blue against high-class foes like Yale Okun, Battling Levinsky, Young Stribling, Dick Daniels, and Osk Till all met with abject failure.

Petrolle spent a week at Madame Bey's health farm in Summit, New Jersey preparing for his June 15th bout against Billy Wallace. While there, Hurley visited with Sam Slotsky, his old friend from their Sioux City days, whose fighter, Joe Schlocker, was helping Petrolle prepare for the fight.[32]

Wallace, 26-years old and a veteran of 89 fights, came up the hard way. Born in Dawson City during the Alaska Gold Rush, Wallace started boxing in California during that state's four-round days prior to the passage of its boxing law. He boxed there almost exclusively during his first six years as a pro, compiling a respectable record, but not earning much in the way of financial remuneration.

When Wallace moved with his manager to Cleveland, Ohio in 1926, his

---

[29] Igoe, Hype, "New Yorker Has Earl on Canvas for Nine Count," *New York World*, May 10, 1927, sports section.
[30] Hurley, *op. cit.*, May 15, 1927, sports section.
[31] BoxRec.com Earl Blue. Box Rec is a work-in-progress website. Records evolve over time as researchers discover more information.
[32] Leonard, Benny, "Benny Leonard Impressed with Style of Petrolle," *Fargo Forum*, June 12, 1927, sports section.

career took off. His breakthrough was a 10-round decision over top-ranked featherweight Babe Herman June 30, 1926. Six months later he scored an upset by stopping ex-feather champ Louis (Kid) Kaplan in five rounds.

As had Petrolle before him, Wallace won over New York fans while losing a close decision to the East Side Phantom, Sid Terris. Wallace floored Terris twice in the first round, once in the third, and had him groggy in the sixth. Only a clean sweep by Terris in the last four rounds salvaged a split-decision victory for the fleet-footed New Yorker.

Wallace's gentlemanly appearance and polished demeanor impressed sportswriters. Always a colorful personality, he was able to regale them with stories of his own experiences as a crooning front-man for a big band in Cleveland, and also with humorous tales about Tex Rickard, who had been his father's partner and next-door neighbor in the Klondike.

Wallace boxed at a high level his entire career, winning consistently until he retired in 1935 with a record of 109 wins, 28 losses, and 27 draws. In his last three years, he won 17 of 19 bouts, posting just one loss and one draw.[33]

The Polo Grounds was bristling with excitement the evening of June 15, 1927. In addition to the four main events, which at least one sportswriter looked upon as "one of the greatest all-star cards ever arranged," it was expected that Charles Lindbergh would be in attendance. Lindbergh had captured the imagination of the entire country three weeks earlier by completing the first solo airplane flight across the Atlantic Ocean.

"Lucky Lindy," as he was affectionately known, had just returned from Europe and was on the first leg of a nationwide coast-to-coast "victory tour" which would end up three months later in Philadelphia. Lindbergh learned to fly in Lincoln, Nebraska, and was attending the show to see his old friend, Ace Hudkins, "the Nebraska Wildcat," go up against former U. S. Army Infantry Sergeant Sammy Baker.[34]

Unfortunately, Hudkins suffered a bad cut over his right eye in the second round. In the seventh round, the referee awarded the fight to Baker on a technical knockout when Ace became blinded by blood and swelling around the eye. Lindbergh, who had other engagements, left after the Hudkins fight, escorted by a contingent of New York's finest. The throng cheered enthusiastically as he strolled out of the Polo Grounds accompanied by New York Mayor Jimmy Walker and a host of other dignitaries.

Petrolle started fast against Wallace, winning the first four rounds and dropping his adversary to one knee for a flash knockdown in the third. After the fourth round, the tide shifted, as Wallace, a tall, deceptively frail-

---

[33] BoxRec.com, Billy Wallace. Box Rec is a work-in-progress website. Records evolve over time as researchers discover more information. Most of Wallace's draw decisions occurred in his California days when bouts were limited to four rounds. Because the bouts were so short, their outcomes were often inconclusive and resulted in many draw decisions.

[34] Morris, William, "Hudkins Promises Action in Battle Against Baker; Terris Tackles Goldstein," *New York Evening Post*, June 15, 1927, sports section.

looking boxer-puncher, figured out the Fargoan's bobbing and weaving style and began to find the mark with brisk left jabs and short, jolting, right uppercuts which straightened up Petrolle.

Although Petrolle staggered Wallace with a right in the sixth round and, by most accounts, easily won the ninth, the Alaska native jabbed his way to win the final round and the fight according to the official scorecards. Scoring by local ringside reporters was split down the middle. Among those expressing opinions one way or the other, three favored Wallace, three leaned toward Petrolle, and two thought a draw would have been fair.[35]

Hurley lodged a protest with the commission because the bell ending the second round rang early, just after Petrolle staggered Wallace with a right. Reporters timed the duration of the round at one minute 42 seconds instead of the normal three minutes. Jack claimed his charge would have knocked out Wallace had the bell not sounded when it did. He argued Petrolle should either be declared the winner or at the very least be awarded a rematch.

At the same hearing, the commission invited the participants on the card to pay back a portion of their purses to the Catholic Boys' Club since the show had not made as much money as anticipated. While each of the other seven headliners except Baker returned varying amounts, Hurley declined.

Hurley reasoned that, since he had originally demanded $10,000 but been paid only $8,000, he and Petrolle had, in effect, already donated the equivalent of $2,000. Furthermore, if the show had drawn more than anticipated, he and Billy would still have not gotten any more than $8,000, so why should they be asked to pay anything back now?

Not surprisingly, after hearing Hurley out on both matters, the commission gave scant attention to the claimed injustice resulting from the shortened round.[36]

On June 27, 1927, Petrolle won a ten-round decision over Basil Galiano in Philadelphia. Afterward, Hurley and Billy returned for a July 19th show in Fargo at the American Legion's state convention. Jack's sister, Abigail, had just married John P. Conmy, commander of Fargo's American Legion post. Conmy was in charge of hosting the convention, and Hurley agreed to make

---

[35] Wilbur Wood of the *New York Sun* (5-4-1), Sid Mercer of the *New York Evening Journal* (6-4), and William Morris of the *New York Evening Post* (rounds not able to be determined) had it for Billy Wallace. George Underwood of the *New York Telegram* (7-3), James Dawson of the *New York Times* ("Petrolle unmistakably"), and Benny Leonard of the wire service (5-4-1) had it for Petrolle. Hype Igoe of the *New York World* seemed to lean toward a draw. Murray Lewin of the Daily Mirror wrote, "at worst Petrolle should have gotten a draw." Ed Frayne of the *New York Evening Journal* and Harry Cross of the *New York Herald Tribune* did not offer opinions about who won. Other New York dailies were not available for consultation. The action account in the text is taken primarily from Wood, Wilbur, "Lindbergh Sees Hudkins Lose," *New York Sun,* June 16, 1927, sports section. Wood, however, saw the ninth round as even.

[36] Wood, "Denies Panic in Sock Market," *New York Sun*, June 21, 1927 sports section. Morris, "Around the Ring," *New York Evening Post*, June 18, 1927, sports section.

his stable available as a special favor to his new brother-in-law.

Luckily, for the sake of peace in the Hurley household, the promotion was a success. More than 3,000 legionnaires and other boxing fans saw Petrolle and Blue knock out their respective opponents, Eddie Brady and Bob Gilbert, in one round. Earl's win was the last he enjoyed with Hurley before they announced their separation in September.

The show's only sour note was LeRoy's poor showing against Al Van Ryan. In a bout, marred by frequent clinching and fouling, Van Ryan used a seven-pound weight advantage to out-maul Russie and win the decision.[37]

After a vacation, Hurley was in St. Paul on August 2 to work with LeRoy in a semifinal against Chicago's Norman Brown and with Petrolle in a main event against King Tut of Minneapolis at a show promoted by Jerk Doran.

Prior to the show, LeRoy asked Hurley to be released from his contract even though their agreement still had a year to run. Jack agreed and told the *Forum* that while he "hoped this day would never arrive ... a change of management may do (Russie) some good ... just like ballplayers who are traded from one club to another and get a new lease on life." Hurley wished LeRoy "luck and success with whoever he decides to cast his lot" and was "pleased to say that we are parting the same friends as when we started."[38]

Although LeRoy won nine of ten rounds in his bout, Petrolle's fight with King Tut was not so easy. In the first three rounds, Billy, a "master boxer and one of the most expert body punchers in the country," mixed up punches beautifully, so that every time "Tut would block a blow directed at his stomach" he would "receive a stiff jolt to head or chin. When he blocked one to the chin he had to take one in the stomach."

Shortly after the start of the fourth round, however, Tut twice landed hard punches below Petrolle's belt-line which drew warnings from referee George Barton. After the second foul, Barton asked if Billy could continue, and he nodded his assent. As soon as they resumed action, Tut drove another right into Petrolle's groin, causing him to sink slowly to the canvas.

Although Petrolle again offered to continue after a short rest, Barton awarded him the fight after an exam by the ringside physician concluded "it would be folly for him to try to do any more fighting for the present."[39]

Tut's fouls were so blatant on-lookers were virtually unanimous in their opinions the blows were intentional. At a commission hearing the next day, Tut tearfully denied any intention to deliberately foul Petrolle and offered to fight him again for free. The commission and promoter Doran accepted the King's proposal. The parties agreed to have the commission withhold his

---

[37] Purcell, "Al Ryan Gets Verdict over LeRoy," *Fargo Forum*, July 20, 1927, sport section.
[38] Hurley, *op. cit.*, August 3, 1927, sports section.
[39] Barton, George, "Petrolle Wins from King Tut on Foul Blow," *Duluth Herald* (special to the *Herald* from the *Minneapolis Tribune* sports editor), August 3, 1927, sports section.

Billy Wallace won a decision over Petrolle at the Polo Grounds.

Petrolle defeated Basil Galiano at Philadelphia in June 1929.

King Tut was Petrolle's archrival, winning three of their six fights. Billy won their August 2, 1929 meeting on a foul.

Tommy Herman stopped Petrolle on a cut, one of only three times Billy failed to go the limit.

$3,500 purse for the first fight until he "made good" on August 16.[40]

The second match was a replay of the first three rounds of the prior fight. As in that affair, Petrolle gradually picked Tut apart with a varied two-fisted attack to the head and body. Billy was credited with winning all but one of the ten rounds. Tut's best round was the second when a solid right hurt Billy and caused him to retreat for a full minute.[41]

Although Petrolle outclassed Tut in these bouts, he by no means had seen the last of the King. In a relatively short period of time, he would display enough improvement to become the No. 1 thorn in Billy's side. Over the next four years, they would engage in four more classic battles which would leave neither warrior with a right to claim superiority over the other.

Petrolle's final match of the summer was against Tommy Herman at Philadelphia on September 8, 1927. The 22-year-old Herman, managed by the notorious Max (Boo Boo) Hoff, had won 10 straight fights in 1926 before losing four tough decisions to Frankie Fink, Bobby Garcia, Billy Wallace and Stanislaus Loayza in 1927. Even so, Tommy was still regarded as a prospect who figured to be a handful to anyone he fought.

Petrolle arrived showing marks from a fight against Harry Kahn 12 days earlier in Milwaukee. Billy won a decision, but suffered a cut near the left eye, and entered the ring with Herman wearing a plaster patch over the eye.

In a bout one reporter saw as "a slashing fight ... which Petrolle had a shade the better of" until "a destructive right hook tore open" the old wound, Herman was awarded a technical knockout when Dr. Abe Barron halted the affair in the break between the seventh and eighth round.

The first four rounds were all Petrolle. At the start of the fourth, he staggered Herman with a right and then "followed Tommy all over the ring, landing hard with both hands." The blows had Herman "bleeding from the mouth and nose," but did "not put him down." Tommy rebounded to win two of the next three rounds, including the seventh and eighth when he "knocked the plaster off Petrolle's eye and the blood poured out of it. This was a tough round, both boxers' faces being covered with blood."[42]

Hurley protested, but Dr. Barron told him Frank Weiner, chairman of the state boxing commission, directed him to stop the fight. Later, Jack said, "There was nothing I could do but accept the ruling, and I did. I am satisfied in my own mind that Petrolle got the worst of the deal, for the fans gave him a great ovation as he left the ring, while Herman was booed."[43]

---

[40] Macdonald, Sandy, "Light Whines and Cheers," *Duluth Herald*, August 5, 1927, sports section.

[41] Purcell, "Minneapolis Pride Wins One Round," *Fargo Forum*, August 16, 1927, sports section.

[42] Rain, Dick, "Cleveland Boxer Puts over His Famous Wallop on Al Gordon in Third," *Philadelphia Record*, September 9, 1927, sports section. Isaminger, James C., "Al on Feet as Battle Is Halted," *Philadelphia Inquirer*, September 9, 1927, sports section.

[43] Fitzgerald, Eugene, "Petrolle Beat Tommy Herman, Hurley Explains," *Fargo Forum*,

Many ringsiders, including three local writers, agreed and "were of the belief that Petrolle should have been given a chance to go another round. He had protected the wound from Herman's punches for six rounds and inasmuch as his handlers were able to stem the flow of blood he should be given a chance to go the limit."[44]

After the fight, Hurley and Petrolle kept their senses of humor. In the dressing room, the question arose as to how to break the news of the fight's outcome to Phil Terk. It was well known in Fargo that, whenever Billy fought out of town, Terk became nervous and could not bear to watch the round-by-round results posted at the Grand Rec.

In discussing the matter, Hurley told Petrolle, "When Terk hears the result of this fight, he will drop dead." "Yes, sir, it'll just kill him," Billy answered. "Are you going to wire him?" "No," Jack replied to Billy, "I think I'll phone him – it's quicker."[45]

Hurley could joke because he was confident that news reports of the bout's controversial outcome would prevent any long-term damage to Petrolle's reputation. Nevertheless, the loss would prove costly. Billy would be out of action three months while the cut healed.

In the interim, Hurley decided to take care of a few health and business matters. Returning home, he underwent a nose operation on October 4, the first of many he would endure for his sinuses. Many years later as an old man, he would dolefully tell anybody who would listen that he'd had 23 sinus operations during his lifetime "and now they decide that it isn't the right thing to do. That's how they found out, by operating on me."[46]

While Hurley was on the road, Terk had been busy arranging for the transfer of the Hurley-Terk boxing business from Fargo to Duluth. Although they had made the decision earlier in the year, they opted to delay the move until the break between the summer and fall boxing seasons. Now, Petrolle's layoff would give Jack time to help with the move and rustle up some fighters from the Duluth area for their new gym.

The move was deemed necessary because recent pro cards at the Fargo Auditorium had been unprofitable, and because Hurley's gym was too small to hold the crowds wanting to see the weekly amateur bouts. With its larger population, Duluth furnished better prospects for growth than did Fargo. Furthermore, since Petrolle was now living in the Zenith City,

---

September 14, 1927, sports section.

[44] Dugan, John, "Wallace Stops Gordon after Gross, Adgie and Herman Win," *Philadelphia Evening Bulletin*, September 9, 1927, sports section. Rain, *op. cit.* Ziekursch, T., "Petrolle Loses by Outrage," *Philadelphia Daily News*, September 9, 1927, sports section.

[45] Hurley, *op. cit.*, September 18, 1927, sports section.

[46] Purcell, "Champion's Crown Not to Be Involved," *Fargo Forum*, October 5, 1927, sports section. Owen, John, "A 'Big City Guy' Finally Goes Home," *Seattle Post-Intelligencer*, November 21, 1972, sports section.

moving the operation made good logistical sense as well.

In addition, Fitger Brewing Company president Victor Anneke agreed to outfit the new gym. Anneke was a sports fan and felt boxing was a good way to publicize a new non-alcoholic beverage the brewery was marketing.

The time had come to see what Hurley could do in a larger setting. The move to Duluth was a logical step up the ladder. Although not a metropolis, it was large enough to allow him to expand his business and still avoid the cut-throat competition which flourished in nearly every major city.

Although Jack would never again reside in Fargo, he would maintain a presence there throughout the next decade, with regular stopovers to visit family and friends and to stage boxing shows featuring Petrolle and ex-heavyweight king Jack Dempsey as both referee and fighter. Billy, for his part, would garner the city more publicity than ever by continuing to bill himself as "the Fargo Express" until his final ring retirement in 1934.

In addition, Hurley would take the habits he learned in Fargo with him wherever he went. The unique perspective and versatility which his small-town roots gave him would enable him to ride out the rough spots while he followed the trail to wherever his roller-coaster profession took him. Jack may have left home with the hope of finding greener pastures elsewhere, but in his heart he would remain a son of Fargo the rest of his life.

CHAPTER 17

NEXT STOP: DULUTH AND A POLISH KILLER

Every sportswriter or editor that I ever ran into said that he was a personal friend and confidante of Jack Hurley's ... He had the ability to make every reporter in America ... Oh, during the course of a year he might talk to over 300 ... He had the ability to make every one of them think he was giving them an exclusive.

He'd sort of talk out of the side of his mouth in almost a whisper, like I'm telling this just to you, and you'd think, "Well, he's really poured this story out to me that he probably doesn't want anybody else to know." You'd put it in the paper, and he'd be down there the next day buying ten copies of the newspaper or a hundred copies and then send them around the country.

... The era he came from was an entirely different era. The ethics of sports writing were not very high at that time. Sportswriters would move into a training camp that would be set up by somebody like Tex Rickard at Miami or somewhere for a title fight. Oftentimes, the promoter would rent a mansion, stock it with liquor, and the sportswriters would live there for two weeks while the training camp was going on. And often, they would put anything in the paper that a promoter wanted them to. This was like in the '20s and '30s.

... You never knew when he was telling the truth and when he was conning you. That was the thing about Jack. Even when you thought, "Well, I really got a fix on Jack. I know now what he is doing." You didn't know what he was doing. And you never would.

... He knew in the last analysis that his best tools were sportswriters and he knew how to keep care of his tools and not abuse them. I think maybe that his secret was that he knew we were doing just what he needed done, and that was creating interest in fights.[1]

– John Owen

****

On September 9, 1927, Jack Hurley and Phil Terk announced they were closing their gym in Fargo and moving to Duluth, Minnesota. The new gym was located at 532 East Superior Street in a building which formerly served as the Fitger Brewing Company's main plant.

The Fitger company, which had relocated to a new site, still owned the building. As part of the agreement, the brewery agreed to have its in-house carpenters convert the main floor into an arena with a seating capacity of

---

[1] "Tales of Jack Hurley," KRAB-FM 107.7, Seattle WA, c. 1980s. John Owen was a sportswriter and columnist with the *Seattle Post-Intelligencer* from 1956 to 1980, a span which included a term as sports editor from 1968-1980.

1,200 and transform the basement into "the best facility northwest of Mullen's gym in Chicago." Equipment worth over $5,000, including steam baths, showers, rubbing tables, lockers, and mats, was being installed.

The new facility was named the "Silver Spray" gym to advertise Fitger's most popular bottled soft drink developed after passage of the Volstead Act. The gym, located in the heart of the downtown area, offered free boxing and fitness training for Duluth's boys and young men. Classes were conducted daily, and amateur boxing cards staged one evening a week, with students being matched according to size and ability.[2]

Emphasis was placed on providing "a clean moral atmosphere." Sportsmanship was "the general keynote of all boxing activities." Notices on the walls warned that "rowdyism is strictly tabooed; smoking is not tolerated; abusive and profane language ... is censored."[3]

In addition to their connection to Fitger's Brewery, Hurley and Terk enlisted the help of Ray W. Hughes, whose National Athletic Club (NAC) owned the city's professional boxing franchise. Jack was to serve as head trainer, Phil as business manager and assistant trainer, and Hughes as matchmaker for the Silver Spray's weekly amateur boxing shows.[4]

Hurley explained at the gym's opening October 24, 1927, that its primary purpose was not to generate income, but to produce boxers who would develop into big-money battlers. "We have 200 pupils attending our daily boxing classes," Jack said, "and from out of this big group we anticipate the development of at least one topnotcher who will be the equal of Billy Petrolle, that is if we are able to make him follow our instructions."

Hurley's first publicity coup occurred at the Silver Spray's second amateur card October 31. Among the prospects attracted to the gym was a young Finnish-American named Wayne "Handsome" Pikka from Virginia, Minnesota, a township in the Mesaba iron range 50 miles north of Duluth.

Pikka was no raw novice. He had been boxing off and on as an amateur in small towns around Duluth for several years. After seeing him box in the gym, Hurley noticed Pikka moved, and had a physique, like Russie LeRoy.

LeRoy was well known in Duluth, having won seven of his eight fights there. The similarities between the two gave Hurley an idea how he could have some fun and create interest in the gym's fights at the same time.

Hurley spent several weeks teaching Pikka all of LeRoy's pet moves and mannerisms until Jack became satisfied that, except for his facial features, Pikka could pass for LeRoy. Hurley matched Wayne in a four-round amateur bout with Leonard Houk, who had impressed Duluth fans the

---

[2] "Hurley Moving Boxing Stable to This City," *Duluth Herald*, September 9, 1927, sports section.
[3] Campbell, Cubby, "The Sport Spigot," *Duluth News Tribune*, October 19, 1927, sports section.
[4] Campbell, "Boxing School Stages Initial Card of Season," *Duluth News Tribune*, October 25, 1927, sports section.

A depiction of the Fitger Brewery buildings on Duluth's East Superior Street where Hurley and Terk opened the Silver Spray gym in September 1927. The city's location at Lake Superior's southern head made it a natural trade and transport center.

An early photograph of the oldest Fitger buildings. The brewery operated from 1881 until 1972 when a state agency mandated the installation of pollution control equipment which the brewery could not afford. As of 2014, the buildings survive as a hotel and retail complex.

previous week by winning his first fight by a kayo.

Before the bout with Houk, Hurley fit Pikka with a mask similar to the one he made a year and a half earlier for Lynn Nelson in Fargo. For good measure, Jack located some ring shorts LeRoy had previously worn in Duluth, put them on Pikka, and sent his Finnish warrior out to battle Houk billed as his new "Masked Marvel."[5]

At this time, Duluth had two daily newspapers. The *Herald* was an evening paper whose sports editor Sandy Macdonald was a seasoned, even-tempered writer who got along with everybody and weighed his words carefully. He was well regarded and had been appointed by the governor to represent Duluth as one of the state's three boxing commissioners.

The *News Tribune* was a morning newspaper whose sports editor was Cubby Campbell, who followed an aggressive tradition of reporting akin to muckraking. Campbell was more suspicious and less reserved than Macdonald and seemed to view the older man's reporting style as complacent and too cozy with the people about whom he was reporting.

In his *News Tribune* fight description the next day, Campbell reported that "the 'Masked Marvel' kayoed Leonard Houk in the first round of [a] headline feature" that was "one of the quickest and most workmanlike knockouts ever executed in the fistic annals of Duluth."[6]

Campbell's main goal after the bout, however, was not to congratulate the new gym owners on uncovering an exciting new prospect. Instead, he charged into the Silver Spray dressing room and in a heated exchange told them, "You got a hell of a nerve. We ought to run you out of town. We know who that Masked Marvel is; he's Russie LeRoy; he's an experienced professional, and you're putting him in against these kids."[7]

In response, both Hurley and Terk "offered to be sworn to a thousand legal oaths apiece" as testament to the fact that the Masked Marvel was not LeRoy, that he was from the Duluth area, that he had "never in his life received a dime for boxing, and that the Duluth fans will be a most surprised lot when the boy unmasks."[8]

The *Herald*'s Macdonald wrote that, even though "the fans, to a man, agreed that the Marvel is [a] professional fighter who has had some professional battles," he nonetheless in the end accepted Hurley's emphatic denials that the Marvel was a professional. Sandy concluded, "Hurley appears to be an up-and-up fellow who is not given to loud conversation. We believe what he says to be true in every detail."[9]

---

[5] Olsen, Jack, "Don't Call Me Honest," *Sports Illustrated*, May 15, 1961, pp. 90-1.
[6] Campbell, "'Masked Marvel' Registers Thrilling One-Round Kayo," *Duluth News Tribune*, November 1, 1927, sports section.
[7] Olsen, *op. cit.*
[8] Campbell, *op. cit.*
[9] Macdonald, Sandy, "Light Whines and Cheers," *Duluth Herald*, November 2, 1927, sports section.

Frankie Petrolle (Billy's brother), Hurley, Phil Terk, and Billy Petrolle at the Silver Spray gym's opening at Duluth in September 1927.

RESEMBLANCES BETWEEN FIGHTERS

Newspaper photographs purporting to show a resemblance between Russie LeRoy and Duluth's Masked Marvel.

Campbell, however, did not believe a word of it. He returned to his office after the fight and, before writing his editorial for the next day's paper, phoned the *Fargo Forum* to ask about LeRoy's whereabouts that evening.

Forum sports editor Pat Purcell confirmed LeRoy had been in Fargo all day and agreed to locate him and have him call Campbell back. Later that evening, "a voice professing to be Russie talked to the writer and assured him that he was in Fargo." Even so, Cubby refused to accept the notion Russie was not the Marvel and insisted that despite his phone call, "'the Unknown' showed so many characteristics of LeRoy that there still remains a lingering doubt that the 'Marvel' is really Russie LeRoy."[10]

After a few more Marvel victories, Campbell, on advice from a referee who knew Pikka, gradually changed his opinion and started dropping hints in his column that the masked one was actually Handsome Pikka.

Hurley was spurred to action after seeing Campbell's article. Each of the Marvel's bouts had sold out, and Jack feared discovery of "the Unknown's" identity might hurt the good thing he had going. With seats selling at four bits for general admission and six bits for ringside, the take for each show was averaging $600-$700. Anything Hurley could do to extend the Marvel's shelf life would put a little extra money in his and Terk's pockets.

Hurley figured a slight adjustment to "the Unknown's" wardrobe would do the trick. Up to this point, the Marvel's black stocking mask had completely covered his eyebrows. For his next fight, Jack enlarged the mask's holes to expose more of Pikka's eyes. Jack then applied mascara to darken Handsome's normally blond eyebrows.

The new ruse worked. After the fight, the referee commented that while he previously thought the Masked Marvel was Handsome Pikka, he must have been wrong because "Pikka had blond eyebrows, but this guy's are black." A few days later the *News Tribune*, at Campbell's direction, was back running pictures of LeRoy and the Masked Marvel side by side and asking readers whether "the Unknown" was Russie or Handsome Pikka.[11]

The Marvel remained undefeated for seven straight fights until he was unmasked by Earl Orton, who knocked him out at Fargo on February 11, 1928. Pikka later explained he was kayoed while adjusting his mask. Even though he was forced to reveal his identity, Wayne would forever-after be billed in Duluth as "Handsome Pikka, the former Masked Marvel."

Setting up the Silver Spray gymnasium, promoting amateur shows, and pulling the wool over Campbell's eyes may have been fun, but they barely covered Hurley's living expenses. Petrolle's eye injury and the defections of LeRoy and Earl Blue from his stable left Jack for the time being without

---

[10] Campbell, *op. cit.*

[11] Olsen, *op. cit.* "Resemblances Between Fighters," *Duluth News Tribune*, *Duluth News Tribune*, November 20, 1927, sports section.

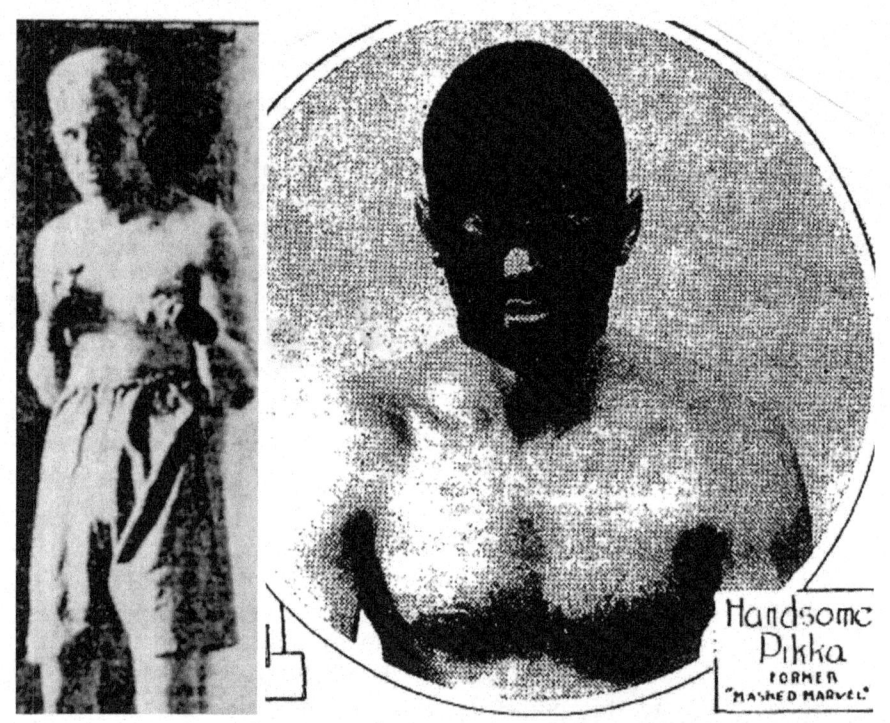

Marvel Wayne Handsome Pikka unmasked (left) and masked (right).

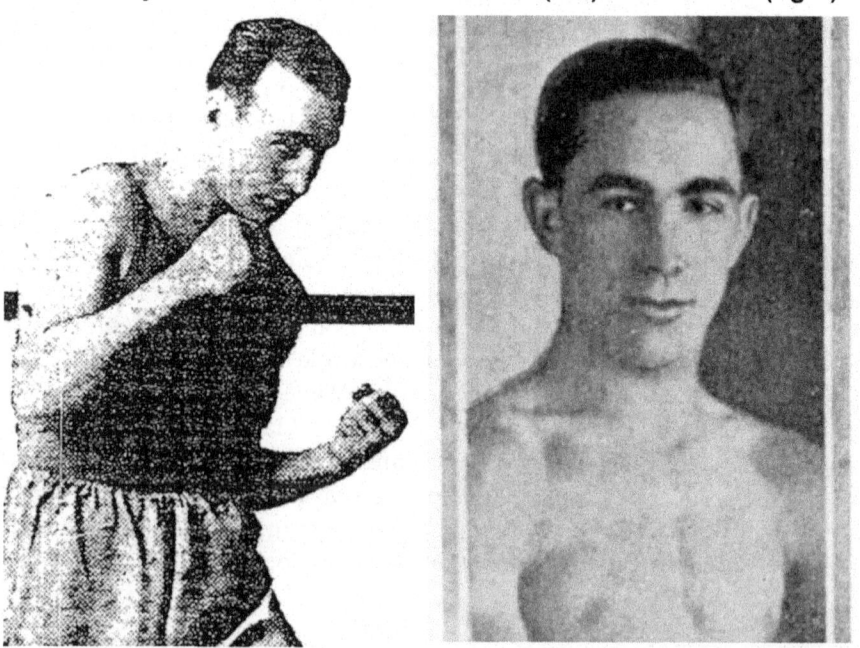

A scandal from Sammy Leonard's (left) bout with Al Van Ryan caused Ray Hughes to sell Duluth's boxing franchise to Hurley and Terk. On the same card, Harry Kahn (right) lost a close decision to Petrolle.

a meal ticket. To partially compensate for these losses, he took over the management of Al Van Ryan from his old friend, Johnny Salvator.

Van Ryan and Salvator had parted ways in August 1927. Al felt that Johnny was too busy handling the affairs of his two fast-rising stars, My Sullivan and Billy Light, to give Van Ryan's own career proper attention.

After the eye injury Petrolle suffered in the Herman fight healed, Duluth promoter Ray Hughes announced he had signed Billy to fight Milwaukee lightweight Harry Kahn in a main event on December 2. In the semifinal, Van Ryan was pitted against Sammy Leonard of Minneapolis, the same boxer who lost to Petrolle in the latter's Twin Cities' debut in 1923.

The Petrolle-Kahn fight was a real donnybrook. Petrolle floored Kahn in the first round for a nine-count, only to later be knocked down twice himself, once in the third for a nine-count and again in the eighth. Going into the last round, Harry had a slight edge in the scoring. Only a strong tenth round, when Billy hammered Kahn from pillar to post to the head and body for a full three minutes, earned Petrolle the close victory.

Van Ryan had little trouble with Leonard, scoring an easy, second-round kayo. The bout's main point of interest was caused by a controversy which raged for days afterward. The excitement stemmed from a rumor which circulated beforehand that the "fight was framed by local gamblers, and that Leonard had agreed to take a flop for a financial consideration."

Commissioner Sandy Macdonald, who first heard about the rumors while sitting at ringside, dismissed them as "the height of foolishness and entirely unfair to both Van Ryan and Leonard." He wrote that "from what we have seen of these so-called tin-horn, ferret-eyed gamblers that make up the local underworld colony, there is not $200 in the whole party, and not one of them would wager a rusty nickel that Pickett's charge was on the square."[12]

In the following days, Macdonald interviewed his contacts in the gambling community. He learned that the day before the fight Leonard had visited a doctor friend in Duluth. That evening, the doctor attended a dinner party and commented that Sammy "looked rather soft" and might be at a disadvantage against the well-conditioned and more experienced Van Ryan. A person at the party overheard the comment, figured it was a good tip, and later in the evening placed a $70 bet on Van Ryan to win by a kayo.[13]

Macdonald also secured Leonard's affidavit swearing the knockout was absolutely legitimate. Sandy wrote in the *Herald* that Sammy sold newspapers as a boy, worked a job all through high school, and was using boxing to pay his way through medical school.[14]

---

[12] "Petrolle Wins over Kahn in Torrid Battle," *Duluth Herald,* December 3, 1927, sports section. Pickett's charge was a major assault at the battle of Gettysburg which ended as a defeat for the Confederacy and proved to be a turning point in the American Civil War.

[13] "Leonard's Own Brother Lost Money on Him," *Duluth Herald*, December 6, 1927, sports section.

[14] "Boxing Moguls to Hold Session in Mill City," *Duluth Herald*, December 7, 1927, sports

Macdonald's article concluded that a "boy who has showed this determination to succeed and make something of himself is hardly the type to be influenced by any betting clique and especially for the penny-ante money that was wagered." On December 8, Sandy presented his evidence at a hearing before the state boxing commission. In a unanimous decision, the commissioners exonerated Leonard of any wrongdoing.[15]

Once again, Campbell found himself opposed to Macdonald. Cubby charged the purpose of the investigation by "the Duluth boxing commissioner and sports scribe" was "to white-wash and gloss over the Leonard-Van Ryan fistic mess." Sandy had prejudged the case and taken sides before all the facts were known. Consequently, his objectivity had been compromised.[16]

To support his allegations, Campbell published a list of 12 questions Macdonald had not addressed. Among them, Cubby asked, "Why did the commissioner not take action before the fight, since he knew of the rumors ahead of time?" "Why had Leonard not been examined by a doctor immediately after he was allegedly knocked out?" "Why was Leonard's purse not held up, as was customary in such situations?"

Campbell also charged that Macdonald's article in the *Tribune* after the bout misstated the facts to make the knockout seem more legitimate than it might have otherwise appeared. Most notably, Macdonald had written that "'Leonard was carried to his corner' when every person who was in the Armory knows that Leonard bounced to his feet and started a fracas with Van Ryan immediately after the count of ten."[17]

Frustrated that the commission ignored his questions before exonerating Leonard, Campbell wrote bitterly afterward that he would "continue on the next lesson of cutting out paper dolls." For Cubby, however, it was no longer going to be business as usual when it came to reporting local boxing news. After the commission's hearing, and without further explanation, he summarily discontinued the *News Tribune*'s pre-fight coverage of both

---

section.

[15] "Leonard's Own Brother Lost Money on Him," *op. cit.* "State Boxing Commissioners Give Mill City Fighter Clean Bill: Did Not Take 'Dive.'" *Duluth Herald*, December 9, 1927, sports section.

[16] Campbell, "The Sport Spigot," *Duluth News Tribune*, December 9, 1927, sports section.

[17] Campbell, "Commissioner Evades Issues," *Duluth News Tribune*, December 7, 1927, sports section. The questions within quotation marks that appear in the preceding paragraph of the text have been rephrased for clarity and simplicity.

Macdonald was frustrated and enraged about Campbell's charges against him. He obviously was convinced there was no question about the legitimacy of Leonard's knockout. On December 6, he had already written for Campbell's benefit: "Any sports editor who is so blind that he cannot see that a boxer is knocked out when the latter is practically knocked right into his lap should lock up his typewriter and get a job making baskets at the Lighthouse." Obviously, Campbell's next day's reference to "cutting out paper dolls" was meant as a mock, self-deprecating reaction to Macdonald's comment.

professional and amateur boxing in Duluth altogether.[18]

The Leonard affair and the *News Tribune*'s resulting war against boxing in Duluth were the straws that broke the camel's back as far as promoter Ray Hughes was concerned. Hughes was the last survivor of a three-man partnership which had been operating the boxing franchise in Duluth for almost six years. During that period, the NAC claimed losses of about $12,000 in its attempt to keep professional boxing afloat in Duluth.

When Hurley and Terk offered $1,300 for the franchise, Hughes jumped at the chance. Since they were the only buyers interested, the commission approved the transfer, and they took over on January 14, 1928.[19]

In purchasing the Duluth franchise, the new owners were bucking a long history of financial misery. Duluth, more than any other city of its size in the entire Midwest, had a reputation as a poor fight town. Even the NAC's very first show in 1922, which featured a city-record gate of $6,500, had lost money, due at least in part to the guarantees paid to its high-cost featured performers, Dave Shade and Morrie Schlaifer.

Hurley's first order of business as promoter was to visit Campbell. On what might be termed, figuratively speaking, bended knee, Jack pledged to conduct boxing at the Silver Spray gym and the NAC "in a manner creditable to the game."

For his part, Campbell promised that the *News Tribune* would "tender its support to the National Athletic Club and the Silver Spray gym, in the promotion of amateur and professional boxing, just so long as there are no unsavory incidents connected with the promotion and conduct of future fights." Based on this understanding, Campbell agreed to resume the newspaper's boxing coverage.[20]

In the meantime, Hurley and Petrolle's two-year chase of Sammy Mandell finally yielded results. Shortly before the new year, Jack announced Billy was set to meet the lightweight champion in a ten-round go at Minneapolis January 13, 1928. Rather than obtaining the bout from a big-time promoter like Mullen or Rickard, the offer came from an unlikely source – Hurley's old St. Paul mentor, Mike Collins.

Collins released his last boxer in early 1927 to take over the Minneapolis franchise, which had been in a depressed state for three years. Within a few months, he surpassed expectations and staged two cards which drew combined receipts in excess of $40,000. Now, by engaging a champion, he was taking another step forward. Mike anticipated a large gate because it was being held in the new Minneapolis Auditorium which seated 10,000.[21]

---

[18] Campbell, "The Sport Spigot," *Duluth News Tribune*, December 8, 1927, sports section.
[19] "New Owner Pays $1,300 for Local Club," *Duluth Herald*, January 15, 1928, sports section.
[20] Campbell, *op cit.*, January 26, 1928, sports section.
[21] Macdonald, *op. cit.*, August 5, 1927, sports section.

Sammy Mandell (left) & Petrolle around the time of their 1928 bout.

Mandell displays his ring wizardry in training (left) and against Luis Vicentini (right).

Mandell accepted the bout only because his crown would not be at stake. Petrolle could not win by decision because Minnesota was a no-decision state. In addition, Billy agreed to weigh two pounds above the 135-pound limit. Even if he stopped Sammy, Billy still could not claim the title.

Experts were in general agreement that Mandell was a likely winner "because of his wonderful speed and skill" and "his ability to shoot snappy punches" from each hand "with unerring accuracy to vital spots." Petrolle's "only chance of beating Mandell lie in crowding continually and shooting punches to the body and face in the hope of delivering a blow, or a series of them, which will turn the tide of battle in his favor."[22]

For seven rounds, the predictions proved accurate. The first four rounds were close with Mandell holding off Petrolle's relentless charges with fast footwork and a darting left jab. In rounds five, six, and seven, Sammy took command, frequently setting himself and jarring Billy with stiff jabs and jolting rights. By the end of the seventh, Mandell was in full control, choosing his spots and making Petrolle fight Sammy's way.

Halfway into the eighth round, the tide of battle changed abruptly. Billy backed Sammy near the ropes and "buried a left hook deep in Mandell's body." The champion dropped his guard and Billy followed with "a leaping right that went squarely to the jaw," driving Sammy backward. But for the ropes, Mandell "would have gone completely down."[23]

The titleholder "was white faced, wobbly, glassy eyed, reeling and groggy. He swayed unsteadily, his face carried a bewildered, puzzled look, and he grasped the top rope to steady himself." As Petrolle moved to the attack, "Sammy wobbled across the ring ending up in the exact opposite corner and again he grasped the ropes to maintain his balance."[24]

Weak and confused, Mandell fended off Petrolle the rest of the round with a combination of reeling retreats, clinches, and gloves planted firmly on Billy's forehead to keep him away. For the rest of the fight, Sammy was never able to fully recover from the effects of that single, right hand punch. Billy kept up the offensive and won the last three rounds, although the lacing he had taken earlier rendered him unable to finish Sammy off.

After the bout, the champion's manager Eddie Kane told reporters, "Petrolle is a great fighter and had Sammy in a bad way when the bell ended the eighth round. I think Petrolle is the class of the challengers." Mandell, offering his own assessment, said, "I agree with Kane that Petrolle is the best of the contenders. He is a great puncher."[25]

---

[22] Barton, George, "Mandell Still Favored to Win Over Petrolle," *Duluth Herald*, January 13, 1928, sports section.
[23] Cullum, Dick, "Titleholder Takes Points in Early Part of Contest," *St. Paul Pioneer Press*, January 14, 1928, p. 8.
[24] Shave Ed, "Petrolle Beaten; Gives Fans Big Thrill in Eighth," *St. Paul Daily News*, January 14, 1928, sports section.
[25] "Petrolle Due Here Monday," *Detroit Free Press*, February 20, 1928, sports section.

Reporters from the Twin Cities, Chicago, Detroit, and Milwaukee all felt Mandell's early lead earned him the win "by a shade." Writers from Petrolle's stamping grounds of Fargo, Grand Forks, and Duluth figured that Billy's aggressiveness, superior firepower, and strong finish warranted a decision in favor of the Fargo Express.

The *Minneapolis Daily Star*'s Charles Johnson, who thought Mandell had carried the day, nevertheless noted that "two-thirds of the fans insist that Petrolle was entitled to the decision and at least no worse than a draw." Johnson predicted Petrolle and Mandell would meet again in a 15-round title bout that would conclusively decide the issue of supremacy between the two battlers. Unfortunately, such a meeting never took place.[26]

The *St. Paul Pioneer Press'* Dick Cullum, who also voted for Mandell, wrote that over a 15-round distance Petrolle would have "at least an even chance of winning the title – perhaps better than even chance." He reasoned that after Mandell was hurt his early lead "was dwindling rapidly ... and there was no indication that he was in condition to keep it from dwindling farther and faster in later rounds, if there had been later rounds."

Cullum also believed that while Mandell was hard pressed to lose weight to make the stipulated 137 pounds, Petrolle had slackened his training before the bout to weigh over 135 pounds. He concluded that if Sammy had to make 135 pounds "it is not likely that it would make him any better," while Billy "probably would have been a little faster and stronger."

Even though he favored Petrolle in a longer return match at the lightweight limit, Cullum observed that "no meeting between these two will be even until Mandell is hit." In other words, if Billy was to have a chance to win a future fight, he would first have to hit and hurt Mandell, as he did in the eighth round of the Minneapolis affair.[27]

February 24, 1928 found Hurley and Petrolle in Detroit where Billy was pitted against Spug Myers in a ten-rounder at the new Olympia Stadium, which was also home for the Detroit Red Wings of the National Hockey League. The two had battled to a draw in their Chicago match a year earlier. Since then, Myers had fought both Mandell and junior welter champ Mushy Callahan and was still recognized as a top contender.

After a furious fight, the referee lifted Petrolle's arm at the end of the battle to signal victory over Myers. All three of Detroit's daily newspapers agreed the bout was either "the Olympia's greatest" or at least "one of the best that has been presented at the Olympia since the arena opened."[28]

The next day, F. J. Carveth described the action in the *Detroit Free Press*:

---

[26] Johnson, Charles, "Lowdown on Sports," *Minneapolis Daily Star*, January 16, 1928, sports section.
[27] Cullum, "The Ring Post," *St. Paul Pioneer Press*, January 15, 1928, sports section.
[28] Greene, Sam, "Petrolle Adds to Ring Rating," *Detroit News*, February 25, 1928, sports section. MacDonnell, Frank, "Fargo Express Wins Great Fight," *Detroit Times*, February 25, 1928, sports section.

"Petrolle took five of the first six rounds, held Myers even in two others, dropped the eighth and ninth, but in a furious tenth round, when the two finely trained youngsters refused to back up or clinch, Myers held Petrolle even again, while the spectators did most everything but break up the chairs....

"It was punch and punch from the first to the last round, with Petrolle's superior generalship and punching power determining the result. Petrolle, agile of limb, strong, courageous, and a driving puncher, boxed like a champion.

"His defense in close was almost perfect and not until Myers caught him with a driving right under the heart in the eighth round did Petrolle slack his pace. The punch plainly hurt the Fargo boxer and he took a beating in the next two rounds, only to recuperate and with Myers make one of the greatest last-round stands seen here.

"Everything that goes to make a great fight was displayed. Boxing skill, punching power, ring generalship and – lion-hearted courage – all these requisites were there in abundance and because Petrolle had more than his clever and rugged opponent he justly earned the decision ...

"Petrolle is a clever ringman. He is an artist in feigning a punch with his left and coming up with a terrific right cross that four times shook Myers to the toes. His work in close was almost perfect, carrying his elbows close to his hips with one or both hands pumping punches in the body ...

"Detroit may or may not see another lightweight fight like this one."[29]

Unfortunately for Hurley and Petrolle, the victory was overshadowed by another bout taking place in New York that evening. In one minute and 47 seconds, "a new fistic sensation – young Jimmy McLarnin of the baby Irish face ... flattened Sid Terris, pride of New York's lightweights, with just two punches" before almost 18,000 spectators who paid a season high $92,000 for an indoor fight.[30]

McLarnin had risen to prominence late in 1927 with a kayo of Kid Kaplan at Chicago, followed by a hairline decision win over Billy Wallace in Detroit. Neither win, however, generated as much excitement as did Jimmy's one-round kayo of Terris. Immediately afterward, Tex Rickard signed Jimmy to fight Sammy Mandell for the lightweight title in New York. The bout, however, was contingent on Rickard signing Mandell.

---

[29] Carveth, F. J., "Fargo Fighter Earns Verdict in Hard Battle," *Detroit Free Press*, February 25, 1928, sports section.
[30] Neil, Edward, "Smiling Young Fighter in Short Fight" (AP), *Duluth News Tribune*, February 25, 1928, sports section.

Petrolle's erstwhile conqueror, Sid Terris, lies on the canvas, the victim of a one-round kayo by Jimmy McLarnin. The victory made Jimmy an instant sensation in New York.

McLarnin signs to fight Sammy Mandell after defeating Terris, just as it seemed Petrolle would land the title fight with Sammy. Back row, McLarnin's manager, Pop Foster, and Jess McMahon. Seated are McLarnin, Tex Rickard, and Mandell's manager, Eddie Kane.

Prior to the McLarnin-Terris fight, experts assumed Mandell's next title defense would be for Jim Mullen in Chicago against Petrolle. McLarnin's sensational win turned those expectations upside-down. Fans formerly abuzz about Billy's near kayo of Mandell, now also were talking about the prospect of a Mandell-McLarnin match.

In the following weeks, papers throughout the country were filled with accounts of the rivalry between Rickard and Mullen as they bid against each other for Mandell's services. Finally, on March 14, 1928, Tex announced he had signed Sammy to defend his title against McLarnin in New York for 37-1/2 percent of gate receipts, which were expected to be over $200,000. The bout was scheduled for May 21, 1928.

Hurley and Petrolle scarcely had time to reflect on the disappointing turn of events. Billy was due on March 16 to enter the ring at Madison Square Garden to fight Bruce Flowers, "the world's Negro lightweight champion." Flowers recently had entered the elite circle of title contenders with wins over Sammy Vogel, Jack Bernstein, Lou Paluso, and Spug Myers.

The day after the fight, the *New York Sun* reported that "Bruce Flowers, rangy negro from New Rochelle, received the decision over Billy Petrolle after their ten-round bout. It was very close ... As usual, Flowers got away to a slow start and finished like a stakehorse."

Most ringside reporters credited Petrolle with a majority of the first five rounds. In the sixth, he had Flowers "badly stung for a few moments when he finally put over his right to the chin." Bruce took charge in the seventh and won three of the last four rounds. His best was the ninth when, rocked by two rights, Flowers "instead of retreating, lashed out in a furious rally that drove Billy around the ring under a shower of punches."[31]

The verdict was split, the referee favoring Billy and the judges Flowers.

Six out of nine sportswriters at ringside agreed with the official verdict. Three disagreed and believed Petrolle deserved the call because he fought for three minutes of each round as opposed to Flowers, who according to one reporter fought "only one minute of each round" and to another who wrote he "might more aptly be termed the 'Minute Man.'"[32]

---

[31] Wood, Wilbur, "Flowers Wins Close Decision," *New York Sun*, March 17, 1928, sports section.

[32] Underwood, George, "Colored Boy Loafs Until Last Minute of Each Round," *New York Telegram*, March 17, 1928, sports section. Wood, *op. cit.* Favoring Flowers: Murray Lewin, *New York Daily Mirror* (5-3-2); William Morris, *New York Evening Post* (6-4); Ed Frayne, *New York Evening Journal* (5-2-3); James Dawson, *New York Times* (4-1-3 at the end of eight rounds); Ned Brown, *New York World* (Brown seems to agree with the verdict); and the Associated Press reporter (rounds not able to be determined). Favoring Petrolle: Wilbur Wood, *New York Sun*, (5-4-1); George Underwood, *New York Telegram* (seems to give Petrolle the first 8 rounds with the caveat that "perhaps in some of the rounds Flowers really did score as many points in the last one-third as Petrolle did in each two-thirds," but he definitely gives Flowers the last two rounds); and Walter St. Denis, *Newark Star-Eagle* (scoring by rounds unavailable). Accounts of other dailies were not available.

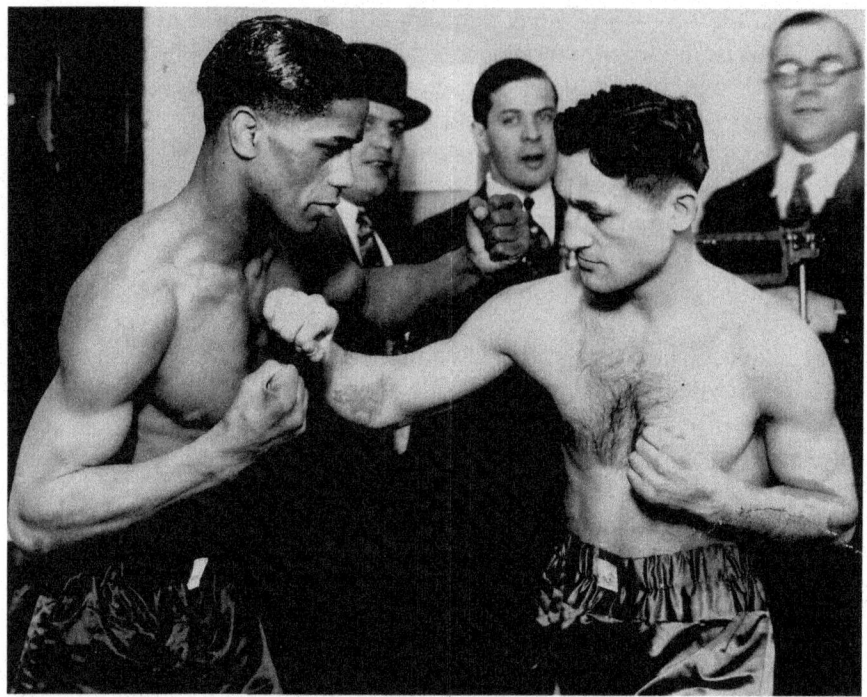

Petrolle & Bruce Flowers (left) face off for their March 16, 1928 bout.

Flowers wins the decision over Petrolle at Madison Square Garden.

On April 27, 1928, Hurley and Petrolle traveled to Omaha, where Billy was matched against the up and coming Tommy Grogan, a 20-year-old native son. Already in his fifth year of pro boxing, Tommy had reached top form in the year's first quarter, defeating in short order such top men as Mike Ballerino, Babe Ruth, Lou Paluso, and Eddie (Cowboy) Anderson.

Petrolle knocked Grogan down in the second round and was far ahead at going into the fifth. Coming out of an exchange with Tommy in the middle of the round, Billy was seen rubbing his right eye. Almost immediately, the eye began to close and puff up abnormally.

Petrolle was unable to see out of the eye in the sixth, but was throwing punches from all angles in an effort to land a hay-maker. Near the round's end, he caught Grogan with a right that split Tommy's lip. By then, the eye was entirely closed, and the puffing had swollen to grotesque proportions. The rest between rounds found "Hurley attempting to stop the fight," but "Billy wave[d] him aside," and persuaded Jack to let him continue.

Petrolle realized the seventh round was his last chance to win, and he tore into Grogan with a vengeance. Although Billy missed a lot of punches, he landed another right which opened a bad gash over Tommy's right eye. The round ended with both gladiators winging away furiously. Petrolle had tried to knock Grogan out, but he was still full of fight. When the bell sounded, Billy was "a ghastly sight," his eye-lid "distended, disclosing a narrow band of white," looking "like a blind man, tapping, tapping, tapping."

Awaiting the eighth round, Petrolle's corner was the scene of a heated discussion. "Billy wanted to go out there and face Tommy again. Billy fought his own handlers to back in there again. But cooler minds prevailed. A towel sailed into the ring." Grogan was declared the winner on a technical knockout in the seventh round.

The results of the examination by Dr. Louis Bushman were frightening. The doctor told reporters that "Petrolle may lose the sight of his eye." An X-ray set for the next morning would "determine if the bone above the eye is fractured." The doctor cautioned that "Petrolle will be confined to the hospital from two days to a week."[33]

Writing his weekly column eight years later, Hurley still remembered the intense emotion he felt after the Omaha fight:

> "Grogan accidentally stuck his thumb in Petrolle's eye and caused the mucous membrane to fill with air. It puffed out little by little, causing the eyeball to turn nearly completely over, which affected the vision of the good eye to such an extent that he was almost totally blind.

---

[33] Wolff, Howard, "Unable to Come Back for the Eighth," *Omaha World-Herald*, April 28, 1928, sports section.

Omaha lightweight Tommy Grogan (left) with manager Roy Feltman. Grogan won by a TKO over Petrolle when their fight was halted due to a severe injury to Billy's right eye.

"I stopped the fight in the seventh round, and those who would have you believe that boxing is devoid of sentiment, should have walked the floor with me for two days and two nights while every specialist in the city fought a winning fight to save a game warrior's sight."[34]

Petrolle was confined to Lord Lister Hospital in Omaha for a full week, but the sight in his right eye was saved. Because the skin around the eye had not actually been cut and no bones were broken, Billy was able to resume training as soon as the swelling subsided. A month after the Omaha fight, Petrolle was well enough to return to the ring. On May 22, Billy kayoed Eddie Dwyer in four rounds in Watertown, South Dakota.[35]

While consecutive losses to Flowers and Grogan normally might have been considered devastating, the Omaha experience caused Hurley and Petrolle to keep their situation in perspective. Even if Billy was no longer next in line to meet Mandell, at least he was healthy and still able to fight. Both Jack and Petrolle still had confidence and believed with a few more fights he would be back knocking on the champ's door.[36]

On June 7, 1928, Petrolle stopped Belgian lightweight champion Armand Schaekels in three rounds at Detroit. Six days later, Billy was in Kansas City, Missouri to take on Chicago fighter Jackie Kane as entertainment for delegates attending the Republican National Convention.

Kane, a shifty, fast, and clever boxer, presented a tough proposition for any lightweight. His record showed wins over King Tut, Joe Azzarella, Tony Ross, Roscoe Hall, and most recently, Russie LeRoy. Jackie's manager, Tommy Walsh, had handled many top fighters including Joe Burman, Charlie White, Joe Mandot, and Jock Malone.

In a fight *Kansas City Journal* sports editor Ed Cochrane described as "worth walking a mile to see," Petrolle and Jackie Kane "stood the fans ... on their excited heads for ten sessions." Billy started slowly and trailed at the end of the fifth round. Kane, however, weakened perceptibly after the sixth round and Petrolle came on strong to have "Kane on the receiving end of a beating in the latter rounds." Cochrane figured that Petrolle had "a shade the better milling" and awarded his newspaper's decision to Billy.[37]

The fight proved so exciting that the local American Legion post, which promoted the bout, immediately signed the fighters to a July 6th rematch. Unfortunately, the card was canceled a week before the date for reasons which later became a topic of heated debate between Hurley and Walsh.

---

[34] Hurley, Jack, "Shadow Boxing," *Fargo Forum*, August 9, 1936, sports section.
[35] "Sight Saved," *Omaha World-Herald*, April 29, 1928, sports section.
[36] Purcell, J. A., "The Sportville Spotlight," *Fargo Forum*, May 17, 1928 and May 27, 1928, sports sections.
[37] Cochrane, E. W., "Chicago Youth Is Weakened in Late Sessions," *Fargo Forum* (special report to *Forum* from *Kansas City Journal*), June 14, 1928, sports section.

Meanwhile back in Duluth, Phil Terk continued to stage amateur shows every week at the Silver Spray gym. Although the club featured quite a few eager youngsters during the indoor season, the novice boxer Terk and Hurley felt most likely to become a pro attraction was a 21-year-old heavyweight who fought under the ring name of Szymka Zabuil.[38]

Standing 6-feet-1-inches tall and weighing 197 pounds, Zabuil, known as the "Polish Killer," made his amateur debut January 23, 1928, with a two-round knockout of Happy Holter. According to Cubby Campbell, Szymka's primary fistic assets were "an abundance of stamina," a "powerful right hand punch, and a promising left."[39]

Although he sported a "splendid boxing physique," it soon became apparent to Campbell that "something about Zabuil's ring personality ... grates against the nerves of the railbirds" and causes "90 percent of the fistic fans attending bouts" to hope he will "be pummeled into jelly." After only a few fights, Poland's pride "was selling the place out, they hate him so much." As Hurley later would later describe it, Zabuil became a "boo fighter," much like today's wrestlers who take the part of a villain.[40]

Zabuil's ability to cause controversy was amply displayed in two bouts against George Asmus, of St. Paul. In their first match, Asmus delighted fans by out-boxing Zabuil and winning an upset four-round decision. In a return bout, George again had the fight well in hand when Zabuil let go "with a vicious right uppercut" which caused Asmus to "topple over [and] stretch out on his face, with both hands clutching at his groin."[41]

The next day in the *Herald*, Sandy Macdonald wrote that the blow which felled Asmus was "a short left to the stomach." Macdonald reported that Dr. D. Murray of the state athletic commission examined Asmus after the fight and "could find no sign of a low blow." Citing the doctor's exam as the basis for his opinion, Sandy found no reason to disagree with the referee's conclusion that the kayo blow had been a legal punch.[42]

The *News Tribune*'s Campbell, on the other hand, was certain the "blow which floored Asmus was not slightly low, rather it was extremely far below the belt line." Not satisfied with the opinions of the referee; the commission doctor; or "Alexander (Sandy) Macdonald, state boxing

---

[38] Macdonald, "Polish Heavyweight Boxer Will Make His Formal Bow at the Silver Spray Gym," *Duluth Herald*, January 23, 1928, sports section. According to Macdonald's research the word "zabuil" in Polish translates into "killer." Szymka's real name was Ben Szymkowski (per his signature on a letter published in Cubby Campbell's "Sport Spigot" column on February 14, 1929). The name therefore actually means "Szymka the Killer."

[39] Campbell, *op. cit.*, April 27, 1928, sports section.

[40] Campbell, *op. cit.*, March 18, 1928, sports section. Olsen, *op. cit.*, p. 89.

[41] Campbell, "St. Paul Boxer Leading Until Sudden Climax," *Duluth News Tribune*, March 21, 1928, sports section.

[42] "Zabuil Stops St. Paul Boxer in the Third," *Duluth Herald*, March 21, 1928, sports section.

commissioner," Campbell sought out Dr. T. L. Chapman, "disinterested ringsider" and "prominent surgeon of Duluth."[43]

To satisfy his own curiosity, Dr. Chapman visited Asmus in his dressing room after the fight and conducted an examination of the fighter in "a more thorough manner" than the commission doctor. Dr. Chapman found "broken and discolored skin low on the left groin" which led him to the inevitable conclusion "that a low blow had been struck."

After summarizing Chapman's findings, Campbell chastised "the commissioner at ringside" for not conducting a more complete investigation and exercising the necessary "timely and fast thinking" which could have reversed the referee's erroneous verdict.[44]

By the middle of May, Zabuil had won ten of 11 amateur bouts and was ready to begin his punch-for-pay career. His first opponent as a pro was Jack Clifford of St. Paul. Clifford was at the tail end of a long career primarily devoted to service as a stepping stone to other heavyweights.

The fight, scheduled for June 1, 1928, was the NAC's second show since Hurley and Terk acquired the pro club in January. Their first promotion in March, featuring Al Van Ryan against Danny Fagan, was poorly attended and lost considerable money. Since the bouts on the upcoming card would feature local boxers, they were hoping it would be well attended and yield a profit. They also were counting on the support of both Duluth newspapers.

When Hurley told Campbell about Zabuil's pro debut, the first thing Cubby did was call Clifford a has-been too far gone to furnish any real competition. Campbell said Clifford "would be unable to stand up over the 10-round route" and should therefore be replaced by a tougher opponent.

Hurley admitted Clifford was on the downgrade, but argued Zabuil had not yet had a single pro bout. Clifford was a wily veteran who was perfect to test whether Szymka had the aptitude and ability to be a fighter. Jack also predicted the match would go a full ten rounds because Clifford was too experienced for a novice like Zabuil to stop.[45]

Privately, Hurley was both exasperated and angry at Campbell's criticism of the impending show. Who exactly did Cubby expect him to obtain as an opponent for Zabuil's first professional fight? Didn't Campbell understand that Jack and Terk were trying to develop young boxers so fans could eventually see a better brand of fighting? How could they accomplish that goal if the *News Tribune* looked at every show with an expectation that something was wrong? No wonder boxing in Duluth had been a bust!

Sandy Macdonald, for his part, could not resist a chance to toss a jab at his journalistic rival. He wrote that "while there are some who apparently believe that Zabuil should be matched with Gene Tunney or Jack Dempsey,

---

[43] Campbell, *op. cit.*

[44] Campbell, "The Sport Spigot," *Duluth News Tribune*, March 22, 1928, sports section.

[45] Campbell, *op. cit.*, May 19 and 20, 1928, sports section.

Romero Quentin Rojas was kayoed by Zabuil at Duluth.

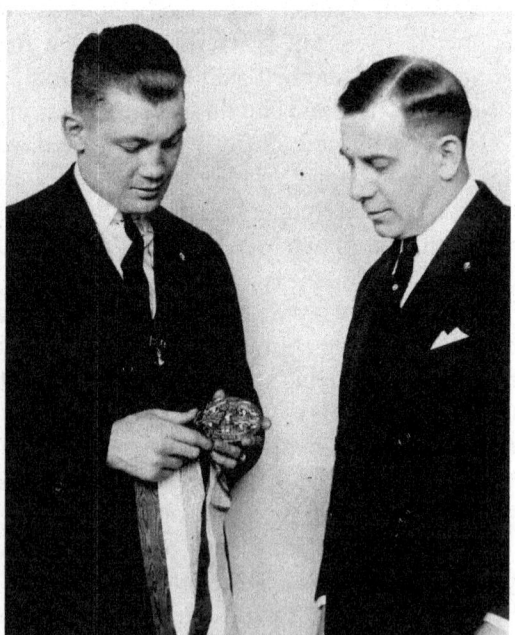

"Polish Killer" Szymka Zabuil, the fighter Duluth loved to hate.

Tom Walsh (right) convinced Campbell to support the Petrolle-Kane/Zabuil-Rojas card. Walsh's favorite fighter of those he handled, Jock Malone, is at left.

there are other wiser critics who are confident that Clifford ... will hit him often and hard enough to test his courage."[46]

As Hurley forecast, the Zabuil-Clifford fight went a full ten rounds. Although Zabuil won a decision and demonstrated he could take a punch, his inability to knock Clifford out showed he had a long way to go before he would be ready for any of the top contenders, let alone Tunney or Dempsey. More than 2,000 fans attended, leaving the promoters a small profit. Even though the main event lacked kayo excitement, a diversified undercard, "jammed with action," left fans in a happy frame of mind.[47]

Hurley and Terk were pleased enough to arrange another card for August. They planned to present separate main events featuring both Zabuil and Petrolle. This time, however, they decided to employ a bit of psychology in the selection of opponents for their headliners.

Campbell's contentiousness almost ruined the prior show, and Hurley was intent on not letting that happen again. If Cubby was fixated on being suspicious, then Jack planned to use this personality quirk to his advantage.

Before announcing the August show, Hurley contacted Jackie Kane's manager, Tommy Walsh, who had been seeking a rematch for Kane with Petrolle ever since their Kansas City fight two months earlier. Jack also was eager for the bout since the first contest had been a good scrap, and the rematch posed little risk to Billy since he had solved Kane's style and figured to have less trouble the second time around.

Hurley told Walsh to write Campbell a letter claiming Kane had actually beaten Petrolle in Kansas City, and that Billy and Jack had run-out on the July 6th rematch which had been previously scheduled.

Next, Hurley tracked down Jack Wrenn, manager of South American heavyweight Quentin Romero Rojas. Rojas made a splash three years earlier by stopping Jack Sharkey and winning decisions over Jack Renault and Johnny Risko, each who had since become top contenders. After these successes, Rojas nosedived, and he had lost 17 of his 20 most recent fights.

Hurley had come across Wrenn's publicity posters extolling his fighter's past glories, but neglecting to mention his recent record. Jack figured Senor Rojas was a good opponent for Zabuil in Duluth, so he negotiated terms with Wrenn and told the manager to send Campbell one of the posters.

A few days later, Hurley visited the *News Tribune* and told Campbell he and Terk were planning an August show. Jack said that while they had not yet signed anyone to fight Zabuil, they had narrowed the field to four opponents. Included were Tiny Herman, of Omaha; Tut Jackson, of Barberton, Ohio; Clem Johnson, of Cleveland; and Farmer Lodge, of Chicago. Hurley also told Cubby he had not yet lined up a foe for Petrolle.

---

[46] "Clifford Will Fight Zabuil in Pro Battle," *Duluth Herald*, May 24, 1928, sports section.

[47] Campbell, "Andy Puglisi Defeats Spencer in Feature Bout of Fight Show," *Duluth News Tribune*, June 1, 1928, sports section.

Campbell's response was just as Hurley expected. Dismissing all four of Jack's candidates for Zabuil as fighters who "had been hovering around the fistic graveyard for half a decade," Cubby suggested Szymka should be tested against "someone who is well-rated in the heavyweight class."

Several days later, Campbell wrote he had found just the man to test Zabuil. His name? "Quentin Romero Rojas, the 'Lion of the Andes' from South America, a fighter who has taken on the best boys in the heavyweight division since his invasion of the United States three years ago." Cubby had received a poster suggesting Rojas might be the one to allow local fans "to witness [their] long cherished desire to see Zabuil sprawling on the floor."[48]

In addition, Campbell had uncovered the perfect adversary for Petrolle. Manager Tom Walsh had written the *News Tribune* claiming his fighter, Jackie Kane, had actually beaten Billy in Kansas City. Walsh wrote that Hurley had skipped out on a rematch scheduled for July 6. Since then, Tom had tried to reschedule the bout, but Jack had given him a runaround.

After publishing Walsh's letter, Campbell commented, "With all this hullabaloo between Hurley and Walsh over the last Kane-Petrolle match at Kansas City and the subsequent 'run-out' by one or the other in the rematch at the same city, we suggest that the boys be matched in Duluth ... A Petrolle-Kane match is about the sweetest fistic morsel matchmaker Terk could round up."[49]

Hurley's responses to Campbell's matchmaking suggestions were masterpieces of incredulous subterfuge. Jack "yelled blue murder" and was "frankly shocked" Cubby would "even suggest matching Zabuil with Rojas." Hurley continued, "I'll put Zabuil in the ring against somebody who will give him a fight, but not against a fighter who will likely crucify him. Six months from now Zabuil will be ready for Rojas."[50]

As for a Petrolle-Kane rematch, Hurley's complaint was only slightly less disingenuous: "What'ya trying to do, make my matches for me with this Kane stuff?" Jack added that even though he resented the insinuation that he was avoiding a Petrolle-Kane match, he was not going to let Campbell rush him into it either.[51]

The very next day, Terk announced he had scheduled a program featuring Petrolle-Kane and Zabuil-Rojas in double main events at the Duluth Curling Club arena August 17, 1928. In his article discussing the show, Campbell took full credit for arranging the bouts, boasting that the "matches were suggested repeatedly in the columns of the *News Tribune*."

Friends, however, soon clued Cubby in that the promoters had arranged

---

[48] Campbell, "The Sport Spigot," *Duluth News Tribune*, August 9, 1928, sports section.
[49] Campbell, *op. cit.*, July 29 and August 5, 1928, sports section.
[50] Campbell, *op. cit.*, August 10, 1928, sports section.
[51] Campbell, *op. cit.*, August 7 and 9, 1928, sports section.

the bouts even before he received the mailings from Walsh and Wrenn.[52]

Campbell sheepishly confessed in his "Sport Spigot" column the next day that "the Silver Spray regime took our breath away Friday afternoon when we received a buzz and were offered the information that the two matches suggested in this column recently had been signed up ... We're convinced that Colonel Hurley was kidding us the past two weeks or more, instead of our ribbing him, about fights for his stable aces ... As both bouts are what we've requested for some time – probably baited very cleverly to do so – we hope they turn out to be just as good as they appear on paper."[53]

On August 18, the "largest crowd that ever attended a local boxing card saw the fastest and most furious heavyweight battle staged here within the memory of the present generation ... when Szymka Zabuil, the 'Polish Killer,' knocked out Romero Quentin Rojas." Zabuil finished off "Rojas for the full count in the early part of the seventh frame when he hooked a right under his heart, which dropped him as if he had been poled."

In the second main event, Petrolle rained "solid shots upon" Jackie Kane "from his belt to his cowlick" to win "every round of a ten-session argument ... The beating which he took about the body was sufficient to kill off any ordinary fighter; but not Kane."[54]

Afterward, matchmaker Terk reported that in addition to the record crowd, estimated at 4,000 people, the box office had taken in over $7,000, also a Duluth record.[55]

The August show ended Terk and Hurley's first year in Duluth on a high note. Overall, however, the year had required them to endure their share of ups and downs. While Petrolle had started out with a bang against Mandell and Myers, the split-decision loss to Flowers and the fluke TKO by Grogan sidetracked the Express' ride to fistic fortune. On the other hand, the Silver Spray's amateur shows were a hit from the start and were the catalyst which raised pro boxing in Duluth to its highest plateau to date.

Even more vital to their future success, Hurley and Terk were able to reach an accommodation with the local press corps. After a rocky start, they had laid a foundation for the *News Tribune* and the *Herald* to become allies upon upon which they could rely in the future. With their assistance, the two men hoped to build on the progress made in 1928 and provide the region's fans with quality boxing entertainment for years to come.

---

[52] "Duluth Boxer Signs to Battle Heavy Chilean," *Duluth News Tribune*, August 10, 1928, sports section.

[53] Campbell, *op. cit.*, August 11, 1928, sports section.

[54] "Greatest Crowd in Fight History of Duluth Sees Zabuil Knock Out Rojas," *Duluth Herald*, August 18, 1928, sports section.

[55] "Boxing Show Draws over $7,000; Record for Local Shows," *Duluth Herald*, August 18, 1928, sports section (over $7,000 gate). Purcell, "Express Proves He Is Master of Chicagoan," *Fargo Forum*, August 18, sports section (some 4,000 fans in attendance).

CHAPTER 18

THE FARGO EXPRESS STALKS A TITLE

In each of his boxing engagements here in Detroit, Billy Petrolle has worn an old Indian blanket. He will wear it again tomorrow night when he goes into the ring at the Olympia. Petrolle has had the blanket for several years. He considers it an essential part of his equipment. He would as soon think of leaving the tape off his hands as of sliding through the ropes without that blanket.

And yet there was one time when Petrolle thought of discarding it. He was in New York for a bout with Hilario Martinez, the Spanish welterweight. Martinez stalked down the aisles of Madison Square Garden, wrapped in a gaudy-colored bathrobe, embellished by a flag of Spain across the back. It was considered an excellent example of what the well-dressed ringman should wear. It aroused considerable comment among both the experts and laity. The next day several metropolitan newspapers referred to the bathrobe as the last word in ring fashion and one of them contrasted it with "Petrolle's horse blanket."

Petrolle did not like that remark. It injured his vanity. He decided he would never wear the old blanket again. It looked older and more faded than ever. He wondered why he hadn't thrown it away long before. For the next two fights, Petrolle left off the "horse blanket" and both bouts proved unsatisfactory. One was with Cuddy DeMarco, and the two fighters were tossed out of the ring on a charge of stalling. In the other, Petrolle simply "couldn't get goin'" and had to be content with a draw with a fighter he regarded as much his inferior.

Petrolle concluded that the absence of the Indian blanket was responsible for his change in luck. He dug it out of the rag pile and has been wearing it to fights ever since. More often than not, it has served him well. He will pin his faith in it tomorrow night although he also intends to carry a rugged pair of fists and a well-conditioned body ring center when the gong calls him into action.[1]

– Sam Greene

****

On May 21, 1928, Sammy Mandell defended his lightweight title with a 15-round decision victory over Jimmy McLarnin at the Polo Grounds. Although 20,290 spectators paid $137,467 see the spectacle, it was the first time in more than 250 shows that Tex Rickard had lost money in New York. As a result, he announced that he was finished promoting lightweights and

---

[1] Greene, Sam, "Boxing," *Detroit News*, April 30, 1928, sports section. Greene was a boxing writer and columnist for the *Detroit News*.

would henceforth devote his efforts to the heavier divisions.[2]

The Mandell-McLarnin fight ended up on the wrong side of the ledger because, in his zeal to outbid Jim Mullen, Rickard miscalculated and guaranteed the fighters too much money. Tex expected McLarnin's popularity after his sensational knockout of Sid Terris to attract more than 40,000 people to the Polo Grounds. He guaranteed the challenger $50,000 and, even with the relatively low attendance, ended up paying Mandell close to that amount for his 37-1/2-percent guarantee.

In the three years since Jimmy Goodrich held the lightweight title, both the cost and the risk of promoting a championship match had risen dramatically. When Goodrich lost the title to Rocky Kansas in Buffalo in December 1925, Jimmy received only $12,000 for the bout. Seven months later, when Kansas lost it to Mandell in Chicago, Rocky asked for, and received, a guarantee of $50,000 plus training expenses.

To help Mullen land the title fight with Kansas, Mandell and his manager, Eddie Kane, agreed to accept 55 percent of the gate and pay Kansas his guaranteed $50,000 from this amount. Unfortunately, rain on the day of the contest kept the attendance low, and total receipts were just "a trifle over $75,000." As result, Mandell and Kane were forced to pay Kansas their entire purse and an additional $14,000 to boot.[3]

Based on this experience, Kane felt justified in setting his minimum price for future Mandell title defenses at $50,000, an exceedingly large purse for lightweights in 1928. Apart from New York, few cities in the country had a fan base capable of supporting such a bout. In addition, building up a contender with drawing power sufficient to make such a show profitable, even in well populated boxing centers, could not be done overnight.

With Rickard bowing out, only two promoters with a serious interest in developing a challenger to Mandell came forward. The first was Mullen who, even though he lost out to Tex for the Mandell-McLarnin battle, was still interested in a title bout for Chicago. The other was Dick Dunn, new manager of the Olympia Stadium in Detroit. In June 1928, both promoters announced plans to independently stage elimination contests, which they hoped would produce a contender popular enough to challenge Mandell.

The announcements of these bouts were good news to Jack Hurley and Billy Petrolle. Although Petrolle had encountered bad luck in his fights with Bruce Flowers in New York and Tommy Grogan in Omaha, Detroit fans

---

[2] Rickard had lost approximately $30,000 promoting the Johnny Wilson-Bryan Downey middleweight championship fight on Labor Day, 1921, but that bout took place in Jersey City, New Jersey. Tex would lose an estimated $400,000 when he promoted the Gene Tunney-Tom Heeney title bout at Yankee Stadium, but that fight would not take place until July 26, 1928.

[3] "Rockford Youth Defeats Kansas in Ten-Rounder" (AP), *New York World*, July 4, 1926, sports section. Fleischer, Nat, "Sammy Mandell, the Shiek," *New York Telegram*, July 28, 1926, sports section.

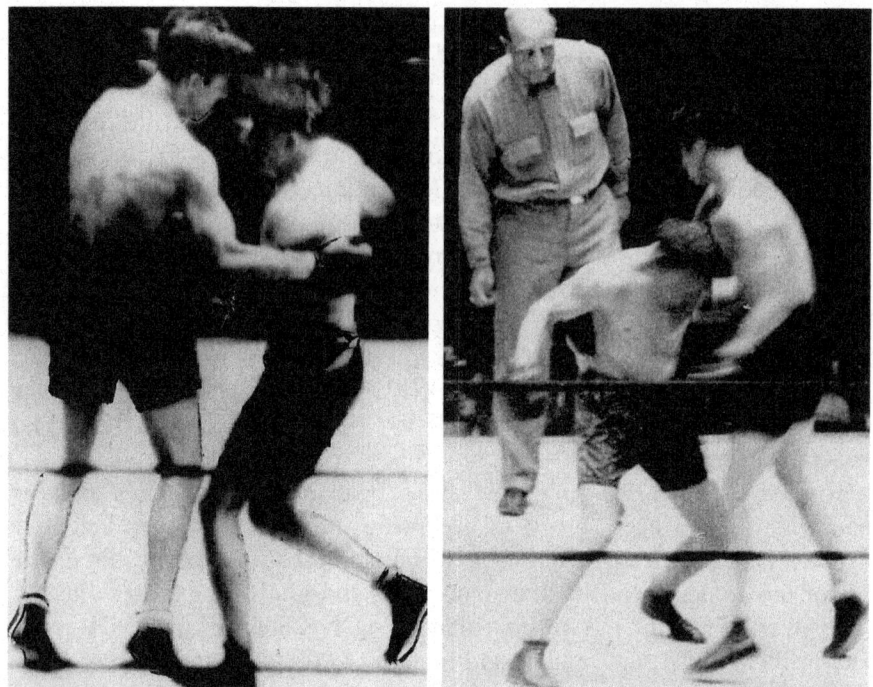

Two views of Mandell's successful title defense against Jimmy McLarnin. Jimmy is the shorter fighter in both photos.

Detroit Olympia Dick Dunn manager and ex-assistant to Tex Rickard.

remembered his exciting contests with Spug Myers and Armand Schaekels. As a result, Dunn was eager to give Billy a place in the elimination bouts. A convincing victory in Detroit would not only enhance his position there, but might also lead to other matches in Mullen's Chicago tourney.

Hurley had met Dunn a year earlier when Dick was serving as Rickard's operations manager at Madison Square Garden. Born into the business of sports promotion, Dunn was the son of John P. Dunn, boxing promoter at the old Coney Island Sporting Club in the first part of the 20th century. Dick's first jobs were delivering press notices for his father in 1911 when he was 12-years old and working as a publicist for P. T. Powers and Harry Pollock, early promoters of six-day bicycle races at a prior Garden building.

Dunn already was on the Garden staff when Rickard took over in 1920, having worked his way up as ticket taker, telephone operator, ticket seller, concessions' manager, timekeeper, and assistant superintendent. Within a few years, Dick became Tex's right-hand man. When Rickard moved the Dempsey-Tunney bout to Philadelphia in 1926, he gave Dunn the hands-on task of accomplishing the chore within a month. Two years later, when the Olympia job became available, Tex recommended Dick for the post.[4]

For Petrolle's first Detroit test, Dunn matched him in a return bout against Bruce Flowers on June 21. Although Billy's encounter with Jackie Kane took place in Kansas City at the Republican National Convention just eight days earlier, he emerged from the bout unscathed and ready for action.

Flowers was also at the peak of his form. In the three months since his first bout with Petrolle, Bruce had maintained his place as a contender by defeating Sid Barbarian and by splitting two bouts with Stanislaus Loayza.

The morning after the Petrolle-Flowers fight, P. J. Carveth filed this report in the *Detroit Free Press*:

> "Fargo's Express was under a full head of steam at the Olympia last night and ... Bruce Flowers, New Rochelle lightweight, was punched around the ring to emerge on the short end ... The Fargo Italian won six of the 10 rounds and held the black shadow even in two others, scored the only knockdown ... and drew the only claret. Flowers looked like championship timber only in brief rallies.
>
> "A smashing left hook that caught the Negro flush on the chin early in the fourth round dropped Flowers to both knees ... It was a perfectly timed punch that traveled only a few inches, but it buckled the Negro's knees and plainly had him in trouble. In the same round a straight left, a weapon that gave Flowers trouble throughout the bout, brought a stream of blood from the mouth ... Again in the ninth, a left hook opened a cut over Flowers' left eye and the claret

---

[4] Dunkley, Charles, Report about Dick Dunn (AP), *Biloxi Daily Herald*, January 29, 1929, p. 3.

dripped from the wound until the bout terminated.

"Flowers looked dangerous when he took a notion to do some fighting, which was much too seldom. When he rallied near the close of several rounds and cut loose a two-handed attack, Petrolle was forced back on his heels but most of the Negro's punches were at random and very few found the mark."

"The decision was greeted by a noisy demonstration from the crowd of about 8,000 people that turned out for the bout, and the verdict was as popular as any rendered here in main events in some time.[5]

Hurley "was all smiles" when he visited the *Fargo Forum* sports desk a few days later to discuss how Billy evened the score against Flowers:

"For the first time in a year and a half, Will was the snarling, punching fighter that made such a big hit with the fans over the entire country. He weaved in and out and around Flowers' punches and landed accurately and forcibly with both hands...

"Bill had plenty of speed, and he needed it, because this Flowers is some fighter. And, in addition to this speed, Bill really was punching. The blow that dropped Flowers didn't travel ten inches. When he fought Mandell, and came mighty near flattening the champion, he was forced to throw from center field in order to get anything behind his blows. He was forced to stay on his heels to retain his balance while hitting and, in short, wasn't near the fighter he was when he licked Eddie (Kid) Wagner, Tommy (Kid) Murphy and that crowd.

"But now, he's fighting like he did before, well, before he got married. Every fighter in history has a letdown at some time in his career, and Petrolle was no exception. But now, he's got his mind on the races again and he's headed right straight for the top."[6]

Although Hurley's euphoria over Petrolle's showing against Flowers was interesting, his remark about Billy's marriage was more revealing. That errant statement is the first instance of Jack's lifelong war against what he perceived as the pernicious influence of women on his fighters. Reading between the lines, the comment leads to the conclusion he believed Billy's marriage was the reason for inconsistency in his then-recent bouts. It also suggests the marriage had caused Jack considerable mental anguish.

Hurley's close friend, writer W. C. (Bill) Heinz, explained years later that

---

[5] Carveth, F. J., "Petrolle Wins Easy Decision over Flowers," *Detroit Free Press*, June 22, 1928, sports section.
[6] Purcell, J. A., "Sportville Spotlight," *Fargo Forum*, June 24, 1928, sports section.

"Jack want[ed] his fighters to be fighters and nothing else." He was "always afraid that some woman [was] going to spoil all his work and wreck all his dreams" and that she was "going to come between him and his fighter."

Instead Hurley told his fighters that "marriage is for women and kids, and it's expensive. You've got to be able to afford it. Your best chance to make a lot of money is to become a good fighter, and then you'll be able to afford marriage."[7]

The close bond Hurley enjoyed with Petrolle before his marriage is illustrated by a story Jack's brother Hank told *Forum* editor Ed Kolpack at the time of Billy's death in 1983:

> "Bill was a real good trainer. He didn't smoke, drink, or stay up late.
>
> "Russie LeRoy was the star of Jack's stable. This was in the 1920s, and one day Russie bought a car. Jack found out and he told LeRoy to sell it. 'You'll be riding when you should be walking,' said Jack. 'The next thing you'll have some dame in the back seat, and then you'll go boozing. It's no good for you.' But Jack couldn't convince Russie to get rid of the car.
>
> "In those days, Petrolle would take a streetcar from Dilworth to Fargo to work out at the Elks club. It cost 5 cents. After his workout, Bill would stop at the Grand Rec for a half-hour or so to see his friends. Everyone knew Bill. About 5 o'clock he'd go home and you wouldn't see him again until the next day.
>
> "One day Jack saw Bill get out of a car. He went over to him and asked, 'Whose car is that?' 'It's mine,' said Bill. 'I just got it.' 'What'ya need a car for?' asked Jack. 'You can ride the streetcar from Dilworth and it only costs a nickel. Sell it.'
>
> "After Bill finished his workout Jack was going to walk over to the Grand Rec with Petrolle. But Bill said he didn't have time. 'I'm going to get rid of the car.'
>
> "That's an example of how much he believed in Jack."[8]

According to Purcell, just a few months after their marriage, Billy's wife, Antoinette, asked him "to retire from the ring and enter business either in Duluth or Fargo." To prevent this catastrophe, Jack "was forced to use his best oratory to convince Petrolle his best chance for a neat fortune rested on his continuing with the boxing profession."[9]

Apparently, Hurley's oratory was convincing, because Antoinette

---

[7] Heinz, W. C., "The Last Campaign of Boxing's Last Angry Man," *Saturday Evening Post*, February 11, 1967, p. 42.

[8] Kolpack, Ed, "Petrolle Lived a Clean Life – and He Listened, Too," *The Forum*, May 19, 1983, sports section.

[9] Purcell, *op. cit.*, December 1, 1927, sports section.

allowed her husband to continue his boxing career until he and Jack mutually agreed Billy should retire in 1934. No further mention was ever made in the Fargo or Duluth newspapers of any interference by Antoinette in the business dealings between Hurley and Petrolle.

While Hurley was not alone in viewing marriage as detrimental to a fighter's career, he would eventually take this notion to great extremes. As time passed, this conviction would grow almost to the level of a vendetta against women in general, even to the point of referring to them as "little creatures." Undoubtedly, the unhappy break-up with his wife in the 1940s contributed to this development, but the seed likely was sewn much earlier.

As we have seen, while growing up, Hurley witnessed the trauma of his father's death while the latter worked 14- and 15-hour days on the railroad. Each week, Jack watched his dad give his pay check to his wife while, before the youngster's very eyes, his father aged at a rate far beyond his 47 years and without any prospect of an end to his labors.

The death of his father caused Jack to spend his teen years growing up in a household of three women: his mother Julia and his sisters Margaret and Abigail, who were one year older and two years younger than Jack, respectively. Jack's sister Katherine and brother Hank were much younger, and were then more like children than siblings to Jack.

After his dad's accident, Jack felt keenly the obligation to support his family, but he was torn between this sense of duty and his desire to follow a line of employment entirely different from his father. Given these circumstances, a fair conclusion is that Jack's suspicion of women likely was rooted in his memory of those years before World War I when he rolled out of bed every day at 5 a.m. to work ten-hour shifts at jobs he hated.

The best evidence this was the case came many years later when Heinz wrote a story about Hurley for the *Saturday Evening Post*. As part of his assignment, Bill met Jack at 7:30 one morning in the lobby of the Olympic Hotel, where he was living in Seattle. While they waited for a cab to take them to the airport, Hurley, almost 70 at the time, gazed out the hotel window as the morning traffic headed into town:

> "Look at the mules. Isn't that terrible? At four-thirty they'll all be heading the other way to take those paychecks back to the creatures. When I started out my mother wanted me to get a steady job. I said 'Mom, a steady job is a jail. I see these fellas I grew up with here, and they're in prison ten hours a day. I want to see something, go somewhere, and I can make a living doing it.'"[10]

After the Flowers fight, Hurley and Petrolle boarded a Great Northern

---

[10] Heinz, p. 47.

Billy Petrolle when he fought Doc Snell in Seattle. Hurley is likely the man standing by in the hat. Courtesy of *Seattle Post-Intelligencer* Collection, Museum of History and Industry.

train in Detroit and headed westward, 2,000 miles to Seattle, Washington where Billy was slated to meet local favorite Doc Snell in a six-round main event on June 29. The show was billed as the region's major boxing attraction of the outdoor season and was to take place at Dugdale Park, home for the Seattle Indians baseball club in the Pacific Coast League.

For an American city as far removed from Eastern boxing centers as a place could be, and which was located in a jurisdiction where the sport was still technically illegal, Seattle was home to a thriving fistic industry. In 1928, fans could choose from shows offered by two separate promotional firms on a year-round basis. Oddly enough, Hurley's fortunes were tied to both of these promoters – one by the past and the other by the future.[11]

The trip west afforded Hurley an chance to renew his acquaintance with Biddy Bishop, former manager of KO Mars. Bishop had helped Jack put over the LeRoy-Mars fight at Fargo in 1924 when Jack was operating on a shoestring. In 1926, Biddy moved to Seattle where he and Lonnie Austin joined forces to promote fights locally and book boxers all over the West. By 1929, Austin and Bishop claimed to operate the world's largest booking agency for fighters, with 436 pro and amateur boxers under their wing.[12]

The head of Seattle's other fistic firm, Nate Druxman, was promoting the Petrolle-Snell fight. Formerly known as "the Boy Promoter," Druxman started promoting fights in 1913 as a 21-year-old matchmaker for the local

---

[11] Washington State's anti-prizefighting law was not abolished until March 1933 (effective July 1933). Prior to that time, the sport was tolerated on a hit-and-miss basis, depending on the policy of local authorities. The rationale for allowing boxing at all was the belief that exhibitions of physical exercise witnessed by members of a private club were not prizefights. As a matter of accommodation to local authorities, bouts were generally limited to six rounds (though on occasion this would be stretched to eight rounds), apparently on a theory that the longer the bout the less it retained the character of "an exhibition."

The volatile nature of enforcement by Seattle authorities over time is best illustrated by a couple of examples. In October 1929, under the administration of Mayor Frank Edwards, authorities attempted to shut down an Austin-Bishop promotion of the Leo Lomski-Jack Willis bout on the basis that it was an illegal prizefight. A trial ensued and a jury found that the bout in question was not a prizefight at all but rather just entertainment for the members of a private club. As each case would turn on its own peculiar facts, there was nothing to stop future prosecutions, but for the time being anyway, the authorities decided not to pursue the matter.

Just three years later in 1932, under a different administration, Nate Druxman promoted a boxing show as a benefit for the Mayor's Fund for the Unemployed. On this occasion, in contrast to the 1929 situation, not only did local authorities fail to enforce the anti-prize fight law, but Mayor John Dore served as an honorary promoter of the show. Times do change, and sometimes very quickly.

[12] "436 Boxers in Stable," *Ring Magazine*, November 1929, p. 15. The *Ring* article claimed Austin and Bishop controlled the affairs of 68 professional, 137 semi-professional, and 231 amateur boxers. The firm claimed to employ "something like 25 persons on the payroll, including a bookkeeper, office men, boxing instructor, professional trainer, porter and other attaches, including road men, clerks, etc."

Seattle promoter Nate Druxman.

Seattle lightweight Doc Snell.

Biddy Bishop with whom Hurley had a reunion in Seattle.

Jackie (Kid) Berg, who gave Petrolle three tough fights.

Elks club. In 1919, Nate left the Elks to start promoting his own shows. By 1928, he felt secure enough in the business to leave his full-time sales position with a cigar distributor and devote all his time to boxing.

When Washington state formally legalized boxing in July 1933, Druxman boldly declared to Seattle sportswriters, "If you think I've done anything up 'til this point, watch me now!" In the next seven years, while the rest of the boxing world languished in the doldrums of "the Great Depression," Natty Nate promoted 11 world title bouts and transformed Seattle into one of the most successful boxing centers in the world.

During this period, Nate would help young fighters like Freddie Steele and Al Hostak, who would win world titles in Seattle, and other stars like Abie Israel, Henry Woods, Tiger Al Lewis, Leonard Bennett, Solly Krieger, and Allen Matthews, who became known to boxing fans all over the world.

More important to Hurley would be Druxman's discovery in 1940 of 18-year-old Harry (Kid) Matthews, then already a veteran of nearly 20 pro fights in his native state of Idaho. In 1950, Jack would move to Seattle, become Matthews' manager, and bring him within one fight of earning a chance at the heavyweight championship. Except for Petrolle, Harry would become the biggest drawing card of Hurley's career.

If Druxman had not established Matthews as a regional attraction, it is likely Harry would have abandoned his boxing career and never connected with Hurley. As a consequence, one of the most interesting chapters in Pacific Northwest boxing history likely would never have happened.

Although rain prevented a sell-out, a goodly number of fans showed up at Dugdale Park June 29, 1928, to cheer Snell to a draw against Petrolle. Alluding to federal laws against train robbery, *Seattle Star* sports editor Leo Lassen left no doubt about who he thought deserved the decision:

> "If Uncle Sam is looking for Harold Jones today, don't be astonished, for the 'Fargo Express' was robbed last night at the ball park when Harold, who was refereeing the main event, handed 'Doc' Snell a draw with Billy Petrolle, a North Dakota lightweight.
>
> "Jones was very big-hearted. Petrolle had a clear edge when the six rounds were in the record book. He's one highly touted visitor who lived up to advance notices, and if you think he can't fight, just page Snell."[13]

The draw had no effect on Petrolle's standing. News that local papers

---

[13] Lassen, Leo, "Petrolle Is Winner, But Still He Isn't," *Seattle Star*, June 30, 1928, p. 8. Leo Lassen would wind up in the radio broadcast booth as the voice of the Seattle Rainiers baseball team in the Pacific Coast League for approximately 25 years. As such, he and his unmistakable staccato baritone are fondly recalled to this day (2014) by area baseball fans in their late 50s and older. The Seattle baseball club discarded the name "Indians" in favor of "Rainiers" when brewery owner Emil Sick bought the team in the 1930s.

favored Billy and awareness of Snell's greater experience in Seattle's six-round game caused experts to discount the result. In addition, Snell had beaten King Tut, Charley (Phil) Rosenberg, Jimmy McLarnin, and Tod Morgan. A draw against Doc under the best of conditions was no disgrace.[14]

Back in Duluth, Hurley found a telegram on his desk from Jim Mullen offering Petrolle a fight against Jackie (Kid) Berg on July 26 as part of the lightweight elimination series Mullen was staging in Chicago. Berg, whose birth name was Judah Bergman, had recently arrived in the U. S. from England and immediately made a hit with three straight wins in the Windy City over Pedro Amador, Freddie Mueller, and Mike Watters.

Born in 1901, Berg grew up in the Whitechapel district of London's East End where ex-welterweight champion Ted (Kid) Lewis was raised. Jackie's parents were among 50,000 Jews who left eastern Europe and migrated to that section of London in the first ten years of the 20th century. While the rest of his family was devout in its faith, Jackie neglected his studies, was passed over for his Bar Mitzvah, and took to roaming the streets.

If ever a fighter could be called a "natural," that fighter was Berg. Learning to fight in the alleys of his neighborhood ghetto, Jackie never had a lesson in his life. The first boxing match he ever witnessed was his own pro debut. In that bout, the 14-year-old Berg was so uninformed about fistic etiquette that when the referee called him to the center of the ring for instructions, he rushed across the ring and immediately started throwing punches.

Berg's seconds had to pull him back to his corner and tell him to wait for the sound of the bell. After the fight began, he never stopped throwing punches, and at the end of six rounds the referee raised his hand in victory. The crowd loved the fight and showed its appreciation by throwing pennies into the ring afterward. Jackie received 15 shillings plus tips for the bout.[15]

Berg's windmill style was his trademark. Ray Arcel, who trained Jackie for his U. S. bouts, probably described this non-stop method of boxing best:

> "Jackie had one style when he came over, and I never change a fellow's style. I might improve it. We had a lot of fighters that fought aggressively but Jackie was a sensational performer, he never stopped moving his arms. I mean, he never held or anything, he was perpetual motion. Punch to the body, then bang bang to the

---

[14] Lassen in the *Seattle Star* had it 3-2 (one round not discussed) in favor of Petrolle ("Petrolle had a clear edge"). Alex Shults in the *Seattle Times* had it 2-2-2 with the comment "Petrolle really shaded Snell just a little, but the margin was slight." Dick Sharp of the *Seattle Post-Intelligencer* agreed with the referee's decision but Sharp's scoring is unclear, the winner of rounds seeming to change depending on what part of the article a person reads. All articles appeared on June 30, 1928 in the sports sections.

[15] Harding, John, with Berg, Jack, *Jackie Kid Berg, The Whitechapel Windmill*, (Robson Books, London, 1987), pp. 13-37.

A dapper Kid Berg returns to visit his family in the Whitechapel district of London after winning the world's junior welterweight championship from Mushy Callahan in 1931.

head and back to the body and keep going ...

"He used to throw a volley of punches and once he got close to you he just kept on throwing punches. His strength was in his determination, his courage, his will to carry on; and even as the fight progressed he was getting stronger. If he had been a good puncher he might have hurt a lot of people. But he wasn't a powerful puncher. But he'd hit you with a series of blows that you had to back up from, you just couldn't stand there and stay with him. It wore you down."[16]

Berg would achieve a level of success in America unprecedented for a British boxer. In 1930, he would win the world junior welterweight title from Mushy Callahan and would defend it successfully ten times. In his 11 years as a boxer in the U. S., he would post a record of 67 wins, 12 losses, and four draws. Against world champions, he would compile a record of six wins, four losses, and one draw. After 22 years in the ring, Jackie would retire in 1945 with an overall record of 157 wins, 26 losses, and nine draws.

The Petrolle fight was Jackie's first against a top-rated contender. Since both fighters were known for their aggressive and exciting styles, it was anticipated sparks would fly when they met in Chicago on July 26, 1928.

At the bell, Billy raced out, and "all but had his English opponent out in the first round when he sent a series of hard blows to Berg's head and body." Jackie "recuperated fast between rounds" and "caught Petrolle unaware" in the second "with an onslaught of telling blows on Petrolle's head, which opened a small cut under Petrolle's right eye."

There was little to choose between the two battlers in rounds three through six, and eight and nine, with each "more than willing to mix it and both suffer[ing] many telling blows." Petrolle won the seventh, and near the round's end "had Berg groggy and hanging after landing several hard rights to the chin and midriff." Jackie finished stronger than Billy in the tenth and "smothered Petrolle with punches to the head and body."

The bout, "one of the best lightweight fights seen in Chicago since boxing was legalized," had "fans roaring throughout the ten rounds." The draw decision was greeted with cheering from the fans, with the judges scoring the bout even and referee Ed Purdy voting for Berg. The throng, estimated at 6,000, paid $14,500 to see the contest.[17]

Berg described the first Petrolle fight in an autobiography he co-

---

[16] Harding with Berg, p. 108.
[17] "Petrolle with Knockout in Grasp, Held to Draw" (AP), *Fargo Forum*, July 27, 1928, sports section. Eckersall, Walter, "Berg Battles Petrolle in 10 Round Draw," *Chicago Tribune*, July 27, 1928, sports section. "Berg on Edge for His Return Bout with Petrolle," *Chicago Tribune*, August 19, 1928, sports section. Eckersall, "Petrolle, Berg, Renew Ring Feud at Mill Tonight," *Chicago Tribune*, August 23, 1928, sports section. The description of the bout was compiled from all of the above sources.

authored with John Harding in 1987:

> "[Petrolle] came into the ring with an Indian blanket over him. He was very superstitious; the blanket was more than just a gimmick. He was scarred up, and he was one of the hardest punchers I have ever fought. Every time he hit me I felt as though his arms were going through my stomach! But I wouldn't give in. You know, he was the first man to make me pass blood. From kidney punches. After the fight I had a shower and I was taking a pee and it was red! I got a shock ..."[18]

Responding to sportswriters' questions following the fight, Petrolle and Hurley agreed Berg was one of the best fighters Billy had faced. "Berg uses about the same style as Ace Hudkins, except that he does not clown like Ace," Jack told writers. "However, he throws as many punches and stands up well under punishment ... He is easily one of the toughest boys Petrolle has ever met. Personally, I thought Billy won, but was satisfied to get a draw in Chicago, and especially as Berg was the favorite with the crowd."[19]

The final bell barely had sounded when Mullen made his way to the dressing rooms with contract forms in hand. Before he left, he had secured their signatures for a rematch August 23, 1928, at Chicago's Mills Stadium.

Afterward, Hurley and Petrolle returned to Duluth for the August 17th show in which Petrolle defeated Jackie Kane, and Szymka Zabuil kayoed Quentin Romero Rojas. Six days later, the duo was back in Chicago for the second Berg fight. At the weigh-in, Jackie tipped the beam at 134 pounds, while Billy scaled 134-1/2. Rain that evening delayed the fight one day. Betting was even money as the fighters entered the ring on August 24.[20]

The Associated Press' opening paragraph of coverage the next day reported that a "relentless two-fisted attack tonight gave Billy Petrolle, the

---

[18] Harding with Berg, p. 90. Berg's observation about Petrolle and the Indian blanket was correct. Years later, Billy discussed the importance of the blanket and its origin in an interview for a boxing magazine:
> "That old Navajo blanket was my trademark for a couple hundred fights. My manager, Jack Hurley, picked it up someplace. Then he gave out a story that a famous Indian chief had given it to me. That Jack ... He sure made things up. The first time I wore it was in Los Angeles. The crowd got a kick out of it and from then on I was never without it. It got all stained with sweat and blood, and it smelled terrible. But I never would send it out to be cleaned because I was afraid all the good luck would be washed out of it." Thornton, Robert J.,"Billy Petrolle's Magic Blanket," Boxing International, June 1965, p. 14.

[19] "Berg-Petrolle Battle Had Fans on Ragged Edge," Duluth Herald. July 27, 1928, sports section.

[20] The weigh-in and the fight were originally scheduled for August 23. The fighters weighed in as scheduled, but when rain caused the fight to be delayed one day, they were not required to weigh in again.

'Fargo Express' a [fifth round] technical knockout over Jack Berg of England and a probable opportunity ... to meet Sammy Mandell for the lightweight championship." It was "the best fight seen in Chicago this season and it had 10,000 spectators on their feet throughout." Gate receipts for the bout were reported as $21,500.[21]

Arcel described the action in Jackie's autobiography:

> "Jack had hardly jumped from his corner when Petrolle streaked across the ring and cut loose with a left hook that caught Jack high on the head and down he went. He went over on his face, and I thought it was all over.
>
> "Frankie Jacobs, who with Sol Gold managed Berg, was seated in the press stand. As Jackie went down, Jacobs yelled to attract his attention. He yelled 'Yiddle!' which is the nickname he had for Jack. Berg seemed to hear above the deafening noise that came from all sides. Jackie suddenly seemed to come to himself and watched Jacobs as he brought his hands together with a loud smack in unison with the timekeeper. I think the count reached eight when Berg came to his feet.
>
> "And then there came one knockdown after another a few seconds between. At least three times it didn't seem that Berg would come up."

The Associated Press reported nine knockdowns in the first round.

> "I remember in one of the knockdowns that Jackie was so badly gone that he couldn't seem to lift his head to look around him and he deliberately dragged his body over the canvas in the direction from which his manager's voice came. And there he listened, apparently unable to see, as Jacobs yelled the count. And at nine he was up once more.
>
> "Berg was in terrible shape in the third and fourth and was so weak at times that he would have gone down from a push. He was knocked down three more times. They wanted to toss the towel in from his corner but Berg wouldn't let them. Finally Goldie could stand it no longer and, in the fifth, in went the towel. They had an awful time trying to quiet Jackie ..."[22]

Mullen told Hurley before the fight he had reached an understanding with Mandell's manager, Eddie Kane, for a title fight. Jim assured Jack an

---

[21] "Fargo Express Sends Berg to Floor 10 Times," *Duluth News Tribune*, August 25, 1928, sports section.
[22] Harding with Berg, pp. 90-92.

impressive showing by Petrolle against Berg would land him the bout as long as they were willing to accept the challenger's minimum guarantee of 12-1/2 percent. Unfortunately, Mullen's assurances were founded more on a hope and a prayer than a written agreement.

In fact, though Mullen had talked to Kane in general terms about the match, they had not reached a final understanding. Jim hoped to bargain down Kane's $50,000 price to a more affordable level. When he refused to budge, Mullen took a long, hard look at whether the bout would draw the $80,000 needed to break even and decided to let the bout die on the vine.[23]

Kane, for his part, was content to wait until a contender emerged who could excite the fans enough for a promoter to pay his demand. He figured Mandell's successful defense against McLarnin in May had bought Sammy at least a year before the various boxing commissions would take action against him for not defending the title. In the meantime, the champion could cut a fat hog touring the country fighting lesser lights in the division for purses of $5,000 to $10,000 a crack without risking the title.

Kane and Mandell were severely criticized by the press and fans alike for this strategy. Although he did not come right out and say it, Kane's philosophy was that his job was to manage Mandell, not please the public. While these tactics made Sammy less popular than he otherwise might have been, they accomplished the main purpose of increasing the size of his purses and extending the duration of his championship reign.

Petrolle's victory over Berg was his most important win since his upset kayo of Eddie (Kid) Wagner in Fargo, which had launched him into national prominence 2-1/2 years before. The Berg knockout completely erased any doubt about Billy's ability lingering from his losses to Bruce Flowers and Tommy Grogan earlier in the year. It also immediately put him back at the top rung of challengers for the lightweight title.

Promoter Dunn was eager to use Petrolle in another elimination bout at the Olympia arena in Detroit, and Hurley readily agreed to a match against Stanislaus Loayza of Chile on September 21, 1928. Loayza had been in the running as a possible foe for Mandell until McLarnin kayoed the Chilean in four rounds on August 2. As a result, the pressure was on Billy to better Jimmy's showing by stopping Loayza in an earlier round.

Hurley told Dunn about the failed negotiations for a Mandell fight in Chicago and offered to help make the bout happen in Detroit. Jack proposed to have Billy fight Sammy for nothing unless the gate exceeded $65,000. Mandell would take the first $50,000, the Olympia the next $15,000 for expenses, with Petrolle to split proceeds above $65,000 with the Olympia. Dunn seemed intrigued, and said he would take the matter under advisement, pending the outcome of the Petrolle-Loayza fight.[24]

---

[23] Purcell, *op. cit.*, August 30, 1928, sports section.

[24] Purcell, *op. cit.*, *Fargo Forum*, September 16, 1928, sports section.

In the presence of a near-capacity 9,000 fans who paid over $22,000, Petrolle "realize[d] his desire to halt the Chilean in shorter time than Jimmy McLarnin," by stopping Loayza in one minute five seconds of round two.

The end came suddenly just after the two fighters had engaged in a furious exchange of body blows. Petrolle charged forward and landed a sweeping right to the jaw that drove Loayza to the ropes. Billy followed with another vicious body attack, capped off by a right uppercut and a left hook to the jaw which traveled less than a foot. Stanislaus was counted out and remained unconscious for almost five minutes.[25]

Afterward, Dunn said he would try to arrange a Petrolle-Mandell bout for the winter, in accord with Jack's proposal, if Billy first could defeat Grogan and McLarnin. Dick figured in addition to providing two more profitable shows, the bouts would build the gate for the title fight.

Dunn called for Petrolle to fight Grogan November 9 with the winner to meet McLarnin later in the month. The later scheduling of the McLarnin fight would give a dislocated thumb Jimmy suffered against Loayza time to heal. Hurley was pleased with the arrangement. He was sure Petrolle could best Grogan and avenge the fluke loss Billy had suffered earlier in the year.

Hurley had seen the McLarnin-Loayza fight in August and devised a plan to beat Jimmy. Back in Duluth, he told Cubby Campbell that if "McLarnin has a sore thumb, he's liable to break it with a swing at Petrolle's head, for Billy will be weaving so much that'll be the only place Jimmy will be able to hit – and of course he can't hurt Petrolle on the head." Future events would bear out the accuracy of Jack's analysis more than once.[26]

In the meantime, King Tut had been on a rampage the past year, with wins over Tommy Cello, Sid Barbarian, Eddie (Kid) Wagner, and Ray Miller. On October 2, Tut defeated junior lightweight champ Tod Morgan in an overweight match at Minneapolis. Promoter Mike Collins was sure a Petrolle-Tut match would to fill the Minneapolis Auditorium.

With a 1-1/2 months to wait for Petrolle's scheduled date with Grogan, Hurley accepted Collins' offer for an October 16th Tut fight. Since Billy had beaten the King twice a year earlier, Jack figured the bout as a welcome opportunity to keep Petrolle sharp and at the same time earn a good payday.

Unfortunately, Hurley's optimism proved to be woefully misplaced.

The day after the bout, the *Fargo Forum* opened its report from Minneapolis with this capsule summary:

> "King Tut, Minneapolis lightweight, tonight gave Billy Petrolle, the Fargo Express, a terrific beating in one of the most sensational

---

[25] Carveth, "Blow to Chin Puts Chilean Fighter Away," *Detroit Free Press*, September 22, 1928, sports section. "Hefty Blows Fly Thickly in 1st Round" (AP), *Fargo Forum*, September 22, 1928, p. 8.

[26] Campbell, Cubby, "The Sport Spigot," Duluth *News Tribune,* September 12, 1928, sports section.

ten-round slugging matches ever seen here, in the opinion of newspapermen. Each fighter gave a rare exhibition of courage and ability to assimilate punishment. Each was on the floor twice and on the verge of a knockout, but Tut, drawing on stronger recuperative powers, outlasted the Express."[27]

Sandy Macdonald, in the *Duluth Herald*, provided a graphic description of the contest's first half when Petrolle dominated most of the action:

"It was a great battle, probably the best ever staged in the Mill City ... Tut had Bill on the floor in the first round from a left chop to the chin which followed a solid right to the same spot. There was no count, but Petrolle was shaky when he went to the corner.

"The Express was running on schedule in the second heat, however, when he gave Tut a terrific pasting to the head and body and should have, by every angling of reckoning known to the great sport of fisticuffs, knocked him colder than a mother-in-law's kiss. Tut was out on his feet, bleary-eyed and with his hands dangling at his sides, yet Petrolle, apparently fresh and going, could not lay a glove on a vulnerable spot. Twice Tut was on the floor, blasted early in the round so that Petrolle had a world of time in which to finish him off in a most workman-like manner, but with his prey wounded and sinking, Billy could not put over a finishing shot. Tut was so far gone when the round ended that he walked to a neutral corner and Referee George Barton had to escort him to his chair.

"Petrolle laid heavy gloves on Tut in the third and fourth rounds, closing his left eye completely and knocking a square inch of skin off of his right cheek.

"Tut and Petrolle were both pretty tired in the fifth inning when little damage was done. But in the sixth Tut began to revive, and using short left and right chops to the jaw forged to the front ... ."[28]

Cubby Campbell's account in the *News Tribune* concentrated on the bout's closing rounds when Tut turned the tide and took the lead:

"From the sixth round on Tut won every round ... Late in the [seventh] round he hammered Billy against the ropes and then as he came off he cracked over a slashing right which dropped Petrolle to his haunches. In plain distress, Petrolle gained his knees, grabbed his head between his two hands and twisted his head this way and

---

[27] "Both Ringmen Down Twice in Great Go," *Fargo Forum*, October 17, 1928, p. 8.
[28] "Petrolle Has Opponent Out on His Feet in Second Heat," *Duluth Herald*. October 17, 1928, sports section.

that to clear his brain. The bell gave him relief at the count of eight.

"... For a time [in the eighth] it appeared Petrolle was rallying. He out-boxed Tut and out-slugged him the first few moments, but Tut again staggered him with those overhand sharp right hand punches, or vicious left hooks, and at the bell Billy was again groggy ... Billy appeared to be somewhat stronger in the ninth, although his punches lacked any semblance of power. Tut was also tiring fast, but shortly before the bell cuffed Billy at will with left hooks and right crosses, but Bill, gamely bobbing staggering about the ring, finished the round. He used the same tactics in the tenth, hardly able to lift his hand to shoot a punch."[29]

In the dressing room, Petrolle sat dazed, his "head dropped down, mumbling between swollen lips time and again, 'I was in good shape – I was in top condition.'" Billy was so disoriented he seemed unaware when his handlers moved "to slash his gloves to ribbons to get them off his hands" because "his puffed up hands ... were twice their normal size."

Concerning these events, Cubby remarked, "After glimpsing Petrolle's hands after the fight, we well realized why ... for the last half of the fight ... his punches lacked any semblance of steam. His left was puffed up like a rubber ball, while a middle knuckle of his right hand stuck up grotesquely, fully an inch back from its normal position."

Campbell guessed Billy injured his hands in the second round when he "was pounding frantically at every portion of Tut's arm-guarded anatomy. Petrolle was slashing lefts and rights in all directions at Tut's crouched body. Solid blows to the head, shoulders or arms may have bruised the hands – for it was clearly apparent as the fight progressed that Petrolle had nothing in either hand that Tut need fear."[30]

A day later, Sandy Macdonald visited a more lucid Petrolle:

> "'Sometimes you win; sometimes you lose,' is the philosophical manner in which Billy smiles off his defeat. 'I beat Tut twice last year. He defeated me last Tuesday. It's all in the game. I feel that I will defeat him if we ever meet again.'
>
> "Petrolle says that after he received the left punch in the mouth in the first round that floored him he did not remember anything until after he had reached his dressing room: 'The newspapers say I floored Tut twice in the second round,' explains Billy. 'I don't remember that. I don't remember anything that happened after the

---

[29] Campbell, "Gameness of Loser Marks Gory Battle," *Duluth News Tribune*, October 17, 1928, p. 12.
[30] Campbell, "The Sport Spigot," *Duluth News Tribune*, October 18, 1928, sports section.

first round. That punch to the mouth was not a hard blow. I remember getting it. I remember going down, but after that my mind was a blank.'"

Macdonald also described Hurley's corner work during the fight:

"Spectators at the Petrolle-Tut fight are still talking about the able manner in which Jack Hurley, Petrolle's manager, handled the latter and brought him through the storm right side up. From the fifth round on, Hurley worked heroically over his boxer, at times slapping his face vigorously to arouse him to a full appreciation of what was going on. It was, to be exact, the work of Hurley that brought Petrolle through to the finish."[31]

Petrolle was not the only one to remember the October 16th bout as a mini-war. Seven months later, Tut recalled the fight in an interview with *Forum* sports editor Purcell:

"Petrolle ... gave me the worst taste of punching I have ever received. He had me out on my feet in the second. Only fighting instinct kept me up. I hid behind my stubby arms, did not know what had happened when I came back for a minute's rest, and was still in a daze for several rounds after that. I saw a dozen or more Petrolles in front of me, but when the storm cleared it was my turn to get busy.

"Billy clipped me again about the sixth or seventh, but I caught him in the eighth, floored him twice and finished the winner. Petrolle hasn't been the same since that slaughter in Minneapolis, although he has often said that he would like to get me again. I'll accommodate him any time he's ready."

Two weeks later, both Petrolle and Hurley were hospitalized. For several months preceding the Tut fight, Billy had experienced discomfort in his left side which he chose to ignore. After the bout, the pain increased. Following an examination, his physician ordered immediate hospitalization, and he checked into St. Mary's Hospital in Duluth October 30.[32]

X-rays showed pieces of a broken rib had created an abscess on a kidney. While still in the hospital for testing, Billy developed a fever and underwent

---

[31] Macdonald, Sandy, "Light Whines and Cheers," *Duluth Herald*, October 18, 1928, sports section.

[32] Campbell, *op. cit.*, October 30, 1928, sports section. "Express Is Pronounced Seriously Ill," *Fargo Forum*, October 30, 1928, sports section. "Billy Petrolle to Undergo Operation at Duluth Today," *Fargo Forum*, November 3, 1928, sports section.

emergency surgery November 3 to clear the kidney of infection.[33]

At first, Petrolle was too weak to talk after the surgery, and rumors circulated that he had died. Worries over his eventual recovery were not eased until two full days after surgery when Billy at last regained his strength enough to murmur to his family that the "Doc had a harder knockout punch than any fighter I ever went up against."[34]

Hurley was in the hospital under observation for stomach pain at Fargo when he heard of Petrolle's illness. Jack's stay, which lasted over a week, apparently alleviated his condition because he did not have surgery at that time. As expected, his ailment was diagnosed as stomach ulcers.[35]

On November 7, Hurley was well enough to discuss Petrolle's condition in a visit to the *Forum* offices:

> "We didn't use Petrolle's illness as an alibi for that beating we took from Tut, but facts are facts and the entire story might just as well be told. The doctor who performed the operation said Petrolle had been suffering from that abscess for more than three months, and it must have eaten heavily into his store of reserve energy. The poor fellow simply couldn't get in shape for that Tut fight, and had I realized how serious his ailment was, Minneapolis never would have seen it.
>
> "But the doctors tell me that Petrolle will be strong as ever in another three months, and then we'll fight a few soft ones and take after big game."[36]

For a second time in two years, injury had ended Petrolle's boxing season early. The loss to Tut was a far more serious setback to Billy's career than the technical kayo suffered a year earlier at the hands of Tommy Herman. The recent reversal came at a time when Petrolle's career was gaining momentum and a title bout seemed to be within his grasp. Now, Billy would have to wait until he was well, and start all over again.

In the meantime, Hurley had plenty to keep him busy, if not make him wealthy, until Petrolle was well enough to fight again. The seeds planted the prior year were beginning to bear fruit. The amateur ranks had produced several promising students who deserved his attention. It was time for "the old Colonel" to return to Duluth for the fall-winter boxing season and give them the tender, loving care they deserved.

---

[33] Campbell, *op. cit.*, November 2, 1928, sports section. "Chipped Rib Likely Cause of Petrolle's Trouble," *Fargo Forum*, October 31, 1928, sports section.

[34] Campbell, *op. cit.*, November 6, 1928, sports section. "Billy Petrolle's Death Rumor Is Branded False," *Fargo Forum*, November 1, 1928, sports section.

[35] Campbell, *op. cit.*, November 2 and 4, 1928, sports sections.

[36] Purcell, *op. cit.*, November 7, 1928, sports section.

CHAPTER 19

HURLEY AND LEROY BURY THE HATCHET

Last night was the last time that the Fargo Express will ever climb between the ropes. It breaks my heart to quit the game but I would rather quit now with the memory of cheers rather than go on a few more years and retire with only jeers as a memory.

I have no alibi for last night. King Tut was a greater fighter than when I fought him last time. He hurt me in the first round and several times during the later rounds. My eyes were both cut badly and this handicapped me although nothing I could have done would have beaten the King last night.

Detroit fans have been great to me. I fought six great fights here. Last night it seemed that I left everything I ever had in the gymnasium. I couldn't get started. I didn't realize it at the time that I was going back down the trail. As the fight wore on and my legs and arms failed to serve me as they had in the past, I tried everything to make it a fight. If I looked bad, I hope the fans will forget the fight, acclaim Tut as a great fighter, and remember me in the great battles I staged here in the past.

Not until I sat in my dressing room at Navin Field last night did I realize that youth does not last forever. Only 24, I must admit that I have reached the end of the trail where I can provide the fans the kind of action I did two years ago. For that reason I am through.[1]

– Billy Petrolle

****

Six days after Szymka Zabuil's kayo of Quentin Romero Rojas on August 16, 1928, the "Polish Killer" dropped a bombshell by refusing to sign the manager's contract which Hurley presented to him after the fight. After reviewing the document at home a few days, Zabuil entered the Silver Spray one evening, and secretly "proceeded to move his effects away. As he was leaving the gym Jack 'cornered him' and demanded an explanation."

The proposed contract called for Zabuil to be placed under Hurley's management on "a 50-50 percent basis." Before deciding to not sign it, Szymka consulted Jack's former pride and joy, Russie LeRoy, for advice. LeRoy had stopped off in Duluth to see the Rojas fight on his way back to Fargo from a hunting trip near Winnipeg. Reportedly, Russie "put a 'bug' in Zabuil's ear on what sort of a contract he should have with Hurley."[2]

In Zabuil's mind, his victory over Rojas assured him a guaranteed path to fame and fortune. Duluth boxing fans, who "had booed the big local boy

---

[1] "Petrolle Will Hang Up Gloves; Strength Gone," *Duluth Herald*, September 13, 1929, sports section.
[2] Campbell, Cubby, "The Sport Spigot," *Duluth News Tribune*, December 4, 1928, sports section.

previously, now joined heartily in cheering him to the echo." His new advisor friends "told him that he was a great fighter and was going to make $100,000" for a single fight "within the next year."

Szymka told Jack he was "undissatisfied" with the proposed arrangement because $100,000 was "a lot of money and you'll get half of it." Hurley "pointed out to Zabuil that he also would make $50,000, but the big Pole refused to accede to the terms and that ended the argument."[3]

In describing his conversation with Hurley, Zabuil told Sandy Macdonald he "had never had so much trouble in my life, so much rowing and never heard such bitter language." Even so, he had "no complaints to make against Hurley, or Terk, either, for they both treated me all right, in fact were fair in every way. However, I did not relish the wording of the contract which Hurley presented me with for my signature and we parted."[4]

Unaware Hurley had carefully orchestrated the Rojas win, Zabuil headed east to Boston and placed himself under the care of Johnny Buckley, manager of future heavyweight champion Jack Sharkey. Buckley, in no-nonsense fashion, quickly matched Zabuil in three preliminary bouts. After winning the first by a kayo, Szymka was himself stopped in the next two.

Deciding the East was not to his taste, Zabuil returned to his family's home at Milwaukee, Wisconsin in January 1929 to recuperate. According to Cubby Campbell, reports from Milwaukee indicated Szymka had been "used merely as a punching bag for Sharkey and other heavyweights" in Boston, and his face would hardly be recognizable by friends in Duluth."[5]

Campbell also noted that "Zabuil, by the way, is still a $100 and less, fighter, whereas he undoubtedly could have made himself a fair-sized stake had he stuck around Duluth for another year or so."[6]

After a three-week rest, Zabuil wrote to Hurley requesting a spot on the National Athletic Club's next boxing show "under the condition that I know who I am going to fight and what I am to get for the fight." Szymka said that Buckley "had been a good manager and got me some fights, but he would not look after me or show me anything, so I left him."[7]

Hurley's response, if any, to Zabuil went unreported, but, under the circumstances, it is unlikely Jack looked with favor upon being dictated to. In any event, Szymka never fought under Hurley's management again.[8]

---

[3] Campbell, "'Polish Killer' Demurs over 50-50 Clause," August 23, 1928, sports section. Campbell, "The Sport Spigot," *Duluth News Tribune*, August 23, 1928, sports section. "Greatest Crowd in Fight History of Duluth Sees Zabuil Knock Out Rojas," *Duluth Herald*, August 18, 1928, sports section.

[4] "Mandell Would Battle Zabuil,," Duluth *Herald*, August 27, 1928, sports section.

[5] Campbell, "The Sport Spigot," *Duluth News Tribune*, February 12, 1928, sports section. Hurley, Jack, "Ring Rations," *Fargo Forum*, April 2, 1933, sports section.

[6] Campbell, *op. cit.*, December 1, 1928.

[7] Campbell, *op. cit.*, February 14, 1928.

[8] Zabuil returned to Duluth to box Jack Dempsey in an exhibition bout in December 1931

The Zabuil incident is the first reference to Hurley's controversial policy of demanding 50 percent as his share of a fighter's purse as opposed to the customary 33-1/3 percent most managers received. This practice would later garner Jack a huge amount of publicity in the early 1950s when he assumed control over the fistic destiny of Harry (Kid) Matthews.

Matthews had fought as a professional for 12 years without financial success when he asked Hurley to be his manager. Jack later recalled their first conversation:

> "When [Matthews] first came to me, he objected to my demand for a 50 percent cut; said he had never paid anybody that much.
>
> "I said how long have you been fighting? 'Ten years.' How much do you have? 'Nothing.' That means 50 percent of nothing for me. You need me, or you wouldn't be coming to me. I don't need you. It costs me $10,000 a year to live. Can you keep me living at that rate? No, I know you can't. I have never seen you fight, but I know you can't or you would have gotten somewhere in ten years.
>
> "I am successful. Remember Billy Petrolle, Vince Foster? And you don't become a success in this business because somebody gives you a diploma and says you are a fight manager.
>
> "I have to be a teacher, a publicity man, trainer (I wouldn't have a trainer ruin my fighter after I make him), a booking agent, everything. I manage you 24 hours a day, pay all expenses; you might fight for me maybe once a month. Hell, I'm not getting 50 percent of you, you're getting 50 percent of me. I'm a going concern; you aren't. If you don't like it, go to some of the other managers."[9]

---

and for several other National Athletic Club fights, but Szymka served as his own manager.

[9] Brady, Dave, "Matthews and Hurley Form Unusual Team," *The Knockout*, February 16, 1952, p. 6. Taken from an article in the *Washington Post* for which Brady was a columnist.

The proposed Hurley-Zabuil contract is the earliest reference to Hurley's 50-percent policy, but exactly when he first implemented it, and how negotiable it was, is open to question. In a 1972 interview, Petrolle told the *Forum*'s Ed Kolpack their agreement initially called for a 25-percent manager's share before they later negotiated a more typical contract calling for 33-1/3 after expenses. Whether this was because the relationship pre-dated Jack's 50-percent days or because of their unique friendship and/or Billy's bargaining position is unclear. The evolution of their relationship suggests Jack started out taking 25 percent after deducting expenses, advanced to a 33-1/3 percent-after-expense arrangement in the mid-1920s, and graduated at the end of the decade to the 50-percent plus expenses formula

It is possible the LeRoy-Hurley break-up in July 1927 occurred over the re-negotiation of a new five-year pact. Jack possibly tried to raise his percentage deal with LeRoy from 33-1/3 to 50 percent at that time, which may have resulted in Russie's refusal to go along with the new arrangement. If so, then LeRoy's advice to Zabuil in August 1928 might have been that most managers extracted only a 33-1/3-percent fee, and therefore Zabuil should not sign the 50-percent deal with Hurley.

Heavyweight Charley Retzlaff, who fought under Hurley's management from 1928-'33,

While at first blush, 50 percent might seem like a lot to pay a manager, closer study offers a plausible argument for a different conclusion. Even apart from any special skills Hurley may have brought to the occupation, just the bare fact that he was a full-time boxing man meant he had more to offer a boxer than the typical managers who either handled a large stable of boxers or engaged in the business as a part-time hobby.

In addition, while other managers claimed to take just 33-1/3 percent of a boxer's purse, they usually deducted substantial amounts for "expenses." Boxing is full of instances where a fighter, having worked his way into his first "big money" fight, was shocked to find his expected share decimated by deductions for long forgotten expenses claimed from years earlier.

In many cases, the expenses charged to the boxer were the kind that in any other line of endeavor would be classified as overhead. Included were charges for items as trivial as stamps to those as important as a trainer or cornerman. An especially "sharp" manager might charge some expenses over and over again to several fighters in his stable.[10]

Taking these factors into consideration, Hurley's practice of taking 50

---

said in a December 1, 1951 interview with Joe Hennessy of the *St. Paul Pioneer Press*, "Yes ... Hurley was a 50-percent manager, and cheap at the price." However, when Hurley tried to sign Retzlaff to a second, five-year contract in 1933, after Charley had become an established attraction, negotiations broke down, apparently over disagreements rooted in the 50-percent clause. Retzlaff's view of the situation must have mellowed over time based on his statement to Hennessy and on the fact that Charley took his son to see Hurley in the 1950s when the young man was thinking of pursuing a boxing career.

Illinois was one state limiting a manager's percentage to 33-1/3 percent of a fighter's purse. When Hurley applied to the commission for a license to manage Vince Foster in 1949, Jack strongly objected to the rule in a meeting before the commissioners. Nonetheless, the commission required Hurley to sign its contract before granting him the license. Foster's only fight in Illinois after the pact was signed was against Chuck Taylor at Chicago in April 1949. Presumably, Hurley abided by the contract in dividing up the purse money after the Taylor fight. Whether he followed the same procedure in May when Foster received a purse approaching $20,000 to fight Charlie Fusari in New York is an open question.

[10] Among managers known for deducting every possible penny from their fighters' purses were such famous pilots as Al Weill and Chris Dundee. Weill was a New York manager, promoter, and matchmaker who managed four world champions. His most famous fighter was Rocky Marciano. Marciano later disclosed he retired as undefeated heavyweight champion in large part to free himself from Weill's management, which Rocky regarded as oppressive. Weill presented his fighters with a written accounting of expenses after each fight. The fighter would have to sign the receipt before receiving his share of the purse. While this was a good business practice, many fighters viewed it as inherently unfair because unless the fighter signed the document he would not be paid. In effect, there was no opportunity to contest the expense figures before signing away their right to object.

Chris Dundee, older brother of famous manager and trainer Angelo Dundee, was a successful manager of fighters in New York until 1950 when he moved to Miami, where he opened a gym and became Miami's most successful fight promoter. In a conversation with the author, boxing historian Hank Kaplan recalled that Dundee made no attempt to conceal his great delight in presenting fighters and managers with an elaborate accounting of expenses that reduced their purses to less than they were expecting.

percent and absorbing the expenses did not compare unfavorably with the practices of 33-1/3-percent managers. Indeed, expenses for a boxer at the start of his career were likely to far exceed his share of purses for quite a while. The fact he might never be reimbursed for those expenses meant a 50-percent manager was accepting a greater risk of loss should the fighter fail, in exchange for the prospect of greater gain in the event of his success.

A 50-percent manager also would not waste his time being bled into bankruptcy by a prospect not likely to succeed. If a fighter was not good enough to make it as a pro, he likely would find out more quickly, and with less likelihood of injury, from Hurley than from a 33-1/3-percent manager, who might extend the young man's career to recoup expenses advanced.

Despite the defection of their first Duluth prospect, Hurley and Terk remained confident the 1928-'29 season would produce at least one or two fighters who would cause local fans to quickly forget about Zabuil. The reason for this confidence lay in the diversity and sheer numbers of aspiring boxers who flocked to the Silver Spray gym seeking free boxing lessons.

Duluth's location in the natural harbor at Lake Superior's southern head, and its proximity to the pine forests, farmlands, and Mesaba iron range of northern Minnesota, led to its development in the 19th century as a major inland port. The new transcontinental railroad further established the township, along with Superior, Wisconsin, its twin-port city across the bay, as major centers for the transfer of goods and services to the East.

In the late 19th and early 20th centuries, factories soon sprung up to process the harvested timber, grain and iron ore for market. Companies like U. S. Steel, McDougall-Duluth Shipbuilding, and Marshall-Wells Hardware built model villages to house their employees. A variety of districts in the city furnished homes to a multitude of Italian, Greek, German, Swedish, Norwegian, Finnish and eastern European immigrants. By 1920, the populations of Duluth and Superior had grown to almost 140,000 people.[11]

As a result of the influx of these foreign-born workers, Hurley and Terk were able to use preexisting neighborhood and ethnic rivalries to stimulate attendance at their amateur shows. Drawing upon a wide array of first-and-second-generation Euro-Americans to fill the spots on the Silver Spray's amateur boxing cards, they fashioned weekly themes for their shows, which at one time or another came to feature nearly every ethnic group in the "Twin-Ports" area.

An "All Nations" card pitted Irish-Americans against German-Americans and Finnish-Americans against Italian-Americans. A special "Italian Night" featured "sons of 'Little Italy'" taking on youngsters from a variety of non-Italian ethnic groups. Rivalries between boxers from adjoining communities

---

[11] "Duluth Comprehensive Plan: Historic Development Patterns," Draft 1, October 21, 2005. The 1920 population figure is rounded to the nearest 10,000. According to 1920 U. S. Census figures, Duluth's population was 98,917 and that of Superior 39,624.

Hurley with amateur recruit Steve Woziak (left) & Billy Petrolle (right), 1929. Woziak, a product of Duluth's Polish community, was one of the boxers who made the "All Nations" ethnic rivalries featured on the Silver Spray's amateur shows so successful. Note the gym's big windows, the high ceiling, the regulation ring, and the extensive bleacher section. Obviously, no expense was spared in outfitting the gym & the boxers.

like "East" and "West" Duluth," and shows matching battlers from enclaves in Superior and Duluth were regular themes for an evening's entertainment.

As time went on, Phil Terk imported teams from outside the "Head-of-the Lakes" region for "inter-city" competitions. Matches pitting Duluth against the "range communities" of Hibbing and Virginia or "the Border City" of International Falls were presented routinely. Boxers from "Twin Ports" competed against teams from the "Twin Cities" of Minneapolis-St. Paul and Fargo-Moorhead. Students from St. Thomas College in St. Paul and soldiers from Fort Snelling were also brought in to box local talent.[12]

During the 1928-'29 indoor season, two boxers emerged from the Silver Spray's fistic melting pot as prospects likely to succeed in the pro ranks.

The first was Angelo (Andy) Puglisi, a 19-year-old Italian-American who already had excelled as a football player for West Denfield High School. Puglisi made his amateur debut for Terk and Hurley in April 1928 when he defeated Handsome Pikka in a four-round decision bout. By September 1928, he had proven unbeatable as a Simon-pure, winning all 12 of his bouts, including nine by kayo. Since he had run out of suitable opposition, he was, in effect, forced to turn professional to keep on boxing.

Puglisi who weighed 145 pounds, was an aggressive battler who patterned his technique after his idol, Billy Petrolle. An exceptionally hard hitter with both hands, he possessed a weaving, bobbing style which made him difficult to hit solidly. A lackadaisical approach to training, however, eventually would prove his undoing. As his career evolved, he tended to become discouraged and run out of gas if he failed to stop his foe early.

Puglisi scored a two-round kayo over veteran Rusty Jones in his first pro fight at Duluth September 25, 1928. Three more kayos followed in quick succession before he was matched to face Russie LeRoy on December 5.[13]

Local experts feared LeRoy was too experienced for Puglisi. "Hurley is going to stir up a lot of ill feeling among Duluth and Superior fans if he starts overmatching Puglisi," cautioned Campbell in the *News Tribune*. "[LeRoy] is a highly rated welterweight, and it seems a bit raw to shove the youngster against this veteran without a little more seasoning."

For once, Sandy Macdonald of the *Herald* agreed with his cross-town rival, and echoed his criticism Hurley was pushing the young Italian along

---

[12] The foregoing synopsis of amateur competition at the Silver Spray gym from a review of the two Duluth daily newspapers from October 1927 through June 1929.

[13] "Andy Puglisi to Make Professional Boxing Debut at Curling Club Show Next Tuesday," *Duluth News Tribune*, September 19, 1928, sports section. As of 2014, BoxRec lists two prior pro bouts for Puglisi, one at Hancock, Michigan and another at Watertown, South Dakota. While the author acknowledges these bouts took place, he has elected to follow the characterization of Puglisi's pro status described in the Duluth newspapers. According to the Duluth press, Puglisi's last amateur bout was at the Silver Spray gym against Ray Greene September 11, 1928. The distinction between "amateur" and "pro" bouts in the 1920s and '30s is blurry at best, and it is beyond the scope of this tome to resolve the issue.

too quickly. "Why Jack Hurley is anxious to stick his welterweight into such fast company so early in his boxing career is past us," Macdonald wondered. "Puglisi is a great fighter considering the short experience he has had, but we believe Hurley is attempting to push the boy too fast." [14]

The fight itself failed to provide any definitive answers to these concerns. After ten rounds of rugged fighting, referee Leo Kossick ruled the contest a draw. Puglisi started out strong and won the early rounds, but LeRoy persevered and evened up the affair by winning the last three innings. The questions of whether, and if so why, Hurley was rushing Angelo Puglisi's career so fast would have to be answered another day.

The Silver Spray's second candidate for pro ranks was (Smilin') Charley Retzlaff, a 24-year-old German-American from Leonard, North Dakota, a farming community near Fargo. Retzlaff was a boyhood neighbor of Lynn Nelson, Hurley's first "Masked Marvel." It was Nelson who recommended Jack to Retzlaff when he showed an interest in becoming a boxer.[15]

Retzlaff began training at the Silver Spray in the winter of 1928, toiling nine months in the shadow of Zabuil prior to his first amateur fight. Charley later recalled those early sessions in a *Fargo Forum* interview:

> "The training period before my first pro fight took longer than I thought it would. Jack got me a job in Superior, and when I got through at night I went over to Duluth and worked out. I did that for more than a year and only had a couple of amateur fights. I couldn't see where I was going to get very far ahead and was disgusted lots of times, but Jack told me to stick. I'm glad I did now.
>
> "I guess I wasn't much of a fighter when I first got to Duluth. Jack used to try and teach me things and I couldn't do them just the way Jack showed me and he used to say some pretty mean things.
>
> "He does that yet when you don't do what he says, but I guess he knows what he's talking about.
>
> "Be set to punch always. I concentrate on having my feet set to punch all the time. I pay a lot of attention to my feet, even in the gymnasium. I see a lot of fellows working out who don't pay attention to what they're doing. But Jack has taken me into a gymnasium where they are working out. He points quickly to a

---

[14] Campbell, *op. cit.*, November 27, 1928, sports section. "West Duluth Welterweight Gets Big Shot," *Duluth Herald*, November 26, 1928, sports section. The "over-matched" claim first was made when Eddie Dempsey was announced as Puglisi's foe on the December 5th card. Dempsey was injured in training two days before the bout, and LeRoy was substituted on short notice. Eddie was a trial horse who was no more formidable than LeRoy, and the comments of reporters before the substitution are equally applicable to Russie.

[15] Leonard, North Dakota 1920 Census. Leonard had a total population of 137. The Retzlaff and Nelson families were neighbors and their census information appeared on the same handwritten page compiled by the census taker. Lynn Nelson was the same age as Charley Retzlaff in the census.

Angelo Puglisi, the first of Hurley's Silver Spray students from Duluth to develop into professional boxer.

Charley Retzlaff, "the Duluth Dynamiter." Originally from Leonard, ND, near Fargo, he followed Hurley to Duluth.

boxer who is doing it wrong and asks me what is wrong with him. He always expects a quick answer. Always, it is they aren't set to punch. That's why I've learned to be set to punch all the time."[16]

When Retzlaff started boxing, he stood six-foot-three-inches tall and weighed 206 pounds. In his first amateur bout October 2, 1928, he knocked out Larry Hunt in the first round. In the ensuing five months, he won 11 out of 12 amateur fights by knockout, while suffering one disqualification loss.

Even as a Simon-pure, Retzlaff impressed experts wherever he fought. "Retzlaff appears to possess everything," wrote Campbell. "He has an easy, graceful movement. He never gets into a tense pose, which so often proves the downfall of fighters, while on the other hand he appears to be solidly set to deliver powerful blows with either hand. And, as he has shown in all his early fights, he carries the well-known sleep-producer in both mitts. Retzlaff has a marvelous temperament for a fighter and possesses a winning personality ... yet his smile cloaks a determined nature when in the ring.[17]

After seeing Retzlaff at the Chicago Golden Gloves in February 1929, Jim Mullen called him one of the best prospects he had ever seen. "Unlike most amateurs," said the promoter, "Retzlaff appears to know how to box. He can feint, and he can hit. He does not tear in like most amateurs do. He maneuvers his man into position and then nails him with either hand. He can take punishment, and he knows something about infighting. He is a promising prospect, who should be heard from in the pro ranks in a short time."[18]

Retzlaff created a sensation at the Chicago tournament by kayoing Al Riebal in 50 seconds. Inexperience, however, resulted in a disqualification loss to Bill Maddux in his next bout. Caught off balance and sent to one knee by a relatively light punch, Charley began to rise, only to return to the knee after remembering Hurley's advice to take a count after going down. Instead of treating the episode as one knockdown, the referee disqualified him on the basis he had gotten up and gone down without being hit.

Despite the loss, Golden Gloves officials selected Retzlaff to represent Chicago in the annual intercity tournament at Madison Square Garden. The tournament, which was set to take place at the end of March, matched Chicago's best amateur boxers against those from New York. Charley was looking forward to the trip as a way to redeem himself after the

---

[16] "Silver Spray Heavyweight Pupil to Make Boxing Debut Tonight," *Duluth News Tribune*, October 2, 1928, sports section (start of Retzlaff's amateur career). Fitzgerald, Eugene, "Injured Hands of N. D. Heavy Fully Mended," *Fargo Forum*, April 5, 1931, sports section (interview).

[17] Campbell, "'Smiling Charley Retzlaff, Andy Puglisi Leading Boxers Developed at Silver Spray," *Duluth News Tribune*, January 13, 1929, sports section.

[18] Fitzgerald, Eugene, "Smiling Charley Retzlaff Is Lauded by Jim Mullen," *Fargo Forum*, February 20, 1929, sports section.

disqualification, but unfortunately he had to bow out when he twisted his ankle on an icy patch while doing roadwork six days before the tournament.

With the end of the tournament season at hand, Hurley decided there was no reason for Retzlaff to continue as an amateur. On April 9, 1929, Charley celebrated his pro debut with a two-round knockout over Gus Kermits at Sioux Falls, South Dakota. By summer's end, he would fight five more times, winning four by kayo and drawing once.

Meanwhile, Hurley had been busy mending a fence in his old stamping ground. The beginning of 1929 found Jack back in Fargo promoting his annual New Year's show. In the main event, Jack engaged King Tut to box Fargo's perennial favorite, Russie LeRoy. In the fifth round, LeRoy showed signs of tiring, and Tut began to mete out a beating. At the end of the round, Russie returned to his corner to find Hurley waiting for him. It was the first time they worked together since parting ways 1-1/2 years earlier.

The *Forum*'s new boxing writer, Eugene Fitzgerald, reported that the "effect of Hurley's advice could not have been more vividly portrayed, for in the sixth round LeRoy made his best showing." Not only did Jack's encouragement re-vitalize Russie in the Tut fight, it "culminated in the resumption of relations between the pair." Although LeRoy lost the decision to Tut, after the fight Russie asked Hurley to manage him again.[19]

After leaving Hurley, LeRoy had enjoyed only mediocre success, with a record of three wins, four losses, and two draws. Recently, matters became worse. In the six months before the Tut bout, his only fight had been the one against Puglisi in Duluth. All things considered, Russie's dream of earning big money without sharing it with a manager remained just that, a dream.

"I made a mistake when I asked Jack to release me," LeRoy admitted after the Tut fight. "I always did my best work under Jack and guess we'll go along now until I'm through. He tied the first [glove] on me and he'll tie the last one on when I make my last start." Hurley's only comment was that everyone "has their arguments, I guess. Russie and I had ours, but I guess the fellow needs me, and I really think I can do him some good."[20]

Shortly before the Tut bout, LeRoy confided to the *Forum*'s Pat Purcell that 1929 would be his last year as a boxer and he hoped to earn a few good paydays before he retired. Apparently, Russie told Hurley the same thing because Jack mapped out an ambitious campaign which included bouts with some of the toughest fighters in the Midwest.

Explaining the strategy, Hurley told Purcell: "I suppose some of the 'wolves' will think I'm overmatching Russie, but he has reached the age where it is too late to pick soft ones when there is an opportunity for a big

---

[19] Fitzgerald, "Pair Started Ring Game Together," *Fargo Forum*, January 3, 1929, sports section.
[20] *Ibid.*

A relaxed pose of "Smilin' Charley Retzlaff," also known as "The Duluth Dynamiter."

purse and an outside chance for a big win."[21]

True to his word, Jack made LeRoy one of the country's busiest fighters. Between February and June, he had 11 fights, winning four, losing six, and drawing once. Among his foes would be rising stars like Paul Pirrone and Tommy Grogan, and tough, old pros like Joe Azzarella and Harry Kahn.[22]

After losing to Azzarella on June 20, 1929, LeRoy took a break before being lured back by a big-money offer for a rematch with King Tut, this time in St. Louis. On February 11, 1930, Tut knocked out Russie in the first round. For the man who in his first bout adopted the ring name of "Kid LeRoy" as a tribute to the memory of his deceased brother LeRoy, it was truly "the Kid's last fight." Shortly afterward, at the age of 27, Russell (Russie LeRoy) Backus announced his retirement from the ring.

By February 1929, Petrolle had recovered sufficiently from his surgery to return to his training regimen. Hurley planned to match him in some tune-ups and, if he did well, go after a leading contender. In the first fight, he kayoed Tony Ross in four rounds March 1 at Grand Forks, North Dakota.

Petrolle's next start was on a March 15th National Athletic Club show put together by Phil Terk against Jimmy Borde, who claimed to be a former French lightweight champion. Billy's return to a Duluth ring, however, was overshadowed by the card's co-featured event, which pitted Angelo Puglisi against St. Paul's Billy Light, managed by Johnny Salvator.

The announcement Puglisi was to meet Light sent shock waves up and down Duluth's sporting rialto. Light was easily the Midwest's highest-rated welterweight at the time, having been ranked as the tenth leading contender for the world title in the *New York Sun*'s most recent poll. Puglisi, at 18 years old was, fistically speaking, still just a baby. In nine professional fights he had won six, lost one, and engaged in two draw decisions.[23]

Puglisi's achievements marked him as a prospect, but one not yet ready for a foe of Light's caliber. The *Herald*'s Macdonald wrote that fans "right away voiced the opinion that Jack Hurley is rushing Puglisi too fast and that Light will take him for a ride just as surely as Grant took Richmond."[24]

Cubby Campbell wrote in the *News Tribune* that the "general comment at the Silver Spray gymnasium ... during workouts of principals ... was, 'it'll be just too bad for Puglisi' ... After watching Light step through the paces ... the opinion was easily formed that Puglisi will be greatly outclassed as far as boxing is concerned. This Light person is a wizard with gloves and feet and Puglisi's only hope for victory will lay in the possibility of

---

[21] Purcell, J. A., "L'Roy Offered Chance to Face Jackie Fields," *Fargo Forum*, February 28, 1929, sports section.
[22] Purcell, "Milwaukee and Chicago Offer Rugged Starts," *Fargo Forum*, June 12, 1929, sports section.
[23] Campbell, "Sports Spigot," *Duluth News Tribune*, March 7, 1929, sports section.
[24] Macdonald, Sandy, "Retzlaff Will Box in Gotham Amateur Show," *Duluth Herald*, March 8, 1929, sports section.

Jimmy Borde (left) fought Petrolle (right) in Duluth March 15, 1929, Billy's first bout after kidney surgery four months earlier.

Billy Light of St. Paul (left) who was matched with Angelo Puglisi (right) on the March 15th show.

'tagging' the St. Paul battler or otherwise slowing him up."[25]

In Hurley's defense, Macdonald commented that since Jack "rarely overmatches any of his boxers, especially the younger ones," he "must feel that Puglisi stands at least an even chance to defeat Light, otherwise the match never would have been made." Sandy suggested, however, that Hurley's judgment was clouded by a desire to even an old score with Light's manager, Johnny Salvator. According to Sandy, Hurley likely felt wronged when Salvator signed My Sullivan to a contract out from under him three years earlier even though Jack had promoted My's first pro fight at Fargo.[26]

In Macdonald's view, the alleged quarrel intensified when in 1927 Hurley took over the management of Salvator's former stable ace, Al Van Ryan, who was thought washed up. Under Jack's guidance, Van Ryan ran off a string of ten straight wins which culminated in a one-sided upset win in February 1928 over My Sullivan at St. Paul.

The disagreement became even more contentious, Macdonald asserted, when Sullivan left Salvator after the Van Ryan fight to go with former St. Paul promoter Jerk Doran as his manager. Now, Sandy implied, the feud had escalated to include the fight between Puglisi and Billy Light.[27]

Over 4,000 enthusiastic fans, Duluth's largest fight crowd in history, "packed the ringside enclosures, hung from the galleries, and jammed its way into every available standing place" at the city armory as Billy Light defeated Puglisi "in a ten-round battle that was hot all the way."

Macdonald described the action:

> "The first and fifth rounds of the fight were even. Puglisi took the fourth and all of the other seven went to Light ... Light outboxed

---

[25] Campbell, *op. cit.*, March 14, 1929.

[26] Macdonald, *op. cit.* The purported feud between Hurley and Salvator had no basis in fact. It is true Hurley promoted Sullivan's first professional bout, but Salvator was already representing My at the time. Whether Macdonald jumped to the wrong conclusion on his own or was fed the wrong information by Hurley or Terk for ballyhoo purposes is unclear.

[27] Although Van Ryan had been on the downgrade, he earned the largest purses of his career under Hurley's management. According to Milwaukee promoter Doc Freeman:
> "Somebody had to tell Al Van Ryan that he was good before he took any stock in such talk, and Jack Hurley had just the sort of blarney to convince him that he was more than an ordinary glove swinger. Where other managers failed, Hurley has succeeded. Had Van Ryan acquired Hurley sooner, he would be a great deal farther ahead now. He was a good boxer, but not sure of himself."

Hurley matched Van Ryan with two future world champions, Tommy Freeman and Jackie Fields, and in both cases was paid an amount commensurate with the risk he was taking. In this regard, Cubby Campbell commented in "Sports Spigot" on March 1, 1929:
> "It speaks well of Hurley's managerial ability to book Van Ryan in the Detroit Olympia against a fighter of Field's ability. Two years ago when Van Ryan shook off the pilot reins held by Johnny Salvator, to join Hurley, he was a $300 fighter. Since joining Hurley, the cut for Van Ryan has been a thousand and more a fight, while for the Fields scrap, his end will total close to three grand."

Veteran St. Paul welterweight Al Van Ryan, as he looked around the time Hurley became his manager in 1927.

Puglisi by a wide margin in the second and third. Puglisi brought the crowd to its feet, cheering and roaring in the fourth round, when he dropped Light twice with right smashes to the jaw. That was Puglisi's golden chance to win the fight right there, but he muffed it and a second opportunity never presented itself ...

"From the sixth round on Light gave Puglisi a bad mauling. Light had Puglisi on the floor twice in the seventh round, once for a count of five and once for a count of nine. Puglisi's mouth and eye were bleeding and the boy looked bad. He was down for two more counts in the eighth, one of nine, and the other had reached two when the gong rang. Pug took another count on nine in the ninth ...

"All of Light's knockdowns were more from the result of fatigue on Puglisi's part than from any hard blows which he caught. He was all in from the sixth round on, flashing only now and then with anything that resembled hitting power. It is odd in a youth like Puglisi to have so little recuperative powers. When he gets tired he just stays tired."[28]

Campbell and Macdonald were encouraged enough by Puglisi's showing in the early rounds to give Hurley's decision to match Angelo with Light the benefit of the doubt. Neither reporter felt the beating Light had given the young Duluthian would have any lasting effect on his physical well being. Both hoped that with more experience and better conditioning, Puglisi might join the top echelon of the welterweight division.

In the other featured bout on the card, Petrolle won all ten rounds against Jimmy Borde, who proved himself "a great showman, but not much of a fighter." Borde was hit "with everything in the book ... but the little Frenchman was right side up at the final gong and still strong as evidenced by the fact that he turned a neat front somersault and then turned a back one. He kissed Petrolle on the cheek at the final gong and, a moment later, ran over to Billy's corner and smacked him on his perspiring forehead."[29]

After Petrolle's kayos of Jose Gonzales in Huron and Norman Brown in Sioux Falls, South Dakota, Hurley announced he had signed Billy to meet Ray Miller at Detroit May 1, 1929, in his first major bout since his surgery.

Promoter Dick Dunn had been seeking Hurley's signature on a Petrolle-Miller contract for three months. Dunn, as Rickard's former chief of operations at the Garden, had seen the two battlers fight a fierce draw at New York in 1927. Dick knew sparks would fly when they met again, and he wanted to be the one to promote the bout. More importantly, the fight was a "natural" for the Motor City since both warriors were undefeated in

---

[28] "St. Paul Boxer Beats Puglisi in Hot Battle," *Duluth Herald*, March 16, 1929, sports section.
[29] *Ibid.*

Detroit, Ray having won all five of his fights and Billy four.

Miller's knockouts of Lope Tenorio and Jimmy McLarnin in 1928 thrilled Detroit fans and launched him into the top ranks of the lightweight division. His stoppage of McLarnin was especially stunning since it removed the aura of invincibility surrounding the baby-faced Irishman. In addition, Miller's sensational fight against Tommy Grogan, when he kayoed Grogan after having been downed six times, also took place in Detroit.[30]

Local experts thought Miller hit harder with his left, but predicted Petrolle would win because he punched more effectively with both hands and was a better all-around ring general. Their major concern was whether Billy had recovered sufficiently from his kidney surgery to go ten rounds at full tilt. At the weigh-in, Billy scaled 133-1/4 pounds and Miller 132-1/4.

A "crowd of more than 12,000 persons" paying nearly $28,000, "protested not only with its lungs but with a shower of newspapers and programs that came flying down from the gallery," as referee Elmer (Slim) McClelland awarded Miller the decision after ten rounds. The verdict was so unpopular that the crowd was still in an uproar at the beginning of the final [walk-out] bout. The ring announcer called for quiet but his efforts were completely drowned out by the audience's "razzberry" response.[31]

The next day's accounts agreed that the first three rounds were even. Miller came on strong in the middle rounds, rocking Petrolle with left hooks several times and causing blood to freely drip from Billy's nose and mouth. By the end of the seventh, Ray was ahead and on his way to victory.

Starting in the eighth round, however, "Petrolle began a brilliant and inspiring stand" which proved "he possesses a wonderful fighting heart and has unlimited stamina." Employing a relentless attack, he completely outfought Miller in the last three rounds, inflicting cuts over both eyes. Afterward, M. F. Drukenbrod of the *Detroit Free Press* wrote that the fight "was one of the most stirring battles ever witnessed here, due largely to the great comeback that Petrolle made against most discouraging odds."[32]

Despite the official decision, experts were divided on whether Petrolle's effort in the last three rounds offset Miller's early lead. Reporters from the *Detroit Times* and the *Detroit Free Press* agreed with the referee's verdict. Writers from the Associated Press, the United Press, and the *Detroit News* sided with Petrolle as the winner.[33]

A half-hour after the bout, Dunn's matchmaker, Scotty Montieth,

---

[30] Greene, Sam, "Boxing," *Detroit News*, April 27, 1929, sports section.

[31] Greene, "Crowd Storms over Decision," *Detroit News*, May 2, 1929, sports section.

[32] Drukenbrod, M. F., "Verdict Fails to Please Big Olympia Crowd," *Detroit Free Press*, May 2, 1929, sports section.

[33] Frank MacDonell of the *Detroit Times* and M. F. Drukenbrod of the *Detroit Free Press* both voted for Miller 6-4. Sam Greene of the *Detroit News* favored Petrolle 7-2-1. Charles W. Dunkley of the AP wire service had it for the Express 6-3-1, and the United Press gave Billy six of the ten rounds.

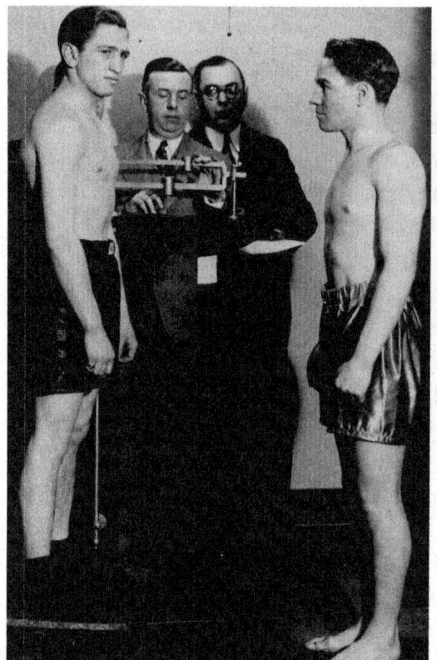

Ray Miller weighs in for McLarnin. Ray's TKO of Jimmy boosted his stock in the lightweight title chase.

After he halted McLarnin, *Ring Magazine* dubbed Ray the "Chicago Knockout King."

Miller was known for a slashing left hook. He and Petrolle fought 3 times with no edge to either. Billy's win in the last bout led to a rating as No. 1 lightweight contender in the *Ring*'s August 1929 issue.

announced he had already signed Miller and Petrolle to a rematch scheduled for June 6, 1929.

On his way home to Duluth after the fight, Petrolle detoured to Fargo where he told Purcell that when the referee McClelland raised Miller's hand to signal victory, Hurley at first thought the referee was kidding. After Jack realized "it was no fooling ... he said some terrible things to McClelland and to everyone who would listen to him."

Petrolle himself "didn't feel so bad about losing the decision as I was too tickled over my fine condition. I had four short fights after a serious operation and was a little nervous about my condition at the start ... When the fight was over I felt strong enough to go for another ten rounds, and I was so pleased over that I didn't care who won."[34]

Although the third Petrolle-Miller fight on June 6 failed to conclusively decide the issue of who was the better fighter, it did balance the account in the record book to accurately reflect the parity existing between the two battlers. This time, referee Al Day raised Petrolle's hand at the end of ten rounds to signal a close decision win over Miller. The verdict evened up the series between the two fighters at a victory apiece with one draw.

More than 12,000 fans paid $35,000 to see the bout. Billy weighed in at 133-3/4 and Ray 132-1/4. On the undercard, Russie LeRoy won a six-round decision over Jimmy O'Brien. Although the decision in the main bout was popular with the crowd, most writers thought Miller rated the verdict. Sam Greene of the *Detroit News* offered this opinion:

> "Last night's decision was open to question. It can be justified on the ground that Petrolle scored [a knockdown in the third round] and on the further ground that Petrolle was the aggressor for the greater part of the distance. But in the matter of rounds won and points tallied, Miller had the advantage. Miller landed more solid blows, he inflicted the greater punishment, and he had Petrolle in distress in the ninth round.
>
> "Miller took the verdict calmly, standing there in his corner, a cynical curl on his lip. He may have remembered that in the last Petrolle fight he himself had received a questionable decision and figured that, even if justice did not prevail at the moment, he had no cause for complaint."[35]

---

[34] Purcell, "Petrolle Believes He Will Be Next Champion," *Fargo Forum*, May 9, 1929, sports section.

[35] Greene, "Petrolle Gets Verdict Because of Knockdown," *Detroit News*, June 8, 1929, sports section. Greene saw the bout 5-4-1 in Miller's favor. Greene thought that even under a point system Miller would have won because Petrolle's third round knockdown was canceled out by Miller's strong ninth round. F. J. Carveth of the *Detroit Free Press* voted for Miller, 7-2-1. Frank MacDonnell said Miller had the advantage, 6-4, on a rounds basis and 25-1/2 to 24-1/2 on a system allocating a total of five points per round between the

In Fargo later, LeRoy offered a different perspective to Pat Purcell. "That fight between Petrolle and Miller was the greatest battle I have ever seen," he said. "I saw Gene Tunney win the championship from Jack Dempsey in Philadelphia, but they were pikers compared to Petrolle and Miller.

"Bill started after him in the first round and forced the fight along at a killing pace. Miller nailed him square on the chin time after time with that left hook, and how he socks with it! But the harder he punched, the harder Petrolle forced his way ahead.

"Petrolle never took one step back in the entire ten rounds. Twice Miller knocked him back a couple of steps, but always he came charging back with both hands, and he set such a pace that it looked for sure like Miller would go out or Petrolle would fall exhausted by the time they passed the eighth heat.

"In the ninth, Petrolle had a mighty hard time of it, but he never quit trying. Then he came back in the tenth with a great finish. I don't know where he gets the strength from, but believe me he certainly had the stuff when the going was the toughest. I've seen and fought some great fighters, but, mark this on your hat, Petrolle's the greatest of them all."

LeRoy's version, though perhaps biased, is interesting, not only for its enthusiasm, but also because it offers a fighter's view of what referee Day, himself an ex-fighter, saw that the reporters might have missed when he awarded the bout to Petrolle.

Specifically, Russie suggested to Purcell that the writers who favored Miller failed to give adequate weight to how Petrolle "had whaled Miller's body unmercifully." Russie completed his analysis with the comment that "evidently referee Al Day [in his boxing days] had caught a few in the body himself like Petrolle had landed on Miller, and he certainly called the fight right when he raised Billy's hand."[36]

Fortunately for Hurley and Petrolle, the controversy surrounding Billy's victory was mostly limited to Detroit. The most important account of the bout was Charles Dunkley's Associated Press wire report, read by boxing fans in newspapers throughout the country. Dunkley wrote, "Petrolle carried the fight to the Chicagoan from start to finish" and "forced Miller to retreat in almost every round." According to Dunkley, "experts credited Petrolle with winning five rounds with four going to Miller and one even."[37]

As a result of his victory, *Ring Magazine* in its August 1929 issue listed Petrolle as its No. 1 contender for Sammy Mandell's lightweight title. The *Ring*'s rating was important because, at the time, it was coming into its own

---

fighters. Charles W. Dunkley of the Associated Press favored Petrolle, 5-4-1.
[36] Purcell, "Petrolle Most Admirable Man, L'Roy Declares," *Fargo Forum*, June 9, 1929, sports section.
[37] Dunkley, Charles W., "Express Beats Ray Miller in Detroit Arena," *Fargo Forum*, June 7, 1929, sport section.

as the most influential boxing periodical in the country.[38]

In the meantime, Jim Mullen had fallen on hard times in Chicago. On May 28, federal revenue agents shut down Mullen's boxing business because big Jim was $44,000 behind in his taxes. In his place, Paddy Harmon, longtime local sports promoter, assumed the mantle as Chicago's leading promoter of big-time boxing shows. Harmon, who had lined up private investors and masterminded the construction of Chicago's new Chicago Stadium, was serving as the Stadium corporation's first president.[39]

The new facility's grand opening was on March 28, 1929, when Tommy Loughran successfully defended his light heavyweight title against Mickey Walker. Now, Harmon was looking for a second boxing extravaganza to fill the stadium and satisfy impatient shareholders, who were looking for an immediate return on their investments.

Three days after the third Miller fight, Harmon approached Hurley with an offer for Petrolle to box Tony Canzoneri in July with the winner to go up against Mandell at the Chicago Stadium in August. Canzoneri had only recently announced he could no longer make the featherweight limit and was entering the lightweight division.[40]

A week later, on June 16, 1929, while Hurley was still weighing this and several other offers, Harmon announced he had gone ahead and signed Canzoneri and Mandell to a championship bout scheduled for the Chicago Stadium on August 2.[41]

Anticipating a complaint from Hurley that the upstart Canzoneri was being allowed to leapfrog over Petrolle to a championship contest before having faced any of the leading lightweight contenders, Harmon's matchmaker, Nate Lewis, contacted Jack. Lewis explained he had signed Mandell for two title defenses before the end of the year, and if Sammy defeated Canzoneri, Petrolle would be his next challenger.

Hurley explained the arrangement to Purcell on a visit to Fargo a few weeks later. "Lewis told me to handle Petrolle carefully for the next two months and to have him in top condition," said Jack. "He said he positively has Mandell's signature on an air tight contract for two fights, and if Petrolle does not blow a decision between now and the first of September, he'll be the one to face the champion in the second fight. In case Canzoneri

---

[38] *Ring Magazine* was founded in February 1922 as a monthly magazine by Nat Fleischer, who cut his teeth in the newspaper business as a sportswriter for the *New York Press* and as sports editor for the *New York Telegram*. By the end of the 1920s, the magazine was the preeminent publication in the sport of boxing. Fleischer carefully fostered an image for himself and the magazine as a champion of fair play. In June 1928, the *Ring* instituted its monthly ratings of the top ten boxers in every division. These ratings soon came to be respected as the most independent system for ranking boxers in the sport.

[39] Macdonald, "Light Whines and Cheers," *Duluth Herald*, May 30, 1929, sports section.

[40] Purcell, "The Sportville Spotlight," *Fargo Forum*, June 9, 1929, sports section.

[41] "Tony Canzoneri to Meet Sammy Mandell for 135 Pound Title," *Fargo Forum*, June 16, 1929, sports section.

wins, Lewis says that he also must defend the title within 60 days.

"Not only has Lewis given his word Mandell is ready to fight twice this season, I have definite assurance Mandell is anxious to retire ... and wants to make two more good purses before retiring. Canzoneri and Petrolle are big cards in Chicago, and Mandell will get plenty for fighting them."[42]

On August 2, Mandell breezed to a convincing ten-round decision win over Canzoneri at the Chicago Stadium to retain his lightweight title. An estimated crowd of 24,500 fans paid $165,000 to see the bout. From the standpoint of stadium shareholders, the venture was a success. Nothing had occurred to upset the plans for the second Mandell title defense against Petrolle, scheduled to take place in the early fall.[43]

Meanwhile, Petrolle fortified his top-rated status by winning a ten-round newspaper decision over former champ Jimmy Goodrich at Duluth on July 26. According to Sandy Macdonald, Billy carried the first seven rounds easily, but "let down" enough in the last three to allow Goodrich to win the eighth and hold Petrolle even in the ninth and tenth.[44]

Hurley announced August 8, 1929 that he had signed Petrolle to a fourth battle against King Tut on September 12, at Detroit's Navin Field, home of the city's major-league baseball team. Jack's agreement with Scotty Montieth, Dick Dunn's matchmaker, called for a guarantee of $7,500 or a privilege of 33-1/3 percent of gross receipts. With an anticipated gate of $50,000, Hurley expected Billy's purse to be the largest of his career.[45]

After signing the contract, Jack visited Fargo to see his family and schedule another sinus operation. While there, he explained to Purcell why he accepted the match:

> "You remember that night in Minneapolis last fall – what a contest that was. That was the only time Petrolle was licked – yes, I mean licked. Several decisions have gone against him, but there were always some who thought Bill had the best of it. That Minneapolis fight was the only time I ever admitted that Petrolle lost, and that means he did.
>
> "The day after that fight, Tut realized he was one of the best lightweights in the world and he has been conducting himself like a champion ever since, and now he is ready to face the man who really gave him the self-assurance to go out and challenge the world ...

---

[42] Purcell, "Petrolle Will Get Chance at Championship," *Fargo Forum*, July 11, 1929, sports section.

[43] Dunkley, "Title Holder Gets Surprise Early in Fight" *Duluth News Tribune*, August 3, 1929, sports section.

[44] "Petrolle Easy Winner in Bout with Goodrich," *Duluth Herald*, July 27, 1929, sports section.

[45] Macdonald, *op. cit.*, August 9, 1929, sports section.

"Tut holds that decisive victory over Petrolle and no doubt he feels that he can beat Bill again or he wouldn't have consented to a rematch. This is sure to count in our favor for it means that Tut will try to be the aggressor. If Tut will charge out after Petrolle like he did ... in his most recent engagements, then he'll make a great target for Billy's right hand. And, don't forget that Petrolle is still the hardest punching 135-pounder in the business.

"I look for Petrolle to knock him out. I hope the fight does not go ten rounds. Should it go the limit, one or the other is sure to be almost a physical wreck. I look for the most grueling fight of the century. It will be nothing more than a slugfest, and the human body cannot possibly stand the wallopings these fellows will mete out and still not suffer later.

"For the past three months, Petrolle has been begging for another crack at Tut. Billy is satisfied that he can top Tut and as he has fought him three times, he should know something about it. I made the match because Petrolle wanted it and because they are paying us a mighty big purse for a non-championship fight."[46]

Two days prior to the bout, Harmon called Hurley to say that he, together with Nate Lewis, champion Mandell, and his manager Eddie Kane, would be making the trip from Chicago to Detroit to attend the fight. Paddy said he was bringing a contract for Petrolle to sign, and the Mandell title bout on November 18, 1929, was theirs "providing Billy wins over Tut."[47]

Despite the fact they were on the threshold of achieving their lifelong goal of a title fight, a sense of foreboding came over both Petrolle and Hurley on the eve of the Tut bout. Although publicly they exhibited confidence, privately each expressed their doubts to Campbell.

After the Goodrich bout in Duluth, Hurley confided to Campbell he was disturbed by Petrolle's tiredness at the end of the battle. Jack was concerned "that Billy had lost 'the zip' in his punches" and that if this meant that "the Express was nearing the end of the line ... he would never allow his pal, as well as stable ace, to continue fighting."[48]

Hurley first noticed a change in Petrolle's endurance after his third fight with Ray Miller on June 6. Although Billy impressed ringsiders with his stamina in the tenth round, he appeared to be more tired afterward than for any of his prior bouts. Following the contest, he told Jack, "I was tired after

---

[46] Fitzgerald, "Champion to Risk Title in Chicago Bout," *Fargo Forum*, August 25, 1929, sports section (Jack had scheduled sinus surgery for the week of August 26, 1929). Purcell, J. A., "Tut's Mental Attitude May Assist Billy," *Fargo Forum*, August 21, 1929, sports section (reasoning behind Tut match).

[47] Campbell, *op. cit.*, September 11, 1929, sports section.

[48] Campbell, *op. cit.*, September 14, 1929, sports section.

Publicity photo of Petrolle ballyhooing the September 12, 1929 fight with King Tut in Detroit. This photo and upper left photo of Billy Petrolle on page 409 courtesy of Walter P. Reuther Library, Archives of Labor and Urban Affairs, Wayne State University.

that fight. Much too tired for my own good."[49]

A few days before leaving for Detroit, Petrolle told Campbell that "in the event Tut turns the trick," the bout might be Billy's "swan song as a ring warrior." Cubby noted that "the Express has wanted to retire from the ring for some time, as he has a sizable bank roll salted away and doesn't relish the thought of absorbing punches when it isn't necessary."[50]

Although only 24 years old, the wear and tear of 121 bouts over a seven-year span had taken its toll. Petrolle's fights the past year against Berg, Miller, and Tut had been the toughest of his career. Billy's comments to Cubby and Jack indicated that fatigue and the money he had salted away had taken the edge off his lust for combat and robbed him of the burning desire to succeed which had been his raison d'etre only a few years earlier.

Petrolle was rated a 10-7 favorite in the betting when he and Tut weighed-in the afternoon of the fight. Billy, at 135 pounds, easily came in under the prescribed 137-pound limit while Tut tipped the beam at 136-1/2. Rain showers threatened during the afternoon, but the promoters decided to go on with the show. The weather held down attendance to a slightly disappointing 10,000, but gate receipts still totaled $30,000.

Those who braved the drizzle saw Tut win "an unmistakable decision" over Petrolle after ten grueling rounds. By all accounts, the King won no less than seven rounds as he out-boxed and out-slugged his listless foe. Tut combined a bobbing, weaving, crowding defense with a left jabbing offense throughout the fight that "completely smothered Petrolle's attack" and "never gave the Fargo-Derailed Limited a chance to get set."

The first five rounds were devoid of sensational features. Tut hurt his right hand in the third round and was able to use only his left hand the rest of the way. In the fourth, the crowd stamped its feet calling for more action.

In the sixth, Tut, by then far ahead in the scoring, opened a cut over Billy's right eye as "Petrolle seemed dead on his feet and rather hazy as to when and where to let go of a punch." The sight of Billy's blood, "in a measure," appeased the crowd, "but the booing did not entirely cease." In the eighth session, a series of lefts tore open the eye further as "new blood in a stream cascaded down over the Express' face and on his chest."

By the end of the fight, Petrolle's face "was a gory smear." Cuts about the nose and mouth and a swollen left eye added further ornamentation to features already colored crimson by the bleeding right optic. Tut's ability to inflict such damage with just his left hand provided the most eloquent witness to Billy's total ineffectiveness and fatigue throughout the evening. Except for "a few rallies," the Fargo Express had completely "exhausted the steam that enabled him to speed through six previous matches here."[51]

---

[49] "Petrolle Will Hang Up Gloves; Strength Gone," *Duluth Herald*, September 14, 1929, sports section.

[50] Campbell, *op. cit.*, September 11, 1929, sports section.

[51] Greene, "Fargo Fighter to Quit the Ring," *Detroit News*. MacDonell, King Loses But One

As if he had resigned himself to the outcome and rehearsed what he was going to say, Hurley leaned through the ropes to speak with reporters after the decision was announced. "[Billy]'s all through," he told the scribes. "He has agreed to it. There is no use in his sticking to the game and getting punched around. I always said that as soon as he started losing to fighters who had no right to beat him, he would quit. And he has."

"I could use more money, but when he can't whip Tut he isn't going to box again under my management. We started together and made a lot of money. He has his sugar, and I haven't anything on account of a bad break.

"I would be a dog to ask him to go on because he is too nice a kid to become one of those punch-drunk relics. I thought he could whip Tut and that's why I made the match. He lost by a wide margin, and I am going back to Duluth and try to find another fellow like him, and you know that's impossible."[52]

Immediately after the fight, Hurley wired three separate articles to the *Fargo Forum* and the Duluth papers for publication in the next day's editions. One was written anonymously as a "Special," one as a column by "Jack Hurley," and the last as a farewell by "Billy Petrolle." Together the articles provide a sentimentalized account of Jack's relationship with Petrolle, the reasons for Billy's retirement, and his farewell to the fans.[53]

The circumstances surrounding Petrolle's precipitous decline in 1929, just when he was so close to realizing his chief aim in life, is hard to fathom. Four months later, Billy would become restless, renounce his retirement, and start a successful comeback. This resumption of ring activity would dispel any notion he suffered any permanent impairment due to ring attrition, as implied by the farewell statements after the Tut bout.

The question then becomes why in the summer of 1929 did Petrolle lose his taste for the ring just when his motivation should have been at its highest? Was there a physical cause, then undetected, for the fatigue that came over Billy during the third Miller, Goodrich, and fourth Tut fights? Or were there external circumstances at work which drained Billy emotionally and either interfered with his training or made him feel tired? Would a simple loss of incentive cause Petrolle to become physically fatigued?

Petrolle's pre-bout conversation with Campbell about retirement and the speed with which Hurley informed reporters at ringside and then dispatched his "Specials" after the fight, lead to a conclusion that Billy's decision had been well thought out prior to the Tut fight.

Round," *Detroit Times*. Bullion, Harry, "Fargo Slugger Plans to Retire," *Detroit Free Press*. All newspapers, September 13, 1929, sports sections. Description and quotes were compiled from all of the above.

[52] Greene, *op. cit.* (first paragraph). MacDonell, *op. cit.* (second and third paragraphs).

[53] "Petrolle Will Hang Up Gloves; Strength Gone," *Duluth Herald*, September 13, 1929, sports section. Hurley, "Billy Petrolle Terminates Career Within Squared Circle Arena for All Time," *Fargo Forum*, September 14, 1929, sports section.

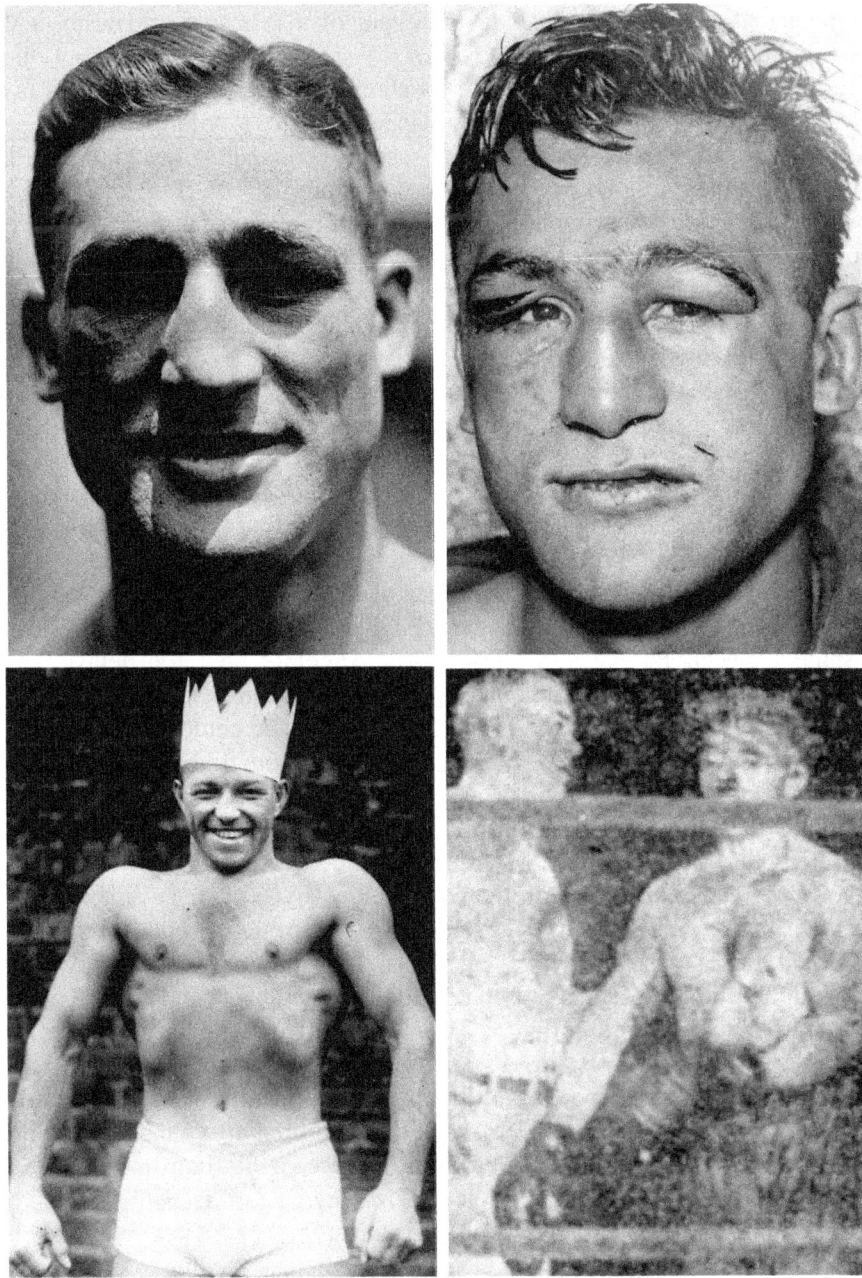

Photos of Petrolle (top) and King Tut (below) before and after their fourth fight, which led to the announcement of Billy's retirement afterward. The newsphoto at right proves that, even though Petrolle lost, he meted out his share of punishment. Taken just before the referee raised Tut's hand, it evidences exhaustion and the marks of a bloody battle on Tut's face.

In fact, it seems likely that, in the event of a loss to Tut, Hurley and Petrolle had scripted in advance what to say, and how to present the decision to the public. Despite Jack's statement to the press that it was his idea, it is more likely that, given the wishes of Billy's wife, the fatigue he was experiencing, and the financial security he had achieved, Petrolle himself was the moving force behind the decision.

It is also evident that while he agreed to fight Tut because of the large purse and because a victory would assure a title bout with Mandell, Billy's heart, for whatever reason, was not in it. Indeed, it does not seem beyond the realm of possibility that Hurley might have found it necessary to coax Billy into "giving it another try" against Tut in exchange for Jack's promise to go along with the retirement if Petrolle lost.

Regardless of the reasons for Petrolle's retirement, the prospect of facing his first season in six years without his close friend and No. 1 meal ticket must have been unsettling to Hurley. Nevertheless, the month of October 1929 found Jack back home preparing for Duluth's first fall/winter show.

Late in the month, Phil Terk announced the National Athletic Club's first pro card of the season would take place at the Duluth Armory November 14. Terk intended to feature Angelo Puglisi in one of the bouts, but a dispute between Puglisi and Hurley over Angelo's next foe delayed its announcement. Puglisi complained Jack had scheduled just two fights for him in the period between April and October, and he couldn't continue to exist on promises alone. "I've been fooling around this fight game for over three years now," he told Cubby Campbell, "and I'm still at a standstill."

Puglisi said he wanted to fight "only topnotchers from now on," like Jackie Fields, Vince Dundee, My Sullivan, and Sergeant Sammy Baker, all who were rated near the top of the welterweight division. "I've either got to make or break right sudden. I showed against Light and a few others that I could hit, but against Light I was up against too smart a fighter. I know this much about the fight game, and that is I have no business fighting a boxer. The kind of a guy I need to fight is a mixer, somebody who likes to sock."[54]

Hurley's first reaction was to laugh. "That's a lot of bosh." he told Campbell, "It's Puglisi's own fault that he hasn't been fighting. I got him a fight early last summer in Detroit, and he injured his hand. Then, he couldn't get in shape for quite a while because of his bum mitt. As for fights, I had him on a card at Hancock, Michigan, just recently, and I've booked him for Calumet on November 4 against Packey Lickar."[55]

The dispute came to a head on October 26, when, according to Campbell, "Hurley and Puglisi were all steamed up in conversation at the Silver Spray

---
[54] Campbell, *op. cit.*, October 24, 1929, sports section. Macdonald, "Murphy, Gollop, Retzlaff to Headline Local Mitt Carnival," *Duluth Herald,* October 28, 1929, sports section.
[55] Campbell, *op. cit.* Puglisi won a decision over Ben Dishau in Hancock on October 15, and he would kayo Lickar at Calumet. Before then, his most recent bout had been in Detroit on May 1 when he lost a decision and broke his hand in a fight with Frank Grover.

gym Friday, during which Puglisi declared emphatically he was going to quit entirely, while his manager told him to go ahead and quit. Just like a couple of half-grown kids quarreling over a back fence."

Hurley ended the discussion by telling Puglisi, "If you can show me where you are entitled to meet some of these real fighters you have mentioned, I'll line up the fight for you, but I'm not going to be responsible for throwing you to the wolves." Afterward, Jack told Cubby "he would sooner give him back his contract than overmatch him."[56]

A few days later, Puglisi visited Campbell with his father, "who desired to make a public appeal for aid in securing a match for his son." Mr. Puglisi told Cubby, "My boy turned down a good job I had for him to go into this fight game. Now he is having trouble in securing matches from this manager. I want to have Angelo given a good bout on this next card and show everybody in Duluth whether he is good enough to continue fighting or whether he should quit and take the job I have fixed up for him."[57]

Hurley's disputes with Zabuil in 1928 and Puglisi in November 1929 are examples of a life-long Hurley "pet peeve" – the fighter's omnipresent "board of advisors." These "advisors" presented themselves to the fighter as friends and were, for one reason or another, always ready to second-guess the fighter's manager and undermine the fighter's confidence in him.

These "board members" usually consisted of one or more persons who ran the gamut all the way from well meaning but misinformed relatives or friends, as in the case of Puglisi, to "know it all" hangers-on, "would-be" fight managers, and disgruntled fighters, as with Zabuil. Also included in this class were rival managers and promoters who poisoned the minds of fighters in order to steal them from their managers.

In Hurley's view, boxing was no place for amateurs. Managing was a craft that took years of experience and headaches to learn. The advice of one calm, competent, unprejudiced, and independent manager was worth more than a boatload of relatives and well-meaning friends. A pro fighter could expect to succeed only with a manager who possessed the expertise to assess his boxer's abilities and weigh them against his potential opposition.

According to Hurley, the world was full of "lots of intelligent people who wouldn't dare tell their wives how to cook a steak, but who can tell a fighter how to throw a left hook and they know equally about both." Jack believed that "people who advise embryo fighters and then laugh when the result of their advice is utter failure, should be put in jail like any other criminal who preys on the unsuspecting minds of weaklings."[58]

---

[56] Campbell, *op. cit.*, October 27, 1929.
[57] Campbell, "Father of Andy Puglisi Asks Aid in Securing Bout for Son," *Duluth News Tribune*, October 31, 1929, p. 15.
[58] Terk, Phil, "Silver Sprays," *Duluth Herald*, October 29, 1929, and *Duluth News Tribune*, October 27, 1929, sports sections. The "Silver Sprays" were page-long columns purchased by Terk and Hurley which appeared on occasion in both Duluth newspapers to assist in the

Hurley's run-in with Puglisi put him between the proverbial rock and hard place. In the normal course of events, Jack would have brought Angelo along slowly, getting him some more wins and experience against less capable young boxers and old-timers. However, Puglisi's headstrong temperament, bolstered by advice of friends and relations, had caused the young Italian-American to put pressure on Hurley for matches with top contenders from the very start of his professional career.

To keep Puglisi happy, Hurley had been obliged to bring him along faster than he liked. Even as critics at the time argued Angelo was in over his head, Jack had still felt justified in matching him with LeRoy and Billy Light. Because Russie's best days were behind him, Puglisi almost beat Russie. And while Light was a good boxer, he was not a puncher likely to hurt Puglisi. Matching Angelo with Billy had been a risk worth taking because Puglisi could hit hard and had a puncher's chance of winning.

Now, however, Hurley was being forced out of his comfort zone, not only by Puglisi, but by his family as well. Angelo was out of control and the only way to rein him in was to give him his chance against a top-ranking fighter "who likes to sock," and let the chips fall where they may. Jack's only other option was to release Puglisi from his contract and let him find some other manager who would do his bidding without regard to the consequences. And this Hurley was not yet willing to do.

Eleven days before the November 14th show, Terk announced he was re-arranging the card to make room for a main event between Puglisi and New York's Sergeant Sammy Baker, the world's fifth-ranking welterweight.[59]

Baker was just what Angelo Puglisi asked for – the real thing. Among the Sergeant's many accomplishments were knockouts over Ace Hudkins and Mushy Callahan, and decision wins over future champions Young Corbett III and Gorilla Jones. In his last ten bouts before meeting Puglisi, Sammy had defeated Georgie Levine, Pete Zivic, Baby Joe Gans, and Joey Silvers, all top boxers, while losing only to Jimmy McLarnin by a knockout. His overall record showed 92 wins, 18 losses, and four draws.

In assessing Puglisi's chances against Baker, Macdonald wrote in the *Herald* that, "Making a fast guess we would say that Pug is well over-matched. If it turns out that way, he has only himself to blame for he has insisted all fall that he would fight no one except a topnotcher, an opponent with a national reputation. Well, he's picked one, all right, and now we will see what he will do against him."[60]

The co-main event featured a contest between Charley Retzlaff and Big

---

promotion of the NAC's professional fight cards. They were nominally penned by Phil Terk, but had all the earmarks of Hurley working behind the scenes as at least co-author or editor.

[59] Campbell, "Sergeant Baker to Battle Puglisi on Mitt Card Nov. 14," *Duluth News Tribune*, November 3, 1929, sports section.

[60] Macdonald, "Serg. Sammy of N. Y., One of World Leading Welters, to Show Here," *Duluth Herald*, November 4, 1929, sports section.

Jim Sigman., a past U. S. Navy heavyweight champion with an undistinguished professional record. Even so, the bout, Retzlaff's seventh as a professional, was a step up in class for Charley since it was his first match scheduled for a full ten rounds.

Appearing on the undercard were two graduates of Hurley's Fargo and Duluth boxing classes. Spud Murphy, a featherweight from Moorhead, had cut his boxing teeth at Hurley's Fargo gym five years earlier. Already a veteran of over 40 pro fights, Murphy was pitted against Ernie North of Waterloo, Iowa in a 10-round semi-final.

Of particular interest to Duluth fans was the appearance of flyweight Louis Gallop in his fourth pro fight. Gallop had caught on as an amateur star at the Silver Spray, and his bout against Buster Madigan was the first opportunity for the locals to see him in a 10-rounder.

In front of "only a fair-sized crowd" which saw "one of the best [shows] ever offered the people at the Head of the Lakes," Sergeant Sammy Baker overcame an early onslaught to score a seventh-round kayo over Puglisi at the armory on November 14, 1929.

As in his previous fight with Billy Light, Puglisi looked like a winner early on as he thrilled the crowd by knocking down his highly touted adversary for a nine-count in the first round. Starting in the second round however, Baker, with right glove held high to ward off Puglisi's left hook, went about the methodical task of wearing down the youthful Duluth native with an assortment of hard rights and lefts to the body and head.

By the sixth round, Puglisi was tiring rapidly and clinching continually, as Baker began shooting home "short rights to the head with nice regularity." This pattern continued into the next round when, after two minutes and 20 seconds, Sammy shot over five successive "short, choppy rights" to the jaw that sent Angelo to the canvas for a final count.[61]

The performances of Retzlaff, Murphy, and Gallop furnished some consolation to local fans. Jim Sigman, at 216 pounds, proved no match for Retzlaff, who weighed in at 197. Sigman, down twice in the first round, lasted only until 1:25 of the second when Charley caught him with a right cross which sent him through the ropes where he took a full count.

The Murphy-North affair was hammer-and-tong all the way until the referee stopped the bout in the third round due to a cut over North's eye. Gallop won a pleasing newspaper decision from an ever-willing Buster Madigan, waging a smart battle by forcing him to lead and then countering with quick rights and lefts to head and body.

As a result of the poor attendance and the extra expense to secure Baker's services, the NAC lost $2,000 on the card. Puglisi, who had agreed

---

[61] Campbell, "Duluth Boxer Thrills Crowd by Flooring Rival in First," *Duluth News Tribune,* November 15, 1929, sports section. Macdonald, "Broadway Will Have to Delay Welcome to West Duluth Fighter," *Duluth Herald*, November 15, 1929, sports section.

For his final 1929 card, Phil Terk signed Sammy Baker (left) to meet Puglisi's demand for tough opposition. Baker kayoed him in 7 rounds.

Spud Murphy, Hurley's Fargo pupil, appeared on the Baker card.

Louis Gallop represented Hurley's Duluth gym on the same card.

to fight for a percentage of profit, received nothing for his losing effort.[62]

It was small consolation to Hurley that his assessment of Puglisi's skills, as opposed to those of Angelo's "advisors," was correct. Jack's reward for proving his point amounted to a promoter's share of losses, a fighter with a reduced market value, and 50 percent of nothing from his fighter's purse.

Given that the stock market had just crashed, and Hurley had just recently lost his best fighter to retirement, it was a fitting way for Jack to close out his 1929 calendar year.

---

[62] Campbell, *op. cit.* (show lost $2,000). Campbell, "Puglisi Fights for Nothing If Boxing Show Is Bloomer," *Duluth News Tribune*, November 8, 1929, sports section (Puglisi fights for percentage of profit).

CHAPTER 20

JACK'S KIND OF TOWN, CHICAGO IS

Chicago, Late November 1929

Dear Phil,

Well, Phil, nothing much happened on the train coming down here. I took your advice and didn't pick up with any strangers. One woman looked like she wanted to talk to me but I remembered what you told me about the 'painted ladies' and I just ignored her. It's a good thing I had that shoe box full of lunch, as I got hungry after we left Superior. The train stopped along the way but I wasn't taking any chances getting off, as it might pull out and leave a fellow. They can't fool me, eh Phil?

I have moved from the first hotel I registered at. It was a small hotel so I walked in and went up to the bar – or, I mean the desk. Nobody came to wait on me so I asked a man there who the proprietor of the place was and he said, "Issy." I said "Issy?" and he said, "Sure he is." I said, "Well by gosh, where is he?" He said, "There he is," and when I looked around there was "Issy" sitting behind a lace curtain.

I finally told them that I wanted a room, so they took me up to the second floor and showed me a room so small you had to back in so you could come out frontwards. It was so small the bed was painted on the wall. I took it, as I was too tired to look any further. My feet were pavement sore and I had the city dust in my eyes. Sometime during the night I stretched out one of my legs and kicked a guy out of bed three doors away. He ran out crying, "Fire." I ran out and made a jump for the elevator – it wasn't there, but I went down just the same. I moved out of that place the next day.

Jim Mullen is back in the limelight here as a promoter. They can't keep him down. Mr. Charles R. Hall, who owns the Chicago Coliseum, paid Mullen a great tribute a few days ago when he said Mullen was the best promoter in the game today. He said anyone can promote when they have unlimited capital behind them but it takes a smart man to promote as Mullen does – on a shoestring.

A short time ago when Mullen was "down" and in trouble, several boxers who got their start from Jim and who are now in the money class, wanted to run a benefit show for him to help him out. They offered to donate their services and give him the entire proceeds.

Mullen thanked them but turned their offer down. He said it was his own fault that he was short. That he got into it himself and that he would get himself out. With Tony Canzoneri, Tuffy Griffiths, Bud Taylor, and several others all boxing on the same show, Mullen's end would have been 40 or 50 thousand dollars. That kind of dough isn't to be sneezed at, but that's

the kind of a guy Jim Mullen is. I hope he gets a break.[1]
Your buddy,
Jack Hurley

****

After Petrolle's retirement September 12, 1929, Hurley made his annual fall excursion to visit family and friends in Fargo. As usual, the trip included a physical exam and a short hospital stay for a sinus operation. Afterward, Jack spent a few weeks recuperating and contemplating a strategy for the indoor boxing season.

The coming year was the first time since 1923 Hurley began a new season without a headline fighter in his stable. Counterbalancing this unhappy circumstance, however, was his possession of one commodity avidly sought after by boxing managers everywhere. This merchandise was a bonafide heavyweight prospect, the first Jack had ever signed to a contract, in the person of Charley Retzlaff.

As Hurley mapped out his campaign, the sports world was muddling along without a heavyweight champion. Jack Dempsey lost the title to Gene Tunney in September 1926, failed to regain it the next year in the famous "Battle of the Long Count," and finally retired as a boxer in late 1927.

Tunney defended the title once after defeating Dempsey. On July 26, 1928, Gene knocked out Tom Heeney of New Zealand in 11 rounds at Yankee Stadium. Two days later, "the Fighting Marine" retired and subsequently married Carnegie steel heiress Polly Lauder. After a honeymoon in Europe, the couple purchased an estate in Connecticut where Gene lived the life of a rich country squire.

In 1928, Tex Rickard announced a tournament to determine Tunney's successor. His announcement sent managers scouring the world to find "a new Dempsey." Newspapers ran daily articles touting the arrival of would-be contenders from Spain, Italy, Germany, Norway, Ireland, Great Britain, and elsewhere, each of whom was a "sure bet" to achieve contender status.

Unfortunately, Rickard died January 6, 1929, from an untreated case of appendicitis in Miami, Florida where he had scheduled the tourney's first bout for February 27. Prior to his death, Tex had invited Dempsey to assist him as co-promoter under Madison Square Garden auspices. Together they supervised the building of an outdoor arena at Miami for the purpose of promoting a ten-round bout featuring Jack Sharkey versus Young Stribling.

Even without Rickard's finishing touch, the Sharkey-Stribling match was a financial success, grossing over $405,000. Artistically, the bout left something to be desired, with Sharkey winning a decision after ten boring rounds. Nevertheless, writers were impressed with the job Dempsey did in staging the show. They speculated the ex-champ might fill the old

---

[1] Hurley, Jack, from letter quoted in Phil Terk's "Silver Sprays," *Duluth News Tribune*, December 9, 1929.

gambler's shoes as the next boxing promoter at Madison Square Garden.

The Garden corporation's new president, William F. Carey, however, had other ideas. Carey decided the corporation did not need Dempsey and instead staged the remaining elimination bouts without his help. On June 27, Germany's Max Schmeling won a 15-round decision over Spain's Paolino Uzcudun at Yankee Stadium, drawing a $378,000 gate. On September 26, Sharkey kayoed Tommy Loughran in three rounds in a promotion which grossed over $254,000.

Although these victories singled out Schmeling and Sharkey as the leading contenders, neither fighter had as yet "caught on" as a worthy heir to the great champions of the past.

Schmeling, though impressive against Uzcudun and against Johnny Risko in an earlier bout, refused to meet British champion Phil Scott in another elimination bout. Max had fought only four bouts in the U. S. since coming over from Germany, and many critics insisted that he had not rightly earned his status as a finalist. As a result, boxing fans remained unsure about his courage and ability.

Sharkey upstaged Schmeling by agreeing to meet Scott, but prior inconsistent performances against Dempsey, Heeney, and Risko, as well as the Stribling fight, led many critics to regard ex-sailor as temperamental and unsuited to be champion. The Sharkey-Scott bout, the last elimination prior to the championship finale, was set to take place February 28, 1930.

Even though revenues generated by these heavyweights did not compare with the million-dollar gates of Rickard's salad days, they still provided far and away the richest purses in the boxing game. By comparison, the top gate among the smaller men in 1929 was the Kid Chocolate-Al Singer fight at the Polo Grounds on August 29 which grossed $215,000. Big money in 1929 remained, as always, in the heavyweight division.

These events formed the backdrop for the scene Hurley was beginning to act out in October 1929. Just as Petrolle's retirement left a vacuum in Jack's life, so did Tunney and Dempsey's retirements and Rickard's death leave a vacuum in the sport as a whole. This void stood out as an opportunity for any heavyweight who could capture the imagination of the boxing public.

Hurley had to know and feel all this as he contemplated his next move. The questions facing him were: "Is Charley Retzlaff the man to fill this vacuum, excite boxing fans, and become the next great heavyweight champion? Should I stick around the Head of the Lakes and wait for something better to come along; or do I roll the dice now, leave Duluth with Retzlaff, and go after the big money?"

In just 1-1/2 years of boxing, which included 12 amateur and six pro bouts through November 1929, Retzlaff had impressed experts in Duluth and Chicago with his speed, punching power, and smooth boxing ability. Those who had seen him fight were saying Smilin' Charley was already the hardest puncher in the heavyweight division.

If there was a weakness in Retzlaff's fistic makeup, it was in his ability to take a punch. Charley had been knocked down or staggered in several of his fights, but his foes were not experienced enough to follow up the advantage. In each of those bouts, Retzlaff was able to come back and kayo his opponent within a round or two. Only time would tell if Charley's problem was an inherent weakness or one that could be corrected by more experience, teaching, and conditioning.

In addition, still to be tested at this early stage was Retzlaff's stamina and fighting heart. So far, his early round kayos had limited the length of his fights to four rounds. How he would respond in later rounds to a tough, well-conditioned foe who could survive Charley's early onslaught and keep boring in was an open question.

One thing, at least, was certain. Retzlaff had gone as far as he could as a novice. To improve, he had to fight and train with better fighters. If the Duluth Dynamiter's career was to move forward, there was only one available option: "Roll the dice and see what happens."

The first indication of Hurley's plans came after a tedious road trip undertaken three days after his return to Duluth from Fargo. Jack had taken Angelo Puglisi and a couple of other Duluth youngsters to a show at Hancock, Michigan, on October 15, 1929, where the Silver Spray stable furnished most of the evening's fistic entertainment.

A tired and irritable Hurley checked in at the *News Tribune*'s sports desk. "I'm through being a traveling man and nurse maid for these battlers here and there and everywhere," he told Cubby Campbell. When told Jim Mullen was promoting again in Chicago, Jack quickly replied that Chicago is "just the spot for me. There's where Charley Retzlaff, Andy Puglisi, Louis Gollop, and Spud Murphy will be doing their stuff in short order."[2]

The news Mullen was back in business was music to Hurley's ears. Jim was his best friend in Chicago. Whenever Jack was in the Windy City, he invariably used Mullen's gym at 180 Randolph Street as his office and training quarters for his boxers. If Hurley ever needed anything, big Jim was always ready to lend a helping hand.

Mullen had promoted two of Russie LeRoy's and all five of Billy Petrolle's Windy City bouts. Even after Petrolle was held to two less-than-impressive draw decisions at Chicago in 1927 against Spug Myers and Freddie Mueller, Jim held steadfast to the belief that Billy was the challenger most likely to defeat lightweight champion Sammy Mandell.

When Petrolle sought to re-establish himself after losing to Tommy Grogan, it was Mullen who matched him against Jackie (Kid) Berg. Billy's five-round kayo of Berg August 24, 1928, was his most sensational win to

---

[2] Campbell, Cubby, "The Sport Spigot," *Duluth News Tribune*, November 17, 1929, sports section.

date. Through all the adversity, Jim continued his efforts to arrange a Mandell-Petrolle title bout, finally giving up only after Billy's loss to King Tut in October 1928 ended Petrolle's title hopes.

Indeed, no person in 1929 could seriously have claimed to have contributed more to professional boxing in Illinois than James C. Mullen.

Mullen became interested in the sport when he met future middleweight contender Eddie McGoorty at an Oskosh, Wisconsin baseball game in 1906. At the time, Jim was a 22-year-old umpire in the Wisconsin State League, and McGoorty was a fan who had been heckling Mullen throughout the game. The two met afterward and, after an initial confrontation, found they liked one another. Eddie, who was just starting out as a fighter, later sought Mullen out in Chicago and asked the former umpire to manage him.[3]

Mullen was working at the time in Chicago as a foreman for the Griffin Wheel Company and later as a deputy clerk for the Cook County Criminal Court. In 1920, he began promoting boxing in Aurora, Illinois, at a location which adjoined the Aurora and Elgin rail lines and provided direct, 40-minute transportation from the Chicago Loop.[4]

Since Aurora law enforcement authorities interpreted Illinois anti-prize fight law less strictly than their Chicago counterparts, Mullen's business flourished. After one year of renting a band-box-sized hall, he leased 27 acres in 1921 and built a wooden, 10,000-seat, open-air arena for $15,000.

In the larger facility, gross receipts leaped from the $2,000-$3,000 range up to $14,000-$18,000. After five shows in 1921, Mullen was able to pay off the cost of the arena from his profits. Irish Jim's fighters prospered as well. Boxers on his cards who had been happy to receive $200-$500 purses now could command $1,000-$2,000 and even more.

In the winter of 1922, Mullen set up a new operation in Chicago using the nebulous description, "suburban club," in his press releases to disguise the fact his fight cards were taking place within the city limits. By this time, a simple word-of-mouth assurance that the event was a "Mullen promotion" was itself enough to fill any building Jim hired.

Mullen's first legal breakthrough in Chicago came when he openly scheduled a Christmas benefit fight card December 23, 1922, at the Dexter Park Pavilion. Anticipating trouble, Jim went to court and asked for an order to enjoin city and county officials from interfering with the show.

Mullen argued the 1869 Illinois law against "prize fights" and "exhibitions" was inapplicable to the "boxing contests" he was staging. He urged that fighters' purses on his shows were fixed ahead of time and that no "prize" was paid to them for winning or losing. He also claimed that the

---

[3] Mastro, Frank, "Death Claims Jim Mullen of Gusty Ring Era," *Chicago Tribune*, June 7, 1945, sports section.

[4] Williams, Joe, "Mullen Is Largely Responsible for Illinois Legalized Boxing," *Fargo Forum*, July 25, 1926, sports section.

"exhibitions" prohibited by lawmakers in 1869 were those staged by the traveling troupes of the era in which non-professionals took on the troupe's house fighter and then were generally knocked senseless.

Cook County Judge Ira Ryner agreed with Mullen and issued the requested injunction against governmental authorities. As expected, the long-awaited Christmas show was both an artistic and financial success. Irish Jim was so delighted that he turned over all profits to a local newspaper for Christmas baskets to give to the needy of the city.

As a result of Mullen's legal triumph, five other promoters began staging bouts in Chicago. For a time, the situation threatened to degenerate into chaos as rival promoters scheduled fight cards on the same dates, and local fighters booked dates so close together that it was physically impossible for them to keep all their commitments.

Once again, Mullen stepped into the breach and organized the Chicago chapter of the National Sports Alliance. The organization exacted dues from boxers, managers, and promoters; it also regulated its members by preventing conflicts in dates and fining members who violated chapter by-laws. As president, Mullen arranged mass meetings and spearheaded a lobbying campaign to convince the legislature to legalize the sport.[5]

Mullen promoted successfully in Chicago until May 29, 1923, when he staged a lightweight title fight between champion Benny Leonard and challenger Pinkey Mitchell at Dexter Park. Unfortunately, the fight ended in a riot as Mitchell's brothers physically attacked the referee when he awarded the fight to Leonard by a knockout. As a result of this affair, Chicago authorities clamped the lid down tightly on all boxing in the city.[6]

After the Leonard-Mitchell bout, Mullen returned to promoting fights at his Aurora arena until the Illinois legislature formally legalized boxing in July 1926. Jim's first show in Chicago under the new law was held at Comiskey Park July 3 when Illinois native Sammy Mandell won the lightweight title from Rocky Kansas in a ten-round decision.[7]

Over the next two years, Mullen experienced a mixture of success and failure. Being more visionary than hard-core businessman, his competitive nature, optimistic outlook, benevolent regard for fighters, and firm belief that Chicago deserved the best often led him to bid more than he could afford for boxers equally desired in New York, Boston, and Detroit.

As a result, Irish Jim was intermittently in and out of trouble with both state and federal taxation authorities. The situation came to a head in November 1928 when the state boxing commission suspended Mullen's

---

[5] Foley, Joe, "Promoter Jim Mullen Gives Chicago Big Boxing Shows Despite Old Laws Against Prize Fighting," *Boxing Blade*, April 7, 1923, p. 4, 13.

[6] Mastro, *op. cit.*

[7] Mullen actually was staging fights in at least two suburban venues just before boxing was legalized in Illinois, including a club in East Chicago which was still outside the city limits of Chicago at this time.

James C. Mullen and a cartoon extolling his virtues as a civic leader.

Mullen's Mandell-Rocky Kansas fight at Comiskey Park July 3, 1926, was the first Chicago show staged under Illinois' new boxing law.

license and foreclosed the mortgage on his gym. Ironically, the man most responsible for professional boxing in Illinois was shut down by the same governmental entity which he had worked so hard to create.[8]

Throughout Mullen's ordeal not a single complaint of non-payment was heard from any fighter or manager. Jim's first concern, as always, was to pay them first and worry about his own predicament second. Now, a year later, he negotiated a settlement to pay off his taxes and was starting over in a 5,000-seat arena located in Chicago's White City Amusement Park.

Hurley viewed the return of Irish Jim to the Chicago boxing scene as a perfect opportunity to take Charley Retzlaff and his other fighters to Chicago. Since both he and Mullen were re-igniting their careers, Jack believed they could help each other by joining forces. Irish Jim needed new attractions to rebuild his business and Hurley needed a venue for his young fighters to start making their marks in the boxing game.

Hurley left for Chicago about a week after staging the November 14th show in which Sammy Baker knocked out Angelo Puglisi. Within a few days, Jack took residence in a Chicago rooming house at 5510 Connell Avenue. By then, Mullen had staged two break-even shows at White City and was looking for an attraction for his third show to lure fans to the arena before he would be forced to close its doors.[9]

Competition among promoters for Chicago's fight dollars was fierce. In addition to Mullen at White City, no fewer than 11 fight clubs would present professional boxing in Chicago during the coming year. Of these, Jim's foremost competitors were the Chicago Stadium Corporation and the newest addition to the Windy City boxing wars, former heavyweight champion Jack Dempsey, who was staging fights at the Chicago Coliseum.

The Chicago Stadium, located at 1800 West Madison Street, was Chicago's answer to Madison Square Garden. With a huge seating capacity of over 22,000, the stadium had an obvious advantage over other local sites in the presentation of major boxing contests. In its first eight months of operation between March and November 1929, the Stadium's 15 boxing shows attracted 211,760 fans and drew gross receipts totaling $780,480.[10]

---

[8] "Boxing in Chicago Faces Crisis" (INA wire report), *Detroit Times*, November 10, 1928, sports section.

[9] Campbell, *op. cit.*, November 29, 1929, sports section. 1930 Chicago Census, Cook County, Chicago Illinois. Hurley was officially listed as a Fargo resident in the 1930 census. However, a Chicago census taker wrote down his name and the Connell Avenue address when he or she took information on April 11, 1930, and then crossed out the information. No notation was made concerning the reason for the cross-out, i. e., whether Hurley or someone else informed the census taker that Jack had moved out or already had been counted in Fargo, but the author has taken the liberty of assuming that Connell Avenue was Hurley's first Chicago address.

[10] Geiger, Edward J., "Sports," *Chicago Evening American*, November 12, 1929, sports section (lists first 14 shows). Kelly, Clair, "Tuffy Earns Shade," *Chicago Evening American*, November 15, 1929, sports section (information for 15th show).

The Stadium's originator was Patrick C. (Paddy) Harmon, a charismatic Irishman from the city's Irish "Valley" neighborhood. Born to immigrant parents from the County of Kerry in 1878, Harmon came up the hard way, selling papers on street corners at age seven to help make ends meet. While still in his teens, Paddy started renting local halls and holding weekly dances. By the early 1920s, he had purchased the Dreamland and Arcadia ballrooms, two of the city's most prominent dance halls.[11]

As he became more successful, Harmon's business interests expanded to include roller-skating rinks, ice hockey, bicycle and motorcycle racing, wrestling, and boxing. By 1926, Paddy' experience in sports promotion led him to see the need for a larger arena in Chicago. To realize his vision, Harmon secured the aid of 27-year-old Cornell University business graduate Sidney Strotz, son of an American Tobacco executive, who had the connections to Chicago's "old money" families which Paddy lacked.

Strotz enlisted as investors automotive industrialist Vincent Bendix, margarine heir John F. Jelke, Jr., auto-manufacturer Clement Studebaker, Colgate-Palmolive vice president B. A. Massee, Sinclair Refining Vice President Sheldon Clark, meat-packer heiress Lolita Armour and her husband Jack Mitchell, and grain-trader James E. Norris.[12]

The new sports facility, called "the Chicago Stadium," was built at a cost of $7,000,000. Harmon, who invested his life savings into the project, reported variously at $500,000 and $2,500,000, oversaw the Stadium's construction every step of the way and was appointed first president of the Chicago Stadium Corporation. Although the initial eight months of operation showed a gross profit of $98,682, the ledger's final entry showed a net loss of $112,025 after paying administrative and other expenses.[13]

On November 19, 1929, just as Hurley was preparing to leave Duluth for Chicago, the Stadium's executive board met at the to determine the corporation's future course. Going into the meeting, Harmon was confident he had the support of leading shareholder James E. Norris, his best friend on the board, and that he would retain his position as president.

Harmon's confidence proved to be unfounded. Norris instead sided with other shareholders and became "the moving spirit in the impending new deal." At the end of the meeting, Paddy was asked to resign his post. Sidney Strotz, secretary-treasurer of the corporation, explained to reporters

---

[11] Newman, Scott A., "Jazz Age Chicago – Urban Leisure from 1893 to 1945: Chicago Stadium," chicago.urban-history.org/ven/sas/chi_stad.shtml.

[12] "Chicago Circus," *Time Magazine*, March 9, 1931, page unknown. James E. Norris was the father of James D. Norris who would inherit his father's interests in a wide variety of sports-related properties including the Chicago Stadium and the Olympia Stadium in Detroit. The younger Norris would go on to co-found and become president of the International Boxing Club.

[13] Fischer, Maurice, "$112,025 Loss by Stadium in Eight Months," *Chicago Daily* News, November 21, 1929, p. 25.

Patrick C. (Paddy) Harmon, first president and leading promoter of the Chicago Stadium Corporation, tallying investors' contributions.

Harmon (right) with Chicago Stadium matchmaker Nate Lewis (left).

that while the directors were satisfied with the returns earned on boxing, they felt "the building should have earned more on other events."[14]

The board approved Sheldon Clark as Harmon's replacement. In explanation, Strotz said, "It was the wish of the committee to obtain a man for this position who is recognized as a big man in business and in sport in Chicago, and the committee believed that Mr. Clark was the best man available." In this regard, the *Chicago Daily News* reported that "Mr. Clark for many years has been identified with sports in Chicago, his hobby being yachting, in which he has been prominent."[15]

Strotz also said that "Paddy's financial interests will be well protected" and that Nate Lewis would be retained as the Stadium's matchmaker.[16]

Meanwhile, Mullen's other competitor, Jack Dempsey, had signed an exclusive lease to hold boxing shows in the Chicago Coliseum at 1513 South Wabash. With seating for 11,175, the Coliseum was the city's second largest indoor arena as well as its oldest. Built in 1899, the facility was a relic of a bygone era with striking Gothic-style exterior walls and castellated battlements which made it seem even more ancient than it was.

Dempsey's Chicago agreement was his third effort at promotion. One month after his success with the Sharkey-Stribling fight in February 1929, the Manassa Mauler had entered into a partnership with Humbert J. Fugazy to promote fights in New York City.

Fugazy at the time was engaged in a war with Madison Square Garden to determine Rickard's successor as boxing's leading promoter. Humbert had signed heavyweight tournament finalist Max Schmeling to a contract and was seeking a credible opponent. Fugazy hoped teaming with Dempsey would lure some major talent their way and produce some profitable shows to dislodge the Garden from its dominant position.

Unfortunately for Fugazy, Garden president William F. Carey and his general manager Frank Bruen outmaneuvered Humbert by securing the services of the rest of the major heavyweight contenders, including Jack Sharkey, Otto Von Porat, Phil Scott, Johnny Risko, Victorio Campolo, and Tuffy Griffiths. Unable to come up with a suitable opponent for Schmeling, Fugazy was forced to sell Max's contract to the Garden.[17]

Dempsey's efforts to sign up talent in the lighter divisions also met without success. Managers were reluctant to sign with an untested partnership and face being blacklisted by the Garden for disloyalty.

---

[14] Geiger, "Ring Post to Dempsey?" *Chicago Evening American*, November 20, 1929, sports section.
[15] Crusinberry, James, "Ask Sportsman to Head Task of Reorganization," *Chicago Daily News*, November 21, 1929, p. 25.
[16] "Harmon Denies Ouster" (subtitle), *Chicago Daily News*, November 19, 1929, sports section.
[17] Neil, Edward J., "Garden Promoter Completes Deal for Fistic Monopoly" (AP), *Duluth News Tribune*, November 13, 1929, sports section.

Consequently, the Fugazy-Dempsey alliance came to an end almost before it began without the firm presenting any major shows.

Despite the failure of the Fugazy arrangement, Dempsey still had the promoter's itch. Although Madison Square Garden had New York sewed up, the Windy City was still an open market, and in early July, Jack signed the pact with owner Charles R. Hall to stage ten shows at the Chicago Coliseum during the indoor season. As part of the deal, Hall agreed to renovate the building so Jack could present it as an updated facility which compared favorably with the new Chicago Stadium in customer amenities.[18]

Dempsey arrived in Chicago on September 14 with his business manager Leonard Sachs and personal secretary Harry Wall to finalize arrangements. After ten days of preparation, which included setting up an office in Room 1306 of the Burnham Building, Jack hosted a gala dinner at the Belford-Stratford Hotel for newsmen and friends. Those toasting the new venture included a host of politicians, bankers, financiers, real estate developers, attorneys, hoteliers, theater owners, restaurateurs, and sportsmen.

At the dinner, Dempsey noted proudly that fans would hardly recognize the old Coliseum. Especially noteworthy were the additions of women's restrooms, men's smoking rooms, and an electrical system which included an electric clock and new lighting and sound systems above the ring. Ticket booths had been moved outside to avoid crowding in the lobby. Other innovations included new uniforms for the ushers and wider aisles to ease access.

The most important improvements concerned seating. Special care was taken to arrange the floorplan so that everyone would have a seat with a clear view. All seats beyond the first 10 rows had been raised to slope on a gradual incline. None of the balcony seats located behind posts would be available for use. The lines of sight for each seat was tested so no one would have to stand "lest somebody else's view be obstructed."

The ring itself would have a red canvas floor to lessen the glare from the overhead lights. The ropes were to be encased in rubber and dusted with soapstone to minimize chafing of the fighters' bare bodies. Stairways to the ring would be covered with rubber tread and built wider than usual so boxers and handlers wouldn't slip when entering or exiting the ring.[19]

Dempsey also introduced Ray Alvis to the guests as his matchmaker. Since his days in Sioux City when he first met Hurley, Alvis had moved to Chicago where he became the Midwest's busiest manager, establishing a booking agency to handle the affairs of over 65 boxers. In just a few years, Ray's skill at finding the right fighter to fill any promoter's need had earned him the reputation as the region's best supplier of boxing talent.

To comply with Illinois law and concentrate on his new duties, Alvis

---

[18] "Dempsey's Presence Booms Chicago Ring" (AP), *Havre Daily News*, July 7, 1929, p. 3.
[19] Geiger, "Sports," *Chicago Evening American*, September 24, 1929, sports section.

Chicago Coliseum promoter, Jack Dempsey, (left) reviewing plans for an upcoming show with matchmaker Ray Alvis in the center of the Coliseum ring. The Coliseum was the Stadium's main competitor when Hurley arrived at Chicago in 1929. Within a few months, Hurley and Alvis would form a partnership to manage fighters.

turned over his entire stable to veteran Chicago manager Barney Abel.[20]

Mullen's first show after Hurley's arrival took place December 9, 1929. After Jim agreed to find spots for Retzlaff and Angelo Puglisi on the undercard, Jack summoned Retzlaff to Chicago so he could have a week to work out with some experienced local heavyweights. Puglisi stayed behind in Duluth to continue his training there until a few days before the show.

In the meantime, Mullen had another project for Hurley. Jim had hit upon a sure-fire gimmick to fill the White City Arena. For the coming show, he secured as a star attraction an athlete already well known in Chicago. The only problem was that this new sensation, although handy with his fists, had never fought professionally. As a result, he needed a short course in both basic boxing technique and the business aspects of the game.

The new find was Charles Arthur ("the Great Man"/"What-a-Man") Shires, Chicago White Sox baseman, whose name had been fixed on the front of the sports pages for the past 16 months. The reasons for his fame was threefold: he was the team's leading hitter, he was unable to avoid controversy, and he was the master braggart and self-promoter of the age.

Dubbed by Chicago writers as "the most talked about athlete in the world" and "one of the five most colorful sport characters of the decade" along with Dempsey, Rickard, Babe Ruth, and Red Grange, Shires joined the White Sox in August 1928. After batting .341 in the season's final two months, Shires instantly became the most popular player on an otherwise lackluster club. Manager Russell (Lena) Blackburne was impressed enough to appoint "Li'l Arthur" team captain at the start of 1929.[21]

It did not take Blackburne long to realize he had made a serious mistake. While still in training camp, Shires slugged Lena in a fit of rage when the manager told the Great Man to remove a red felt hat he wore to the plate as a lark during batting practice. Shortly after the season began, the two had another altercation when Blackburne found Art returning to the team's hotel drunk at 1:30 a.m. This time Lena suspended What-A-Man for a week.

After a couple more flare-ups, the situation came to a head in Philadelphia when Blackburne caught Shires drinking again, this time in his hotel room. In the ensuing confrontation, the Great Man punched not only Blackburne, but the White Sox traveling secretary and two hotel detectives. After this fracas, Shires was fined and suspended for the rest of the season, his ultimate fate on the team to be determined at a later date.[22]

Despite all these distractions, What-A-Man still managed to post a .312 batting average for the 1929 season in 353 trips to the plate.

Obviously, the sport world's fascination with Shires was based on more

---

[20] "Fistic Facts," *Chicago Evening American*, September 18, 1929, sports section.

[21] Whitney, Eli, "Great Art's Story Told," *Chicago Evening American*, January 24, 1930, ("most talked about"). MacNamara, Harry, "Shires Meets Trafton in Ring Tonight," *Chicago Herald and Examiner*, December 16, 1929, sports sections ("five most colorful").

[22] "'Base Ball Too Sissy,' Says Shires," (AP), *Detroit News*, June 22, 1929, sports section.

Arthur (What-A-Man) Shires.

Photo inscribed by Art recognizing Jack's boxing lessons. Courtesy of the Hurley family.

Art Shires, the boxer, in training. A bare-headed Jack Hurley can be seen in the back row in the right half of the crowd, peering between customers who are wearing hats.

than clubhouse fights and hotel brawls. *Chicago Herald and Examiner* sports editor Harry MacNamara noted that, while the Great Man boasted far and wide about his multi-faceted prowess, "up to date, Mr. Shires had made good in whatever he has tried, be it baseball, plain and fancy fisticuffing, or basketball. He has demonstrated that he can and will do all three."[23]

Even before playing organized baseball, the 22-year-old Shires demonstrated uncommon versatility as an athlete. In his teens, he made headlines in Texas as a member of the celebrated Waxahachie high school baseball team which won three state championships and 65 straight games in 1924-'25-'26. The team boasted three other future major-leaguers, the most notable being future manager and executive Paul Richards.[24]

At Westminster College in Texas, Shires was a standout quarterback in football, capable of completing "uncannily timed and accurate" passes "short or long, from any conceivable angle and position." His kicking exploits were legendary, with news accounts cataloging dropkicks successfully executed from the 50 yard-line. As a punter, the Great One averaged 53-1/2 yards per kick, including several ranging as far as 80 yards.

In basketball, Shires played center as a teenager for the Gulf Oil Company team in Port Arthur, Texas. The Gulf team, whose competition included strong Southwest Conference major colleges like Baylor and Texas A&M, lost only one game the entire season. Even after he joined the White Sox, Art continued to play semi-pro basketball for the Chicago Goldes and the Philadelphia Sphas in the off-season.[25]

In the fall of 1929, Mullen heard Shires was short of funds and was seeking ways to pay off some bills and pad his bank account. Although Shires' salary for the White Sox called for $8,500 annually, his fines and suspensions reduced his income from baseball to little more than $5,000.[26]

Mullen convinced Shires he could make big money in the off-season by cashing in at the prize ring box office on the notoriety gained from his off-field exploits. Jim proposed to have Arthur engage in a couple of tune-up fights and then match him with Hack Wilson, star of White Sox's cross-town National League rival, the Chicago Cubs.

Wilson, like Shires, was near the height of his popularity. During the 1929 season, he guided the Cubs to the National League pennant, hit 39 home runs, and drove in a league-leading 159 runs. Also like Shires, Wilson

---

[23] "There'll Be Cheers, Too, for 'Fearnot Shires,'" *Chicago Herald and Examiner*, December 8, 1929, sports section.

[24] Information provided in an email letter to author by sports researcher J Michael Kenyon.

[25] Untitled, *Mexia* (Texas) *Daily News*, October 2, 1925, sports section (drop-kicking exploits). "Football Star Praised When Students Vote," *Mexia Daily News*, November 6, 1925, sports section (quarterbacking, punting, and basketball exploits). Wire Service reports from Chicago, December 18, 1929 (Shires playing basketball).

[26] MacNamara, Harry, "'May "Carry" Trafton Round or Two,' Says Great Shires," *Chicago Herald and Examiner*, December 14, 1929, sports section.

had engaged in several extra-curricular fights and owned a reputation among ballplayers as being handy with his dukes. Mullen was sure a match between these two Chicago ballplayers would draw over $100,000.

Although Shires had a business manager, Mullen provided a team of experienced boxing people to prepare him for his fistic career. Barney Furey, trainer of world champions Bud Taylor and Sammy Mandell, was hired to get Art into physical condition. To acquaint him with the rudiments of pugilism, Jim solicited Hurley to serve as the Great One's instructor.[27]

Shires' opponent for his December 9th debut was one Dan Daly, of Cleveland, who according to Mullen was a close friend of Lena Blackburne out to seek revenge. Phone calls to Cleveland soon revealed no one had heard of Daly or of any boxer who knew Blackburne. As a result, Chicago writers immediately took to calling Shires' foe "Mysterious Dan" Daly.[28]

Such petty discrepancies, however, were not enough to spoil the festive atmosphere at White City on the gala occasion of What-a-Man's debut. Within 11 seconds of the first bell, Shires threw a bevy of lefts and rights which landed with "furious speed ... squarely on the jaw," and "'Mysterious Dan' hit the canvas." Ten seconds later it was all over, as the referee counted Daly out in an official time of just 21 seconds.[29]

In their Chicago debuts, both Retzlaff and Puglisi scored convincing knockouts. Puglisi stopped Kurt Prenzel of Germany with one punch in 55 seconds while Retzlaff also finished off Larry Serratti in less than a round.

Surprisingly, none of the 5,000 fans in the sellout crowd which paid $13,000 were a bit disappointed with the brevity of the bouts. Shires' kayo was a smash hit. The *Chicago Evening Post* reported that even "Mack Sennett, in his heyday ... never got more howls of delight out of an audience than did Charles Arthur's glove slinging. The customers stood on their seats, cheering madly as Cleveland's Daniel went kerplunk."[30]

For his 21 seconds, Shires received a very satisfactory $1,000. What-a-Man had proven conclusively that he could pack fans into the arena as a boxer. In his next bout a week later on December 16, Sir Arthur would receive 20 percent of the gross receipts.[31]

Not all Chicago newspapers viewed Shires' fistic fling with the same enthusiasm as the *Evening Post*. Edward Geiger of the *Evening American* called Shires' bouts "burlesque matches." Geiger feared that rewarding

---

[27] *Ibid.* Campbell, *op. cit.*, January 3, 1930, sports section.
[28] MacNamara, "Mullen to Box Shires? "'It's a Lie, I Want Arthur to Win' – Jim," *Chicago Herald and Examiner*, December 6, 1929, sports section.
[29] Murphy, Mike, "Makes Hit with White City Fans," *Chicago Daily News*, December 10, 1929, sports section.
[30] Whaley, Vernon E., "Art Shires Kayoes Foe in 1st Heat," *Chicago Evening Post*, December 10, 1929, sports section.
[31] MacNamara, "Shires Meets Trafton in Ring Tonight," *Chicago Herald and Examiner*, December 16, 1929, sports section.

JACK'S KIND OF TOWN, CHICAGO IS   433

Shires kayos "Dangerous Dan" Daly in 21 seconds of the first round.

"What-A-Man" looks to his corner after sending Daly to the canvas.

players for throwing punches on the ball field by giving them lucrative opportunities to make money in the prize ring could lead to chaos. He felt such bouts could set baseball's reputation back 20 years, to the time when it was perceived as a rowdy sport.[32]

With an eye to again filling the White City arena, Mullen chose as Art's next opponent George Trafton, one of several Chicago Bear football players who had issued challenges to fight the Great One. Like Shires, the burly, 33-year-old, 6-foot-2-inch, 230-pound Trafton was a Chicago favorite, being the only remaining member of the original Bear team of 1921. Although he had never fought professionally, George claimed to have had 15 amateur bouts and was known as the toughest man in pro football.

While Mullen was preparing for the December 16th show, he was also waving money under Hack Wilson's nose in an effort to convince him to fight Shires in early January. Jim's earlier pleas had failed because Wilson's wife and Chicago Cubs' president Bill Veeck had persuaded him not to box.

Wilson had turned down Mullen's offers of $5,000 and $10,000, but when Jim upped the ante to $15,000, Hack boarded a train from his home in Martinsburg, West Virginia and headed to Chicago. Wilson told reporters Irish Jim's most recent proposal was too much money to turn down and he was going to accept it despite the continuing opposition from his wife and Veeck. Hack had received $17,000 as regular season pay from the Cubs in 1929, and Mullen's latest offer represented almost a full year's salary.[33]

At this stage, even the baseball commissioner, Judge Kenesaw Mountain Landis, seemed to relish the prospect of a Shires-Wilson bout. The *Chicago Daily News* reported on December 14, 1929, that when "Landis was asked what he thought of the fight between Wilson and Shires he laughed heartily and then shouted, 'Let them fight!'"[34]

Wilson's acceptance sent Mullen scurrying around to find an indoor site large enough to hold the crowd. The White City arena was obviously too small, and the city's huge outdoor stadiums were unsuitable for boxing in the winter. Finally, after extensive negotiations, Chicago Stadium officials assured Jim that a revenue-sharing arrangement could be worked out.[35]

Just as everything seemed to be coming together, the hand of fate intervened. For the Shires-Wilson bout to be a success, Sir Arthur still had to defeat George Trafton on December 16.

In making the Shires-Trafton match, Mullen apparently convinced

---

[32] Geiger, "Sports – Trafton Does Boxing A Big Favor," *Chicago Evening American*, December 18, 1929, sports section.
[33] "Hack Comes to Chicago; $15,000 in the Air," *Chicago Evening Post*, December 16, 1929, sports section.
[34] Stanton, Bob, "Hack Assures World He'll Box Art the Great," *Chicago Daily News*, December 14, 1929, sports section.
[35] Brown, Warren, "So They Tell Me," *Chicago Herald and Examiner*, December 16, 1929, sports section.

himself the Great One's trim physique and superior athleticism were enough to overcome the rather crude ring technique and somewhat blubbery 35-pound weight advantage of George Trafton.

Unfortunately, on this occasion Mullen's usually reliable intuition was proved wrong.

According to the *Daily News*, Shires began the first round "with a rush, peppering rights and lefts to George's face and body but the blows had little effect on the big Bear center. Then Art ran afoul of a right to the jaw and went to his knees while holding onto George's knees in a feeble tackle." Although Shires was knocked down once more in the first round and again in the second, the fight soon became "a farce not a fight" as both athletes became so tired that they found it difficult to lift either arms or legs.[36]

At the end of the scheduled five rounds, both Trafton and Shires were exhausted, and it was impossible to tell by looking at them who had won. On the basis of his early knockdowns, George was awarded the decision.[37]

---

[36] Crusinberry, "Art, the Great, Floored 3 Times by Huge Center," *Chicago Daily News*, December 17, 1929, sports section.

[37] At this point, the author finds it impossible not to engage in a bit of speculation and second-guessing about Mullen's actions. Why did Jim jeopardize the Shires-Wilson bout by matching the Great One with a customer as tough as Trafton? Couldn't he have found someone else to build up a Shires-Wilson gate?

One explanation is that Mullen was trying to get two bites out of the apple. It may have been that, except for Wilson, there was no one other than Trafton who could have drawn as big a gate in Chicago with Shires. If that was the case, Mullen's thinking might have been, "Why not try and sneak in another lucrative bout with Shires before the big one with Wilson?" Even though the gate for a Shires-Trafton fight would not be as large as for the Wilson fight, the purses of the fighters and the cost of a larger stadium than the White City arena would have been much less.

Mullen might have figured his take after expenses for the Shires-Trafton bout would likely be almost as much as for the Shires-Wilson bout. Because of the relative amount of monies at risk, he might have seen the Shires-Trafton bout as a safer investment than Shires-Wilson. Then, if Shires defeated Trafton, the Shires-Wilson bout would have become that more attractive to both boxing and baseball fans and, at the same time, more lucrative and less of a risk to Mullen. If, on the other hand, Shires lost to Trafton, as did in fact happen, Jim at least received a payday almost as good as if Arthur had fought Hack without having met Trafton first. Indeed, Jim may have been feeling the financial crunch enough so he needed the stake from a Shires-Trafton match to finance the up-front costs of the Shires-Wilson affair.

Another scenario is more sinister and requires an interpretation of Mullen's actions which seems out of character with what we know about him. That is, unless we give credence to Dan Daly's later accusations that Daly "took a dive" in his December 9th fight with Shires and that Mullen knew about it (See remainder of this chapter's text and footnote 43). Mullen is on record as wanting to promote the Shires-Wilson match more than he did any other in his career. The question then becomes, "Did Mullen want to promote the bout so much that he would have attempted to influence the outcome of the Shires-Trafton bout on December 16, and maybe even the outcome of the Shires-Daly fight a week earlier?"

Jim Dent in his biography of football great Bronko Nagurski writes that Trafton was approached by two hoodlum-types before the Shires fight and told he would have to lose the fight or else. According to Dent, Trafton was trying to decide whether to go ahead with the match when another underworld personage, Machine Gun McGurn, also paid him a visit and

On the undercard, the best Hurley's stable could do was break even. Retzlaff scored another one-round, this time against Jack Castello, while Puglisi dropped a five-round decision to Patsy Pollock. Once again, the show was a sellout, as over 5,000 satisfied fans paid in excess of $15,000.

Although the consensus among sportswriters was that the Shires-Wilson fight was dead and C. Arthur's ring career was over, the Great One corrected that erroneous notion in an interview the next day:

> "Fight again? Say, I've just begun to fight. I can't quit now. There's no hound in me, and I'm not going to fold up just because George Trafton belted me around a little. I gave away too much weight for an experienced fighter, but I guess I showed the fans I could take a punch as well as throw 'em. Say, I was cuckoo for two rounds after George hit me that right hand smash on the jaw in the first round.
>
> "I made up my mind that they wouldn't carry me out of there, and I went out on my own power, didn't I? Sure, I'll fight again, but the next time I step into the ring the fellow in the other corner will be somewhere near my weight.
>
> "I want to give Trafton the credit due him for the fight he put up. He can take a punch, and I am here to testify that he can sock."[38]

After the bout, Shires met with Hurley and Mullen to plan a strategy for the future. According to Jack's Duluth partner, Phil Terk, who was visiting in Chicago at the time, Sir Arthur told them "that he really wanted to fight

---

told him to go ahead and try to win the fight on its merits. McGurn, who was known to be Al Capone's bodyguard, said if "those bums" come around again "just give me a jingle."

Exactly who "those bums" were and who sent them was either never known, or at least never disclosed, by Trafton. Most likely, they were connected with gamblers who wanted to rig the outcome of the fight in order to make a killing by placing some bets. To support this proposition, Denton cites a wild shift in the odds from Shires to Trafton the day of the fight.

The other possibility is that Mullen sent the two men to see Trafton. Jim clearly had a motive to guarantee a Shires' win, but the "evidence" against him is at best remote and circumstantial. The only "evidence" is the similarity in circumstances between the alleged visits to both Dan Daly and Trafton; and Daly's subsequent claim to reporters that Mullen knew at the time that Dan's bout with Shires was being fixed. If Daly's claim was true, then by inference the same conclusion might be true for the Trafton bout, i. e., Mullen might have known about or even orchestrated the attempt to "fix" the Trafton bout.

On balance, in light of his otherwise unblemished reputation it would seem unfair to conclude Mullen either "fixed" the Daly match or attempted to "fix" the Trafton bout. However, since Daly was never given a chance to explain his allegations at the hearing which took place a few weeks later, the possibility cannot be entirely discounted. *Dent, Jim, Monster of the Midway: Bronko Nagurski,* (MacMillan, 2004), pp. 46-47. Burns, Edward, "Illinois Chiefs Clear Great Shires; Dan Daly Set Down for Life Suspension; Verdict Stuns Daly (AP)," *Chicago Tribune,* January 9, 1930, sports section.

[38] MacNamara, "'Quit Ring? I've Only Begun to Fight.' – Shires," *Chicago Herald and Examiner,* December 18, 1929, sports section.

The "Great Man" shows off his new ring robe at his pro debut.

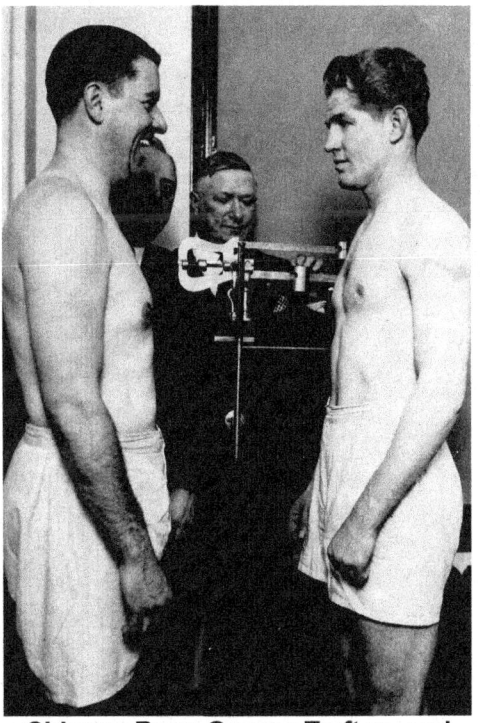

Chicago Bear, George Trafton, and Shires weigh in before their bout.

Trafton scores his first of two knockdowns against the "Great One."

Trafton's second knockdown of Shires, at the end of the first round.

Boxing hopeful, Arthur (the Great Man) Shires in Chicago, 1929.

Chicago Cub Lewis (Hack) Wilson.

guys who were in some other profession like himself. He knows he isn't a fighter, but he realizes his 'gate' appeal and wants to go through with a lot of fights booked with fellows in baseball, football, hockey or other sports who don't know anything more about the game than he does."[39]

Terk left with the impression "Shires is nobody's fool. He's in the racket for dough and he's going to get it." Shires agreed with Mullen and Hurley that if he could get a few quick wins under his belt and redeem his stature after the Trafton fight, they might still be able to pull off a Hack Wilson fight in Chicago. A major consideration, however, was they were running out of time. Baseball's spring training was set to start in late February.

Getting busy, Hurley helped put together as many fights as he could for Shires as quickly as possible. By Christmas Day, Shires had lined up five bouts: at Buffalo December 26 against wrestler Bill Bailey; at Detroit on New Year's Day against fledgling boxer Battling Criss; at St. Paul January 7 against former Cleveland Indian pitcher Tony Faeth; at Davenport, Iowa January 9 against Pacific Coast League umpire Louie Kohl; and at Boston January 17 against Al Spohrer, catcher for the Boston Braves.[40]

What-a-Man had an easy time in Buffalo, kayoing Bill Bailey in two rounds, but he ran into trouble in Detroit against Battling Criss at the Western Athletic Club. On the morning of the fight, Shires reportedly woke up with a severe head cold, and after an examination by the commission doctor, the bout was canceled.

In the next few days, all hell broke loose. On January 2, 1930, Criss' manager, Vandes Gildersleeve, complained to the Michigan athletic commission that promoters Benny Ray and Scotty Strachan told him a day before the fight that they "can't let Shires get beat." Gildersleeve refused "to be a party to any fix," and the next day Ray got in touch with him and said that a fighter named Heinie Groves would take Criss' place on the card.

A few hours later, the bout was canceled because of Shires' reported cold.

The Michigan commission and the National Boxing Association took swift action, and immediately suspended Shires, his business manager Nessie Blumenthal, and the two promoters pending a hearing on January 4. Five days after the hearing, the commission ruled the Great One had been unaware of the shady dealings going on around him and lifted his suspension. With respect to Blumenthal and the two promoters, however, the suspension remained in force pending further inquiry.[41]

On January 4, Mysterious Dan Daly, apparently emboldened by the disclosures in Detroit two days earlier, confessed to a reporter from his

---

[39] Campbell, *op. cit.*, January 7, 1930, sports section.

[40] "Shires Is Back in Form Again; Will Do Battle," *Chicago Daily News*, December 23, 1929, sports section.

[41] "Shires to Fight Criss at Chicago Stadium Jan. 24, 1930," *Chicago Evening Post*, January 17, 1930, sports section. Carmichael, John P., "Shires Cleared by Michigan, to Fight Spohrer Tonight, Quit," *Chicago Herald and Examiner*, January 10, 1930, sports section.

home in Columbus, Ohio, that he "did a nosedive" in his fight against Shires on December 9, 1929. Daly claimed he had "been taken for a ride" the day before the fight and was instructed that he had to "take a dive or else." For agreeing to cooperate, Daly was paid $150 plus expenses for the fight instead of the $100 originally promised.[42]

The Illinois commission reacted even more quickly to Daly's accusations than had the Michigan commission to those of Gildersleeve. Summoning Daly, his Cleveland manager Eddie Meade, Shires, Blumenthal, and Mullen, the Illinois body held hearings in Chicago on January 7 and 8, 1930, to determine the truth of Daly's allegations.

In addition to hearing testimony from Shires, Mullen, and Meade that the Shires-Daly fight had been entirely legitimate, the commission called upon George Bricker, a surprise witness from Columbus, Ohio, who formerly had been Daly's manager. Bricker testified that Daly's real name was Jim Gerry, that he was 18 years old, and that he had been previously knocked out twice, most recently in 17 seconds. Bricker also described Gerry as "an irresponsible, publicity-craving youth" who was "subject to daydreams."[43]

Notably absent from the hearing was Daly/Gerry himself who, it was reported, could not afford train fare to Chicago to attend in his own defense.

The Illinois commission exonerated Shires, Blumenthal, Mullen, and Meade from any wrongdoing and instead unleashed the full measure of its wrath on the absent Mysterious Dan. The commission found that the charges filed by Daly/Gerry were "as false as the affidavits filed here in which his name, age and previous experience were misrepresented." As a result, the commission ruled that "Mr. Daly be suspended in Illinois boxing circles, for the rest of his natural life."[44]

---

[42] Burns, "'Daly' Says Art Won Bout Here on a Frameup," *Chicago Tribune*, January 5, 1930, sports section.

[43] "Continue Investigation," *Chicago Tribune*, January 8, 1930, sports section. "Daly Knockout May Prove Genuine," *Fargo Forum*, January 8, 1930, sports section. The Illinois commission scheduled a special second session on January 8 to accommodate Shires who was fighting in St. Paul on January 7. At this time of his life, Shires was bouncing around like a rubber ball, attending commission hearings in Detroit and Chicago, fighting in St. Paul and Boston, playing basketball and giving a speech in Philadelphia, and addressing a congressional delegation in Washington D. C., all during a ten-day span.

[44] "Shires Meets Faeth in St. Paul; Clinnin Quiz Opens Today," *Chicago Herald and Examiner*, January 8, 1930, sports section. Carmichael, "Art the Great Tells Board Story of Rise to Ring Fame," *Chicago Herald and Examiner*, January 9, 1930, sports section. Although the Illinois commission's decision ending the investigation was accepted without much critical comment from most Chicago papers, *Tribune* sportswriter Edward Burns was openly skeptical of the affair.

Burns hinted that the commission treated Daly/Gerry's charges too lightly and rushed to exonerate everyone else too quickly. To support this position, the *Tribune* ran directly below Burns' article an AP wire account from Columbus, Ohio of an interview with Daly/Gerry at his home a day after the Illinois ruling. Mysterious Dan explained he didn't attend the hearing because he was told by Eddie Edwards, an agent of Eddie Meade, "it would 'not be

Throughout this turmoil, Shires continued to fight in front of sellout crowds. On January 7, he stopped former Cleveland Indian pitcher Tony Faeth in one round at St. Paul. Three days later, in Boston, he kayoed Boston Brave catcher Al Spohrer in four rounds. The bout in Beantown, originally set for January 17, was moved ahead a week when Davenport promoters, upset by the controversy, canceled their January 9th show.

After his Boston victory, the Great One said, "I've known Spohrer two or three years, he's a great kid but he can't fight. He needed the money just like I did. I didn't want to fight Al Spohrer, anyway. I wanted to fight Hack Wilson."[45]

When Wilson heard what Arthur had said, he responded immediately that "I want Shires just twice as bad as he wants me." Sensing a renewed opportunity, promoter Mullen quickly wired Hack and reinstated his prior offer of $15,000 to meet Shires. The contest, which had seemed dead just three weeks earlier, was once again a hot topic.[46]

Before he could stage the match, however, Mullen wanted the Great One to set the record straight on one matter. The debacle in Detroit over Shires' canceled fight with Battling Criss was still on the minds of boxing fans. If What-a-Man could defeat Criss before fighting Wilson and erase any lingering doubts about the legitimacy of Arthur's fights, then Irish Jim was sure the Shires-Wilson bout would be a financial blockbuster.

With this in mind, Mullen contacted Criss' manager, Vandes Gildersleeve, and rescheduled the Shires-Criss bout for White City on

---

necessary' for him to go to Chicago to speak before the commission." According to Daly/Gerry, Edwards visited Columbus two days before the commission hearing and accompanied Mysterious Dan and his wife to Cleveland for the next two days for a "conference," giving them spending money and entertaining them.

In the meantime, Eddie Meade attended the Chicago hearing and testified against his fighter Daly/Gerry. If Mysterious Dan's version of Edwards' actions were true, it would have inevitably led to the conclusion a cover-up was taking place. It would also have lent considerable credence to Daly/Gerry's charges his fight with Shires was fixed. No further mention of the incident appeared in the Chicago newspapers, however. It also is worth noting that in the AP account Daly/Gerry "charged for the first time that promoter Jim Mullen and Shires knew of the bout being 'fixed.'" Burns, "Illinois Chiefs Clear Great Shires; Dan Daly Set Down for Life Suspension; Verdict Stuns Daly" (AP), *Chicago Tribune*, January 9, 1930, sports section. In these articles "Gerry" is now "Gary."

It should be noted in defense of Shires and the Illinois commission's decision that despite the brevity of the Shires/Daly fight, virtually all sportswriters at ringside were convinced at the time Daly/Gerry had been legitimately knocked out. All reports indicated Shires actually landed hard punches and it took a full five minutes to revive the fallen gladiator. Consequently, the reporters and commission members who saw the fight were reluctant to believe a claim by Daly/Gerry initiated almost a full month after the fact. Otto, Wayne K., "Shires Bubble Bursts," *Chicago Herald and Examiner*, January 6, 1930, sports section.

[45] "Shires KOs Spohrer; Plans 3 More Bouts," *Chicago Daily News*, January 11, 1930, sports section.

[46] "Hack, Artie Pining for Each Other," *Chicago Evening Post*, January 13, 1930, sports section.

Shires attacks Boston Braves catcher Al Spohrer January 17, 1930. His business manager Nessie Blumenthal looks on next to ring post.

It was an easy decision when Commissioner Landis forced the Great One to make up his mind between boxing and baseball. It took just three minutes for Art to choose baseball.

January 24, 1930. If Art could defeat Criss, then the Wilson fight would be on again in early February just before the start of spring training.[47]

Once again, fate, this time in the form of a summons from baseball commissioner Kenesaw Mountain Landis, intervened to dash Mullen's carefully plotted plan.

Judge Landis, while vacationing in California, had been monitoring the twists and turns of Shires' saga as closely as a kid listening to his favorite team's baseball game on the radio. Scheduling a Chicago stopover on his return to the East Coast, the commissioner set up a meeting with the Great One to "talk things over about all the things he has been doing and find out all about his boxing business and what he intends to do."[48]

Landis had undergone a change of heart since his December 14th statement when he seemingly approved the bout. After Michigan's investigation of Battling Criss' fight-fixing charge on January 3, the judge said his "personal opinion" that "Shires' attempt to gain fame, or whatever it was, as a fighter is a disgrace to baseball. Whether Shires is innocent or not his appearance as a fighter is not for the general good of baseball."[49]

Landis' January 18th meeting with Shires lasted exactly three minutes. Leaving the commissioner's office, Arthur told reporters the judge had ordered him to make no comment except to say that he was still first and foremost a baseball player and was through with boxing. Two hours later, the commissioner issued a prepared statement declaring that any player "who engages in professional boxing will be regarded by this office as having permanently retired from baseball. The two activities don't mix."[50]

The person most upset by the judge's ruling was Mullen. Apart from any money he might have made, Jim was enchanted with the idea of staging what would then have been the most improbable match in boxing history. In the promoter's opinion, a Shires-Wilson fight at the world's largest indoor boxing arena would have been the crowning achievement of his career.

The depth of Mullen's disappointment was amply demonstrated years later when he was promoting one of his last shows at the Chicago Coliseum in December 1938. In a column which reminisced about Jim's career as "the best matchmaker who has yet operated in Illinois," *Chicago Herald and Examiner* sports editor Warren Brown asked Mullen what was the best match among all the crowd-pleasers he had presented.

In response, Mullen indicated he really could not choose a favorite, but the bout he remembered best was the one that got away. His biggest regret

---

[47] "Shires to Fight Criss at Chicago Stadium Jan. 24," *Chicago Evening Post*, January 17, 1930, sports section.

[48] "Commissioner to 'Talk Things Over' with Art," *Chicago Daily News*, January 15, 1930, sports section.

[49] "Quiz Proves Great Arthur Not in on Deal Says Brown," *Chicago Herald and Examiner*, January 3. 1930, sports section.

[50] "Shires Case Brings Ban," *Chicago Evening American*, January 18, 1930, sports section.

was that he had been prevented from staging the Shires-Wilson match.[51]

****

In the early 1950s, Hurley's campaign to obtain a championship fight for Harry (Kid) Matthews made Harry's home base of Seattle, Washington, "heavyweight crazy." After Matthews passed out of the picture, the idea of bringing a title match to Seattle began to grow in Jack's mind. His first effort in 1955, an attempt to promote the Rocky Marciano-Don Cockell bout, met with ridicule.

Critics asked, "How can Seattle support a heavyweight title fight?" Instead, the IBC and the powers controlling champion Rocky Marciano awarded the match to San Francisco.

In December 1956, a 28-year-old army lieutenant by the name of Pete Rademacher surprised the amateur boxing world by capturing a gold medal in the heavyweight division at the Melbourne Olympics. As it turned out, Rademacher was well-known to boxing fans in Seattle, having won several Golden Gloves tournaments there in the early 1950s.

Rademacher's win gave Hurley an opportunity to fulfill his ambition of promoting a heavyweight title fight, and at the same time stage a match that, for pure originality and boldness, would rival any that had ever been held. Six months after his Olympic victory, Pete told Jack he had acquired enough backing from private investors to finance a fight that would capture the imagination of the entire country. And Pete wanted Jack to promote it.

The bout was a contest between Rademacher and Floyd Patterson. The affair's improbability was based on the fact that it would be the first contest ever between a reigning amateur titleholder and a reigning pro champion for the world heavyweight title. To further upset boxing purists' keen sense of decorum, the bout was to be held at a minor-league ballpark in Seattle; a city located in, of all places, the far northwest corner of the United States.[52]

While Hurley was busy arranging the bout, he could not have missed the obvious parallels existing between his tribulations in 1957 and those faced by his mentor, Jim Mullen, for the ill-fated Shires-Wilson fight in 1930.

As with the earlier match, the sheer novelty of the Patterson-Rademacher fight met with resistance. Boxing's most ardent advocate, Nat Fleischer, editor of *Ring Magazine*, declared the bout was "silly" and "a detriment to the better interest of boxing." Fleischer was "amazed" Hurley "would dream up such a match" and said Jack "should have (his) head examined."[53]

---

[51] Brown, "So They Tell Me," *Chicago Herald and Examiner,"* December 20, 1938, sports section.

[52] It sometimes has been alleged that Pete Rademacher was the first fighter to fight for a heavyweight championship in his first pro bout. This is actually not true because neither Rademacher nor his trainer, George Chemeres, received any money for the fight except training expenses. Pete was arguably therefore still an amateur when he fought Patterson.

[53] Fleischer, Nat, "Nat Fleischer Says," *The Ring,* September 1957, p. 29.

Just as Mullen had struggled to find a suitable site for his show, Hurley had to look hard for a location to hold his heavyweight title fight. The University of Washington's board of regents denied Jack his first choice, Husky Football Stadium, which seated 55,000. Hurley nevertheless was eventually able to secure Sicks' Stadium, Seattle's minor-league ballpark, which had seating capacity large enough for only 20,000 attendees.

Much like Mullen in 1930, Hurley endured interference from boxing commissions all over the country. Both the National Boxing Association and the New York State Athletic Commission urged Washington state authorities to ban the contest because it was detrimental to boxing. Luckily for Jack, two of Washington's three commissioners voted to allow the bout.

Whether or not Hurley dreamed of promoting a contest as unlikely as the one that got away from Mullen 27 years earlier, when Jack's chance came, he made the most of it.

The Patterson-Rademacher fight, which took place August 22, 1957, surpassed expectations. Pete thrilled the crowd when he knocked Patterson down in the second round with a right hand just above the champion's jaw. Floyd, clearly stunned, was down four seconds. Had the punch landed two inches lower, Rademacher likely would have been champ. After regaining his feet, Patterson gradually wore Pete down before sending him to the canvas seven times and finally kayoing him in the sixth round.

Most important to Hurley was the vindication provided by the financial returns. The next day's newspapers reported that 16,961 people had crammed into the ballpark and paid $243,030. By comparison, the Marciano-Cockell fight in San Francisco, which Jack had previously tried to obtain for Seattle, drew only 15,235 fans and receipts of just $196,720.[54]

When it was over, Hurley had promoted a match experts said should not have been allowed, in a city that would not be able to support it, and before a crowd larger than could possibly be assembled. Despite all advice to the contrary, Jack had persevered and presented an improbable spectacle which had been an overwhelming success.

His old friend, Jim Mullen, had he lived to see it, would have been proud.

---

[54] Fleischer, "1958 Ring Record Book," (The Ring Book Shop, Inc., New York, New York, 1958), p. 71, 97.

CHAPTER 21

BUMPY RIDE ON THE GRAVY TRAIN

After Jimmy Borde of France boxed Billy Petrolle at Duluth more than a year ago, he asked me to be his manager as well. I couldn't use Borde, and tried to talk him out of the idea and still retain his friendship. He asked if I was interested in a heavyweight. I said I was, and he showed me a picture of the biggest human I ever looked at. He said the man was more than 6 feet 6 inches tall and weighed 275 pounds. Borde added the man was working in a circus in France, and he could get him for me if I would advance $1,000.

Thinking that Borde was trying to slicker me out of the grand or else use the big fellow as a club to force me to manage him (Borde), I made excuses that I was too busy, but would think it over and let him know about it later on. Perhaps you have guessed by this time that the heavyweight Borde wanted to get me was none other than Primo Carnera.

Now, all the eyes of the boxing world are on the Man Mountain from France, Italy, and points east. The main question in the minds of the fans is just how good a fighter he is.

I have seen the big fellow in action on two different occasions, and can truthfully say that he is a better fighter than he is being given credit for. The man is so big his size actually frightens you the first time you see him. If there ever was such a thing as a giant, Carnera is that, but he is wonderfully proportioned, except for his feet, which look like a couple of violin cases. The size of his "dogs" do not seem to handicap him, as he is as fast, if not faster, than any heavyweight around today.

The general opinion seems to be that Carnera is fighting no one unless they are handcuffed. I mean by this that his opponents are not supposed to win. This is not the case. He has fought a number of "bums," and he has knocked every one of them out, reports to the contrary notwithstanding. Some of these "bums" may have entered the ring with the express purpose of taking a "dive," but I know that they never get a chance, as Carnera, who really punches dynamically with either hand, stopped them in their tracks. He will prove to the satisfaction of all concerned this summer that he is as good a heavyweight as there is in the world today.[1]   – Jack Hurley

****

Boxing promoters were the first branch of the sport to suffer from the economic pinch caused by the stock market crash of October 29, 1929. Up

---

[1] Hurley, Jack, "Ring Rations," *Fargo Forum*, April 13 and 27, 1930, sports sections. The introduction is a combination of selections taken from two different Hurley columns as published in the *Fargo Forum*.

to then, they had been promising fighters and managers large purses with confidence, knowing almost any attractive show would be well supported.

The big guarantees continued a few months after the crash, as promoters, still in an optimistic frame of mind, refused to believe the effects of "Black Tuesday" would last for long. However, by year's end, realization the downturn was more than just a temporary blip in the economy's radar was beginning to hit home.

Jack Dempsey's Chicago promoting business was impacted by the economic tidal wave more than most. As the new kid on the block, he sought to take the city by storm by presenting shows he hoped immediately would surpass in fan appeal those presented by the Chicago Stadium.

Dempsey and his backers invested heavily in renovating the Chicago Coliseum and securing such all-star performers as Tony Canzoneri, Jackie Fields, Vince Dundee, Louis (Kid) Kaplan, and Bud Taylor for his first three shows in 1929. While these cards averaged paid attendance of 7,600 and gross receipts of $31,000, the return failed to cover operating expenses, let alone up-front outlays for office, staff, and improvements.[2]

The Chicago Stadium was also feeling the pinch. Although boxing there operated profitably in 1929, by March 1930 deficits in three of the new year's first four shows forced officials to announce they could no longer pay the "exorbitant" flat guarantees asked for. Boxers on future cards would be paid a strict percentage, in proportion to what they "draw at the gate."[3]

From April through June, Stadium cards were cut from a biweekly to a monthly schedule. In July, management implemented an even more drastic measure – for the first time since its opening two years earlier, summer boxing shows at the Stadium were suspended altogether.[4]

---

[2] Jackie Fields v. Vince Dundee (10/2/1929) – paid attendance 7,269/receipts $31,574; Tony Canzoneri v. Stanislaus Loayza (10/30/1929) – paid attendance 7,848/receipts $31,556; Bud Taylor v. Santiago Zorilla (11/15/1929) – paid attendance 7,678/receipts $30,646. As an example of costs for shows like these, Tony Canzoneri was guaranteed $12,000 and Stanislaus Loayza $4,000 for the 10/30 show. A fair guess is that former champ Louis (Kid) Kaplan likely received $5,000 and his opponent, Eddie (Kid) Wolfe, $2,000 for the semifinal. Tony Herrera and Jackie Pilkington in the third feature bout were pretty good names, so $1,000 apiece does not seem out of line.

These items bring the cost of the card up to $25,000 with no allowance yet added for two more prelims, referees, security, etc. Those items also do not include the cost of the stadium, state and federal taxes, etc. A fair estimate, then, is that Dempsey lost at least $5,000 on the show before allocating amounts to overhead, i. e., secretaries, business manager, and matchmaker Alvis, et al. Geiger, Edward, J., "Sports," *Chicago Evening American*, November 7, 1929, sports section.

[3] Geiger, "Club to Cut Guarantees," *Chicago Evening American*, March 28, 1930, sports section.

[4] "Fight at Stadium in August," *Chicago Evening Post*, July 24, 1930, sports section. The article explains that Chicago Stadium directors were closing up shop after the July 2nd show, but were allowing the facility to be rented to an outside promoter for a show August 7. The Stadium corporation itself promoted no further boxing shows until September, however.

Dempsey's first show in 1930, on January 17, featured James J. Braddock against Leo Lomski in a match billed as the first in a series of elimination bouts for the light heavyweight title, which Tommy Loughran recently had vacated. Newspapers predicted a sellout, but a cold weather snap limited attendance to 6,500. Unfortunately, the $18,000 realized at the gate failed to even cover the boxers' minimum guarantees.

The Braddock-Lomski show caused Dempsey to reconsider whether he was really cut out to be a boxing promoter. While trying to get the Coliseum on its feet, Jack had refused several lucrative vaudeville engagements the previous fall. Now, three months later, the operation had lost $50,000 and was in danger of going deeper in the red. Prospects for success on future shows planned for the spring did not look any better.

Dempsey was locked into a lease agreement to promote fights at the Coliseum through May 1930. To avoid going broke, he decided to change course and accept some of the personal-appearance offers he was receiving. At the same time, he quietly transferred day-to-day operations of his boxing enterprise to his business manager, Leonard Sachs, who remained behind in Chicago until the expiration of the Coliseum contract.

As a further result of the squeeze, Ray Alvis stepped down as Dempsey's matchmaker on January 19, 1930. Alvis gave his reasons for resigning in a statement to the *Chicago Evening American*: "Although my relations have always been cordial with Jack Dempsey and his business manager, Leonard Sachs, I have the urge to go back to the managing end. Like the old cobbler who always goes back to the last, I have the managerial fever. It is my ambition to establish a champion in one of the divisions."[5]

Alvis' decision to return to managing had significant consequences for Jack Hurley. Since December, he had been helping Barney Abel book fights for the huge boxing stable Alvis entrusted to Abel. Barney, at 70 years of age, found the duties to be too much for him. Hurley, new in town with extra time on his hands, was only too happy to help out.

Two days after leaving Dempsey, Alvis announced he was resuming control over the boxers he had placed in Abel's custody and was taking on Hurley as a full partner in the business, which would oversee "the largest stable in the country – 65 boxers" as well as exercise a "booking interest in some 30 others." As part of the arrangement, Alvis and Hurley would assume a 50-percent interest in each other's stables.

The firm of "Alvis and Hurley – Pugilistic Brokers," located in Room 506 of the Burnham Building, promised "24-hour service to promoters throughout the country" with "Cowboy Alvis on hand during the day and Hurley [on] the night shift." The firm's slogan was "a fighter for every town, every occasion, and every pocketbook."[6]

---

[5] "Alvis Leaves Dempsey," *Chicago Evening American*, January 18, 1930, sports section.
[6] Whaley, Vernon E., "Alvis Rejoins Stable Boys," *Chicago Evening Post*, January 21,

In their positions as "fistic booking agents," Alvis and Hurley were in effect "managers for managers of fighters." On the one hand, the new firm performed the service of locating matches for managers who were otherwise unable to find bouts for their fighters. On the other hand, Alvis-Hurley worked with promoters all over the country to find battlers to supply unfilled spots on their cards. In this way, the two partners worked both ends of the game, obtaining bouts for fighters and fighters for promoters.[7]

Alvis' statement to the *Chicago American* concerning his ambition to manage a world champion was not mere window dressing. In 1928, he had purchased the contract of leading welterweight contender Young Jack Thompson. One of the main reasons Alvis wanted Hurley as a partner was so Ray could more spend time touring around the country with Thompson in an effort to track down a title bout with champion Jackie Fields.

Born on a Wood County, Texas farm in 1895, Alvis received his boxing baptism doing publicity work for a Fort Worth promoter in 1920. Before long, he caught the "boxing bug" and started managing boxers for a living.[8]

By 1924, Alvis had gathered together a stable of 13 boxers and moved to Chicago with his wife, Crystal. Working as a partner with her husband, Crystal remained in the Windy City to handle correspondence and pay bills while Ray took his fighters on the road. The two communicated by telegram on such a frequent basis that one writer was moved to dub the transplanted Texan "Telegram Ray."[9]

Other journalists more commonly referred to the energetic young man as "Reckless Ray." Joe Ryan of the *Sioux City Journal* wrote that Alvis "radiates personality." Alvis himself admitted that as a boy he been given the nickname "Boss" "because of a desire to always lead and manage." Ray also confessed his favorite sport apart from boxing was horse racing, and that it was "the uncertainty of the game" that attracted him to boxing.[10]

1930, sports section. Kelly, Clair, "Kelly's Fight Gossip," *Chicago Evening American*, February 11, 1930, sports section. Powers, Francis J., "Hurley, Alvis Have Largest Stable of Boxers in World (Syndicated)," *Duluth Herald*, April 7, 1930, sports section.

The author has been unable to track down all of the alleged 65 fighters under Hurley's and Alvis' management during the firm's seven-month existence. He has, however, been able to confirm the following by researching Chicago's daily newspapers, particularly the *Evening American* and the *Evening Post:* Meyer Grace, Tony Herrera, Rex King, Seal Harris, Pete Zivic, Jack Zivic, Ray Kiser, Cowboy Dula, Mike Dundee, Charley Arthurs, Young Jack Thompson, Billy Petrolle, Spug Meyers, Bobby LaSalle, Cowboy Dula, Morrie Sherman, Jimmy Mahoney, "Milk Man" Kohler, Russie LeRoy, Angelo Puglisi, Jim Sigman, Vernon Jackson, Charley Retzlaff, Angus Snyder, Jack McCarthy, Bearcat Wright, Otto Von Porat, and Larry Udell.

[7] Campbell, Cubby, "Sport News Gossip," *Duluth News Tribune*, March 23, 1930, sports section.
[8] Ryan, Joe, "S. C. Bantam Has Had Rapid Rise in Ring," *Sioux City Sunday Journal*, July 20, 1924, p. 14.
[9] *Ibid.* Cuddy, Jack, "Chicago Boxing Notes," *Boxing Blade*, October 18, 1924, p. 3.
[10] Ryan, *op. cit.* "Who's Who in Fistiana," *Boxing Blade*, August 8, 1925, p. 15.

True to his reputation as a risk-taker, Alvis was not one to nurture a boxer and bring him along slowly. Ray's theory of management was a shake-the-tree kind of approach – assemble a bunch of fighters, throw them in the ring against tough opponents, see how they do, and keep the best ones. This aggressive strategy was attractive to some boxers because, when it worked, it brought quick results. In addition, in those instances when it failed, the youngster at least knew he had received a shot at the big-time.[11]

Some old hands argued this method was tantamount to murder because Alvis risked serious injury to young prospects by bringing them along too fast. Managers who had not secured their fighters' services in writing also complained that Ray was just another fast talker out to steal their fighters. Admirers, on the other hand, asserted Alvis was simply a fine judge of talent who recognized a good opportunity when he saw one. When he joined Dempsey in 1929, the former Texan was widely regarded as one of Chicago's most capable post-World War I boxing managers.

Just as the new partners were setting up shop in the Burnham Building, Windy City boxing fans were preparing to greet a man who one sportswriter called "Italy's latest and by far largest gift to boxing." On January 27, 1930, that man, Primo Carnera, with "feet the size of gondolas," and hands requiring boxing gloves the size of "twin sofa pillows," arrived in Chicago and proceeded to "take the city by storm."[12]

Carnera was a 23-year-old, 6-foot-6-inch, 275-pound "man mountain" who had left his home village of Sequals, Italy, at the age of 12, because he ate so much his family could not afford to feed him. For a time, he held jobs as apprentice to a cabinet-maker and a stone mason, but after he became

---

[11] An example of a Ray Alvis success story was his discovery of Connie Curry. Alvis first spotted Curry working out at a gym in April 1924 when Ray was handling another fighter for a bout in Sioux City. At the time Connie had just seen Bud Taylor fight on a card in Sioux City. Curry was sure that he could beat Taylor, a top contender who would later win the bantamweight championship.

Alvis promised Curry a fight with Taylor within six weeks if Connie would let Ray manage him. Within a few months after casting his lot with Alvis, Curry had not only won a newspaper decision over Taylor but had also defeated two other top bantamweight contenders, Johnny McCoy and Herb Schaefer. Ryan, op. cit.

Similarly, Chicago bantamweight Eddie Shea was going nowhere until he went with Alvis. After taking control, Ray put Shea in the hands of Chicago trainer Art Winch, who transformed Shea from a cautious to an exciting fighter. Three months later, Shea had won five straight and earned a non-title match with then-bantamweight champion Abe Goldstein. Shea later engaged in two fights for world championships. Winch, Art, "Chicago Boxing News," Ring Magazine, December 1924, p. 41.

[12] Walsh, Davis J., "Carnera Weighs 269-1/2 for First U. S. Bout Tonight," *Chicago Evening American*, January 24, 1930, sports section ("Italy's latest and by far largest gift to boxing"). Murphy, Mike, "Record Crowd Jams Gym to See Man-Mountain," *Chicago Daily News*, January 27, 1930, sports section (feet the size of gondolas). Armstrong, Anne, "Primo Proves Sequals' First Gift to Ring," *Chicago Daily News*, January 28, 1930, sports section (hands compared to sofa pillows). Murphy, "Carnera Packs 'Em in at Gym; Breaks Marks," *Chicago Daily News*, January 29, 1930, sports section ("taken the city by storm").

full-grown at 18, he found that work as a circus strongman and wrestler was more suited to both his physique and his appetite.

According to publicity circulated by Carnera's European manager, Leon See, Primo lost his circus job when a young bull elephant gave him a playful push. Carnera mistook the push as an act of aggression and picked up the elephant and threw it against a cage wagon. The wagon was destroyed, and he was fired as a result. Later, Primo started boxing after a chance encounter with Paul Journee, a heavyweight boxer from France.[13]

Carnera's Chicago Stadium debut on January 31 against Montreal's Elizear Rioux was only his second fight in the United States since his arrival from Europe January 1, 1930. Primo's first bout, a one-round knockout over Big Boy Peterson at Madison Square Garden in New York a week earlier, had been so short that spectators were not sure what had actually happened. Experts hoped the coming fight in Chicago would answer any questions which remained about Primo's boxing ability.

Accompanying Carnera to Chicago "was the most colorful retinue of managers and attendants that has ever hit the city." Primo's party consisted of nine men, all standing between eight and 16 inches shorter and weighing at least 100 pounds less than the towering Italian. Most noteworthy in this regard was former French jockey, Maurice Eudaline, the big man's second trainer, whose primary job was to stand on a stool and reach up from his tiptoes to wipe Carnera's perspiring brow after workouts.

Included in the entourage were Leon See and American managers Broadway Bill Duffy and Walter (Good Time Charley) Friedman, both associates of mobster Owney Madden, rumored to be a silent partner in the Carnera enterprise. Primo also brought along a personal valet and French cartoonist Louis Bering, who, with some success, was teaching the big fellow to draw. Rounding out the group was head trainer, Abe Attell, the former featherweight champ, and two French sparring partners.[14]

Although the boxing world had seen "giants" before, Primo Carnera was more than just a big man. Spectators who came with the idea of viewing a physical freak were surprised to see that Primo, for all his enormous size, was a perfectly proportioned athlete who moved with surprising speed and

---

[13] "A Massive Man Is Mr. Carnera; Look Him Over!" *Chicago Daily News*, January 28, 1930, sports section. The story is apocryphal. Carnera later admitted he left the circus only after it shut down.

[14] Kelly, "Primo Moves Fast (subtitle)," *Chicago Evening American*, January 27, 1930, sports section. Not surprisingly, Carnera's trainer, Abe Attell, the former longtime (1901-1912) featherweight champ, also had underworld connections, having been an associate of Arnold Rothstein, reputed head of the Jewish mob in New York. Attell was indicted in connection with the 1919 scandal in which members of the Chicago White Sox baseball team were accused of throwing the World Series to the Cincinnati Reds, but the charges were dismissed before trial. Rothstein was murdered in 1928, reportedly for refusing to pay a debt arising out of a fixed poker game. Attell lived to a ripe old age, dying of natural causes at the age of 86 in 1970.

grace. Unlike the ungainly former champion, Jess Willard, with whom he was often compared, Carnera was beautifully muscled and endowed with well-developed arms and legs, as well as tremendous shoulders.[15]

In addition to providing a picturesque background for reporters, Carnera's experience in the circus had prepared him for the fistic limelight. Journalists who expected to see a sullen-faced Primo, emotionally jaded by early years as a sideshow attraction, instead found him to be pleasant and cooperative. The big man willingly posed at length and endured the most ridiculous requests with a playful sense of humor and unfailing grace.

The first testimony to the gold awaiting those who cooperated in the ballyhoo of the "Ambling Alp" came from Hurley's friend and mentor, Mike Collins. Mike stopped in Chicago on his way back to Minneapolis from New York where he had just offered up Big Boy Peterson as the first sacrifice at the altar of Primo's buildup. Collins had managed Peterson for years and had never before earned any real money with him.

Collins collected $10,000 for Big Boy's 70 seconds of service against Carnera on January 24 and was "tickled pink" over his good fortune. On his arrival in Chicago, Mike told columnist Harry Hochstader of the *Chicago Evening Post* that "New York is a great place. Just imagine, I finally filled the Garden with Big Boy Peterson! God sent the angels down to me when they picked Primo for Peterson."[16]

Exactly 21,304 boxing fans paid $60,141 to Madison Square Garden's coffers to see Carnera kayo Peterson. Of this amount, Primo and his backers received approximately $18,000. Boxing experts anticipated a similar gate on January 31 when Carnera faced Elizear Rioux at the Chicago Stadium.

The New York success served as a clarion call for boxing entrepreneurs to jump aboard and get a piece of the Carnera action. Promoters and managers from all over the Midwest congregated in Chicago for the Rioux fight in hope of convincing Primo's managers to visit their cities or use one of their fighters as an opponent. They all prayed the big man would be the tonic to help pull the sport out of the doldrums into which it seemed headed and to boost their bankrolls, even if for just one show.

While Carnera was in Chicago, Hurley renewed his acquaintance with Primo's main strategist, Bill Duffy, whom he had met on several occasions while living in New York a few years earlier. Jack introduced Bill to Ray Alvis and explained that he and Alvis had just joined forces to form the largest brokerage firm for fighters in the Midwest.

Carnera was fighting in Newark on February 6, but after that Primo would be returning to the Midwest to fight as often as he could, wherever he could. Duffy assured Hurley and Alvis that if their firm could provide a

---

[15] Geiger, "Sports," *Chicago Evening American*, January 27, 1930, sports section.
[16] Hochstader, Harry, "Hoch's Blues," *Chicago Evening Post*, January 28, 1930, sports section.

Carnera greets Young Stribling who he fought in London before coming to the U. S January 1930.

Carnera weighs in for a bout against Jim Maloney of Boston.

Carnera cavorts with an undersized quartet to emphasize his size.

Carnera stops Elizear Rioux in one round, Chicago, February 2, 1930.

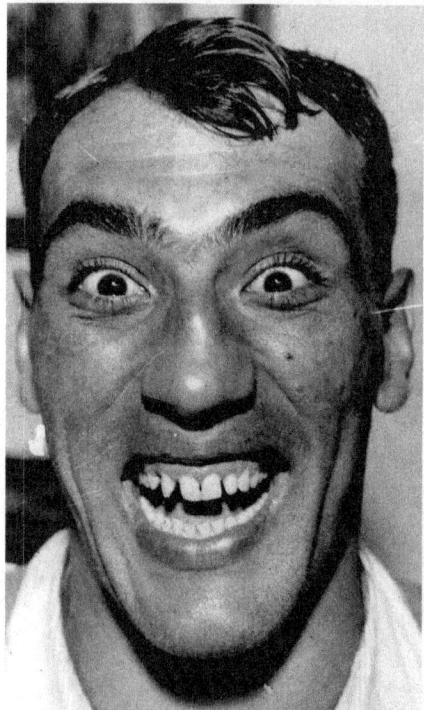

Primo after winning heavyweight title from Jack Sharkey in 1933.

"Da Preem" celebrates at a New York bistro after his title victory.

steady supply of opponents for Carnera on short notice over the next few months, they could do a lot of business. The new partners told Bill they could furnish whatever opposition Primo would need without any problem.

On January 31, 17,349 customers paid $59,626 to see Carnera stop Elizear Rioux in one round. Rioux, apparently in awe of Primo's reputation, hit the canvas six times in 47 seconds without being struck solidly until the last knockdown. Carnera received 30 percent of the gate and Rioux a flat $3,000. Although the inconclusive ending disappointed the crowd, a chance to see Primo plus a strong undercard sent fans home reasonably satisfied.[17]

A subsequent investigation by the Illinois boxing commission ruled that although there was no evidence of fraud, collusion, or conspiracy, Rioux had fought when he was "scared stiff" and as a result had not given the fans an honest exhibition. The commission fined Elizear $1,000 and suspended his boxing license indefinitely. The commission found no evidence of wrongdoing on the part of Carnera or anyone in his entourage.[18]

Meanwhile, Hurley's leading prospect Charley Retzlaff continued his winning ways by kayoing veteran Art Malay at the Jai Alai Fronton arena January 23. Although the bout lasted only one minute 25 seconds, Retzlaff had a scare in the first few seconds when he ran into "a vicious left hook to the head" which sent him "toppling back into the ropes." Pulling himself together, he tore into Malay and promptly ran into another haymaker, this time "a stiff right hand," making him groggy and forcing him to hold on.

After his head cleared, Retzlaff found the range with a ripping right hand to the chin, causing Malay to topple forward. Charley deftly stepped aside and landed "a short cuffing jab" which sent Art to the floor where he was counted out.[19]

On February 14, 1930, Hurley was in Detroit where Retzlaff was boxing Tony Talarico on a show at the Olympia Stadium featuring middleweight champ Mickey Walker in a non-title bout against Leo Lomski, the Aberdeen Assassin. Talarico, a Lomski stablemate from Walla Walla, Washington, figured to give Charley his toughest test to date. Tony had been boxing five years and reportedly had lost only four bouts. Lately, he had been on a victory binge, winning five straight fights, including two in Detroit.

The fight was particularly important because it was Retzlaff's first appearance on a major fight card, and it was in a city where he had never fought before. An impressive victory would likely open the doors to additional appearances, not only in Detroit, but in other Eastern fight centers as well. The bout also was the first of his fights to be picked up by a

---

[17] Kelly, "Ring Board Plans Quiz," *Chicago Evening American*, February 1, 1930, sports section.

[18] Eckersall, Walter, "Hand Elizear $1,000 Fine for Being Scared," *Chicago Tribune*, February 5, 1930, sports section.

[19] "Retzlaff Wins Third Kayo in Chicago Arena," *Duluth News Tribune*, January 24, 1930, sports section.

major wire service. The next morning, thousands of boxing fans from coast-to-coast would read about "Charley Retzlaff of Duluth" for the first time.

A record crowd watched Retzlaff blast Talarico to the canvas eight times before he was counted out in one minute of the second round. The fight was the evening's last bout, and the 17,000 fans, most of whom stayed to watch, stood cheering at their seats a full five minutes after the match ended. Prior to the contest, Charley weighed in at 193-1/2 pounds and Tony 195-1/4.[20]

Hurley, "so excited that he was jumbling his words," called Duluth sports editor Cubby Campbell on the phone from Detroit immediately after the fight. Campbell reported that "some of his coherent remarks were: 'What a hit he made here' – 'He stole the show' – 'Jim Mullen of Chicago wants him back in Chicago right away. Says he's a sure comer' – 'They gave him one of the best ovations I ever heard' – 'Wait until those mugs up there [in Duluth] get a glimpse of Charley now, their eyes will pop out.'"[21]

Scotty Montieth, Dick Dunn's matchmaker at the Olympia, barged into the dressing room afterward, offering $10,000 for Retzlaff to box Carnera in Detroit. After thinking it over on the train to Chicago, Hurley phoned a reply the next day. "That's a lot of money, Scotty," said Jack, "but in a year or so it will not be pocket money for him ... What he needs is experience, and he is going to get all he can within the next 12 months. After that, bring on all the Carneras, Sharkeys, Scotts or Striblings you can dig up."

Another dressing-room visitor was Jack (Doc) Kearns, famous as the manager who led Jack Dempsey to the heavyweight title. Kearns handled Walker during his winning effort against Lomski and then watched afterward as Charley pummeled Talarico into submission. After introducing himself and chatting with Retzlaff a while, Kearns took him to Mickey's dressing room, presented him to the middleweight titleholder, and told Walker: "Here's the best looking heavyweight around, Mick."[22]

Before leaving the dressing room, Kearns confirmed that Charley had signed a five-year contract with Hurley. Later that evening, Doc approached Jack and hinted he was interested in purchasing the contract. A week later, Kearns showed up at the Burnham Building in Chicago and reportedly offered $10,000. Hurley thanked Doc, but declined the offer.[23]

Kearns was in Chicago not only to ask about Retzlaff, but also to check out the local boxing scene in general. Doc was still under suspension in New York for counseling Dempsey to not fight Harry Wills five years

---

[20] "Duluth Boxer Stops Pacific Coast Heavy," *Duluth Herald*, February 15, 1930, sports section.

[21] Campbell, *op. cit.*, February 15, 1930, sports section.

[22] "Jack Kearns Reported Keen About 'Big Charley Retzlaff,'" *Duluth News Tribune*, February 16, 1930, sports section.

[23] Macdonald, Sandy, "Hurley Refuses to Turn over Retzlaff's Contract to Kearns," *Duluth Herald*, February 22, 1930, sports section (proposed meeting in Chicago). Campbell, *op. cit.* February 25, 1930, sports section (offer was $10,000).

earlier. He recently had decided it was too difficult for Walker to make the middleweight limit. As a result, Kearns was temporarily using Chicago as a base from which to direct Mickey's campaign for a heavyweight title shot.

One of the first people Kearns contacted after his arrival was Jim Mullen. Jim had done Doc and Walker a favor in 1926 by promoting Mickey's fight against Tiger Flowers when Mick won the middleweight title. Kearns had heard the big Irishman was down on his luck. If he could arrange a tune-up fight for Walker on short notice against "a fair opponent," Doc would "throw him in at White City and make that show an outstanding one."[24]

Mullen accepted the offer and matched Walker in a St. Patrick's Day show against Jim Mahoney, a local journeyman from the Alvis-Hurley stable. In the first round, Mickey, in typical fashion, teased the crowd by letting Mahoney be the aggressor. In the second, however, Walker decided the fun was over and landed "a corking left hook to the chin" which knocked Mahoney cold at 1:07 of the round. In a preliminary, Retzlaff, 196-1/2 pounds, stopped John (Man Mountain) Erickson, 216-1/2, in one round.

The card drew 4,000 fans who paid approximately $7,500. Afterward, Kearns and Walker donated their purse to Mullen in gratitude for the help he had previously given them.[25]

Among those in attendance that evening were New York sportsman Anthony (Tony) J. Drexel Biddle and his boxing advisor, Jimmy (Bow-Tie) Bronson. Afterward, Biddle reportedly offered Hurley $15,000 for Retzlaff's contract. As with Kearns' offer, Jack declined, this time with the response that he placed a value of at least $25,000 on "Smilin' Charley."[26]

Opinions about Retzlaff at this time ranged from the "he can't miss" positive-thinking variety to the "he sure punches hard, but can he take it?" school of skeptical thought. Mullen thought that, of the fighters he had seen in the recent past, "Retzlaff looks better to me than any of them. I have watched fighters come and go for 30 years, and I do not hesitate to say that Charley Retzlaff is the greatest puncher of all-time. Give him one more year's experience and there isn't a man that can go four rounds with him."[27]

Detroit promoter Joey Malone said "fans are positively 'hot' for Charley in Detroit and if his manager, Jack Hurley, don't make that match with

---

[24] Geiger, "Sports: Kearns Loyal to Jim Mullen," *Chicago Evening American*, March 12, 1930, sports section.

[25] Hurley, *op. cit.* April 20, 1930, sports section.

[26] Kelly, "Clair Kelly's Fight Gossip," *Chicago Evening American*, March 14, 1930, sports section. "Levinsky Bout Tops Card," *Chicago Evening American*, March 24, 1930, sports section. "Levinsky Gets Tough Bout," *Chicago Evening American*, March 22, 1930, sports section. Biddle was really serious about Retzlaff since he also sent Bronson to Fargo for the Retzlaff-Italian Jack Herman fight on April 26, 1930. After watching Charley kayo Herman in one round, Bronson reportedly upped Biddle's offer to $20,000.

[27] "Duluth Heavy Stops Buckeye Boxer in Hurry," *Duluth Herald*, March 25, 1930, sports section.

Retzlaff (left) made a hit in Detroit by stopping Tony Talarico (right) in one round on the undercard of the Walker-Lomski boxing show.

Retzlaff was introduced to Jack Kearns (left) and Mickey Walker (right) after the show. Kearns reportedly was so impressed he offered Hurley $10,000 for Charley's contract.

Tuffy Griffiths in Detroit ... he is a dumber bozo than I've given him credit for being ... The trouble with Hurley is that he don't realize how good a fighter he has. I'll lay my money on the line right now that Retzlaff is the equal of any of the best five heavies in the game today. All he needs is to win one or two big fights, and he will be ready to challenge for the title."[28]

Veteran manager Barney Abel was more cautious. He felt that "Retzlaff is a wonderful prospect" who has "one of the most terrific right-hand punches I ever saw" but "his chin isn't as strong as it should be." Abel guessed that this weakness was "why Hurley don't match him with some of the top-notchers. He has been shying away from these matches for some time now, and the word going around the fistic rialto of Chicago that the reason is Retzlaff can't take 'em. There isn't anything else to think."[29]

Duluth sports enthusiast Neil MacKenzie, fresh from a trip to the Windy City, told Cubby Campbell: "The reason Chicago fans are so wild about Retzlaff, is that they've seen him clipped on the chin and knocked down a couple of times, and then watched him get up off the floor and step in and finish the other guy. They know when Charley fights they are going to see plenty of action, with the possibilities of a knockout almost inevitable."[30]

Hurley was happy with Charley's progress, but advised caution. "Retzlaff is an especially well-made human, who may train into a really great fighter," Jack told Sandy Macdonald: "He has everything to fight with. Age, power, speed and a wonderful disposition are all in his favor. His habits are the best. Retzlaff's tremendous hitting power is his strong appeal. He has developed a left hook to the body and jaw which, when he has it perfected, will be highly dangerous. He is hitting straight and hard with his right.

"I am hopeful that we can land him in the first division within the next year or so. So far he has done everything we have asked of him. How well he will travel as the going gets tougher remains to be seen. Personally, I think he has a fine future."[31]

A question arises at this point. If Hurley was worried Retzlaff's career might be threatened by an inability to take a punch, why didn't he sell

---

[28] Campbell, *op. cit.*, June 19, 1930, sports section. Joey Malone was the promoter at the Fairview Athletic Club in Detroit. Although he talked about a possible Retzlaff-Griffith fight in Detroit, he was not interested in promoting it himself because, in his own words, "My club is too small to handle this fight." He did, however, support the idea of the fight occurring at the Olympia Stadium because it was "the only spot (in Detroit) which could handle the card." He also said that he knew "positively that Scotty Montieth, matchmaker of the Olympia, is keen for the match."

[29] Campbell, *op. cit.*, July 20, 1930, sports section.

[30] Campbell, *op. cit.*, *Duluth News Tribune,*, March 23, 1930, sports section.

[31] Macdonald, *op. cit.* Macdonald,, "Retzlaff May Have Real Opposition in Bout with Castano," *Duluth Herald*, May 16, 1930, sports section. The quotation is a combination of Hurley's comments from both articles.

Charley's contract to Jack Kearns or Tony Biddle when he had a chance?

The obvious question begs an obvious answer. Hurley was confident he was a good enough manager to overcome Retzlaff's deficiencies, at least to the extent of being able to make more money by handling Charley than by selling his contract. In addition, Jack also probably thought that, given the fluid state of the heavyweight division at the time, Retzlaff was still a good gamble to earn some reasonably large purses before he was through.

Another answer, however, though less obvious, offers a better insight into how Hurley viewed his role a manager. A review of his career demonstrates that whenever Jack and one of his boxers parted, the reason was invariably because of mutual agreement, expiration of the contract period, or retirement. Although at times the "mutual agreement" would be the result of a bitter argument or difference of opinion, not once in 50 years as a manager did Jack ever sell a fighter's contract.[32]

In Hurley's mind, his fighters were not commodities to be bought and sold but were instead his own special creations – products not only of his effort to teach them how to fight, but also products of his own special brand of ballyhoo and matchmaking – molded in the image of what he thought a fighter should be, and then protected by matching them against foes who would best showcase their talents.

Hurley perfected his methods as a teacher and promoter in North Dakota during the wild and wooly era when the fans, untutored in the sport's niceties, demanded non-stop action. As a result, Jack taught his men to be sensational fighters, not fancy-dan boxers. He disdained "hit, grab, and run" boxers, as "thieves" and "agony fighters," who who put boxing fans to sleep with their defensive ways. These types of boxers did not fit into his view of what a fighter should be and were, if at all possible, to be avoided as opponents because they made his boys look bad.

Hurley knew that, by virtue of the style he taught, his battlers needed a manager who understood how to match and market them. Jack taught his fighters to stand their ground, to sidestep, slip, or roll with punches, and to plant their feet so they could deliver hard, counter blows to an opponent's lead. They were at their best against rivals willing to move forward and trade blows instead of flicking out jabs and then holding or running away.

The answer, then, to the question why Hurley refused to sell Retzlaff's contract is that, in Jack's view, it would have been unfair to place him in the hands of a manager who did not understand the constraints imposed by the style Charley had learned. Retzlaff had put himself in Hurley's care and learned the specialized style he taught, a style more suited to some types

---

[32] The lone technical exception to this statement was in August 1930 when Jack terminated the partnership with Ray Alvis. However, even in this case, both men took back the boxers they originally owned and relinquished only those which the other brought into the partnership.

of foes than others. In return, Jack undertook to oversee Charley's career and present him in the best possible light. Selling his contract to anyone else would have violated Hurley's sense of duty to the fighter he created.

At the same time Hurley was moving Retzlaff's career along, his partner Ray Alvis was working hard to guide the ace of his half of the stable, Young Jack Thompson, to the welterweight championship of the world.

Thompson, born Cecil Lewis Thompson, was 24 years old and already a veteran of six years in the professional ring when Alvis bought his contract from Ace Hudkins' brother, Clyde, in the spring of 1928. Young Jack, campaigning in his home state of California, was unhappy with Hudkins because Clyde had refused an offer for a fight at Madison Square Garden since he was "too busy" with his brother's affairs to make the trip.[33]

At first, Thompson, a black man, hesitated to go along with the sale because Alvis had been a member of the Ku Klux Klan in Texas. A meeting between Ray and Young Jack's father, Scipio Thompson, relieved the family's anxieties and the deal was completed.

Scipio, or "Slick" as his friends called him, himself had become a boxer in the early 1900s after he put on too much weight to continue his career as a jockey. Fighting under the name of Bob Johnson, his most noteworthy contest was against a long-forgotten fighter named Montana Dan, who Scipio knocked out in the 18th round after having himself been knocked to the canvas 17 times. Slick also had served as Joe Gans' head sparring partner for many of the famous champion's fights on the West Coast.[34]

Although Scipio did not want his son to be a boxer, he finally gave in to Cecil's pleas and started teaching him when he reached age 16. When the youngster turned pro two years later, Slick assumed a role as his son's trainer and continued to serve in that capacity even after Young Jack took on a manager. Contract terms with Alvis called for Young Jack to receive 50 percent, his father 15 percent, and Alvis 35 percent of the fighter's purses.[35]

After winning his first four bouts under Alvis' management, Thompson

---

[33] Most sources have Young Jack's birth name as "Cecil Lewis Thompson," but Ed W. Smith had it as "Cecil Bayard Thompson." Smith, Ed W., "Ed Smith Tells about 'Slick,'" *Chicago Evening American*, July 10, 1930, sports section. Unlike many who adopted names of former fighters and added the prefix "Young" to call to mind a great fighter of the past, Thompson's father, Scipio Thompson, changed his son's fighting name to "Jack" because he felt "Cecil" did not evoke a proper image for a fighter. Scipio then added the prefix "Young" to set his son apart from others who had previously fought as "Jack Thompson," but without notable distinction.

[34] Smith, *op. cit.*

[35] "He Didn't Raise His Boy to Be a Ring Warrior," *Detroit News*, May 6, 1930, sports section. MacDonell, Frank, "Sports – Alvis Had Great Faith in His Fighter," *Detroit Times*, May 10, 1930, sports section (agreement of Scipio Thompson and Alvis; purse split; Thompson cannot get along with Clyde Hudkins). Busch, Noel, "Colored Fighter Veteran of 259 Tough Battles," *New York Daily News*, March 27, 1930, sports section (Scipio Thompson's boxing history).

was matched with welterweight champ Joe Dundee in a non-title fight at Comiskey Park in August 1928. In a stunning upset, Young Jack kayoed Dundee in the second round and was immediately catapulted into a position as one of the leading contenders. After the National Boxing Association (NBA) rescinded its recognition of Joe's title for failing to defend it, Thompson met Jackie Fields for the NBA version of the crown at the Chicago Coliseum March 25, 1929.[36]

Thompson lost a ten-round decision to Fields, but afterward was grateful to have survived with his life. A riot started in the seventh round when someone hollered a racial slur, resulting in injury to over 100 people.

Young Jack became aware of the disturbance only when white ringsiders started climbing into the ring. Realizing that Fields was a Chicago native and 75 percent of the crowd was white, Thompson feared the worst, but after the injured were attended to and order restored, the fight continued.[37]

Thompson's next big break came on March 28, 1930, when he made a long-delayed debut at Madison Square Garden against New York idol Jimmy McLarnin. Young Jack came into the bout a 6-1 underdog and was even money to be kayoed by the Irishman. At the time, McLarnin was universally recognized as the No. 1 welterweight challenger.[38]

The day after the fight, Hype Igoe of the *New York Evening Journal* described the McLarnin-Thompson brawl as "a savage encounter" and "one of the best duels of little men that I ever looked at." It was a contest that "took your breath away" and in which "there wasn't an Adam's apple in Madison Square Garden that wasn't swallowed a dozen times or more, how swiftly they moved, and always within striking distance of each other, feinting, side-stepping, parrying, doing the beautiful in boxing."[39]

In the end, McLarnin's busier left hand and steady aggressiveness impressed officials more than Thompson's potent right hand and sharper, all-around punching. Albeit disputed, the decision went against Young Jack.

"Thompson's spectacular work won the approval of the crowd and there was considerable booing when the Irish lad's hand was lifted in victory," wrote the AP's Alan Gould. Young Jack was "one of the smartest playmates McLarnin had chosen in a long while. He kept circling [to] Jimmy's left and reversing himself when the Irishman set himself to throw it. He varied his attack, shooting from long range in one round and shortening his sights

---

[36] The National Boxing Association (NBA) was an organization composed of boxing commissions from 32 states in the U. S. which had legalized boxing. Membership was voluntary for each state. New York and California had chosen not to join the NBA.

[37] "Guns and Razors Flash About in Balcony Scene" (INS), *Waterloo Daily Courier*, March 26, 1929, sports section.

[38] Wood, Wilbur, "McLarnin Wins Close Battle," *New York Sun*, March 29, 1930, sports section.

[39] Igoe, Hype, "Clever, Open Fight Waged by Welters," *New York Evening Journal*, March 29, 1930, sports section.

Thompson squares off with welter champ Joe Dundee before their non-title fight in 1928. Left to right: trainer Heinie Blaustein, Dundee, referee Eddie Purdy, Thompson, unidentified, and manager Ray Alvis.

Thompson kayos Dundee in two.   Young Jack with his father, Scipio.

Young Jack Thompson and Jackie Fields square off in the gym prior to their NBA welterweight championship bout at Chicago, won by Fields on March 29, 1929. It was at this match that a racist remark incited a riot causing injury to more than 100 people.

the next. This ... confused [McLarnin] no little."[40]

An informal poll of reporters showed that ten favored McLarnin, seven Thompson, and one called it a draw. Even those backing Jimmy, however, expressed amazement that it had taken a fighter as good as Young Jack so long to show his wares in New York.[41]

Although there was no hard evidence that race influenced the bout's outcome, several reporters raised that possibility in post-fight articles. Jim Burchard of the *New York Telegram*, who scored the bout in Thompson's favor, wrote that Jimmy seemed to believe he had lost and "was suitably shocked when his hand was raised in token victory. Young Jack Thompson won, but sportively shrugged his shoulders as he realized that a Negro boxer is two strikes gone before he climbs through the ropes."[42]

James W. Jennings, of the *New York Evening Graphic*, commenting about six low blows McLarnin landed, wrote "had it been a white boy boxing the Irishman, Jim might have been disqualified ... The Negro never complained and is a splendid example of gameness for our fleet of boxers who howl 'foul' when tapped on their middle ... Before they left the ring Thompson was the vocal choice of the fans." Had the referee penalized McLarnin for his fouls, Jennings argued, the decision might have been different.[43]

Ironically, the loss to McLarnin, together with the sportsmanlike way Young Jack accepted it, worked in his favor. In this regard, the case of Tiger Flowers bears a striking similarity to Thompson's situation. Flowers, also a black American, had lost a universally reviled decision to Mike McTigue in 1926. The unjust result created so much sympathy for Flowers that he was

---

[40] Gould, Alan, from Hurley-Alvis flier, AP story first published on March 29, 1930 (first quote). Farrell, Jack, "Broken Hand Jimmy's Alibi for Showing," *New York Daily News*, March 28, 1930, sports section (second quote).

[41] Wilbur Wood of the *New York Sun* (McLarnin-4, Thompson-3, Draw-3). Jim Dawson of the *New York Times* (M -7, T-3). Jack Farrell of the *New York Daily News* (M-5, T-4, D-1). Jim Burchard of the *New York Telegram* (T-5, M-4, D-1). Jack Kofoed of the *New York Evening Post* (McLarnin winner). Ed Frayne of the *New York American* (McLarnin winner). Ned Brown of the *New York World* (Thompson winner – "The worst Thompson should have had was a draw"). Don Skene of the *New York Herald* (T-5, M-3, D-2). Bill Corum of the *New York Evening Journal* (Thompson winner). Hype Igoe of the *New York Evening Journal* (McLarnin winner). W. S. Farnsworth of the *New York Evening Journal* (Thompson winner – "a draw was the worst that the negro should have received"). James W. Jennings (Draw – "So close was the encounter that a draw would not have been amiss," but he goes on to suggest that McLarnin should have been disqualified). Grantland Rice of the *New York Sun* (Thompson winner – "if Thompson lost then Man o' War never won a race"). Joe Williams of the *New York Telegram* (T—5, M-3, D-2). Alan Gould of the *Associated Press* (M-5, T-3, D-2). Edward Van Every of the *New York World* (McLarnin-winner). Davis J. Walsh of the *International News Service* (McLarnin-seemed to go along with decision). Herbert W. Barker of the *Associated Press* (M-5, T-3, D-2). Other newspapers unavailable.

[42] Burchard, Jim, "Coast Puncher Lays Poor Showing to Injured Hand," *New York Telegram*, March 29, 1930, sports section.

[43] Jennings, James, W., excerpt from Hurley-Alvis flier, *New York Evening Graphic*, March 29, 1930.

Thompson ducks as McLarnin's right to the top of the head in round one lifts his foot off the canvas. Hurley advised Jack in the maneuver after seeing Jimmy hurt his hand in similar fashion in a 1928 bout. This very blow is possibly the one which broke Jimmy's hand.

Thompson slips to the canvas against McLarnin at Madison Square Garden. Young Jack lost the decision, but the uproar about the verdict led to his title bout with Jackie Fields.

Hurley's flier following the McLarnin fight helped land Thompson a second welterweight title fight against Jackie Fields in Detroit.

given a title bout with middleweight champ Harry Greb. Flowers made the most of the opportunity and defeated Greb to win the title.[44]

At any rate, the publicity generated by the McLarnin fight turned out to be better for Thompson than any victory he could have won in the ring. Hurley was with Alvis in Young Jack's corner during the fight. The next day he bought copies of every newspaper which reported the fight. Before he left New York, Jack had mailed out hundreds of 18"x 28" fliers to sports editors and boxing experts throughout the country with quotations describing how Thompson had been robbed of the decision.

---

[44] At this point it is appropriate to point out how representative the stories of Scipio and Young Jack Thompson were of the problems facing African-American boxers in America generally during the first half of the 20th century. Unless a black fighter was lucky enough to find a manager, almost invariably a white manager, who actually took an interest in him, he was done before he started. At the same time, the Thompson story is a truly special one of how the bond between a father and son was able to overcome the prejudice and bigotry which threatened to prevent Young Jack from achieving his full potential.

Although details about Scipio Thompson's ring career are sketchy, it appears he was a self-taught boxer, whose ring career was probably spent fighting in the open fields, back barrooms, and dance halls of various small towns and western mining camps. Scipio's story of being knocked down 17 times in one fight illustrates the plight of black fighters who fought in those types of venues in the rough and tumble days at the early part of the century. Such fighters usually fought for white promoters and at the pleasure of white audiences who had absolutely no regard for the fighters' safety or welfare. Often, aspiring black fighters would be called on to provide "comic" preliminary entertainment for the amusement of well-liquored white patrons. On other occasions, a large group would be turned loose in the ring to fight brutal "battle royals" in which the last man standing would be declared the winner.

Black fighters on such ugly occasions were more often than not forced to endure the most vile racial epithets, and worse, in an atmosphere encouraged and cultivated by the rough and ready mores predominant in the "lower echelons" of America's sporting subculture.

It is no wonder, then, that Scipio Thompson discouraged his son from a career in the prize ring. And it is also no wonder that when his son persisted in wanting to be a fighter that the elder Thompson, as a conscientious father, would elect to remain with him as a trainer, advisor, and all-around "guardian angel."

Young Jack made a strategic mistake when he signed to have Clyde Hudkins manage him. At the time, Clyde was also managing his brother, Ace Hudkins, who like Thompson was also a top welterweight. Clyde was preoccupied with managing Ace and certainly was in no hurry to advance Young Jack's career while his brother was doing so well. This conflict of interest was no doubt behind Clyde's indifference to Thompson, and his refusal to take him to New York, since Ace was already a big favorite there.

Unfortunately, Young Jack's situation was like that of any indentured servant. He was tied to Hudkins until either their contract expired or he was sold to another manager. His only protection was that his father retained a small interest in his contract and therefore exercised some influence over the selection of a potential purchaser. In effect, Scipio was "part of the package" that went along with Young Jack.

The true measure of the Thompsons' desperation at the time, and of how limited their options were, is gauged by their decision to go along with the sale of Young Jack's contract to a former Ku Klux Klan member from the South! It is hard not to sympathize with the misgivings they must have felt in having to choose between making this pact with the devil or instead allowing Young Jack's chance for success to continue withering on the vine.

One source of consolation to Young Jack was likely the realization he was not the only

As it turned out, for once luck was with Thompson. Welterweight champ Jackie Fields, who had erased any doubt about his right to the title by defeating Joe Dundee in June 1929, was himself in violation of the NBA's six-month time limit for defending the title. McLarnin had broken his right hand against Young Jack in the first round and was therefore unavailable to fight the champion. Rather than be stripped of his title like Dundee, Fields agreed to defend it against Thompson in Detroit on May 9, 1930.[45]

Although Alvis believed the fight could draw more money in Chicago, he nonetheless agreed to accept a lesser guarantee so Dick Dunn could promote the contest at the Olympia Stadium. Michigan lawmakers had legalized 15-round title fights whereas Illinois still limited all bouts to ten rounds. While Thompson had lost a ten-round decision to Fields in Chicago a year earlier, he had been coming on strong in the later rounds. Alvis figured the longer distance would be to Young Jack's benefit.[46]

---

person facing this situation. Thousands of other African-Americans were forced to make similar choices in their lives every day. The Thompson story turned out better than most at least in part because Ray Alvis kept his word to give his best efforts on Young Jack's behalf and did an excellent job in positioning him for a title fight.

As a postscript to this note, Young Jack's fight against Leonard Bennett in Seattle, Washington, on May 25, 1932, is worthy of mention, if only to bring the Thompsons' father-son saga full circle. Thompson, by then a 27-year-old ex-champion back on the small-time circuit, was taking on Bennett in a six-round bout. Young Jack also by this time had become a free agent, having ended his contractual relationship with Ray Alvis.

As Young Jack finished his first workout after his arrival in Seattle, a newsman took note of an older gentleman who was working alone as trainer to Young Jack. The reporter approached the man and asked how long he had been with Jack. The trainer introduced himself as the fighter's father, and replied he had been with his son for all his 326 amateur and professional bouts and had in fact been the person who had taught him how to box and given him the ring name of "Young Jack" before his first fight.

Three days later, Young Jack Thompson won a six-round decision over Bennett in his 327th fight. As it turned out, the bout was the last of his career, since he announced his retirement just a few months later.

After the bout, father and son climbed through the ring ropes and down the steps for the last time, alone against the world but together to the end, just as they been since the very beginning of Young Jack's career. "Thompson's Jack Was Cecil Once: Ex-Welter Champ Goes Wednesday," Seattle Times, May 22, 1932, sports section. (Note: the author passes no judgment on Scipio's claim that Young Jack had 326 fights.)

[45] McLarnin's broken hand was not the result of a random accident. As discussed in Chapter 18 of the first volume of this set, Hurley had seen Jimmy hurt his right hand on the head of Stanislaus Loayza at Detroit in 1928. As part of the game plan for the McLarnin-Thompson fight, Jack coached Thompson to lean forward as Loayza had done when Jimmy threw his right so that it would land on the hard part of Young Jack's head. Later in 1930, Hurley would give Billy Petrolle the same advice while preparing for his November 21st fight with McLarnin, and Jimmy would break his hand again.

[46] MacDonell, Frank, "Sports – Fields Favorite, Alvis Confident, New Fouling Rule," Detroit Times, May 5, 1930, sports section. Hurley disagreed with Alvis and thought Young Jack would have a better chance against Fields at the ten-round Chicago distance than the 15-round Detroit distance. While working in Thompson's corner for his ten-round fight with McLarnin, Hurley noticed Young Jack tired badly in the last few rounds. This experience

Alvis' analysis proved to be on the mark. Fields jumped out to an early lead and won a majority of the first six rounds. Starting in the seventh round, Thompson came on and progressively took the play away from the champion. By the 11th round, it looked like he might score a knockout, but Fields managed to weather a number of storms to finish on his feet. At the end of the bout, most reporters' scorecards gave Thompson nine rounds and Fields six. The referee, and sole arbiter, Elmer McClelland, had it 10-3-2.

Young Jack Thompson was the new welterweight champion. For the fight, Fields weighed 145-3/4 pounds and Thompson 142-3/4. A "crowd exceeding 10,000" paid gross receipts "close to $70,000 to see the show" with net receipts "in the neighborhood of $55,000." Fields received a guaranteed purse of $37,500, while Young Jack's share amounted to just $2,500. Profits to the Olympia were figured at $5,600.[47]

Before the contest, the Michigan commission ruled each boxer could have no more than three handlers in his corner for the fight. For Thompson, Alvis, as head second, was to be assisted by Hurley and cutman Charley Moore. Scipio Thompson was not chosen because Alvis thought he would be nervous about his son and interfere with the corner work.

On the eve of the fight, Hurley wired to say an emergency had come up, and he could not be present. Scipio was selected to take Jack's place.

The late substitution turned out to be both unfortunately ironic and singularly appropriate. While Hurley was unable to see his first, and what would prove to be his only, champion win a world title, Scipio Thompson received the once in a lifetime opportunity to work in the corner with his son for the fight. Significantly, the next day the *Detroit News* reported that "last night Scipio was the coolest second of the Thompson trio."[48]

---

convinced him Thompson would have a harder time going 15 rounds. Thompson took the McLarnin bout on eight days notice and told reporters afterward that he not had time to get into condition for the bout. Alvis, based on his greater experience with Young Jack, knew his ways better than Hurley and apparently agreed he was not at his best endurance-wise for the McLarnin fight. As noted in the text, Alvis was in Thompson's corner for his ten-round bout with Fields in 1929, and had seen Fields tire while Thompson came on strong in the latter rounds. Hurley had not seen the 1929 fight.

In any event, Hurley, in his boxing column a week before the bout, predicted that Thompson, a fighter in whose earnings Hurley held a 17-1/2 percent interest, would lose his bid to win the championship because of the 15-round distance. Although nothing was mentioned about his difference of opinion with Alvis in Jack's column, it is not difficult to imagine that the matter was privately the subject of a heated discussion between the two managers before Alvis accepted a match for Detroit instead of Chicago. Fortunately for all connected with the Thompson camp, Alvis' judgment proved correct.

[47] MacDonell, "New Welter Champ in Hospital," *Detroit Times*, May 10, 1930, p. 1, continued in sports section. Shaver, Bud, title unavailable, *Detroit Times*, May 15, 1930, sports section (profits $7,500 less $1,900).

[48] "To General Scipio It Was Just Another Fight," *Detroit News*, May 10, 1930, sports section. Hurley's emergency resulted from problems with the May 16th Louisville show he and Alvis were promoting with the American Legion to take advantage of trade generated by the Kentucky Derby the next day. The episode is described at the end of this chapter.

Thompson hooks a left to Fields' kidney in the fourth round of their welterweight championship bout at the Olympia Stadium in Detroit.

Another Detroit scene as Fields advances & Jack seeks an opening.

The two Jacks in the 15th round just before the bell ends the battle.

Slim McClelland declares Thompson new champ. Walter P. Reuther Library, Archives of Labor & Urban Affairs, Wayne State University.

Young Jack Thompson, two-time world's welterweight champion, 1930 and 1931.

One of the steadiest sources of income enjoyed by the Alvis-Hurley partnership during this period came from furnishing opposition to Primo Carnera on his much-ballyhooed tour across the United States. As he had promised at the time of the Carnera-Rioux fight in Chicago, Bill Duffy contacted Hurley in early February and told Jack to be ready to supply as many as two different heavyweight opponents per week for the tour.

From February 11 through March 28, Carnera would engage in ten fights. Of these, Alvis and Hurley provided seven of Primo's foes: Jim Sigman at Memphis on 2/14; Man Mountain Erickson at Oklahoma City on 2/17; Farmer Lodge at New Orleans on 2/24; Sully Montgomery at Minneapolis on 3/11; Chuck Wiggins at St. Louis on 3/17; George Trafton at Kansas City on 3/26; and Jack MacAuliffe at Denver on 3/28.[49]

All of these bouts ended as either one- or two-round kayos for Carnera.

Although at first some promoters thought it would be easy to find their own foes for Carnera, it soon became evident the task was more difficult than it seemed. The pool of local heavyweights husky enough to at least appear able to furnish credible opposition to Primo was generally small. If a candidate did exist who had a local reputation, he might be reluctant to risk it for what the promoter would be willing to pay. In other cases, a likely foe for Carnera might already be engaged to fight someone else.[50]

Primo's fight in Oklahoma City was a good example of these difficulties. On February 13, Hurley received a panicked phone call from promoter Lou Cutler. The promoter had made a deal with Duffy on February 7 for a fight featuring Carnera on February 17 with a minimum guarantee of $7,500.

Cutler told Hurley that in the six days since committing to the bout, he had contacted Pete Wistort, a 192-pounder, and Big Sid Terris, a 200-pounder, who were both well known in Oklahoma boxing circles. Wistort had declined because he felt Carnera was too big for him, and Terris had demanded more money than the show could afford. Now, just four days before the fight, Duffy had given the promoter Hurley's name. Could Jack find an affordable opponent on short notice to meet Carnera?[51]

Luckily for Cutler, Hurley said he had just such a man. His name was John (Man Mountain) Erickson, also known as "the Big Swede." He was 6-feet 3-inches tall and weighed 220 pounds. Erickson had won four of his last five fights in Chicago and had previously defeated Big Boy Peterson, Carnera's first opponent in the United States.

Hurley guaranteed that Erickson could be on the ground at Oklahoma City in two days. Erickson did not have a manager, but to make sure nothing went wrong, Hurley accompanied the Big Swede on the train ride

---

[49] Hochstader, *op. cit.*, April 29, 1930, sports section.
[50] Ray, John, E., "Ray's Column," *St. Louis Post-Dispatch*, Feb. 10, 1930, sports section.
[51] "Man Mountain Will Come to City Saturday – Cutler Still Seeks Opponent," *Oklahoma City Times*, February 12, 1930, sports section.

to Oklahoma City. Unfortunately, Jack's efforts were not enough to salvage the show. Largely because of confusion over Carnera's foe, only 3,000 fans were present to see Primo kayo Erickson in two rounds.[52]

The experience was enough for Duffy, however. To help Cutler out, he reduced his guarantee to a straight percentage of the gate. In the future, if a promoter did not have a foe lined up, Bill would insist he contact Hurley at once so the show would have time to be properly publicized.

As Carnera piled up a string of early-round knockouts over a parade of mostly unknown opponents, reporters started questioning both the quality of his opposition and the sharp practices of his handlers. Criticism generally fell into two camps: those who thought the Primo's fights were fixed in advance by his managers; and those who thought his bouts were honest, but that he was being matched with pushovers.

To answer these questions and make recommendations about how to handle the situation, the NBA appointed a special committee on March 28, 1930, to investigate the Carnera tour. Questionnaires were sent out to the commissioners in each of the states where Primo had fought to see if they had noticed any irregularities in the big fellow's fights.

When the committee finally issued its report on May 15, it found that Carnera's managers had employed a campaign to "build up" Primo without matching him with a single legitimate contender. Although the committee unearthed no direct evidence of criminal conspiracy, it concluded such a practice was not in the best interests of boxing. As a solution, the committee recommended that Carnera and his managers be indefinitely suspended.[53]

Although Alvis and Hurley's work as booking agents for a majority of Carnera's foes was not the basis for its recommendations, the committee noted that their involvement was a "circumstance, if true, which might be considered suspicious."

In reply, Hurley told the *Fargo Forum* that he and Alvis "made no secret of the fact that [we] were booking fighters for Carnera. Booking fighters is the business of Hurley and Alvis." Jack emphasized that in each case "the promoters knew the qualifications of Carnera's opponents" and the "commissions knew far in advance who they were." If the promoters or the commissions had questions about the quality of Primo's opposition, they should have raised them before, and not after, the fights had occurred.[54]

What the NBA and other critics failed to realize was that their concerns were largely irrelevant to most sports fans. The Carnera phenomenon was giving a financially ailing sport a shot in the arm. Wherever he went, the

---

[52] Hurley, "Shadow Boxing," *Fargo Forum*, July 22, 1934, sports section. Raspberry, Charles W., "In the Sports Spotlight," *Oklahoma City Times*, February 18, 1930, sports section.

[53] "N.B.A. Acts to Bar Primo, 4 Managers," *Louisville Times*, May 15, 1930, sports section.

[54] Fitzgerald, Eugene F., "The Sport Whirligig," *Fargo Forum*, May 18, 1930, sports section. The words are Fitzgerald's paraphrase after talking with Hurley.

big man stirred up new interest, giving not only boxing enthusiasts a reason to part with their increasingly scarce dollars, but attracting persons who normally would not otherwise think of attending a boxing card.

Fans were less interested in who Carnera fought or how good a fighter he was, than in simply watching the "man mountain" with the oversize hands and feet perform. Whether he properly "snapped a punch" or just bowled a foe over by the sheer force of muscle and weight did not matter. Leave the intricacies of the sport to the experts. The fans just wanted to see a show.

The professionals in boxing, i. e., the promoters, managers, boxers, and even local sportswriters, understood the situation very well. Carnera's popularity afforded more work and better pay for not only Primo's opponents and their managers, but also for everyone associated with one of his shows, from the promoter, to the publicists and concessionaires, all the way down to the preliminary fighters and their managers.[55]

---

[55] The matter of Primo Carnera's "build-up" and "exploitation" has been an on-going subject of biography, fiction, and movies ever since Carnera became a public figure. Regarding the question of whether the build-up involved fixed fights or outside influence, the author subscribes to a view much like the one Hurley expressed in the introduction to this chapter, i. e., that Carnera was capable of beating most of the fighters he met during his barnstorming tour without outside influence. Nonetheless, given the men handling Primo, the specter of such illicit assistance was lurking behind the scenes for ready use whenever the need might arise. The Leon Chevalier incident discussed later in this chapter seems to have been this type of occasion.

Surviving boxing films (albeit filmed from a later period in Carnera's career) show Primo handling with ease foes far more capable than those he met in his initial tour of the U. S.

Fights against Jimmy Maloney (which Primo lost by a close decision), Tommy Loughran, Paolino Uzcudun, K. O. Christner, and the ill-fated Ernie Schaaf show a fighter who was reasonably fast and in most cases just too darn big and strong for most of the good heavyweights of the era. He may have pushed his punches, but they still had a clubbing effect. Because of his size and strength, he was able to manhandle and maul most of his opponents into near exhaustion. And Primo could take a pretty good punch, especially from smaller foes who lacked the leverage to reach his chin with their best shots.

To the author's eye, even Carnera's first fight against Jack Sharkey, which Primo lost by a decision, was close, contemporary accounts to the contrary notwithstanding. In watching the most complete version of his losing fight with Max Baer, Carnera fights the lazy Baer to a standstill in those rounds where Primo is not knocked down. One judge even had Carnera ahead in rounds won until Baer finally knocked Carnera out in the 11th round).

Rumors of Carnera's exploitation were no doubt true. Primo had three managers of record: Leon See, Bill Duffy, and Walter Friedman; and at least one not of record, Owney Madden. According to contemporary news accounts, these managers together took 72-1/2 percent of Carnera's earnings, leaving him with just 27-1/2 percent. Even if one accepts the unlikely fact that an honest set of books was maintained, it is doubtful Primo would have saved much of his 27-1/2 percent. Carnera was trusting by nature and at that time was undoubtedly unschooled in the ways of finance. His handlers wanted to keep him happy and as carefree as possible, and probably gave him whatever he wanted as long as it didn't interfere with his training routine. He had specially tailored clothes that must have cost a bundle. It is likely nothing was too good for Primo as long as he was raking in the dough from his boxing and paying for it all out of his share.

It was widely publicized when Carnera became champion in July 1933 he already had

The Midwest boxing promoter who benefited most from Carnera's build-up was Mique Malloy. Mique had been a fixture in the Chicago sports scene since his days as a fleet-footed baseball player in the Wisconsin-area leagues in the early 1900s. In 1912-13 he managed the Wausau Lumberjacks before retiring to become a scout for several major-league teams, including the Chicago Cubs. His most notable find was Charley Grimm, who became a long-time big-league first baseman and manager.[56]

Malloy began promoting in 1926 at the White City arena and also at various outdoor sites around the Windy City area. Although he staged quite a few successful shows in the halcyon years before the market crashed, like many others, he was struggling in Chicago during the winter of 1929-'30.

When it became apparent Primo was going over big, Malloy contacted the owners of the new 21,000-seat St. Louis Arena and offered to bring the Ambling Alp to St. Louis. During the next few months, Mique promoted two Carnera shows at the Gateway City to houses of 11,000 and 18,130 spectators, and gates of $29,551 and $48,157, respectively. For his efforts, Malloy earned nifty profits of $5,000 and $15,000.[57]

In similar fashion, Mike Collins did well with Carnera in the smaller Minneapolis market. Already enriched in his capacity as a manager by Big Boy Peterson's appearance against Primo in New York, Collins, as a promoter, brought Carnera to the Minneapolis Auditorium on March 11, 1930. In front of 11,000 people, Primo kayoed Sully Montgomery in two rounds. The show's gate of $17,000 ended up as the city's second largest of the year, surpassed only by a later card refereed by Jack Dempsey.[58]

In late March, Dempsey's Chicago office recommended Alvis and Hurley to the Jefferson Post of the American Legion in Louisville as likely promoters to stage a boxing show. Would Ray and Jack be interested in joining with the post in promoting a card on the eve of the Kentucky Derby featuring Carnera as the star attraction? The answer from the fistic brokers was a resounding yes. Since Hurley was already a legion member, not only

---

filed for bankruptcy. It is curious that the New York State Athletic Commission did not investigate Carnera's affairs then. The commission had a rule which purportedly prevented a manager from taking a share greater than 33-1/3 percent of a fighter's earnings. Reports that Carnera's managers were taking 72-1/2 percent had circulated since 1930. The New York commission never hesitated to investigate, levy fines, and issue suspensions in other less pernicious situations. Had the commission conducted an investigation it might have saved Carnera future grief. Apparently, that potato was just too hot for the commission to handle.

[56] "Who's Who in Chicago Sports," *Chicago Evening American*, March 4, 1930, sports section.

[57] McGowan, W. J., "Malloy After Other Matches," *St. Louis Post-Dispatch*, March 3, 1931, sports section (11,000 fans paid $29,551 at St. Louis on 2/11/30). "18,130 Persons Attend Arena Show; Receipts, $48,157," *St. Louis Post-Dispatch*, March 18, 1930, p. 6-C. Geiger, Edward J., "Sports – They Go for Mique Malloy," *Chicago Evening American*, March 22, 1930, sports section (profit of $5,000 and $15,000).

[58] Macdonald, "American Fight Fans Will Expect Carnera to Meet Real Boxer," *Duluth Herald*, March 19, 1930, sports section.

would they help out, they would consider it an honor to do so.[59]

Alvis and Hurley could hardly believe their good fortune. They had made a few dollars supplying Primo with opponents, but nothing like Malloy and Collins had made as promoters. Now, as promoters during the Kentucky Derby, they could ride the Carnera gravy train in style.

Jefferson Post had already reserved the local armory and secured approval for the May 16th date from the Kentucky Athletic Board of Control. With thousands of sportsmen staying overnight to see the next day's Derby, the show could not miss being a success.

All Hurley and Alvis had to do was sign up Carnera and assemble the other boxers for the show. Jefferson Post would handle all other arrangements. Jack and Ray's major concerns were to nail down the two most important fights on the card as early as possible so that press releases could be distributed before out-of-town Derby goers made travel plans.

By April 9, the card was set. As anticipated, Carnera had been signed and was scheduled to meet Bearcat Wright in the main event. Jack (Doc) Kearns also had agreed to send his heavyweight hopeful, Al Fay, into the ring against Al Friedman of Boston. Unfortunately, within a week the carefully laid plans of Alvis and Hurley would begin to unravel on multiple fronts at an ever-accelerating pace as Derby day approached.

On April 15, Carnera was credited with a kayo of Leon (Bombo) Chevalier in six rounds at Oakland, California, when Chevalier's second, Bob Perry, inexplicably threw in the towel even though many ringsiders felt Leon was winning the fight. Afterward, Bombo claimed that, in addition to stopping the fight when he was not hurt, Perry had threatened to kill him if he did not "lay down." Chevalier also claimed Perry had rubbed an irritant in his eyes and impaired his breathing between rounds.

On April 18, the California boxing commission conducted a hearing during which it learned Perry had East Coast connections of a dubious nature and had met with Carnera's California representative, Frank Churchill, in the seats behind Chevalier's corner just before the fight. The commission also discovered Perry had worked as a second for Primo's prior opponent in Los Angeles just seven days earlier.

On April 22, the commission ruled Carnera and Chevalier had put in honest efforts, but "that the action of second Perry had been inspired by some person connected with the management of Carnera." As a result, the commission suspended Primo, his manager Leon See, Bob Perry, Frank Churchill, and Chevalier's manager, Tim McGrath.[60]

On April 25, the Kentucky Athletic Board of Control notified Jefferson

---

[59] "Seek Carnera for Derby Eve Go," *Chicago Evening Post*, March 27, 1930, sports section.

[60] "Carnera Bout Is Probed by Board," *Louisville Times*, April 16, 1930, sports section. "Fight Body to Suggest Suspension," *Chicago Evening Post*, April 19, 1930, sports section. "Rule Monday on Carnera," April 17, 1930, sports section.

Post it would not allow Primo to fight in the state because of the California ruling and "because of the questionable bouts in which Carnera has been engaged." Three days later, Hurley reached an agreement with Kearns to have middleweight champ Mickey Walker replace Primo as a headliner. Walker would fight Al Friedman, who had been slated to box Al Fay. Fay's new foe in the semifinal would be Frankie Wine of Butte, Montana.[61]

Three days before the card, Hurley learned Friedman recently had broken his hand and was unable to fight Walker. The next day, Jack's first substitute, George Cook of Australia, was rejected as unsuitable by the Kentucky commission.

After a hectic night spent burning up the phone lines, Hurley announced he had secured the services of light heavyweight Paul Swiderski, the "Sad-Eyed Pole," as Walker's opponent for the following evening's festivities. Swiderski, who was managed by Tom Walsh, had defeated George Hoffman and King Levinsky in his last two fights. A win over Walker would place him in the front ranks of the light heavyweight division.[62]

On the morning of the fight, Hurley arrived on the scene in Louisville to find the Derby show, which had once shown such promise, in complete shambles. Walker had skipped a light-training photo session scheduled for publicity purposes the day before in favor of attending pre-Derby races at the track. As a result, instead of boosting the show, angry reporters were speculating that Walker, a notorious playboy, had avoided the session to hide the fact he was in no condition to wage a good fight against Swiderski.

To add to his troubles, Hurley learned at the last minute that Swiderski was Walker's former sparring partner. Jack worried that a secret deal might be in the works between the two fighters to "take it easy" on each other and not give their best efforts. Even if this were not the case, Hurley feared that if word of their prior relationship leaked out, the gate might still be adversely affected by rumors of such "an arrangement."

As a final obstacle, the pre-fight agreement to have Ed Cochrane, of Kansas City, referee the main event was set aside by Kentucky authorities, who insisted that a local man perform the honors. Doc Kearns, who originally requested Cochrane, threatened to call off the fight, but then backed off when he saw that the Kentucky board would not budge.

A tally of ticket sales, once thought likely to exceed $40,000, showed that less than $4,000 had trickled into the till by the morning of the bout. As fight time neared, Kearns, sensing that Walker's $7,500 guarantee was in jeopardy, told Hurley that neither Mickey nor Al Fay would enter the ring without being paid in full before the fight.

---

[61] "Carnelian-Wright Scrap at Louisville Canceled," *Duluth News Tribune*, April 26, 1930, sports section.

[62] The foregoing chronology of events prior to the Walker-Swiderski fight is taken from the sports pages of the *Louisville Times* from April 5 through May 16, 1930.

Kearns and Hurley finally reached a settlement late in the afternoon when Doc agreed to reduce Mickey's purse to $5,000. In the course of these negotiations, Kearns, as a ploy for Hurley's benefit, turned to Walker and said, "Okay, Mick. No fight tonight. Go out and have a good time."[63]

Unfortunately, Walker took Kearns seriously. On his way out, Mickey ran into some newsmen in the lobby and told them the fight was off and, by the way, did they want to join him for a few drinks at a nearby speakeasy?

When Kearns finally located him, Mickey was four sheets to the wind. Returning to the hotel room, Kearns and trainer Teddy Hayes threw Mickey into a cold shower. By the time they arrived at the Louisville Armory at 9 p.m., Mick's condition had just about progressed to the hangover stage.[64]

In contrast to the days and hours leading up to the contest, the Walker-Swiderski fight itself was recalled by those in attendance as one of the great ring spectacles of all-time.

The fight started slowly with Walker biding his time for just the right moment to counter one of Swiderski's leads. After about a minute of sparring, both boxers let go with right hands simultaneously. Each hit the deck, but the tall Polander's punch was much the harder. Paul was up immediately while Mickey stayed down for a nine-count.

Sensing the chance of a lifetime, Swiderski threw caution to the winds and downed the reeling Walker again with another terrific right hand. Overeager, Paul hit Mickey with a left hook while he was on the canvas, but the referee ignored the punch. Up again at nine, Walker was met by a flurry of blows that left him draped helplessly over the ropes as a bell rang to end the first round. Mick appeared to be completely "out."

In the terrific din, Swiderski failed to hear the bell. Paul continued to pummel Mickey with both hands as he remained against the ropes. In a flash, Kearns jumped into the ring to protect Walker, while Teddy Hayes pushed Swiderski away from Walker and threw a punch of his own at the flailing Pole. Instantly, Paul's handlers entered the fracas, followed by members of the state boxing board, the police, and a score of spectators.

About four minutes elapsed before the ring was cleared, as Kearns and Hayes worked desperately to revive Walker. Even with the extra rest, Mickey was in tough shape for round two. Before the heat ended, Swiderski had knocked Mick down two more times. Again, Paul struck Walker while he was down without a warning from the referee. When Mickey went to his corner, it hardly seemed possible he could go on much longer.[65]

In round three, those present witnessed a remarkable metamorphosis. Walker began, in the words of one disinterested observer, to shake off the

---

[63] McNeil, Louis P., "Legion Is $5,000 Loser on Fight," *Louisville Times*, March 17, 1930, sports section.

[64] Walker, Mickey and Reich, Joe, *Mickey Walker, the Toy Bulldog and His Times*, (Random House, New York, 1961), pp. 201-202.

[65] McNeil, *op. cit.*

effects of both the alcohol and the punches he had absorbed, as he literally "fought his way into condition." By round's end, Walker had knocked Swiderski down three times and taken complete charge of the bout. From then on, Mickey gave Paul a thorough pasting until the bout was over. After ten rounds, Louisville newspapers all awarded their decisions to Walker.[66]

Years later, Kearns took credit for having "happened to hit the bell" with a water bottle before the first round officially ended to save Walker from certain defeat. For his part, Mickey told Damon Runyon that after the first punch he "didn't know much about anything for about seven heats."[67]

After the fight, while remnants of a "woefully small crowd" lingered in the armory to relish the shared experience of having seen "one of the greatest fights ever," Hurley and the American Legion officials counted gate receipts amounting to a grand total of $7,045.

According to the final accounting, the show lost $5,000. Legion officials considered the loss "only temporary" because the fight was "underwritten by Ray Alvis and Jack Hurley, Chicago boxing brokers and promoters," and it was "up to them to make good." The officials also promised that "we are going to collect, even if we have to resort to the federal courts."[68]

As far as Alvis and Hurley were concerned, if the Jefferson Post was arguing that the two Chicago-based fistic brokers were responsible for the full amount of the loss as "underwriters," then Ray and Jack would take the opposite position. In their view of it, they had been hired as matchmakers and bore no responsibility as promoters of the show. If Jefferson Post felt otherwise it would have to make good on its threat of legal action.

Alvis and Hurley's ride on the Carnera "gravy train" had run its unfortunate course. They had "hopped aboard" and ridden it to the end of the line, but had fallen short of their destination. Now, it was time to go back to work and earn their money the hard way.

The day after the Derby, a sadder but wiser Hurley and Alvis purchased pullman seats on a real train and headed home to Chicago.

---

[66] McDonnell, "Sport – Lack of Condition Nearly Defeats Walker," *Detroit Times*, May 17, 1930, sports section.
[67] Kearns, Jack (Doc) as told to Oscar Farley, "The Million Dollar Gate," (The Macmillan Company, New York, 1966), p. 242. Runyon, Damon, "Damon Runyon Recites Fun Had at Louisville Fight," *Detroit Times*, May 22, 1930, sports section.
[68] McNeil, *op. cit.*

CHAPTER 22

MA AND THE MANASSA MAULER

I predict Jack Dempsey will return to the ring. No doubt you are wondering why I say so, and I am going to try to explain just that. Dempsey earned more than $2,000,000 as his end of the big gates he drew. Dempsey is a free-spender and gives away more money than a lot of bank presidents earn. His wife, Estelle Taylor, is a woman with big ideas. She wants to be a movie and stage star, no matter what the cost may be. She cost Dempsey plenty, and I'll tell you why.

Dempsey and Estelle made several pictures on the Pacific Coast that never were released. Dempsey paid for these. How long does it take to spend a million dollars in pictures? Dempsey and Estelle financed a road show, "The Big Fight," in which they co-starred last fall, and after running six weeks the show closed down. Jack paid these losses, also. He dropped $50,000 promoting boxing shows in Chicago. He pulled out of this two months ago, although they still use his name as the promoter.

Dempsey played at the Avalon and Capitol theaters in Chicago a week ago. I had several visits with him during this time, and incidentally, arranged to have him referee the boxing show at the Fargo Auditorium next Saturday. I rode in the taxicabs with Jack as he jumped back and forth between the theaters, doing six and eight shows a day. He ate sandwiches in the cab, as he didn't have time to sit down to an evening meal. He confided in me that he was tired of hopscotching around the country playing one-night stands, and was anxious to retire and live the life of a private citizen.

It is my contention that Dempsey isn't as well fixed financially as most folks are led to believe. If he were, he would not be engaged in his present occupation. They say he has a million-dollar trust fund, but no one has been able to find out what company it is with, or when it was taken out. Babe Ruth has a trust fund, and the company he has it with advertises it plenty. If Dempsey really has a trust fund, why doesn't his company advertise the fact? Personally, I think Dempsey is a little bit financially embarrassed; that's why I say he is going to return to the ring.

When Dempsey leaves Fargo next Saturday he is going to Chattanooga, from there to Nashville, and then on to Los Angeles to start training. I think this explains the entire situation. However, I am going to try to have Dempsey say a few words from the ring at the Fargo Auditorium next Saturday night regarding his future plans. Incidentally, this will be Dempsey's first appearance in North Dakota.[1]

— Jack Hurley

---

[1] Hurley, Jack, "Ring Rations," *Fargo Forum*, April 20, 1930, sports section. Hurley's

****

No sooner had Hurley gathered his belongings together, left behind his Duluth lodgings, and moved to Chicago in December 1929 when he began to hear rumors that Billy Petrolle was back training at the Silver Spray gym.

At first, Petrolle claimed his gym appearances were "just to keep the weight down." Billy said a return to the squared circle was the furthest thing from his mind because he was "a family man now and can't be bothered with fighting any more."[2]

When Petrolle retired in September 1929, he was physically and mentally exhausted. After his first loss to King Tut at Minneapolis in August 1928, his friends began dropping hints his days as a top performer were over, and he should retire before he was seriously injured. His subsequent surgery for an abscessed kidney only increased their pleas he give up the ring.

The grueling fights with Ray Miller and Jimmy Goodrich and the non-stop training grind leading up to his September 1929 bout with Tut in Detroit left Petrolle stale and lacking in stamina and determination. The beating Tut subsequently gave him was final straw which convinced Billy his friends were right. And so, following their advice, he retired.

Indeed, at the time, Petrolle saw no reason to continue his boxing career. He had built and paid for a beautiful $15,000 residence in an upscale neighborhood in Duluth. He also had purchased a home for his parents in Dilworth and established a trust fund so they would not have to worry after his father retired.

Petrolle somehow resisted the temptation to buy stocks during the boom leading up to the October 1929 stock market crash and instead invested his entire $75,000 savings in gilt-edged bonds. Rather than losing money like most people, his ultra-safe investments increased in value during the crisis. Consequently, as 1930 approached, he was well-fixed financially.

What Petrolle did not expect was how heavily his leisure time would weigh upon him. After a few weeks of hunting and roaming the North Dakota prairies, he returned to Duluth and found himself getting restless. Billy had no desire to hold an office job and no hobbies apart from boxing. To keep busy, he obtained a referee's license and started to train a few amateur prospects for their weekly bouts at the Silver Spray gym.

With 2-1/2 months of rest and relaxation under his belt, Petrolle began to

---

specific prediction was that Dempsey would fight Primo Carnera on his comeback. Dempsey did try a comeback, engaging in over 100 exhibition bouts between 1930-32, but by the time it was underway the clamor for a Carnera bout died down. Consequently, the author has edited out and modified the parts of Hurley's article referring to Primo. After being decisively beaten by King Levinsky in a four-round exhibition at Chicago on February 19, 1932, Dempsey abandoned his comeback without ever actually taking part in a "regulation" bout.

[2] Purcell, J. A., "Little Action Necessary for Top Condition," *Fargo Forum*, December 15, 1929, sports section. Campbell, Cubby, "Billy Petrolle Decides to Try Ring Comeback," *Duluth News Tribune*, December 13, 1929, sports section.

feel like his old self again. A few weeks of hard workouts and a couple of sparring sessions at the Silver Spray convinced him he still had the stuff to be a successful fighter. After all, at just under 25 he was hardly an old man, even by the rigorous standards of the prize ring.[3]

On December 12, 1929, Petrolle phoned Hurley in Chicago after a workout at to say he wanted to return to the ring and would be ready for a fight in two weeks. While still on the phone, Jack outlined a plan for Billy to engage in a series of warm-up bouts before challenging Tony Canzoneri, then recognized as the leading lightweight contender, in a bout to determine the right to meet the champion.[4]

The announcement of Petrolle's return proved to be a bit premature. The next day, after a conference with his wife, Billy said he would stay retired. It took another four weeks, until a second announcement on January 9, for Petrolle to convince Antoinette to allow him to fight again.[5]

By this time, Hurley was comfortably settled in Chicago and fully immersed in brokering the affairs of more than 60 fighters. Since Petrolle was essentially starting all over with fights paying only $200 to $250 per bout, they agreed that for the time being that Petrolle would remain in Duluth, and Jack would book Billy's fights out of his Chicago office just as he was doing for his other fighters.

Petrolle lost a close, ten-round newspaper decision to Jackie Purvis in his first comeback bout (two local newspapers had it for Purvis and one for Petrolle) at Indianapolis on January 28, 1930. Three weeks later, however, Billy got back on track with a three-round kayo of Joey Brooks in Louisville. Over the next seven months, Billy would engage in ten more fights against ordinary competition, winning nine by kayo and one by decision before achieving his goal of a bout with Canzoneri in September.

Meanwhile, Charley Retzlaff's success in the first quarter of 1930 had boxing fans in his native North Dakota and his adopted home of Duluth clamoring to see him fight. Retzlaff's one and only pro appearance in Fargo had been January 1, 1929. Charley's last fight at Duluth had been five months earlier on November 14, 1929, just before moving to Chicago.

In addition, Phil Terk had been struggling mightily to hold things together with his weekly amateur shows at the Silver Spray gym. Terk figured it was time for Hurley to bring Retzlaff home to give "ol' buddy Phil" a chance to earn a couple of decent paydays.

The National Athletic Club's first pro card of the year at Duluth on April 11, 1930, featured Retzlaff against Ludwig Haymann. Herr Haymann, the reigning German heavyweight champ, came to the United States in 1929

---

[3] McKenna, Lou, "Strain of Inactivity, Not Crash of Stock Market, Sent Petrolle on Comeback Trail," *St. Paul Pioneer Press*, January 25, 1931, sports section.

[4] Campbell, *op. cit.*

[5] Purcell, "Petrolle to Try Comeback," *Fargo Forum*, January 9, 1930, sports section.

with a respectable record, but failed to live up to his advanced billing. Even so, because of his prior ring experiences against such fighters as Paolino Uzcudun, Phil Scott, Tuffy Griffiths, and Franz Diener, local fans expected the German to provide a good test for their hero.

As Terk hoped, the spectacle of welcoming home the city's first heavyweight contender was an irresistible attraction. A record crowd of 6,000 paid an unprecendented $9,000 to see Retzlaff beat the German into submission with three seconds left in the opening round. Although it was a short fight, fans were satisfied they had seen a much better Retzlaff "than before he left to train in Chicago. He looks more like a fighter, moves around better, and shoots his punches faster and harder from all angles."[6]

On April 26, Hurley took Retzlaff to Fargo to fight veteran heavyweight Italian Jack Herman, of New York. Of particular interest to local fans was Petrolle's return to the Gateway City after an absence of more than two years. Billy was boxing Chicago lightweight Tony Sanders in the fifth bout of his comeback. In addition, as a special attraction, Hurley had arranged to have Jack Dempsey referee the Retzlaff-Herman bout.

Hurley first met the former champ in June 1927 at the signing of contract articles for Dempsey's fight with Jack Sharkey, which Hurley covered on special assignment for the *Fargo Forum*. The Fargo man was impressed with the ex-champ's congenial nature and the fact that Dempsey knew who he was when they were introduced. Hurley left with the sense that he had just met a compelling and forceful personality who "seems to know a little about everybody's affairs and always has a good word for everybody."[7]

Hurley got to know Dempsey better in Chicago when Alvis was the ex-champ's matchmaker the prior year. At the time, Hurley was helping Barney Abel furnish boxers from Ray's then-former stable to fill the empty slots in the preliminary bouts of Dempsey's Chicago Coliseum shows.

After Alvis left Dempsey to team up with Hurley, the partners continued working closely with the ex-champion and his business manager Leonard Sachs. Since both firms were located in the Burnham Building, they shared information on almost a daily basis. As mentioned earlier, it was Dempsey's office which recommended Hurley and Alvis to the American Legion for the Kentucky Derby boxing show.

At the time Hurley hired Dempsey for the Fargo show, the Manassa Mauler was in a period of transition. When he retired as a boxer in 1927, the former champion assumed his drawing power would fade rapidly and he would have to return to the task of "working for a living." With this in mind, he envisioned a future for himself as a boxing promoter along the lines of fistic impresario Tex Rickard.

---

[6] Macdonald, Sandy, "6,000 Customers Pay over $9,000 to See Local Boxing Show," *Duluth Herald*, April 12, 1930, sports section.

[7] Hurley, "Broadway Breezes," *Fargo Forum*, July 3, 1927, sports section.

Jack Hurley, flanked by Charley Retzlaff (left) and Bearcat Wright and Jackie Williams (right) prior to the April 11, 1930 show at Duluth. Retzlaff fought Ludwig Haymann in the main event. Wright and Williams were also featured on the card.

Jack Dempsey enjoys tea with Hurley's mother, Julia, on one of his Fargo visits.

Now, three years later, it was becoming clear that, even though his promoting career was at an end, he was still popular enough to make a comfortable living by just being Jack Dempsey. Instead of risking his own capital in a financially uncertain environment, the ex-champ could rake in the dough with virtually no risk by collecting fat guarantees in exchange for personal appearances, either as a vaudeville artist or as a guest referee.

In 1930, this phenomenon was still a novelty to the retired champion. As a former hobo who since had become accustomed to an extravagant lifestyle, Dempsey was obsessively driven by unpleasant memories from his hungry past and fear of losing all he had gained over the past decade. He still felt it necessary to look over his shoulder and ask "just how long will this popularity last? When will I have to go out and get a real job?"

Indeed, how long a sports idol could ride the crest of past glories and live in comfort was uncharted territory in 1930. Though ex-champs like John L. Sullivan, Jim Corbett, Jim Jeffries, and Jack Johnson had capitalized on their fame, none had relied on past reputation alone to accumulate wealth, at least not on the scale Dempsey aspired to and would eventually achieve.

The former titleholder, at this stage in his career, was inventing a formula to extend the shelf life of his fame beyond those of his predecessors and enable him to amass a fortune from personal appearances the rest of his life.

Dempsey arrived at Fargo on April 26 about six hours before the 9 p.m. boxing show was set to begin. Knowing the ex-champ to always be a "good sport," Hurley arranged to have him "picked up" in the city's only "paddy wagon." Eugene Fitzgerald, the *Fargo Forum*'s newly installed sports editor, described the scene:

> "Dempsey ... upon his arrival in Fargo Saturday afternoon ... was transported to his hotel in Fargo's 'Black Maria' from the Great Northern station. The 'Black Maria' is the police department's patrol wagon – or automobile, if you please. The car, driven by Andy Quinn, detective, was 'let out' with siren wide open. As the top heavy car swayed, Dempsey remarked: 'This guy's takin' us for a ride, eh?'
>
> "'Well, back home again,' Dempsey remarked as he stepped into the car. He greeted Chief of Police Madison with a 'Glad to know you Chief.' Upon alighting at the hotel, Dempsey attempted to remunerate the Fargo police head for the ride but was informed that 'Your money is no good in this town.' He thanked the chief for the ride and went direct to his quarters ...
>
> "Dempsey chatted about Fargo, inquiring how big the town was, what the people did for a livelihood and was this the best hotel in town. He went on to explain that he was a farmer once himself, having been reared on a farm where he 'jerked juice' and drove a

milk wagon.

"The reason for Dempsey's great popularity is not amazing after chatting with him. He is even greater than anticipated. Pictures don't do him justice. He really is 'better looking' than the camera shows him to be ... Dempsey was weary from the train ride and laid down for a short nap before dinner."[8]

On his way to dinner, Dempsey met privately in the hotel lobby with an elderly friend of Hurley's mother who was "just dying to meet Jack Dempsey." Years later, Hurley recalled the incident in a conversation with Seattle sportswriter Paul Rossi. Hurley watched from a distance as Dempsey, following instructions perfectly, found the lady waiting patiently to meet him in a remote alcove. The ex-champ greeted her "like a long lost friend" and "you could see the years melt off her face as she talked to him."

Hurley told Rossi that "Dempsey was always doing things like that."[9]

In the main bouts, both Retzlaff and Petrolle scored one-round kayos over Jack Herman and Tony Sanders, respectively. Despite "hurried endings in the two main events," Fargo fans went home happy because they had seen Dempsey in action as a referee and because the rest of the card was "exceptionally well balanced" and "crammed with action."

Financially, the program proved to be "by far the most successful fistic venture in North Dakota history." Approximately 3,900 fans paid $12,000 to see the show. To house what was probably the "greatest throng" that would ever pack the Fargo Auditorium, Terk and Hurley had supervised construction of special bleacher seating on the stage and along the walls, all at locations where seats had never been installed before.[10]

After paying Dempsey's standard $2,500 rate plus expenses for a small city show (shows in larger cities commanded up to $5,000), the promoters still realized a substantial profit. As a result of the success of his Fargo appearance, Hurley and Terk hired Dempsey to referee the main event

---

[8] Fitzgerald, Eugene, "Dempsey Given Novel Ride on Arrival Here," *Fargo Forum*, April 27, 1930, sports section.

[9] Author's conversation with Paul Rossi January 25, 2008. Rossi was a sportswriter for the *Seattle Post-Intelligencer*. Although not usually assigned to write about Hurley, Paul and Jack were close friends who spent a lot of time together socially in the 1960s.

[10] Fitzgerald, "New Yorker Is Disqualified in Opening Round," *Fargo Forum*, April 27, 1930, sports section. The *Forum* described the ending as a disqualification because Herman struggled to his feet at the count of nine and then lost his balance without being hit. A fighter is subject to disqualification if he goes down without being hit, but the better view in this case would seem to be that Herman was still feeling the effects of the original punch and the count would be regarded as continuing after the second "fall." In any event, the 1941 edition of the *Ring Record Book* lists the result as a one-round knockout.

The claim that the Retzlaff-Herman card was the most financially successful card in history may be true, but the Russie LeRoy-Pinkey Mitchell bout on January 14, 1926, which also reportedly drew over $12,000, was at least a close second.

between Retzlaff and Andres Castano in Duluth on May 16, 1930.[11]

After his Fargo engagement, Dempsey checked into the Mayo Clinic at Rochester, Minnesota to undergo surgery for an intestinal growth that had been troubling him for more than seven years. The Duluth card had to be postponed for one week as Jack took longer than expected to recover from the procedure. Doctor Charles Mayo, founder of the clinic, was one of several physicians who accompanied the ex-champ to Duluth.[12]

A week before the re-scheduled show, Dempsey's secretary, Harry Wall, and his last boxing manager, Leo P. Flynn, both died unexpectedly. At first, Terk feared he would have to cancel the card so Jack could attend the funerals in New York. This concern was relieved, however, when Dempsey wired that "though deeply grieved at death of former associates, I feel you have already been greatly inconvenienced by first postponement of your boxing program due to my illness. The 'show must go on,' you know."

Terk told the *News Tribune* "whatever has been my opinion of Jack Dempsey in the past, his thoroughbred adherence to the trouper's creed, 'on with the show,' makes me worship the man. I don't know of a more

---

[11] As a footnote to the introduction of Andres Castano in the text, and to sports history in general, the author offers a slightly edited portion of an email penned by eminent sports historian J Michael Kenyon:

"There is no doubt that the Andres (or Andre) Castana (or Castano), who fought Retzlaff in Duluth was the fellow who wrestling promoters throughout the Americas described, during most of the 1920s and 1930s, as 'Andreas Castano, the Spanish wrestler and boxer.' The records of famous wrestlers like Jim Londos, Stanislaus Zbyszko, Wladek Zbyszko and Stecher, among others, contain matches with Castano.

"Whether billed as Don Andreas Castano, Pedro Castano, Don Jose Castano, or just plain Andreas Castano, this 203 to 210-pounder was a first-cabin 'jobber,' or 'fall guy' in the mat trade, working for the top promoters in the U.S. (Lou Daro in Los Angeles, Julius Sigel in Texas, Tom Packs in St. Louis, Ray Fabiani in Philadelphia, Jack Curley in New York) until he wandered down to Cuba in 1927 and began his 3-4 year stint as an 'opponent' – and not even a very stout one – for heavyweights of all stripes.

"The only fighter of note he ever 'beat' was Harry Wills, who made the mistake of hitting him after the first-round bell in Mexico City. Castanos thought about it a few seconds, probably was coached by his corner, and took a dive. The referee went along with the nonsense and disqualified Wills, who flattened Castano in a return match after punishing him, horribly, for seven minutes.

"It is a good thing that Hurley and Phil Terk somehow got Jack Dempsey to miss Leo Flynn's funeral and show up in Duluth May 23, 1930 – otherwise the two promoters might well have been arrested and sent to jail. The only people resembling fighters on the show were the referees: Billy Petrolle on the undercard and Dempsey in the main event.

"But Castano, who probably got tired of diving to the canvas to lose boxing matches, went back to the mat game and enjoyed his finest years in the 1930s. A longtime ally and associate of the famed Zbyszko brothers, Stanislaus and Wladek, he followed them to Argentina in 1933-34 and became a box-office sensation while winning a major international wrestling tournament. As far as I know, he never came back to North America to wrestle. Who knows? He may have been a romantic and gone back to Spain to get his ass shot off in the civil war."

[12] Menke, Frank G., "Drops Summer Bouts Here," *Chicago Evening American*, May 15, 1930, sports section (surgery was for an intestinal growth). "Doctor May to Accompany Dempsey to Duluth Friday," *Duluth News Tribune*, May 21, 1930, sports section.

heartbreaking 'spot' to be in than Dempsey found himself in today, but he was still big enough not to forget a measly boxing promoter like me."[13]

On the night of May 23, 1930, Dempsey entered the Duluth Amphitheater before his official duties were to begin, took a seat in the bleachers during one of the preliminary bouts, and patiently spent the entire time before the main event "inscrib[ing] his signature on business cards, photos and what not" for all who approached.

The main event itself turned out to be a virtual repeat of Dempsey's refereeing duties in Fargo. Jack once again tolled out the fatal "ten" count over Charley Retzlaff's opponent for the evening, Andres Castano, in the first round. A couple of rights to the body, followed by "a right cross high to the jaw ... sent the Spaniard crumbling to the canvas" where Castana remained until the count was finished.

After the fight, it was a full 15 minutes before Dempsey was "able to get out of the ring, as the mob swept upward through ropes with eagerly stretched hands ... Jack, smiling as if he were enjoying the reception, exchanged a lot of banter with the fans" and "grabbed one and all within reach, with a 'Glad to know you,' for each handshake."

The chaos continued as Hurley, along with several ushers and handlers "vainly attempted to keep the crowd back to get Dempsey out of the ring. They finally eased him out one corner, half lifting and half carrying the big fellow, with hands still clawing about for the Mauler's great 'kayo right.'"

A crowd of over 6,000, which "filled all but two small corners of the Amphitheater," paid $12,000, shattering records set a month earlier when Retzlaff defeated Haymann. Despite another disappointing main event, the fans again went home in a happy frame of mind. The Dempsey magic had saved a second Terk and Hurley show. The ex-champ had more than earned his hefty fee, which this time amounted to $2,750 plus expenses.[14]

---

[13] Campbell, "Jack Promises to Fulfill His Date in Duluth," *Duluth News Tribune*, May 20, 1930, sports section. It is likely that if Phil Terk had any prior ill feelings toward Jack Dempsey, they were connected with the charges that Dempsey had been a draft dodger during World War I. Jack was acquitted of the charges in a celebrated trial, but some anti-Dempsey sentiment still lingered in certain circles up until World War II. These sentiments were pretty well laid to rest at that time when Dempsey, well into his 40s, volunteered for service in the Coast Guard where he served honorably for four years.

The distress and insecurity that Dempsey felt as a result of these charges and his desire to overcome their stigma undoubtedly contributed to Jack's almost compulsive need to meet new people and make new friends. These factors, together with his fear of poverty and the underlying restlessness which was part of his nature, all had much to do with his ease in being able to adapt to life as a barnstorming referee and personal appearance specialist. Unfortunately, Dempsey's domestic life suffered as a result and he went through three marriages and numerous relationships until he settled down to a less nomadic lifestyle after his fourth marriage in 1958.

[14] Campbell, "Charley Retzlaff Kayoes Castana Within 2 Minutes," *Duluth News Tribune*, May 24, 1930, section. "Record Crowd Sees Retzlaff Stop Castana," *Duluth Herald*, May 24, 1930, sports section. Since both Fargo and Duluth realized record high gross receipts of

A few days later, Cubby Campbell explained why Hurley tried to protect Dempsey from the crowd. The *News Tribune* sports editor wrote that "the enthusiastic fans who fairly 'mobbed' Dempsey at the end of the fight card did not realize that they were causing him considerable anguish and physical pain." When the Manassa Mauler "finally managed to reach the dressing room," one of his doctors made "a hurried examination of the stitches from [his] recent operation" to make sure they had not torn loose.[15]

Before leaving Duluth, Dempsey told Sandy Macdonald of the *Herald* that he had earned $60,000 as a part-time referee during the past year, more than enough to cover losses he had incurred in the promoting business. Jack figured if he devoted himself to refereeing and personal appearances full-time, he could gross $200,000 a year, from which he would deduct $60,000 in expenses. Dempsey reasoned if he could net $140,000 a year for personal appearances, his days as a promoter were probably over.

In addition, Dempsey said he would not rule out a return to the ring, especially if Max Schmeling of Germany defeated Jack Sharkey in the upcoming heavyweight title bout. The fight, set for June 12, 1930, was the final elimination to decide Gene Tunney's successor. If Max won, Dempsey might try and win the crown back for the U. S. Macdonald felt Jack was "loathe to let the impression get out he is never going to fight again, for that would dim the limelight of popularity in which he is presently basking."[16]

The events in Fargo and Duluth presented a full picture of the charisma

---

approximately $12,000 for the shows Dempsey refereed, it is interesting to contrast how the two cities set their new records.

In 1930, the Duluth/Superior area had more than a three-fold advantage in population (256,000 versus 72,000) and an arena with seating about twice the capacity (Duluth Amphitheater at 7,000 versus the Fargo Auditorium at 3,900 "with help from a shoehorn") of the Fargo/Moorhead area. Despite these disparities, the smaller community around Fargo was able to draw as large a dollar gate as the more populated Duluth area.

Obviously, Hurley's eight years as a promoter in Fargo had not been without beneficial effect. Over the years, the Fargo boxing public had become accustomed to seeing good boxing and was willing to pay for it. As we have seen in prior chapters, by presenting increasingly good shows over a long period of time, Hurley, and later Phil Terk, had gradually raised the price of their shows from a $3-$2-$1 scale to the $5-$3-$1 level. The goodwill that the promoters developed over the years paid off.

Duluth presented a different proposition. Years of poor quality boxing shows haphazardly presented by prior promoters had dampened patrons' interest in boxing. After less than three years with Hurley and Terk as promoters, the sport had not yet generated the same enthusiasm in Duluth as it enjoyed in Fargo. Consequently, ticket prices for the Dempsey show in Duluth still were scaled at $3-$2-$1. The larger arena allowed promoters to make up the difference in price with a larger volume of ticket sales. Both cities hosted successful shows with Dempsey as referee, but differences in history, population, and size of the arena had required the promoters to devise independent marketing strategies for each.

[15] Campbell, "Sport News Gossip," *Duluth News Tribune*, May 25, 1930, sports section.
[16] McDonald, "Will Box Schmeling if the Latter Defeats the Boston Orator," *Duluth Herald*, May 24, 1930, sports section. This article is also the source for information that Dempsey was paid $2,750 to referee in Duluth.

and charm that so endeared Dempsey to fans and promoters alike.

Dempsey knew he was being well paid for what he was doing, and he went out of his way to give value to the promoter. To Jack, an appearance was more than just an appointment to be at a particular place at a particular time. Wherever he agreed to appear, Dempsey lent himself wholeheartedly to whatever the promoter had in mind. The agenda might include publicity stunts, radio appearances, visits to schools or orphanages, or just allowing the promoter to be a "big shot" as he hosted Jack around the city.

The Manassa Mauler truly enjoyed meeting new people, making friends, and seeing they had a good time in his presence. The ex-champion had a way of connecting with whomever he met and finding a common experience they shared. He had the ability to convey the feeling that every handshake was an event just as important to him as it was to the person whose hand he was shaking. In Jack's mind, he was making a new friend with each handshake given, each picture posed, and each autograph signed.

There was none of the prima donna in Dempsey. Having been a promoter himself, he understood that a promoter was at the mercy of a countless number of potential events that were out of his direct control. As a result, once Jack signed a contract, he did his best to honor it. Promoters came to know that Dempsey kept his promises and could be counted on to be there and exert his best efforts to help "put the show over."

As time went on, Dempsey's celebrity status would rise to a level akin to that of a natural resource upon whom sports promoters and sponsors all over the world could call to boost sales for any show they had planned.

With the arrival of 1930's summer season, Hurley became disenchanted with the monotonous tedium of overseeing the affairs of 75 fighters in Chicago while Ray Alvis basked in the limelight as pilot of welterweight champion Young Jack Thompson. Alvis was out of the office from June 1 until the middle of July, taking Thompson west for lucrative non-title fights in Omaha, Portland, Los Angeles, and San Francisco. In Ray's absence, Jack was left in full charge of the partnership's boxing stable.

Hurley had never been a man to stand for routine either in his business or personal affairs. Now, with Alvis taking Thompson on tour, Jack felt like an office boy, chained to a desk where he was constantly on the phone in an effort to keep his ungrateful boxers busy, lest they hit him up for advances on earnings that might never materialize.

Given Hurley's penchant for wanting to control a fighter's every move, it is easy to picture how difficult it was for him to jump into a nerve-wracking situation where he had to handle 75 different personalities coming from so many diverse backgrounds. To meet expenses, Jack had to schedule 20 to 25 fights for his battlers every week. Just keeping the percentage cuts of all the fighters in good order was almost a full-time task in itself.[17]

---

[17] Campbell, "Cubby Campbell's Column," *Duluth News Tribune*, September 15, 1930,

The situation came to a head in June when two of Alvis' fighters, Tony Herrera and Spug Myers, refused to accept bouts Hurley had booked for them. The first dispute was settled when Herrera cooled down and finally agreed to the contest Jack had offered. Myers, however, refused to accept two fights scheduled within a week of each other on the grounds the bouts were too close together. Hurley disagreed and figured Spug would have little trouble because both fights were against mediocre competition.

Hurley long had held the opinion that "Alvis spoiled and babied the fighters, while I make them fight and gather in the coin." Jack gave Myers the option of either accepting both fights or not fighting at all. When Spug refused to accept them both, Hurley ordered Myers out of the office until Alvis returned from his tour with Thompson in July.[18]

At the same time he was having trouble with his partner's fighters, Hurley's own assets, Billy Petrolle and Charley Retzlaff, were going strong. Petrolle had won eight straight bouts and was scheduled to box Paddy Walthier on August 12 at the Congress Arcade Stadium in his first Chicago-area appearance since his retirement. It was rumored a Petrolle victory against Walthier might land Billy the first major bout of his comeback campaign, a fight against Tony Canzoneri at the Chicago Stadium.[19]

On June 5, 1930, Retzlaff created a minor sensation in Detroit by kayoing Tom Sayers in one round on the undercard of a show which headlined Primo Carnera's four-round knockout of KO Christner. In the dressing room afterward, matchmaker Scotty Montieth offered Charley a main event against a leading contender, but Hurley declined on grounds that Retzlaff still needed a few more fights before he would be ready.

With Petrolle and Retzlaff on the verge of major breakthroughs, Hurley decided the time was right to end his partnership with Alvis. Jack sensed that Ray, too, was ready for the break-up, not only because of the friction between Jack and the members of Alvis' stable, but also because Young Jack Thompson was preparing for his first title defense.

Hurley knew Alvis would welcome not having to share his end of Thompson's first big purse with Jack. While Ray felt his charge would retain the title for a couple of defenses, Hurley doubted Young Jack would hold the crown long enough to make a lot of money. Now that Petrolle was fit once again, Jack figured he could do better with Billy and Retzlaff by

---

sports section. Hurley, "Sports Editor's Mailbox" (letter from Hurley to Cubby Campbell), *Duluth News Tribune*, June 10, 1930, sports section (having to hustle to keep fighters busy to avoid loans; stable at 75 fighters at this time). Campbell, "Sport Gossip," *Duluth News Tribune*, May 23, 1930, sports section (have to keep 20 to 25 battlers busy every week and difficulty of keeping percentage cuts in good order).

[18] Campbell, "Cubby Campbell's Column," *Duluth News Tribune*, September 21, 1930, sports section.

[19] Petrolle would win two more fights after the Walthier bout to raise his winning streak to 11 straight up to the Canzoneri bout.

himself rather than splitting the purses of all three fighters with Alvis.[20]

On August 7, Hurley announced "Ray Alvis and myself have parted company ... just as we started, each taking his own men ... we are and always will be friends." Although the exact terms of the dissolution were not announced at the time, Jack commented that "I got a lucky break when Jack Thompson won the title because when we broke up, my end on Thompson's earnings amounted to ten-grand."

Three weeks later, Hurley elaborated on the break-up with *Fargo Forum* sports editor Eugene Fitzgerald: "I simply made a good deal with Alvis. I retained my original stable of fighters and sold him a half interest back in his own stable." It is likely if Jack did receive $10,000 from Alvis, the sum was intended as a full settlement of the partnership's dissolution, encompassing the liquidation of Jack's interests in Thompson and the rest of Ray's stable as well as Alvis' interests in Petrolle and Retzlaff.[21]

As expected, Petrolle had no trouble against Walthier August 12, kayoing the game Chicago youngster in the fourth round. A week later, matchmaker Nate Lewis announced he had signed Billy and Tony Canzoneri to a ten-round bout on September 11, 1930, as part of a show arranged to honor Chicago Stadium builder Paddy Harmon.

Harmon had died virtually penniless on July 22 in a tragic auto accident, after having invested all his money in the Stadium. At the time of his death, he still owned shares in the Stadium corporation but, due to economic conditions, the stock's value was problematic. Officials of the corporation promised to donate all profits from the show to a trust fund set up for Paddy's four-year-old daughter, Patricia.[22]

Landing the match with Canzoneri was a coup for Hurley and Petrolle. Tony, destined to be remembered as an all-time ring great, was an ex-featherweight champ who had outgrown that division in 1929. He quickly cut a wide swath through the lightweight division and had already signed for a lightweight title match with new champ Al Singer before agreeing to fight Billy. Tony's only defeat in his last 15 bouts had been a decision loss to Jackie (Kid) Berg, who Petrolle had kayoed at Chicago in 1928.

Al Singer, a 21-year-old slugger from New York's Lower East Side, had annexed the title in a sensational upset by knocking out champion Sammy Mandell in 1:46 of the first round on July 17, 1930. A product of the same Jewish ghetto as the revered former champion Benny Leonard, Singer was being touted as the "new Leonard." His first title defense against Canzoneri was expected to sell out Madison Square Garden because of the natural

---

[20] Campbell, *op. cit.*, September 15, 1930, sports section.
[21] Fitzgerald, "Petrolle Has Big Ring Chance of Career Ahead," *Fargo Forum*, August 31, 1930, sports section. Hurley, "Sports Editor's Mailbox" (letter from Jack Hurley to Cubby Campbell dated August 7, 1930), *Duluth News Tribune*, August 10, 1930, sports section.
[22] "Paddy Harmon Died Penniless, Friends Reveal," *Chicago Daily News,* August 12, 1930, sports section.

ethnic rivalry between the Jewish and Italian communities.

Critics were at a loss to figure out why Canzoneri had taken the fight with Petrolle when Tony had already signed to fight the champion. Though most predicted a Canzoneri victory because they thought Billy was on the downgrade, they still regarded the Fargo slugger as a dangerous foe and the hardest hitting lightweight in the business. A win over Petrolle would gain Tony nothing, while a loss would jeopardize the Singer title fight.[23]

Reporters believed Petrolle, on the other hand, had everything to gain and nothing to lose. A victory would immediately put Billy back in the middle of the lightweight title picture, while a loss would leave his position in the rankings unchanged.

In response to the critics, Canzoneri explained he took the bout because the money was good and the match was sure to make him sharp for the Singer fight. Tony was grateful to Paddy Harmon for promoting his three most important Chicago bouts, including his 1929 lightweight title fight with Sammy Mandell. In addition, Tony was angry over the split decision he had lost to Jackie (Kid) Berg in New York and wanted to prove his superiority over Berg by defeating the man who had knocked the Kid out.[24]

Despite the opinions to the contrary, Hurley and Petrolle did not share the view Billy had little to lose. To them, the Canzoneri fight was a moment of truth. After four months of retirement and eight months of fighting for chump change on the backwater circuit, it was time to find out if the Fargo Express was ready for the main track. If he did not show well against Tony, then there was no reason for Petrolle to continue fighting.

A crowd of 13,260 who paid $45,668 watched as 6-to-5 underdog Petrolle, weighing 134-3/4 pounds, decisively whipped Canzoneri, at 132-1/14, "after ten torrid rounds" by standing "in as close as possible with Tony and slugg[ing] away punch for punch." Canzoneri wobbled Billy with two left hooks in round two, but "after that Petrolle steadily forged ahead, banging away with both fists, meanwhile protecting himself cleverly with a weaving, bobbing style of boxing."[25]

In the third round, Petrolle opened a gash over Canzoneri's right eye. In the fourth round, a "left to the body, followed by a left and a right to the head" shook Tony up badly. Canzoneri rallied to win the sixth and seventh

---

[23] "Punchers May Spill Dope at Stadium on Thursday," *Chicago Evening Post*, September 6, 1930, sports section.

[24] Murphy, Mike, "Canzoneri and Lomski Favored to Win Battles," *Chicago Daily News*, September 10, 1930, sports section. Smith, Wilfrid, "Canzoneri Bout Opens Stadium's Fistic Campaign," *Chicago Tribune*, September 7, 1930, sports section.

[25] Fry, Kenneth D., "Petrolle, Levinsky, Win Bouts," *Chicago Evening Post*, September 12, 1930, sports section. Murphy, "Veteran, Floored in Fifth, Unable to Continue; Tony Slipping?" *Chicago Daily News*, September 12, 1930, sports section. Dunkley, Charles, W. (AP), "Express Batters New Yorker During Six Out of 10 Rounds," *Duluth News Tribune*, September 12, 1930, sports section.

rounds, but Billy came on in the last three rounds to insure his victory. "Tony seemed to be staggering at the end of the battle, and he was bleeding badly at the mouth and from the cut over his eye."

According to the *Chicago Evening Post*, "One of the judges gave the fight to Canzoneri by a slight margin, but Referee Phil Collins and the other judge ruled for Petrolle. Canzoneri tossed more punches but Petrolle was landing cleaner and harder blows." The Associated Press and all six Chicago daily newspapers scored the fight for Billy.[26]

Stadium officials announced slightly over $10,000 had been raised for Patricia Harmon. For their efforts, Canzoneri received 25 percent of the net gate and Petrolle 15 percent.

Afterward, Cubby Campbell explained the strategy Hurley had devised to help Petrolle win the fight:

> "'Canzoneri was a smarter fighter than I figured he was,' stated the Colonel, 'but nevertheless Petrolle fought one of the smartest fights of his career ...'
>
> "According to Hurley, Canzoneri is the type of fighter who leans forward, with hands swinging inertly at his sides, inviting a punch. When this ruse works, Tony swarms in with a flurry of blows. Petrolle stepped into the ring under orders to make Canzoneri fight Billy's style of fighting instead of his own. When exchanges started Billy was ordered to be sure and throw more blows than Tony, never back up, and maneuver him into a corner before attempting a solid knockout punch.
>
> "... Billy followed orders perfectly, cuffing and mauling and outpunching Tony at every exchange. These tactics were followed during the early rounds with the result that Petrolle was outscoring the eastern flash. It was not until the ninth and tenth rounds that 'Petrolle was told to try for a knockout ... Canzoneri took a terrific beating, but he never allowed Billy to get set for a finishing punch."[27]

Petrolle's victory over the leading lightweight contender immediately returned him to the top echelon of the division. Four days later, Hurley announced an agreement with matchmaker Tom McArdle for Billy to fight a ten-rounder against Jackie (Kid) Berg on October 10, 1930, at Madison Square Garden. According to McArdle, if Petrolle defeated Berg, Billy would take Canzoneri's place as challenger in the lightweight title bout scheduled in November against Al Singer.[28]

---

[26] Fry, *op. cit.*
[27] Campbell, *op. cit.*, September 17, 1930, sports section.
[28] Fitzgerald, "Petrolle Will Meet Berg in Title Contest," *Fargo Forum*, September 16, 1930,

The Berg fight was Petrolle's first Garden appearance since March 1928.

Almost unbelievably, Berg had won 26 of 27 fights since Billy stopped him two years earlier, with only a draw against Stanislaus Loayza spoiling his otherwise perfect record. Jackie's crowning achievement during the period was a ten-round decision victory in London over Mushy Callahan in February 1930 to annex the world's junior welterweight title.

Although New York state did not recognize "junior" titles, Berg's grim determination, non-stop punching style, and ability to absorb punishment nevertheless made him the darling of New York boxing fans and writers. Disputed wins against Canzoneri and Kid Chocolate had proven that most local boxing judges favored Berg's cuffing, windmill approach over the less busy but sharper punching of more conventional boxers.

On the afternoon of October 10, both fighters weighed in well under the junior welterweight limit of 140 pounds: Berg at 135-3/4 pounds and Petrolle at 137 pounds. Jackie's world title would be at stake. If Billy won, he would be the new junior welterweight champion in all parts of the world except New York.

In a bout which "easily could have been called a draw, or, as many thought, a victory for Petrolle," 11,646 customers paid $35,633 to watch Berg receive the official decision over Billy. It was "a stirring affair with plenty of lusty, unrestrained socking, but little progress was made in settling the question of supremacy between them ... The official ballots were not released ... but it is safe to say that Berg's margin was as narrow as a back alley in the Limehouse district of his own London town."[29]

Although scoring was not disclosed at the time, it was later learned judges George Patrick and George Kelly favored Berg, while referee Arthur Donovan scored the bout for Billy.[30]

Even as a narrow majority of ringside reporters agreed with the judges' decision, some writers voiced their astonishment in no uncertain terms. Harry Grayson, of the *New York Telegram*, was especially outspoken in his displeasure with the verdict:

> "The system of winning a fight by taking a terrific beating was introduced at Madison Square Garden last night. Jack Kid Berg could not have possibly been given the verdict over the battle-scarred Billy Petrolle for any other reason. The Italian with the tattooed forearms was the Fargo Express of old, but was the victim of what is known as a local decision ...
>
> "The Whitechapel Windmill took a solid licking in a battle as

---

p. 11.

[29] Dayton, Alfred, "Berg Takes Close Verdict," *New York Sun*, October 11, 1930, sports section.

[30] Fitzgerald, "Sport Whirligig," *Fargo Forum*, October 19, 1930, sports section.

savagely fought as any the old-timers could recall. How he stood up under it is a mystery. Petrolle clearly captured six of the ten rounds – the second, fourth, fifth, seventh, eighth, and ninth. The other four went to Berg, but only the opener was credited to him for any other reasons than crowding and mauling.

"Decided as a boxing match should be decided – on the number of clean punches and actual damage done, the contest was one-sided ... Petrolle, a corking hitter, gave a remarkable exhibition of sharp shooting. He chiefly concentrated his heavy attack on the Briton's body. He buried his left fist there repeatedly, pumped his right hand to the heart and scored with both weapons to the head all the way along the route ...

"Although jarred and rocked time after time, the stout-hearted boy from London's ghetto never stopped charging. He threw more punches than Petrolle, but they were light taps and cuffs after the early rounds."[31]

Paul Gallico, *New York Daily News* sports editor, attended the Berg-Petrolle fight with his newspaper's boxing writer, Jack Farrell, who was scoring the bout for publication in the next day's sports section. In a remarkable discussion with his editor, Farrell admitted he was scoring rounds for Berg, not because Berg was winning them, but to keep his article in line with how he believed the judges were going to score the fight! Two days later, Gallico wrote about the fight and his discussion with Farrell:

"In Madison Square Garden I was more impressed with the bravery of young Berg than I was with his prize fighting. I had a great argument with Jackie Farrell all through the brawl. I was scoring rounds for Petrolle and he was giving them to Berg and then we'd wrangle and I'd point out Petrolle's clean, sharp hitting, his volleys of left hooks to the middle that never missed their mark, his uppercuts that were straightening Berg up as he came in as compared to Berg's taps and cuffs and those silly pattings in the face he would give Petrolle in the clinches, and Jackie (who was doing the round by round and had to be careful) would say, 'Lissen; these chumps around here think that's fighting. If Berg were fighting outside of New York, he'd lose tonight, and he'd have lost the Chocolate fight too. You can score rounds for Petrolle, enough to give him the fight, same thing, stepping around and pasting Berg both hands, but those guys just glue their eyes on Berg's arms and every time he moves them they score points for

---

[31] Grayson, Harry, "Petrolle Deals Berg Solid Licking but Loses Decision," *New York Telegram*, October 11, 1930, sports section.

Petrolle (right) hooks a left while Jackie (Kid) Berg jabs in their 1930 fight at Madison Square Garden, won by Berg in a disputed decision.

Berg's jab falls short as Petrolle pulls back.

him.'

"What I did admire however, was Berg's courage in the face of a relentless and painful attack to his body. One lost track of the left hooks that Petrolle dug into his belly, but one couldn't lose track of that pale determined face. I realize that a pugilist is, by the very nature of his calling expected to be brave, but Berg's feat of never taking a backward step in the face of ten rounds of punching from the hardest hooking lightweight in the ring was, in its way, a minor epic in determination. I didn't think he won, but he certainly gave a thrill."[32]

Gallico's prose called into question not only the correctness of the Berg-Petrolle verdict, but also the competency of the commission-appointed judges. It also went a long way to explain the trouble that Petrolle had experienced in winning a decision in New York. In seven prior decision bouts in the Garden State, Billy had never been returned a winner.

In particular, Farrell's observations lent support to Hurley's long-held belief that boxing judges were in the same class as the politically chosen commissioners who appointed them. Both were amateurs who did not know the first thing about boxing. In Hurley's experience, judges were usually "high-grade politicians" who either did not understand the finer points of the game or were afraid to render a decision as they saw it. Instead, they usually listened to the crowd and rendered their decisions accordingly.

According to Hurley, the solution for bad verdicts was to eliminate judges and leave the business of rendering decisions to the referee who usually had to know something about the sport to receive his appointment.[33]

As a result of Berg's victory, Madison Square Garden officials decided to go through with plans to have Canzoneri, rather than Petrolle, fight Al Singer for the lightweight title on November 14, 1930. In a remarkable upset, Tony stunned boxing fans by knocking Singer out in 66 seconds of the first round to become the new champ.

In losing to Canzoneri, Singer earned the dubious distinctions of having the shortest reign of any titleholder to date (three months and 28 days) and being the only champion to win and lose his title by first-round knockouts.

Although he lost the decision, Petrolle's performance convinced Garden matchmaker Tom McArdle that the Fargo Express' two-fisted, walk-in style of fighting could still send New York's boxing fans flowing through the turnstiles. As a result, he signed Billy to face Jimmy (Baby Face) McLarnin November 21, 1930. In signing the match, McArdle guaranteed McLarnin 27-1/2 percent and Billy 22-1/2 of net receipts.

---

[32] Gallico, Paul, Gallico's Sunday column (title unavailable), *New York Daily News*, October 12, 1930, sports section.

[33] Hurley, "Ring Rations," *Fargo Forum*, November 9, 1930, sports section.

After a losing bid against lightweight champion Sammy Mandell 2-1/2 years before, McLarnin had defeated Mandell twice in non-title bouts and won 11 of 12 fights against the best fighters in the lightweight and welterweight divisions. His lone loss, a technical knockout to Ray Miller in Detroit, had subsequently been avenged by a decision win. In the course of this stretch, McLarnin had moved up to the welterweight class and won all eight of his New York fights, including five by early-round knockouts.

McLarnin was widely regarded as the best boxer in the world and, along with Kid Berg, New York's greatest drawing card among the smaller divisions. Jack Kofoed, of the *New York Post*, called Jimmy "the greatest little bit of fighting machinery in the world." Don Skene in the *Herald Tribune* agreed, terming him "the greatest fighter, pound for pound, in the game." The *American*'s Ed Frayne went even further, pegging him "the greatest fighter of all time" and "the super-fighter of the ages."[34]

Boxing experts agreed McLarnin had all the qualities of a truly great fighter – experience, punch, stamina, heart, speed, and generalship. He was an expert boxer, able to move swiftly or stand his ground as the situation demanded. A master at feinting, Jimmy had perfect judgment of distance which allowed him to slip punches by inches and step in with crushing counter punches with either hand. His best punch was a straight right-hand which he delivered flat-footed, leveraged with the entire weight of his body.

Hurley previously had a chance to match Petrolle against McLarnin in Detroit for a guarantee of $15,000 or 25 percent of the net gate when both fighters were "hot" two years earlier. Jack had held out for $20,000 or a privilege of 30 percent, and negotiations broke down. At the time, Jack thought the match would draw a "hundred grand," and he wanted to make as much as possible for a bout he feared Petrolle might lose.[35]

This time, Hurley again was reluctant to rush into the match. It was not until Petrolle begged for the bout that Jack decided to accept it. Billy argued that even though McLarnin outweighed him a few pounds, Jimmy could not hit hard enough to hurt him. In fact, Petrolle believed he punched much harder than Jimmy, and his 51 kayos opposed to McLarnin's 15 proved it. In Billy's words, "He'll never come up to my half-a-hundred or more knockouts if he keeps on fighting until he is 80."[36]

In the end, Petrolle's confidence was the deciding factor which convinced Hurley to accept the match. Jack's only question to Garden

---

[34] Kofoed, Jack, "Petrolle Offers Second Miracle to Fight Patrons," *New York Evening Post*, November 22, 1930, sports section. Skene, Don, "Fighting Heart Enables Irish Boxer to Last," *New York Herald Tribune*, November 22, 1930, p. 16. Frayne, Ed, "Knockout of Billy Tonight Is Not Unlikely," *New York American*, November 21, 1930, p. 10.

[35] Campbell *op. cit.*, November 23, 1930, sports section.

[36] *Ibid.* (Petrolle had to beg Hurley for the McLarnin match). Igoe, Hype, "McLarnin Go Sought by Petrolle," *New York Evening Journal*, October 9, 1930, sports section (Petrolle's comparison of his punching power with that of McLarnin).

officials before he signed was whether McLarnin had used an uppercut in his last fight. When he heard Jimmy hadn't, Hurley signed on the dotted line. Jack had a strategy in mind to beat the Irishman which was more likely to succeed if an uppercut was not a regular part of Jimmy's repertoire.[37]

The consensus was that Petrolle was a lamb being led to the slaughter. Joe Williams of the *New York Telegram* figured Billy would be "a soft one" and that "the Irisher shouldn't have much trouble pounding his way to victory." Harry Grayson, also of the *Telegram*, said that the fight was "another striking mismatch stuffed down the public's throat." Jack Kofoed predicted that "Petrolle will finish on the floor in about the same state as a Bismarck herring after having been packed in a barrel for several weeks."[38]

The minute Hurley signed the contract New York writers accused him of making the match just for the money. In their opinion, he was carrying on in the grand tradition of that lowest form of boxing vermin – the greedy manager who would offer his fighter to the lions just to turn a quick buck.[39]

Stung by the publicity about what a mismatch the bout would be, Hurley lashed back with a vengeance, claiming McLarnin was a quitter. "We know how to fight McLarnin and, believe me, Billy will be right on him from the opening bell," Jack told reporters. "He won't box, but he'll fight.

"Everybody laughed when I came in here with Jack Thompson and said he would beat McLarnin. The officials didn't give the fight to Thompson but of lot of people thought he won. And Thompson had to take off ten pounds in eight days to get the fight. What did McLarnin do in that fight? He dogged it. What's more, he sent in several low ones. If he hits Petrolle low Billy will hit him back in the same spot. You can print that, too.

"Billy will out-game McLarnin. You wait and see. They don't come any gamer than my boy. He won't call it a night if he's cut under an eye, like McLarnin against Miller in Detroit. Billy went along with King Tut, a good puncher if there ever was one, when he had two eyes worse than McLarnin's in Detroit.

"Who did McLarnin ever lick to become such a great fighter? Only a lot of scared kids and veterans ready for the scrap heap. McLarnin has gained

---

[37] Frayne, "Petrolle Wins Decision over Jim M'Larnin," *New York American*, November 22, 1930, sports section. Hurley last had seen McLarnin fight Young Jack Thompson in May 1930. Since then, Jimmy had engaged in just one bout, a sensational kayo over Al Singer in September. As the text will discuss, Jack planned to have Petrolle use a bob-and-weave defense against Jimmy, a style vulnerable to an uppercut. Hurley felt Jimmy's failure to use the uppercut tilted the odds in Billy's favor against the Irishman, and he wanted to make sure before he signed the contract that McLarnin had not added the uppercut to his arsenal.

[38] Williams, Joe, "Garden Fans See Epic Fight," *New York Telegram*, November 21, 1930, sports section. Grayson, "Fistic Stars Permitted to Choose Garden Opponents," *New York Telegram*, November 17, 1930, p. 15. Kofoed, *op. cit.*

[39] Campbell, *op. cit.*

such a reputation as a killer that most of the boys who fight him are scared to death when they get into the ring; beaten before the bell rings.

"Petrolle doesn't scare. He thinks he can hit just as hard as the Irishman, and he is sure he can take it better than McLarnin. What if Billy is giving away a few pounds? He has been doing that all his life. When he was just a 128-pounder he whipped tough lightweights and made them like it. McLarnin won't be the first 140-pounder he has beaten.

"You may think I'm shooting off just to ballyhoo the show. That's what they thought when I said Thompson would beat McLarnin. I still think Thompson won that fight. Wait and see if I'm not giving you the straight dope. I hope they make McLarnin 4 or 5 to 1. If they do, I'll get mine."[40]

Sportswriters were quick to defend "the Belfast Spider" and rebut Hurley's shocking assertions about their fistic idol. The *Evening Journal*'s Hype Igoe disputed Jack's contention that McLarnin's opponents had been washed-up veterans or scared kids. Igoe listed Al Singer, Ruby Goldstein, Sid Terris, Joey Sangor, Jackie Fields, Kid Kaplan, and Joe Glick, all as worthy opponents who were neither "toddlers" nor "old men."[41]

Wilbur Wood, of the *New York Sun,* took issue with Hurley's claim that McLarnin was a quitter. Wood recalled seeing Jimmy get up off the floor, and fight harder than ever, to kayo Kaplan in eight rounds at Chicago. He had seen McLarnin, weakened at efforts to make the lightweight limit, never take a backward step against Mandell even though Jimmy had to know that he was going to take a beating. And, it "was a known fact" that McLarnin had beaten Thompson after breaking his hand in an early round.[42]

Hurley continued to get under McLarnin's skin while Jimmy and his manager, Pop Foster, were exercising their rights to be present when Petrolle's hands were being taped. For this bout, the taping of the fighters was done under the supervision of a state inspector in the presence of not only the managers, but both fighters as well.

New York law limited the tape on a boxer's hands to two feet. As he taped Petrolle's hands Hurley needled Foster, who was known as a stickler for rules, by asking if Pop would let Jack use more than the two feet on Billy's hands. The dispute heated up and, as Foster began to get angry and McLarnin became nervous, Billy piped up in a relaxed drawl, as if bored by the whole discussion, "Ah, let's fight without bandaging our hands at all."

When it came time to oversee Foster's bandaging of McLarnin's hands, Hurley slipped in a few more digs, "It's a tough break for you, kid, that Pop won't allow more tape on your hands. You're going to break those mitts

---

[40] Wood, Wilbur, "Petrolle Talks Great Fight," *New York World*, November 18, 1930, sports section.

[41] Igoe, "Igoe Defends M'Larnin from Hurley Tirade," *Duluth Herald*, November 19, 1930, sports section.

[42] Wood, *op. cit.*

Petrolle prepares for his test with McLarnin.

McLarnin shows Pop Foster his trusty right before his fight with Billy November 21, 1930.

Third-round action in the stirring Petrolle-McLarnin fight. A full 25 years later the *New York World-Telegram*'s Joe Williams still termed the fight the greatest he had ever seen.

some day. Remember how you hurt the dukes on Young Jack Thompson's head. That wouldn't have happened had you had your hands properly bandaged. Be careful, now, that you don't bust them up on Petrolle."[43]

On the afternoon of the bout, McLarnin weighed 141 pounds to Petrolle's 138. Odds, which had held steady in the 3-to-1 and 4-to-1 range all week, jumped to as high as 8 to 1 for Jimmy immediately before the fight.

The contrast between the two warriors was never more evident as when they climbed into the ring a few minutes after 10 p.m. Petrolle entered first, "a swarthy-skinned veteran," wrapped like a hooded mummy from head to ankle in a crusty old Indian blanket, except for his long, lean face with bent nose and scarred brow. After ducking inside the ropes, the rough-hewn Fargo Express made a couple of half-bows to the crowd, which responded tepidly with "a faint pounding of palms, and a few shrill whistles."

A minute later, "the Garden boiled and seethed with that deafening medley of noise that is peculiar to packed thousands surrendering to primitive emotions." McLarnin, resplendent in a shimmering emerald green robe with trunks to match, "bounced into the ring from an opposite angle. Baby Face McLarnin, the great little Irish battler from the West, the idol of New York's army of fight followers." In gratitude, Jimmy waved and turned 360 degrees on his heels before going to his corner to await the first bell.

In the fight's early moments, McLarnin appeared in control, peppering Petrolle's head with short lefts and rights, waiting for a spot to plant his potent straight right hand. Then, as the tick of the clock neared the one-minute mark, Jimmy thought he saw his chance and ripped the right in the direction of Billy's head. Deftly, Petrolle weaved under the punch and countered with a left hook that momentarily staggered McLarnin.

Stung, McLarnin quickly responded with two hard lefts which caught Petrolle squarely on the chin. Billy, wavering for an instant, blinked "his deep-set eyes," and threw a blistering right hand that landed high on Jimmy's cheekbone just under his left eye.

The blast "was a slashing blow coming from nowhere as far as McLarnin was concerned, and it scrambled Jimmy's mental apparatus." It "carried enough force to split the skin and bring a stream of blood. From that moment McLarnin was never in the fight, never within a mile of winning, never dangerous." The punch "transformed the angelic murderer of the ring into a startled, stunned, despairing figure who looked no more like the destructive genius he is popularly supposed to be than Albie Booth

---

[43] Campbell, *op. cit.*, November 30, 1930, sports section. For the purpose of storytelling, Hurley probably simplified his tale somewhat for the benefit of Cubby Campbell and his readers. At the time of the Petrolle-McLarnin fights, New York allowed a maximum of six feet of gauze to protect the hands and two feet of tape to go over the gauze. Thus, the dressing room discussion probably included references to New York's limitations on both gauze and tape.

Petrolle scores first of two 4th-round knockdowns against McLarnin.

McLarnin taking a nine-count after the first knockdown. Hurley can be seen in the white sweater yelling instructions to Petrolle from the first row just to the left of the ring post.

resembles Primo Carnera."[44]

Petrolle followed up his advantage and pummeled a retreating McLarnin severely with both hands, landing two more rights on the button as the first round ended and sending Jimmy to his corner in a daze. In the second round, Billy pursued McLarnin furiously, landing punch after punch to Jimmy's head and body. Twice, McLarnin stopped Petrolle's rush by shooting right hands to the head. On one of those occasions, Jimmy landed a punch to the top of Billy's head which broke the Irishman's hand.

McLarnin flashed his old form in the third round, and for a while it looked like he might come back and make a real fight of it. But in the fourth, Petrolle again stepped in under Jimmy's right hand and landed a terrific left hook that sent him sprawling to the canvas.

Referee Patsy Haley sent Petrolle to the corner and then returned to the center of the ring to count over the fallen McLarnin. After the toll reached nine, the gray-haired Haley appeared to hesitate for a full second, "as if the 'ten' count had got up as far as his front teeth and lodged there." At the last possible instant, just as the referee's hand was starting its downward arc, McLarnin arose, wobbly and glassy-eyed, to barely beat the count.

McLarnin's hands were down as Petrolle rushed in for the kill, and Jimmy was powerless to defend himself against a crushing right-left-right combination that sent him down again for a second nine-count. Once more Jimmy rose to his feet, "swaying unsteadily and making grotesque fighting gestures" as Billy chased McLarnin around the ring, raining blows from all directions at the tottering Irishman.

For a full two minutes, McLarnin called upon stumbling legs and unresponsive arms to give "as perfect an exhibition of generalship as any ring ever saw." Jimmy made the overeager Petrolle miss again and again until Billy punched himself weary and slowed to a walk with about 45 seconds left. By that time, McLarnin's eyes had cleared and he had begun to dance around. As the round ended, Jimmy was beginning to fight back.

By the eighth round, McLarnin's face was "a crimson smear" from the cut under the left eye and a deep laceration below his lower lip. During a

---

[44] Albert James (Albie) Booth was a 5-foot-6, 144-pound halfback, punter, and drop-kick specialist who played college football for Yale from 1929-1931. His most famous game was against Army on October 26, 1929, when he came off the bench with his team trailing 13-0 and scored two touchdowns to give Yale the lead. He capped off his performance by returning an Army punt for 70 yards as Yale ended up winning 21-13. Booth had accounted for all of his team's 21 points.

Booth went on to star in football in each of his three years, though he was injured for much of his junior year. An all-around athlete, he was captain of the Yale basketball team in his senior year and was a starting baseball player on the varsity as well. In his last appearance as a college athlete, he hit a grand slam home run to lead Yale to a 4-3 victory over arch-rival Harvard. Booth was elected to the College Football Hall of Fame in 1966.

The appearance of Booth and Carnera's name in the text is an obvious reference to the contrast in size between the 6-foot-6-inch, 270-pound Carnera and Booth.

Jimmy takes another nine-count after second 4th-round knockdown.

Another view of the second knockdown.

pause in the action, referee Haley stepped in and asked Jimmy if he wanted the fight stopped. "A mingled expression of anger and fear flashed across the little gamester's distorted features, and through bruised and swollen lips, he mumbled, 'No, please, no.'"

The tenth and final round saw both fighters dead tired, but still punching. Twice Petrolle landed left hooks that almost dropped McLarnin, but the game Irishman finished upright, though reeling and staggering at the bell.[45]

The decision in Petrolle's favor was a foregone conclusion. The crowd, which had been so one-sided in McLarnin's favor before the fight, cheered both gladiators equally as each in his own time left the ring afterward. As columnist Bill Corum wrote the next day, "this was one time there was honor and glory enough for both, for this was such a fight as comes only after much waiting. You are lucky if you see ten such in a lifetime."[46]

A total of 12,512 fans paid $56,624 in gross receipts and a net of $47,903 to see the affair. The terrific pace kept the crowd in a frenzy throughout the match. The excitement was too much for one ringside observer, who died from a heart attack.

After the bout, Petrolle gave full credit to Hurley. "I never knew of a fight in which a man had another fighter figured out as Jack had McLarnin gauged," said Billy. "Jack planned the fight, mapped it out, blow for blow, move for move, step for step. I was there only carrying out orders."

"He schooled me about getting away from McLarnin's right hand. Only one way – duck straight down in front of him when he shoots it, and either it goes over your head or lands on top of it. I would then be in position to deliver a left hook to body or head. In camp we practiced this ducking all through training. Jimmy cracked up alright, on top of my head. If he broke his right hand he can thank Hurley for it, for he's to blame more than me."[47]

---

[45] The foregoing description of the first Petrolle-McLarnin fight was a blending of accounts from various New York daily newspapers in the days after the match. The basic framework for the account borrows liberally from Joe Williams' classic column in the *New York Telegram*. Williams was obviously moved by the bout and his article must rate as one of the most stirring accounts of a fight ever written. Years later, Williams still remembered it as the best he had ever witnessed in his 25 years of watching fights at the Garden. Williams, "By Joe Williams – Garden Fans See an Epic Fight," *New York Telegram*, November 21, 1930 (all quotations except those listed below). Kieran, John, "Sports of the Times – The Fine Italian Hand in Boxing," *New York Times*, November 28, 1930, p. 32 ("slashing blow coming from nowhere..."). Kofoed, "Petrolle Offers Second Miracle to Patrons," *New York Evening Post*, November 22, 1930, p. 11 ("as perfect an exhibition of ring generalship..."). Igoe, "Billy's Left Hook Beats McLarnin," *New York Evening Journal*, November 22, 1930, p. 12 ("a crimson smear"). Williams, Joe, "By Joe Williams," *Pittsburgh Press*, December 21, 1950, p. 42.

[46] Corum Bill, "Sports – The Fargo Express Rolls to Town," *New York Evening Journal*, November 22, 1930, sports section.

[47] Campbell, *op. cit.*, November 30, 1930, sports section. Igoe, "Petrolle Ready for Two Champs," *New York Evening Journal*, November 22, 1930, sports section.

Petrolle jolts McLarnin with his left in the eighth round.

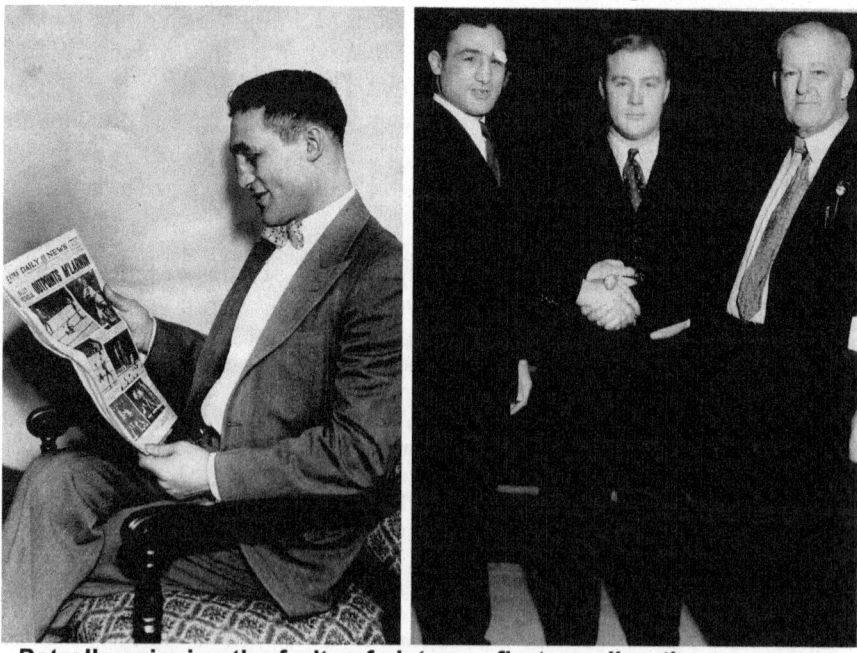

Petrolle enjoying the fruits of victory – first, reading the newspaper headlines the day after his victory (left) and then, accepting congratulations on his return home to Duluth.

Hurley's tactic for countering McLarnin's right ran contrary to the way most boxers were taught. Jack instructed Petrolle to duck down and weave to his left toward the same side from which Jimmy would be punching so Billy would be in position to counter with a left hook. Orthodox teaching, and instinct, would have a fighter shift inside and away from the attacking hand, putting himself in position to counter with his own right hand.

Years later, Hurley recounted to columnist W. C. Heinz in great detail his instructions to Petrolle before the McLarnin fight. "With this guy you have to resort to an amateur trick," Jack recalled telling Billy. "He won't expect it from you because he knows you're a good fighter, and he thinks you know too much. What you got to do, is drop the left hand. He'll throw the right, and you lean down under it and counter with the left instead of the right. He won't be looking for it, and you can't miss him with it."[48]

As planned, Petrolle dropped his left to draw McLarnin's right, ducked down, leaned to his left (Jimmy's right) and countered with a left. At first, McLarnin didn't know where the punch was coming from, but he figured it out, and Petrolle reversed tactics to reflect orthodox strategy. The result was "Billy walked out there and started jabbing and missing, jabbing and missing. Jimmy thought he had him all figured out, and he tried to anticipate Petrolle and moved in. He came in – right into a right Billy had been building up all the time."

As Petrolle intimated, when Jimmy broke his hand, it was no accident. As discussed previously, Hurley realized McLarnin's right hand was vulnerable to Petrolle's hard head after watching Jimmy box Stanislaus Loayza at Detroit in 1928. Hurley tested his theory by teaching Young Jack Thompson a modified bob and weave style prior to his fight with McLarnin in March 1930. Jimmy broke his hand on Thompson's head then.[49]

With Petrolle, a natural bob and weaver, Hurley had the opportunity to take his theory one step further. He not only taught Billy the ducking maneuver as a defense against Jimmy's potent but vulnerable right hand, he trained him in a tactic that would entice McLarnin into throwing it at Petrolle's head, so Billy could counter. In Petrolle, who was probably the best in history at offering his head as a decoy in exchange for a chance to land a hard punch, Hurley had the perfect vehicle to execute this strategy.

After the fight, Petrolle learned Hurley had won three thousand dollars by betting $500 at 6-to-1 odds before the bout. When he heard this, Billy approached Jack and, with a grin on his face, asked if he was going to get his "usual cut" of the proceeds. Unable to conceal his displeasure, Hurley replied, "There's too much larceny in you, Billy. And besides, you wouldn't

---

[48] Heinz, W. C., "The Man Who Makes Fighters," *Esquire Magazine*, May 1951, p. 103.

[49] Hurley's observation after the McLarnin-Loayza fight about the vulnerability of Jimmy's right hand to a hard-headed opponent (two years before the first Petrolle- McLarnin bout) was discussed in Volume One, Chapter 18 of this set.

bet on yourself." Laughing, Billy answered, "Oh yeah?! If you'd lost, I'd been 'cut in' alright. Right off the top of our purse!"[50]

The McLarnin fight in 1930 was a landmark for both Petrolle and Hurley.

For Billy, the bout was the culmination of a career of hard work, blood, sweat, tears, and self-sacrifice. After eight fights and five years of failed attempts to break into the ranks of New York's boxing elite, Billy finally made it into the inner circle on his ninth try. From this time forward, instead of having to take what was offered in terms of both money and opposition, Petrolle would exercise the leverage earned by his new popularity to command large purses and have a say in the selection of his opponents.

Considered washed-up only a year earlier, Petrolle had now taken his career to a level far higher than before his temporary retirement. In the last three months, Billy had defeated the best men in two divisions: Tony Canzoneri, the lightweight champion, and Jimmy McLarnin, the world's leading welterweight. For the next three years, though he would have some ups and downs, he would remain a leading contender in both divisions and reign as New York's most popular fighter and consistent drawing card.[51]

For Hurley, the victory had exactly the same significance as it did for Petrolle, and a whole lot more. Whereas before Jack had been recognized as a personable young man with a gift of gab and a steadfast, if irritatingly strident loyalty to his fighter, he now was regarded as a shrewd manager

---

[50] Campbell, *op. cit.*,, December 2, 1930, sports section.

[51] Because of the lack of a popular heavyweight champion and also because of a feud that champion Max Schmeling had with Madison Square Garden officials during part of the 1930-32 period (until Jimmy Johnston replaced William Carey as MSG president), the lighter divisions were more active in New York than the heavier divisions. If the second Schmeling-Jack Sharkey heavyweight championship bout on June 21, 1932 is excluded (receipts $432,000), combined net receipts for Petrolle's fights were the highest of any fighter who appeared in New York in the period between his first McLarnin fight on November 21, 1930, and his second Canzoneri fight on November 4, 1932:

Petrolle-McLarnin #1	$47,992
Petrolle-Tut #6	39,296
Petrolle-McLarnin #2	70,184
Petrolle-Suarez	23,826
Petrolle-McLarnin #3	40,763
Petrolle-Townsend	40,103
Petrolle-Ran	45,558
Petrolle-Battalino	65,959
Petrolle-Canzoneri #2	<u>78,568</u>
Total	$452,249

Inclusion of the second Schmeling-Sharkey fight would hand honors to Sharkey, who also drew gates of $238,831 against Mickey Walker July 22, 1931, and $129,325 against Primo Carnera October 12,1931, both non-title fights at Ebbets Field. Note these figures from the 1957 edition of the *Ring Record Book* are net receipts. Gross receipts were on average about ten to 15 percent higher. Additionally, looking at just Madison Square Garden, as opposed to New York fights as a whole (i. e., excluding fights at outdoor venues), Petrolle drew the Garden's second largest gate (with McLarnin #2) in 1931 and its two largest gates (with Battalino and Canzoneri #2) in 1932.

and a master strategist. Henceforth, he would be regarded as wise beyond his years, a man whose word, though maybe slanted with an eye to promoting his fighter, was always taken seriously and never ignored.

For the rest of his life, Hurley would remain a favorite of both New York's boxing scribes and the city's boxing cognoscenti at large. Whenever he spoke, they would listen and, whenever he had a fighter to show, they would watch. Over the next few years, those same journalists would write enough good things about Jack and Billy Petrolle, his Fargo Express, to insure their place as one of the most memorable teams in boxing history.

CHAPTER 23

AN OLD EGYPTIAN JINX

I suppose the fellows in the boxing game in New York think I do everything backward. Well, I guess I do, according to their ideas. But I work along the lines I have found best suited to me.

I never want to be babied, either in or out of the ring. I want to do things for myself, and I don't want to rely on anyone else. You know, when you're in the ring, you're in there alone, and you have to rely on no one but yourself to help. Having a flock of trainers and assistants hanging around to comb your hair and hand you your tie and collar or tie your shoes is all right for the baby scrappers, but I can't be that way.

As to getting a rubdown. Good fighters don't need rubs, and bums shouldn't have 'em. I tried the rub-down stunt, but it didn't work, so I cut 'em out. I've found they do me no good, and even take a little out of me. I guess maybe it's because I was brought up without any fancy stuff. The fancy trimmings never appealed to me. I get along better just being myself.

I don't have a regular trainer except for my manager, Jack Hurley. I believe I know more about what's good for me than any trainer who doesn't know me. I know myself better than any one, except Hurley. Whatever he says I'll do, because I feel that he's right when he says something.

Sometimes, I kid Hurley by telling him he is my trainer only because he causes me to do a lot of road work running up and down stairs trying to get him out of bed in time to go to the gym with me.

I've bandaged my hands, and am ready to start working out, but right now I'm waiting for Hurley to show up before I begin. I always like having him around when I work out. I don't feel right without him. That's why I left Gus Wilson's training camp up the country in Orangeburg, New Jersey, to train here in town – so Hurley can be with me.[1]   — Billy Petrolle

****

At the end of 1930, the full impact of what was increasingly being called a "depression," as opposed to a "recession," was continuing to work its way through the American economy. Although business had slowed after the "Great Crash of October 1929," hope still lingered that the country's financial outlook would improve during the coming year.

Unfortunately, the bitter reality was things would get much worse before

---

[1] Wood, Wilbur, "No Frills on Billy Petrolle," *New York Sun*, May 15, 1931, sports section. Hurley, Jack, "Ring Rations," *Fargo Forum*, June 28, 1931, sports section. Corcoran, Jimmy, "'No Help Wanted' Is Petrolle's Slogan," *Chicago American*, May 19, 1932, sports section. The opening vignette is a compilation of Petrolle quotes from all three sources.

they got better. In fact, the effect of the stock market failure was only beginning to make its presence felt in American homes. Even though the country had been alarmed at the abrupt failures of 1,700 banks in the past year, 1930 would later be regarded as just the tip of the iceberg.

In 1933, the number of bank failures would exceed 4,000. Before the bloodletting finally could be staunched, the "Great Depression" would cause 10,763 of the nation's 24,970 commercial banks to fail. As a result, America's financial system would lose over 30 percent of its money supply. Consumers would deplete their savings and spend less money. Countless businesses, crippled by lost sales and lack of credit, would go bankrupt, and 25 percent of the country's workers would lose their jobs.

Like the rest of the economy, boxing also was feeling the pinch.

At New York's Madison Square Garden, annual gross receipts between 1929 and 1933 would fall from $1,480,734 to $305,809. A reported loss of $315,000 in the first eight months of 1931 would result in the firing of matchmaker Tom McArdle by Garden officials and his replacement by veteran manager and promoter, James J. Johnston.

Proceeds from heavyweight championship bouts presented at New York between 1930 and 1933 would mirror perfectly the dramatic decline in boxing revenue for the sport as a whole: $711,668 for the Schmeling-Sharkey bout in 1930; $432,465 for the Sharkey-Schmeling bout in 1932; and $184,000 for the Carnera-Sharkey bout in 1933.

In Illinois, the athletic commission would report a decline in receipts of $242,536 and in attendance of 219,363 between 1930 and 1931. Whereas, in 1930, revenues from the Mandell-Canzoneri and Mandell-McLarnin bouts had totaled $136,002 and $102,355, respectively, comparable championship attractions in 1931 featuring Canzoneri-Berg and Battalino-Mastro, would draw only $54,675 and $42,017. The state's largest show for 1931 would be the Carnera-Levinsky card with receipts of $56,428.[2]

Ironically, during this same period of economic upheaval, Jack Hurley would enjoy the most financially successful years of his life.

Hurley's apprenticeship as a small-town promoter in the 1920s was a perfect training ground for survival in the constricted economic environments of Chicago and New York in the 1930s. Promoting in Fargo and Duluth had always provided Jack the unique challenge of presenting entertainment which would appeal to the maximum number of limited fans available and at the same time still not cost too much to present.

The circumstances Hurley overcame in coaxing scarce dollars from the tight fists of fans in Fargo were similar to those that he would face in larger cities during the economic hard times. Indeed, the quest for "sensational

---

[2] Fleischer, Nat, "The 1957 Ring Record Book," (The Ring Book Shop, 1957), pp. 63-65, 74-75. Conklin, Les (INS), AP report on Madison Square Garden financial situation, *Duluth Herald*, September 19, 1931, sports section. Dunkley, Charles, "Illinois Bouts Draw 200,000 Less Patrons," *Duluth News Tribune*, December 15, 1931, sports section.

attractions" at a low cost early in his career had led Jack to develop the unorthodox teaching methods that would go on to produce exciting fighters like Billy Petrolle and Charley Retzlaff.

Now that both fighters were at the peaks of their popularity, Hurley was perfectly situated to present an exciting brand of entertainment of particular appeal to the value-conscious, big-city boxing fan of the 1930s.

Furthermore, Hurley's early experiences endowed him with a "sixth sense" for aligning himself with established performers and entrepreneurs who had a knack for showmanship and self-promotion. Jack's alliances with Jack Dempsey, Primo Carnera, Art Shires, and Ray Alvis already provided ample testimony to his ability to identify and work with the most popular and imaginative boxing practitioners wherever he went.

Petrolle's first 1931 ring appearance was at the annual New Year's Day show in Fargo. Billy won a six-round newspaper decision over Johnny Salvator's ace welterweight, Billy Light, who outweighed Petrolle by seven pounds. Hurley arranged the card as a favor to his friends in Fargo, who wanted to see Billy after his big win over McLarnin. It proved to be Petrolle's last fight in his namesake city.

In addition, Billy's comeback and sensational victory rekindled excitement in the Twin Cities over the championship prospects of their favorite son, King Tut. Despite his wins over Petrolle in 1928 and 1929, Tut had not yet captured the fancy of boxing fans outside the Midwest. Billy's resurgence as a legitimate contender presented a new opportunity for the King to make an impression on the national scene.

Although Hurley realized that Tut, more than any other fighter, had the strength and style to cause Petrolle fits, he accepted St. Paul promoter Jerk Doran's offer to fight the King on February 2, 1931. Doran was offering a guaranteed purse of $12,000, which would be Billy's largest for a fight to date. Petrolle was fighting better than ever and was confident he could beat Tut. If Billy was ever to even the score with Tut and avoid charges that he was "ducking 'the Egyptian,'" now was the time.

The fight on February 2 was the pair's fifth encounter. Petrolle had won the first bout on a foul and then out-punched Tut for a victory in their second fight. Twin Cities' fans still recalled their third fight at Minneapolis in August 1928 as "one of the greatest battles ever staged in the Northwest." Tut had gotten off the floor in the second round and come back to give Petrolle a decisive licking. Tut duplicated this feat in their fourth bout at Detroit in September 1929 in the fight which led to Billy's first retirement.[3]

Even in the midst of a depression, the Tut-Petrolle fight caught the Twin Cities' fancy as had no other since the area's two favorite fighters, Mike O'Dowd and Mike Gibbons, fought for the middleweight title at St. Paul in

---

[3] McKenna, Lou, "King Tut Hurts Hand in Drill; Will Be Ready," *Saint Paul Pioneer Press*, February 1. 1931, sports section.

1919. Two days before the bout, advance ticket sales totaled $20,000, and it was estimated that gate receipts might reach as high as $30,000. Remarkably, final figures surpassed even these optimistic estimates.

According to a final accounting, receipts set a state record of $38,546.[4]

Despite expectations the battle would test to the limit the endurance of each gladiator, the fight was over almost before it started. At the gong, Tut "hurtled from his corner, tore across the ring at full speed and half way over started hurling punches." Billy never even left his corner. "The King covered the 22 feet with such a terrific headlong cyclonic rush that Petrolle did not take two full steps before the storm broke."

The first blow Tut landed was a left hook which Petrolle blocked with his right glove, but the blow's force, aided by the King's terrific forward momentum, jammed Billy's glove against the side of his head and drove him backward and off-balance. Tut missed with a couple of rights that flew over Petrolle's head and then, crouching down, he unloaded a devastating left hook to the ribs that lifted the Fargo Express entirely off his feet and flung him back into his corner right up against the ropes.

Tut was on top of his injured foe, winging punches "like an enraged wildcat." He "lashed out another left hook and caught Petrolle flush on the jaw. As Billy started to sink to the canvas, Tut crashed over a right cross that landed on the button. The force of this blow draped Petrolle over the lower strand of the ring ropes, and it was there that he was counted out." Except for two left hooks to the body, Billy failed to land a single punch.

The time from the opening bell to the final count was just 34 seconds.[5]

The next day, Petrolle, though at a loss to explain what happened, was adamant in wanting a rematch as soon as possible. "One punch doesn't prove to me that Tut is a better fighter than I am," he told Cubby Campbell. "I want another chance – I've got to have it, whether Hurley consents to it or not. I'm ready right now for a rematch later this week, next week, next month or whenever Tut will agree to meet me in the ring again.

"My mind is still a blank as to how it all happened. I barely remember being backed into the corner. They say I never tried to get out of the corner.

---

[4] "Record Gopher Ring Dates," *St. Paul Pioneer Press*, February 3, 1931, sports section:

RECORD GOPHER RING DATES

Attraction	Date	Receipts	Attendance
Tut-Petrolle, St. Paul,	2/2/1931	$38,546	10,249
Gibbons-O'Dowd, St. Paul	11/21/1919	37,461	6,579
Gibbons-Ahearn, St. Paul	1/18/1916	23,618	6,357
Von Porat-Stribling, Minneapolis	7/12/1927	19,105	7,686
Okun-Daniels (Dempsey referee), Mpls	4/25/1930	18,864	8,673
Gibbons-Smith, St. Paul	3/17/1916	17,169	5,204
Mandell-Petrolle, Minneapolis	1/13/1928	16,971	7,274
Carnera-Montgomery, Minneapolis	3/11/1931	16,863	8,398

[5] Shave, Ed L., "Record Crowd Gasps at Cyclonic Onset of Midget Battler," *St. Paul Daily News*, February 3, 1931, sports section.

Well, maybe I didn't want to, for I've always been able to take care of myself before, when in a corner. In fact, lots of times I've purposely let a fellow get me in there, just to turn the tables on him. I don't know now whether that was my intention or not last night, for the second punch of the fight numbed my brain. I guess I didn't work very well last night."[6]

Hurley needed to act quickly to contain the damage from the one-round kayo before it permanently affected Billy's future money-making prospects. Fortunately, matchmaker Tom McArdle was eager to stage the return bout at Madison Square Garden. On February 7, McArdle announced he had signed the fighters to a ten-rounder at the Garden on February 27, 1931, with Tut to receive 30 percent and Billy 20 percent of gate receipts.

To secure the match, Hurley made a secret side agreement to guarantee the King a minimum of $15,000, with any shortfall to be paid from Petrolle's percentage. The fight was Tut's first at Madison Square Garden.[7]

Despite the fact Petrolle had lost three bouts in a row to Tut, Hurley told the *New York Sun*'s Wilbur Wood that Billy was sure to beat the King. After hearing Jack explain that Petrolle was weakened for the 1928 fight at Minneapolis by an undiagnosed kidney abscess, and that he lost the 1929 match at Detroit because he had already decided to retire beforehand, Wood asked Hurley why he expected Billy to beat Tut on February 27.

"That brings us down to the recent affair in St. Paul," replied Hurley, "I don't say the knockout of my boy then was an accident, but I do say it was one of those breaks that come once in a lifetime. Tut nailed Billy before he was out of his corner. It was all over before Petrolle knew it had started.

"You ask me why I think Petrolle will win tonight. Because he is the better boxer, because he is the harder puncher, because he can take it better than Tut, because he is determined to win this one if he never wins another, because New York is his spot.

"You ask me how Billy will win. Tut is a weaver, who gets down so low his chin almost scrapes the floor. Petrolle will get down with him, straighten him up with left uppercuts and then cross him with the right. Petrolle is a short puncher; Tut is a clubber who lets 'em go hoping they will land. Billy will beat him to the punch. That's my story. Check up on me tonight."[8]

A reported 14,193 fans paid $43,860 to see the fight. The next day, scribes expressed surprise that two Midwestern lightweights accounted for the Garden's largest gate in the first two months of 1931, outdrawing heavyweights like Ernie Schaaf, Tommy Loughran, Max Baer, Tom Heeney, and Jimmy Braddock. The February 27th gate would stand as the

---

[6] Campbell, Cubby, "Cubby Campbell's Column," *Duluth News Tribune*, February 4, 1931, sports section.

[7] Fitzgerald, Eugene, "Northwest Rivals Meet in Feature Garden Go Feb. 27, Hurley Says," *Fargo Forum*, February 8, 1931, sports section. Wood, Wilbur, "Penalty for Boxers Unlikely," March 4, 1931, sports section.

[8] Wood, "Petrolle Drops Tut Four Times," *New York Sun*, February 28, 1931, sports section.

largest of the Garden's 1931 weekly shows until the same Petrolle would draw over $80,000 for his fight three months later with Jimmy McLarnin.

In a time of economic hardship, Petrolle indisputably had "arrived" as New York's most popular fighter, a post he would hold the next two years.[9]

At the bell, Tut rushed across the ring, slinging punches just as he had in St. Paul. Petrolle, who had not heard the faintly sounding gong, was again caught flatfooted, but this time was able to block Tut's blows and work his way out of the corner. The rest of the round, Billy kept out of Tut's way as much as possible, content to survive the round which caused him so much grief in their most recent bout. Tut won it easily, landing "several jolting stabs to the mouth and cross[ing] a couple of rocking rights to the head."

In the second session, Billy went to work. "Like a sculptor chiseling carefully at a piece of marble," Petrolle "started hammering home rights and lefts to head and body" soon after the round started. "When Tut weaved close to the floor Billy would go down with him, then bring the King's head with a left uppercut and cross his right to the chin. This was the style mapped out by Hurley before the fight and drilled into Petrolle in a sizzling pep talk before he entered the ring."[10]

Before the knockout, Billy scored three knockdowns against Tut, one in each of the second and third rounds, and another in the fourth just prior to the end. On each of these occasions, the King sank slowly to one knee apparently more to take a rest from the constant pounding of his body rather than from any one punch. Each time, Tut arose at a count of nine, seemingly refreshed and full of fight, and took the battle back to Petrolle, only to be met by another barrage of lefts and rights to head and body.

In the fourth round, Billy came charging at Tut after the third knockdown and caught him flush on the jaw with a long, swinging right. For the fourth and final time, the King dropped to the canvas where he rolled over in an attempt to rise before he fell flat on his face and was counted out.

Even as fans in New York were raving about what a great fight it had been, Minnesota's boxing commission a thousand miles away was busy casting doubt on the bout's validity. Information had come to its attention from a disgruntled Minneapolis gambler that the fight had been fixed. Relying on this unconfirmed source, the Minnesota board wired the New York commission and urged an investigation because of "evidence so strong against the participants that quick and decisive action is imperative."[11]

The next day, the New York commission announced an investigation into

---

[9] Wood, *op. cit.*

[10] Vidmer, Richards, "Physicians Fear Defeated Boxer Is Seriously Hurt," *New York Herald Tribune* February 28, 1931, sports section ("... several jolting stabs to mouth ..." and "... hammering home rights and lefts ..."). Burton, Lewis, "Boxing Solons Holding Purses Pending Probe, *New York American,* February 28, 1931, p. 11 ("Like a sculptor chiseling ..."). Wood, *op. cit.* ("When Tut weaved ...").

[11] "Petrolle, Tut, Hurley Barred by the State," *Duluth Herald,* February 28, 1931, p. 1.

Sweet Revenge! Billy Petrolle scores one of four knockdowns on his way to a kayo victory over his archrival King Tut February 27, 1931, at Madison Square Garden.

Another knockdown of King Tut for the Fargo Express.

Announcer Joe Humphreys raises Petrolle's hand in victory over Tut. Johnny Salvator tends to Billy as Hurley joins with the towel.

the matter, citing as reasons the Minnesota commission's concerns, a sudden shift in odds before the fight, the curious nature of Tut's three knockdowns, and the complete reversal in outcome of the St. Paul and New York fights. In response, the Minnesota commission summarily revoked Petrolle's and Tut's licenses pending the results of the New York inquiry.[12]

Hearing of the commissions' actions the next day, most knowledgeable fight fans in the Big Apple were hard pressed to understand the reason for suspicion. Mayor James J. Walker, a regular patron at the Garden, reacted by saying: "If that fight was a fake let us have more of them." One veteran manager, when asked if the bout looked shady, could only whisper a reply: "I lost my voice yelling for the first time since the Dempsey-Firpo fight. I suppose that also was a fake, as well as the first battle of the Marne."[13]

In the meantime, anticipating the matter would be resolved quickly, Hurley signed a contract for Petrolle to fight Tony Canzoneri for the lightweight championship at Madison Square Garden on March 27, 1931.[14]

The New York commission heard testimony on March 3, 1931. Despite the Minnesota commission's promise to forward "strong evidence" of a "betting coup," none was offered. Evidence was presented that if the odds had been influenced at all, it was due to information from a friend of Tut who knew about the King's prior treatment for appendicitis. Betting on the bout had been light and no evidence of a "coup" was found.

The commission heard evidence confirming post-fight reports that Tut was treated for appendicitis at the Mayo Clinic in Rochester, Minnesota, several months before the February 27th bout. Petrolle's body blows had aggravated this condition and caused Tut's legs to give way several times during the bout. Blood tests after the bout at the Polyclinic across the street from the Garden were consistent with appendicitis. Tut testified he planned to have an appendectomy as soon as he returned to Minnesota.[15]

At its regular monthly meeting on March 13, the New York commission

---

[12] Farrell, Jack, "Hospital Holds the King While Boxing Papas Hold the Purse," *New York Daily News*, February 28, 1931, p. 32.

[13] Wood, *op. cit*. The first battle of the Marne was a famous battle in World War I when Allied forces stopped the German army on the outskirts of Paris in September 1914 and forced it to retreat and abandon its plans to take over the city. The battle resulted in more than 500,000 casualties and led to four years of trench warfare on the Western Front, a stalemate which continued until the United States forces arrived at the front in 1918.

[14] "Billy Petrolle Opens Training for Title Bout," *Fargo Forum*, March 10, 1931, sports section.

[15] Wray, John, "Wray's Column," *St. Louis Post-Dispatch*, April 3, 1931, sports section (no evidence presented by Minnesota commission; no betting coup; information from a friend of Tut). Wood, "Penalty for Boxers Unlikely," *New York Sun*, March 4, 1931 (re-creation of New York commission's closed-door hearing; plans to have Tut's appendix removed). Morris, William, "Purse Withheld, King Tut Is Taken to Polyclinic, Ill," *New York Evening Post*, February 28, 1931, sports section (blood test). As he told the New York commission, Tut did undergo surgery in Minnesota for removal of his appendix March 10, 1931. "Tut Undergoes Operation at Mayo Clinic," *Duluth Herald*, March 11, 1931, sports section.

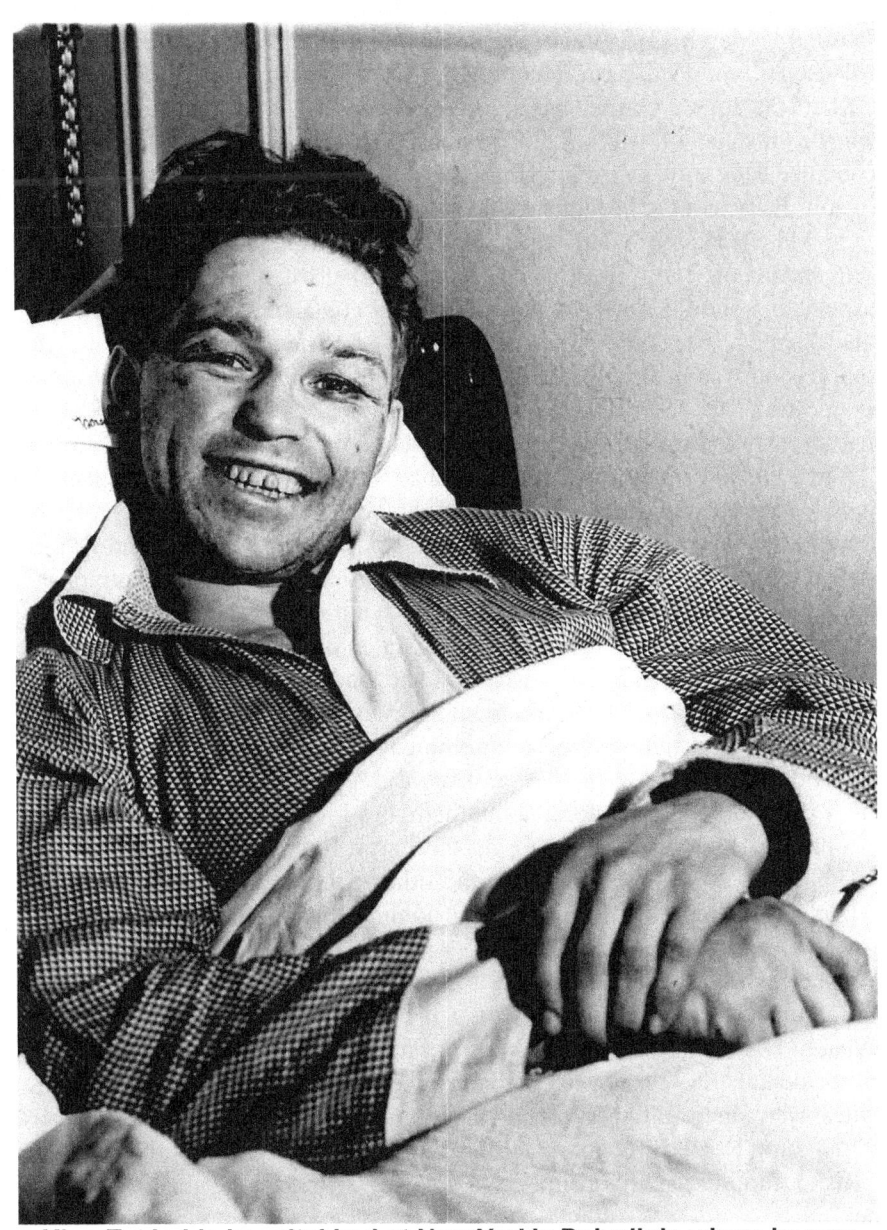

King Tut in his hospital bed at New York's Polyclinic where he was diagnosed with appendicitis after his fight with Petrolle February 28, 1931.

exonerated all concerned and ordered the purses of both fighters to be released in full. Unfortunately, the commission declined to authorize Petrolle's March 27th lightweight championship fight with Canzoneri because Billy's license was technically still under suspension in Minnesota.

Madison Square Garden officials lost no time in finding a substitute for Petrolle. Instead of waiting for Minnesota to reinstate Billy, the Garden scheduled Jackie (Kid) Berg to fight Tony for the title on April 24, 1931. As a result, Billy lost the best chance he would ever have to win a world title.[16]

On March 31, the Minnesota commission summoned Tut, Petrolle, and their managers to a meeting in Minneapolis to show cause why the suspensions should not be made permanent. In a remarkable turnaround, Chairman Dr. Alexander Sivertsen opened the meeting by admitting the commission was unable to produce any evidence of wrongdoing and it had no questions to ask. The chairman also said the commission had voted unanimously to drop all charges and reinstate all concerned.

When the chairman asked if Hurley had anything to say, hr produced the signed contract for Petrolle's title fight with Canzoneri. Jack told the commission that, because they had taken stock in false rumors and hearsay evidence, a Minnesota boy had lost an opportunity to win a championship and the more than $100,000 that went with winning a world title.

The commissioners reviewed the contract, and while they said nothing, it was apparent the gravity of what they had done finally began to sink in. Jack told the *Duluth News Tribune* an attorney advised him he and Petrolle had a good case against the commission for slander, but he decided "the less said about the case the better. They did a lot of talking about us, and now I could do a lot of talking about them, but I have decided to drop it."[17]

While Hurley was working to get the Fargo Express back on track after his February 2nd loss to King Tut, the other anchor of his stable, Charley Retzlaff, was preparing for a fight with Johnny Risko, "the Cleveland Baker Boy," at Detroit, February 6, 1931.

Since his knockout of Andres Castano at Duluth in May 1930, Retzlaff had continued his winning ways over the lesser lights of the heavyweight division. His only loss in eight bouts during that time, a disqualification for an accidental low blow, was later avenged by a first round kayo. Boxing critics were increasingly voicing the opinion, however, that Hurley was mishandling Retzlaff by not matching him against better opposition.

Risko, though past his prime, was Charley's first test against a topnotch foe.

Olympia Arena matchmaker Scotty Montieth had been after Hurley to show his tiger again in Detroit ever since his kayo of Tom Sayers in June

---
[16] Wood, "Berg ready for Canzoneri Bout; Board Releases Purses of Petrolle and Tut," *New York Sun*, March 14, 1931, sports section.

[17] Hurley, *op cit.*, April 13, 1931, sports section.

1930. A Retzlaff-Risko bout figured to be attractive since Johnny had always drawn big crowds in the Motor City. In addition, Montieth hoped that a new scale for tickets – featuring 50-cent gallery seating – would help to increase lagging attendance and benefit patrons who could no longer afford high-priced seats.

Demonstrating the wisdom of Scotty's new policy, a surprisingly large crowd of 13,836, paid $15,337 to watch 9-5 underdog Retzlaff win seven out of ten rounds against Risko. It was the first time Charley, who was now being called the "Duluth Dynamiter," had gone ten rounds. To the surprise of many, he finished the bout much stronger than his veteran opponent.[18]

Upon his return to Duluth, Hurley brandished "a nice green check ... totaling $3,435.75, which represented Retzlaff's end of the purse in Detroit last Friday night." Showing it to Cubby Campbell, Jack brashly remarked, "We're in the money now with the big fellow, and I'm not going to be too hasty about who, when and where we fight."[19]

As it turned out, Hurley did not have to wait long. Montieth wanted Retzlaff back in Detroit on March 6 against another trial horse, Tom Heeney of New Zealand. Heeney was well known for having fought Gene Tunney for the heavyweight championship 2-1/2 years earlier.

Once again Montieth's bargain-basement prices proved to be good business. This time, 15,405 fans paid $18,975 to see Duluth's "Dynamiter" knock out the "Hard Rock from Down Under" in the seventh round.

Up until the knockout, the fight was "a rather dull exhibition, marked by tugging and clinching by both gladiators." Although Retzlaff dominated the early action, he was unable to find the range with his right-hand haymaker. By the fourth round, Heeney had solved Charley's style and was holding his own by ducking under the straight right hands and banging away with his own left hooks to the body.[20]

Hurley told Retzlaff in the rest period between the fourth and fifth rounds that whenever Heeney ducked, he was an easy mark for a right uppercut. Charley said he understood, but nonetheless went out in the next two rounds and threw nothing but straight rights, which Tom continued to duck and cause to fly harmlessly over his head.[21]

Returning to his corner amid a chorus of boos after the sixth round, a tired and discouraged Retzlaff recieved no sympathy from his enraged pilot. Listening from ringside, reporter Sam Greene transcribed the exchange between the manager and his fighter for the next day's *Detroit News*:

---
[18] Shaver Bud, "Victory Sends Duluth Boy Up Ladder," *Detroit Times*, February 7, 1931, p. 13.
[19] Campbell, *op cit.*, February 11, 1931, sports section.
[20] Greene, Sam, "Retzlaff's Hard Right Finishes the Hard Rock," *Detroit News*, March 7, 1931, sports section.
[21] Heinz, W. C., "The Man Who Makes Fighters," *Esquire Magazine*, May 1952, pp. 43, 100.

"'You're the worst fighter I ever saw,' began his manager, Jack Hurley, in a husky voice that could be heard three rows back. 'Yes, the worst fighter in the world.'

"'He keeps holdin',' countered Retzlaff. 'Holdin,' shouted Hurley. 'You're holdin' more than he is. He's an old man in there trying to stay the limit, and the way you're fightin' he could stay a hundred rounds. Why don't you use the uppercut like I told you?'

"'My hands are sore,' said Retzlaff. 'I think this one is broke.' And he held up the right glove. 'Broke or not, go in there and punch,' insisted the manager. You might as well have it broke right.'"[22]

"'Listen to me,' he said to Retzlaff ... 'Either you throw the uppercut this round or when you come back I am going to hit you over the head with this water bottle.

"So help me, I'll do it. It will be the end of everything. You and I will be through. I'll lose my license, I'll be done in boxing, but I'll do it. You're a disgrace.'"[23]

Doing as he was told, Retzlaff "rushed from his corner and started punching." A right uppercut, followed seconds later by a right cross, knocked Heeney down for a nine-count. After Tom struggled to his feet, Charley was on him with two more rights that sent the New Zealander "tumbling to the floor for the second time. The referee counted him out and the fight was over 53 seconds after the seventh round had opened."

Retzlaff's decisive finish "made the 15,405 paying clients forget the dreariness of the first six rounds and sent them home satisfied." Afterward, Montieth tendered Hurley a check for $4,337.50 for Charley's share of the evening's proceeds.[24]

As a result of his Risko and Heeney victories, both *Ring Magazine* and the National Boxing Association listed Retzlaff as the eighth-rated contender for the heavyweight title. Unfortunately, Charley would have to wait two months, until May 1930, for his bruised hands to heal before continuing efforts to advance higher in the rankings.[25]

---

[22] Greene, *op. cit.*

[23] Heinz, p. 100.

[24] Greene, *op. cit.* Net proceeds for the Retzlaff-Heeney fight were reported as $17,250 in the *Detroit Times* sports section on March 7, 1931. Since the check Hurley had received for the Retzlaff-Risko fight had amounted to 25 percent of the net proceeds from that fight, i. e., 25 percent of $13,743 = $3,435.75, the author is assuming that Hurley and Montieth had the same arrangement for the Retzlaff-Heeney fight, i. e., 25 percent of $17,250 = $4,337.50.

[25] Campbell, *op cit.*, May 31, 1931, sports section. Borden, Eddie, "Ratings for the Month of March," *Ring Magazine*, April 1931, p. 47. The National Boxing Association's first-quarter ratings for 1931 lists Retzlaff as the 9th best heavyweight and champion Max Schmeling as No. 1, thus making Charley the 8th leading contender. The April 1931 issue of *Ring Magazine* lists Schmeling separately as champion and Retzlaff as the No. 8 contender.

Retzlaff finally throws an uppercut at Heeney with Hurley's urging.

One of the rights that led to Retzlaff's 7th-round kayo of Heeney. Both photos this page & top photo on p. 528, courtesy of Walter P. Reuther Library, Archives of Labor & Urban Affairs, Wayne State University.

Heeney on his way to the canvas for a knockdown.

Another knockdown for Retzlaff against Heeney.

While in Detroit, Hurley ran into Sam Slotsky, his old friend from Sioux City. Slotsky had been helping out at the Olympia Stadium while Montieth had surgery. With Scotty just out of the hospital, Sam was seeking a new business opportunity. He had just met with Missouri boxing commissioner Seneca Taylor, who gave Slotsky a green light to promote in St. Louis. Would Jack be interested in partnering there with Sam?

After the Retzlaff-Heeney fight, Hurley high-tailed it to St. Louis to check out the situation. On March, 11, 1931, the *St. Louis Post-Dispatch* announced he and Slotsky had reserved four dates at the St. Louis Coliseum to promote shows during the spring under auspices of the American Legion. As a show of good faith, Hurley and Slotsky posted $100 for each date.[26]

The new promoters' inaugural show March 25 featured St. Louis heavyweight hopeful John Schwake in a main event against Johnny Risko. Much to the delight of local fans, Schwake was able to eke out a ten-round decision against the veteran "Baker Boy."

Adopting the pricing practices of Detroit's Olympia arena, the promoters reduced the price of gallery tickets to 55 cents. The idea was a decided hit as all the gallery seats were sold out. The card drew paid attendance of 6,450 and gross receipts of $7,934.00, netting a $1,200 profit.[27]

Although the show was a success, a disagreement arose between the promoters and commissioner Taylor that spelled doom for the partnership's survival. The source of the dispute was Missouri's boxing law, which obligated promoters to issue an unlimited number of free passes to city and state officeholders and to any other guests authorized by the commissioner.

The generosity the Missouri law imposed upon promoters and the discretion it gave the boxing commissioner far surpassed that of any other state in the country. Under the law, not only were promoters obligated to give away tickets, they were required to furnish prime seats to free pass-holders and pay the 15-cent state tax on each ticket. Moreover, the promoters suffered added injury when many of the passes ended up being scalped at cut-rate prices by original freeholders to secondary purchasers.

As a result, the promoters were forced to issue the incredible number of 517 free passes to politicians and "special guests" of the commission. The situation came to a head the night of the fight when Slotsky flatly refused Commissioner Taylor's last-minute request by emissary for 15 more tickets.

The next day, Taylor told Hurley and Slotsky he was done dealing with them, and in the future would funnel all commission business through the local American Legion post. He said that in refusing to grant free passes the promoters had jeopardized the state's boxing law because "some members

---

[26] "New Promoter Asks Dates for Four Shows at the Coliseum," *St. Louis Post-Dispatch*, March 11, 1931, sports section.

[27] McGoogan, W. J., "St. Louis Heavy Staggers Rival Several Times, in Hard Battle," *St. Louis Post-Dispatch*, March 26, 1931, sports section.

of the Legislature who were in the city were unable to see the bouts without paying, and they are the ones to who I must look to protect my law."

Hurley did not hesitate to take issue with the commissioner. "I am the man behind the business who supplies the funds with which the bills are paid," he argued. "When anybody wants to give away my money, I should have something to say about it. I am not so much interested in providing free entertainment for public office-holders as in seeing that the fans who paid their way into the performances receive their money's worth."

Commissioner Taylor ended the "wrangle which lasted for some time," by telling Hurley and Slotsky "he was running things the way he saw fit and if they didn't care to abide by his rulings, 'You can get out of my town.'"

Although the outlook for cooperation from the commissioner remained bleak, Charles Cunningham, chairman of the city boxing commission, agreed too many passes were being issued. As a show of good faith, he told the promoters his office would forego any such demands in the future.[28]

Despite the onerous law, the success of their first card prompted Hurley and Slotsky to go ahead with a second show April 10, 1931, featuring Billy Petrolle in a ten-round bout against Lope Tenorio of the Philippines. The fight was noteworthy in that it marked the first appearance of Harry Kessler as the referee of a major main event. Kessler later was to become known as the "millionaire referee" who, as a hobby, would referee many important matches all over the world during a long career.

The Petrolle-Tenorio bout produced more than its share of controversy when Billy knocked Lope to the canvas with a right to the head in the fifth round. Kessler, convinced Tenorio was not hurt and was about to take "a dive," refused to count and, in a highly unusual move, pulled the Filipino fighter to his feet and told him to continue or he would not be paid. Lope performed as directed and went the distance before losing the decision.[29]

---

[28] McGoogan, "Action Follows Row over Free List; Byrne to Run Next Show," *St. Louis Post-Dispatch*, March 27, 1931, sports section.

[29] In the opening 11 pages of his autobiography entitled "The Millionaire Referee" (Harkness Publishing, St. Louis, Missouri, 1982), Harry Kessler discusses the Petrolle-Tenorio fight in detail. Kessler claims that up until the fifth round both Petrolle and Tenorio were engaging in a fake fight with the apparent knowledge and acquiescence of Hurley. According to Harry, for the first four rounds "all Petrolle did – when he did it, which was seldom – was pepper the Filipino's shoulder and upper arms with powder puff blows that wouldn't have raised a welt on a gnat's hide." Lope, for his part, "cowered behind his raised forearms, protecting his face and head" while "hiding from Petrolle, me and the ever-maddening throng."

According to Kessler, midway in the second round, the crowd began clapping for more action "in a rhythmic thunder [that] spread quickly and built to a crescendo that reverberated off the ceiling." Harry said the crowd's reaction "left the fighters unfazed. Petrolle's blond hair, which he wore parted in the middle in the style of the times, wasn't mussed in the slightest; Tenorio was still hiding behind his gloves."

Kessler warned both fighters during the course of the third and fourth rounds to make an honest effort to pick up the pace. Harry says he went to Petrolle's corner at the end of the

Unfortunately, though filled with action, the card failed to show a profit. Paid attendance of 5,080 fans and gross receipts of $5,859 resulted in a loss of $2,500 after expenses.[30]

Hurley and Slotsky decided to go ahead with a third show on May 1 relying on the same format which had been such a success in March. Local hero John Schwake was slated to meet another veteran, this time KO Christner, in ten rounds. Unhappily, the card was canceled after several attempts to re-schedule due to injuries suffered by Christner. At the time of the cancellation, the other dates reserved with the commission had expired,

---

third and fourth rounds to tell Hurley he knew the fighters were not trying and that, unless they started to fight soon, neither of them would be paid. Kessler alleges that both times Jack replied, "Sez who, you Jew bastard!" and then told him to "remove my person to some distant place and there fornicate myself." Harry also claims that on one of these visits to the corner Billy spit at him, just missing his right shoe.

According to Kessler, when Tenorio was knocked down in the fifth round, "he sagged like a wet gunny sack when an ineffectual blow barely grazed his left temple. He lay face down in the ring, stretched out in feigned semi-consciousness." As Harry looked at the fallen figure on the canvas, he was certain that he "was looking at the prostrate form of a fake named Lope Tenorio."

Kessler responded to the allegedly faked knockdown by "kick[ing] Lope Tenorio in the ass" while at the same time giving him a "soft nudge to the buttocks," then lifting him to his feet by the armpits, and finally warning him in Spanish that he would not receive his purse unless he started fighting. After this incident, Harry claims Petrolle still tried to "follow the script" but that Tenorio got the message and started to fight in earnest. Pretty soon, in order to defend himself, Billy began fighting hard as well and "the more savagely Tenorio attacked, the more punishing was Petrolle's retaliation." By the end of the fight, the action had gotten so hot that "10,000 wildly enthusiastic and thoroughly satisfiefight fans tendered Petrolle and Tenorio a standing ovation." The bout ended up being "one of the greatest fights St. Louis had ever seen."

Afterward, Kessler, who in accordance with Missouri law was the sole arbiter, raised Petrolle's hand as winner because he had landed "the sharp, telling blows." According to Kessler, his own "actions in the ring ... turn[ed] a fix into a great fight."

Kessler wrote that the reason Hurley "had rigged a rinky-dink in St. Louis" was because he did not want to jeopardize the big-money fight Jack had scheduled for Billy with Jimmy McLarnin at Madison Square Garden a month later.

While the author is not so naïve to suppose Kessler's scenario is a complete impossibility, the fact Harry published this story for the first time ten years after Hurley's death requires a rebuttal on Jack's behalf. For the portions of the rebuttal pertaining to the fight action itself, the author relies heavily on contemporaneous eyewitness accounts of two writers from the *St. Louis Post-Dispatch*, W. J. McGoogan and John Wray.

With respect to Kessler's claims the first 4-1/2 rounds were boring and were faked, McGoogan wrote:

"**All through the contest** Petrolle waded in, trying to get close enough to do some real damage, and he presented a good target to the retreating Filipino, with the result that Billy took some stiff right-hand punches on the chin. These blows failed to stop him, however, despite the fact that he was bleeding from the nose, a cut over one eye and a cut ear."

Wray observed:

"The bout was one of **continuous action**. Tenorio was knocked to the floor, but retaliated by shaking Petrolle to his toes on frequent occasions with straight, solid rights to the head. At the close of the bout Petrolle's mouth was cut, his nose was bleeding and his ear was

and the two promoters decided to abandon the St. Louis venture altogether.

Several months later, Hurley admitted that after paying off all bills, including expenses advanced for the canceled third show, he had blown "$4,200 ... to help a pal get a start" at St. Louis. When asked later why the operation failed, Hurley just shrugged his shoulders and said, "It was just too hard to make any money in St. Louis."[31]

Meanwhile, after Petrolle was reinstated by the Minnesota boxing commission on March 31, Hurley signed for Billy to meet Jimmy McLarnin in a re-match at Madison Square Garden May 8, 1931.

---

split; Tenorio was gashed over both eyes and roughly used.

"And yet there were expressions heard that Petrolle had 'carried' Tenorio! To this writer it appeared that Petrolle, at the risk of losing a highly lucrative fight with McLarnin, took desperate chances by forcing the battle and by leaving himself open, in his effort to penetrate the baffling guard of the Filipino.

"Petrolle probably was a victim of his own reputation. The 'man who beat Jimmy McLarnin and who knocked out King Tut' was expected to display far more stuff than he seems to possess. As a matter of fact Petrolle has plenty of blowholes in his record, having been beaten NINE TIMES officially by decisions, knocked out twice and had the worst of couple of no-decision fights with King Tut." (bold emphases added by the author)

With respect to Kessler's claims a lack of action by the fighters prompted booing by the crowd and that his actions warning the fighters and Hurley in the third and fourth rounds came after the crowd's reaction, McGoogan's account indicates Kessler's actions warning Petrolle against low blows were what actually incited the crowd to boo Billy:

"Tenorio proved a very tough nut for Petrolle to crack. The Filipino showed that he is a good boxer with a fine left jab and a perfect defense. He kept body and chin pretty well covered and backed and jumped away from the advancing Petrolle with the result that several of Petrolle's punches landed low. Tenorio, however, noticed only one of them, but Kessler's ire was raised, and **his warnings to Petrolle caused the fans to 'ride' the Fargo lightweight** ... (bold emphasis added by the author)

"Petrolle was disgusted with the 'razzing' he took from the fans and asserted that he felt it was undeserved. He said he knew that Tenorio would not lead, so it was up to him to do so, and he therefore waded in, trying to land his punches. He said he was considerably worried by the referee's tactics and couldn't understand why Kessler thought he was trying to 'carry' Tenorio."

With respect to Kessler's claim that Petrolle's knockdown of Tenorio was faked, McGoogan felt that Harry entered the ring with a pre-conceived notion there was something wrong with the contest. McGoogan wrote that when Lope was knocked down, Kessler did not even begin to count before taking his remedial action against Tenorio:

"The Petrolle-Tenorio contest, however, was handicapped from the start by the cloud of suspicion which surrounded it from the time Seneca C. Taylor, Missouri Boxing Commissioner, (at first) refused to sanction the bout when it was first presented to him. Harry Kessler, the referee, judged by his handling of the bout, carried the thought of suspicion to the ring with him ...

"Then in the fifth round, when Petrolle did hit Tenorio on the head with a right-hand punch and the Filipino went to the floor, **Kessler refused to count** on the ground that Tenorio had not been hit hard enough to go down and pulled Lope to his feet and told him to go on with the fight, which Tenorio did ...

"After the contest, Tenorio declared that he had not noticed any of Petrolle's low blows except the one which struck him on the left leg and after which he was granted a rest. He said the blow which Petrolle struck him in the fifth round hurt, but did not daze him, but **he**

Hurley returned to New York in late April to secure training quarters for Petrolle and to ballyhoo the re-match. Boxing fans remembered the first Petrolle-McLarnin bout as the most exciting contest of 1930, and Madison Square Garden had hopes that the return bout might draw as much as $60,000. Attendance at Garden shows for the year were down drastically from 1930. Of its 14 cards up to then, the most profitable of the Garden's shows in 1931 was the Petrolle-King Tut bout 2-1/2 months earlier.

Hurley's return to Gotham found him reaching a much larger audience for his pre-fight prophecies than ever before. His accurate predictions of

---

went to the floor in the hopes of taking a count for a breathing spell." (bold emphases added by the author)

In this connection, it should be mentioned that, as long a fighter is hit with a significant punch, there is no rule against, or even any particular dishonor in, going down "for a breathing spell" as long as the action does not detract from the fighter's overall performance. The practice, judiciously used, has even been cited in some instances as a mark of good ring generalship.

Even if Tenorio had been planning on taking the "easy way out" by staying down for a full ten-count, it does not necessarily mean his action was pre-arranged with Hurley and/or Petrolle. Tenorio had lost quite a few bouts in the previous two years and had reached the stage of his career where he may have not wanted to take an unnecessary beating. It is even possible that this expectation was why Jack selected him as an opponent. However, absent an agreement about a fight's outcome, the mere fact a manager or a promoter has an expectation about how an opposing fighter might or might not perform does not make the fight a fix. If this were the case, more than 50 percent of all bouts could be termed "fixes."

Kessler's suggestion that Hurley might stage a fake fight so as to not jeopardize Petrolle's pending match with McLarnin has some logic, but it ignores the fact that Jack had invested a lot of money and effort trying to establish his promotional business in St. Louis on a sound footing. Why would he chance turning fans against him by staging an obviously fixed fight as Harry claimed Hurley had? Wouldn't he instead try and match Billy with a tough but less skilled opponent like Tenorio who could be expected to put up a good show but finally fall short of winning? Petrolle needed a tune-up fight against a good "opponent" before taking McLarnin on anyhow. It might as well be in St. Louis as anywhere else.

Finally, we come to Kessler's allegations of spitting by Petrolle and anti-Semitic remarks by Hurley. With respect to the claim Bill spat at Kessler, this physically would been very difficult for Billy to do because by this time fighters were wearing mouthpieces which remained in place from the beginning of the fight until it was over. In addition, it is hard to believe that Petrolle, who was trained to let Jack handle all the non-combative aspects of their partnership, would jeopardize the outcome of the fight itself and the proposed McLarnin bout by antagonizing the referee. The Tenorio bout was Billy's first in St. Louis, and he undoubtedly would have been on his best behavior in an effort to make friends and not rock the boat, especially since his manager had so much at stake as a promoter there.

All this is in addition to the fact that Kessler's allegation is entirely out of character with everything anyone else has ever said about Petrolle.

As set forth in the second paragraph of this note, Kessler remembers Petrolle having "blond hair" that was "parted in the middle." As almost everybody who has ever seen a picture of Billy knows this was about as wrong a description as could possibly be made. Petrolle was a swarthy Italian whose coal black hair was not parted in the middle. One is almost left with the impression that Harry is talking about someone else. Could he have in fact confused Billy with some other fighter or the entire incident with some other event?

With respect to Hurley's alleged anti-Semitic remarks, the corollary question to why

Petrolle's wins over McLarnin, Tut and Canzoneri, coupled with advance explanations which had detailed exactly how Billy was going to do it, had raised Jack's stature. Those same reporters who previously viewed his forecasts with obvious skepticism now treated them as opinions to be valued and featured as centerpieces in the next day's sports pages.

From this time forward, the open door Hurley enjoyed at sports desks in New York would include not just boxing writers, but also columnists whose beat included all types of sports. As a result, Jack's future declarations would reach an expanded market of readers, who, though not avid boxing

---

would Petrolle want to antagonize Kessler is why, for the same reasons, would Jack want to unnecessarily offend the referee? In addition, a less obvious but even more important point is that Hurley had more close associations, both personal and business, with Jewish people than with any other ethnic group. His banker Bill Stern, his Duluth promoting partner Phil Terk, and his St. Louis promoting partner Sam Slotsky were all of Jewish heritage. Jack's first and closest friend among New York sportswriters and the man upon whom he usually relied to wire stories from New York about Petrolle's fights back to Fargo and Duluth, Hype Igoe, was a Jewish-American. Billy McCarney's partner Joe Jacobs, a man with whom Hurley shared an office in New York, was a Jewish-American. As the author will shortly develop in the text, Jack had hired a Jewish-American woman as secretary and stenographer for the Hurley-Alvis operation in Chicago and for a while had apparently become romantically involved with her. Finally and most tellingly, at the time of the Tenorio fight, Jack very likely already had begun dating a Jewish-American woman in NewYork, the very woman who in August 1932 would become his wife.

Such associations with persons of Jewish heritage do not prove Hurley did not call Kessler "a Jew bastard," but they at least put the matter into question. Would Jack have wanted to risk offending his Jewish friends and his partner in the St. Louis venture, Sam Slotsky, by making a racial slur against the referee of the promotion? Hurley had to figure that Slotsky would hear about it after the fight. And even if Jack did make the remark, doesn't the nature of his many relationships with Jewish people help put the statement into the context of the era and Hurley's own social situation at the time? Indeed, knowing Jack as they did, would the Jewish people who knew him even have been offended at all by these remarks? And given the era and the context in which the remark allegedly was made, was it really intended to demean Jews at all, or just Kessler? The author will develop this last point a little more in his conclusion at the end of this note.

Kessler's motivation in presenting his version of the Petrolle-Tenorio fight at the beginning of his biography was to set a framework for establishing himself as a fearless square-shooter both in life and as a referee. Writing the story as an octogenarian 51 years later, and focusing on it as a defining moment in his life, likely left in Harry's mind a heightened sense of self-righteousness about what had happened, and even may, in fact, have distorted his view of what had actually occurred. After all, Hurley wasn't around any longer to give his version. Why not interpret the facts he remembered in a way most advantageous to the points he was trying to make? Also, Kessler admittedly was bitter about having lost the job as referee of the Matthews-Marciano fight in 1952, an assignment he was about to receive, but which he believed had not been proffered because Jack at the last minute had exercised his right to veto the commission's selection of Harry. When he lost the job to referee the Marciano-Matthews fight, Kessler missed out on one of his first opportunities to referee a major contest in New York.

Having summarized Kessler's account of the Petrolle-Tenorio bout and, given Hurley's inability to defend himself, having constructed from available news articles a rebuttal on his behalf, the author offers the following points as his opinion of what actually happened:

fans, regularly read the columns of such all-around sports journalists as Damon Runyon, Paul Gallico, Westbrook Pegler, Bill Corum, Joe Williams, Joe Vila, and Davis Walsh to satisfy their need for sports information.

With his pool of journalistic allies now encompassing a much broader segment of New York's "fourth estate," Hurley expanded his repertoire of stories as well. Part of this process required him to know the special interests of the specific writer he was visiting and to shape his stories accordingly. Indeed, Jack's experience with his own weekly column gave him a better idea than most about what went into making a good story.

---

1) Kessler more likely than not misread the situation and was wrong in his opinion that Hurley and/or Petrolle were trying to "fix" the bout. This conclusion is based on the other eyewitness accounts of the fight and on an analysis of the incentives that both Hurley and Petrolle had to make the card a success as opposed to the benefits of engaging in a "fix."

2) Tenorio would have been able to get up after being knocked down in the fifth round, but it is uncertain whether he was planning to stay down or not because Kessler did not even start to count over him. In any event, whether or not he would have gotten up is an issue independent of whether Hurley or Petrolle had any part in a "fix" (see answer to (1) above).

3) Hurley and Kessler exchanged words, likely between rounds and probably even after the fight. Jack would have been indignant at being accused of having told his fighter not to make an honest effort and at claims his fighter was making a bad fight. He would have looked upon Kessler as the worst of all possible referees – an amateur hobbyist who caters to the emotions of the crowd and incites it against the fighters rather than exercising his independent judgment about what is actually happening in the ring.

Hurley would have viewed Kessler as an interloper in the corner between rounds who interfering with his ability to minister to the needs of his fighter.

Since Hurley was well known for having a sharp tongue, it is possible and maybe even likely that at some point in the evening Jack called Kessler "a Jew bastard," not out of any deep-rooted feeling of anti-Semitism, given Hurley's close personal and business ties at the time to other Jewish people, but instead out of the very personal motivation to get under Harry's skin. Kessler's claim that Jack had "fixed" the Petrolle-Tenorio fight would have hit Hurley where it hurt most, his reputation and potentially his pocketbook, and in his mind it would have deserved retaliation in kind.

Hurley knew Kessler would take offense at the remark and Jack, in the heat of that moment, may have wanted to offend Harry in the quickest and most efficient way he could so he could get back to tending to Petrolle during the very short rest period between rounds. In Hurley's mind, the epithet would have been an accurate description of Kessler, at that particular instant, anyway: Harry was Jewish and he was acting like a bastard, at least in the popular if not literal sense of the word. Indeed, Jack himself would have taken less offense at being called "an Irish bastard," "a Catholic bastard," or a "fish-eating bastard" who should go and perform an unnatural sex act on himself, than at being charged with fixing a fight or telling his pride and joy, Billy Petrolle, to give anything less than his best effort.

4) Kessler exercised fairness when he awarded the decision to Petrolle over Tenorio. McGoogan of the *St. Louis Post-Dispatch* scored the fight a very close five rounds for Billy four for Lope, and one round even (the Associated Press had it 5-2-3 for Petrolle). Given the tension between Hurley and Harry that night, it would have been an easy matter for Kessler to have awarded the decision to Tenorio out of spite and thereby upset Jack and Billy's plans for the big payday with McLarnin in May.

[30] McGoogan, "Petrolle Is Victor over Tenorio in Close Bout," *St. Louis Post-Dispatch*, April 11, 1931, sports section.

[31] Runyon, Damon, "Pure Grit Gave Impetus to the Man from Fargo," *New York American*,

On April 29, Petrolle came down with a case of influenza requiring his May 8th bout with McLarnin to be moved to May 27. The postponement left Hurley with extra time on his hands. In the interim, he decided to make the rounds to a few New York sports desks before focusing his ballyhoo on the upcoming fight. Three visits to New York's most widely read sports columnists in early May provide glimpses as to how Jack tailored his approach to suit the particular journalist he was calling upon.

Hurley first met Damon Runyon when the *New York Evening Journal*'s Hype Igoe and the *Newark Star-Eagle*'s Walter St. Denis introduced him to the celebrated *New York American* columnist in May 1931. Although Runyon had not as yet warmed up to Petrolle, a situation which would change after Billy kayoed Justo Suarez in June, he was well known as having a special fondness for heavyweight fighters, even to the point of having shared a financial interest in several with Jack Kearns

The topic which most interested Runyon was Retzlaff. Damon as yet had never seen him fight, but had heard that Hurley refused Tony Biddle's $25,000 offer for Charley's contract. Runyon was, to say the least, intrigued. Just how in the world could Jack justify not selling Retzlaff for that much money? Charley couldn't possibly be that good. In fact, Runyon wrote, he doubted that any heavyweight prospect was that good and, if Damon himself had 20 heavyweights, he would sell them all for $25,000.

During the course of their conversation, which coincidentally filled a day's column, Hurley ended the discussion by revealing that, while Retzlaff agreed with Jack "that a single fighter can go farther than a married fighter," Charley also maintained that a "manager ought to be single, too." Consequently, Hurley said, "I made an agreement with him to that effect."

Runyon, obviously amused, ended the piece with his own comment, "'I insist that you sell the guy ... He does too much thinking to be a fighter.'"[32]

Hurley next visited the *Evening Journal*'s Bill Corum to take issue with an article in which the columnist described "young Mr. Hurley" as a "Johnny come lately." Jack showed "Mr. Corum a few gray hairs which have started to crop out proving that I wasn't as young as he thought," and then described his experiences as a small-town "manager, promoter, trainer, second, announcer, publicity man and whatnot." Hurley argued it was tougher to promote in Fargo with a limited budget than in New York "where the cream of the crop [is] knocking at [the] door daily asking for work."[33]

Afterward, Corum admitted Hurley was not such a novice after all. More importantly, Corum became one of Jack's biggest boosters.[34]

August 19, 1931, sports section.
[32] Campbell, *op. cit.*, May 9, 1931, sports section. Hurley, "Shadow Boxing," *Duluth News Tribune*, July 27, 1931, sports section. Biddle's highest offer for Retzlaff's contract which the author has found was for $20,000, not $25,000 as stated by Runyon.
[33] Hurley, "Ring Rations," *Fargo Forum*, May 24, 1931, sports section.
[34] Corum, Bill, "The Harp That Was Twanged," *New York Evening Journal*, May 26, 1931,

When he called upon *Evening Graphic* sports editor Davis J. Walsh, Hurley decided it was time to plug the upcoming Petrolle-McLarnin fight. Even on this occasion, however, his comments were offered as much to entertain as to promote the fight. For Walsh, the bait was a few borrowed lines from a comic strip of the day, "Joe Jinks," which was about a fight manager of the same name who managed a boxer named "Dynamite Dan."

As luck would have it, Jinks, in the episode the day before Hurley met with Walsh, had phoned a reporter and said his fighter would name "the round, the minute, the punch, and the spot" in which Dynamite Dan would knock his foe, Ole Bashum, for a loop. During his real-life interview with the *Evening Graphic* columnist, Jack relied heavily on Jinks' catchy jargon to describe "how, when, and where Billy was going to park a sleeping potion on Jimmy McLarnin's chin when the two meet on May 27."

The similarity between Hurley and the comic-strip character was not lost on Walsh. The columnist, whose forte was breezy, humorous, and slightly irreverent prose, could not resist the temptation to poke fun at Jack as a real-life Joe Jinks in his next day's column.[35]

Hurley's cultivation of columnists like Runyon, Corum, and Walsh reaped longer-term benefits than he ever could have anticipated. Each of their columns were syndicated to newspapers all over the U. S. Over a working life that lasted another 40 years, their columns made Jack and his entertaining idiosyncrasies familiar to sports fans for generations to come.

In the week prior to the May 27th fight, Hurley abandoned light-hearted banter and focused all his energies on the Petrolle-McLarnin rematch itself. Jack claimed their prior fight proved Billy's fighting style was made-to-order for anything McLarnin had to offer. Jimmy's best punch was a straight right, and Petrolle had nullified it by stepping in and aggressively throwing left hooks to the head. According to Hurley, Billy figured to "beat him again and make an even more decisive job of it this time."[36]

Oddsmakers, however, disregarded McLarnin's earlier defeat and ruled him an 8 to 5 favorite. Experts anticipated "one of the best fights of the spring season, unless Jimmy puts on his Ray Miller act." In that bout, McLarnin waged a boring fight at the Garden against Miller, who had previously kayoed Jimmy in Detroit. Despite expectations of a slam-bang affair, McLarnin disappointed the crowd by playing it safe and boxing carefully as he jabbed his way to a lackluster decision.

At the morning weigh-in, Petrolle scaled 138 pounds and McLarnin 142.

---

sports section.

[35] Campbell, *op. cit.* Unfortunately, the microfilm for the *Evening Graphic* is very hit and miss and, as far as the author can ascertain, Walsh's original article does not survive (at least in library microfilm copies of the *Graphic*). The author's information comes from Campbell's account of Walsh's article and the Joe Jinks strip itself. Forythe, Vic. "Joe Jinks." *New York World*, May 7, 1931, p. 12.

[36] Wood, "Heavy Situation Still Puzzle," *New York Sun*, May 26, 1931, sports section.

The crowd which piled into Madison Square Garden the evening of May 27 exceeded everyone's greatest hopes. "It looked like the good old days, with the paid attendance amounting to 17,846 and the gross receipts reaching $82,377.38. Winner and loser each receive 25 percent of the net gate of $70,184.98. All of which goes to show that there is no depression in the sock market when the fans are given a fight that appeals to them."

After two slow rounds, Petrolle started the action in the third by jumping in with a left hook to the head. Billy held the advantage most of the way in this session, but McLarnin landed a left and then a cracking right to the jaw that had Petrolle woozy at the bell. It was one of McLarnin's few rights and it was his hardest punch of the fight.

The fourth round "was one of the best seen in the Garden this year." The fighters "went from one rally to the other in an amazing avalanche of blows." Although the round was scored as even on most scorecards, it was the turning point of the fight. From then on, McLarnin surged ahead and won every round, except the seventh, when Petrolle landed frequently with his left on Jimmy's head and body.

Petrolle tired in the final rounds, as "Jimmy was a shifting shadow that was hard to hit, and [he] counter-punched with blows that almost always found a mark." At the end, Billy's right eye was almost closed, his nose bleeding, and his face a mass of bruises.

McLarnin, who later said he felt "twinges" in his right hand in an early round, relied almost entirely on his left throughout the bout. With that hand, Jimmy "poked, propped, hooked and uppercut ... religiously." For the most part, he boxed carefully and "gambled only when he had been clipped himself and had to fight back in order to survive."

At the final bell, "Petrolle's courage earned him the unstinted plaudits of the mob. No matter how he suffered ... the Fargo Express kept tearing in, punching with both tireless fists ... Though Jimmy McLarnin fought an intelligent fight, the abysmal courage of the Dakotan caught the fancy of everyone who admires reckless daring ... and when Petrolle dragged his battered body back to his corner the cheers for him were quite as much as for the victorious Baby Face."[37]

---

[37] Wood, "Seven Rounds Go to Jimmy," *New York Sun*, May 28, 1931, sports section ("It looked like the good old days ..."). Kofoed, "Fargo Boy Wins Plaudits with Display of Courage" (subtitle), *New York Evening Post*, May 28, 1931, sports section ("one of the best seen ..."; "Petrolle's courage ..."). Walsh, Davis J., "Vancouver Bearcat Gets Revenge for Trouncing Suffered Six Months Ago," *New York Daily Graphic*, May 28, 1931, sports section ("gambled only when ..."). Vidmer, "McLarnin Wins over Petrolle in Bout at Garden," *New York Herald Tribune*, May 28, 1931, sports section ("shifting shadow ... always found a mark"). Igoe, Hype, "Garden Battle Round by Round," *New York Evening Journal*, May 28, 1931, sports section ("... amazing avalanche of blows"). Igoe, "McLarnin Whips Petrolle with Left Alone," *New York Evening Journal*, May 28, 1931, sports section ("poked, propped, hooked, and uppercut ...").

Petrolle avoids McLarnin's left during their May 27, 1931 contest.

Petrolle and McLarnin head-to-head.

Petrolle loops a right to McLarnin's chin.

McLarnin's left forces Billy to turn away as Arthur Donovan watches.

Petrolle offered his take on the fight in the dressing room: "I don't want to take one bit of credit away from Jimmy McLarnin. He fought a clever fight. He didn't fight my kind of fight. If I hadn't chased him there wouldn't have been a fight had I not gone to him. If I had laid back like he did, there would have been another Ray Miller-McLarnin squawk.

"I think my recent attack of flu left me sluggish. My head told me what to do but I was always off time. I just wasn't there. I lacked something and I don't know what it was. McLarnin seemed much stronger than before. He had the good sense to conserve his strength. I lost energy going after him."[38]

Hurley had his own opinion about the evening's entertainment. He argued Petrolle deserved the decision because most of McLarnin's punches had not been in accordance with the rules. "I am a believer in living up to the rules of boxing," Jack told the *New York Sun*'s Wilbur Wood the day after the fight. "The rules distinctly state that any punch not delivered with the knuckles is illegal. Most of McLarnin's lefts were delivered with the front side of his fist. They were cuffs or slaps, but not punches.

"Either a fighter should be made to live up to the rules and punch with the knuckles or the rules should be changed. Look at Maxie Rosenbloom. According to the rules, it [should be] impossible for him to win a fight. Tiger Flowers was another fellow who used the illegal slapping style. Yet when a referee in Chicago had the courage to call him the loser in a fight with Mickey Walker, he was given the gate and has not worked since. If the officials are not going to live up to the code, the rules should be changed.

"... Anyway, you have to give Petrolle credit. He still had some of the flu in his system, but he kept on walking into McLarnin. If he hadn't, it would have been no fight. Don't overlook that when handing out credit. McLarnin was in there looking out strictly for McLarnin, taking no chances. Petrolle was fighting to revive the boxing game by making it a pleasing bout. If he had been content to lay back and wait for McLarnin, like McLarnin waited for him, it would have been another black eye for the game."[39]

Although boxing writers generally disagreed with Hurley that Billy deserved the decision they did concede that "the blue jowled Petrolle carried ... the fight to the heavier McLarnin every step of the way. For this he deserved a world of credit, for otherwise it might have been a repetition of McLarnin's agonizing second edition with Miller."[40]

Indeed, rather than hurting Petrolle's prospects, most reporters believed "sentiment for a fight between Petrolle and Canzoneri is on the increase. The Fargo Express made such a gallant attempt against McLarnin that

---

[38] Igoe, *op. cit.*
[39] Wood, "Garden Has Outdoor Problem," *New York Sun*, May 29, 1931, sports section.
[40] Williams, Joe, "By Joe Williams," *New York Telegram*, May 28, 1931, sports section.

everyone seems to be pulling for him to get a shot at the lightweight title."[41]

Garden matchmaker McArdle agreed Petrolle deserved consideration, but first wanted him to fight Justo Suarez of Argentina on June 25, 1931. In actual fact, McArdle was more interested in building up Suarez than in helping Billy. Justo was the new lightweight sensation, never having lost in 48 amateur and 24 pro bouts. Fistic experts generally agreed that the man from the Argentine ranked right up there with Petrolle and Jackie (Kid) Berg as a logical contender for Canzoneri's lightweight crown.

In his first United States campaign a year earlier, the 22-year-old Suarez took New York by storm. In short order, Justo won five consecutive bouts, registering decision wins over Herman Perlick, Joe Glick, Ray Miller, and Kid Kaplan, plus a six-round knockout of Bruce Flowers, in the latter's first kayo loss. In addition, wins in Argentina over such contenders as Luis Vicentini (W 12), Hilario Martinez (TKO 5), Stanislaus Loayza (KO 3), and Babe Herman (KO 1) gave added luster to Suarez's bid for recognition.[42]

Suarez returned to Argentina at the beginning of 1931 as a national hero. There, he registered three more kayos before heading back to New York to resume his quest for a title shot. For his fight with Petrolle, several Buenos Aires newspapers pooled their resources and put up $25,000 to sponsor a live radio broadcast of the bout for transmission back to Argentina.

Suarez was figured as a 9-to-5 favorite over Billy, odds which increased to 13-to-5 when they entered the ring. Not surprisingly, Hurley dismissed these reports with the remark that odds never meant much to Petrolle: "It is just when everybody expects to see him licked that Billy contributes his best fights. You could write your own ticket on Canzoneri when Tony boxed Petrolle in Chicago. Everybody said Billy was just going in to pick up a chunk of dough. As it happened, he gave Canzoneri a terrific pasting.

"It was as high as 8 to 1 against Petrolle when he met McLarnin in their first fight. I guess everybody still remembers what Billy did to James. I only hope the odds go sky high on Suarez. If they do it will be a sure thing for Petrolle to win."[43]

A total of 9,394 fans paid $23,826 to see Petrolle, 139-1/2 pounds, beat the odds and score a ninth-round knockout over the pride of the Argentine, Justo Suarez, 138-pounds, "in a thrilling fight from beginning to end."[44]

---

[41] Wood, *op. cit.*

[42] BoxRec, www.boxrec.com as of May 2014.

[43] Wood, "Poll Shows Suarez Favorite," *New York Sun*, June 24, 1931, sports section.

[44] Generally, Madison Square Garden shut down its weekly indoor shows during the summer and limited its promotions to two or three major outdoor events at Yankee Stadium or the Polo Grounds. The theory was fans were too busy in the summer to attend weekly shows, but would pay more to see a few especially attractive shows at a larger venue. The Petrolle-Suarez show on June 25 was therefore an experiment to see if Depression-era fans could be lured to a reasonably priced indoor show. The Garden corporation viewed the Petrolle-Suarez fight as an attractive, if not major, show. The relatively small turnout of 9,394 at the fight ended the Garden's plans to stage more indoor shows during the summer.

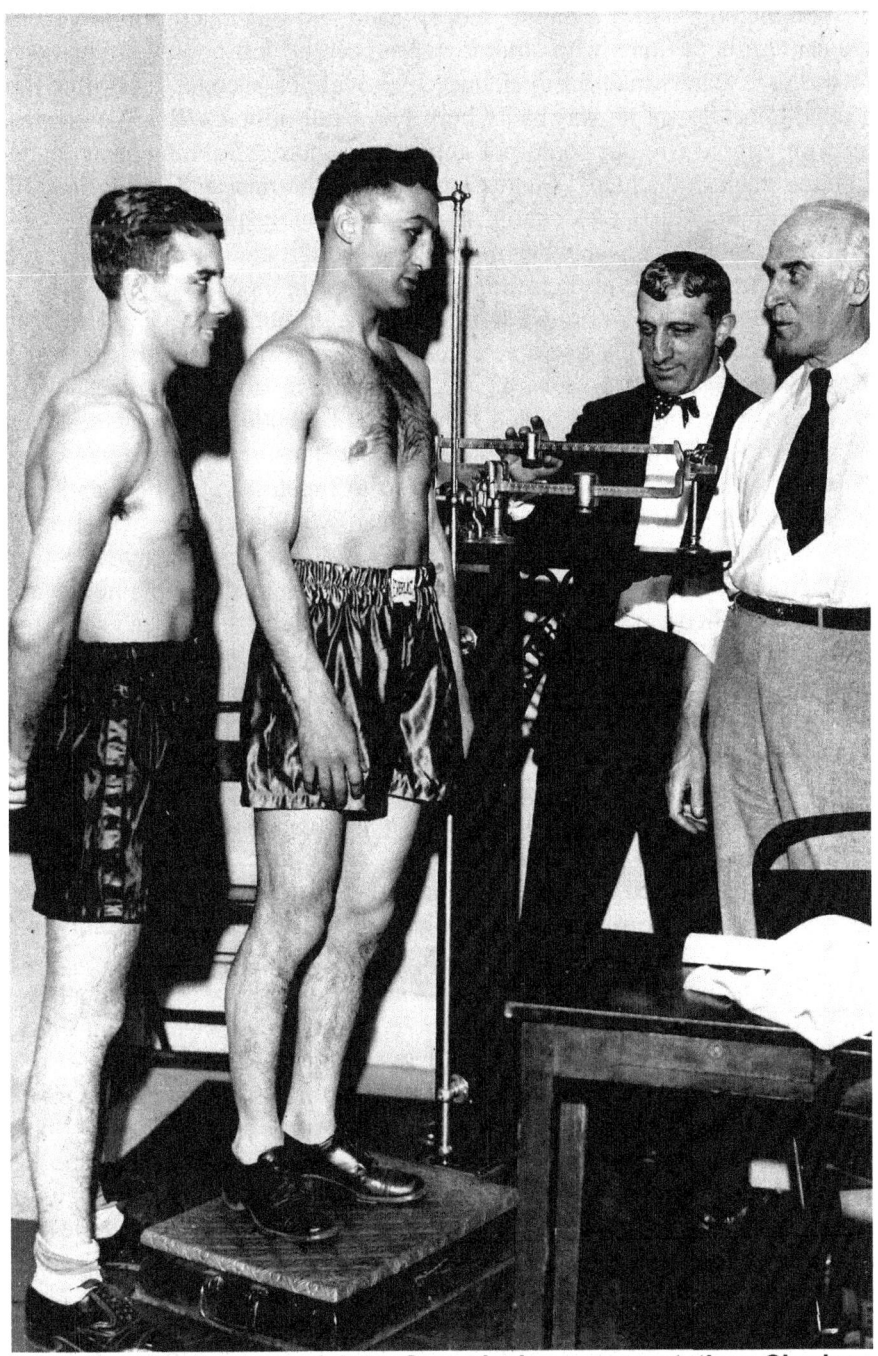

The Petrolle-Suarez weigh-in. Commission representatives Charles Goodman and John McNeil officiate. Petrolle weighed 139-1/2 pounds and Suarez 138.

With the bout barely a minute old, Petrolle sent Suarez crashing twice to the canvas, both times with similar right-uppercut, left-hook combinations to the jaw. Each time, Justo bounced up without a count, but after the second knockdown, he was badly hurt. For a full minute, "Petrolle opened up with a rapid fire but could not get a clean shot." "Bobbing around and fighting back undaunted," Suarez survived the barrage and in the last 30 seconds miraculously took charge and put Billy on the defensive.

Suarez fought like "a wildcat in the second round." For a full three minutes, he "lunged at Petrolle, swinging wide hooks, left and right, without stopping. A reformed left-hander, he frequently reverted to that style of boxing, but his fists never ceased making wide arcs that beat the Fargo Express steadily backward," forcing him to break ground repeatedly.

When the second round ended, "Suarez had 10,000 customers standing on chairs and throwing hats" up in the air. To those fans, it seemed clear Billy "had shot the works in his vain effort to finish it in the first, and that the youth and strength of the South American would carry him to victory." Justo "punched Petrolle all over the ring and ... looked like a winner."

When Petrolle returned to his corner, Hurley was ready with a new plan. Jack had watched the iron-chinned Suarez absorb Billy's best head shots for two rounds and keep rushing in recklessly for more. Unless Petrolle could slow the Argentinean down, he risked being overwhelmed by Justo's wild charges and even nailed by one of his unpredictable roundhouse swings.

After having Petrolle relax and take a few deep breaths, Jack advised him to not hit Suarez on the chin again until later, and instead, "When you leave this corner you bend over and you punch up with both hands to the body."

Round three found Suarez back using the same attack which had been so successful the previous round. The strategy was effective in the first half of the round until he "rushed Billy to the ropes and tried to measure him with a right. As Justo fired the right, Billy slipped under it, sunk his own right to the stomach, and shook up the Buenos Aires boy with a two-handed attack. Toward the close, two especially vicious rights to the wind bent Justo double. It was a close round, but Petrolle was entitled to the edge."

The third round was the turning point. Starting in the fourth, Petrolle became the aggressor and the bout gradually turned into a rout. "Body punches robbed Suarez's blows of their steam and much of the time he merely was making a bluff at fighting. Justo tried every trick he knew to escape that murderous attack. At times he broke into a run. Sometimes he turned southpaw. But there was no way he could get away from those terrific wallops in the breadbasket."

At the end of the seventh round, Petrolle said Justo was ready for a kayo, but Hurley remained adamant Billy should limit his attack to Suarez's body. Jack's answer was, "No, not yet. Stay right down there and punch up."

Justo Suarez, who never tasted defeat until beaten by Petrolle.

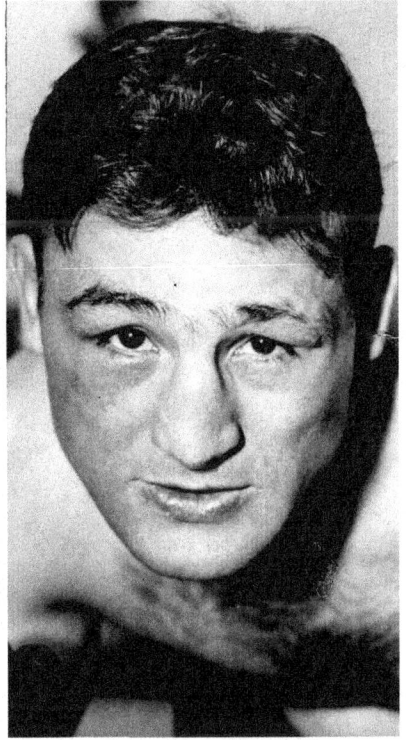

A close-up of Petrolle.

Petrolle (left) and Suarez each look for an opening in the 7th round.

Petrolle slips inside a looping left to deliver a right to Justo's body.

Petrolle's ninth-round kayo of Suarez.

After the eighth, Hurley gave Petrolle the go-ahead: "All right, now is the time. Start this round the same way and after three or four punches to the body, raise up and hit him a right hand on the chin. If he don't go, get down again and then raise up and hit him a left hand on the chin. If he don't go then, you stay down."

Petrolle came out "with determination written all over his face and started to slaughter Justo with left hooks and overhand rights to the face and body. He feinted a left and hit Suarez with a terrific right to the chin, staggering him against the ropes where "he sunk a series of lefts and rights to the stomach." An instant later, "a right uppercut almost sent Suarez out of the ring, and when he straightened, Petrolle hooked a left to the head and shot a right to the jaw and the battle was over." The end came at 1:51 of the ninth round.

After the fight, even the most experienced boxing writers agreed the fight was one of the most exciting they had ever witnessed. Two weeks later, the *New York Sun*'s Wilbur Wood was still marveling that "Petrolle's masterful demonstration of the value of body punching" had been "one of the finest exhibitions of that type of mixing seen in years."[45]

---

[45] The author's description of the fight was a synthesis of articles from the following sources: Heinz, "The Man Who Makes Fighters," *Esquire Magazine*, May 1952, p. 103 (all discussions between rounds). Wood, "Petrolle Wins in Ninth Round," *New York Sun*, June 26, 1931, sports section (all quotations pertaining to the action except those which follow in this note). Frayne, Ed, "So. American Champ Puts Up Valiant Fight," *New York American*, June 26, 1931, p. 19 ("Suarez had 10,000 customers standing on chairs ..."). Igoe, "Petrolle Finds Flaw in Suarez Defense; Bang!" *Duluth Herald*, June 26, 1931, sports section ("had punched Petrolle all over the ring ..."). Byrne, Tim, "Suarez Battered to Knockout by Petrolle's Onset," *New York Evening Post*, June 26, 1931, p. 16 ("Bobbing around and ..."; "wildcat in the second round ..."; "lunged at Petrolle ..."). Simon, Jack, "Fargo Express Earns Right to Meet Tony in Outdoor Lightweight Title Bout," *New York Evening Graphic*, June 26, 1931, sports section ("with determination written all over his face ..."). Dawson, James P., "Suarez Is Stopped by Petrolle in 9th," *New York Times*, June 26, 1931, sports section ("a right uppercut almost sent ..."). Wood, "Body Punching Coming Back," *New York Sun*, July 10, 1931, sports section.

The Petrolle-Suarez fight must have been truly exciting. The next day's hyperbole in the New York papers was, in the author's experience, unsurpassed in the annals of ring literature. Even some of the usually more conservative members of the boxing writers' corps like James Dawson and Richards Vidmer could not restrain themselves. Some examples, all from June 26, 1931 –

Ed Frayne of the *New York American*:
> "Roll all the great fights you remember into one, throw in a keg of dynamite and a ringful of cannon crackers and there you have Bill (Fargo Express) Petrolle's knockout victory over Justo Suarez at Madison Square Garden last night."

Richards Vidmer of the *New York Herald Tribune*:
> "They advertise battles of the century, but sometimes the real battles bob up unexpectedly and the best of the year, at least, was fought in Madison Square Garden last night when Billy Petrolle, the Fargo Express, with a deep desire to meet Tony Canzoneri for the lightweight title knocked out the favored Justo Suarez, of Argentina, in 1:51 of the ninth round.

Twenty years afterward, Hurley told W. C. Heinz the Suarez bout was Petrolle's greatest fight. Billy's memories of the epic battle were equally vivid. He recalled Justo as the toughest man he ever faced: "I knocked him out because I could hit him in the belly. Hitting him on the chin was like trying to break concrete with a toy hammer."[46]

After the Suarez fight, McArdle offered Hurley the choice of a big show at Yankee Stadium for Petrolle in July or August against either Canzoneri for the lightweight title or against McLarnin in a second rematch. Since Billy would receive 22-1/2 percent of the net gate against McLarnin as

---

"Here was a scrap that had 10,000 customers clinging to their seats and yelling themselves hoarse from start to finish – a fight without a second that wasn't packed with action and flying fists. It had all the elements of drama from the first to the last of the count which Referee Patsy Haley tolled over the flattened form of the South American in the ninth session."

James Dawson of the *New York Times*:

"In one of the most spectacular ring battles seen here in recent years, Petrolle knocked out his rival in one minute 51 seconds of the ninth round, after subjecting Suarez to a beating that few boxers of the current era would have or could have withstood for so long ...

"The bout had crowded into it all the thrills known to the sport: the spectacle of Suarez being floored twice in the opening round to rally gallantly and press a desperate, untiring attack over the two succeeding rounds, a fighter who knew no restraining influence."

Hype Igoe of the *New York Journal American*:

"The 'Fargo Express' is roaring toward Duluth today with Justo Suarez smeared all over the cow-catcher. Billy Petrolle is at the throttle, and what an engineer! He flayed the invading Argentine champion within an inch of his life in Madison Square Garden last night, and yet the sloe-eyed Buenos Aires boy fought back with such tigerish fury that one of the greatest battles in the history of lightweights resulted.

"Petrolle fought with the cunning of an old pit dog. Courage was the banner which each flung to the wind, and Suarez's was only lowered when he fell over backward with his colors tangled about him. They don't mold braver boys."

Harry Grayson of the *New York World-Telegram*:

"Billy Petrolle, a broken warrior going blind two years ago, today had contributed another absorbing chapter to one of the most amazing comeback stories in ring history. He dealt young Justo Suarez a cruel beating at the Garden last night, the tragic ending of which saw the pride of the Argentine dumped on the canvas a helpless heap in the ninth round.

"It was an upset almost as astounding as the savage lacing the old warhorse with the wobbly legs handed Jimmy McLarnin, the killer, last November. And blasé Broadway, used to the unusual, was babbling again and shaking its head in wonderment as the outmoded Fargo Express shouted for another crack at McLarnin and chances at the championships held by Tony Canzoneri and Young Jack Thompson."

Tim Byrne of the *New York Evening Post*:

"It was a thrilling lightweight fight from beginning to end. There was constant, hair-raising action every second on one side or the other. First it was Petrolle, then Suarez, raging back and forth in a ceaseless flailing of fists."

Wilbur Wood of the *New York Sun*:

opposed to 12-1/2 percent as the challenger's end against the champion, Hurley chose "the rubber match" with McLarnin.

Asked by Cubby Campbell why he was passing up an opportunity for Petrolle to fight for a championship, Hurley explained that since McLarnin was a welterweight, even if Billy lost to Jimmy his prestige as a lightweight would not be affected to any great degree. As a result, Petrolle could fight McLarnin first in August and still fight Canzoneri for the lightweight title later on, thus insuring two large purses instead of just one.[47]

Hurley spent five years working to make Petrolle a drawing card in New York, and had finally succeeded. Billy earned almost $18,000 in the second McLarnin fight, and he stood to make as much, if not more, in a third fight.

Now that Petrolle was at the apex of his popularity, he could have a bout with Canzoneri any time he wanted. Since Billy boasted a win over Tony, the champion, because of his competitive nature, wanted to "square" things with Petrolle and eliminate the cloud he cast over Canzoneri's title. Tony also knew he could draw a bigger gate with Billy than any other challenger.

In Hurley's opinion, the longer he put off Canzoneri the better. As long as Petrolle remained unbeaten as a lightweight, he would remain the leading contender and a major drawing card. Given the state of the lightweight division, he could make more money by fighting upcoming youngsters than challenging Tony. Each of these fights could be expected to realize $7,000-$12,000, about the same as a challenger's share against the champion.

Even if Petrolle defeated Canzoneri, he might not be able to hold the title long enough to make significant money. The various boxing commissions would to a large extent dictate when, where, and who Billy could fight. With Petrolle's extraordinary drawing power as the leading lightweight contender, Jack figured he could handpick whatever opponents he wished.[48]

"The hatchet-faced Fargo Italian turned in one of the gems of his career in handing the swaggering South American one of the worst beatings any fighter ever has taken in the Garden ring. Suarez was so badly broken up by the terrific body punching he absorbed from the third on that he scarcely could speak over the radio hookup to South America."

[46] Payton, Ralph, "The Fargo Express," *Boxing Illustrated*, May 1959, p. 33. The beating Suarez took from Petrolle effectively ended his career. He would have three more fights before retiring in 1932. A one-fight comeback in 1935 would prove unsuccessful, and he would die of tuberculosis in 1938 at the age of 29.

[47] Campbell, *op. cit.*, June 26 or 27, 1931, sports section.

[48] At first blush, gamesmanship such as Hurley was engaging in might be thought of as outdated nowadays. New weight divisions proliferate, and self-styled sanctioning bodies have created multiple titles within each weight division, giving rise to at least 128 "world champions" as of May 2014. Being No. 1 contender in any of the divisions lacks the stature it once had until 1970 or so when there were only ten divisions. A fighter must become recognized as a champion by at least one of the sanctioning bodies or he has no hope of making any real money. However, upon closer reflection, the situation of the champion and No. 1 contender in the 1930s is analogous to the situation of two champions from different sanctioning bodies today. Can a champion today make more money by limiting himself to

The third Petrolle-McLarnin bout was set for August 20, 1931, at Yankee Stadium. The card was Madison Square Garden's first outdoor show of the year and gate receipts well in excess of $100,000 were anticipated. The Garden was so confident of the match's appeal that the price of ringside seats were set at $9.10, which was top dollar for a non-title fight in a lighter weight division, even in the balmy days before the Depression.

Unfortunately, the fight did not catch on as expected. A week out, only $1,800 in ticket sales had been reported. Critics attributed fan apathy to the exorbitant ticket prices and to the belief that McLarnin would likely employ the careful boxing style of the second fight rather than the risky punching style of the first. The opinion of fans and experts alike was that if the battlers chose to slug it out, Petrolle had an even chance, but if Jimmy refused to mix it up, the third fight figured to be a repeat of the second.

On August 13, Hurley appeared before the state athletic commission with a copy of its own rule book in hand, ready to argue that McLarnin had persistently fouled Billy in the second fight by cuffing and slapping his way to a decision. Jack's plan was to urge that if Jimmy used such tactics in the third fight, the ring officials should penalize McLarnin by deducting rounds from him on their scorecards.

The commission's response, after informing Hurley in no uncertain terms it was not his business to dictate how boxing was run in New York, was to order Jack out of the room even before he finished the opening paragraph of his statement. Hurley's argument did not go to waste, however. After being shown the door, he made his case about McLarnin's unfair tactics to a host of boxing writers waiting outside on the steps leading up to the commission offices. The next day's sports pages were packed full of Jack's charges.

A day later, Hurley ratcheted up the attack by telling matchmaker McArdle that unless the Garden convinced the commission to reconsider, Jack was going to pull Billy out of the fight: "I can see the writing on the wall. I have too many offers for Petrolle to get tossed around like this. All I ask is that McLarnin fight according to the rules. They make Petrolle do it, but McLarnin makes up his own as he goes along. McLarnin has always been the favorite son in this town. All I ask is the same treatment for Petrolle that they give McLarnin. If I don't get it, the fight is off."[49]

Hurley backed away from his threat after McArdle told him "that none of his fighters will show in this state for many a day" if Petrolle pulled out.

---

fights against the challengers rated by his own sanctioning body or by taking a chance and fighting the champion of another sanctioning body in a unification bout? Managers (and/or the promoters/heads of the competing sanctioning bodies) of champions in the same weight class, but from different sanctioning bodies, must make a risk analysis similar to the one Hurley made with Petrolle in the 1930s when they decide whether or not to match their fighters against each other in "unification" bouts.

[49] Frayne, "Hurley to Have His Way or Quit," *New York American*, August 14, 1931, sports section. Hurley's quote has been condensed.

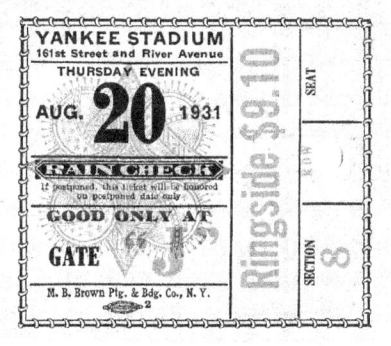

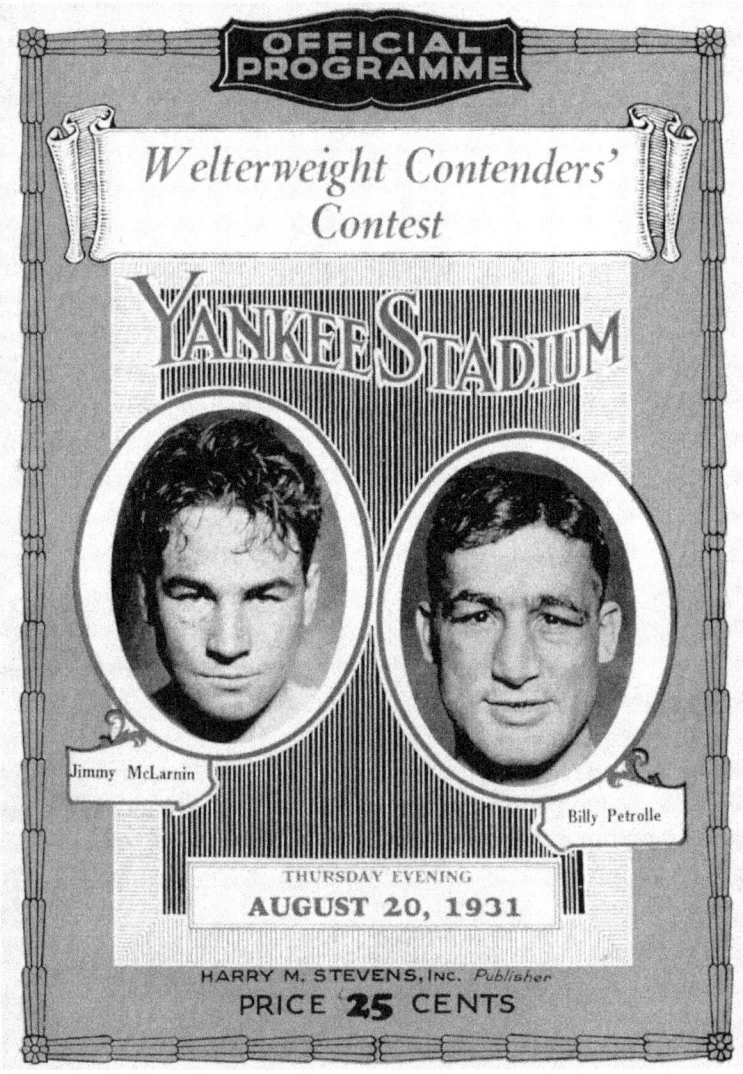

Program and ticket for the third Petrolle-McLarnin fight.

Jack, however, was not finished stirring the pot.

Hurley went after the commission again. In a "public apology," he said he was sorry for trying "to persuade that august body to force McLarnin to stand up and fight, punch for punch, when he meets Petrolle." He now realized "in refusing to entertain my plea the commissioners merely were admitting it was beyond their power to make McLarnin open up ... Neither the New York commission nor all the other commissions put together can make a boxer fight if he has made up his mind not to get hurt."[50]

On August 15, Hurley told Davis J. Walsh of the *Evening Graphic* that not only did McLarnin physically quit without good reason in his Detroit fight with Ray Miller, but he also mentally quit in his first fight with Petrolle. Jack claimed Jimmy purposely stayed down until he thought the count had reached ten and "then got up with the idea of claiming that he hadnt heard the count." In Hurley's view, Jimmy did this to avoid taking a beating, but "they fooled him," and "he had to take the beating anyhow."[51]

Hurley's oratory made no impression on the boxing commission, but it did help generate interest in the fight. According to the *Sun*'s Wilbur Wood:

> "At last the fans are talking about that third meeting between McLarnin and Petrolle. The fiery outbursts of Jack Hurley ... have instilled some life into the attraction. When Hurley started to squawk against what he terms McLarnin's sneaky tactics in the second fight with Petrolle, nobody took him seriously. But Jack emitted such long and loud blasts that he finally got under the skin of old Pop Foster, who considers any reflection on McLarnin as nothing short of treason.
>
> "Judging from the style McLarnin has displayed in his sparring sessions during the last few days he also has been annoyed and will take a chance on slugging with the Fargo Express. That is just what Petrolle would like him to do, for Billy realizes that if Baby Face keeps the contest on a boxing basis McLarnin will have a considerable advantage."[52]

In addition to trying to build the gate and annoy McLarnin so he would swap punches with Petrolle, Hurley's verbal attacks against Jimmy had other strategic purposes. Even if the commissioners did not listen to him, Jack hoped his protests about slapping might either convince the referee and judges to penalize McLarnin for such violations or else cause him to alter his fighting style. Whatever the effect, if baiting Jimmy and his

---

[50] Wood, "Hurley Talks a Good Fight," *New York Sun*, August 18, 1931, p. 35.
[51] Walsh, "Petrolle's Manager Says Baby Face Quit Physically in First Encounter Here," *New York Evening Graphic*, August 15, 1931, p. 17.
[52] Wood, "Busy Week in Sock Market," *New York Sun*, August 17, 1931, sports section.

manager would give Billy a better chance to win, it was worth the effort.

By fight time, feelings in both the McLarnin and Petrolle camps were strained. Not only had Pop Foster cogently defended Jimmy in the press against Hurley's accusations, he had also, in moments of pique, threatened Jack with bodily harm, even to the extent of offering on one occasion to bite off Hurley's ear and nose.

When Hurley greeted McLarnin at the weigh-in, Pop stepped between them and snapped, "You have no business talking to Jimmy. We haven't anything to say to you." Jack, answering, "O. K., Pop," shrugged his shoulders and walked away. Even the fighters refused to speak to each other when they squared off to pose for photographers and met at the scales to be weighed. McLarnin registered a surprisingly heavy 146 pounds, while Petrolle was a full seven pounds lighter at 139.[53]

The first half of the fight was fought on even terms, with ringside reporters about evenly divided in their opinions as to whether Petrolle or McLarnin had won either two or three rounds of the first five rounds.

Petrolle rushed out in the third round and staggered McLarnin with a left to the head, followed by a left to the body and a right to the head. Another left to the body doubled Jimmy up and he almost went down, but he pulled himself together and outboxed Billy, landing "deft left hooks and jabs" for the greater part of the round. A vicious exchange at the bell also ended in Jimmy's favor. "It was close, but McLarnin was entitled to a shade."

The fifth round was Petrolle's best. Fighting out of his customary crouch, he literally "turned McLarnin around with resounding lefts to the face ... four times during this wild round." In between these blows, Billy bulled his way inside with left hooks to the body and right uppercuts to the jaw. Jimmy's most effective punches were solid right hands to the head, but they were not enough and the round "went to Petrolle with plenty to spare."

The turning point came in the sixth. Petrolle came out aggressively in an effort to maintain his advantage of the previous round, but with each attack, the Irishman would strike back, "hitting faster and harder. Near the close, Billy sent over a jarring left to the jaw. McLarnin came back with left, right and left to the head, winning the round by a wide margin."

---

[53] Frayne, "M'Larnin 2-1 Favorite in Betting at Ringside," *New York American*, August 21, 1931, sports section. The *New York American* also reported Hurley and Foster almost came to blows shortly before their fighters entered the ring. As in the case of the first McLarnin-Petrolle fight, the managers had been arguing about the amount of tape being used on the fighters hands. Foster had cut a piece of tape 25 inches long, one-inch longer than the legal limit of 24 inches, and Hurley had made him cut off the extra inch.

When it came time for Hurley to tape Petrolle's hands, Foster objected that the tape Jack was using was thicker than the rules prescribed. "It took all the inspectors in the ball yard to convince (Foster) that Petrolle's tape came off the same roll as McLarnin's. Two or three times bystanders had to separate them."

Frayne, "Gate Indicates Passing of $10 Tops at Ball Parks" (subtitle), August 22, 1931, p. 17.

McLarnin feints to draw a lead from Petrolle in their third fight.

The Fargo Express looks for an opening, but it never came.

The rest of the contest belonged to McLarnin since Petrolle tired as it wore on. Jimmy boxed beautifully and, though plainly "out to win without taking unnecessary chances, he stood flat-footed to punch with Petrolle when shaken up and usually had the better of these exchanges." Billy "took quite a pasting" in the eighth when Jimmy forced him "for the first time in this series of three bouts ... to actually break ground under the power of punishing punches."[54]

In the final rounds, "McLarnin tried with every ounce of his strength, with every trick of the trade and every punch at his command to stop Petrolle. And he failed only because Petrolle simply refused to budge even under McLarnin's best punches." Billy "felt enough savage rights carom off his jaw to topple a dozen ordinary fighters. But this reincarnated Petrolle ... is no ordinary fighter. And if he felt McLarnin's blows he gave no heed, because he was too intent on an attempt to accomplish McLarnin's downfall."[55]

At the conclusion, Petrolle was by far the more battered warrior. His "right eye was almost closed ... and the crimson flowed freely from his mouth and nose. The only trace of conflict exhibited by McLarnin was a slight cut on the lower lip." The decision in Jimmy's favor was unanimous.

Afterward, Petrolle explained McLarnin's weight was too much for him. "A few years ago I might've been able to give away ten pounds or so but not today at least not against such a good fighter as McLarnin," Billy told reporters. "For five rounds I went along fine but then that extra weight McLarnin carried began to tell and I started to slow up ... I lost fairly and squarely and I don't want that weight business used as an alibi. I'm just explaining how I failed to win. You've got to hand it to Jimmy – he is a great boxer. He knows all the tricks and is as clever as they come."[56]

Hurley had no qualms about using McLarnin's weight advantage as an excuse. According to Jack, "weight and nothing else beat Petrolle tonight" and it was "too much to ask of any man to spot as good a puncher as McLarnin seven pounds." Hurley said he was "through letting out those blasts about barring no one." Instead, Billy will be "a lightweight from now on," and "we'll pick our spots in the future."[57]

---

[54] Wood, "McLarnin Wins Seven Rounds," *New York Sun*, August 21, 1931, sports section (all quotations except the ones which follow in this note). Dawson, "McLarnin Defeats Petrolle on Points," *New York Times*, August 21, 1931, sports section ("deft left hooks and jabs"). Walsh, "Vancouver Irishman Wins Off by Himself, Taking 6 of 10 Rounds," *New York Evening Graphic*, August 21, 1931, sports section ("turned McLarnin around ...").

[55] Dawson, *op. cit.*

[56] Dayton, Alfred,"Weight Told, Says Petrolle," *New York Sun*, August 21, 1931, sports section.

[57] Mercer, Sid, "Weight Only Beat Petrolle, Says Manager," *New York American*, August 21, 1931, sports section (first two quotes). Dayton, *op. cit.* (last two quotes).

Although Garden officials publicized an unofficial attendance of 15,000, Ed Frayne, sports editor of the *New York American*, estimated that the crowd was really just "slightly over 10,000, making it one of the smallest crowds ever recorded at a New York ball park fight." Gross receipts were not disclosed, but the show reportedly netted $40,763.

After taxes, miscellaneous expenses, and paying McLarnin $11,210 (27-1/2%), Petrolle $9,507 (22-1/2%), Yankee Stadium $5,095 (12-1/2%), and the prelim fighters $5,000, the Garden was able to realize a profit of $3,000. The figure was not nearly as much as hoped for, but at least the show turned out not to be the financial disaster everyone feared before Hurley took things into his own hands and started blasting away at everyone in sight.[58]

Summer's end in 1931 found Petrolle with money in the bank, a firm hold on his rating as the leading lightweight contender, and an established position as a first-tier New York fistic attraction. Understandably, after three hard fights in four months against the best fighters of two divisions, it also found him tired and in need of a breather. After talking the matter over with Hurley, Billy decided to take a couple of months off. The plan was for him to return to New York in time for the start of the winter boxing season.

Petrolle's rest came at a convenient time. While Billy was scaling the fistic heights, Charley Retzlaff had been busy working in the trenches. For most of July, he had fought at an outdoor club in Queens, knocking all opposition dead. Word had it that he was the best young heavyweight around. While hopeful, Hurley was not sure whether it was true or not.

For better or for worse, he was about to find out.

---

[58] Frayne, *op. cit* (all information except as below). Morris, "Around the Ring," *New York Evening Post*, August 21, 1931, sports section (estimate of amount paid to preliminary fighters).

CHAPTER 24

THE DYNAMITER FROM DULUTH

Best of all these new heavyweights is Charley Retzlaff, of Duluth – Retzlaff, the Ripper. I'll tell you why. He is a ruthless, wicked fellow inside those ropes. There is no mercy in his heart. At long range he blasts away with both hands, and he is a mighty puncher with a left hook, or a right cross. In close – and that's where he loves it – he is a butcher knife of a man. He carves 'em up.

He uses his powerful arms, and elbows, and wrists and hands in a most unorthodox, but deadly manner. He is guilty of what they used to call "ripping" in the old days, working his sinewy hands and wrist across an opponent's face with terrific violence.

He mauls and hauls, and pounds and chugs. He never gives his opponent a second's peace. He hits him on top of the head, back of the neck, and everywhere else. They come out of his embrace all chopped up. I like this fellow because when the bell bangs, he leaves politeness at home. He seems to know that prize fighting is a mean, vicious pastime, and that the other guy is in there to knock his ears down if, he can, and Retzlaff, the Ripper, tries to do the knocking down first.

... This tall, lean-flanked, lathy fellow from Minnesota has as much ring ferocity as Jack Dempsey. He has a magnificent physique, with the waist of a girl. His face is thin, and his eyes glitter with cruelty when the smoke of battle gets in his nostrils. I think he has the makings of a tremendous fighter. I hold out but one reservation at this time. I want to see him tagged hard, and in distress. I want to see him on the floor. I want to know how he reacts to these situations before I pass final judgment on him. You can't tell anything about a fighter until you see him hurt.

... Retzlaff has the color necessary to make him a great drawing card ... Retzlaff tries to win his fights right off the reel. He doesn't fiddle and stall around. He takes the battle to his opponent at once, a slow beginner is in a tough spot with him immediately. If he can take a punch proportionately to his own punching power, he is bound to be a championship contender inside of the next year.

A month ago, Retzlaff was unknown in New York. Today he is a sensation. He has had about 34 battles, of which perhaps 15 were with fighters of little account. Since he has been eased into stronger competition, he has whipped Johnny Risko, Bombo Chevalier, and a number of other fair fighters. He is ready for such as Ernie Schaaf, Max Baer, and the other members of what you might call the second flight of heavyweights, right now. In another year, he is apt to go far beyond that kind. I haven't seen a fighter in a long time who has impressed me so favorably.[1]

– Damon Runyon

****

A pair of bruised hands forced Charley Retzlaff to take some time off after his knockout win over Tom Heeney at Detroit in March 1931. In May, he returned to action and scored four- and one-round kayo wins over Jack Gagnon in Duluth and Tiny Debolt at Chicago.

Even before the Heeney kayo, Jack Hurley was fielding questions about when he would take Retzlaff to New York. In reply, he told the *Duluth Herald*'s Sandy Macdonald, "When I start him there I will be certain that he is right. New York folks are funny. If they like a boxer the first time they see him they will always like him." On the other hand, Hurley implied, if they didn't, it was almost impossible to change their minds later on.[2]

Consequently, Hurley was waiting until he was sure Retzlaff had progressed far enough to make a good impression. Charley's victories at Detroit made Eastern boxing experts curious about "the Duluth Dynamiter," and they also convinced Jack that Retzlaff was as ready as he ever would be to take the plunge in a Gotham City ring.

On May 30, 1931, Hurley announced Retzlaff would meet 23-year-old Marty Gallagher in the semi-windup to the Victorio Campolo-Roberto Roberti show at Madison Square Garden on June 11. Gallagher's record of 31 wins, 11 losses, and four draws included victories over George Hoffman, Pietro Corri, Al Friedman, Salvatore Ruggirello, and ex-light heavy champ Battling Levinsky. Marty, with 14 kayos against only one kayo loss to his credit, figured to be a fair test for Charley in his New York debut.[3]

For a while it looked like the Gallagher-Retzlaff match would not happen at all when the Garden canceled the Campolo-Roberti card because of a Roberti scheduling conflict. Instead of dropping the match altogether, however, Garden officials rescheduled it as a five-round preliminary bout on the July 3rd Cleveland, Ohio show in which Max Schmeling was defending his heavyweight title against Young Stribling.[4]

Schmeling had won the title on June 12, 1930, in the final bout of the tournament to determine Gene Tunney's successor. In a controversial outcome, Max was declared the winner on a foul when Jack Sharkey hit him below the belt in the fourth round, and Schmeling was unable to

---

[1] Runyon, Damon, "Runyon Thinks Retzlaff Best of New Heavies," *New York American*, July 29, 1931, p. 19.
[2] Macdonald, Sandy, "Retzlaff Will Show in Gotham When He's Fit," *Duluth Herald*, February 12, 1931, sports section.
[3] BoxRec as of 2014."Billy Petrolle to Meet Suarez in N. Y. June 25," *Fargo Forum*, May 31, 1931, sports section.
[4] Campbell, Cubby, "Cubby Campbell's Column," *Duluth News Tribune*, June 7, 1931, sports section. "Retzlaff Gets Semiwindup Go on Title Card," *Fargo Forum*, June 21, 1931, sports section.

continue. After the fight, the New York commission recognized Max as the new champ on condition that he meet Sharkey in his first defense.

Schmeling was contractually bound to fight for Madison Square Garden as promoter of his next bout. Although the commission ruled Sharkey should be Max's first challenger, Garden officials were adamant that unless Sharkey defeated a contender in a build-up contest, the Schmeling-Sharkey rematch would be a financial disaster.[5]

When Sharkey refused the Garden's offer to fight a contender and instead chose to stand pat and rely on the New York commission's ruling, Garden officials signed to have Max defend his title against Young Stribling instead. In their view, while Sharkey was resting on his laurels, Stribling's victories over contenders Otto von Porat, Phil Scott, and Tuffy Griffiths had made him a more attractive challenger than Sharkey.[6]

In response, the New York commission declared the heavyweight title vacant in New York and barred the Schmeling-Stribling bout from the state until such time as Schmeling would first fight Sharkey. As a result of all these circumstances, Madison Square Garden was forced into the awkward position of having to promote the Schmeling-Stribling bout at Cleveland, rather than at the Garden's home base in New York City.[7]

The transfer of the Retzlaff-Gallagher fight to the heavyweight championship card meant that virtually every important boxing writer east of the Mississippi River would have a chance to see Retzlaff in action for the first time. In a real sense, Charley held his entire future in his own gloved hands. A good showing against Gallagher would lead to money-making dates in larger cities throughout the East.

For most of the bout against Gallagher, Retzlaff looked anything but impressive. Marty, a good defensive boxer, was able to easily avoid all of Charley's straight right-hand punches by simply turning away from them. Rather than devising an alternate attack, Retzlaff surrendered to his frustration and continued to throw more and more right hands. By the fourth round, Gallagher was well on his way to making Retzlaff look "like a bum" and thoroughly embarrassing Hurley in front of his reporter pals.

Returning to his corner at the end of the fourth, Retzlaff had only one round left in the five-round bout to prove himself. As he had done when Charley fought Tom Heeney, a desperate Hurley threatened his reluctant tiger with bodily harm: "Can't you see you're disgracing me? You can't hit him with a right hand. It must be a left hook, but you can't throw that from the open. Left jab, and he'll pull away. A right hand, and he'll turn away,

---

[5] "To Visit Commission" (subtitle), *Fargo Forum*, May 24, 1930, sports section.
[6] "Heavy Champ Returns to U. S. in Fine Shape" (AP), *Duluth News Tribune*, January 28, 1931, sports section.
[7] Hurley, Jack, "Ring Rations," *Fargo Forum*, January 11, 1931, sports section.

Jack Hurley (left) and Charley Retzlaff, circa 1931.

Retzlaff ready for his New York debut, circa 1931.

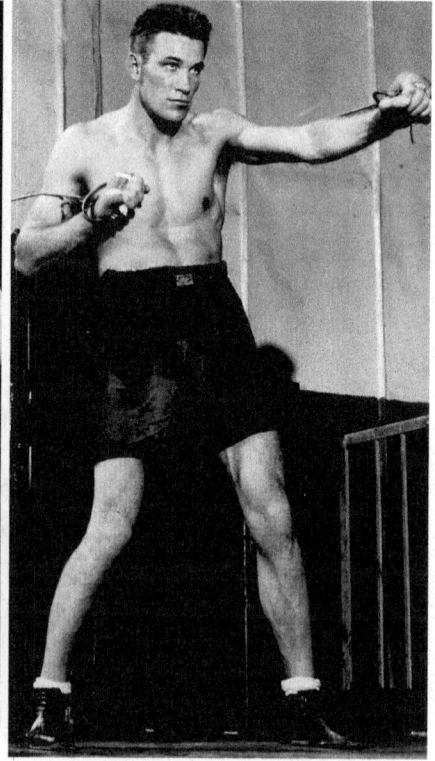

Looking lean and hungry.

and then hook. If you don't do it this round, you know what you'll get."[8]

Hurley's harsh words had the desired effect. A single left hook to the chin, thrown just as Jack had prescribed, finished off Gallagher for good. After the punch, Marty fell and rose three times during the referee's toll. Although on his feet at ten, "his muscles were as loose as putty" and he "could hardly hold himself together." Without any hesitation, the referee stopped the fight and led Gallagher to his corner. For the bout, Charley had weighed 195 pounds to Marty's 207.[9]

In the main event, Schmeling proved worthy of the heavyweight championship by stopping Stribling in the 15th and final round. In his boxing column published the previous week, Hurley had been among the minority of boxing experts who had predicted a Schmeling victory.[10]

Retzlaff's performance on the undercard came in for special mention in many of the accounts of the show which appeared in the next day's papers. Bill Corum's description for the *New York Evening Journal* best captures the flavor of what reporters seated in the first press row saw and felt:

> "Now, let's not laugh at Retzlaff. The Duluth farmer boy came into the ring for the preliminary bout immediately preceding the Schmeling-Stribling heavyweight championship fight at Cleveland looking for all the world like a misplaced undertaker, what with his solemn pan, his big black sweater and black trunks.
>
> "He was quite crude at the outset and plainly startled at seeing so many folks gathered together in one place, and he had Messrs. Hype Igoe, Damon Runyon, James J. Johnston, Harry Grayson and others giving Jack Hurley the birdie in pantomime during the first four rounds of his engagement with the shopworn Marty Gallagher.
>
> "Hurley, you see, had been around for some time telling the boys to keep an eye out for Charley. And, then, while all of us were in the midst of a wide yawn, it happened.
>
> "Retzlaff let 'er go Gallagher with a point-blank left, and Gallagher went. With one punch he knocked Marty kicking, crazy, cuckoo, and out. And with that punch he proved that not all the things young Mr. Hurley had been saying about him were the pure fabrications of an agile mind. Patently, he can punch, and so far as anybody knows he can take it."[11]

After the Gallagher fight, Hurley booked Retzlaff into the Queensboro

---

[8] Heinz, W. C., "The Man Who Makes Fighters," *Esquire Magazine,* May 1952, p. 100.
[9] "Retzlaff Wins Technical K. O." (AP), *Duluth News Tribune,* July 4, 1931, sports section. Kofoed, Jack, "Thrills in Sports," *New York Evening Post,* July 13, 1931, sports section.
[10] Hurley, "Shadow Boxing," *Fargo Forum,* June 28, 1931, sports section.
[11] Corum, Bill, as excerpted by Eugene Fitzgerald from Corum's *New York Evening Journal* column, "The Sport Whirligig," *Fargo Forum,* July 19, 1931, sports section.

Stadium in Long Island City on July 16, 1931, for his first New York appearance. Charley's opponent was Ralph Ficucello, a former national amateur champion with a pro record of 30 wins, 5 losses, and two draws. Although Ficucello was regarded as a solid performer, Retzlaff's reputation as a prospect "'hotter' than any ... who has come to town in years" had preceded him, and Charley was made a betting favorite to win by a kayo.[12]

Hurley chose Queensboro's outdoor stadium rather than Madison Square Garden for Retzlaff's Gotham debut so Charley could become accustomed to the big city and establish himself as a winner. In addition, Jack figured to have more control over the selection of Retzlaff's opponents at Queensboro than at the Garden. At the end of the Queensboro's season in October, Hurley planned to take Charley indoors and roll the dice against the stiffer opposition the Garden would require him to meet.

Starting Retzlaff out in Queensboro was Hurley's first opportunity to work with matchmaker Al Weill, who would figure significantly in Jack's future dealings in Chicago and New York. Most significantly, the two men would lock horns in 1952 when Jack's contender, Harry Matthews, would fight Al's fighter, Rocky Marciano, in a heavyweight elimination bout for the right to meet champion Jersey Joe Walcott.

Weill moved with his family to New York in 1908 at age 14 from his native Gebweiler, Alsace in France. His first contact with boxing was in 1915 when he went to work in a barbershop as a porter for John (The Barber) Reisler, an early manager of Jack Dempsey.

Al left Reisler after a few years to assemble his own stable. Queensboro Stadium owner Si Flaherty thought enough of his ability to hire him as the stadium's matchmaker in 1929. Within a year, he built the arena into New York's most profitable outdoor boxing club. After his Queensboro run ended, Weill managed three champions before Marciano: featherweight Joey Archibald; lightweight Lou Ambers; and welterweight Marty Servo.[13]

Weill, whose real first name was Armand, was nicknamed "The Vest," partly due to his penchant for three-piece suits, but also because he was a crafty businessman and driver of hard bargains, known for "playing it close to the vest." Described by one writer as "often rude, crude and abrasive," Al reputedly was a sloppy eater who liked thick soups, leading to the widely circulated, multi-layered, inside joke that "the Vest gets all the gravy."[14]

As expected, Retzlaff, at 192 pounds, had little trouble disposing of

---

[12] Wood, Wilbur, "What Price Against Retzlaff," *New York Sun*, July 16, 1931, sports section.

[13] "Al Weill Is Dead; Guided Marciano," *New York Times*, October 22, 1969, p. 47. Meany Tom, "Boxing at Queensboro Assured with Flaherty and Weill Again at Helm," *New York World-Telegram*, June 12, 1931, sports section.

[14] Daley, Arthur, "Sports of the Times: Mitt Machiavelli," *New York Times*, October 24, 1969, p. 57. Loubet, Nat, "Al Weill Was Master Manager, as He Proved with Marciano," *Ring Magazine*, January 1970, p. 30.

Ralph Ficucello, 192-1/2. After two minutes, Charley nailed Ficucello with a straight right which sent him stumbling to the ropes, badly shaken. Moments later, the Duluth Dynamiter sent in another right that ripped a cut alongside Ralph's left eye. As the round ended, blood was literally spurting from the wound. When the cut re-opened after action resumed in the second session, the referee stopped the bout at 50 seconds of the round.[15]

Approximately 8,000 fans paid $12,609 to see the bout, a figure the *New York* American's Ed Frayne termed "unusually high for these times." Frayne predicted that if Retzlaff were matched against Steve Hamas, another outstanding heavyweight prospect, "the Queensboro [capacity 18,000] will not be large enough to accommodate the crowd."[16]

In his next outing at the Queensboro July 28, 1931, Retzlaff, 194-1/2, was pitted against Spain's Mateo Osa, 185, who also had kayoed Ficucello in Osa's most recent New York appearance seven months earlier.

In the words of the *New York World*-Telegram's Harry Grayson, "Retzlaff and Mateo gave the crowd everything but a revolution." The first highlight came when Osa struck Charley after the bell at the end of the first round. Retzlaff tore after Mateo, and when the referee jumped between the fighters to pin Osa, Charley kept punching over the referee's shoulder. The extracurricular milling continued for almost 30 seconds and ended only when Hurley jumped into the ring to pin his infuriated battler from behind.[17]

With scarcely enough rest for a quick sponging-off, the maulers were back at it for the second round. Osa, fighting in a crouch, landed a low left hook for which he was cautioned. A second low left drew another warning and made Retzlaff grimace, but he did not complain. Instead, Charley, exhibiting "the required fighting spirit ... lost no time in curing Osa of the habit, making a believer out of him with the same kind of a punch."[18]

The end came at 2:30 of the third round. Though at first, "Osa's turtle-like defense nullified the long armed Retzlaff's attack," Charley "continued to fire rights and gradually wore down the Basque. A long right put Osa on the ropes and as he came off Retzlaff uppercut him with a right to the chin. Osa fell on his face and remained there for the full count." As Grayson commented afterward, the fact that Charley "found openings in (Osa's shell defense) raised him in the estimation of schooled boxing men."[19]

---

[15] Wood, "Retzlaff and Hamas Victors," *New York Sun*, July 17, 1931, sports section.

[16] Morris, William, "Around the Ring," *New York Evening Post*, July 17, 1931, sports section (fans paid $12,609). Frayne, Ed, "Retzlaff Kayoes Ficucello in 2nd," *New York American*, July 17, 1931, p. 21.

[17] Grayson, Harry, "Fighting Days Return with Young Blood," *New York World-Telegram*, July 29, 1931, sports section.

[18] Frayne, "Retzlaff Knocks Out Osa in Third Round Before 14,000 Crowd," *New York American*, July 29, 1931, p. 17.

[19] Wood, "Retzlaff Stops Osa in Third," *New York Sun*, July 29, 1931, sports section ("continued to fire."). Grayson, *op. cit* ("Osa's turtle-like defense ..." and "found openings ...").

According to *New York Sun*'s Wilbur Wood, "12,000 paid admissions, putting a total of approximately $22,000 in the box offices at one, two and three dollars," witnessed Retzlaff's knockout. The show had furnished "proof enough that there is no panic in the sock market when the customers are given the right sort of entertainment at the right sort of prices." For his work, Charley received 22-1/2 percent of the net proceeds.[20]

Although Retzlaff had yet to meet a contender, praise for Hurley's "Ripper" flowed from the pen tips of almost every boxing writer in New York. Grayson wrote that he "captured the imagination of ringworms to a greater extent than anyone since Max Schmeling." Jack Kofoed of the *New York Evening Post* called Charley "a tough looking boy" and "one of the best of the younger heavyweights."[21]

Retzlaff's most enthusiastic booster was the *New York American*'s Damon Runyon, at the time the most influential sports columnist in the country. After the Osa bout, Runyon discussed what he liked about Charley:

> "When Mateo Osa slugged him low the other night at the Queensboro, Retzlaff promptly whaled Osa plenty low. When Osa showed a disposition to keep fighting after the bell, Retzlaff didn't hesitate an instant. He just kept blasting away, and it took Danny Ridge, the referee, and Retzlaff's manager, Jack Hurley, to pull 'em apart. Hurley just barely ducked a wicked punch let fly by his own fighter, and Ridge got a pop on the chin from one or the other gladiator, and came out of the melee covered with Osa's gore.
>
> "... I saw Retzlaff flatten Marty Gallagher in Cleveland with a left hook to the chin that made the 200-pound Gallagher bounce twice as he hit the floor, and knocked him absolutely cock-eyed. I saw Retzlaff carve the stocky Ficucello until the referee had to stop the fight, and I saw him pound out Osa the other night, and each time my opinion that Retzlaff will go a long way has been strengthened. He's got what it takes – viciousness.
>
> "The first time Retzlaff appeared here, another likely heavyweight prospect was on the same card in the person of Steve Hamas, the former Penn State athlete, and at the close of the proceedings the talk was all Hamas. I thought Hamas looked good, at that, but I didn't think he showed the promise of Retzlaff ...
>
> "Hamas hasn't got that wickedness and fire that Retzlaff has. I allow Hamas hasn't had half Retzlaff's experience, either, but experience doesn't give them that man-killer instinct. That's born in 'em. Hamas can't punch with Retzlaff. He hasn't Retzlaff's

---

[20] Wood, *op. cit.*
[21] Grayson, "Retzlaff Like Dempsey, but Tunney Is His Model," *New York World Telegram*, August 25, 1931, sports section. Kofoed, *op. cit.*

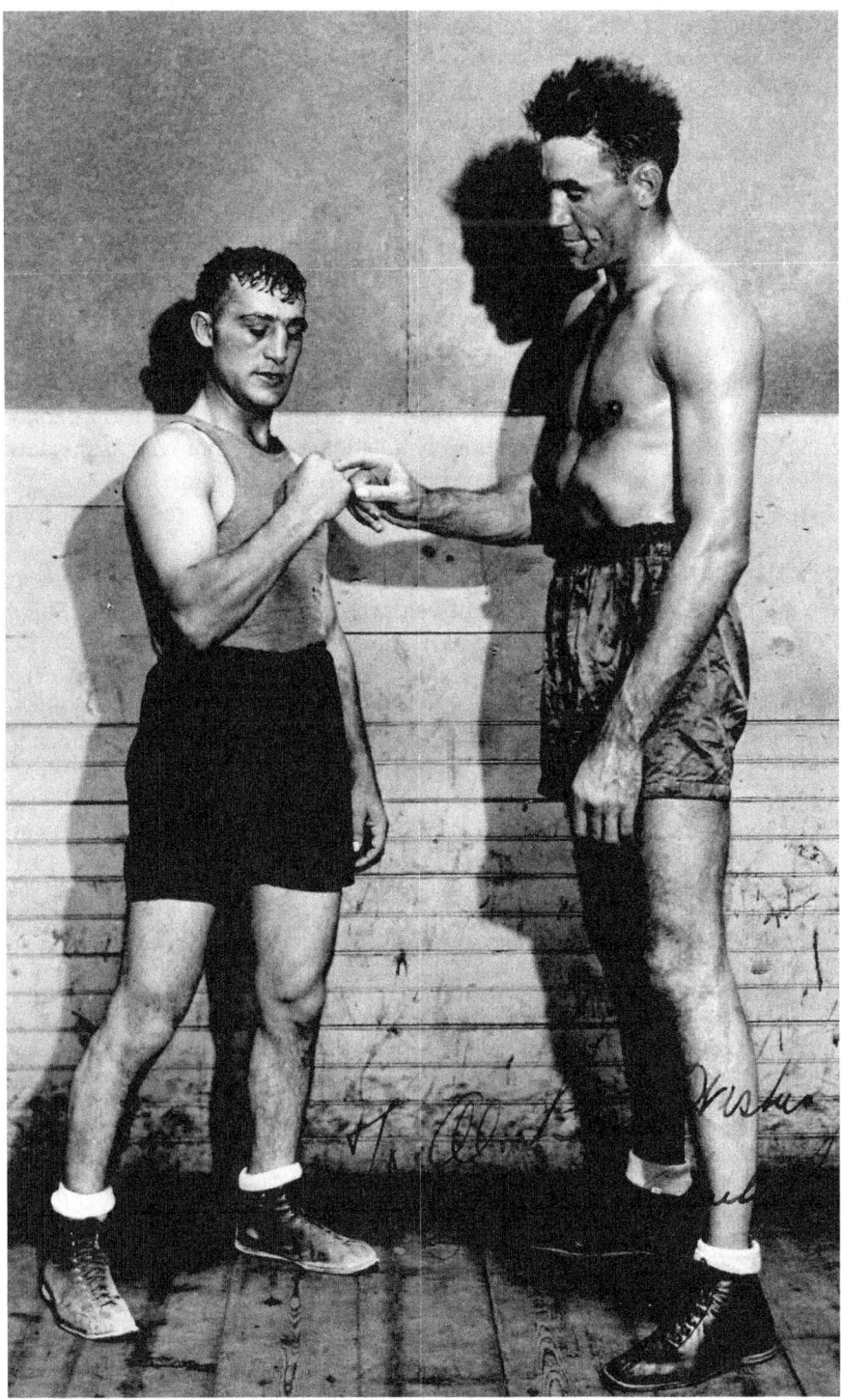

Petrolle and Retzlaff at the Pioneer Gym in New York City, 1931.

stamina. I think Hamas will make a mighty good fighter some day, and earn lots of money, but I've seen 50 Hamases the past few years and only one Retzlaff. This kind comes along at rare intervals.

"I think he is a better fighter than his manager, Jack Hurley, realizes, unless Hurley knows something about Retzlaff that hasn't been disclosed in his recent fights. I says this, because Hurley is inclined to be a trifle cautious about Retzlaff's opponents, while I believe the lean chap from the Northwest is ready for the best competition he can get."[22]

At the beginning of August, Hurley interrupted Smilin' Charley's New York campaign for an August 7th fight in St. Paul against Riccardo Bertazzolo, of Italy. The bout was the main event on the first professional show promoted by Johnny Salvator, who had just been approved as the new promoter in the saintly city by the Minnesota Boxing Commission.

In addition to making Retzlaff available to Johnny, it was "pretty well known" Hurley had provided the financial backing "behind Salvator" and his new club. The pair were forced to keep publicity about the arrangement to a minimum, however, because of a new commission policy prohibiting a promoter from using any boxers that he managed on his own shows.[23]

The firm was christened "the Capitol City Boxing Club" to evoke the memory of St. Paul's glory days when the Gibbons brothers boxed for a club with the same name 15 years earlier. To comply with the law, evidence

---

[22] Runyon, *op. cit.*

[23] "New Boxing Commission Rules Against Promoters Being Interested in Fighters" (AP), *Duluth News Tribune*, May 24, 1931, sports section. Campbell, *op cit.*, August 9, 1931, sports section ("It is pretty well known that Hurley's money is behind Salvator and the Capitol City Boxing club.").

Although fleeting references to Hurley having promoted in St. Paul pop up in subsequent articles about Jack's career, the author has been unable to determine whether his involvement with the Capitol City Boxing Club was an equity or a loan interest. Certainly by the time Salvator went broke promoting in the mid-1930s, Hurley already had dropped out of the financial picture. Salvator's son, John Salvator II, when asked by the author, did not know about Jack's financial role in the business, but was not surprised because "Hurley always seemed to have a little money." John II, who was nine years old in 1931, did remember, however, that Jack was usually present at his father's St. Paul shows.

The younger Salvator recalled that at some point his father mortgaged the family's summer property at Big Sandy Lake in an attempt to save the boxing business. When it finally failed, Johnny was forced to turn the property over to Billy Petrolle, who had loaned him the money. John also remembered that his maternal grandfather offered to loan his father money to save the lake property, but Johnny declined, telling his father-in-law, "I owe so much money I don't know when I'd ever be able to pay you back."

It is just as likely Hurley never had any direct financial interest in the club at all, but instead merely facilitated the loan arrangement between Salvator and Petrolle. Even so, Jack was still identified closely with the club by the members of Minnesota's boxing colony and was motivated to work with Johnny both as a friend and as a person who would benefit from the venture's success, if not as an investor, then as a paid consultant and supplier of talent.

of Hurley's part in the venture was absent from documents filed with the commission. Instead, the club's officers and owners of record were listed as Johnny Salvator; Jerry O' Connor, Salvator's father-in-law; J. W. Winter, his brother-in-law; and Tom Walsh, his St. Paul attorney.[24]

Salvator and Hurley had continued to collaborate both as friends and business associates after Jack's move to Duluth in 1927. Johnny had made welterweight Billy Light available to Hurley for bouts against Angelo Puglisi in 1929 and Petrolle in 1931. Though Light beat Puglisi in Duluth, Petrolle defeated Light at the annual New Year's Day card in Fargo.

Hurley also had worked in Light's corner as a favor to Salvator on October 24, 1930, when Light scored the most important win of his career over Frank Battaglia. Afterward, Jack interceded on Johnny's behalf with matchmaker Tom McArdle and arranged for the St. Paul welterweight's first Madison Square Garden appearance against Eddie Ran in the semifinal bout on the Petrolle-Tut card on February 27, 1931.

Light was way ahead in the Ran fight until Eddie floored him three times in the ninth round and scored a knockout. Even so, Light was impressive enough to merit a rematch against Ran in the semifinal of the second McLarnin-Petrolle card three months later. Unfortunately, Light's second Garden performance was also his last. In a bout not nearly as exciting as their first, Ran won an easy ten-round decision.

For several years prior to his acquisition of the St. Paul franchise, Salvator had been an outsider in boxing affairs there. Johnny had feuded with Jerk Doran, the previous promoter, over the managerial rights to star welterweight My Sullivan. Hard feelings resulted when Sullivan went with Doran. Afterward, Salvator had trouble obtaining bouts for his fighters from Doran, except for Billy Light who was a big drawing card.[25]

Hurley also had been on "the outs" in St. Paul. After trying to earn a living there for six months in 1922, Hurley returned to Fargo when he was unable to break into the clique which controlled boxing at the time. His most recent effort to crack the St. Paul nut had also failed when King Tut kayoed Petrolle in 34 seconds of the first round. Baseless rumors still persisted in the Twin Cities that Jack had been behind a "betting coup" in connection with the Petrolle-Tut return bout in New York.

Now, with the acquisition of the franchise, Salvator and Hurley were eager to prove they could do a better job of running boxing in St. Paul than their predecessors who had locked them out of the business.

Unfortunately, vindication did not come with their first show on August 7. Instead, the main event ended with over 5,000 jeering spectators watching in disgust while referee Ed Shave stopped abruptly in the middle

---

[24] Campbell, *op cit.*, June 13, 1931, sports section. The Tom Walsh who was a St. Paul attorney was not Tom Walsh, the well-known Chicago fight manager.
[25] *Ibid.*

of his count over a downed Riccardo Bertazzolo and awarded the fight to Retzlaff by a knockout when Bertazzolo made no effort to rise.

From the start, it was evident Bertazzolo was too frightened to fight. For the entire first round, Retzlaff chased him around the ring and was able to land only one solid punch, a left hook. At the end of the round, and again shortly after the start of the second, Riccardo went down without being hit. The "kayo" came later in the session when Charley rushed the Italian into a corner, and he crashed to the floor after a punch brushed his shoulder.[26]

The Minnesota commission met immediately after the fight and voted to allow Bertazzolo to keep his purse, but banned him from the ring for life. Minneapolis scribes Charles Johnson of the *Daily Star* and Dick Cullum of the *Journal* suggested the Retzlaff-Bertazzolo bout was another "'one of those things'" like the Petrolle-Tut bouts "engineered by Jack Hurley."[27]

Hurley was indignant that the Minneapolis writers "intimated that [he had] arranged a 'Barney.'" Jack explained that promoter Salvator had "selected Bertazzolo because he had all the qualifications" and "was known as a tough, game fellow who had been never been knocked off his feet." Hurley concluded, "Retzlaff's reputation as a terrific puncher scared the big Italian" but "how was anybody to know that in advance?"[28]

After their rough reception by the fourth estate in the Twin Cities, Hurley and Retzlaff were only too happy to return to New York and leave St. Paul to Salvator. For Charley's third fight at Queensboro Stadium, Al Weill arranged for "the Ripper" to face Joe Sekyra in a ten-rounder on September 1, 1931.

Hurley originally signed Retzlaff to face Ernest Guhring on August 25, but the German backed out and signed to fight Pat Redmond at Ebbets Field instead. Next, Italy's Giacomo Bergomas agreed to meet Charley, but then changed his mind, deciding he needed more time to prepare for such a big test. In the Italian's stead, Weill chose Sekyra, who had performed creditably against the world's best heavyweights and light-heavyweights, but was thought to be on the downgrade.[29]

In accepting the Dayton Ohio light heavyweight, Hurley was matching Retzlaff against a different style fighter than he had ever been up against.

---

[26] "Foreign Boxer Suspended for Poor Showing," *Duluth News Tribune*, August 8, 1931, sports section.

[27] Campbell, *op. cit.*, August 9, 1931, sports section.

[28] Hurley, *op. cit.*, August 23, 1931, sports section. A review of Bertazzolo's ring record supports Hurley's view that while Ricardo figured to be a classic "opponent" in the sense of having lost most of his recent fights, he had nonetheless stayed the distance rather than taken the "easy way out." According to BoxRec, Riccardo had lost six straight fights, but all except a three-round kayo loss to Primo Carnera had been by decision. Bertazzolo had gone the distance in losing ten-round efforts against Jose Santa and Jack Redmond in his most recent fights before meeting Retzlaff at St. Paul.

[29] "Second Fighter Refuses to Mix with Retzlaff," *Duluth Herald*, August 20, 1931, sports section.

Previously, Charley had fought mostly heavy men eager to trade punches. With Sekyra, however, "Smilin' Charley" was encountering a stripe of another color – a lighter and more experienced adversary who used speed and cleverness rather than heft and power as his main method of attack.

The Retzlaff-Sekyra bout initially was slated to fill the August 25th date, but rain postponements set the bout back to September 1. Newsmen speculated the delay might hurt Retzlaff since it was something new for him. Hurley admitted as much a day before before the fight, conceding "the task of keeping Retzlaff on edge has been none too easy."[30]

Most critics figured Charley would have little trouble with Sekyra, but a few dissenting voices hinted Hurley was making a mistake. Among these was the *Sun*'s Dayton:

> "Heretofore, there have been few shafts of criticism aimed at Hurley for the manner in which he has brought the lanky youngster from Duluth to the front. In fact, few better examples of managerial acumen have cropped up in recent years, for Hurley has brought Retzlaff along without the necessity of tossing him in with too many set-ups. Numbered among his victims have not been any truly big timers, but he has taken on several formidable and sturdy opponents to score 30 knockouts in 34 engagements.
>
> "However, in this triumphant march to the spotlight of serious consideration, Retzlaff for the most part has taken on slow, lumbering fellows who either get their man early or go out themselves ... The target has not swayed and dodged in a tantalizing and baffling manner, and so Retzlaff has been hitting at more or less stationary marks. This is the main reason why some of the critics are questioning the wisdom of the bout with the Bohemian battler from Ohio this evening.
>
> "Another argument they produce is that Sekyra is much lighter than Retzlaff, and rather than working as a disadvantage for him will serve as an asset. Retzlaff has little experience against light, faster men ... They point out that Sekyra, with about the same difference in weight against Max Schmeling, made the heavyweight champion appear in none too glorious a light before the German finally got the decision after ten rounds.
>
> "Hurley refuses to be bothered by these moaners. He smiles confidently and says that he has not made any mistakes so far and does not intend to start making them at this late date ... Last year Sekyra was beaten by Charley Belanger, Joe Banovic and Larry

---

[30] Dayton, Alfred, "Heavies Up for Inspection," *New York Sun*, August 31, 1931, sports section.

Queensboro matchmaker Al Weill introduced Retzlaff to New York.

Ralph Ficucello, Retzlaff's first kayo victim in New York City.

Ralph Bertazzolo, whose poor effort in St. Paul set boxing back.

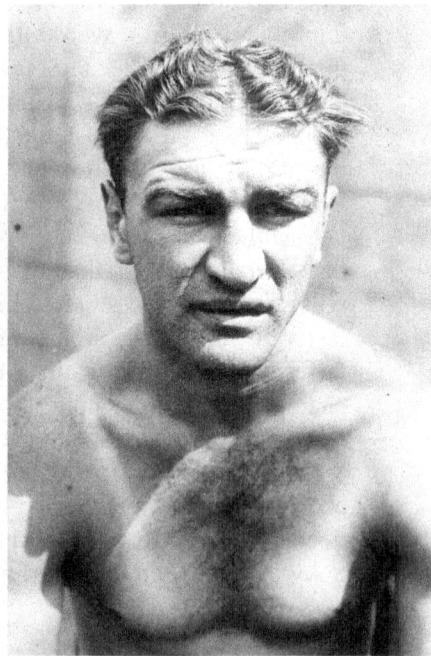

Veteran Joe Sekyra upset Retzlaff at Weill's Queensboro club.

Johnson, which sort of bears out the contention, which, no doubt, is planted firmly in Hurley's mind, that Sekyra has slipped considerably. But, on the other hand, these bouts are used to build up the question over the wisdom of this bout for, they point out, Belanger, Banovic and Johnson are light-heavyweights. Against such heavyweights as Matt Adgie and others, Sekyra did very nicely."[31]

In a fight the *New York World Telegram*'s Grayson termed "the biggest upset in years," Sekyra, 176 pounds, won a unanimous decision from Retzlaff, 193-1/2. The show drew 6,822 fans and a gross gate of $13,832.[32]

Although close when judged by number of rounds won, there was no question of the verdict's fairness. While Retzlaff forced the fighting, he clearly was out-boxed and his face was a gruesome sight at the bout's end. A right in the second round raised a lump over his left eye, a left in the fourth resulted in a purple egg that shut his right eye, and by the fifth his nose was smashed and bleeding. In addition, a looping right at the tail end of the seventh knocked Charley down and left him temporarily senseless.[33]

Afterward, Hurley raised no complaints about the decision, but he did explain that multiple postponements caused by the bad weather had upset Charley's training regimen. Jack also claimed a Sekyra headbutt rather than a punch caused Retzlaff's right eye to swell up and close tight. Hurley was encouraged Charley "kept fighting back under a terrific handicap and in the face of certain defeat." He predicted that "Retzlaff will overcome this temporary setback" and would beat Sekyra in a rematch.[34]

Given the care Hurley usually exercised in matching Retzlaff, it is difficult to understand how he let a clever boxer like Sekyra slip through the cracks, especially since it was so obvious to others Charley was in for a rough night. The most likely explanation is Jack was so busy preparing Petrolle for McLarnin that he gave less thought to Retzlaff's schedule than he otherwise might have. According to news reports, Al Weill slipped Sekyra in as a substitute August 19, a day before Billy and Jimmy tangled.[35]

As a result of the defeat, plans for a remunerative Retzlaff fight in mid-September against Boston's Ernie Schaaf evaporated. Experts had predicted a match between the two young heavyweights would draw in excess of

---

[31] Dayton, "Joe Sekyra to Test Retzlaff," *New York Sun*, August 27, 1931, sports section.

[32] Grayson, "Retzlaff Bubble Bursts, Blasting a $100,000 Shot," *New York World-Telegram*, September 2, 1931, sports section ("biggest upset in years"). Taub, Sam, "Ernie Willing to Box Walker or Loughran for Experience," *New York Evening Graphic*, September 3, 1931, sports section (attendance and gate information).

[33] Frayne, "Sekyra Drops Retzlaff and Wins Decision," *New York American*, September 2, 1931, p. 17.

[34] Hurley, *op. cit.*, September 6, 1931, sports section.

[35] "Second Fighter Refuses to Mix with Retzlaff," *op. cit.*

$100,000. Promoter Jimmy Johnston already had offered Hurley $15,000 for the fight at Ebbets Field if Charley defeated Sekyra. Rumor had it that Tom McArdle of the Garden had been ready to top Johnston's offer.[36]

Although discouraged at the loss of the big money opportunity, Hurley lost no time in getting Retzlaff back into the Queensboro ring. If Charley could pick up a couple of quick wins in the few remaining weeks of New York's outdoor season, he might still earn a shot in one of the heavyweight elimination bouts the Garden was planning for the fall and winter. In anticipation, the Garden had already signed up several other young hopefuls, including Schaaf, Max Baer, Stanley Poreda, and Steve Hamas.

At Queensboro on September 15, Retzlaff, 195-1/4 pounds, kayoed Gene Stanton, 197-1/2, a protégé of Johnny Risko, in four rounds. A week later, Charley fought again on the undercard of the Tommy Loughran-Joe Sekyra show and knocked out Germany's Dick Onken, 206, in two rounds.

Damon Runyon was one of the writers who saw Retzlaff lose to Sekyra and then come back to defeat both Stanton and Onken. The Hearst columnist still believed Charley was the best of the young heavyweights:

> "Sekyra's defeat of Retzlaff was the big upset of the pugilistic year hereabouts. He fairly slaughtered the best looking heavyweight prospect that had bobbed up in a long time, and in doing the job, Sekyra turned in one of the best fights he ever displayed in New York ...
>
> "I still like that Retzlaff as a prospect. It took a game fellow to return to the same ring where he got such a battering from Sekyra, and endure the jeers of the mob. The crowd that saw him flatten Gene Stanton, of Cleveland, didn't realize that Stanton was accounted something of a prospect himself ...
>
> "Retzlaff is still green, but he can hit, and he can hit with both hands. He showed me in the Sekyra fight that he can take punishment, and I insist that he has a bright future. Poreda is far ahead of Retzlaff in boxing ability, but Poreda cannot punch like Retzlaff."[37]

As a result of the Stanton and Onken kayos, Hurley landed a ten-round semifinal for Retzlaff against Italy's Giacomo Bergomas at Madison Square Garden on a November 13th show featuring Tommy Loughran and Paolino Uzcudun. The bout was Charley's debut at the Garden, and experts predicted an easy kayo for the Duluth Dynamiter. If any additional

---

[36] Grayson, *op. cit.* "Sekyra Gives Retzlaff Test," *New York World-Telegram*, September 1, 1931, sports section.

[37] Runyon, "Loughran Has Picked Himself Dangerous Job," *New York American*, September 19, 1931, p. 21.

incentive was needed, matchmaker McArdle promised a convincing win by either man would earn the victor a main event a few weeks later.

Unfortunately, an excruciatingly poor performance by Retzlaff and Bergomas eliminated both fighters from consideration. The lead sentence describing the fight for the *New York American* said Retzlaff and Bergomas "were simply too terrible for words." The *Sun*'s account was no better, depicting the action "as a new low for heavyweight fighting. It was no more than an international necking party."

Although Bergomas outweighed Retzlaff by almost 30 pounds, 226 to 196-3/4, the Italian refused to fight and "wrapped himself around Retzlaff with the ardor of a Boa Constrictor and he hung there for the rest of the evening. It was one long clinch." Although "Retzlaff did what little fighting there was, the officials called it a draw."[38]

This time even Hurley's most animated tongue-lashings between rounds failed to coax, shame, or otherwise lift Charley out of an uninspired, lethargic effort. Afterward, Jack was so upset that he scarcely even bothered to challenge the decision or defend Charley's performance. Sure, it was true he had "tried to fight," and Bergomas had done nothing but "wrestle, hold, and run," but even so "Charley should have put him away easily." According to Hurley, the bout was "putrid ... [and] I mean terrible."[39]

A disgusted Hurley told Lester Conklin of the International News Service he was "tired of fooling around" with Retzlaff: "No more set-ups for Charley. I'm going to find out right soon whether he's a championship prospect or a bum ... Retzlaff has been fighting for three years now and it's about time he learned to box. I'm going to send him against Loughran, and if Tommy knocks him out it will be nothing less than a public disgrace."

At the time of the interview with Conklin, Hurley was trying to match Retzlaff against Tommy Loughran in a charity show at Detroit. Jack went on to say if he could not land the Loughran bout, "there are plenty of other good opponents available," and he would "go after all of them."[40]

Obviously, Hurley's patience with Retzlaff was wearing thin. Twice in three months he had maneuvered Charley to within one win of a big-money fight – close enough for Jack to taste it. While losing to a cagey veteran like Sekyra was excusable, it was quite another matter for Retzlaff to fail to defeat an inept boxer like Bergomas with so much at stake.

---

[38] Frayne, "Loughran Wins from Uzcudun," *New York American*, November 14, 1931, p. 23 ("simply too terrible for words" and "...Boa Constrictor..."). Wood, "Loughran Wins Close Fight," *New York Sun*, November 14, 1931, sports section ("as a new low for heavyweight fighting ..." and "Retzlaff did what little ...").

[39] Hurley, "Ring Rations," *Fargo Forum*, November 22, 1931, p. 14 (all quotes except for following citation). Conklin, Les, "Retzlaff Will Be Thrown In with Fast Boys" (INS), *Duluth Herald*, November 16, 1931, sports section "Charley should have put him away easily.").

[40] Conklin, *op. cit.*

To Hurley, Retzlaff's poor showing proved the beating he received from Sekyra had stripped away Charley's zest for battle. Gone was the hunger and ambition he showed when he first started boxing. Although he still possessed "the weapons and ability to earn hundreds of thousands of dollars," Charley had lost the desire "to cash in on them" because he already had "made enough money to buy a farm and is satisfied."[41]

One of the side effects of finding Petrolle so early in Hurley's career was that it forever spoiled his ability to handle other fighters without becoming openly frustrated with their mistakes. While Retzlaff's fistic qualities were no worse than most of the boxers Jack would ever handle, Billy was something special – that rare combination of ability, physical toughness, and fighting heart which is characteristic of only truly great fighters.

When Hurley discovered Petrolle, he found a man whose temperament, courage, and physical equipment was perfectly suited to the style of boxing Jack taught. Indeed, after a few years, Hurley made Billy into the fighter Jack himself dreamed of being – a fighter who executed Hurley's moves to a "T" – like an idealized extension of Jack himself.

When measured against Hurley's memories of Petrolle, all of Jack's future boxers could only suffer by comparison. Forever after, he could never be entirely happy with any other fighter. Retzlaff, as the first of his contenders after Billy, suffered more than most by the comparison. At that stage, Hurley's high expectations had not yet been tempered by the realization of just how special Petrolle really was.

In any event, after the Bergomas fight, Hurley and Charley began to lose the rapport they had shared earlier. Jack's intimidating pep talks between rounds, so effective in the Heeney and Gallagher fights, no longer motivated Retzlaff. As a result, he became less aggressive than earlier, and he began to clinch more and fight back less when hurt or tired.

When the Retzlaff-Loughran bout fell through, Hurley decided to send Charley home to rest for a couple months until after the New Year.

Retzlaff would return for another chance at Madison Square Garden against journeyman Joe Woods, 185-1/2, on the undercard of the January 29, 1932 King Levinsky-Max Baer show. In an unimpressive performance, Retzlaff, 193-1/2, would barely survive a nine-count knockdown in the fourth round before coming on later to kayo Woods in the seventh.

Although Retzlaff would continue to fight in main events at regional boxing centers for the rest of his career, he would never again be considered a serious contender for the heavyweight championship.

Meanwhile, with both Retzlaff and Petrolle taking breaks from serious ring action until after the 1931 Christmas season, Hurley turned his efforts toward re-energizing the rest of his boxing empire. Boxing fans in Fargo who had been without a Hurley card since New Year's Day were clamoring

---

[41] Hurley, "Shadow Boxing," *Fargo Forum*, February 18, 1934, sports section.

for the big-time action which only Jack could provide. In addition, the National Athletic Club (NAC) in Duluth and the Capitol City Boxing Club in St. Paul were in need of help as well.

In Duluth, the NAC was hit hard when new Governor Floyd B. Olson replaced all three members of the boxing commission in April 1931. Minnesota's 1915 boxing law limited the state's boxing franchises at St. Paul, Minneapolis, and Duluth to a maximum of 12 shows each per calendar year. While earlier commissions had applied the law so as to limit the number of both pro and amateur shows, the most recent commission had rejected the prior interpretation and applied the law to allow franchisees to stage up to 12 pro shows and as many amateur cards as they wanted.

The new commission reversed the liberal interpretation of its immediate predecessor and returned to the conservative application employed by the prior commissions. The effect on Terk's Duluth operation was immediate and devastating. While Phil had presented 27 boxing cards (18 amateur, four professional, and five mixed "pro-ams") in 1930, complying with the new interpretation had forced Phil to limit the NAC to just ten programs (eight amateur and two professional shows) in the first 10 months of 1931.

Fortunately, the two professional shows, featuring hometown favorite Charley Retzlaff, had drawn well, and the NAC had managed to remain in the black for the first ten months of the year. While Duluth legislators were seeking to change the law and provide long-term relief for the problem, Terk was counting on Hurley to come up with an attraction for at least one of the season's last two shows so the NAC could end the year profitably.[42]

In St. Paul, Salvator's Capitol City Boxing Club was experiencing problems typical of most start-up businesses. The Retzlaff-Bertazzolo show in August had shown a fair profit, but the controversy surrounding its outcome made boxing fans leery about attending subsequent cards. Shows in September and October featuring Frank Battaglia and Prince Saunders, new talents who augured well as future attractions, barely covered costs.

With all this in mind, on the day after the Retzlaff-Bergomas fight, Hurley left New York and boarded a train for Kansas City. Although his main purpose for the trip was to second Petrolle in a four-rounder against Indian Joe Rivers November 18, another reason for the stopover was to meet with Jack Dempsey, who was headlining the show.[43]

The Manassa Mauler was in the midst of an exhibition tour with a stated objective of seeing whether he could get in good enough shape to challenge

---

[42] The preceding five paragraphs are based on the author's review and distillation of the *Duluth Herald* and the *Duluth Tribune* 1930 and 1931 sports pages.

[43] As a four-round bout, Petrolle's fight with Rivers (also known as Jack Reyna) was more in the nature of an exhibition. Petrolle knocked Rivers down in the first round and then coasted to victory the rest of the way without trying for a knockout. For the bout, Petrolle apparently made no effort to be in top fighting form since he weighed 145 pounds, the heaviest he would ever be for a match in his entire career.

heavyweight champion Max Schmeling. Dempsey began the tour in Reno, Nevada on August 19, 1931, after a year of indecision about whether he should attempt a comeback. In finally going ahead, he was operating under the theory that a series of exhibition fights against all kinds of competition was the best way to reach a decision.

Prior to Kansas City, Dempsey already had fought in 17 cities against a total of 45 different opponents. During that time, Jack had taken on all comers, from shivery-kneed novices, whom he sometimes carried for the crowd's benefit, to seasoned pros like Tony Talarico, Big Bill Hartwell, Bearcat Wright, Pete Wistort, and George Neron, some of whom provided Jack stiff opposition. In Kansas City, Dempsey's opponents were veterans Jack Roper and Charley Belanger for two rounds each.[44]

Before leaving New York, Hurley already had secured a verbal promise from the former champion for appearances in Fargo, Duluth, and St. Paul. The reason for their meeting was to finalize December 4, 7, and 11 as dates for the shows in each of the cities. Like Dempsey, Hurley arrived in Kansas City ahead of time, and their business went off without a hitch.[45]

Dempsey's arrangement usually called for four rounds of fighting. While the ex-champ encouraged the use of local favorites to build up the gate, the promoter was free to hire whomever he wished. Whether Dempsey fought one man for four rounds or a greater number of foes for fewer rounds was entirely up to the promoter. On some occasions, the former titleholder was matched against four different fighters for one round apiece.

As far as Dempsey was concerned, every bout had the potential of being a real fight. "I don't care who you get," Jack told promoters, "as long as they can fight." Once he was in the ring, favors were neither sought nor given. "I'm barring no one," he told one writer, "It's fighting I need to get into real form again, and it's fighting I intend to do in every bout ... It's me or them. I'm out to defend myself. My future is at stake."[46]

Dempsey admirer Damon Runyon wrote that Jack's tour recalled the 1880s when John L. Sullivan toured the country offering $1,000 to any man who could last four rounds against him. Runyon was of the opinion that the Dempsey's tour was "an astounding display of courage and confidence in one's own ability" and "a remarkable exhibition of honesty with the pugilistic public." Damon felt that by meeting real professionals Jack was taking far greater risks with his reputation than had Sullivan.[47]

---

[44] Fleischer, Nat, "1957 Ring Record Book," (Ring Book Shop, Inc, New York, New York, 1957), p. 155.
[45] "Former Champ Is Booked for Duluth Battle," *Duluth News Tribune*, November 16, 1931, sports section.
[46] Martin, Ellis, "Jack Looking for Crown He Used to Wear," *Duluth Herald*, August 24, 1931, sports section.
[47] Runyon, "Dempsey Making History with Comeback," *New York American*, December 22, 1931, p. 19.

By the time Dempsey arrived in Kansas City, the tour was already a fabulous success. Records for attendance had been set at almost every stop including Boise (6,500), Seattle (13,000), Portland (17,300), Tacoma (11,000), Salt Lake City (7,500), Omaha (9,000 indoors), Eugene (8,500), Aberdeen (4,500), and Vancouver, B. C. (10,000).

Dempsey's going rate for an appearance was 50 percent of net receipts. According to his manager, Leonard Sachs, Jack had already pulled in combined totals of 145,000 fans and gross receipts of $288,000. Of this, Dempsey's share had amounted to about $123,500.[48]

Following the pattern established by Dempsey's appearances in other locales, Hurley assembled at each of his three cities a mixture of native talent and outside professionals to oppose the ex-champ. Hurley's hope was that such combinations would satisfy the public's sometimes conflicting

---

[48] Kirksey, George, "Dempsey Tour Grand Success in Northwest," *Duluth Herald*, October 30, 1931, sports section. The following quote from Kirksey's article is based on information provided by Dempsey's manager Leonard Sachs:

"In 14 appearances in the far Northwest and West, Dempsey attracted approximately 118,000 customers and gate receipts of about $232,000 (net). Dempsey's end was slightly more than $100,000.

"... The paid attendance figures and net receipts on the first stage of the tour as announced by Sachs, follow: Portland, 17,800 persons, $28,000; Seattle, 13,000, $22,000: Spokane, 11,000, $21,000; Vancouver, B. C., 10,000, $18,000; Tacoma, Wash., 8,500, $14,000; Eugene, Ore., 8,500, $15,000; Salt Lake City, 7,500, $19,000; Boise, Idaho, 6,500, $13,000; Rock Springs, Wyo., 5,000, $10,000; Aberdeen, Wash., 4,500, $10,000; Logan, Utah, 5,000, $11,000; Reno (first appearance, indoors), 5,000, $17,000; Reno (second appearance, outdoors), 11,000, $22,000; Wenatchee, Wash., (author's note: Wenatchee on August 29th was an appearance as referee, not an exhibition), 5,500, $17,000."

The first stage of Dempsey's tour started in Reno on August 19, 1931, and ended September 17. The second stage had been scheduled to start in October, but was postponed when Jack caught the flu. That stage finally got its start at Provo, Utah, November 6 and ended at Sioux Falls, South Dakota on December 18. The Kansas City and Fargo-Duluth-St. Paul engagements were therefore in the middle of the tour's second stage. In between the Kansas City and Fargo stops, Dempsey staged exhibitions at Wichita, Tulsa, and Phoenix. A third stage was started on February 1, 1932 and continued at least through March 31, 1932.

After the end of the third stage, Dempsey ended his comeback because he felt he could not get in good enough shape to engage in real ten-round fights. Jack's losing effort in a four round exhibition at Chicago against King Levinsky on February 18, 1932, was the bout that made him decide to quit. For a while, Sachs and Dempsey talked of a new tour starting in August 1932, and Dempsey actually did have exhibition fights at Seattle and Portland, but this tour apparently never got off the ground.

To arrive at the figures in the text, the author has added the following second stage figures to Sach's figures as reported in Kirksey's article: Des Moines, Iowa (11/9), 7,500, $11,000; Omaha (11/11), 9000, $12,000 (gate receipts figure is author's conservative estimate); and Moline, Illinois (11/13), 10,000, $23,000. These second stage figures are from wire reports that likely used figures submitted by Sacks. The text understates the total attendance and gate receipts realized by Dempsey prior to the Kansas City appearance because the author did not have at hand figures for the 11/6 Provo, Utah appearance. The author has double-checked Sachs' figures from Portland, Seattle, Spokane, and Tacoma against local sources, and they are accurate.

desires to see how "one of their own" would do against Dempsey and at the same time see him perform against meaningful opposition.

In contrast to his visit as a referee a year earlier, Dempsey's public appearances during his comeback tour were infrequent, owing to the greater rest and exercise required by his fighting regimen. In both Fargo and Duluth, he headed to his hotel for a short rest after arriving, followed by a brisk walk before proceeding directly to the gym for a workout.

In Fargo and Duluth, the former titleholder's workouts were closed to the public with only a few invited guests present. Training sessions were timed by his trainer, Jerry "the Greek" Luvadis, and lasted less than 40 minutes, just long enough for 12 rounds of strenuous exercise with 20 second breaks between rounds. Afterward, the ex-champ chatted with reporters, showered, had a rubdown, and returned to his hotel room for the evening.[49]

Upon his arrival in St. Paul four days before he was scheduled to fight, Dempsey found "scores of invitations" waiting, but he declined "most of them, 'for this comeback business is serious with me.'" Even so, "Jack's suite at the Hotel St. Paul was a busy place," and "between callers in person and on the telephone, the former champion was kept constantly occupied." One caller who met with Dempsey was his old adversary, Tommy Gibbons, with whom Jack had a nice "chat about old times."[50]

Dempsey did attend two noontime luncheons sponsored by business leaders, as well as an evening dedication for a new school gym where he shared the dais with Mayor Gerhard J. Bundlie and Governor Olson. The former champ also donated autographed boxing gloves for an auction which was raising money for Christmas gifts to needy children.[51]

Another event Dempsey attended was a party hosted by promoter Johnny Salvator at St. Paul's Lowery Hotel on December 9, 1931, in joint celebration of his son's ninth and Jack Hurley's 34th birthdays. Seventy-six years later, Salvator's son, John II, still relished the memory of Dempsey inquiring at dinner as to the youngster's favorite song, and then afterward making a special request for the hotel's orchestra to play it. The band was the Johnny Hamp Orchestra, and the song "Just One More Chance."[52]

Dempsey fought four opponents for one round each December 4 at Fargo and three opponents December 7 at Duluth, two for one round and one for

---

[49] Campbell, "Dempsey Set for Exhibit of His Skill," *Duluth New Tribune*," December 7, 1931, sports section.
[50] O'Phelan, Jim, "Notes Improvement as He Battles with All Comers," *St. Paul Pioneer Press*, December 9, 1931, sports section.
[51] "Dempsey, Gibbons Talk over Shelby Battle at Luncheon" *St. Paul Pioneer Press*, December 10, 1931, sports section. "Minnesota Club to Be Dempsey's Host Today," *St. Paul Pioneer Press*, December 10, 1931, sports section. "Gym Dedicated, Dempsey Guest," *St. Paul Pioneer Press*, December 10, 1931, sports section. "Jack Dempsey Offers Gloves to Aid Santa," *St. Paul Pioneer Press*, December 9, 1931, p. 1.
[52] Author's Visit with John Salvator II at St. Paul, September 29 and 30, 2007.

THE DYNAMITER FROM DULUTH

Dempsey training with Jerry (the Greek) Luvadis for his comeback.

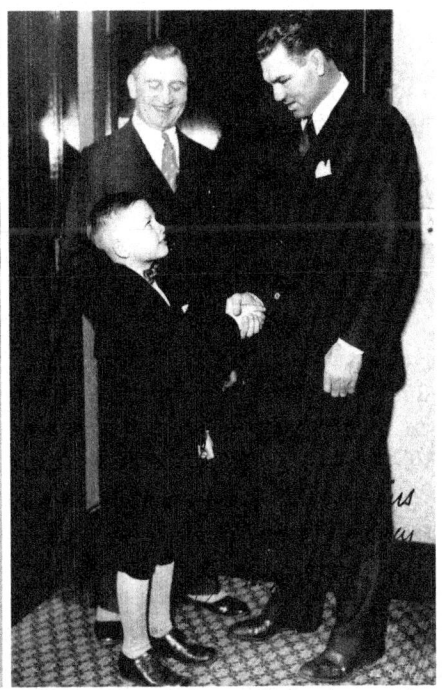

Promoter Johnny Salvator and son greet Dempsey in St. Paul.

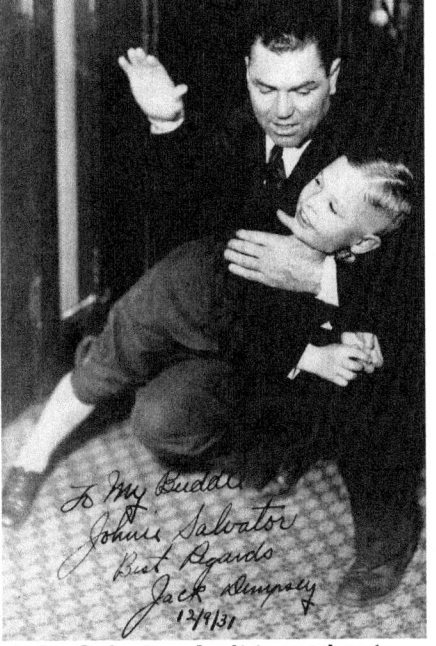

Dempsey hams it up with young John Salvator. As it turned out, Jack's one day off in St. Paul coincided with John's ninth birthday.

two rounds. Since he had ties to each city, Retzlaff faced Dempsey in one-rounders at both shows. Surprisingly, Retzlaff was booed in both cities when he failed to land a significant blow in either fight, choosing to stay on the defensive as Jack chased him around the ring.

Dempsey did not go entirely unchallenged at Fargo, however. Tommy Davenport of Little Rock, Arkansas, boxed smartly and landed several solid lefts to last out the round in good style. In the other fights, Jack had it easy, stopping both Swede Gransberg of Fargo and Johnny Korada of Chicago in less than a minute.[53]

The return of boo-fighter Szymka Zabuil, the man boxing fans loved to hate, saved the show in Duluth. Dempsey alternated between landing hard punches and playfully tapping and cuffing at Zabuil when he threatened to quit. After Szymka was downed by a particularly hefty punch, Jack picked Zabuil up as he clung desperately to the ropes in a comical effort to stay down. When Szymka got to his feet, Jack, playing to the crowd, prolonged the humiliation by forcing Zabuil to finish the full two rounds.[54]

Dempsey met the stiffest opposition on his swing through the Upper Midwest on December 11 at St. Paul. Minneapolis prospect Art Lasky did not flinch for an instant when the Manassa Mauler, in his patented bob and weave style, stepped to the center of the ring in the first round and immediately landed his famous left hook. From then on, it was a hammer and tong affair. For a full two rounds, fans were in an uproar as Art refused to break ground and on occasion was even able to beat Jack to the punch.

After the Lasky bout, Dempsey tired, and Jack Roper of Los Angeles and Angus McDonald of Winnipeg each stayed one round with the ex-champ.[55]

According to local reports, 3,911 people contributed $7,975 in Fargo, slightly more than 6,000 paid more than $12,000 at Duluth, and 10,360 chipped in with $21,853 at St. Paul. Attendance was at or near building capacity at each location, although, because of depression ticket prices, only Duluth set a record gate for a boxing show. According to news articles, boxing fans in all three cities "seemed to have a whale of a time."[56]

For the three shows, Dempsey received about $20,000. When added to prior earnings, his income from the tour up to and including the St. Paul exhibition totaled around $200,000. Remarkably, these earnings for 1931 would be greater than those of any other boxer, even exceeding the income

---

[53] Edmond, George, "Retzlaff Fails to Throw Punch but Goes the Limit," *St. Paul Pioneer Press*, December 5, 1931, sports section.
[54] Campbell, "Manassa Mauler Displays Former Fistic Technique," *Duluth News Tribune*, December 8, 1931, sports section.
[55] McKenna, Lou, "Lasky Gives Former Champ 2 Furious Opening Cantos," *St. Paul Pioneer Press*, December 12, 1931, sports section.
[56] Macdonald, "Dempsey Draws over 6,000 Fans to Amph Arena," *Duluth Herald*, December 8, 1931, sports section.

of heavyweight champion Max Schmeling.[57]

Notwithstanding the ex-champ's big percentage, each of the shows made money for promoters Hurley, Terk, and Salvator. At St. Paul, a happy Dempsey accepted $10,000 even though he was entitled to $618 more, telling Salvator to "keep the change" as a Christmas present.

Runyon, traveling from New York to see Dempsey in St. Paul, summed it up best when he wrote that Jack had "been the savior of the promoters in the Northwest." The comeback tour, Runyon continued, demonstrated the depth of Jack's popularity because "in a time of depression, in towns where they wouldn't pay a dime to see an earthquake, he is playing to packed houses and to gates that are establishing new records in the regions he is covering. The fellow is a wonder. That's all. Just a daggone wonder."[58]

Hurley could only agree with Runyon's assessment and thank his lucky stars for Jack Dempsey. For two years in a row, the Manassa Mauler's barnstorming tours, first as a referee and now as a fighter, had helped keep the promotional ventures of Hurley and his cronies operating in the black.

With business in Duluth and St. Paul healthy for the time being, Hurley could return with a clear conscience to his most remunerative endeavor, managing the fortunes of Billy Petrolle. During Billy's time off, Madison Square Garden's new boxing director Jimmy Johnston had uncovered a couple of prospects he wanted to try out on Petrolle. On December 12, Johnston wired, "Can Billy be ready for a fight December 30, 1931?"[59]

Hurley lost no time responding, "You bet he can." Two weeks later, Jack and Billy were back in business, riding first class on a Great Northern train. They were on their way for yet another run at New York City.

---

[57] Runyon, *op. cit.*
[58] Runyon, "Dempsey's 12th Manager Good Business Man," *New York American*, December 19, 1931, p. 20.
[59] "Petrolle to Box Townsend," *Fargo Forum*, December 13, 1931, sports section.

CHAPTER 25

FIRST ENCOUNTER WITH A BOY BANDIT

Billy Petrolle is a throw-back and a glorious one, to the old days when fighters fought with brains, as well as arms and legs ... Petrolle has one of the greatest fighting brains this generation has known. The boys go into raptures about his hitting power, but the big point is that Petrolle uses his head to trap the other fellow into position where he can hit him with a paralyzing blow. Other men, perhaps, can hit as hard as Petrolle – if they can find the spot. But Petrolle finds it. They can't, and he has become the modern knockout sensation among the little fellows. — James J. Corbett

Petrolle's ... the greatest little ring warrior of these times ... And when I say fighter, I mean just that. He is the grandest "crowd pleaser" the game has seen in many years. Petrolle's idea of a fight is to get in there and throw leather, and that's what the clients pay to see ... He is as plain as an old shoe. He goes and comes quietly, minding his own business. There is no swank or swagger to William Petrolle. He is just an everyday fellow.
— Damon Runyon

You see, Willie ... has been both down and up and knows how to take it the hard way, which is maybe why he is my favorite fighter. To be a trifle ungrammatical about it: He don't shake hands with himself – he don't blow kisses at the crowd – he don't wink at customers in ringside chairs – he don't affect a sickly smile when he is hit – he don't croon – he don't dance – and he can't play the piano. He just fights. And if the other guy will fight, too, when you go to see him you are in for a lively evening. — Bill Corum

I dislike to write again about Petrolle, but he happens to be my favorite fighter of the moment, and on top of that I think he is one of the most underrated fighters that has come into the game in a number of years. I don't think he would have any trouble winning the welterweight championship ... and if he cared to it probably would be easy for him to win the lightweight title ... — Joe Williams

It's too bad Billy Petrolle isn't a heavyweight. The world's championship would be returned to America quicker than you could say "Donnerwetter," if the job was assigned to him. He doesn't hold any titles and he never may acquire one but, for my dough, this little pisan from Fargo with the pushed-in face, is the greatest fighter now in the ring ...

Petrolle has everything a fighter needs. He has a devastating left hook, a wicked right cross, a concrete jaw, a heart of steel, and a head that is of

some use besides as a place to which cauliflower ears could attach themselves like barnacles ... I've been watching Petrolle perform for a long time now and never have seen him turn in a dull fight. – Dan Parker

Now, I've long since given up waxing sentimental over fighters, but one does get the feeling while watching William in there throwing them that at least here is honest endeavor and a pure fighting heart. I don't know much about him outside the ring, but inside he does his stuff. He gives a show. He takes chances. He fights. Oh my friends and countrymen, how he fights. And how many others do?[1] – Paul Gallico

****

The appointment of James Joy (Jimmy) Johnston as boxing director and head matchmaker at Madison Square Garden marked the first major shake-up in Garden management since William (Bill) Carey assumed control as president after the death of Tex Rickard three years earlier.

While the depression and the resultant downturn in attendance at boxing shows was the first and most obvious reason for Carey's decision to replace Tom McArdle with Johnston, there were at least two other reasons as well.

One reason had to do with boxing politics in New York State. The state athletic commission viewed the Garden's refusal to arrange a Schmeling-Sharkey bout for New York and its subsequent staging of the Schmeling-Stribling match in Cleveland as open defiance of its authority. As a result, the commission had in subtle ways undertaken to work against the Garden.

Choice dates for shows sought by the Garden were mysteriously granted to competitors. Approvals for bouts the Garden requested were delayed and sometimes refused without explanation. License applications by out-of-state fighters the Garden wanted to use were denied. Garden officials hoped that Johnston's close personal ties to Mayor Jimmy Walker and William Farley, who was one of the boxing commission's three members, would reverse this trend and cause the commission to view the Garden more favorably.

Although the depression and upper management politics were matters largely out of his control, the third reason for McArdle's ouster was because of an old feud he could not let go. As early as 1915, McArdle and Johnston had worked as opposing matchmakers for the two largest boxing clubs in New York City. As a result, there had been no love lost since then.

Their dislike for one another came to a head in 1931 when McArdle

---

[1] Menke, Frank G., "Billy's Victory Analyzed by Corbett," *New York Evening Journal*, March 25, 1932, sports section. Runyon, Damon, "Runyon Exposes the Engineer of Fargo Express," *New York American*, January 25, 1932, pp. 19, 21. Corum, Bill, "Sports," *New York Evening Journal*, January 23, 1932, sports section. Williams, Joe, "By Joe Williams," *New York World-Telegram*, January 23, 1932, p. 8. Parker, Dan, "Not a Champ, but Better Than One," *New York Daily Mirror*, January 24, 1932, sports section. Gallico, Paul, "Discussing W. Petrolle," *New York Daily News*, January 24, 1932, sports section.

refused to use fighters managed by Johnston and his brother Charley on any of the Garden's shows. In an effort to reach a peaceful solution, Jimmy brought the matter up directly with McArdle's boss, President Bill Carey.

After looking into it, Carey told Jimmy over dinner that McArdle's stated reason for not using Johnston's fighters was that they were not good enough to appear at the Garden. Bill further explained he could not help Jimmy since Tom had been hired as the Garden's boxing director, and it would be bad policy for Carey to interfere with McArdle's judgment.

After finishing his meal in relative silence, Jimmy told Carey on the way out of the cafe that Bill's decision to back McArdle left Jimmy no choice but to declare war and to promote boxing in direct competition with the Garden. Johnston told Carey that not only would Jimmy be putting fighters from the Johnston stable to work at the new boxing club, but he would also be going after fighters normally used by the Garden itself.

Carey pointed out the Garden already had two major ballparks, the Polo Grounds and Yankee Stadium, under lease for the summer and the only option, Ebbets Field, was at a disadvantage because of its Brooklyn locale. To these bits of information, Jimmy's only response was, "We'll see."[2]

In arousing the ire of James Joy Johnston, Carey and McArdle had upset not just any fight manager, but instead a man generally regarded as the shrewdest and most resourceful of all operatives to emerge from the boiling stewpot that was New York's boxing scene in the early 20th century. Fifty-five years old in 1931, Johnston had started out as a flyweight boxer in the late 1890s before working his way through every job the sport had to offer as trainer, second, manager, press agent, matchmaker, and promoter.

Christened "the Boy Bandit" because of his youthful appearance, diminutive stature, and his knack for always coming out on top in his business dealings, the "cocky little bantam with the tilted derby hat" coupled a keen intellect and bold courage with "a jaunty bearing and raven black hair that few of youthful age could rival."

James Dawson of the *New York Times* described Jimmy as "a master of ballyhoo in a field where ballyhoo climbed to its dizziest heights." He was "possessed of an extensive and well-exercised vocabulary" which he liberally seasoned with "colorful invective and lashing sarcasm. Nothing delighted him more than to be provocative."[3]

Johnston was born in Liverpool, England November 28, 1875, and came to the United States with his family at the age of 12. While working full-time in an iron foundry and fighting for extra money on the side, Johnston caught the eye of boxing manager Charley Harvey. The older man was interested in Jimmy not as a fighter, but rather as a potential assistant to help in the details of managing boxers in Harvey's stable.

---

[2] Griffin, Marcus, "Wise Guy," (The Vanguard Press, 1933), pp. 298-299.
[3] "J. J. Johnston Dies; Ring Promoter, 70," *New York Times*, May 8, 1946, p. 25.

A major part of Harvey's business was importing top fighters from the British Isles to box in the U. S. Specifically, Charley thought the energetic young "Joimes," as the Liverpool native then was called, to be the perfect choice to make Harvey's newly arrived attractions feel comfortable in a strange land. After a few years, Jimmy left Harvey and branched out on his own, while continuing to specialize in handling imported boxers.

In the 1910s, Johnston alternated as a manager and promoter/matchmaker at several of New York City's leading boxing clubs. His most famous fighters during this period were George (Boer) Rodel, Owen Moran, and welterweight champion Ted (Kid) Lewis. As promoter, he staged fights at St. Nicholas Arena and operated under lease as boxing director at Madison Square Garden from 1915 until the legislature made boxing illegal in 1917.

The return of the sport to legal status after the passage of the Walker Law in 1921 found Johnston back promoting fights. In 1923, he staged the Benny Leonard-Lew Tendler lightweight title bout at Yankee Stadium. The match attracted 58,500 spectators who paid $452,648. Both figures stood as records in the lower weight divisions until 1951 when 61,370 fans paid $767,626 to see the Ray Robinson-Randy Turpin middleweight title bout.

Later in the 1920s, Johnston specialized as a manager in reviving the careers of ex-champs Johnny Dundee, Mike McTigue, and Pete Latzo. Jimmy also served as an advisor to heavyweight challenger Jack Sharkey and was instrumental in restoring the ex-sailor's reputation after his loss to Dempsey in 1927. His most impressive feat of the decade, however, and his final undertaking before challenging the Garden, was the manipulation of an inept, glass-jawed British heavyweight named Phil Scott into a place of prominence in the tournament to determine Tunney's successor.

Following his fateful meeting with Carey, Johnston enlisted Humberto (Jack) Fugazy as a financial backer to co-promote outdoor boxing shows at Ebbets Field. Fugazy, it will be recalled, had been competing off and on against the Garden since 1925. Most recently he had partnered with Jack Dempsey to unsuccessfully challenge Madison Square Garden's supremacy in 1929. Fugazy obviously had little affection for the Garden, and he was eager to join with Jimmy in challenging its management.[4]

For his first major outdoor promotion, Johnston had no trouble convincing Jack Sharkey to fight Mickey Walker in a main event at Ebbets Field. Sharkey still blamed Garden officials for not giving him the title fight with Schmeling instead of Young Stribling. As a result, Jack was happy to thumb his nose at the Garden and sign with his former advisor. Walker and his manager, Jack Kearns, who both had been shunned by New York's boxing establishment, were also eager to get back into the limelight.

On July 22, 1931, ex-middleweight champ Walker, weighing 169 pounds, stunned the sports world by holding Sharkey, 198-1/2, to a 15-round draw

---

[4] Humbert Fugazy's prior career as a promoter was discussed in Chapter 14.

Portrait of a youthful Boy Bandit, James J. (Jimmy) Johnston, inscribed many years later to Archie Moore, whom Johnston was managing at the time of his death in 1946.

in front of more than 30,000 fans who paid $212,095. Incredibly, although few had given the much smaller Walker a chance to win, most writers thought afterward he had beaten Sharkey handily.

Jack Hurley was one of the few who favored Walker. The day before the match, the *New York Sun*'s Wilbur Wood devoted a full column to Hurley's pre-fight analysis. Jack felt that Mickey, who possessed more determination than Sharkey, proved his ability to handle bigger men in fights with Paul Swiderski and Bearcat Wright. Sharkey, on the other hand, Hurley urged, was temperamental and likely to become discouraged when facing a foe like Walker who would keep coming at him.[5]

The success of the Sharkey-Walker show encouraged Johnston to try again. Sharkey was eager for a chance to work his way back into the good graces of the boxing public. Jimmy believed the quickest way to do this would be for the Boston Gob to fight Primo Carnera.

While Carnera already had been signed by the Garden to fight Schmeling for the heavyweight title later in the summer, Johnston had a feeling that Max, who had returned to Germany after his July 3rd fight with Stribling, did not want to fight again in 1931. Playing his hunch, Jimmy decided to keep pressure on the Garden and sign Primo to fight Sharkey anyway.

Although the Garden obtained a court order enjoining Carnera from fighting Sharkey, Johnston's hunch proved correct. In August, Schmeling wired that he would not return to fight Carnera in 1931. As a result, the injunction was lifted and Jimmy scheduled the Sharkey-Carnera fight for the tail end of the outdoor season on October 12, 1931.[6]

Johnston's show was another artistic and financial success. Sharkey, boxing beautifully, redeemed his rating as the No. 1 heavyweight challenger by winning a clear 15-round decision over the huge Italian. At the box office, 24,014 cash customers paid $129,325 to see the event.[7]

To further cramp the Garden's style, Johnston announced plans to promote boxing at two locations during the indoor winter season. Jimmy told reporters he already had secured the 6,000-seat St. Nicholas Arena and was in the midst of negotiations to take over one of the largest armories in the city, an indoor facility which could seat 30,000 persons.[8]

"I do not intend to allow Madison Square Garden, Bill Carey, the '600 millionaires' or anyone else drive me out," vowed Jimmy. "I'm in the business of promoting professional boxing to stay, as Madison Square

---

[5] Wood, Wilbur, "Hurley Rates Walker a Cinch," *New York Sun*, July 21, 1931, sports section.
[6] Pegler, Westbrook, "Speaking Out on Sports," *New York Evening Post*, July 24, 1931, sports section.
[7] Morris, William, "'I Did My Best,' Carnera Says; Sharkey Praises Beaten Rival," *New York Evening Post,* October 13, 1931, sports section.
[8] "Johnston Beats Garden in Lining Up Talent," *Minneapolis Star*, August 12, 1931, sports section.

Mickey Walker shakes hands with Jack Sharkey after they signed contracts presented by promoter Jimmy Johnston (center). Standing are (left to right) Billy Lahiff, Jack Kearns, Damon Runyon, Dan McKetrick, Bill Farnsworth, and Humbert (Jack) Fugazy.

Primo Carnera and Sharkey sign for their 1931 bout as matchmaker Sam McQuade presides (center). Standing (left to right) are Bill Duffy, Leon See, Fugazy, Bert Strand, Johnston, and Jimmy Buckley.

Garden and 'Square Shootin' Bill' will discover if they stick around long enough. However, if the Garden continues to go downhill the way it has for the past year, they'll have to turn the place into a garage."[9]

Outmaneuvered at every turn during the outdoor season and now facing the prospect of continued competition during the fall and winter, Carey and the Garden waved the white flag of surrender and asked for a truce. On October 14, 1931, just two days after the Sharkey-Carnera fight, Carey called for a meeting and offered Johnston the job as Garden boxing director.

The offer provided a hefty annual salary of $25,000 and an opportunity to earn additional income through performance bonuses pegged to increases in the price of Garden stock. After a period of negotiation, a contract was drafted and signed by Carey and Johnston. The war was over. Matchmaker Tom McArdle was out, and boxing director Jimmy Johnston was in.[10]

And so, in December 1931, Hurley and Petrolle went to work for a new matchmaker, a man equally experienced, but more strong-willed than his predecessor. Although he had never met Johnston, Jack expected no problems because of Jimmy's reputation as a knowledgeable boxing man.

Johnston's first foe for Petrolle was "the Blond Tiger" Billy Townsend, a hard-punching 22-year old from the coal mines near Vancouver, British Columbia, Canada. Townsend turned pro in 1926 and gained acceptance as the West's best welterweight by beating Tony Portillo, Johnny LaMar, Joe Medill, Tod Morgan, Doc Snell, Tommy Herman, and Wildcat Carter.

Undefeated in his most recent 15 bouts, Townsend's two-fisted style already had made him a New York favorite. In prior outings, he impressed fans and experts alike with wins over Eddie Ran and Andy Saviola. In the Ran fight especially, the crowd warmed to Billy when he came back from an early knockdown to earn a close verdict. In a third go with local welter Paulie Walker, the Canadian battler was a victim of a draw in which "the gathering almost to a man thought Townsend was entitled to the decision."[11]

The left hook which sealed Townsend's fate against Petrolle December 30 was a "wicked smash ... one of Petrolle's very best," delivered midway in the first round. The impact sent Townsend to the canvas, but the knockdown was delayed, "the punch not taking full effect until a couple of seconds later." Townsend "stiffened in his boots ... then he seemed to snap

---

[9] "'They'll Have to Turn Garden into Garage,' Says Warring Jim Johnston" (UP), *Minneapolis Journal*, August 12, 1931, sports section. The term "600 millionaires" was a figure of speech coined by Tex Rickard to describe the team of wealthy backers he assembled to finance construction of the third Madison Square Garden, for which ground was broken on January 9, 1925.

[10] Wood, "Johnston May Get $100,000 A Year," *New York Sun*, October 10, 1931, sports section. Neil, Edward J., "Jimmy Johnston Plans New Series of 'Heavy Battles,'" *Duluth Herald*, October 14, 1931, sports section.

[11] Dawson, James P., "Townsend Draws in Bout at Garden," *New York Times*, October 17, 1931, p. 19.

Billy Townsend, "the Blonde Tiger," from Vancouver, B. C.

An earnest looking Petrolle as he looked against Townsend.

Townsend down the first time for a nine-count in the opening round.

out of it" and "was about to strike a new stance" when finally "he settled toward the floor, slowly, easily, without again being punched."[12]

The blow seemed to anesthetize Townsend's brain and delay not only his reaction to the punch itself, but also his response to the referee's count. According to the *New York American*'s Ed Frayne, "Townsend was so thoroughly numbed he almost forgot to get up. [Referee Willie] Lewis was halfway down on the final stroke of the last second when Townsend's knee left the floor. The blond Canadian never recovered from that blow."[13]

When he arose, Townsend folded his arms around his head and covered up. Instead of rushing in, Petrolle was cautious and deliberate. Afterward, he explained to reporters he did not want to unnecessarily hurt his hands. "All he gave me for a target was arms and elbows," Billy told them, "and I wanted to open him up rather than take a chance on breaking a hand."[14]

Townsend's head cleared sufficiently during the rest period to win the second round. In that session, the Blond Tiger made a stand and threw everything he had into turning the tide of the fight, consistently out-punching Petrolle in vicious exchanges. Near the end of the round, "a booming right to the head" shook the Fargo Express to his heels, and for a short while "the old engine rocked on the rails."

Returning to his corner, Petrolle was grinning as he sat down to tell a concerned Hurley, "See that kid swingin', Jack? Let him swing. He'll get tired. He's like Suarez. He got tired, too, Jack. Five or six years ago I'd have swung with this kid, but I'm too foxy now."[15]

As Petrolle predicted, Townsend's monumental effort in the second round sapped his vitality. In the third and fourth, the Express regained control and carefully picked his spots with bursts of lefts and rights which gradually wore the Canadian down. At the end of the fourth, Townsend rallied and landed some effective blows, "but was very, very wild."

A left hook, and Townsend was down for a nine-count again midway in the fifth. His wild flurries of punches kept Petrolle at bay for the rest of the round, but the effort resulted in a perceptibly slower Townsend coming out for round six. Another left floored him at the end of that round, and his seconds had to drag him to his corner for an attempt at revival.

Toeing the mark for the seventh, "Townsend was too weak to protect himself and was pounded hard until he finally went down after receipting for a left and right to the jaw. Referee Lewis then stopped it. The weights

---

[12] Frayne, Ed, "Fargo Express Knocks Rival Down 4 Times," *New York American*, December 31, 1931, sports section ("wicked smash ..."). Wood, "Petrolle Wins in the Seventh," *New York Sun*, December 31, 1931, sports section ("the punch not ..."). Igoe, Hype, "Crushing Left Hook of Petrolle Puts Townsend Out," *New York Evening Journal*, December 31, 1931, sports section ("stiffened in his boots...being punched").

[13] Frayne, *op. cit.*

[14] Wood, *op. cit.*

[15] Igoe, *op. cit.*

The Fargo Express slips a punch and charges forward during a middle round. Townsend recovered after a rough first round to win the second, but it was all downhill after that.

FIRST ENCOUNTER WITH A BOY BANDIT

A left hook sent Townsend down for nine midway in the fifth round.

Townsend stretched out for a final ten-count in the seventh round.

were: Petrolle, 140-1/2; Townsend, 142." The time was 1:58 of round seven.[16]

After the fight Petrolle was asked about the seemingly delayed effect of the first knockdown. Billy compared Townsend's reaction to that of King Tut in their fight at the Garden ten months earlier: "They thought they had shaken off the punches and suddenly everything went blank including their legs. When I hit them, I hit them."[17]

Accounts in the New Year's Eve editions of the next day's newspapers were enthusiastic and replete with elaborate hyperbole giving full scope to Petrolle's ring persona as "the Fargo Express" and "the grand old veteran" of the squared circle. Though Billy was still ten days shy of his 27th birthday, most scribes wrote as if "the old battle-scarred stager from the wilds of North Dakota" had already spent a lifetime rattling back and forth on railroad tracks between New York and the Midwest.

The four-month interlude since Petrolle's last New York appearance led New York's hard-boiled journalists to unleash a torrent of praise. It was as if their admiration for his efforts over the past year had been subconsciously building during his absence, waiting for an excuse to be released like bubbly spirits from a freshly uncorked bottle of vintage champagne.

From matchmaker Johnston's perspective, the most impressive part of the show had been the 14,623 people who paid gross receipts of $40,103. Jimmy had originally viewed the program as "a filler" arranged to maintain the Garden's schedule of weekly fights during the traditionally slow Christmas and New Year's season. He even went so as far as to use only out-of-town fighters for all bouts on the show, not wanting to waste strong local drawing cards for an event that he thought would be poorly attended.[18]

As it happened, except for the Tony Canzoneri-Kid Chocolate lightweight title bout on November 20 (19,001/$83,408), the Petrolle-Townsend show was the most lucrative of the ten cards on the Garden's fall/winter calendar. While the Al Singer-Bat Battalino (17,250/ $46,918) and the Carnera-Vittorio Campolo (10,000/$41,307) cards had registered larger grosses, both were charity shows. After paying donations to charity from net receipts, both cards realized less profit than Petrolle-Townsend.[19]

---

[16] Wood, *op. cit.*
[17] Igoe, *op. cit.*
[18] Wood, "Garden Has Out-of-Town Card," *New York Sun*, December 26, 1931, p. 29. Wood, "Sharkey's Chances Brighter," *New York Sun*, December 28, 1931, sports section. Grayson, Harry, "Petrolle Scales 140-1/4, Townsend 142, for Garden Headliner Tonight – Fargo Express Looms as 2-1 Choice over Youngster," *New York World-Telegram*, December 30, 1931, sports section. Frayne, "Petrolle 8 to 5 over Townsend," *New York American*, December 30, 1931, sports section.
[19] To support conclusions about the profits of the shows, the author has relied on figures published in the *New York American* for the Singer-Battalino show and in the *New York Evening Post* for the Petrolle-Townsend card. Frayne, "Referee Stops Xmas Fund Go Before 18,000," *New York American*, December 12, 1931, pp. 19, 21. Frayne, "Battalino's Pete

The success of the show was a boon for Johnston, who was still working to justify the big salary Bill Carey and the "600 millionaires" were paying him. With Petrolle now a hot item, Johnston could rely on sportswriters to go to bat for almost any show as long as they could continue to indulge in whimsical metaphors comparing "the squeaking old 'Fargo Express'" to another "round-house-swinging youngster" like Billy Townsend.

Fortunately, Johnston had just such a candidate in 145-pound welterweight Eddie Ran, a 23-year-old native of Warsaw, Poland whose real name was Edouard Fiszmajster. Ran had studied engineering in Poland, but left in 1929 for Paris because he could make more money fighting. After scoring half a dozen kayos in France, he arrived in the United States in the spring of 1930, via Havana, where he stopped off and won three bouts.

Ran made his U. S. debut in Tampa, Florida, and then won five of six bouts at Milwaukee and Chicago before heading to New York. Eddie scored a three-round knockout over Tommy Jordan in his first Empire State bout at the Broadway Arena in Brooklyn on October 27, 1930. Over the next 17 months, he established himself as a New York favorite by winning 10 of 12 bouts, including five by knockout.[20]

Reilly Put 'Wise' Boys on Spot," *New York American*, December 13, 1931, sports section. Morris, "Around the Ring," *New York Evening Post*, December 31, 1931, sports section.

The *American* was the sponsoring newspaper for the Singer-Battalino show, which supported the Christmas Fund, a charity organized to distribute gifts to poor children. According to the *American*, the show drew a gross gate of $46,918,24. Net receipts, after deducting for security, ticket takers, referees, taxes, etc., amounted to $41,493.24. Out of this, the Christmas Fund was given "more than $7,000," leaving approximately $34,400 left to pay the fighters and the Garden. Of this amount, Battalino received approximately $9,000 (whether this was a percentage or flat guarantee is not stated). The amount Singer received was unreported but a good guess is somewhere in the 20-25 percent range. The remainder ($16,800-$18,600) presumably would go to the Garden and to other fighters on the card.

In comparison, the Petrolle-Townsend show grossed $40,102.78 and netted $36,146.58. No further deductions had to be made before distributions to the fighters and the Garden. Petrolle received 25 percent ($9,037) and Townsend 20 percent ($7,229). The remainder ($19,829) presumably went to the Garden and the preliminary and semi-main event fighters.

Although the author did not have information at hand to do the same calculations for the Carnera-Campolo fight, the *New York Sun* estimated attendance at 10,000 and gross receipts at $40,000. The *Ring Record Book of 1957* reported gross receipts at $41,306.57, which seems correct. The record book's attendance figure of 31,682 is obviously wrong since the Garden held barely 20,000 tops. Could the *Ring* have meant attendance at 10,682 or 11,682? Unfortunately, the author has found that *the Ring Record Book*'s Madison Square Garden figures (all editions) are sometimes wrong. Apart from typos, the book frequently confuses net and gross receipts, making accurate comparisons impossible without independent verification. In any event, since the Carnera-Campolo show benefitted the Federation for the Support of Jewish Philanthropic Societies, it is clear that after deducting expenses and a charitable contribution from gross receipts of $41,306.57, the Garden would have realized less profit from that show than from either the Singer-Battalino or Petrolle-Townsend shows. Wood, "Carnera Stops Campolo in 2d," *New York Sun*, November 28, 1931, sports section. Fleischer, Nat, *1957 Ring Record Book*, (The Ring Book Shop, 1957), p. 75.

[20] Grayson, "Ran Qualifies for Petrolle by Kayo over McNamara," *New York World-*

Even though Ran lost a close decision to Townsend in October 1932, he figured to be a tougher rival for Petrolle. Not only was his list of New York foes longer and more formidable than Townsend's, but Eddie had knocked out Louis (Kid) Kaplan in one round. At the time, the former featherweight champ was No. 2 contender for the lightweight title.[21]

Known as "the Polish Thunderbolt," Ran had impressed experts with the power of his straight right hand. The *American*'s Ed Frayne saw him throw a right in the Kaplan fight that "crashed to Kaplan's jaw," knocking him "colder than a hound's nose." Wilbur Wood of the *Sun* termed Ran "a dynamic right hand puncher" after watching him kayo Jimmy McNamara in the second round. In winning the fight, Eddie knocked Jimmy down three times with right hands inside 35 seconds of the second round.[22]

Johnston scheduled the Petrolle-Ran bout for January 22, 1932. Wood summed up expectations about the fight: "Petrolle is one of the best left hook artists of modern times. Ran has a peach of a right cross. It will be a duel between Billy's left hook and Eddie's right cross. There is dynamite in each. It looks like a large evening."[23]

Before the bout, Hurley and Petrolle planted a notion Billy would use his left hook to counter Ran's right. Billy told the *World-Telegram*'s Harry Grayson he expected Ran to carry the battle to him and if he did, Billy would be ready: "The secret of my success in my old age is most of these fellows cannot understand why I am not washed up. Anybody who thinks I am and just tries to whip me is just a cousin of mine. Those who run away give me the most trouble. They tell me Ran is right-hand crazy. I'll beat the right-hand specialist to the punch with a left hook every time."[24]

In making this statement, Petrolle was engaging in a neat bit of subterfuge. While Billy would certainly make every effort to land his left hook whenever he could, he and Hurley had come up with a plan that focused more on Petrolle's right hand than his left.

Years later, Hurley told columnist W. C. Heinz that Petrolle's ring artistry reached its peak against Eddie Ran: "The funny thing about Petrolle is that people never knew how good he was. They thought he was a lucky fighter. He wasn't a lucky fighter. What he did, he did because it was planned that way. It wasn't an accident when he won a fight.

Telegram, January 12, 1932, p. 32.

[21] Borden, Eddie, "Ratings for the Month Ending October," *Ring Magazine*, December 1931, p. 47.

[22] Frayne, "Champ Fights Himself 'Out' in 15-Round Go," *New York American*, November 21, 1931, p. 19. Wood, "Ran Scores Early Knockout," *New York Sun*, January 12, 1932, sports section. Wood, "Fargo Express I in Again," *New York Sun*, December 30, 1931, sports section.

[23] Wood, "Punchers Meet in Garden Ring," *New York Sun*, January 22, 1932, sports section.

[24] Grayson, "Opponents' Belief He Is Through Aid to Petrolle," *New York World-Telegram*, January 21, 1932, sports section.

"Petrolle, you know, wasn't easy to hit. He gave the impression he was easy to hit. Sure he did. He invited you to hit him. Do you know why? Because then he could hit back. Petrolle would go in there, and put it right up there where you could hit it. He'd take two or three jabs, and then slip under and let go with the heavy artillery. That's a good trade, any time you can take three light punches to let go with the heavy stuff.

"What gave people the impression that Petrolle was easy to hit was that he was always on the edge of danger. That's the place to be. Be in there close where you can work, where you can take advantage of it when the other guy makes a mistake. You're inside where you may get your block knocked off if you don't know what you're doing, but if you know what you're doing it's a cinch.

"You look so easy. The other guy has to try to hit you. Don't you see? He can't help himself, and then, when you've got him coming, you work your stuff, you let the heavy stuff drop. Like the night Petrolle fought Eddie Ran."[25]

The plan was to lure Ran into throwing his right so Petrolle could slip or duck under it and counter with his own right hand. Eddie would not be looking for a right-hand punch because of Billy's reputation as a left hooker. In order for the plan to work Petrolle had to make it look easy for Ran to hit him. Billy would have to take two or three jabs and maybe even a right hand to give Eddie confidence enough to really let go with it so Billy could slip it and have an open shot at Ran's jaw with the "heavy artillery."

Petrolle landed the fight's first punch, a hard left hook to the body, as he rushed Ran to the ropes. Eddie came back with two left jabs to the face and missed a right. Ran scored with three more solid lefts and sent in a hard right that pushed Billy back on his heels. Eddie moved in to follow up with another right, but Petrolle saw a chance to throw his own right, and he beat Ran to the punch with a sock that landed on his neck, and Eddie was down.

The knockdown was the first of three during the round. Ran was on his feet at three, much too early since he arose on wobbly pins and immediately fell back against the ropes. Petrolle, still following the plan perfectly, launched another right to the jaw which put the Polish Thunderbolt down again, this time for two. When he got up, Eddie tried to fight back, but he caught "a whistling left hook" and hit the canvas for a full nine-count. They were mixing in the center of the ring at the bell to end the first round.[26]

Between rounds, Ran's seconds drenched him with water in a frantic effort to revive him. When the bell rang, he "went back after his tormentor in the second round as if the first had never been fought." Eddie "pegged

---

[25] Heinz, W. C., "Plan to Conquer," *Ring Magazine*, August 1950, p. 36.
[26] Simon, Jack, "Fargo Express Ends Bout in 6th Round with Hard Right on Rival's Chin," *New York Evening Graphic*, January 23, 1932, sports section. Simon's article was the main source for the description of the first-round action with assists from the Igoe and Wood articles cited in two notes immediately following.

away with his right, but the hard-bitten veteran worked under or away from the punches," hammering the body with both hands, and "was not tagged until just before the bell. It was Petrolle's round, but not by much."[27]

Ran was a smart fighter, and during the second round he had figured out what was happening. Although Eddie still was relying on his right-hand money punch, he was no longer falling for Petrolle's invitation to throw the right when Billy was set to counter. As a result, after this round Petrolle put aside, for the time being, the plan of trying to set up Ran for the right hand.

In the next three rounds, Ran continued his remarkable recovery and fought Billy on almost even terms. Eddie had his best round in the third when he opened up "and crossed Billy time and time again with straight rights that shook Petrolle, but couldn't keep him from coming in." In the fourth round, Billy administered a ferocious body beating that had Ran "back[ing] around the ring and try[ing] to escape the terrific punishment."[28]

In the fifth round, Petrolle changed tactics and laid the foundation for a return to his original strategy. According to Paul Gallico of the *New York Daily News*, it was "an even and hard-fought round with Petrolle bent on getting Ran to watch that left. He poked it into his face; he poked it into his stomach – it was left, left, left, until [Billy] finally sold Ran on the idea that that was the hand to watch."[29]

By this time Ran was seeing so much of Petrolle's left hand he had forgotten about the right. Coming out for the next round, Billy felt Ran was ready to be taken. Hurley described the end to Heinz: "Do you know that we had to wait until the sixth round for [another] chance for Petrolle to get that opening for his own right? He went out there, jabbing and hooking light and sticking it right out there, and Ran wouldn't do anything. All of a sudden, though, he fired that right and Petrolle slipped it and let his own go.

"It was really a hook with the right, and Ran went down like he had been cut down at the knees with a scythe. After the fight everybody said Petrolle was a lucky fighter. They said, 'My, how lucky that Petrolle is.'

"It wasn't luck. It was the work of an artist, and none of them knew it, none except Ran. After he was dressed, Petrolle went into Ran's dressing room and Ran was sitting there with his head down, and then he looked up.

"Ran said, 'Billy, I'm ashamed.' Petrolle said, 'Why, Eddie?' Ran said, 'I'm ashamed of Eddie Ran, Billy. I knew you were going to do that to me, but I couldn't help myself. You made it look so easy I just had to throw that right.'"[30]

---

[27] Igoe, "Left Worries Ran, Right Kayos Him," *New York Evening Journal*, January 23, 1932, sports section ("went back after his tormentor ..."). Wood, "Petrolle Stops Ran in Sixth," *New York Sun*, January 23, 1932, sports section.

[28] Wood, *op. cit.*

[29] Gallico, "Straight Right to the Chin Ends Stirring Battle," *New York Daily News*, January 23, 1932, sports section.

[30] Heinz, *op. cit.*

When Hurley told Heinz everybody thought Petrolle was lucky, he was going overboard to make a point almost 20 years after the fact to a writer who had never seen Billy fight. In actual fact, boxing experts who saw the Ran fight were lavish in praising the Fargo ringster as a fighting marvel.

The *Evening Journal*'s Hype Igoe wrote that a "ten-year stretch of hard service has made Billy Petrolle one of the most remarkable warriors in the history of the ring ... a tricky old general who knows fighting backwards." Igoe commented that as a welterweight Ran was "the best youngster of the lot" and it "was no disgrace to be beaten by a genius like Petrolle."[31]

The *World-Telegram*'s Harry Grayson was equally enthusiastic in his admiration of Petrolle's ring talent:

> "Broadway, the street hardest to sell, today doffed its hat to William Michael Petrolle. The old bloke in the blanket knocked Eddie Ran stiffer than Grover Whelan's wing collar in the sixth round at the Garden last night, and left for his Duluth home today generally regarded as the finest fighter for his inches in the business.
>
> "He had everything last night. He never stopped coming in, called every shot and put something on each one, paid strict attention to defense, and showed a superb spirit to win. He had to have everything to score over the younger and ambitious Ran. It is little wonder that old-timers today were comparing him with other greats of the smaller divisions, McGovern, Lavigne, Gans, Leonard and the rest.
>
> "Petrolle has been around longer than he cares to remember, and the boys are wondering what is going to become of the younger generation. His business seems to be baptizing youngsters with fire ... And they said the Fargo Express was rusted stock that could roll no longer."[32]

The show had played to a near-capacity crowd of 17,000 paid admissions. The gross gate was $43,557.79 and the net $39,246.79. On the afternoon of the bout, Petrolle weighed in at 140-1/4 pounds and Ran 145.

Following the bout, Petrolle's status as boxing's hottest attraction placed him in the unusual but enviable position of being a challenger pursued by

---

[31] Igoe, *op. cit.*.

[32] Grayson, "Petrolle Voted Best Boxer for Inches after Ran Kayo," *New York World-Telegram*, January 23, 1932, sports section. Grover Whelan (1886-1962) was for years a dapper and affable fixture around New York known for his service as a public official and organizer of various public events. His positions of service included: president of the 1918 Committee to Welcome Home the Troops; New York City police commissioner; head of the Mayor's Commission for Protocol (i. e., the official greeter for New York City, a position he held for 34 years); and president of the New York World's Fair Committee (1939-40).

"Polish Thunderbolt" Eddie Ran, of Warsaw, Poland.

Petrolle, as he appeared when training to box Ran in the Garden.

A cagey Fargo Express (right) bides his time against Eddie Ran.

FIRST ENCOUNTER WITH A BOY BANDIT 601

Referee Patsy Haley yells into Ran's ear while Petrolle relaxes in a corner after one of four knockdowns Eddie suffered during the fight.

Haley tolls the fatal "ten" over a dazed Ran in the sixth round.

the titleholders in two divisions. Upon conferring with the managers of both champions, Johnston approached Hurley with the option of a bout for Petrolle with the monarch of his choice, either Tony Canzoneri, the lightweight champ, or Lou Brouillard, the new welterweight titleholder.

After talking it over with Petrolle, Hurley said Billy preferred to fight Brouillard in March at the Garden and then Canzoneri in the summer at a New York ballpark. Jack's reasoning was that Petrolle, who had done all his recent fighting above 135 pounds, could make the lightweight limit more easily during the hot summer months. In addition, he felt Tony was a better drawing card in New York than Lou, and that a Petrolle-Canzoneri outdoor show would draw more fans than the Garden's indoor seating could handle.

Unfortunately, plans for a welterweight title bout were dashed on January 28, 1932, when Brouillard, who had won the title from Young Jack Thompson four months earlier, lost it by decision to Jackie Fields in Chicago. Johnston's efforts to replace the Petrolle-Brouillard match with a Petrolle-Fields fight were likewise stymied when Fields' manager, Jack Kearns, who at first seemed interested in the fight, demanded an under-the-table ownership interest in Petrolle in exchange for giving Billy a title shot.

When prospects for the championship match fell through, Johnston cast his eyes toward Christopher (Battling) Battalino, of Hartford, Connecticut, as an opponent for Petrolle. Battalino, who reigned as featherweight champion for two years, had been forced to abdicate his title in Cincinnati on January 27 just prior to a scheduled title defense against Freddie Miller because he could no longer make the division's 126-pound limit.[33]

Battalino, in fact, was having trouble making even the lightweight (135-pound) limit and was jumping past that division into the welterweight (147-pound) class. As a result, Johnston signed the "Hartford Tarzan" to fight Petrolle in a ten-round bout on March 11, 1932. Three days before the date, Billy hurt his neck in his final training session and the bout was canceled.

Johnston signed Petrolle's recently vanquished foe, Eddie Ran, as a substitute to meet Battalino. Jimmy was taking a chance because a Ran victory would have ruined prospects for the Battalino-Petrolle bout. Fortunately, Bat, an underdog against Ran, won the decision even though he weighed just 138 pounds as compared to Ran's 146. A greatly relieved Johnston then re-scheduled the Petrolle-Battalino fight for March 24.

As it turned out, Battalino's victory made his bout with Billy more desirable than ever and gave matchmaker Johnston an excuse to extend the contest's distance to 12 rounds and raise admission prices to pre-depression levels. For the first time in almost a year, tickets for a non-title affair at the Garden were priced from $2 to $8 instead of $1 to $5.74. The effect of this

---

[33] The unsavory circumstances surrounding Reilly's attempt to fix the outcome of the Cincinnati fight so the featherweight title would pass from Battalino to Miller were discussed in Chapter 14 of this volume.

increase was to raise the potential scale of the house from a capacity of approximately $54,000 to $75,000.[34]

Battalino initially was regarded as a "cheese champion" after winning the featherweight title in September 1929 from the aging French titleholder, Andre Routis. Since then, however, five straight defenses against the division's leading contenders had won the fans over and proven to them that Bat was one of boxing's worthiest champions in recent years.[35]

As in the case of Petrolle, acceptance of Battalino in New York had been a slow process. An underdog in each of his four Empire State fights, Bat beat the odds every time, decisioning Kid Chocolate and Fidel LaBarba in title defenses and kayoing ex-lightweight champ Al Singer in an overweight bout just prior to his win over Ran. Although he did not possess Petrolle's punch, Battalino was an exciting fighter admired for his swarming style, iron jaw, and fighting heart.

Leading up to the fight, reporters made much of the strategic duel they expected to see between the managers of the two fighters. Battalino's manager, Pete Reilly, the old "Silver Fox," had mapped out the tactics that had led Bat to victory in each of his prior New York bouts. Although Reilly was barred from working with Battalino in New York, he nevertheless continued to serve behind the scenes as Bat's main "advisor."[36]

Following Reilly's orders against hard-punching but china-chinned Al Singer, Battalino simply walked in, absorbed the best that Al had to offer, and overpowered his man. Against the more elusive Chocolate and LaBarba, Bat adopted a rushing, bob and weave style to get inside and corner his lighter foes. Against the heavier and harder punching Ran, Reilly taught Bat a cautiously aggressive, crouching style where he moved forward with gloves and arms positioned to fully protect his face and body.

Hurley told reporters Petrolle was ready for whatever type of attack the Hartford Tarzan chose: "Justo Suarez was a dead ringer for Battalino, and

---

[34] Frayne, "Scalpers Reap Profit on Bat-Billy Battle," *New York American*, March 23, 1932, sports section. Frayne, "18,000 Expected at Battle Between Featherweight Champ and New York's Favorite," *New York American*, December 11, 1931, p. 23. Frayne, "Bat Assails Referee for Stopping Bout," *New York American*, March 26, 1932, sports section. Albertanti, Francis, "Loser's Nose Broken, Gate $62,000," *New York Evening Graphic*, March 25, 1932, sports section. Ticket prices for the show as originally scheduled on March 11 were at the $1 to $5.74 scale. Interestingly enough, demand to see the fight was so strong that almost all the higher priced tickets sold out with scalpers even realizing as much as $15 for ringside seats. Most of the unsold tickets were for the lower priced $2 and $3 seats.

[35] In addition to the defenses at New York against Kid Chocolate and Fidel LaBarba referred to in the next paragraph of the text, Battalino also successfully defended his title against Frank Mastro at Chicago, Freddie Miller at Cincinnati, and Ignacio Fernandez at Hartford.

[36] Igoe, "Experience, Punch Makes Billy Favorite," *New York Evening Journal*, March 24, 1932, sports section. The New York commission barred Reilly from managing in New York due to the improprieties arising from the Battalino-Miller fight at Cincinnati on January 27,1932 (See note 33). Even so, Pete continued to work behind the scenes and take his cut from Battalino's purse.

stronger, too. Billy stiffened him. King Tut weaved like Battalino, and the old man stretched him. If Battalino will meet Petrolle halfway it will be a good fight. If he comes out with his arms wrapped around his head, Bill will have to use up more time. It's a tough fight, but anyone who can take McLarnin's punches shouldn't have to worry about Battalino."[37]

Another topic discussed prior to the bout was "Why did Petrolle seem to be fighting so much better in 1932 than prior to his 'retirement' in 1929?"

Wilbur Wood observed that everyone referred to Petrolle as "an old man," even though he was just 27 years old, "because in his early years he seldom had a soft fight, taking considerable punishment every time he went to the post." In those days, Billy had been "purely a slugger, willing to take two or three punches to get in one." Wood speculated Petrolle must have done some thinking during his layoff and adopted a different system of fighting so that he would not "burn out [so] rapidly."

Wood noticed that, starting with the fight against King Tut at New York in February 1931, and continuing through the Suarez, Townsend, and Ran fights, Petrolle had been able to "ripple his opponent quickly, and finish him at leisure." Wood concluded that in such cases, Petrolle had adopted "a system of watchful waiting" where "he was content to keep" [his opponent] under control until he found the proper opening for a final smash."

By not rushing in wildly to finish off his man, Petrolle was able to conserve his energy and avoid receiving needless punishment and injuries to his hands. The question to be answered in the Battalino fight was, in Wood's view, whether or not Billy would "find it much more difficult to keep him under control than was the case in other fights."[38]

Petrolle told Joe Williams of the *World-Telegram* that it was caution in his comeback fight with Tony Canzoneri which caused him to slow down and change his style of fighting: "This (waving his fist to indicate his punch) really did not come to me until I met Canzoneri in Chicago a year ago last September. I had brought myself back gradually in the sticks after my layoff, but wasn't sure how I would go against a speedy kid like Tony.

"When my legs were good I waded in, hitting so rapidly that I wasted half my punches and had little leverage on most of those that I landed. Uncertain about my ability to step along with Canzoneri for ten rounds, I decided to gait myself carefully for five or six rounds, figuring that if I got that far I could give him both barrels in the stretch.

"Therefore I shuffled in, instead of springing forward as I did in the days when I had more bounce than brains. I, perhaps, was more surprised than Canzoneri the first time I socked him squarely. 'Where has this been all my life?' I asked, when Tony reeled into the ropes. I was gripping the canvas

---

[37] Frayne, "Scalpers Reap Profit on Bat-Billy Battle," *New York American*, March 23, 1932, sports section.
[38] Wood, "Petrolle Is a Fast Starter," *New York Sun*, March 23, 1932, sports section.

with my toes – a change, and in doing so I perfected timing – the secret of hitting."[39]

One person who planned to attend the Petrolle-Battalino fight was former heavyweight champ James J. Corbett, considered by many as the father of modern boxing. Three days before the bout, Gentleman Jim, then 66 years old and battling the liver cancer and heart disease which would take his life within the year, made a surprise visit to the Garden ticket office to make sure he got a good seat. Corbett had just been discharged from the hospital and reportedly was still too weak to make it up the stairs to his apartment.

Doctors advised against his attending the show, but Gentleman Jim told boxing writers he would not miss it for anything in the world: "I couldn't bear to think about the old Fargo Express coming in without being at the station. Petrolle is my favorite fighter today. He knows what it's all about. He wastes no motion ... This Battalino boy is plenty tough, and I'm not making any predictions, but I do know it is going to be some fight, one like we used to have in the old days. Let 'em try to keep me away."[40]

On the afternoon of the fight, Petrolle weighed 139 pounds to Battalino's 135. At the weigh-in, Bat was nervous and became visibly upset when he learned the boxing commission had assigned him purple instead of his customary black boxing trunks. With the announcement, Hy Malley, Bat's manager of record, "turned white" and "rushed across the room to Petrolle and anxiously inquired if Billy would mind swapping trunks."

Petrolle appeared genuinely amused, and his reply was a good-natured, "What's the difference? Go ahead, take the black ones."[41]

Although the Fargo Express rated a slight 7-to-5 favorite to defeat Battalino, both fighters were regarded equally courageous and as "game as a pebble." Each had proven in the past to be a superb "money fighter" who was "at his best in the pinches." Petrolle was viewed to have an edge in punching power, experience, and ring generalship. Battalino's assets were "youthful vim and vigor" and "boundless stamina" which would help him go the full 12 rounds at top speed and possibly wear down his adversary.[42]

For once, a bout touted as a battle between two titans surpassed expectations of even the most optimistic boxing fans. The next morning, the *Daily News*' Francis Wallace was one of many writers who stretched the limits of boxing's rich lexicon in search of words to describe the fray:

> "No more tales of the savage battles of olden days; no more stories of the prowess of Battling Nelson and Joe Gans; no more talk of the

---

[39] Williams, "Joe Williams," *New York World-Telegram*, December 31, 1931, sports section.

[40] "Jim Corbett Fighting Desperately for Life," *New York American*, March 18, 1932, sports section. Wood, "Contrasting Billy and Bat," *New York Sun*, March 22, 1932, sports section.

[41] "Petrolle Enters Ring 7 to 5 over Battalino," *New York American*, March 25, 1932, sports section.

[42] Wood, "Fargo Express Made Favorite," *New York Sun*, March 24, 1932, sports section.

Battling Battalino's manager, Pete Reilly, "the Silver Fox."

Petrolle in a makeshift headdress and his famous Navajo blanket.

Publicity shot of Bat "batting" at Billy's image on the heavy bag.

Square-off at the physical exam a few days before the fight.

days when fighters were men; no more of any of that for the 18,000 persons who last night saw Madison Square Garden receive its real baptism of blood – the blood of Battalino.

"It was one of the most sensationally fought battles of modern times; by all odds the best the new Garden has ever seen. It was opened on a note of savagery and for eleven rounds it continued on that plane.

"It ended on a note of bitter tragedy – for, with only one minute and 29 seconds to go in the 12th and last round, Bat Battalino was counted out on his feet, and Billy Petrolle was declared the winner by a technical knockout.

"For Petrolle it was a glorious and dramatic climax to the campaign which he began two years ago after having gone into retirement, apparently washed up. For Battalino it marked the first check in a meteoric career – and perhaps a serious check. Men do not often come back to their full power after taking such a relentless beating as Petrolle administered last night."[43]

To Wilbur Wood, it was "a fight unparalleled in recent years for savage intensity." The *Evening Graphic*'s Francis Albertanti called it "one of the bloodiest battles waged between little men in 22 years ... a duplicate of the 20-round Tommy Murphy-Abe Attell massacre, which Californians to this day agree was the last word in pugilistic warfare." Ed Frayne of the *American* termed it "a thriller that has seldom been matched."[44]

Paul Gallico in the *Daily News* likened it to a "small war" with Bat advancing in the face of "short, jarring punches" which gradually wore him down "the way a barrage wears down the nerve and resistance of the men who are subjected to it." The 12th round was Bat's "zero hour" when it became clear that "the 11-round pounding by Petrolle had practically gutted Battalino ... When the final showdown came, Battalino crumbled quickly and thoroughly – the way the Germans crumbled at the end of the war."[45]

The *Post*'s Jack Kofoed called the bout "the most desperately sensational and bloody battle ever seen within [the] historic walls" of the Garden. W. J. Macbeth of the *Herald Tribune* wrote it was "one of the most thrilling so-called lightweight battles of a generation ... reviv[ing] memories of the historic duels between Joe Gans and Frank Erne, Kid Lavigne and Joe

---

[43] Wallace, Francis, "Sensational Battle Thrills 18,000 Fans," *New York Daily News*, March 25, 1932, p. 54.
[44] Wood, "Uppercuts Ruin Battalino," *New York Sun*, March 25, 1932, sports section. Albertanti, "Loser's Nose Broken, Gate $62,000," *New York Evening Graphic*, March 25, 1932, p. 32. Frayne, "Petrolle Stops Battalino in 12th," *New York American*, March 25, 1932, p. 17.
[45] Gallico, "All the Elements of War," *New York Daily News*, March 26, 1932, sports section.

Walcott, Benny Leonard and Lew Tendler." James Dawson of the *Times* labeled it a "sizzling battle ... that had few if any parallels for slugging."[46]

From the clang of the first gong in the opening round until the last volley of punches which finally sent him lurching helplessly to the ropes in the 12th round, Battalino never took a backward step. Fighting from a crouch and facing Petrolle squarely most of the time, "the Battler" moved relentlessly forward with both gloves raised to protect his face.

Battalino crowded Petrolle on the theory the best way to beat him was to keep him off balance and moving backward to rob his blows of their leverage. Rather than wear himself out by challenging the younger man's forward march, Billy's response was to bend like a reed in the wind. He met Battalino's march with a steady "advance to the rear," all the while raking face and body with short, precise right uppercuts and left hooks calculated to wear Bat down in stages rather than finish him off with one punch.[47]

Battalino's offense as he rushed ahead, consisted mostly of side-arm swings to Petrolle's ears and jaw. Though many of these landed, Billy's shorter and more accurate blows usually beat Bat to the punch and prevented him from establishing a rhythm for landing damaging combinations. Petrolle was also often able to duck or roll with these swings to take some of the sting out of their impact.

Petrolle drew first blood in the third round when he "crashed over a right that sent blood spurting from a deep rip" on Bat's nose. Later in the round, Hartford's Tarzan partially evened the score by opening a cut over Billy's left eye. For the rest of the night, the crimson flowed freely at ringside, as first row patrons used their notepads and the canvas apron of the ring to shield shirts and ties from the splatter.[48]

As the fight wore on, each succeeding round resembled the preceding frame with both battlers throwing countless punches, but with Petrolle gradually taking control with harder and cleaner blows. By the end of the 11th round, Billy was in full command, beating Battalino to the punch at every turn. Still, Bat kept coming forward, "always dangerous and always willing ... It was an almost unbelievable continuation of swinging, with never a dull second, with never a moment that might not contain disaster."[49]

When Bat came out for the 12th and final round, he knew he was behind in scoring and had to do or die. In a last valiant effort to turn the tide, he abandoned his crouching shell defense and left his corner intent on trying to

---

[46] Kofoed, Jack, "Hartford Boxer Hammered Down by Savage Attack," *New York Evening Post*, March 25, 1932, p. 12. Macbeth, W. J., "Referee Stops Fight to Save Groggy Loser," *New York Herald Tribune*, March 25, 1932, sports section. Dawson, "Referee Ends Bout in Final Chapter," *New York Times*, March 25, 1932, p. 24.

[47] Pegler, Westbrook, "Speaking Out on Sports," *New York Evening Post*, March 25, 1932, p. 12.

[48] Wood, *op. cit.*

[49] Wallace, *op. cit.*.

Battalino (right) sways neatly to avoid a left in the fifth round.

Petrolle hooks to the side of Bat's head.

Petrolle digs a left hook deep into Battalino's rib cage.

Referee Gunboat Smith stops the bout with 1:29 left in the 12th round.

knock Petrolle out. Bat immediately rushed Billy to the ropes and landed a solid left and right to the head, blows representing, as it turned out, the former featherweight titleholder's last meaningful offensive effort.

Petrolle, "craftiest of all ringmen, caught the change even before the crowd. He had been punching his best before, but now he redoubled his efforts. Right hands, left hands, uppercuts, [and] hooks rattled against Battalino's face and body," causing him to break ground "for the first time during the night." A terrific right sent Bat reeling into the ropes, his hands dangling helplessly at his sides, as referee Gunboat Smith stepped between the warriors to stop the fight and save Battalino from permanent injury.[50]

As ring announcer Joe Humphreys raised Petrolle's weary right arm to signal his victory, Billy was greeted by "the greatest storm of applause that ever rewarded a fighting man."[51]

In a dressing room interview, Petrolle praised Battalino for his courageous performance: "I have never met a gamer foe. And if I fight another 10 years I will never meet a gamer boy. I blasted him with everything I had, but I never could make him back up."[52]

After the battle Frank G. Menke interviewed James J. Corbett at ringside for an INS wire service article. In a glowing tribute, the past heavyweight champion analyzed the fight and praised the efforts of both fighters:

> "Battalino fights from out of a shell. This method was successful when he went up against other fellows who tried to beat him with long swings. But it was a failure against the smart Petrolle. Before the first round was half over, Petrolle had learned all he needed to learn about Battalino, and from that time on he made but little use of long punches.
>
> "Petrolle resorted almost exclusively to short jolts and uppercuts. He rarely missed, whereas a less intelligent fighter would have been throwing leather over Bat's head and leaving himself wide open for a counter-punch from Bat.
>
> "I have rarely seen a more masterful exhibition than Petrolle displayed. He was cool and calm through every round. He knew every second of the way what should be done, and he did it. Unable to nail Bat flush on the chin with his wicked left or his savage right, he battered Battalino's face to wreckage, then he shifted to the body, came back to the face again – waiting and waiting for the golden opportunity to finish his rival.
>
> "Bat came out in the final round hoping that a cyclonic rush might enable him to break down Petrolle's resistance and that he might

---

[50] Frayne, *op. cit.*.
[51] *Ibid.*
[52] Wood, *op cit.*

A common scene at Madison Square Garden in the early 1930s. Joe Humphreys raises Petrolle's hand as ring seconds tend to his battered foe, in this case Battling Battalino.

Petrolle's phenomenal popularity peaked in 1931-'32 and led to two cover spots in *The Ring*.

slip across a knockout punch. He came out unprotected and that was doom for him. This was the chance that Petrolle wanted. He reached Bat's jaw with a left, then a right and another left.

"... I never saw a greater display of raw courage, nor more ability to take punishment than Battalino's ... My hat is off to both of them, because they both fought with every ounce of power within them and no men who are warriors of the prize ring can do more."[53]

The next day paid attendance was reported as 14,679. Due to the increase in ticket prices, gross receipts amounted to a season high $65,960 and a $56,104 net. For his share, Billy received $15,429 and Bat $14,026.[54]

****

Over the years, boxing writers have traced the start of Battalino's ring decline to the terrific beating he took from Petrolle in New York. Certainly, the evidence is there to support the proposition. The knockout was the only kayo Battalino would ever suffer during his entire career. In the years immediately following, Bat boxed on the fringes of the big-time with only modest success. Thereafter, he finished out his career as an ordinary club fighter when he returned home to Hartford for most of his final fights.

The Battalino fight and other Petrolle bouts point to a broader conclusion that Billy was the most devastating puncher of his era in the lighter divisions. As far back as 1926, Pat Purcell wrote in the *Fargo Forum* that Billy's wicked punching was feared throughout the featherweight ranks. Purcell argued that because he was a body puncher, Billy had trouble winning decisions he deserved. In Pat's opinion, the blows Petrolle "delivered to the body were just as effective as blows landed on the head but they are not quite as spectacular."[55]

One of the toughest fighters Petrolle fought during his early years was Joe Jawson of Milwaukee, Wisconsin, a man whom Billy ended up fighting three times. At the time of their first bout in October 1925, Jawson already had engaged in no less than 76 fights against the best lightweights in the world and had never been knocked out. Two months after his first fight with Petrolle, Joe was an interested spectator along with Purcell when Billy fought Jawson's fellow townsman Joe Azzarella in Milwaukee.

Near the end of the sixth round, Petrolle dropped Azzarella with a tremendous right hook under the heart. Jawson, who was sitting near Purcell at the time, was overheard to say that Azzarella would not last the round: "I know that he is through. I fought a draw with that fellow

---

[53] Menke, "Corbett Pays Grand Tribute to Duluth Boy" (International News Service), *Duluth Herald*, March 25, 1932, sports section.
[54] Frayne, "Bat Assails Referee for Stopping Battle," *New York American*, March 26, 1932, sports section.
[55] Purcell, J. A., "The Sportville Spotlight," *Fargo Forum*, January 16, 1926, sports section.

(Petrolle) and since that time I have found it almost impossible to get in shape. I have met some of the hardest punchers in the game but never did I face such a terrific body puncher as that fellow Petrolle."

Petrolle's last fight with Jawson took place February 25, 1927. Billy scored four knockdowns in the seventh round, and for the first time in his career Joe was counted out. Ironically, the fight hastened the end of Jawson's career. After losing his next two bouts, he retired from the ring in February 1928.[56]

An analysis of the records of other prominent boxers Petrolle fought after kayoing Jawson bears out Joe's observation that a dose of Billy's body punching was sufficient to interrupt or even ruin a previously successful boxing career. Such a review also supports the claims of Hurley, Purcell, and other boxing experts of the era that if Petrolle's body punching had been valued by boxing judges in accordance with the degree of punishment administered, Billy might have won many of the close decisions he lost.

Petrolle's first two fights at New York against Sammy Vogel and Sid Terris in 1926 are cases in point. According to ringside reports, Billy dealt heavy body punishment to both New Yorkers, but lost close decisions to each because of their flashy boxing. While Vogel and Terris had averaged almost one fight a month before their fights with Billy, afterward they both found it necessary to take long layoffs. For Terris, it was a full seven months before his next bout. Vogel's return to fistic endeavor was only slightly more energetic. In the next eight months, Sammy had just one fight, a losing effort four months later to Tommy (Kid) Murphy, a future Petrolle knockout victim. After Murphy, Vogel took another four months off before returning to his normal fighting regimen.

Johnny Adams' big bid for fame and fortune came against Petrolle at Chicago in July 1926. In 68 bouts fought during the 37 months between June 1923 and July 1926, Adams had only twice been inactive during a calendar month. When Billy kayoed him for just the second time in a career of 99 professional fights, Johnny had to discontinue fighting a full three months. Although he had previously defeated such men as Mushy Callahan and Ace Hudkins, Adams afterward was never able to beat a top contender.

The decision awarded Jackie Berg in his third bout with Petrolle at New York in October 1930 rankled Billy more than any other. Petrolle never could understand why the officials awarded the fight to Berg when Billy hit Jackie harder and more often than he had hit any other fighter. Apart from never winning a world title, the biggest regret of Petrolle's career was that Berg's managers never would agree to another match.[57]

---

[56] Jawson had been stopped by Dick (Honeyboy) Finnegan on a sixth-round technical knockout, but in that instance the referee stopped the fight without a count either because Jawson was cut or else to protect Jawson from further punishment.

[57] Frayne, *op. cit.*

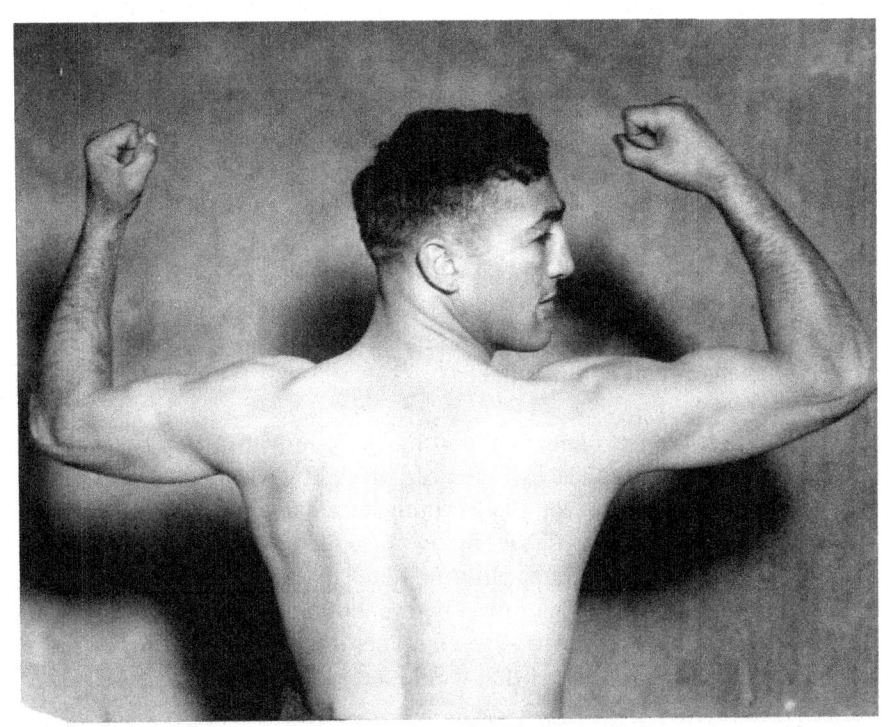

The upper half – front and back – of Billy Petrolle's power package.

Trainer Ray Arcel worked in Berg's corner for the fight. Years later, Arcel told Berg's biographer that during the course of the fight, "Petrolle hit Jackie with a left hook to the belly and I swear to you I saw that left hook go right through Jackie's body and come out the back! That's how hard the punch was. When Petrolle hit him I thought sure that was the end of it – but he fought back with such fury that he actually made Petrolle back up ..."[58]

Berg, one of the toughest fighters ever to grace the squared circle, refused to admit after the fight that he had been hurt at all. However, in the days that followed, Petrolle's body punches caught up to Jackie, and he was forced to take extra rest before he could fight again. Prior to their third bout, Berg had fought 25 times in 17 months without a loss, for an average of almost 1-1/2 fights a month. Jackie's slow recovery after the fight disrupted this rigorous schedule and required him to lay off a full 3-1/2 months.

It is likely that the punishment delivered by Petrolle to Berg had an even longer-lasting effect on Berg's fighting efficiency. The *Evening Journal*'s Hype Igoe was one writer who reconsidered his prior opinion that Berg had been entitled to the decision over Billy at New York. Writing shortly after Tony Canzoneri kayoed Jackie in the third round at Chicago in April 1931, Igoe indicated he agreed with those who said the beating Berg had received seven months earlier from Petrolle had softened Jackie up for Tony:

> "Billy did give Jackie quite a whaling that night, though Jackie got the duke. I said at the time that though I knew that Berg had received a dreadful body drubbing, through some queer optical illusion, I, like the referee, thought that Berg deserved the decision.
>
> "Now I'm convinced that it was all wrong; that I was seeing things, and things in this instance happened to be Berg ... Berg never will be able to shake off the body thumping Petrolle gave him that night. At least, I've seen few of them who have been able to come back and be the same."[59]

The final pieces of evidence supporting Petrolle's case as a devastating puncher are his fights against Justo Suarez, Billy Townsend, and Eddie Ran.

As we have seen, each of these youngsters came up against Petrolle boasting an impressive record, seemingly poised to earn whatever riches the ring had to offer. In each fight, Billy battered his foe severely for several rounds, scoring multiple knockdowns before landing a kayo wallop. In each case, the destruction wrought was so complete it marked the beginning of a downward trajectory in a career that would never regain its former stature.

---

[58] Harding, John with Jack Berg, "Jack Kid Berg – The Whitechapel Windmill," Robson Books, London, England, 1987), p. 134-5.
[59] Igoe, "Petrolle Bout Ruination of Jackie," *New York Evening Journal*, May 8, 1931, sports section.

The most precipitous of these nosedives was the downturn in fortune experienced by Justo Suarez of the Argentine. When he faced Billy in June 1931, Suarez was unbeaten in 72 amateur and pro bouts and stood out as the world's number two lightweight contender. In addition, matchmaker Tom McArdle was grooming him for a title bout against Tony Canzoneri in what was expected to be the marquee match of Madison Square Garden's fall season. Entering the ring against Billy, Justo rated a 13-to-5 favorite.

As it turned out, the brutal body beating Suarez endured prior to his ninth-round kayo ended not only his championship hopes, but also his career. Afterward, Justo engaged in one ten-round draw with journeyman Emil Rossi at New York in August 1931, lost two of three uninspired bouts in Argentina over the next three years, and retired from the ring. He died in poverty at home, age 29, in 1938.

****

Although Hurley and Johnston were both eager to strike while the iron was hot and put the Fargo Express to work as soon as possible after Petrolle's sensational effort against Battalino, an urgent personal matter prevented them from doing so.

In late February, Hurley had spent a week at the Mayo Clinic in Rochester, Minnesota, undergoing tests and examinations for sinus trouble and severe pain from his long-suffering ulcerated stomach. As Jack expected, the doctors told him both conditions were serious, and that treatment sooner would be better than later.

Hurley was forced to delay the procedures when the Battalino fight was set back because of Petrolle's neck injury. Now, his condition had reached the stage where he risked life-threatening consequences if they were put off any longer.

The day after the first Petrolle-Battalino fight, Hurley boarded a train bound for Minnesota. Jack was due to check in at the Mayo Clinic in Rochester on March 28. He would be there a total of 40 days and 40 nights.

CHAPTER 26

AN ATTRACTIVE, DARK-HAIRED WOMAN

Rochester, MN – The Mayo Clinic. *Did I tell you about my operation? No? Well, you haven't heard the half of it. I reported to the clinic at 7 a. m., which is the middle of the night for me. Under orders, I came with an empty stomach. But on my arrival they handed me eight small cookies and two glasses of water, which I was told to consume as quickly as possible.*

After sitting around for an hour, I was called into a very small room. In this room, two nurses forced me to swallow three feet of hose. Then they walked me down the hall into another small room, where a nurse attached a stomach pump to the hose and took back the cookies and water they had given me an hour earlier. The old meanies!

I was as bad off now as when I arrived. But, empty stomach and all, I was examined and X-rayed for every possible ailment. Finally, at 2 p.m. they X-rayed my stomach. And while doing so some heavyweight doctor made me drink a quart of white stuff that tasted like chalk. I managed to escape out of there with my life, and on the outside a nurse informed me I could now eat whatever I wanted. Can you beat that? How could I eat anything when I was so full of that chalk stuff it was running out my ears?

At any rate they found plenty wrong with me, and the first operation they performed was on my nose. Dr. Hempstead, who did the job, said that never in all his experience had he removed so much stuff from one person's nose. I was just about to start accepting congratulations for establishing a record, when some smart-aleck orderly said something about not counting the record because I had a bigger nose than anyone else who had gone through the same operation, and that it wasn't fair.

Well, that orderly can go smoke a herring. I did establish a record, and I think it will stand for some time to come. Of course, if Jimmy Durante or Phil Terk decide to enter into competition, then I am licked. I'm a game guy, but I can't beat a cinch.[1]

– Jack Hurley

****

If you were an attentive reader of either the nation's leading sports magazines or the sports section of almost any daily newspaper in the United States during the 1960s and early '70s, you knew all about Jack Hurley and his huge inventory of physical ailments.

Hurley was living at the Olympic Hotel in Seattle. In those years, friends and journalists from all over would visit him either at the hotel or else on the road when he was pitching a fighter or acting as a front man for the

---

[1] Hurley, Jack, "Ring Rations," *Fargo Forum*, April 10, 1932, sports section.

Harlem Globetrotters. Inevitably, the first question they asked was how he was feeling. In most cases, his reply would range all the way from an uncommonly optimistic, "Not so good," to the more usual, "Terrible."

If the visitor were courteous, curious, or foolish enough to inquire further, the then-thin, pale, wizened-faced Hurley would squint through his wire-rimmed, bottle-bottom lenses and launch into a detailed description of his ailments with all the aplomb of an old vaudevillian. "I brought Harry Matthews out here from Chicago for a fight, and we drew pretty well," Jack would say, as a way of introducing his topic. "I thought maybe I'd stay here for six months, a year. But I've been stuck here ever since.

"I've got two of the worst things a person living in Seattle can have – rheumatism and sinus trouble. I had 22 sinus operations. Now, they've decided that isn't the right thing to do. That's how they found out, by operating on me. Two-thirds of my stomach has been cut out, my appendix and prostate gland, too. Let a new disease spring up overnight and I'll have it in 24 hours.

"Now, I've got cataracts, so I decided to go for the operation. So what happens? When it's over, I ask the doctor, 'Now, Doc, I understand after 90 percent of these operations, the patient's sight can be corrected with glasses to 20-20. Is that right?' So he says, 'Well, that's about right.' So I say, 'But Doc, I'm not gonna have 20-20, am I?' He says, 'Well, no.' So I say, 'All right. How good is my sight gonna be?' He says, 'Well, pretty good.'

"Now, wouldn't you know that? Ninety percent are successful, but I have to be in the other ten percent. Why? Now tell me something else. What does he mean by 'pretty good'? Just how good is 'pretty good'? I can't see a damn thing. Oh hell, I can see some, but at the hotel I've already fallen down the stairs twice, and now I've gotta have the other eye done. How about that 'pretty good' though?"[2]

Despite a slick veneer of folksy showmanship and an obvious desire to entertain his listeners at the expense of the character he had created for himself, Hurley's descriptions of aches, pains, and other insults to his well being were all real enough.

While medical treatment by and large provided relief for his appendix, prostate, and cataract conditions, Jack's other maladies were more resistant to cure. Since before 1930, severe rheumatism, stomach ulcers, and chronic sinus problems had ravaged his body without respite. Together, these ailments gave rise to chronic insomnia, a condition which plagued Jack the rest of his life and caused him to adopt a regimen that Seattle writer John

---

[2] Owen, John, "First Sports Citizen Is Worst Fan," *Seattle Post Intelligencer*, November 6, 1961, sports section. Washington Post Service, "Fight Manager Jack Hurley Quitting after Only 50 Years," *Fargo Forum*, March 26, 1972, sports section. Watson, Emmett, "Look Out Cassius Clay," *Seattle Magazine,* October 1966, p. 42. Heinz, W. C., "The Last Campaign of Boxing's Last Angry Man," *Saturday Evening Post*, February 11, 1967, p. 38. The quotation in the text is a blending of quotes from all the above sources.

Owen later called "the most regularly irregular life imaginable."

For sleeplessness, Hurley adopted a pattern of not going to bed until 4 a.m. Since he had only a part of his stomach left, his body was unable to store nourishment. As a result, Jack needed to eat six meals a day. Typically, he would take brunch at 10 a.m., followed by meals at noon, mid-afternoon, evening and midnight, before completing the cycle with a bedtime snack.[3]

The rheumatism wracking Hurley's limbs was a result of circulatory problems dating from his World War I army service in France when his feet froze in the trenches. His stomach ulcers and sinus trouble sprang up a few years later after Jack started managing and promoting fighters.

Hurley told the *Omaha World-Herald*'s Robert Houston he first experienced stomach trouble in late 1925 while preparing for the Pinkey Mitchell-Russie LeRoy fight at Fargo when Mitchell canceled his appearance at the last minute. At the time, Jack had sold more tickets for a fight than ever before. Up until then, he had been barely making ends meet, and refunding all that money caused his stomach to do a "flip-flop."[4]

The first account of Hurley receiving treatment for ulcers was in October 1928 when the *Fargo Forum* reported he was "undergoing observation at a local hospital for stomach trouble." Interestingly enough, this confinement came less than two weeks after Billy Petrolle's fourth fight with King Tut when Petrolle suffered his worst beating up until then. Shortly thereafter, Billy underwent surgery for an abscessed kidney. Apparently, the doctor felt that Jack's condition did not warrant surgery at the time.[5]

Hurley often said, "When you manage a fighter, you end up with cancer, heart trouble or ulcers. I took the least." He elaborated for the *World-Herald*'s Houston: "It's a tough business to succeed in. You live in hope and die in despair. There are a lot of ingrates among boxers, about nine-tenths of them.

"When a fellow won't listen to reason you get kind of fed up. They think they've discovered gold and it will last forever. And they pick up a lot of advisers, jerks who can't run their own businesses. You teach a fellow how to fight, you get him in shape for a bout. But while he's doing roadwork he might step on a stone or in a hole. In the ring he might not follow instructions. You worry all the time, and it takes a lot out of you.

"... I work 24 hours a day for [my fighter]. If I had devoted 35 years to another business, I'd have done as well. I'm a hustler."[6]

At first hearing, Hurley's assertion he underwent 22 sinus operations

---

[3] Owen, *op. cit.*

[4] Houston, Robert, "Hurley: One of Boxing's Great Figures," *Omaha World-Herald*, January 13, 1952, p. 10-G.

[5] Campbell, Cubby, "The Sport Spigot," *Duluth News Tribune*, October 30, 1928, sports section.

[6] Crittenden, John, "Even at the End, Hurley Had a Plan," *Miami News*, December 14, 1972, sports section ("... cancer, heart trouble or ulcers"). Houston, *op. cit.*

might seem like a preposterous claim advanced merely for comic effect. A closer look, however, dispels the notion he was joking. Repetitive surgeries in the era of Jack's youth were often the only relief available for patients with chronic sinusitis. Even with today's advances, multiple surgeries are on occasion the only effective treatment for some sinus sufferers.[8]

The first account of a Hurley sinus surgery appeared on October 5, 1927, when the *Fargo Forum* reported Jack was "going into a hospital today for a nose operation." Two years later on October 11, the *Duluth Herald* reported he was "in Fargo convalescing following an operation on his nose." Two years after that, another story, this time in the *St. Paul Daily News*, reported had been in the hospital for his sinuses on October 16, 1931.[9]

After Petrolle retired, and Hurley left Duluth to live in Chicago, references to the personal details in Jack's life, including his visits to the hospital, rarely made it into the news. As a result, information about his post-1935 surgeries is only sporadic.

However, with few advances occurring in treatment for chronic sinusitis until the development of combination antibiotic therapies late in Hurley's life, there is no reason to believe his surgeries would not have continued at about the same rate as in Fargo and Duluth. Consequently, Jack's claim of 22 sinus operations during the period between the mid-1920s to the late 1960s seems right on the mark.

On March 28, 1932, Hurley checked into the famous Mayo Clinic at Rochester, Minnesota for a thorough examination of his sinus and stomach ailments. Apparently, the treatment helped because the clinic remained Jack's facility of choice for most of his adult life. Hurley told columnist Emmett Watson in 1967 he had been a patient at the clinic for extended periods on six occasions. As a general rule, he would have a complete check-up, and often would undergo several procedures during each stay.[10]

Typically, Hurley took a room at the Kahler Grand Hotel across the street from the clinic where he continued to conduct business by letter and phone when not actually hospitalized. During his time there in 1932, he continued to write his weekly newspaper column and even picked up an additional outlet by convincing the *Rochester Post-Bulletin* to run the series.[11]

Hurley became acquainted well enough with the Rochester editor to be

---

[8] Lane, Andrew, "Weakened Immune System in Chronic Sinusitis Reveals New Treatment Targets," Johns Hopkins Medical Institutions Press Release, September 15, 2006.

[9] Purcell, J. A., "Champion's Crown Not to Be Involved," *Fargo Forum*, October 5, 1927, sports section. "Hannigan Will Tackle St. Paul Fighter Here," *Duluth Herald*, October 11, 1927, sports section. "State Ring Body Bans Foul Rule," *St. Paul Daily News*, October 27, 1931, sports section.

[10] Watson, *op. cit.*

[11] Hurley, *op. cit.*, April 3, April 10, April 17, April 24, May 1, and May 8, 1932, sports sections. John Salvator II recalled that Hurley would stay at the Kahler during a series of conversations with the author at Salvator's home in St. Paul on September 29 and 30, 2007.

asked to write his autobiography for the paper after Petrolle retired in 1934. Apparently, Jack declined because no such articles were published.[12]

Hurley's "Ring Rations" column for April 10, 1932 was interesting as an early first-hand description, from a patient's perspective, of the then-new diagnostic procedure called "contrast radiology," which was used by the doctors to view the ulcers in his stomach. Jack relates in detail the process of having his stomach pumped, drinking a quart of barium, and then being X-rayed. The basics of the procedure are still used today although a CT scan has replaced the X-ray, and a stomach pump is no longer necessary.[13]

Hurley was healthy enough during his stay to announce he had closed bouts for Charley Retzlaff against James J. Braddock on May 13 at Boston Garden and for Petrolle against Battling Battalino on May 20 at the Chicago Stadium, but he was unavailable when reporters tried to contact him for further details about the matches.[14]

On Sunday May 8, 1932, the *Duluth News Tribune* reported Hurley "left a hospital at Rochester Saturday and is reported to be in the proverbial 'pink.'" During his 40 days at the clinic, Jack had undergone two courses of treatment, first for his sinuses and then for his stomach. According to his doctors both treatments had gone well.[15]

---

[12] Jack Hurley's Secretary, "Ring Rations," *Fargo Forum*, March 25, 1934, sports section.
[13] Hurley, *op. cit.*, April 10, 1932. The relevant portions of this article are reproduced in italics as the introduction to this chapter.
[14] "Petrolle and Battalino Are Matched Again," *Fargo Forum*, April 22, 1932, sports section.
[15] Campbell, *op. cit.*, May 8, 1932, sports section. Although Hurley's April 10th column describes his sinus surgery and a battery of stomach X-rays (contrast radiology), he apparently had not yet started actual treatment for his stomach condition. In the 1930s treatment for peptic ulcers was based on the simplistic theory that ulcers were caused by excess acid in the stomach. Treatment followed two alternative paths: control of diet over an extended period of time to limit and absorb stomach acid secretion and give the ulcers time to heal, known as the "Sippy diet;" or removal of the lower half of the stomach in hopes of reducing acid secretion. Obviously, the surgical option was more drastic and was usually employed only after the dietary option had failed.

It is therefore unlikely Hurley had stomach surgery at this time. Jack returned to action at full speed when he was discharged by the clinic on May 7, about 30 days after he wrote his April 10th column (probably actually written around April 7). Thirty days would hardly have been long enough for a full recovery in 1932 from such major surgery. Although Hurley talks about the nose operation as his "first," he likely did not know exactly what type of treatment he would be receiving for his stomach when he wrote the column. In addition, if he had required stomach surgery at the time, he would have not been able to continue writing his column without missing a single week. In contrast, when Jack had the surgery in 1934, he was off for a longer period of time and he had a stand-in "secretary" write the column.

On the other hand, 30 days seems about right for the Sippy diet. This treatment required the approximately four weeks of bed rest. For the first few days, nourishment was limited to hourly doses of milk and cream between 7 a.m. and 7 p.m. Gradually, soft-boiled eggs and soft-cooked cereals would be added to the regimen. In addition, the patient would typically be given antacids with each meal and every half-hour in between.

In the 1950s, the Sippy diet was discredited when studies showed that ulcers of patients using it took longer to heal than ulcers of patients who followed the same program of bed

While Hurley knew he would have to undergo future sinus treatments, he hoped his stomach renovation had cured his ulcers once and for all. Unfortunately, Jack would be disappointed. Within two years, his stomach pain would recur, more virulent than ever, and he would return to the clinic again, this time under emergency circumstances requiring major surgery.

On the day of his discharge, Hurley hopped a train to Chicago where he signed a contract for the Petrolle-Battalino rematch before continuing on to Boston for Retzlaff's match with Braddock six days later.

After the disastrous draw the previous November against Giacomo Bergomas, which had derailed Retzlaff's quest for a big-money bout in New York, Charley rang up three straight kayos, the most impressive being a four-rounder over Jack McCarthy at Boston Garden on March 18, 1932. McCarthy, a local favorite from nearby Roxbury, had been a winner in all 11 of his previous fights in Beantown, including seven by knockout. As a result, Retzlaff's showing drew rave reviews from the city's press corps.

---

rest and antacids with a regular diet which included only moderate amounts of milk. Later, it was determined that milk products had no beneficial effect on ulcers. The Sippy diet was not totally without medical effect, however. According to at least one report many patients developed cardiovascular disease because of the very fatty "ulcer diets" prescribed by their doctors. (Author's note to note: Hurley often was described as having a bottle of milk and a banana with him as a late-night meal before going to bed. One of the causes of Hurley's death in 1972 was said to be heart disease. If the ulcers did not get him in the end, maybe it was the treatment his doctors prescribed for the ulcers that got him instead!).

In the 1980s, a study found that bacteria called *Helicobacter pylori* (*H. p.*) was present in the stomachs of every person tested who had ulcers (and conversely the same bacteria was not found in the stomachs of persons who did not have ulcers). As a result, most people can now be successfully treated for stomach ulcers as outpatients with a seven-day program of combination therapy (an anti-acid secretory drug and at least two antibiotics). Surgery is rarely indicated.

Although stress alone is no longer considered to cause stomach ulcers, Hurley's belief his ulcers were stress-related is still consistent with modern thinking which cites stress as a possible factor in producing acid which aggravates the ulcers resulting from the presence of *H. p.* bacteria in the stomach.

Before the discovery of the *H. p.* bacteria, it was thought removing part of the stomach gave relief to people with ulcers because the stomach would then produce less acid. Doctors now think the reason such surgery worked in the past was because the part of the stomach usually removed, the distal stomach, was typically the favorite habitat of the bacteria and therefore the usual site of infection. This, then, was probably the reason Hurley's ulcer problem was alleviated by the removal of "2/3" of his stomach when he finally did have surgery in 1934. Marshall, Barry J., "Peptic Ulcers, Stomach Cancer and the Bacteria Which Are Responsible," *Heinekin Lectures 1998*, (Royal Academy of Arts and Sciences, Amsterdam, 1999), pp. 28-38. Paradowski, Leszek; Blonski, Wojchiech; and Kempinski, Radoslaw; "Twenty Years After Introducing Proton Pump Inhibitors. What Have We Achieved in Peptic Ulcer Disease Conventional Treatment?" *Advances in Clinical and Experimental Medicine, 2004*, Volume 13, Number 5, pp. 737-747. Chu, KM, "Helicobacter Pylori Infection: the Reduced Need for Ulcer Surgery," *Hong Kong Medical Journal*, Volume 5, Number 2, June 1999, pp. 158-161.

At right is the then new Mayo Clinic building in Rochester, as it was in the late 1920s when Hurley began going there. The clinic's original building is in the center, and the Kahler Grand Hotel is on the left.

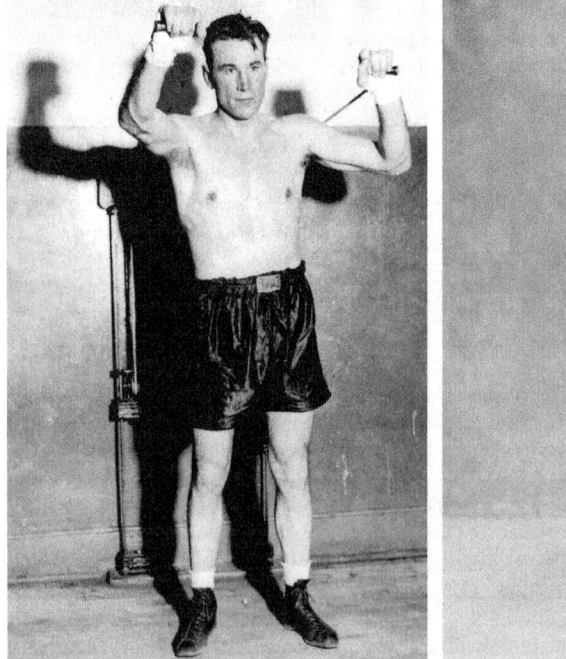

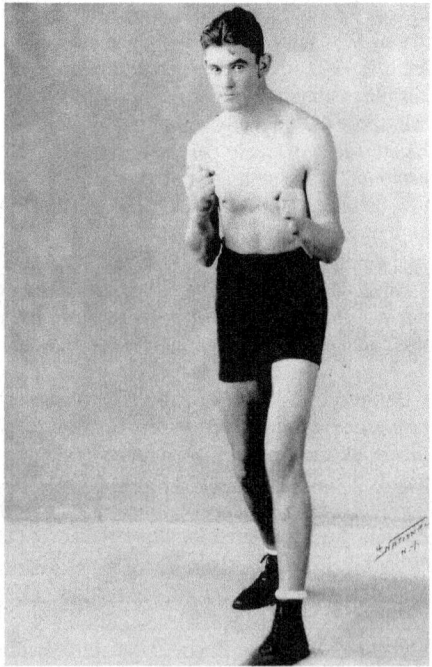

After his discharge from the clinic, Hurley hustled to Boston where Retzlaff (left) was fighting Jimmy Braddock (right). Charley eked out a decision, but failed to impress the fans.

Boston Garden general manager Dick Dunn had been after Hurley for another chance to show Retzlaff ever since the McCarthy bout, but Jack's illness delayed Charley's return. Dunn had taken the job at Boston in January 1931 after having served in the same capacity at the Olympia arena in Detroit since 1928. It was Dick who had built Retzlaff into an attraction at the Motor City with big wins against Johnny Risko and Tom Heeney, and now he was hoping Charley would catch on in similar fashion at Boston.

Based on his sensational showing against McCarthy, Boston reporters predicted a kayo for Retzlaff over Braddock. At the time, Jimmy had lost three of his last four fights, and his career appeared to be on the downgrade. If Charley could come through with another impressive victory, Dunn planned to match him with Ernie Schaaf, another local favorite, in a bout expected to sell out the Boston Garden.

Although Retzlaff, 195, won a decision over Braddock, 181, by a margin of five rounds to four with one round even on most scorecards, the crowd jeered as he left the ring. Despite the hoopla about his vaunted power, the Duluth Dynamiter fought cautiously, using his longer reach to hold off and jab his way to victory without closing in on his lighter foe. The official decision was split. One judge, Toby Lyons, voted for Braddock while Al Bates and referee Johnny Brassil thought Retzlaff had done enough to win.

In the next day's *Boston Herald*, W. A. Hamilton called "a dismal failure compared to the slashing, two-fisted fighter he was when he knocked out Jack McCarthy here several weeks ago. He looked worse in victory than Braddock did in defeat." The fact Jimmy was a dangerous puncher who never had been kayoed meant nothing to the action-hungry Boston crowd, which expected to be entertained by a kayo.[17]

With scarcely enough time to clear his head from the catcalls of the prior evening, Hurley boarded a train for Chicago the next day to prepare for the May 20th Petrolle-Battalino fight. Matchmaker Nate Lewis told reporters he expected a turnout of 14,000 fans and a gate of $50,000. Instead, just 10,800 people paid $31,000 to see a fight which was largely a repeat of the first, with Bat absorbing ever-increasing doses of punishment as the rounds rolled on. Billy won a unanimous decision, and likely was denied a kayo only because the go was set for ten rounds rather than 12 as in New York.[18]

---

[17] "Retzlaff Wins from Braddock in Boston," Fargo Forum, May 14, 1932, sports section. Hamilton, W. A., fight report (title unavailable), May 14, 1932, sports section. Three years later, the reason for Retzlaff's caution against Braddock became clear when Jimmy proved what a good fighter he really was by putting together a string of wins which landed him a heavyweight championship bout with Max Baer in June 1935. Braddock, in one of the great upsets in boxing history, defeated Baer and became heavyweight champion. Unfortunately for Retzlaff, his own rating had taken a downturn by then, and his earlier victory over Braddock was no longer relevant to the heavyweight picture.

[18] Brown, Warren, "So they Tell Me," *Chicago Herald and Examiner*, May 14, 1932, p. 12. Murphy, Mike, "Petrolle Wins Hard Fight, but Gets No Money," *Chicago Daily News*, May 21, 1932, sports section.

The contest's most exciting moment, and the only time its action varied from the prior fight, came in the first round when Bat landed a left hook that dropped Petrolle in the center of the ring. Billy took a long nine-count, barely rising in time to avoid a kayo, and came back fighting. By round's end, he had taken charge and bloodied Battalino's mouth. From then on, Petrolle battered his foe severely and won every round until the tenth when an exhausted but still flailing Bat staged a desperate, two-fisted rally which earned him the round by a shade on the scorecards of most reporters.[19]

Although Petrolle's knockdown startled fans, his dominant performance in succeeding rounds caused them to forget about it afterward. In 1953, however, Hurley had occasion to recall the knockdown after witnessing a similar situation in the second Rocky Marciano-Jersey Joe Walcott heavyweight title fight when Walcott was knocked down, lost track of the count, and was a second late getting up. Drawing a parallel between Jersey Joe's knockdown and Petrolle's 21 years earlier, Jack explained how close Billy had been to not getting up before the ten-count:

> "He waited in that position for the count of eight, as I always had coached him to do in the event of a knockdown. But he didn't get up at eight. [Referee Dave] Barry counted nine and then, taking it for granted that Petrolle was getting to his feet, turned around to signal Battalino to resume the fight. When he realized that Petrolle hadn't gotten up, he turned around with his arm upraised, to count ten. But before he could do so, Petrolle jumped to his feet.
>
> "When it was over, he told me that he suddenly had blacked out for an instant at about the count of eight. The next thing he knew the referee was coming toward him with his arm upraised and he jumped to his feet. 'How many times was I knocked down?' he asked me."[20]

Despite Petrolle's close call, the incident did nothing to detract from the lofty status he had achieved in the eyes of boxing critics. Eddie Borden, who compiled the *Ring Magazine*'s ratings for July 1932, wrote, "Petrolle still remains the dominant figure in three divisions. He clinched his supremacy in the lightweight class with his victory over Battling Battalino." Remarkably, Borden rated Billy as the No. 1 contender in the lightweight, junior welterweight, and welterweight divisions, all at the same time.[21]

---

[19] MacNamara, Harry, fight report (title unavailable), *Chicago Herald and Examiner*, May 21, 1932, sports section.

[20] Anderson, Lenny, "Walcott's K.O. Reminds Hurley of Tunney's Sitdown," *Seattle Times*, May 24, 1953, sports section.

[21] Borden, Eddie, "A Corner on the Fistic Market; Ratings for the Month of May," *Ring Magazine*, July 1932, p. 48.

Petrolle and Battalino maneuver for an opening during their Chicago battle in May 1932.

Battalino advances as Petrolle looks ready to counter.

Petrolle steps inside Battalino's left hook.

The Fargo Express lands a left hook flush on Battalino's jaw.

Hurley returned to Duluth two days after the fight, and took his first real vacation in two years. Phil Terk staged his last boxing card May 18 and was not planning any more shows until the fall. For two weeks, Jack conducted a little business by phone, called on friends, and played a lot of golf.[22]

The *News Tribune*'s Cubby Campbell reported Hurley and Terk had taken lessons in 1928 from Ralph Kingsrud, house pro at the municipal golf course in Fargo. At the end of their lessons, Jack and Phil were feeling pretty good about their games, and they bet Ralph he could not beat them playing with one hand. After losing "plenty" to the Fargo pro in a challenge match, they learned he was an expert one-hand player who had made a specialty of winning several national one-hand tournaments.[23]

Campbell recalled that before Hurley started golfing he "always had a sneering remark for anyone taking up the game." Jack at first denied rumors he was taking instruction in Fargo, countering that "the only lessons he had so far were with a broom" from his mother who had taught him "the follow-through swing." Finally, however, Jack was forced to admit that he had paid "55 bucks for a set of five clubs and bag and $15 for golf shoes," but that "as yet he refuses 'to go around in those there knee britches.'"[24]

As might be expected from a boxing manager, Jack was more competitive as a dressing-room handicap negotiator than as a course golfer. According to Campbell, who played in a foursome with Hurley and Terk, Jack "was free and easy with the amount to be played for – anything from two bits to a buck a hole – but the terms were too mercenary."

Cubby explained that Jack's negotiating technique was to downplay his own abilities and "continually pester" his opponents to "'give me a little handicap,'" namely "'two strokes on the long holes, and one on the short.'" Describing his own talents, Hurley called himself "'a revolutionary war golfer – out in 75 and back in 76.'"[25]

When Petrolle took up the sport in 1929, he was able to beat Hurley at his own game. Billy told Jack and Phil he was a complete novice. In sporting fashion, they agreed to spot him one stroke per hole with a side bet of a buck a hole. For the rest of the afternoon, Billy won almost every hole, all the while repeatedly denying he had ever taken golf lessons.

At one of the last tees, Petrolle hit an especially long drive down the middle of the fairway. In admiration of the perfect shot he had just seen, Billy's caddy commented loud enough for everyone to hear, "Mr. Petrolle, those lessons are certainly helping your game." As Hurley later told the story, the game ended right on the spot. Neither Jack nor Phil ever got their

---

[22] Campbell, "The Sport Spigot," *Duluth News Tribune*, May 26, 1932, sports section.
[23] Campbell, *op. cit.*, July 17, 1929 and June 30, 1929, sports sections.
[24] Campbell, "Sport News Gossip," *Duluth News Tribune*, June 1, 1930, sports section.
[25] Campbell, "Cubby Campbell's Column," *Duluth News Tribune*, June 1, 1932, sports section. Hurley, *op. cit.*, August 30, 1931, sports section.

money back, and they never played golf with Billy again.[26]

Campbell provided another glimpse of what a joy it was to play 18 holes with Jack when he wrote: "Hurley's idea of a real life with ease is to have enough money to construct his own golf course. He would eliminate all hazards and limit the guests on the course so that there would be no players barring his way in front and no vexing cries of 'fore' from the rear."[27]

Hurley and Petrolle were in Pittsburgh on June 15 for Billy's bout with Tommy Grogan. Although Grogan was no longer the fighter he had been in 1928 when he cut Petrolle's eye and scored a technical knockout, both Jack and Billy were happy for the chance to even accounts. As expected, Petrolle won the ten-round decision, knocking Tommy down twice in the process.[28]

After Pittsburgh, it was on to New York for Hurley where Retzlaff was battling Hans Birkie June 21, 1932, in a preliminary bout to the heavyweight title rematch between champion Max Schmeling and Jack Sharkey. In contrast to his impressive demonstration on the undercard of the Schmeling-Stribling show a year earlier, Charley's performance against Birkie was only mediocre, and he had to settle for a 5-round draw.

In the title bout itself, Sharkey became the new heavyweight champion by winning a split, 15-round decision over Schmeling. Hurley, who had predicted a Schmeling victory in his weekly column, was among the vast majority of writers who felt Max was robbed. Although Jack wrote that it was "a terrible fight," more like a fencing duel than a boxing match, he thought Schmeling was entitled to at least eight of the 15 rounds because he had chased Sharkey around the ring and at least tried to make a fight of it.[29]

While in New York, Hurley met with Garden matchmaker James J. Johnston to finalize the verbal agreement they made three months earlier for a summertime lightweight title bout between Petrolle and champion Tony Canzoneri. After the meeting, Johnston announced the 15-round fight would take place at Madison Square Garden's new outdoor bowl in Long Island on August 8, 1932. To properly publicize the fight, Hurley agreed to arrive in New York two weeks ahead of time.[30]

Within a day or two, Hurley was on his way to Chicago where Retzlaff was fighting ex-college football star Les Marriner in a ten-round main event on June 28. On the same train as Jack, also on their way to the Windy City, were Damon Runyon, celebrated columnist for the *New York American*, and Chicago Stadium matchmaker Nate Lewis.

Since all three were all night owls, they stayed up until the morning's wee hours discussing everything from "politics to ski jumping." When

---

[26] Hurley, *op. cit.*, December 31, 1933, sports section.
[27] Campbell, *op. cit.*
[28] "Duluth boxer Evens Account with Old Rival" (AP), *Duluth News Tribune*, June 16, 1932, sports section.
[29] Hurley, *op. cit.*, June 26, 1932, sports section.
[30] "Aug. 8 Is Set for Petrolle's Shot at Title," *Fargo Forum*, June 24, 1932, sports section.

Runyon suggested going to bed at 4 a.m., Hurley agreed, but Lewis became indignant and claimed Damon and Jack were lightweights when it came to staying up. Lewis, whose normal routine was to sleep from 10 a.m. until 6 p.m., was still muttering to himself when Jack went to sleep.

When the train arrived in Chicago at noon the next day, Hurley and Runyon "hit the floor a-runnin" but Lewis was nowhere to be seen. After searching the train, a crew member found Nate still asleep, and so groggy he either refused or was unable to get up. Before long, the train had to be cleared out of the station and moved to the yards to make room for oncoming trains. Jack learned later Lewis had arisen at his usual time just as the cleanup crew was going home and had to hitchhike back to the city.[31]

After Retzlaff stopped Marriner in one round, Hurley again found himself with extra time on his hands. Since he was not due in New York for three weeks, Jack accepted an invitation to be the guest of Johnny Salvator and his wife at their Big Sandy Lake beach cottage in northern Minnesota.

Before leaving Chicago, Jack served as best man for Al Sweeney at his wedding with Berenice Peltz. Hurley met Sweeney two years earlier when Jack was booking fighters with Ray Alvis, and Al was helping handle the 65 boxers who fought under the agency's banner. The friendship of the two men continued to work to their mutual benefit after the Alvis-Hurley breakup since Hurley taught Sweeney a lot about the boxing game while Al watched over Jack's interests in Chicago whenever he needed help.

Sweeney, a Chicago native, began as an 18-year-old promoter of amateur boxing shows at the Union Park Temple in 1925. Over the next few years, he helped sportswriter Walter Eckersall put together the first Chicago Golden Gloves tournament and served as assistant matchmaker for Mique Malloy in his promotions at Mills Stadium, the Coliseum, and the Rainbo Fronton arena. It was after his stint with Malloy that Al became associated with the Alvis-Hurley combine in 1930.

At the time of his wedding, Sweeney's main occupation was managing lightweight Prince Saunders, who had headlined several of Salvator's fight cards in St. Paul. In 1933, he quit managing to take a job as Nate Lewis' assistant matchmaker at the Chicago Stadium. Shortly afterward, Al hit upon the idea of staging midget auto races at the Stadium. His first venture was a financial success, but the arena's ventilation system was unable to properly evacuate the exhaust, so he shifted his next race outdoors.

Sweeney's decision to pursue auto racing proved to be a life-changing event. His flair for showmanship led Alec Sloan, then the Midwest's leading auto-race promoter, to hire him in 1934. After Sloan died in 1937, Al founded National Speedways Inc. with partner Gaylord White. Sweeney operated the company until he retired in 1972. In 1971, Al was inducted into the International Motor Contest Association's Hall of Fame based on a

---

[31] Hurley, *op. cit.*, July 3, 1932, sports section.

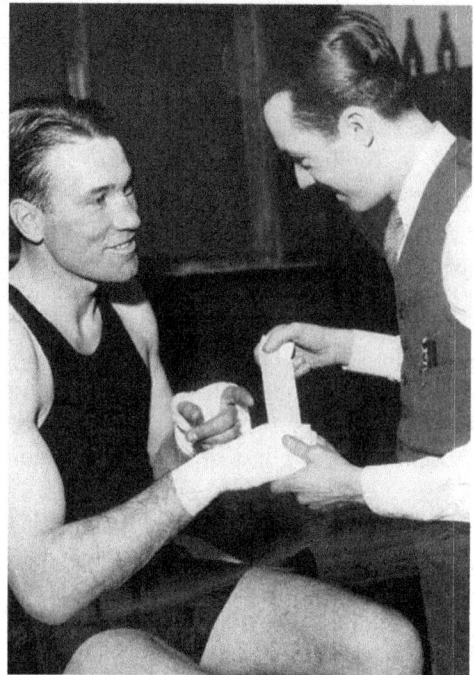

Al Sweeney (right), helping with Charley Retzlaff's handwraps.

Al Sweeney's stable ace, Prince Saunders.

Bertha, John II, and Johnny Salvator at their Big Sandy Lake residence.

The Big Sandy Lake cabin where Jack and Reggie stayed. The man is unidentified.

lifelong reputation for integrity and concern for the safety of his drivers.[32]

Al and Berenice (pet name – "Brunch") Sweeney were married June 27, 1932, at Our Lady of Lourdes Catholic Church in Chicago. To finance the event, Al borrowed $200 from Hurley, rented an apartment, paid the first month's gas, electric and telephone bills, made a down payment on some furniture, and bought a marriage license. After paying for a post-wedding breakfast for a party of four accompanied by Xavier Cugat's orchestra, including Jack and the matron of honor, Al still had money left for carfare.[33]

Three days later, Hurley took a train to Duluth and touched base with Terk and the sports editors of the city's two newspapers. Jack filled them in on the details of the upcoming title fight and promised that if Petrolle became champion, his first ring appearance as a titleholder would be in Duluth at the National Athletic Club sometime in the fall.[34]

When he arrived in Duluth, Hurley was accompanied by an attractive, well-dressed, dark-haired, woman from New York named Regina (Reggie) Grossman. The couple had been maintaining a long-distance romance for over a year. The offer to vacation at the Salvators' Big Sandy Lake cottage undoubtedly was their first chance to spend a solid block of quiet time together, away from the bustle of the big city nightspots, sports arenas, train stations, and hotels where their courtship had of necessity been nurtured.

From Duluth, Jack and Reggie (rhyming with Peggy) took a train 60 miles west to MacGregor, Minnesota, where Johnny and Bertha Salvator, along with their ten-year-old son John, picked them up and drove to Big Sandy Lake.[35]

The Salvators purchased the property in 1922 and built two cottages on a hill above the lake. The main house was a log cabin with five rooms and a porch. The guest cottage was similar to the main cabin except it had only three rooms. Later, the Salvators added a tree house built of logs for their son. The addition of a 100-step stairway provided direct access to the lake.

---

[32] Dotten, Herb, "Auto Race Promoter Al Sweeney Started Out to Become a Jockey," *Billboard Magazine*, May 13, 1950, p. 53. "Al Sweeney" National Sprint Car Hall of Fame web page. Interestingly, Sweeney also served as advance man for Jack Dempsey's 1931 comeback tour, a duty which included among its responsibilities lining up opponents for Dempsey's exhibition bouts.

[33] Weitzel, Tony, "Along the Trail," *Naples Daily News*, May 28, 1983, p. 2-A.

[34] Campbell, *op. cit.*, June 30, 1932, sports section.

[35] The author has been unable to determine exactly when Hurley and Reggie connected on this trip. Reggie might have been with Jack on the train from New York along with Damon Runyon and Nate Lewis or she could have joined Jack on a later train in Chicago, Minneapolis, or Duluth. The one fact which suggests she may have hooked up with Jack after the Sweeney wedding is that "the party of four" which Al describes as being present at the post-wedding breakfast did not include Reggie since Brunch's matron of honor was a Mary Flood of Lake Zurich. It seems likely Reggie would have been at the breakfast if she was traveling with Jack, and the breakfast would have become a party of five. All that is known for sure, however, is that Reggie was with Jack at the train station in MacGregor when the Salvators picked them up.

Young John Salvator remembered that when Reggie arrived at Big Sandy Lake, his father already knew her from a previous trip to New York. Johnny had returned to St. Paul with a gift of two pairs of pajamas for his wife that Reggie had helped him pick out at the shop where she worked in New York City. John recalled his mother saying one of the pairs was okay, but that the other was too sporty, prompting her to comment, "That'll never do."[36]

Although the exact circumstances and date of Jack and Reggie's first meeting are likely lost forever, the timing of Johnny Salvator's trip to New York suggests they had known each other for at least 13 months and probably longer. Salvator was in New York with Hurley to handle Billy Light for his fight with Eddie Ran on the Petrolle-McLarnin undercard at Madison Square Garden on May 27, 1931. It was in all likelihood during this trip that Johnny met Reggie while shopping for Bertha's gift.[37]

During this same period in 1931, topics other than sports find their way into Hurley's "Ring Rations" column for the first time. Something obviously had changed, because suddenly Jack was going places and doing things he had never mentioned before. It is hard to believe that his increased interest in the non-boxing aspects of popular culture were caused by anything other than his burgeoning courtship with Regina Grossman.

In June 1931, Hurley attended two revues at the Palace Theater featuring Eddie Cantor, Cab Calloway, Georgie Jessel, and Jack Benny. Later that summer, he took in three more shows starring Lydia Roberti, Lew Pollack, Edward G. Robinson, Kate Smith, Lou Holtz, as well as "the best band I ever heard," the Horace Heidt Orchestra. Jack also saw Mae West in "The Constant Sinner" at the Royale Theater. There, he noted "the stagehands were as important as the actors … for their fast work in shifting the scenes."

During this time, Hurley also started writing about other attractions like the Empire State Building and major-league baseball. On Memorial Day, he was "one of the 60,000 spectators" who saw Brooklyn win a doubleheader from the New York Giants. In June, he saw Babe Ruth go hitless at Yankee Stadium when the Detroit Tigers beat the Yankees in extra innings.[38]

Hints more directly suggestive of a courtship surfaced around this time as well. In late August 1931, sportswriter William Morris of the New York Evening Post dropped the tidbit in his boxing chitchat column that Hurley and a lady friend had dropped by his office on the way to catch a train.[39]

---

[36] Conversations with John Salvator, August 31, 2007. Visit with John Salvator, September 29 and 30, 2007.

[37] Salvator also had been in New York to handle Billy Light for a preliminary fight on the undercard of the Petrolle-Tut fight on February 27, 1931. It is possible he first met Reggie at this time instead of the later date. Whichever date is correct, the point is that Jack and Reggie had known each other for quite some time before their vacation at Big Sandy Lake.

[38] Hurley, op. cit., June 5, June 21, September 6, and September 27, 1931, sports sections.

[39] Morris, William, "Around the Ring," New York Evening Post, September 24, 1931, sports section.

In "Ring Rations," Jack mentions he postponed a return to Duluth after Petrolle's fight with Billy Townsend on December 30, 1931, to help welcome in the New Year the next evening at Times Square on Broadway. During the following week, he attended a hockey game at the Garden and a "George White Scandals" stage show at the Apollo Theater where he saw Ray Bolger, Ethel Merman, Everett Marshall, and Rudy Vallee.[40]

On February 17, 1932, Cubby Campbell wrote that Hurley was returning to Duluth the next day from New York where he had lingered to combine romance with managerial duties for 3-1/2 weeks after the January 23rd Petrolle-Ran fight.[41]

Although Hurley's travel schedule and his passion to succeed as a boxing manager often prevented him from staying in one place long enough to look for a mate, his pursuit of Reggie was not his first serious courtship. Two years earlier, his seven-month stretch in Chicago as office manager for Alvis-Hurley afforded him an opportunity to seek and almost find a wife.

In September 1930, Campbell reported on a rumor that a wedding was in the works for a "former secretary of the recent Alvis-Hurley firm of booking agents" and Jack Hurley, "the manager of Silver Spray fighters and an avowed 'woman hater.'" Cubby called the romance a "version of 'Abie's Irish Rose,'" in that Hurley was Irish-Catholic and the lady was Jewish.[42]

Hurley never discussed the affair while it was on, but when it was over he offered an explanation why it did not work out: "The girl informed me I would have to show at least $200,000 and her folks would expect me to change. I advised her I had hopes of making that much, but I didn't see why I had to change my religion. 'Who said anything about religion,' she said. 'What my folks said was for you to quit fooling around this boxing game and go to work for a change.' My answer to her was, 'The deal is off.'"[43]

Hurley's explanation was presented in his usual pithy, tongue-in-cheek style, but like many of his stories, it had an aura of truth. In any event, it is the only description of the relationship he or anyone else ever offered.

At the time of her visit to Big Sandy Lake in July 1932, Regina Grossman was a 33-year-old working woman, employed as a manager in a New York City dress shop. She was the daughter of Morris and Sarah Grossman, Jews from Russian Poland who had immigrated to America via England in 1899, the same year Reggie was born. Reggie was the eldest of six children and the only one born in England rather than the United States.

---

[40] Hurley, *op. cit.*, January 10, 1932, sports section.
[41] Campbell, *op. cit.*, February 17 or 18, 1932, sports section.
[42] Campbell, *op. cit.*, September 30, 1930, sports section. "Abie's Irish Rose" was a stage comedy of the period telling the story of an Irish Catholic woman who marries a Jewish man over the objections of both of their fathers. The play ran for 2,327 consecutive performances on Broadway from 1922 until 1927 and was made into a successful movie in 1928.
[43] Hurley, *op. cit.*, September 21, 1930, sports section.

In census records from 1910 through 1930, Morris Grossman is listed as a self-employed tailor. In 1910, Sarah supplemented the family income by working as a hairdresser, but in later years is listed as having no occupation. In 1910, Reggie's name is reported as "Rachel Grossman."

Between 1910 and 1930, the Grossmans were shown living in different apartments during each ten-year cycle, but always renting, presumably moving to a nicer flat each time as the family became more prosperous. However, in 1930 things were not so flush that Morris and Sarah felt averse to taking in lodgers and subletting rooms left vacant as their children left the roost. Reggie was definitely brought up to count her pennies.

By 1920, Reggie was married to Harry Nadel, a 23-year-old clothing salesman. Reggie is described as 20-years old and having no occupation. Harry and Reggie were living in the same building as Morris and Sarah, but in an adjacent apartment. Reggie's name is reported as "Regina Nadel."

By 1930, Harry Nadel was no longer living with Reggie, who again was living with her folks, her youngest brother, and a Mr. and Mrs. Golden, who possibly might have been a sister and brother-in-law or else two lodgers. Presumably, at this time Reggie was either divorced or separated. Reggie is listed as 31 years old and her name again is reported as "Regina Nadel."

The 1930 census also shows Reggie employed as a manager in a dress shop. It is possible she obtained the job through her ex-husband, the clothing salesman, or her father. As a tailor's daughter, she was accustomed to wearing fine clothes and was probably well prepared to sell them. Running a dress shop also would feed the passion she apparently had for stylish clothes when she met Hurley and a very young John Salvator II.[44]

John II remembered that Jack and Reggie's visit to Big Sandy in 1932 lasted for at least two weeks. He recalls that instead of sending them to the guest cottage, his parents "gave up their bedroom to Jack and Reggie." His parents were naturally tolerant and had no qualms about letting an unmarried couple use it. According to John: "People in the fight game did not go by all the rules of the rest of the public, anyway."

Apart from a liberal attitude, there was another reason the Salvators gave Jack and Reggie their room. John explained: "Jack was a favorite of my mother, and she would do almost anything for him. When he came through in the 1950s and '60s to plug the Globetrotters, he had my folks pick him up. On the way, dad also picked up Don Riley, of the *St. Paul Pioneer*, who interviewed Jack in the backseat. This upset my mom. She complained that Riley 'took up all of Jack's time and I didn't get a chance to talk to him.'"

---

[44] U. S. Census Records, 1910, 1920, 1930. The appearance of the name "Rachel" in the 1910 census and "Regina" in the 1920 and 1930 censuses supports the recollection of John Salvator II that Jack addressed her in both names. Conversations with Jack's nieces and nephews elicited different recollections about which name was used, with both names coming up. Most of those who met her, however, seemed to favor Reggie, and John Salvator, who knew her best among those interviewed, always referred to her as Reggie.

Studio portrait of a chicly groomed Regina (Grossman) Hurley, taken in Chicago at about the time of her marriage to Jack. Note the conspicuously displayed wedding ring.

Reggie was obviously comfortable around children. She spent a lot of time with John Salvator at Big Sandy and was nice to him. He recalled one incident in particular: "A song about Paradise from a movie starring Pola Negri was popular on the radio. Reggie transcribed the words for me off the radio because I liked the song so much. I think she used some kind of shorthand, so she must have had some secretarial training."

To the young Salvator: "Reggie was very dramatic looking, even theatrical; and very attractive and well dressed. She had very dark hair and she dressed in black a lot, probably because it made her look thinner. She was also dramatic in her actions."

John remembered that "Reggie never got up until noon and she would not come to lunch until one or 1:30 p.m. because she had to have time to make herself up. She would take the time to put on very long fake eyelashes every day and remove them every night. This was in the days before they made eyelashes that could be put on one eye at a time. She put them on slowly, one eyelash at a time. I watched her do it. Looking back on it, she put on a helluva lot of makeup."

Bertha Salvator and Reggie got along well. Again, John recalled: "Mother was a bit hefty and for a long time weighed about 190 pounds. My father joked that if she ever reached 200, he would trade her in for two girls who weighed 100 pounds each. After that my mother never talked about weight at all." Reggie was apparently sympathetic to Bertha's situation because as John put it: "They were always going on diets together."

While at Big Sandy, the adults played a lot of cards. John remembered on occasion, both at the lake and afterward, substituting for his father in games of bridge with Jack, Reggie, and his mother when Johnny was away attending to his promoting business. Later on, the couples took turns hosting card parties at their homes in Duluth and St. Paul. Later still, after Jack and Reggie moved to Chicago in 1935, Al and Brunch Sweeney often joined them to make up a third couple at cards.

John recalled Big Sandy Lake as a happy time for Jack and Reggie. To all appearances, they got along well and enjoyed each other's company. He remembers Jack called her by the names of both "Rachel" and "Reggie," but that she addressed him just as "Jack."[45]

John confirmed Reggie was Jewish and she had divorced before she met Jack. He also volunteered that Hurley was Catholic and was sure that even after their marriage, the family never told Jack's mother Julia about Reggie.

The accuracy of John's observation about the secrecy of the marriage was brought home to the author with remarkable clarity and force when, on the same trip, he interviewed Carol Olson, daughter of Jack's oldest sister, Margaret; and Gail Hafner, daughter of his second oldest sister, Abigail.

---

[45] Conversations with John Salvator II, August 31, 2007. Visit with John Salvator II, September 29 and 30, 2007. Conversation with John Salvator II, February 12, 2009.

While discussing family history, the author questioned Gail about her uncle's marriage. Hesitating, Gail looked at her elder cousin and asked, "Is it okay to talk about this?" Carol nodded it was okay, the conversation continued, and they confirmed Julia was never told about the marriage to spare her the pain of learning Jack had married a Jewish divorcee.

It had been just a brief hesitation by Gail, but the fact it had happened at all, 64 and 35 years after Julia and Jack's respective deaths, spoke volumes about how important it had been to the family to keep the marriage a secret from Jack's mother. Julia died in 1943.

Hurley's attitudes regarding women were complex, and are not easily woven into coherent explanation. In fact, uncovering information about his relationships with women, and especially about his marriage, has been one of the author's biggest challenges in writing these volumes.

Chapter 18 touched on the idea that the experience of seeing his father work and die while supporting a wife and kids made Jack question whether the traditional notions of work, marriage, and family life were paths to his own happiness. The chapter also discussed his view of women as a threat to his relationships with his fighters, even to the point where he eventually referred them as "little creatures."

With such deep-rooted notions about the opposite sex, it was unavoidable Hurley would experience a conflict between the natural attraction he felt toward women and his innate prejudices which made him suspicious of them. Unless these negative feelings could be overcome, it was almost inevitable they would retard his perception of women and interfere with any future long-term relationships which Jack might later develop.

Before marriage, this ambivalence often manifested itself in a tendency for Hurley to joke about his marital prospects as if there were none in sight, and to deny or hide the fact that he had any when a relationship was serious. It was almost as if he perceived his attraction to the opposite sex as a weakness in character or a betrayal of his inner self which made the entire topic of his relationship with women embarrassing to talk about.

Any hope for a change in Jack's attitude after marriage could not have been helped by the decision to hide it from his mother. Exclusion from such a major part of his life could only have exacerbated any doubts or insecurities Reggie may have brought to the relationship. As a result, the likelihood that either of them could cope with, compensate for, or otherwise remedy the deficiencies of the other was significantly reduced.

After two weeks of enjoying life at Sandy Lake, Jack and Reggie boarded a train at MacGregor and headed east. Hurley was anxious about Petrolle's lightweight title fight with Tony Canzoneri on August 8, 1932. Jack needed to finalize arrangements for Billy's training facilities at the Pioneer Gym in New York and to keep his promise of arriving two weeks early to ballyhoo the fight.

Jack's niece Carol (Comrie) Olsen with her husband, Dick Olsen, 2007.

Jack's niece, Gail (Comny) Hafner with her husband, Yates Hafner, 2007.

John Salvator II, 2011

Hurley's mother, Julia, circa late 1930s.

While Jack and Reggie vacationed at Big Sandy Lake, Petrolle was doing roadwork in Duluth's northern hills. On July 23, he left Duluth for Chicago to train under the supervision of Al Sweeney and begin his boxing work with Prince Saunders. After two days, the trio left for New York where Prince would continue to serve as Billy's main sparring partner.

For Petrolle, the Canzoneri bout was the climax of a ten-year pro career. According to widely circulated reports, he had accumulated over $175,000, invested wisely, and was set for life. His primary reason for boxing was no longer to earn money. He was fighting for his legacy. Billy wanted to win a world title before he retired.

The main topic of discussion when Petrolle checked into the Pioneer Gym in downtown New York City was his weight. He had weighed between 138 and 140 pounds for all his recent fights, and it had been almost two years since he fought at 135 pounds. The question was, "Can Billy make the lightweight limit and still be strong enough to defeat Canzoneri?"

After watching Billy work a few days, experts remained uncertain of his ability to "make weight." Some said he was already down to 140 pounds and could easily trim off five more, while others said he actually weighed 146 pounds and would not be able lose any more without starving himself.[46]

Hurley claimed Petrolle's weight ten days before the fight did not matter at all. Billy was really a natural lightweight and would have no difficulty making the limit. His only reason for weighing more in recent bouts was because all the boxers he had fought were welterweights and junior welters.

Hurley was asked why Billy chose such a modestly equipped downtown gym while others preparing for a major fight preferred the peace, quiet, and cool country air of fancy resorts like Madame Bey's or Pompton Lakes.

Hurley responded with an extended list of reasons. First, Petrolle liked the Pioneer Gym. He had prepared for all his major New York bouts there, knew its staff and clientele, and had established a comfortable routine. Billy found from past experience the hot city weather tended to curb his appetite and helped sweat off any weight he needed to lose.

Secondly, food intake was easier to monitor in the city where Billy ate privately with his trainer from an individually served plate. At a training camp, country air increased a boxer's appetite, and everyone sat at the table and helped himself to whatever food he wanted, served family style on huge platters. This made it hard for a fighter trying to lose weight because he might be seated next to another boxer who who wanted to gain weight.

Finally, Petrolle relaxed more easily in the city. A fighter at a camp has too much time on his hands. He starts worrying about the upcoming fight, about making weight, about being hungry, about his wife or girl friend, and about all his other problems. In the city, a fighter, like Billy, who enjoys

---

[46] Campbell, *op. cit.*, July 24, 1932, sports section. "Billy Petrolle Must Take Off 11 Big Pounds," (AP) *Fargo Forum*, July 31, 1932, sports section.

movies, can go to a show and pass away the time. His mind is distracted from the weight question, and his appetite is kept under control.[47]

Unfortunately, six days before the fight's scheduled date, questions about Petrolle's weight were rendered temporarily moot when he aggravated a chipped bone from an old elbow injury during a training session and became unable to move his arm. After X-rays and a doctor's examination confirmed the obstruction, Petrolle underwent surgery on August 3 to remove the chips and uncoil a nerve which the loose bone had disturbed.[48]

After the operation, Petrolle's doctors said he could resume training in six weeks. When Canzoneri's manager Sammy Goldman heard that Billy would be ready to fight before the end of the fall season, Sammy rejected Jimmy Johnston's offer to match Tony against Kid Chocolate in place of Petrolle. Since Billy was the leading contender, Canzoneri would wait until he recovered from surgery.[49]

Billy later told the *Fargo Forum*'s Eugene Fitzgerald his weight was 136-1/2 pounds when he hurt his arm, and he easily could have made 135 by the day of the fight.[50]

On August 9, only seven days after Petrolle's injury, Isadoro Gastanaga knocked Retzlaff out in one round at Queensboro Stadium. The bout was the semifinal on a show in which Ernie Schaaf defeated Paolino Uzcudun. Charley never landed a punch and was knocked down three times before being counted out by the referee after just two minutes and 45 seconds.

At this time, Jack and Reggie decided to get married. Since their differing religions did not allow them a church wedding, their easiest option was to be married by a justice of the peace. The privacy of a civil ceremony also reduced the chance of Jack's mother finding out about the marriage.

With Hurley due in Chicago to handle Retzlaff in a bout against Paul Pantaleo August 19, the couple took an express train out of New York City after the Gastanaga fight. After their arrival, they boarded a commuter train to Waukegan, Illinois, 40 miles north of the Loop. They were married August 18 by Justice of the Peace Harry Hoyt in a ceremony witnessed, as far as is known, by employees of the Lake County clerk's office. No notice of the event appeared in any of the Fargo, Duluth, or Chicago newspapers.[51]

Though detailed accounts, either written or remembered, about Jack's state of mind at the time have not surfaced, circumstantial evidence suggests his decision to marry was well thought out and not solely the result of mere whim, impulse, or unreasoning passion.

---

[47] Hurley, *op. cit.*, July 31, 1932, sports section.
[48] Hurley, *op. cit.*, August 7, 1932, sports section.
[49] "Canzoneri's Manager Prefers to Wait for Petrolle to Recover," *Duluth News Tribune*, August 9, 1932, sports section.
[50] Fitzgerald, "Sport Whirligig," *Fargo Forum*, October 8, 1932, sports section.
[51] "Marriage License – John Hurley and Regina Grossman," August 18, 1932, copy certified for genealogical purposes only on September 26, 2006 by Lake County Clerk.

As early as November 1928, Cubby Campbell wrote that Hurley was "contemplating marriage," but had not as yet "picked out his other '99 per cent.'" Campbell explained that Jack was tired of eating in restaurants which made his "tummy revolt," and was ready to settle down to meals of "the home-cooked brand."[52]

As his cronies married and began raising families, Hurley's self-imposed pressure to find a wife became more apparent. In October 1929, Cubby observed: "Hurley is like a man without a country. His sidekick, Phil Terk, has turned family man, and there's no one to stay up until the wee sma' hours of the morning with the colonel. Therefore, Hurley is pondering about pulling stakes to Chicago."[53]

Marriage was still on Hurley's mind in Chicago in 1930 when he told the *Evening Post*'s Vern Whaley in 1930 he was "waiting for the 'right girl' – one with a Hundred Gs preferred." Ten days later, he updated Whaley about the results of his offer by revealing he had as yet "received no replies to his offer to marry the girl – if she has 100 Grand." A fair interpretation of these remarks, even though made in jest, is that Jack viewed at least some degree of financial independence as a desirable quality in a future wife.[54]

By the time Jack and Reggie began to get serious, most of Hurley's closest friends already were married, and he was in greater danger than ever of becoming odd-man-out in his social set. After Al Sweeney's wedding, a week before Jack's vacation with Reggie, he joked that he had been a best man so often that if the economy worsened, he still had his "regular trade to fall back on, that of a professional stander-up (best man to you)."[55]

Another Hurley friend whose marriage at this time may have influenced Jack's decision was Damon Runyon. It seems likely he and Hurley discussed the pros and cons of matrimony during their late-night chat on the train ride to Chicago at the end of June. The topic was very much on Runyon's mind because his own wedding was taking place two weeks later on July 7, 1932. It was widely known Damon had fallen hard for actress Patrice Amati del Grande and was elated when she agreed to marry him.[56]

It is doubtful Hurley fretted for long about whether his mother Julia would approve of his marriage. Jack had chosen to please himself rather than his mother in matters of personal happiness years before, when he chose to follow his own star and pursue the dicey life of a boxing man. Marrying Reggie was just another path connected to the same trail.

---

[52] Campbell, "The Sport Spigot," *Duluth News Tribune*, November 27, 1928, sports section.

[53] Campbell, *op. cit.*, October 20, 1929, sports section.

[54] Whaley Vern, "Knockout Drops," *Chicago Evening Post*, January 6 and 10, 1930, sports sections.

[55] Hurley, *op. cit.*, July 3, 1932, sports section.

[56] "Damon Runyon Marries Actress in New York" (AP), *Fargo Forum*, July 8, 1932, sports section.

Marriage was in the air during 1932. Damon Runyon supports the hand of his new bride, Patrice Amati del Grande, with George Marshall, owner of the Washington Redskins' football team.

For readers skeptical that a critic of women like Hurley would ever marry, here is a copy of his marriage license.

The Holland Hotel, 501 West Superior St., downtown Duluth, where Jack and Reggie lived after they were married.

At the same time, Hurley loved his mother and did not want to ruin their relationship or cause her unnecessary distress. He obviously figured if he spared Julia from knowledge about his marriage to Reggie, he would avert a confrontation that could have no mutually satisfactory resolution. Apparently, the family agreed because no one else ever did, either.

On August 19, the day after he and Reggie were married, Jack was in Retzlaff's corner when he stopped Paul Pantaleo in the seventh round at the White City Arena. Afterward, Hurley sent Charley home for a rest.

The next two weeks found the newlyweds relaxing in a luxury suite at the Lowery Hotel in St. Paul, Minnesota. Hurley had arranged for Primo Carnera to appear on a September 1, 1932 show Johnny Salvator was staging. Primo's opponent was Art Lasky, who had been a sensation a year earlier in his two-round exhibition bout against Jack Dempsey.

Carnera's appearance was Hurley's effort to pump life into Salvator's Capitol City club, which was suffering the same economic woes as the rest of the country. Unfortunately, Primo was no longer the novelty he once had been, and the show barely broke even.[57]

After the St. Paul show, the Hurleys leased a suite at the Holland Hotel in downtown Duluth, located on the corner of West Superior Street and North 5th Avenue West. According to John Salvator, the Holland was Jack and Reggie's residence until they moved to Chicago three years later.

Hurley's first order of business in Duluth was to check on Petrolle's elbow. At the time of his surgery, the hope had been that it would heal in time for Billy to fight Canzoneri before the end of the outdoor season ended October 12. Unhappily, the elbow was too tender to meet the target date.

Instead, Jack wired James J. Johnston at Madison Square Garden that Petrolle would be ready to fight by November 1. After checking with Canzoneri's manager, Sammy Goldman, Johnston wired back: "Canzoneri agrees. Fight a go. Nov. 4."

Billy Petrolle was finally getting his chance at the lightweight title.

---

[57] Campbell, "Cubby Campbell's Column," *Duluth News Tribune*, September 4, 1932, sports section. Campbell's account provides a nice summary of the financial aspects of the Carnera-Lasky fight:

"Fistic promotion has become extremely difficult with the addition of the ten-percent federal tax. Johnny Salvator drew close to $8,000 for the Carnera-Lasky fight last Thursday, but realized little or nothing on the card. In addition to the federal tax, the St. Paul promoter had to give ten percent to the state, a license fee; ten percent to the St. Paul auditorium where the bouts were staged and 50 percent of the net to Carnera and Lasky. With about $2,000 remaining, Johnny had to pay the other fighters on the card as well as for advertisements, police officers, ushers, ticket sellers and other incidentals."

CHAPTER 27

'HOW'S THE GAS WITH YOU, BILL?'

In this day of peacock-feathered press agentry it is only with the greatest reluctance this department arouses itself from its dolce far niente *and advocates your attendance at the Polo Grounds Wednesday evening July 12, 1933.*

There in a marquee, pitched in an exotic setting near second base, Mynheer Bep van Klaveren of Rotterdam and the Duluth veteran, Monsieur Guilluame Petrolle, le rapide de Fargoo, as we say along the Second Avenue Riviera, will meet in combat mortal.

Along de Bois de Broadway, Monsieur Petrolle, he of the formidable left wallop, is quoted at 7 to 5, or, if you prefer it, the messieurs and mesdames will lay seven bucks against your five that Monsieur Petrolle will still live to eat pressed duck in the Café des Bons Enfants after the battle.

Your correspondent was at Hasbroucks Heights, N. J., today where a clambake was being held in conjunction with van Klaveren's final workout. He was like a dike without a thumb stuck in it. In other words, he was a slapsy-slapsy, wham-wham of a fellow, in magnificent condition prepared to go 20 rounds where the agreements call for but ten.

Joe Frisco, with hives in his heels, never showed the footwork the Dutchman's got. And Lionel Strongfort, with four Indian clubs in each hand, couldn't outpop a man – if he hit him – any quicker than Bep. He apparently is one of these guys – like Maxie Baer – who fights for the pure unleavened joy of fighting.

But for all that, picking a guy to whambo the old Petrolle wagon is risky business. He's not a champion and never will be, but he's whipped the best of his weight – McLarnin, Townsend, Suarez, Ran and a covey of others. When he has to give weight the Fargo Express is just a milk wagon, making all the whistle stops. But with his natural poundage under a full head of steam, he's old 97 coming round that mountain when he comes.

Old Man Petrolle has got a left hand that sort of swishes when he lets it loose. And there's not many people who can see a swish coming. The old man may fall apart after five rounds, but those five rounds in which he is still together figure to be as sweet and low down as any New Yorker has seen in a long, long time. [1]

– Henry McLemore

---

[1] McLemore, Henry, "Duluth Boxer Has Great Left Hand; Both Boys Ready" (UP), *Duluth Herald*, July 11, 1933, sports section. Joe Frisco was a famous vaudevillian, comedian, and jazz dancer of the era. Lionel Strongfort (real name Max Unger) was a strongman who first became famous as the "Human Bridge" for supporting a bridge-like platform with an automobile and six passengers on his back, all purporting to weigh 3-1/2 tons. Later, he established a famous mail order course that touted the virtues of physical

****

The question boxing experts were asking on October 23, 1932, as Billy Petrolle strolled into the Pioneer Gym for his first workout in preparation for his November 4th lightweight championship fight, was the same one they asked before he injured his elbow. Could he make the 135-pound lightweight limit and still be strong enough to defeat Tony Canzoneri?

After reading a news article to the effect that the champion would likely defeat him because of weight difficulties, an edgy Petrolle, who usually let manager Hurley do all his talking, could not contain himself. "I read one story to the effect that Canzoneri has every advantage," said Billy, "but I know he can't hit as hard as I can, and I'd like to know when they quit taking punches into consideration. He also is to climb into the ring knowing that I beat and cut him up at 134-1/2 pounds two years ago.

"The majority is brushing me aside because they fear I can't do 135, but I'll cross them as well as Canzoneri. I weighed 145 when I started work last Friday and 141 yesterday. Poundage will come off gradually like that until I'm down to 134-1/2 the day of the fight.

"... Ask yourself whether Canzoneri could give Jimmy McLarnin three stiff fights and knock out Justo Suarez and a welterweight like Eddie Ran. If you do not think so, wager that if there is a knockout, Petrolle will score it. And don't let them tell you that I'm a broken down old man at 27."[2]

Canzoneri's camp was quick to point out Tony was not at his best against Petrolle in 1930. At the time, he just had engaged in hard battles with Benny Bass and Goldie Hess, and was still recovering. Against Hess, Tony suffered an ugly cut through his right eyebrow that had not entirely healed.

Though manager Sammy Goldman and trainer Lou Fink had begged him to cancel his first fight with Billy, Canzoneri stubbornly refused. The show was a benefit for the family of Paddy Harmon, the Chicago promoter. Tony told his handlers, "I'm going through with it. I know Petrolle is tough, but when Paddy Harmon was alive he made a lot of money for me putting on my fights. I wouldn't dream of turning down his lady. The fight is on."

Fink claimed that before the fight he had installed a skin-like coating over the cut, painted over it with pigment, and fashioned a new eyebrow from burnt cork until it appeared normal. Unfortunately for Canzoneri, a Petrolle left hook delivered in an early round made a direct hit on Fink's

---

fitness. Unger apparently walked the walk as he lived to a ripe old age of 92.

McLemore's "old 97" is a reference to a song entitled "the Wreck of the Old 97", a musical rendering about the legendary last ride of locomotive engineer Casey Jones, who crashed his train at full throttle going down a mountain attempting to make up time lost on the route by a prior engineer. Country western singer Vernon Dahlhart sold over one million copies of the song on a wide variety of record labels.

Petrolle pronounced his name "patrol." Ergo, McLemore's use of the phrase "the old Petrolle wagon."

[2] Grayson, Harry, "Canzoneri Talk Puts Petrolle on Ring Stump," *New York World-Telegram*, October 27, 1932, sports section.

Rembrandt creation and busted the wound wide open. Tony, bothered by the injury, took a beating the rest of the bout. Even so, the fight was close enough that one of the three officials gave him a slight edge in scoring.[3]

After the loss to Petrolle, Canzoneri never looked back. Instead, he assured himself a spot among the all-time greats by becoming the first man in boxing history to hold two world titles at the same time. In November 1930, Tony was crowned lightweight champ when he scored a first-round kayo over Al Singer. Five months later, he also acquired the junior welterweight title with a three-round knockout over Jackie (Kid) Berg.[4]

In addition to winning the aforementioned titles, he previously had held the featherweight championship and successfully defended his lightweight title twice and his junior-welterweight title four times. All told, in the 26 months since he first fought Petrolle, Canzoneri had won 17 of 20 fights against the elite of two divisions. His only losses during that period were to Sammy Fuller in a non-title bout at Boston in 1931 and to Johnny Jadick in two junior welter title bouts at Philadelphia earlier in 1932. Ringsiders had been quick to denounce all three of these verdicts as hometown decisions.[5]

---

[3] Igoe, Hype, "Billy Won't Sit Him Down, Says Tony," *New York Evening Journal*, November 1, 1932, p. 23.

[4] Some may dispute the contention that Canzoneri was the first person to hold two titles simultaneously by arguing that Ruby Robert Fitzsimmons held the middleweight titles and heavyweight titles at the same time. Fitzsimmons won the middleweight championship from Nonpareil Jack Dempsey on January 14, 1891, and later the heavyweight title from James J. Corbett on March 17, 1897. In between these two events, Fitz last defended his middleweight title by knocking out Dan Creedon on September 26, 1894, 2-1/2 years before he would defeat Corbett for the heavyweight title. After defeating Creedon, Ruby Robert lost interest in the middleweight title and concentrated on winning the heavier title. In the author's opinion, Fitzsimmons had for all intents and purposes abandoned the middleweight title when he defeated Corbett.

A potential sub-issue to this discussion centers on the question of just when did Fitz actually acquire the heavyweight championship. Confusion exists because for a time during this period, Corbett declared himself retired before having second thoughts about the matter and deciding to defend the title against Fizsimmons. In the middle of Corbett's period of indecision, Fitzsimmons claimed the championship by scoring a one-round knockout victory over Peter Maher on February 21, 1896.

A consequence of accepting the Fitzsimmons-Maher fight as part of heavyweight title lineage is that it wreaks havoc with present notions of who was heavyweight champion during this period and when was he the champion. The reason for this is that Fitzsimmons was disqualified in the eighth round in his very next fight against Sailor Tom Sharkey on December 2, 1896. If Fitzsimmons were to be regarded as champion by defeating Maher, then Sharkey should be regarded as champion for defeating Fitzsimmons and the Corbett-Fitzsimmons fight should not be regarded as having been a title fight at all.

In any event, even if one recognizes Fitzsimmons as a simultaneous two-time champion, Tony Canzoneri was without question the first title-holder who as champion actively defended multiple titles during his tenure as a holder of concurrent championships.

[5] Canzoneri won the junior-welterweight title from Jackie (Kid) Berg on April 23, 1931. He lost it to Johnny Jadick on January 18, 1932, and lost to Jadick again when he tried to regain it on July 18, 1932.

Any doubts about Petrolle's ability to make weight were removed at a special preliminary weigh-in conducted Tuesday (Nov. 1), three days before the fight. When Billy stepped onto the scales, the beam leveled at 136-1/2 pounds, just 1-1/2 pounds above the lightweight limit.

Petrolle said he would easily lose the extra weight through exercise and by "drying out" before the bout. He planned to scale a fraction less than 135 at the 1:30 weigh-in on the afternoon of the fight, eat a steak immediately afterward, and weigh about 138 when he entered the ring at 10 p.m.[6]

Even after the special weigh-in, scribes continued to disagree over how making 135 pounds would affect Petrolle. The *World-Telegram*'s Harry Grayson felt that, "after watching Billy closely for several days," he would "be as formidable as ever." Hype Igoe of the *Evening Journal* agreed. In his view, "Any man who arrives at 1-1/2 pounds above the title mark four days before the bout is going to make the weight and be strong."[7]

The *Daily News*' Paul Gallico saw the end result of the weight-reducing process differently than Grayson and Igoe. He believed Billy's performance could not help but be affected by the ordeal he just had endured:

> "When Shylock demanded his pound of flesh from Antonio, the Merchant of Venice, he meant to cut it from the region of the heart. When a fighter claims his pound of flesh from an opponent, he extracts it from approximately the same region. Beware of the fighter who has to make weight. He isn't a whole man ...
>
> "The human body is a delicate mechanism. Consider the slight stimuli needed to throw it out of gear – temperature, the failure of the sun to shine, a thought, the sight of something horrible. Consider likewise, then, the damage that must be done to the system by the effort of making an unnatural weight and the climax of that effort to be followed immediately by intense physical effort. Add to this the further harm to the system done by the hasty throwing into it of quantities of food in the effort to regain in hours what it took weeks of diet and labor to pare off ...
>
> "Once Petrolle gave Canzoneri a bad thrashing. But it wasn't at weight. Tonight the conditions are different. Canzoneri enters the ring as champion of the lightweight division. Petrolle challenges him to fight in that class. Canzoneri is a lightweight. Billy isn't. That's the entire handicap I would ever ask of any man. Sweat out, dry out, starve, labor, worry, upset the normal metabolism of the body. Throw every organ out of gear so that it no longer functions

---

[6] Grayson, title unavailable, *New York World-Telegram*, November 1, 1932, sports section.

[7] Grayson, "Petrolle Gives No Sign of Tilt with Poundage," *New York World-Telegram*, October 31, 1932, sports section. Igoe, "Tony Will Find Billy Strong at 135 Lbs.," *New York Evening Journal*, November 2, 1932, p. 21.

normally. Then get in the ring and fight me. Half my battle is won.

"When he is fighting those heavier loogans, when his heart and compact little body are sound, when he comes into the ring brimming with energy and whistles those steaming lefts for their heads, when his eye is clear and sharp and his senses acute so that the counters slip by his chin, a fraction of an inch from disaster, I pick Petrolle, my friends, against anybody whose chin he can reach. But at weight, and against the champion, how do I know which Petrolle is coming into the ring tonight?

"...You can gamble if you like. I'll stick to form and take the champion, the younger man, and the fellow who hasn't had to make weight."[8]

Odds that favored Canzoneri by as much as 2 to 1 a week before the bout narrowed to 7 to 5 when Petrolle, as he promised, weighed in at 134-1/2 pounds the day of the fight. In a rare occurrence, an informal poll of sportswriters revealed that a majority of their opinions differed with those of the oddsmakers. A review of articles from 16 New York boxing writers showed that six favored Billy as a likely victor, four thought Tony would win, while six hedged their bets and offered no opinion as to the outcome.[9]

Madison Square Garden officials were hoping for a near-capacity crowd. With tickets priced at a depression-reduced championship scale of $2.20, $5.50, and $11, a sellout would realize a gate of approximately $90,000. According to reports around ringside, both Canzoneri and Petrolle were receiving premiums for their services. Tony was guaranteed 40 percent of net receipts and Petrolle 17-1/2 percent. Normally for a fight at the Garden, a champion's share was 37-1/2 percent and a challenger's 12-1/2 percent.[10]

The pattern of the bout was set from the clang of the first bell. As expected, Petrolle came out fighting from a crouch and looking for an opportunity to push the attack. In contrast, Canzoneri stood upright, bouncing on his toes, hands held low, prepared to counter Billy's forward charges but also ready to lead with an occasional sally of his own.

[8] Gallico, Paul, "The Pound of Flesh," *New York Daily News*, November 4, 1932, sports section.
[9] Writers favoring Petrolle: Frank Menke of the *International News Service*; Hype Igoe of the *New York Evening Journal*; Francis Wallace of the *New York Daily Journal*; Richards Vidmer of the *New York Herald Tribune*; and Harry Grayson and Joe Williams of the *New York World-Telegram*. Writers favoring Canzoneri: Jack Kofoed of the *New York Evening Post*; Paul Gallico of the *New York Daily News*; Davis J. Walsh of the *International News Service*; and Dan Parker of the *New York Daily Mirror*. Writers expressing no opinion: James Dawson of the *New York Times*; Wilbur Wood of the *New York Sun*; Ed Frayne of the *New York American*; Damon Runyon of the *New York American*; Edward J. Neil of the *Associated Press*; and Bill Corum of the *New York Evening Journal*.
[10] Morris, William, "Around the Ring," *New York Evening Post*, November 5, 1932, sports section. Revenue realized by the Garden after federal was $2, $5, and $10 per ticket. The scale for a pre-depression championship show normally started at $20 or more for ringside.

Champion Tony Canzoneri and Petrolle sign contracts July 27, 1932, for their lightweight title match. Left to right: Canzoneri; his manager, Sammy Goldman; matchmaker Johnston; Hurley; and Petrolle.

Petrolle advances in an early round of his 15-round title tilt.

The first four rounds were hotly contested as Canzoneri scored to the head with both hands, and Petrolle blended two-handed body attacks with a random left or right to the head. Scoring was divided in these rounds, but by the end of the fourth, Tony had a one-round edge on most writers' cards.

Petrolle came on strong to win a majority of rounds five through eight. His best rounds in this stretch were the sixth and the eighth. In the sixth, he mixed his punches well, shaking up Tony with a left-right combination to the head and landing several lefts to the body. In the eighth, Billy at one point hooked with ten straight lefts to the body, leaving Canzoneri in some distress. Tony came back with a strong combination of lefts and rights near the end of the round, but Billy retained an edge for the round on most cards.

The two men split rounds nine and ten. Petrolle took the lead in the ninth with a two-fisted body attack, but his advantage was overtaken by two jolting rights followed by a dozen left hooks and jabs to the head delivered by Canzoneri with the skill of a master swordsman. Billy nullified Tony's attack in the tenth by pressuring him with left hooks to the body and by landing two left-right combinations which rattled Tony's head back and forth like a bouncing ball tethered to a short leash.

The fight was dead even after ten rounds. Of the 11 reporters whose accounts of the fight included round-by-round scoring, five at that stage scored the bout for Canzoneri, five for Petrolle, and one had it even.[11]

---

[11] Listed in this note is the scoring by rounds of the 11 boxing writers referred to in the text. Scoring as of the end of ten rounds is shown first followed by the scoring after the full 15 rounds. The author's account of the fight is taken both from the reports of these writers published the day after the fight and from a review of rounds one, six, eight, and ten through 15 of surviving film footage of the fight.

Writers giving Canzoneri the edge at the end of ten rounds: James Dawson of the *New York Times* (6-3-1 and 11-3-1); Ed Frayne of the *New York American* (4-3-3 and 8-4-3); Jack Kofoed of the *New York Evening Post* (5-4-1 and 9-5-1); Richard Vidmer of the *New York Herald Tribune* (7-1-2 and 11-2-2); and Frank Neil in collaboration with Alan Gould of the *Associated Press* (7-2-1; 12-2-1). Writers having Petrolle ahead at the end of ten rounds: Hype Igoe of the *New York Evening Journal* (6-3-1 and 6-8-1); Wilbur Wood of the *New York Sun* (5-4-1 and 5-9-2); Francis Wallace of the *New York Daily News* (6-3-1 and 6-7-2); Davis Walsh of the *International News Service* (6-4 and either 6-8-1 or 6-9 – Walsh is unclear about his scoring in the 14th round); and Nat Fleischer of *Ring Magazine* (5-3-2 and 5-8-2). Paul Gallico of the *New York Daily News* had the fight even at the end of ten rounds (3-3-4 and 8-3-4).

For those readers whose only access to footage of the Canzoneri-Petrolle fight is through the "Greatest Fights of the Century" version, which shows just the first, sixth, eighth, tenth and fifteenth rounds, the author suggests they turn off Marty Glickman's narration for the first four of these rounds and view the film without sound so they can form their own opinions as to who was winning the rounds shown. Apparently, the producers of this film only had footage from these rounds available when they made the film. Lacking the footage from most of the later rounds which Canzoneri dominated, the writers of the script necessarily had to anticipate the fight's outcome in their narration of this earlier footage. Consequently, in the author's opinion, the narration does not always reflect the action happening on the screen.

In round 11, the tide of battle turned in Canzoneri's favor. At the bell, both men came out, exchanging fierce lefts and rights. Petrolle let fly with a right uppercut that missed and paid the price when Tony shot home a solid right while Billy was still wide open. Before he had a chance to recover, Tony quickly pressed forward and methodically pot-shotted Billy almost at will with accurate and telling lefts and rights to head and body.

Petrolle weathered the storm, but was unable to regain his earlier form. As some had predicted, the strain of making weight seemed to rob Billy of his recuperative powers.

Canzoneri dominated the action and won the last five rounds on most scorecards. Every round after the 11th was much like the previous one as the rapidly fading Petrolle, with little sting left in his punches, plodded forward only to be met by Tony's faster and crisper punching.

When Petrolle returned to the corner at the end of the 12th round, Hurley asked, "How's the gas with you, Bill? Going all right?" Petrolle replied simply, "Going okay." Again, at the end of the next round Hurley inquired, "Only two more, Bill – can you make it?" This time, Billy merely looked at Jack and nodded his head to indicate a "yes" answer.[12]

In the final two rounds, it became obvious Petrolle's only chance to win was to knock out Canzoneri. His best chance came in the waning moments of the 15th round when a hard right staggered Tony for a moment, but by then Billy had neither the time nor the energy left to follow his advantage.

When the unanimous decision in favor of Canzoneri was announced, there was not a dissenting voice raised. Petrolle, obviously leg-weary at the finish, had a mass of facial bruises and a right eye nearly swollen shut. Canzoneri's face was unmarked, but his body showed multiple red marks from the beating it had received.

Francis Wallace, boxing writer for the *Daily News*, wrote: "It was a hard but practically bloodless fight – a fine exhibition of boxing and hitting by masters of the art. It lacked the explosive climax of a knockout but carried the continuous threat of one."[13]

Wallace's sports editor Paul Gallico agreed, and commented:

> "It has been a long time since there has been such an hour of honest effort on the part of two prizefighters in Madison Square Garden. There were no more than eight clinches at most during the entire 15 rounds. If there is any justification for boxing as a sport or a spectacle, it is contained in such a battle.

---

[12] Igoe, "Title Quest of Petrolle Is Over," *New York Evening Journal*, November 5, 1932, pp. 11, 13.

[13] Wallace, Francis, "Lightweight Champ Flags Wobbling Fargo Express," *New York Daily News*, p. 24, 27.

The champion wings a left to Petrolle's heart in the eighth round.

Petrolle (left) and Canzoneri play cat and mouse in the ninth round.

Petrolle (left) kept pace with Canzoneri for 10 rounds, but ran out of gas in the last five.

In the late rounds, Canzoneri dug deep into his bag of cute tricks. Here, a tired Petrolle is slow to react as Tony turns his back and dances away after landing a quick combination.

"For ten rounds it was an even fight. Up through the tenth I had scored three for Petrolle, three for Canzoneri and four even. It might have been a shade this way or a shade that, but there was little to choose between them. They were evenly matched, equally strong, skilled at defense, and lightning fast on the attack.

"It was the most explosive punching I have seen in many months. They threw them so fast that the eye could not follow the motion of the arm. You just saw gloves suddenly detonating, crisply and sharply."[14]

After the fight, Canzoneri was quick to acknowledge Petrolle gave him a tussle: "A tough old guy, I tell you. I don't want to meet a tougher one. I hit him with my best, yet he was squinting and swinging right up to the end. I could feel him slipping badly after the 11th, but he was still hoping to nail me with one good right.

"Don't forget that he is always a dangerous puncher. He was dangerous to the last bell, and one of the best punches he hit me with was a solid right to the chin in the last round. Outside of that his best punches were left hooks to the body."[15]

Billy tried to take a philosophical view, but had trouble hiding his disappointment. "I guess everyone could see I wasn't as strong as usual," he said afterward, "but I don't want to make an alibi. We were in there fighting for the lightweight title, and if I didn't want to fight at 135, I should not have taken the match. Tony's a great champion. I take my hat off to him. I hit him often enough. I felt fine at first and about as fast as usual, but I didn't have the stuff in my punch and my legs were gone after ten rounds.

"I'll never do 135 again. Jack Hurley wasn't in favor of my doing it, but I wanted to win a title if I could. They forget good fighters, but they remember champions. A title is about the only thing I could ask from boxing that it hasn't given me. But that fellow was stubborn. He didn't seem to want to go over when I nailed him.

"I made the weight two years ago. I thought I could do it again. I was wrong. It's back to the welters where I belong, I guess. I'll have to give them weight. I can do that. But I can't spot them my strength. I'll never be that silly again."[16]

Garden officials reported paid attendance at 17,183, gross receipts at $78,521, and net receipts at $69,973. It was later disclosed that, except for a major mix-up, the show would have been a sellout. Hundreds of choice

---

[14] Gallico, "The 'It' Was Out of Bill's Punches, The Old Gentleman Is Mortal" (subtitle), *New York Daily News*, November 6, 1923, sports section.

[15] Igoe, *op. cit.* Corum, Bill, "Sport – Yessir, He's Right Tony!" *New York Evening Journal*, November 5, 1932, sports section. Wood, Wilbur, "Petrolle Fades at Finish," *New York Sun*, November 5, 1932, sports section. Canzoneri's quote is a blending from all three sources.

[16] Wood, *op. cit.* Corum, *op. cit.* Igoe, *op. cit.* Petrolle's quote blends all three sources.

tickets placed with outside agencies were not returned to the box office in time for sale to the general public. As a result, many purchasers stayed away because of false reports that there were no seats left.[17]

Even so, with the Depression now nearing its bottom, gross receipts from the Canzoneri-Petrolle bout were not exceeded by a Garden indoor show for more than three years, until December 3, 1935, when the Joe Louis-Paolino Uzcudun fight drew $128,395.[18]

Following the fight, Hurley told Cubby Campbell via telephone that, although Petrolle's cheeks and nose were puffed from Canzoneri's jabs, Billy suffered no major bruises or cuts as he had in some of his other fights. Jack already had received several lucrative offers for Petrolle's services, and he expected Billy would be back in action as soon as he rested up.[19]

Returning to Duluth, Petrolle told Campbell he did not realize the extent of the ordeal he had endured to make weight until a few days after the bout: "It was the first fight I ever had that left me 'dog' tired afterward. I was too tired to eat that night, and I went right to bed after having a glass of ale. After all my other big fights, I never could sleep as the letdown always left me nervous. But that night I dropped off into a 'dead' slumber.

"I had breakfast – cakes, bacon and eggs, and milk – at eight o'clock, but at 11 I was hungry again. I had a full course spaghetti lunch, including soup, meatballs, spaghetti and topped off with good wine. At three o'clock, I was hungry again. I had a big steak with all the side fixings. I thought surely that would carry me through the day, but at seven that evening I was hungry again, so I tackled some more spaghetti. I went to bed early, but after a short nap I awoke and found myself hungry again. I sent down and munched a clubhouse sandwich and a glass of milk and went back to bed.

"The next morning, I was as hungry as ever and I had a good breakfast. At 11, I had my favorite dish of spaghetti again. Then along about two p.m., I had a mess of stew. It seemed that my body simply craved wet foods. Before leaving for the train late that afternoon I stepped on my scales and tipped the beam at 150 pounds. I could hardly believe my eyes, but tested the scales as I had done dozens of times before and found them true.

"When I got on the train that night, I ate a steak dinner and retired early. By ten p.m., I was up again and coaxed a sandwich out of the dining car steward. I was up early and had another substantial breakfast and had another spaghetti dinner upon reaching Chicago. I was finally 'fed up' when reaching home early Tuesday and consider myself back to normal again, although I'm considerably overweight.

---

[17] Igoe, *op. cit.* Borden, Eddie, "Along the Great Fight Way," *Ring Magazine*, January 1933, p. 42.
[18] Fleischer, Nat (editor), "Garden Promotions Under William F. Carey and James J. Johnston," *1958 Ring Record Book*, (Ring Book Shop, NY, NY, 1958), p. 84.
[19] Campbell, Cubby, "Cubby Campbell's Column," *Duluth News Tribune*, November 5, 1932, sport section.

"Another unusual post-fight incident is the stiffness of my muscles. After no other fight have I ever experienced this same feeling. The soreness didn't develop until about the second day after the fight, but it now seems that every 'bone' and muscle in my body is 'raw beef.' I don't recall being hurt at any time during the entire fight, so it couldn't have been the blows which brought on this soreness. It was probably due to straining the muscles in making the weight"[20]

The first offer Hurley accepted for Petrolle's next bout was from Jimmy Johnston to fight Bep van Klaveren of Holland at Madison Square Garden on January 20, 1933. Van Klaveren, who was the former 1928 Olympic featherweight champion, had been fighting professionally for 3-1/2 years. During that time he had won the European lightweight title and defended it successfully three times before losing it on a decision to Cleo Locatelli of Italy in his final bout before coming to the United States.

The Locatelli bout convinced Bep he was no longer strong at the 135-pound limit, and he came to the U. S. billed as a welterweight. Victorious in his first three New York contests, the "Flying Dutchman" impressed critics as the best European welterweight to cross the Atlantic since the arrival of former world champ Ted (Kid) Lewis more than 15 years earlier.

Hurley arrived in New York a week before the fight. On January 15, he visited Madison Square Garden to check on ticket sales when, on his way out, he passed the office of Garden president Bill Carey. Carey, who was meeting with his executive board to discuss ticket prices for the coming year, spotted Jack in the hallway and waved him inside.

Although the price of a ringside seat for an average non-title fight at the Garden had already been reduced once during 1932 from $9.10 to $5.75, attendance at Garden shows during the depression continued to fall dramatically. The proposal under discussion by the Garden board was whether or not ticket prices should be reduced even further.[21]

Ed Frayne of the *New York American* happened to be at the Garden office at the time and reported the next day on what happened at the meeting:

> "Incredible though it may sound, it was a fight manager who helped Carey decide upon the reduction at a meeting of Garden executives on Sunday afternoon. Carey, a strong believer in lower

---

[20] Campbell, *op. cit.*, November 13, 1932, sports section.

[21] The prices of $5.75 and $9.10 were typical prices for ringside seats at ordinary non-title Garden shows in the periods before Carey's determination to uniformly set non-title prices at $3.30 during the 1933 indoor season. In earlier periods, the Garden had tended to price each fight individually according to its estimated worth rather than at a uniformly set price. At $9.10 for ringside, which was the most typical price before 1932, other tickets would scale at around $3.30 and $5.75 for side arena and floor sections, and $2.20 for the entire balcony. At the $5.75 ringside price adopted during 1932, other tickets would scale at around $2.20 and $3.30 for side arena and floor sections, and $1.10 for the entire balcony.

prices, was being outargued when Jack Hurley of Duluth, manager of Petrolle, was announced. Hurley was indignant: "'I think you people are making a terrible mistake, Mr. Carey. I was under the impression the prices for our fight were to be $3 ringside, plus tax. I think it's an outrage to charge more than that in these times.'

"Carey, taken by surprise, looked at his dumbfounded executives, laughed and ended the discussion. 'That will be all, fellows,' he chuckled. 'The new scale will be $3.30 for all fights, and have the box office make rebates on all tickets sold for this week's bouts.'"[22]

Unfortunately, van Klaveren suffered a broken bone in his right hand three days before the fight. In an effort to salvage the card, Johnston offered Hurley seven substitute opponents: Eddie Ran, Paulie Walker, Eddie (Kid) Wolfe, Andy Callahan, Baby Joe Gans, Johnny Jadick, and Ted Yarwitz.

Hurley would have none of the fighters on the list. Petrolle had already beaten Ran. Walker, at 148 pounds, was too heavy. Wolfe and Callahan were not good enough drawing cards. Gans and Jadick had styles that would not make for an interesting match. Yarwitz was a jabber who fought like "a circus clown" and would not stand up and fight. As a result, Johnston dropped Billy from the card and arranged on two days notice for Hans Birkie and Jimmy Braddock to face off in a substitute main event.[23]

Although from Johnston's perspective Hurley's actions were unreasonable, Jack saw things differently. He and Petrolle were the ones with the most to lose. Billy had told Jack 1933 would be his last year in boxing unless he was able to win a world title. Petrolle was still recognized in Eastern circles as the leading welterweight contender. For him to be happy, every match Jack accepted had to be made with Billy's goal in mind.

Hurley in fact was close to landing a title bout for Petrolle. After a year of cashing in on the welterweight championship with a series of non-title bouts, Doc Kearns, manager of champion Jackie Fields, was ready to have his charge defend the title. Doc was weighing two offers – one from matchmaker Nate Lewis to box Billy in Chicago and another to meet Young Corbett III at San Francisco. A poor showing by Billy at this critical stage would take him out of the running and end his title hopes for all time.[24]

---

[22] Frayne, Ed, (as quoted in the *Duluth Herald* on January 24, 1933) *New York American*, January 16, 1933, sports section. The scale was reported as $3.30 ringside, $1.10 and $2.20 for side arena and floor sections, and 55 cents for the entire balcony. "Garden Prices Are Cut," *New York Times*, January 16, 1933, p. 20.

[23] Igoe, "Hurley, Petrolle's Pilot, Tough 'Un to Satisfy," *New York Evening Journal*, January 19, 1933, sports section. Dawson, James P., "Petrolle Bout Off; Rival Boxer Hurt," *New York Times*, January 19, 1933, p. 22. Wood, "Braddock Will Box Birkie," *New York Sun*, January 19, 1933, p. 27.

[24] Fitzgerald, Eugene, "The Sport Whirligig," *Fargo Forum*, March 5, 1933, sports section.

Hurley had been around long enough to know that many an applecart had been upset by a manager's easy acceptance of a late substitute. Only a year earlier, he himself had made the mistake of allowing Joe Sekyra, who was thought to be washed-up, to be inserted as a last-minute opponent for Retzlaff. The veteran soundly thrashed Charley, who then was just one fight away from a big money main event at the Garden. The loss to Sekyra unnerved Retzlaff and derailed what had looked to be a promising career.

Besides, Hurley did not trust Johnston, who had not been nicknamed the "Boy Bandit" without reason. Friends told Jack that Jimmy had "openly bragged he would get Billy Petrolle licked." In Hurley's opinion, Johnston's selection of substitutes, "none of (whom) could draw their breath at the box office ... with their safety-first styles," only confirmed that Jimmy was out to either embarrass Billy or see that he was defeated.[25]

Hurley even harbored a suspicion that Johnston, who was a close friend of Sammy Goldman, had stacked the deck against Billy in the Canzoneri bout. Shortly before the fight, Jimmy brought commissioner John J. Phelan to the dressing room to convince Hurley to allow Tony to wear a set of five-ounce Sol Levinson gloves that had been custom-made for Canzoneri's small hands. Billy was forced to wear the regulation six-ounce Everlast gloves because his hands were too large for the Sol Levinsons.

In addition, Johnston had without explanation rearranged the order of fights at the last minute so the main event came on at 9:10 p.m. instead of the announced time of 10. Hurley suspected Jimmy's reason for the change was related to Billy's weight-making ordeal. Johnston likely figured that limiting the length of Petrolle's rest after he had just finished his first full meal in a week would allow less time for Billy's vitality to return.[26]

---

[25] Hurley, Jack, "Shadow Boxing," *Fargo Forum*, February 17, 1935, sports section.

[26] *Ibid*. Hurley also had his suspicions about two of the officials for the Petrolle-Canzoneri fight, referee Gunboat Smith and Judge George Kelly. These men had voted for Jack Sharkey in the much-reviled split decision over Max Schmeling which gave Sharkey the heavyweight title five months earlier. Johnston had formerly managed Gunboat Smith and was still on friendly terms with him. Johnston also had owned part of Sharkey's contract. Sharkey was still Jimmy's friend and had helped him out by signing to fight Mickey Walker and Primo Carnera for Johnston rather than for Madison Square Garden when Jimmy was feuding with the Garden in 1931.

Hurley suspected Johnston may have influenced the commission's choice of Smith and Kelly as officials and through them the outcome of the Sharkey-Schmeling fight. Jack believed it was more than just a coincidence that these same two men had been appointed to judge the Canzoneri-Petrolle contest. Although as it turned out, he had no quarrel with the verdict rendered in the bout, he had suspicions that if the fight had been closer at the end of 15 rounds, then the presence of these same officials might have worked to Petrolle's detriment.

Hurley pulled no punches concerning Johnston in his "Shadow Boxing" column:

> "I'll say one thing for Johnston, he is very strong politically and doesn't stop at anything, where he is trying to protect his or his friends' interests ... Johnston wasn't taking any chance of Petrolle having the best of it. He was protecting his friend, Sammy Goldman, manager of Canzoneri, who is one of the few managers

And so, rather than face a second-tier replacement who could do little to further Petrolle's title ambitions, Hurley decided to wait for van Klaveren's hand to heal. In Jack's mind, the Flying Dutchman was the perfect opponent for Petrolle. Like Eddie Ran and Billy Townsend before him, Bep was a new face who had caught the fancy of New York's boxing public. Hurley had seen van Klaveren fight and was certain his crowd-pleasing, walk-in style was made to order for Billy's aggressive counter-punching attack.

If Billy could be the first U. S. fighter to defeat van Klaveren, Hurley's "Old Man" would likely rekindle the excitement generated by his victories over Ran, Townsend, and Battalino and earn a shot at the welterweight title.

As soon as the Petrolle-van Klaveren match was called off, Hurley asked Johnston for the $250 expense money which the contract stipulated. Canzoneri had been paid expenses in the same situation when Billy's elbow injury necessitated a postponement of their fight, and Jack was of the opinion the present instance should be treated the same way.

Johnston denied Hurley's request, arguing that his refusal to accept a substitute relieved the Garden of responsibility. Jack pointed out Petrolle's fights had netted the Garden $400,000 in receipts over the past two years, making him the facility's No. 1 meal ticket. When this approach failed, Hurley "blew up" and vowed to "get even" by making sure Billy "would never fight in the Garden again." No one took Jack seriously at the time, but later events proved he meant every word, because Petrolle never did.[27]

At the same time he was bickering with Hurley, Johnston was experiencing even greater difficulties in maintaining control over Madison Square Garden's most precious asset, the heavyweight division. While the Garden still held the contract for champion Jack Sharkey to defend the title on or before June 30, 1933, the Boston sailor's two leading challengers, Max Schmeling and Max Baer, had refused to sign the Garden's contract for an elimination battle and instead agreed to fight for another promoter.

At the beginning of the 1932 fall season, Johnston's plans had called for Baer to meet Carnera in November and for Schmeling to face Young

---

stringing along with him today. You might ask why he was allowed to get away with this. Well, this is a funny business, and if Petrolle or any other fighter that I hope to manage wanted to show in New York State, it was best not to defy the commission, or they would suspend us for so long it would put us out of business.

"If you ask me or anyone else connected with boxing what's wrong with the game in New York, I can only give you one answer – Jimmy Johnston. How long they will tolerate him and his ethics is problematical. New York City hasn't one drawing card today. Where are the Singers, Goldsteins, Bergs, Chocolates, and Jebys? Johnston got them all bumped off and bragged about it."

Hurley, Jack, "Shadow Boxing," *Fargo Forum*, February 17, 1934, sports section.

[27] Campbell, *op. cit.,* September 26, 1933, sports section. Fitzgerald, "Keeping in Line," *Fargo Forum*, October 12, 1933, sports section.

Stribling in a warm-up bout in February. The winners were to then fight for the right to challenge Sharkey during the summer of 1933.[28]

Johnston's agenda unraveled soon after Schmeling's victory over Mickey Walker on September 26, 1932. After the fight, Max and his manager Joe Jacobs flatly refused Johnston's offers for bouts with other challengers. In their opinion, Schmeling's victory over Walker entitled Max, as the former champion who had lost the title to Sharkey by a questionable decision, to a rematch with the champion without having to face further opposition.

The next day, Johnston returned to Jacobs with a contract offering Schmeling ten percent for the Sharkey fight as opposed to the champion's 42-1/2 percent. When Jacobs saw the offer, he exploded: "You think you're going to club Schmeling into fighting for what you want to give him, do you? Well, Mr. Wise Guy ... what would you say if I told you that I've already closed to fight Baer in June? Well, I have. How do you like that?"

Jacobs explained to reporters Schmeling was angry at Garden president Bill Carey for an incident which occurred before Max's fight with Walker. Schmeling learned Carey had visited Mickey's dressing room just before he entered the ring and said: "Mickey, knock him into my arms, my boy." Afterward, Max had words with Bill and told Jacobs he had no intention of boxing for the Garden again while Carey and Johnston were in power.[29]

Johnston had gone into the meeting with Jacobs believing that with champion Sharkey under contract he was holding all the aces. Apparently, Jacobs' revelation that Baer's managers already had signed to meet Schmeling shook up the old Boy Bandit more than he let on, because that same evening he sent a wire directly to Baer in California.

The telegram informed Baer that Johnston would send him transportation to New York if he would ignore his present managers and allow himself to be placed under the control of Jimmy's brother, Charley Johnston, "who will make you world's champion." The wire went on to say that Charley "will also attend to your managerial duties, as well as legally attend to your other managers." It ended by requesting Baer to "Answer immediately."

As a publicity ploy, Johnston's telegram was a smashing success. Sports pages in every paper across the country featured extensive coverage about Jimmy's attempted theft of Max Baer. Reporters who were offended openly reviled Johnston as deserving of the "all-time, All-America championship" for "18-karat effrontery and brazen disregard of pugilistic, legal and moral conventions." Those who refused to take the matter seriously viewed it as just another annoying example of the Boy Bandit's crude sense of humor.[30]

---

[28] Neil, Edward J., "Schmeling and Baer Included in Ring Plans" (AP), *Fargo Forum*, September 28, 1932, sports section.

[29] Frayne, "Schmeling to Fight Baer in June, Joe Says," *New York American*, October 20, 1932, pp. 21, 23.

[30] Frayne, "Jimmy Makes Bid on Behalf of his Brother," *New York American*, October 21, 1933, p. 17. Runyon, Damon, "Mr. Johnston Is Having Fun with Poor Old Scribes," *New*

As a device calculated to induce Baer and Schmeling to sign with the Garden or otherwise tangibly benefit the Garden or Johnston, however, the telegram was an utter failure. Its only effect was to further alienate Max and convince Baer's managers to accept Jacobs' offer for a Schmeling fight and to help Joe find a promoter other than the Garden to stage it.

The man they came up with was Jack Dempsey, the old Manassa Mauler. Dempsey already had promoted two of Baer's fights in Reno, Nevada with movie star Wallace Beery. While Beery was not interested in promoting in New York, Jack enlisted Big Tim Mara as financial backer. Mara was well known as a successful bookmaker and owner of the New York Giants football team. By March 1933, Dempsey and Mara had targeted early June as the best time to stage the Baer-Schmeling fight at Yankee Stadium.[31]

Dempsey's reasons for going up against Johnston were founded in a desire to help his friends and to protect his own interests. While serving as Baer's promoter, Jack became close to Max and his manager Ancil Hoffman. As payment for his help in advancing Baer's career, they gave Dempsey a share in Max's contract. Jimmy's move to take control was therefore a direct threat to Jack's economic well-being.[32]

In addition, Dempsey had no particular liking for Johnston. On Jack's first trip east as an unknown fighter in 1915, Billy Roche, a respected referee of the era, tried to introduce the young westerner to Johnston as a likely prospect. Jimmy, then New York's leading matchmaker, was "too busy" to talk to Dempsey. Needless to say, this experience left an impression which remained with Jack the rest of his life.[33]

Losing the heavyweight division's two best attractions to Dempsey and Mara left Johnston in a tough situation. Under Sharkey's Garden contract, Jimmy was required to furnish a challenger's name to Jack by June 1 and schedule the fight for no later than June 30. Failure to meet either deadline would release the champion from the contract and make him a free agent.

Johnston could sign Sharkey to meet Carnera, but the champion had already beaten Primo once in better economic times two years earlier, and the fight had barely drawn a net of $100,000. There was little reason to believe a second fight would draw much more, if any, unless fans could be

---

York American, October 24, 1933, p. 17. Frayne was the reporter who took offense at Johnston's actions. Runyon viewed it as just business as usual for the Boy Bandit.

[31] The two fights Dempsey promoted with Beery were Fourth of July extravaganzas at a racetrack in Reno. Baer lost to Paolino Uzcudun in 1931 and defeated King Levinsky in 1932 with both battles going a full 20 rounds. Interestingly enough, these two fights were among the last major matches of the "modern era" to actually go more than 15 rounds.

[32] Dempsey's financial interest in Baer's contract was kept quiet at the time or else Jack would not have been allowed to promote the Baer-Schmeling fight by the New York State Athletic Commission. According to his last autobiography, Jack owned a seven-percent interest in Baer's earnings. Dempsey, Jack, with Barbara Piatelli Dempsey, "Dempsey," (Harper and Row, New York, 1977), p. 243.

[33] Dempsey, with Piatelli Dempsey, pp. 43-4.

convinced Carnera had improved. Apart from Baer or Schmeling, credible candidates for a build-up fight with Primo were in short supply.

Johnston chose New Jersey heavyweight Ernie Schaaf to fill the breach as Primo's opponent in a Garden "elimination" bout on February 10, 1933. Although most experts thought Schaaf had already been eliminated when Max Baer beat him decisively six months earlier, Ernie resurrected his career by placing himself under the management of Jimmy's brother Charley. This arrangement qualified Schaaf as "family" and therefore as an ideal contender in the eyes of the Garden matchmaker.

As expected, Carnera defeated Schaaf by stopping him in the 13th round. Afterward, Ernie lapsed into a coma and died in a New York hospital from a brain injury. Writers were united in the opinion that the beating he received from Baer earlier, as much as Primo's blows, had caused Schaaf's death.

After the Carnera-Schaaf bout, Johnston signed Primo and Sharkey to a heavyweight title bout to take place June 29, 1933, at Long Island Bowl, three weeks after Dempsey's Baer-Schmeling match. In an effort to add luster to the event, Johnston announced that part of the proceeds would be donated to Mrs. William Randolph Hearst's Free Milk Fund for Babies.

Meanwhile, misfortune continued to plague Petrolle's dream of winning a world title. San Francisco promoters outbid Chicago's Nate Lewis in the competition to land a welterweight title fight. On February 22, Young Corbett III, of Fresno, California, became champion by winning a ten-round decision from Jackie Fields at San Francisco.

The effect of Corbett's win was to shift the locus of interest in the division from Chicago and points east, where Fields was based, to California where the new champion lived. From a West Coast perspective, a match in California between the new champion and Jimmy McLarnin, who had begun his pro career in Oakland, was seen as "a natural." As a result, any hope Petrolle had for a title bout was put on hold until after Corbett's defense against McLarnin, which was set for Los Angeles in May 1933.[34]

During this same period, events of far more importance to the country than the sport of boxing were unfolding on the national political and economic scene. On March 4, 1933, a worried nation, in the midst of a financial panic, watched in hopeful anticipation as Franklin D. Roosevelt took the oath of office to become President of the United States.

Pent-up anxiety caused by three years of high unemployment, depreciated asset values, and 5,000 bank failures had come to a head in February when the governor of Michigan declared an eight-day banking

---

[34] McLarnin did have a couple of semi-pro fights at his birthplace of Vancouver, B. C., before moving to California with his manager Pop Foster in January 1924. These took place at Jack Allen's gym while Allen was in California with his fighter, Vic Foley. Allen had left the gym in the hands of former Australian heavyweight, Jim Tracey, who was living in Vancouver at the time. Tracey held a couple of semi-pro shows at the gym in December 1923 and re-matched McLarnin with a couple of his former amateur foes.

holiday to save his state's two largest banks from ruin. Soon, the hysteria became nationwide as panicked depositors demanded their money all at once, and cash-strapped banks shut down their operations in all 48 states.

On March 5, 1933, the new president declared a four-day national banking holiday and ordered a special session of Congress to address the crisis. On March 9, Congress passed an emergency bill calling for the banks to reopen as soon as federal inspectors declared them financially secure. On March 12, Roosevelt, in the first of his many radio fireside chats, explained to an information-hungry nation what was being done and why.

On March 13, banks in the country's major cities started to re-open. Within weeks, most of the federal inspections had been completed and two-thirds of the nation's banks were adjudged to be sound. Afterward, depositors returned and, for the first time since the start of the Depression, banks began to take in more deposits than they paid out in withdrawals.

Although Roosevelt's election and his administration's efficient response to its first crisis restored a measure of confidence, the real start of the nation's recovery was yet to come. The economy would continue its downward course until later in the year when unemployment would reach a high of 25 percent and industrial output a low at 50 percent of its 1929 peak. Even then, pre-depression levels of employment and production would not be restored until after the start of World War II in 1941.

With his options limited by van Klaveren's injury in New York, the prevailing welterweight situation in California, and the sad state of the economy everywhere else, Hurley accepted an offer from Nate Lewis for Petrolle to meet Barney Ross at the Chicago Stadium on March 22, 1933. Since Ross was a lightweight, Hurley was forced to agree that Billy could weigh no more than 138 pounds in order to make the match.

The reason Hurley accepted the bout under such terms was that it offered the only lucrative payday available. As a local star who had captured the imagination of Chicago's boxing public, Ross was one of the few lighter division boxers anywhere in the distressed economic climate of 1933 who could still attract a decent gate for a non-title bout.

Chicago, too, was experiencing hard times. Although the Stadium's boxing showed a small operating profit during 1932, overall revenues were not enough to pay overhead, and the corporation lapsed into receivership. To defray expenses while a new owner was being sought, the receiver appointed an operating company to rent out the stadium. Pursuant to the terms of this temporary arrangement, the operating company required renters to post money to eliminate the possibility of loss to the Stadium.[35]

In the midst of this bad news, the emergence of Ross was a breath of fresh air to Chicago boxing fans. A 1929 national Golden Gloves champ,

---

[35] Macdonald, Sandy, "Hurley Demands Salary 'Cut' for Stadium Job" (subtitle), *Duluth Herald*, January 27, 1933, sports section.

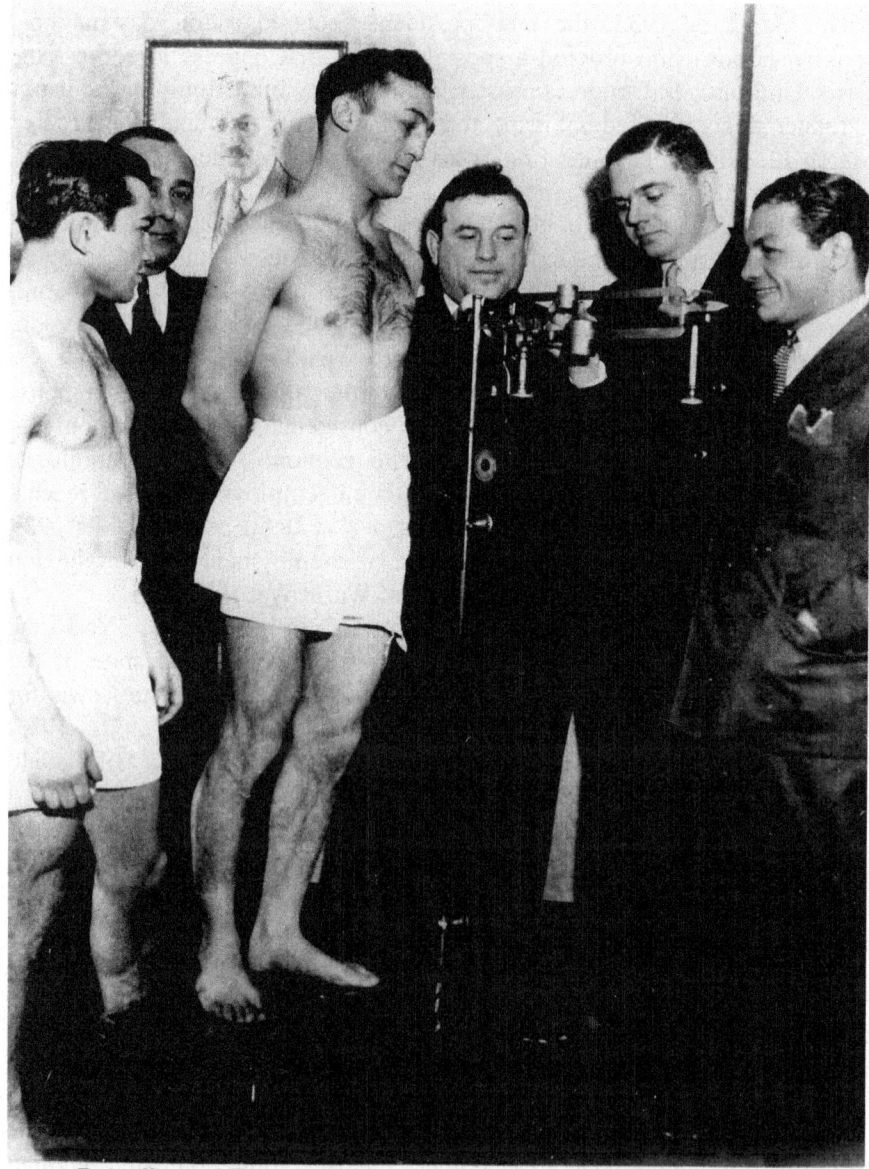

Petrolle and Barney Ross weigh in for their March 22, 1933 elimination battle at Chicago as champion Tony Canzoneri (right) watches. Officiating are commissioners Packey McFarland (left) and Joe Triner. The man between Ross and Billy is unidentified.

Barney came into prominence as a pro by defeating Ray Miller in August 1932. Over the next year, Ross followed up with wins over Goldie Hess, Johnny Farr, Johnny Datto, and Bat Battalino. By the time he signed to box Petrolle in March 1933, Barney had compiled a record of 42 wins, two losses, and two draws, and was rated as the leading lightweight contender.

Ross' bouts at the Stadium against Battalino and Hess had attracted over 11,000 customers each and gates of more than $20,000. Matchmaker Lewis scaled seating at the Stadium for the Petrolle-Ross bout so a full house would realize receipts of over $30,000. Realistic estimates predicted a turnout at the fight of 15,000 fans and a gate in excess of $25,000. As added incentive for both Ross and potential patrons, Lewis promised Barney a lightweight title bout with Canzoneri if he could defeat Petrolle.

Ross did not disappoint his Windy City followers. Boxing beautifully, Barney kept Petrolle from setting himself to throw his vicious left hooks. When Billy tried to punch, Barney met him with stinging left jabs as fast "as a serpent's tongue." When Petrolle backed off and waited for an opening, Ross moved ahead with piston-like combinations that overwhelmed Billy before he could launch a counter-attack.[36]

At the end of ten rounds, the officials awarded a unanimous decision to Ross as 14,068 onlookers who had paid $25,698 shouted in approval. After deducting expenses, the operating company realized a profit of $3,000.[37]

Canzoneri, who came from New York to see the bout, agreed Barney was "a good man," and that "he out-boxed Billy and hurt him several times." Tony also told Nate Lewis he "would be glad to meet [Ross] for the title."[38]

Three months later, on June 22, 1933, Ross won a ten-round decision and the title from Canzoneri at Chicago. A disappointing crowd of 11,204 paid gross receipts of $46,306 and net receipts of approximately $36,000. This time, the result was disastrous for Lewis and the operating company. After paying guarantees of $30,000 to Canzoneri and $7,200 to Ross, as well as other expenses, the promoters lost nearly $10,000.[39]

If the boxing business was in bad shape in New York and Chicago, things were even worse in Minnesota when Hurley returned to the Gopher State in March 1933 after the Ross-Petrolle bout.

At Minneapolis, Hurley's former mentor Mike Collins and his partner Jim McCarthy surrendered their franchise in May 1932 after a year of losses. After that, Collins had kept busy hustling up odd jobs. Among other

---

[36] Fry, Kenneth, D., "Ross Not Great Boxer; Will Do for Time Being" (UP), *Duluth Herald*, March 23, 1933, sports section.
[37] Murphy, Mike, "Chicago Lad Derails Fast Fargo Express," *Chicago Daily News*, March 23, 1933, p. 18.
[38] Dunkley, Charles, "Chicago Scrapper Outboxes Billy in Elimination Bout" (AP), *Duluth News Tribune*, March 23, 1933, sports section.
[39] AP Report, *New York Sun*, June 23, 1933, sports section. Frayne, "$30,000 Guarantee" (subtitle), *New York American*, July 8, 1933, sports section.

Ross fends off Petrolle's left jab and launches a counter of his own.

Barney ducks nimbly as Billy fires a left hook intended for the body.

things, Mike booked a Northwest exhibition tour for Carnera which had to be canceled before it started when Primo became homesick for his native Italy. Another Collins' project during this lean period was a lecture tour showing old-time fight films to boxing fans in small Minnesota towns.[40]

After Collins and McCarthy gave up the franchise, boxing in Minneapolis lay dormant until Billy Hoke and Frank McCormick took a run at promoting in October 1932. In the six months which followed, they staged just three shows and lost money on each one.

In St. Paul, Johnny Salvator ran shows grossing a total of $60,000 in 1931-'32 and lost $7,000. The next season, Salvator drastically scaled down his shows and managed to stay out of the red for the year by offering less costly but still pleasing local talent. Even so, he had to borrow funds to make up the 1932 deficit so he could continue to make payments on the Big Sandy Lake property he had mortgaged when he bought the franchise.[41]

Salvator drew his largest crowd of the 1933 winter season on March 7 during the bank holiday when he allowed fans to attend even if they lacked currency. In addition to cash receipts of $2,585, Johnny accepted in trade a quarter of beef; a case of malt syrup; separate orders for a woman's dress and a pair of shoes; four bushels of potatoes; eight pounds of butter; ten dozen eggs; ten neckties; $5.50 in groceries; a large number of post-dated checks; and $173 in IOUs. A crowd of 3,132 paying customers attended.[42]

The most successful Minnesota promoter was Phil Terk. Duluth boxing was by no means flourishing, but Terk adjusted to the depression early on and reduced the scope of his shows accordingly. For a six-month period during 1932, Phil stopped his boxing programs altogether. In the early months of 1933, he hit upon a formula of presenting small bi-weekly cards which created fan interest by using mostly young, inexpensive talent focusing on action fights rather than star attractions.

Whereas receipts for Terk and Hurley's cards in the 1929-'31 period normally ranged between $4,000 and $7,000 (save for special attractions like Jack Dempsey), gates for shows in 1932-'33 ranged from $800 to $1,500. For these events, Terk reduced both his ticket prices and his costs. Typically during this period, Phil paid main-event fighters $100 to $250, depending on his ability to draw fans into the auditorium. If a boxer could not fight for those amounts, then Phil could not afford to use him.[43]

Terk also benefited from the fact he and Hurley had opened a large billiard room and café/cigar store called "The Ringside" in conjunction with the boxing franchise. This business was primarily Phil's responsibility, and

---

[40] Macdonald, *Duluth Herald*, December 2, 1932, sports section (Carnera tour). Hurley, *op. cit.*, April 2, 1933, sports section (lecture tour).

[41] Shave, Ed L., "The Sport Trail," *St. Paul Daily News*, April 29, 1933, sports section.

[42] "Might Not Be a Bad Idea, John" (A.P.), *Fargo Forum*, March 9, 1933, sports section.

[43] Macdonald, "Game Booming Here" (subtitle), *Duluth Herald*, March 9, 1933, sports section.

Promoter Salvator trades tickets for produce during the bank holiday.

Retzlaff kayoed by King Levinsky in Chicago, nine days before his bout with Art Lasky in St. Paul.

Retzlaff, circa 1933.

its existence afforded Terk both a steady income and the flexibility to cut back on his boxing shows to fit the lean times.[44]

Hurley's main contribution to Salvator's St. Paul operation was to make Charley Retzlaff available for a bout against Minneapolis' pride and joy, Art Lasky, on May 12, 1933. Since his embarrassing kayo loss to Isidoro Gastanaga in August 1932, Retzlaff had regained some of his lost luster by running off an unbeaten string of six bouts, including wins over relatively well-known fighters like Tom Heeney, Jack Roper, and Walter Cobb.

Retzlaff had won the Minnesota heavyweight championship in March 1932 by stopping Dick Daniels, and a title defense was overdue. Salvator was counting heavily on the Retzlaff-Lasky showdown to register a profit so he could make payments on his debts. Based on early ticket sales, he anticipated gate receipts between $8,000 and $10,000. To stimulate further interest, he even ordered a championship belt to present to the winner.

Eight days before the show, Salvator's plans suffered a setback when King Levinsky unexpectedly kayoed Retzlaff in the first round at Chicago. Charley claimed Levinsky landed a lucky punch and that the experience made him more determined than ever to defeat Lasky to prove he was not a has-been. Even so, the defeat dampened interest in Johnny's program.

As fate would have it, the match was "one of the most vicious ring encounters of all Minnesota boxing history." After six rounds of battling, Charley redeemed his honor and kayoed Lasky with a right to the jaw.

Since it followed in the wake of a dismal showing against Levinsky, Retzlaff's effort was of no help to Salvator. Net receipts after deducting ten percent for state taxes came to about $4,200. Payment of Charley's 30 percent, Lasky's 25 percent, and the arena's ten percent left Johnny with $1,470 to take care of prelim fighters, railroad fares, advertising, tickets, help, and other expenses. As a result, Salvator lost money again.[45]

On June 1, 1933, Hurley left Duluth for New York to report on the June 8th Baer-Schmeling fight for his "Ring Rations" syndicated column. Like a majority of experts, Jack thought Schmeling would defeat Baer. While admitting that Baer was a big, tough, hard puncher, Hurley felt Schmeling's systematic body attack would wear Baer down and leave him vulnerable to the German's sharpshooting right cross in the later rounds.[46]

When Hurley arrived at New York, it was apparent the fight had caught on, and attendance would be on a par with a world championship bout. Promoter Dempsey was everywhere, racing from camp to camp, shaking hands, selling tickets, making public appearances at horse shows and amateur fight cards, and even sparring one round each with both Schmeling

---

[44] Shave, *op. cit.*, December 14, 1932, sports section.
[45] Shave, "Any Time, Any Place Is Challenge," *St. Paul Daily News*, May 13, 1933, sports section.
[46] Hurley, "Ring Rations," *Fargo Forum*, June 4, 1933, sports section.

Promoter Jack Dempsey and his fighter, Max Baer.

A pale-skinned Dempsey spars with Maxes Schmeling (left) and Baer (right) to publicize their fight which Jack was staging with Tim Mara.

and Baer during visits to their training quarters.

The contrast between the two fighters was obvious in these mini-bouts with Dempsey. Schmeling took his session seriously and traded blow for blow with the Manassa Mauler until Jack tired at the end. At Baer's camp the next day, the scene was quite different as "Madcap Maxie" laughed and clowned throughout while Dempsey spent most of the time chasing him around the ring. Only in the last ten seconds did Baer get serious and cut loose, landing a left hook to the stomach that doubled Jack over.[47]

Baer's casual attitude raised doubts in Dempsey's mind whether Max would be ready for Schmeling. The following day Jack returned to Baer's camp to convince him to buckle down and get serious. Standing on a platform next to the ring, Dempsey coached Baer to move forward with his chin down and bang Schmeling's body with both hands. Jack's plan was for Baer to wear Schmeling out and deny him room to land his deadly right.[48]

Although at the time Dempsey's coaching was thought to be just another effort at pre-fight ballyhoo, Baer's performance against Schmeling proved Jack's lessons must have been effective. For one of the few times in his career, Baer put clowning aside and fought according to a plan. Mixing his punches and pacing himself beautifully, Baer pressured Schmeling for most of the fight, waited for him to tire, and then pounded him relentlessly with rights and lefts in the tenth round to score a knockout.

A crowd of 55,000 fans paid gross receipts of over $244,000, and a net of $201,000, to see the fight. Afterward, Edward J. Neil, of the Associated Press, described the fight as "one of the greatest upsets that the modern ring has seen." Neil termed Baer "another Jack Dempsey" whose knockout of Schmeling was administered "with such savagery as the ring hasn't seen since the departure of the old 'Man Mauler'" himself.[49]

Hurley was as excited as Neil. He called Baer "a new star ... who bids fair to put boxing back on the same plane as it was when Jack Dempsey occupied the heavyweight throne ... Everything goes with Baer, the same as it used to go with Dempsey. He considers fighting a rough and ready business and thinks the rules should be made accordingly."[50]

On June 16, Hurley announced Dempsey and Baer were teaming up to go on a barnstorming which would include appearances in St. Paul and Duluth June 22 and 23. In both cities, Max would spar with one of his stablemates in an exhibition which Dempsey would referee. For each show, Baer's entourage was to receive $3,500 plus $300 in travel expenses.

---

[47] Neil, "Mauler Pokes Baer, Worried His Partners" (AP), *Duluth News Tribune*, May 29, 1933, sports section.
[48] Neil, "Dempsey Assumes Coaching Job in Training of Baer" (AP), *Duluth News Tribune*, May 30, 1933, sports section.
[49] Neil, "West Coast Youth Surprises Fans by Savage Punching" (AP), *Duluth News Tribune*, June 9, 1933, sports section.
[50] Hurley, *op. cit.*, June 11, 1933, sports section.

Unfortunately, the excitement Hurley felt in New York did not translate into economic gain for either Salvator in St. Paul or Terk in Duluth. Whether because of the Depression, the lack of credible opposition for Baer, or a once-too-often trip to the Dempsey well, attendance was disappointing. Accounts from Duluth described the crowd as only "fair sized," while in St. Paul the *Daily News* reported the show lost $1,000.[51]

Afterward, Hurley hurried back to New York to cover the June 29th Jack Sharkey-Primo Carnera heavyweight title bout for his "Ring Rations" column. Jack predicted a win for Carnera despite Sharkey's victory two years earlier. Hurley reasoned that Primo had been fighting regularly since then and was much improved. Sharkey, on the other hand, had fought only once during the same period and was not as good as he once had been.

Hurley had seen Carnera box many times and had a better idea than most of his abilities. In Jack's view, Primo was fast for his size, had developed into a pretty good boxer, and was too big and strong for Sharkey. Hurley, in fact, not only thought Carnera would beat the champ, but figured he might even win by kayo.[52]

In an interview just before Hurley left New York to attend Baer's exhibitions in Duluth and St. Paul, boxing writer Ike Gellis of the *New York Evening Post* asked Jack if he really thought Carnera had any chance of knocking Sharkey out. In reply, Hurley had said: "You bet he has. If he uses that right uppercut more often. He gets a lot of leverage and power in his uppercuts, but I don't think he throws 'em enough. Jess Willard used it and stopped most of his opponents. Carnera has it, but doesn't favor it."[53]

When Hurley returned from Minnesota, he visited Carnera's training camp and was called aside by Bill Duffy, Primo's manager. Duffy had read Gellis' article and wanted to thank Jack for his suggestion about the uppercut. Bill told Hurley that they "had been trying to polish up the punch" and planned to use it against Sharkey.[54]

Although Sharkey outboxed Carnera the first five rounds, Hurley's prediction of the fight's outcome proved to be the most accurate of any sportswriter in the country. The end came in the sixth round when Primo pushed Sharkey into the ropes and caught him as he bounced off with a sweeping right uppercut that one reporter wrote "must have felt like a cobblestone wrapped in a leather sack." The champion fell face first to the canvas and was counted out while he lay flat on his face.[55]

---

[51] Macdonald, "Erjavec to Box Simpson Here Friday," *Duluth Herald*, June 16, 1933, sports section. Macdonald, "Baer Looks Part of Real Boxing Man," *Duluth Herald*, June 24, 1933, sports section. "Baer Shows Wares to 2,500; Rest of Card Disappointing," *St. Paul Daily News*, June 23, 1933, sports section.

[52] Hurley, *op. cit.*, June 4, 1933, sports section.

[53] Gellis, Ike, "Around the Ring," *New York Evening Post*, June 17, 1933, sports section.

[54] Hurley, *op. cit.*, July 8, 1933, sports section.

Attendance and gate receipts for the fight did not reach the level of the Baer-Schmeling bout, but they did produce a nice profit for the Garden. A crowd of 31,753 paid gross receipts of $198,289 and a net of $163,798. After paying Sharkey's 42-1/2-percent share of $69,000, Carnera's ten-percent share of $16,379, a rental fee for the use of Long Island Bowl of $16,000, and other expenses, the Garden netted $39,000.[56]

Apart from the Carnera camp, the people happiest over his triumph were Bill Carey and Jimmy Johnston. Primo's victory assured the Garden continued control of the heavyweight title. Prior to the bout, the matter had been in doubt because the Garden's option on Sharkey's services was expiring and Jack had announced he was open to future offers from other promoters. Carnera's contract, however, injected new life into the Garden's hold over the title because it bound him to the Garden for a year.[57]

Carnera's win also saved Johnston's job as matchmaker. Jimmy's standing at the Garden had been weakened significantly when Schmeling's manager Joe Jacobs blindsided him by arranging the German's match against Max Baer directly with Baer's manager. If the Garden had lost the heavyweight title as well as the Baer-Schmeling bout, fault would have been assigned to Johnston and, according to contemporary reports, Carey would likely have removed Johnston from his Garden post.[58]

Although the Garden retained control over boxing's biggest prize, Jacobs' bold stand encouraged other boxing men to challenge Johnston's dictatorial methods. The success of the Baer-Schmeling fight inspired the bout's financial backer, Tim Mara, to form his own Aram Athletic Club (Aram A. C.) to compete with the Garden in the promotion of major fights during the summer of 1933. Mara hired Al Weill as matchmaker and secured leases on the Polo Grounds and Yankee Stadium.[59]

Johnston long had been criticized for blatantly using his political connections and Garden position to further his personal and family interests. As a friend of Mayor James J. Walker and politician James A. Farley, who also served as chairman of the boxing commission, Jimmy always seemed to receive favored treatment in matters before the commission. Indeed, as we saw at the beginning of Chapter 25, these connections were the reasons why the Garden hired him in the first place.[60]

After becoming matchmaker, Johnston "sold" his stable to his brother Charley to comply with the commission's conflict-of-interest rules. Though

---

[55] Neil, "Italian Delivers Mighty Uppercut to Capture Title" (AP), *Duluth News Tribune*, June 30, 1933, sports section.

[56] Frayne, "Carnera, Happy to Sail Home," *New York American*, July 19, 1933, p. 17.

[57] "Carey Resigns as Head of Garden," *New York American*," July 1, 1933, sports section.

[58] Wood,, "Rumor Garden Seeks Jacobs," *New York Sun*, June 23, 1933, sports section.

[59] "Aram" was the last name of its owner, Tim Mara, spelled backwards.

[60] Pegler, Westbrook, "Speaking Out," *New York Post*, October 31, 1932, sports section.

this transfer technically met the regulations, Jimmy made no bones about granting Charley preferential treatment. Replying to a claim he recommended his brother as manager to a boxer whom Jimmy wanted to use at the Garden, he offered no apology: "What's wrong with that …? There is no law against recommending my brother as manager of a fighter, is there? He's managed fighters for years, and I shouldn't discriminate against him just because he's my brother, should I?"[61]

The third piece of the Johnston boxing empire, in addition to Jimmy's lofty position at the Garden and his brother's stable of fighters, was the family's control of St. Nicholas Arena which, second only to the Garden itself, was New York's largest year-around boxing club. Before taking the job at the Garden, Jimmy and another of his brothers, Ned, had leased St. Nick's with the intention of operating it jointly. Afterward, Jimmy bowed out from active ownership and turned the club over to Ned.[62]

The power exerted collectively by the Johnstons far exceeded the control any one of them wielded individually. Charley served as primary broker who supplied fighters to the farm team, i. e., Ned's St. Nicholas Arena, and to its parent club, i. e., Jimmy's Madison Square Garden. Although the Garden presented other boxers of merit, those handled by Charley and built up by Ned at St. Nick's dominated the Garden's cards in disproportionate numbers and enriched the Johnston family coffers accordingly.

Apart from the allegations of favoritism and unfair profiteering, the most common complaint against Johnston was his arrogant and high-handed dealings with managers and their boxers. In most cases, Jimmy presented them contracts on a take-it-or-leave-it basis without a chance to negotiate either terms or opponents. Failure to accept a contract meant a manager and his fighter were shut out of New York's two most important fight clubs.

With dissatisfaction against Johnston mounting steadily, it was not surprising that the Aram A. C.'s entry into the field of boxing promotion was greeted with enthusiasm. Almost before Jimmy knew what happened, Aram's matchmaker Al Weill had taken advantage of the situation and signed up the three best outdoor bouts of the season. As a result, Johnston and the Garden, with the best organization and the nation's most prestigious boxing arena, were left without a major show for the rest of the summer.[63]

---

[61] Frayne, "Jimmy Makes Bid on Behalf of His Brother," October 31, 1933, p. 17.

[62] Parker, Dan, "Keeping Bat from Getting Batty," *New York Daily Mirror*, March 30, 1932, sports section. The Johnstons also controlled the Broadway Arena in Brooklyn. Charley Johnston would be suspended in 1934 for mixing his managerial and promotional endeavors against boxing commission rules. At the time, commissioner Bill Brown called the Johnstons "a detriment to the sports of boxing and wrestling." Hurley, "Shadow Boxing," *Fargo Forum*, February 18, 1934, sports section.

[63] Campbell, *op. cit.*, August 6, 1933, sports section.

Success at the Baer-Schmeling fight led Tim Mara to enlist Al Weill as matchmaker and form the Aram Athletic Club to challenge Johnston and Madison Square Garden. Here, (left to right) Weill and Mara welcome Jimmy McLarnin and Pop Foster to New York for a prior pilot promotion of the McLarnin-Lou Brouillard fight August 4, 1932.

The first bout Aram signed was the long-delayed fight between Petrolle and Bep van Klaveren, scheduled for July 12 at the Polo Grounds. As the first to sign with Weill, Hurley was leading the charge of managers in revolt against Johnston. As a further incentive to Jack, Al pledged to exert his best efforts to arrange a title bout for the winner against McLarnin, who had defeated Corbett on May 29 to annex the welterweight title.

The most important fight Aram wrested from the Garden was the Ross-Canzoneri lightweight title rematch, set for September 12 at the Polo Grounds. Landing the bout was important because Tony was a proven attraction and Barney was the first Jewish boxer of superior ability to show at New York in years. Receipts of over $100,000 were expected.

Weill's success in obtaining the bout was largely due to the dislike that Sam Pian, Ross' co-manager, had for Johnston. Pian had tried to arrange a fight for Barney in New York before he won the title. Jimmy had offered Sam just two opponents, Sammy Fuller and Benny Bass. Pian had not wanted either foe for Ross at that stage of Barney's career and had returned to Chicago with Ross, vowing never to work with Johnston again.[64]

Aram's third coup was signing a bout between Ben Jeby and Lou Brouilliard for New York's version of the world middleweight title, also set for the Polo Grounds, August 9.

Petrolle was a 7-to-5 favorite over van Klaveren. Since their previously scheduled bout in January, Bep had recovered sufficiently from his broken hand to defeat Baby Joe Gans, Jimmy Phillips, and Herman Perlick in warm-up bouts, to run his string of stateside wins to six. When he entered the ring, van Klaveren wore a plaster patch over his right eye to protect a cut not yet completely healed after the Perlick match 5-1/2 weeks earlier.

Amidst a storm of boos, Petrolle, 144, was awarded a fourth-round technical kayo over van Klaveren, 145-1/2, when commission physician Dr. Joseph Sheridan ordered the fight stopped. The action was taken at the end of the round after Sheridan examined the cut over Bep's right eye and found he risked permanent injury if the fight continued.

The abrupt ending stunned the 10,000 fans who had paid around $15,000 to see the fight. Although Petrolle's left hook re-opened the old cut early in the second round, van Klaveren's seconds stopped the bleeding during the rest period. The blood bothered Bep in the third, but Dr. Sheridan examined the eye between rounds and let the bout continue. The cut hardly bled at all in the fourth, and onlookers were unprepared when Sheridan changed his mind and advised the referee to stop the bout at the end of the round.

Promoter Mara complained afterward that the fans were cheated by Dr. Sheridan's premature stoppage. Bill Brown, who had just replaced William Muldoon on the boxing commission, agreed and said that if he had been the referee he would have disregarded Dr. Sheridan's advice. Even Dr. Vincent

---

[64] Frayne, "$30,000 Guarantee" (subtitle), *New York American*, July 8, 1933, sports section.

'HOW'S THE GAS WITH YOU, BILL?' 679

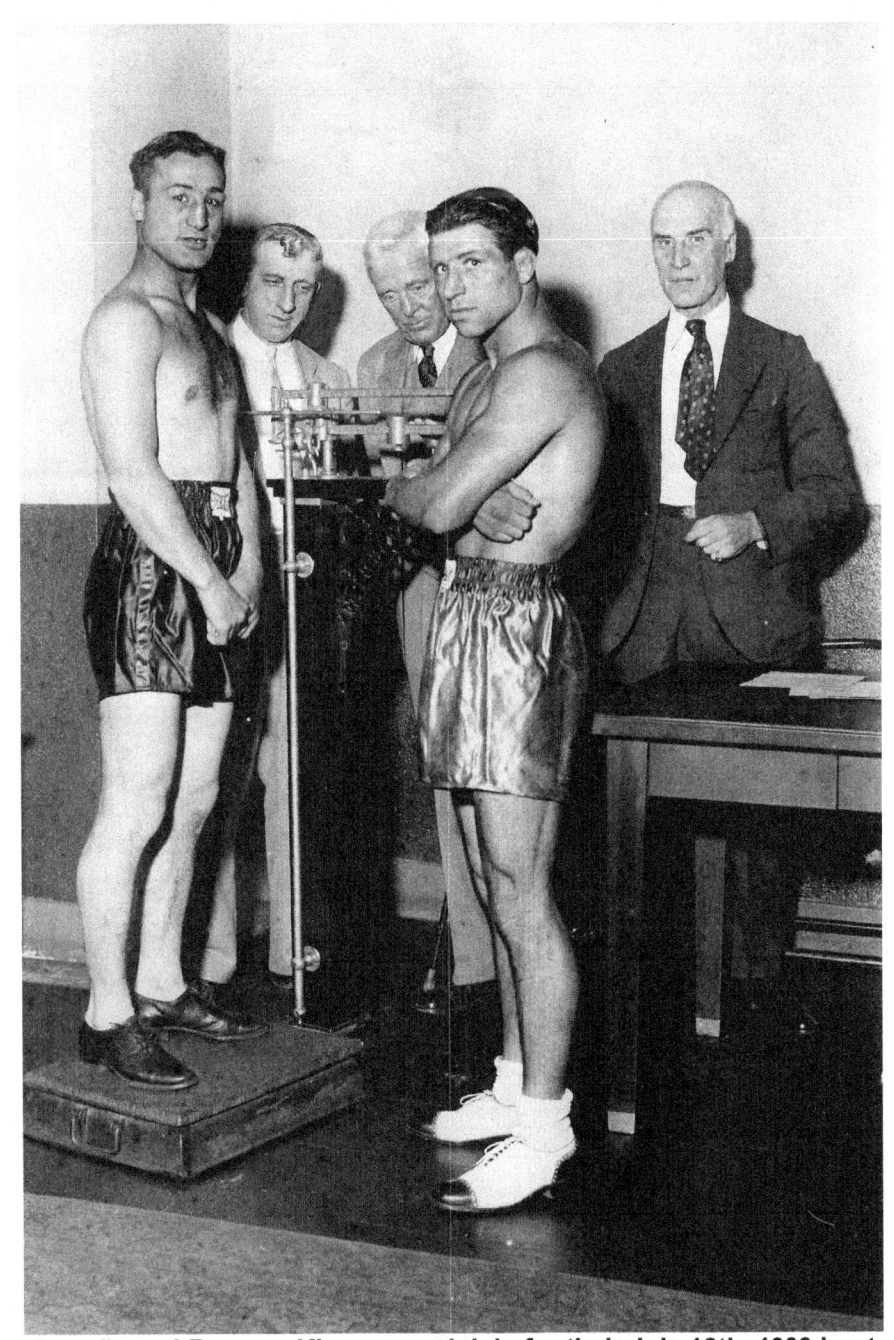

Petrolle and Bep van Klaveren weigh in for their July 12th, 1933 bout at the Polo Grounds promoted by Tim Mara's Aram Athletic Club.

Petrolle lands a hard left to van Klaveren's shoulder.

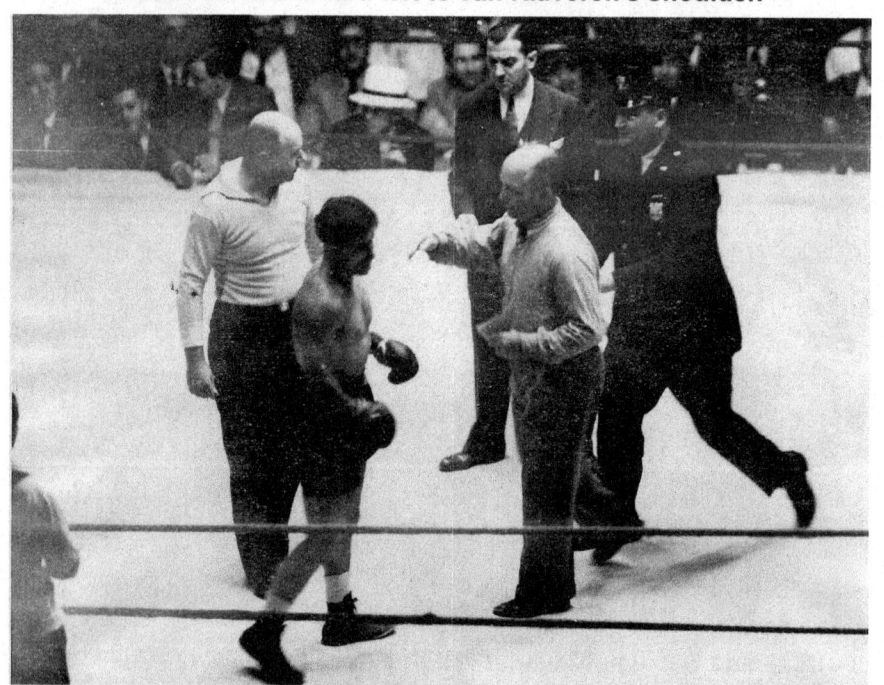

A policeman enters the ring to help calm down a disappointed van Klaveren after the referee stopped the bout.

Nardiello, an alternate commission physician seated beside Sheridan at ringside, took issue with the actions of his colleague.[65]

Sheridan explained that the cut was located at a dangerous spot over the eyelid. The *Evening Journal*'s Hype Igoe, who looked at the eye after the match, confirmed the "cut was two inches long and ran through the eyebrow, in a downward slant, finally ending on the upper lid itself." Igoe noted that the controversy set the stage for "a corking return match."[66]

After deducting taxes and rent for the Polo Grounds, the boxers were paid off on a net of $9,700. Billy received 30 percent and Bep 20 percent.[67]

In the following days, critics shifted their scrutiny away from the doctor to questions about why Bep was allowed to box with an eye that was not completely healed. In reply, the commission ruled that any contestant in a future main event must must report to New York five days before a match and submit to an exam by a commission doctor 48 hours before the bout.[68]

With this rule, it was hoped injuries to boxers could be discovered early enough to give promoters time to change their cards and for fans to adjust their ticket-buying plans. In addition, the doctors would be faced less often with the situation of having to decide whether to pass a marginally fit boxer on the day of a bout to avoid disappointing promoters and fans who had already purchased tickets and made travel arrangements.[69]

---

[65] Grayson, "Safety First Medic Ruins Petrolle-Van Klaveren Tilt," *New York World Telegram*," July 13, 1933, sports section.

[66] Dayton, Alfred, "Bad Eye Ruins Van Klaveren," *New York Sun*, July 13, 1933, sports section. Igoe, "Calling Halt to Petrolle Go Wise Move," *New York Evening Journal*, July 13, 1933, sports section. Hurley, "Ring Rations," *Fargo Forum*, July 23, 1933, sports section. Though Hurley's opinion could hardly be called unbiased, it is interesting because it provides a context for what happened. Jack believed Dr. Sheridan was justified in his action:

> "Mara wasn't the only one in the arena who thought the doctor erred in stopping the Petrolle-Van Klaveren match. The majority of fans and newspapermen shared his opinion. They felt a main-event fighter should be prepared to take hard knocks and wounds. And the day after the fight, one newspaperman suggested that before the next boxing show, it might be a good idea to have the announcer enter the ring just before the first bout and ask, "Is there a doctor in the house?" And then if one answers, have a couple of robust cops throw him out and proceed with the show.
>
> "I don't blame Mara in a way, or the fans either, for that matter, but after all they were in no position to contest the judgment of a medical man. To hear them yell you would think those seated in the upper stands knew the fighter's condition better than the doctor examining the wound ...
>
> "When the doctor's order ended hostilities, I did not think van Klaveren's eye was bad enough to incapacitate him. But upon close inspection in the dressing room afterward, I changed my mind. The cut was very deep and down into the eyelid. The Flying Dutchman continued to beef, claiming that Dr. Sheridan broke his string of consecutive victories, but you could see that he was just 'putting on an act.' Down in his heart he knew that the doctor was right in stopping the bout."

[67] Frayne, "Commissioners Plan to Curb Ring Doctors," *New York American*, July 14, 1933, sports section.

[68] Capossela, Fred, "Around the Ring," *New York Post*, July 18, 1933, sports section.

[69] Dayton, "Ring Officials on Watch Again," *New York Sun*, July 15, 1933, sports section.

Five days after the affair, matchmaker Weill announced he had signed Petrolle and van Klaveren to a return bout at the Polo Grounds on August 23, 1933. The commission provisionally approved the match but issued a special order that Bep would have to pass an exam by three commission doctors before the fight could take place.[70]

While Hurley and Weill were negotiating a rematch, Johnston dug out the contracts for the Petrolle-van Klaveren bout canceled the prior January. Although he had not tried to stop the July 12th show, Johnston now said the Garden would seek to enforce the old contracts and block any future match Aram sought to make between the two fighters. Jimmy argued that "contracts are contracts and both fighters will have to live up to them."

Asked about the threat, Hurley laughed. "The contracts Johnston holds aren't worth the paper they are written on," said Jack. "Billy was ready to fight the Dutchman for the Garden in January. The fight was called off because Bep hurt his hand. It wasn't postponed; it was called off. A new set of contracts would be required. And we haven't signed any. Besides, as long as Johnston has anything to do with the Garden, none of my fighters will be booked there. I don't like his attitude."[71]

As a result of Johnston's assertion the Garden could enforce its old contracts, the members of the newly constituted state athletic commission issued a ruling which established that a boxing club wishing to retain the services of any fighter after a postponed fight had to claim him within five days. Since it made no such claim, the Garden had lost the match.[72]

Whether Johnston really believed he could use old contracts to bend Hurley to his will or whether it was just the Boy Bandit's way of showing he could not be intimidated was unclear. What was clear, however, is that Jack and Jimmy had crossed swords and joined each other in battle. There would be no turning back for either of them.

---

[70] Capossela, *op. cit.*

[71] Gellis, Ike, "Klaveren Matched with Petrolle," *New York Evening Post*, July 13, 1933, sports section.

[72] Grayson, "Bep-Petrolle Bout Off Indefinitely," *New York World-Telegram*, July 25, 1933, sports section.

The members of the New York State Athletic Commission in July 1933 were: Brigadier General John J. Phelan, appointed in 1930 after the resignation of George E. Brower; Colonel D. Walker Wear, appointed in March 1933 when Farley resigned to accept the position of postmaster general of the United States from President Roosevelt; and Bill Brown, the replacement for William Muldoon after the latter died in June 1933.

The resignation of Farley and the appointment of Brown substantially weakened James J. Johnston's influence with the commission. Farley, who was one of Johnston's best friends, was a long-time Tammany politician and practitioner of patronage politics who regarded taking care of his friends as one of his duties as a government official. Brown, who had a lifetime background in the sport of boxing as a boxer, manager, and small-club promoter, came onto the commission with grassroots ideas how to improve the sport. Managers, sportswriters, and small-time operatives all welcomed his appointment.

CHAPTER 28

THE OLD MAN REACHES THE END OF THE LINE

Nightfall on a bleak Dakota farm . . . A sprawling barn . . . Kerosene lanterns swaying from the rafters . . . A straw-covered splotch of ground . . . A sub-zero wind whistling through the boards . . . A thin, ribby youngster trying out punches with his kid brother.

That was the beginning of the ring career – the laboratory work – of Billy Petrolle, who in due time came on to Broadway to become one of the great favorites of the Big Town ...

Petrolle may not go much further. They are calling him Old Man Petrolle now. He is 29-years old, and he's been in the ring 11 years. Petrolle is here to fight Barney Ross, the lightweight champion. They fight Wednesday night in the Bronx Coliseum ten rounds. This fight should be in the Garden. But the stars no longer fight in the Garden. This fine temple that the Great Believer, Rickard, reared to glorify the bloody arts is now a cheap mission house where only the renegades, the misfits, and the unanointed gather to worship before ghostly audiences in empty pews. The rebellion against the Garden high priests appears to be complete. Their administration has been neither wise nor wholesome. Their losses have been heavy, both in caste and currency. Most of the star fighters prefer to fight elsewhere and for less money. Their bitterness is deep rooted.

... I say the Petrolle-Ross fight belongs in the Garden and not on the outskirts of Yonkers because there is every prospect it will be a fine fight. Petrolle will stand up and throw punches until the cows come home – and they can come all the way from Fargo as far as he is concerned. Ross twice whipped Canzoneri. That shows he belongs. For that matter Ross has also whipped Petrolle. But the Old Man says it was a mistake. "I trained down from 160 pounds to 138 for the fight and I was weak ... Still, he hit me with everything he had and didn't hurt me ... At 142 I will be myself, and generally that is enough." Your correspondent wishes to add that generally it is too much ...

We got to talking about that old Indian blanket the Old Man wraps his battered torso to when he comes into the ring. His manager, Jack Hurley, bought it for him a long time ago to make him distinctive ... "All fighters wear bathrobes," said Hurley. "You are going to be different." The Old Man laughed, showing a perfect set of strong, white teeth. "You know the reason Hurley bought that blanket? Well, it was too much trouble for him to pull a bathrobe over my gloves in the ring. It meant a little work, and managers don't like to work."

The Old Man has worn the blanket a number of years now. It has never been washed. A tubbing might offend the gods and bring evil luck. It is dirty, bloodstained and frayed, but it will always be draped around the shoulders of the twisted-nosed veteran when he climbs into the ring.

"What are you going to do with it when you finish fighting?" "I'll probably have to give it back to Hurley. He paid for it. And you know how managers are."[1]
— Joe Williams

****

Although it received scant notice, an examination of Bep van Klaveren at the commission office two weeks after his bout with Billy Petrolle completely vindicated Dr. Joseph Sheridan's order to stop the fight. Three doctors looked at the wound July 25 and found it still was not fully closed.

In accordance with the findings of its doctors, the commission refused to approve the August 23rd return bout and told Bep to come back for another exam in two weeks to seek approval. After thinking the matter over, Aram A. C. matchmaker Al Weill decided to give the injury an extra month to heal and rescheduled the bout for September 27.[2]

While awaiting the Petrolle-van Klaveren rematch, Jack Hurley arranged a bout for Billy at Boston against local favorite Sammy Fuller in a ten-rounder on September 8, 1933. Jack also matched Charley Retzlaff on the same card against Gene Stanton of Cleveland.

Fuller, whose birth name was Sabino Ferullo, was a chunky 27-year-old Italian who in nine years of boxing had met and defeated some the best fighters in the lightweight and junior-welterweight divisions, including Bruce Flowers, Billy Wallace, Tony Canzoneri, Ray Miller, Andy Callahan, and Jackie (Kid) Berg. At the time he faced Petrolle, Fuller boasted a record of 45 wins, 12 losses, and two draws.

The most notable of Sammy's wins was a ten-round decision over Berg on May 20, 1932. Afterward, Fuller claimed Jackie's disputed world junior-welterweight title. Berg's claim had come into question after his kayo loss in a lightweight championship bout to Tony Canzoneri on April 24, 1931. Although Tony claimed both laurels after the fight, Jackie maintained his title had not been at risk because in seeking the lighter title he had been required to weigh five pounds under the 140-pound junior-welter limit.

As it turned out, Petrolle was less concerned with staking a claim to a "junior" title than with entering the ring at a comfortable weight. Billy scaled two pounds over the junior welter limit at 142 the day of the bout while Fuller weighed 138. Since both battlers were hard punchers with

---

[1] Williams, Joe, "From a Barn to Broadway, That's Petrolle's Career, Garden Loses More Class," *New York World-Telegram*, January 22, 1934, sports section. Williams' article has been edited for space and context. His opening paragraph, though evocative, is inaccurate. As described in Chapter Eight, Petrolle grew up in Berwick, Pennsylvania, and Schenectady, New York. Billy never actually lived in Fargo, but at age 17 moved with his family to Dilworth, Minnesota, approximately six miles east of Fargo. After moving to Dilworth, Petrolle worked as a car checker at the Northern Pacific Railroad's maintenance facility.
[2] Gellis, Ike, "Around the Ring," *New York Evening Post*, July 26, 1933, sports section.

walk-in styles, experts predicted a knockout was likely.[3]

Hurley had dickered for the Fuller bout for several years, but always insisted it be staged in New York or some city other than Sammy's hometown. Boston was one of several other cities, like Syracuse, Philadelphia, and Buffalo, which had the reputation of awarding "hometown decisions" to local fighters when undeserved.

Now that Petrolle was competing as a welterweight instead of directly against Fuller for a lightweight title shot, Hurley accepted the bout, figuring a hometown verdict would not harm Billy's career to any great extent.[4]

According to reports appearing in the next day's newspapers, Fuller held his own against Petrolle in the first three heats, but thereafter failed to win a single round. Sammy's best session was the second when he scored with hard right uppercuts to the jaw and left hooks to the body. Billy came on strong after the third round, and for the rest of the fight landed almost at will with stinging overhand rights to the head and heavy lefts to the body which backed Fuller around the ring and had him looking like a novice.

Fuller was cut under the right eye in the sixth round, and the wound bled off and on until the end of the bout. A hard right to Sammy's jaw in the tenth sent him to the canvas, but the Boston lad jumped up without a count.

The *Boston Globe* reported that when referee Johnny Brassil "gathered the votes at the end of the fight he had a puzzled look on his pan. Johnny thought, as did most everyone, that Petrolle had won – and voted so. But the judges disagreed." Judge Tom Brady cast his ballot for Fuller while John Glackin, the other judge, declared the bout a draw. With each of the ring officials dissenting, the contest went into the record books as a draw.[5]

The next day boxing writers in each of Boston's seven daily newspapers openly expressed their opinions Petrolle was a victim of one of the worst decisions in the city's history. In their efforts to overcome the injustice of the verdict, they showered upon Billy as much praise as he had ever received for any of his most widely acclaimed wins. A listing of headlines

---

[3] The junior-welterweight title and the junior-lightweight titles were the only "junior" titles in 1933 (as opposed to the more-than-can-be-counted "junior" and "super" titles in the post 1970s era). As the very name "junior" connotes, these two titles did not have the stature of the championships of the other eight "legitimate" divisions. Evidence of this is the fact that by 1935 both these junior titles would lapse into long periods of disuse as a result of the general lack of public interest. Making a weak claim for a "junior" title ould not have held much appeal for a top-level competitor like Petrolle, especially since Fuller himself did not take his own claim very seriously at the time. The distinction of having been a claimant for 'junior' title in 1933, when there were so many fighters and so few champions (two "junior" and eight "legitimate"), holds more significance to boxing enthusiasts today than fans in the past, particularly when the present-day dilution of what a title means is taken into account.
[4] Campbell, Cubby, "Cubby Campbell's Column," *Duluth News Tribune*, September 10, 1933, sports section.
[5] Hurwitz, Hy, "Fuller Given Draw to Surprise of All," *Boston Globe*, September 9, 1933, sports section.

from the Boston newspapers serves to illustrate the point:

- FULLER GIVEN DRAW TO SURPRISE OF ALL
- PETROLLE WINS EIGHT ROUNDS, BUT FULLER RECEIVES DRAW
- FULLER IS GIVEN BREAKS WITH PETROLLE AS MASTER
- DULUTH PUNCHER TAKES NINE HEATS, CROWD HOOTS
- FULLER FORTUNATE TO GET DRAW WITH PETROLLE
- SANTA CLAUS IN EARLY FLIGHT TO PUGILIST FULLER
- FOUND – A CLEVER BOXER; SELF DEFENSE AN ART; PETROLLE SCIENTIST OF RING.[6]

Among the articles, Victor O. Jones of the *Boston Globe* wrote perhaps the most eloquent description ever written about Petrolle's ring abilities:

"After a good many years of wondering, I finally found out last night what's wrong with boxing. The trouble seems to be that there are not enough Billy Petrolles. Having seen Petrolle, I came to the conclusion that I had seen for the first time something which might be called by the grandiloquent title which the old timers bestowed upon the sport – The Noble Art of Self Defense.

"With Petrolle you have something more than just a fine physical specimen trying his hardest to inflict corporeal punishment on a rival. The man has a skill and a technique which none of the other fighters I have ever seen had. With Petrolle, boxing is both an art and a science, while with the others it is merely a case of well-meaning but misdirected pushing, hauling, clinching and swinging.

"Mere physical exertion – and that's about all I ever got out of fighters – does not constitute sport. The thing which distinguishes an athlete and a non-athlete is his skill. Anyone can go out on a golf links and hit a golf ball with a golf club. But it isn't until you can make the golf ball go where you want it to go with a reasonable degree of accuracy that you can call yourself a golfer. The trouble with boxing, as I see it now very clearly, is that most of the boxers don't know how to box.

"There was a glint in various faded eyes at the Garden last night which I haven't seen before at any of the fight cards. The old-timers, for once, felt that they were getting their money's worth. One of them said to me: 'Well, son, now you've seen an old-time fighter. You think Petrolle was wonderful? Well, compared to what

---

[6] Boston's seven daily newspapers were the *Boston Daily Record*, the *Boston Evening American*, the *Boston Evening Transcript*, the *Boston Globe*, the *Boston Herald*, the *Boston Post*, and the *Boston Traveler*.

we've got these days, he's good. But I've seen the day when every main bout boxer was that good and some of them were lots better.'

"If this is so – and I have no doubt it is – I can see where boxing was a great thing. Last night's fight was great, but think what it would have been if Sammy Fuller had been as good as Petrolle! For if last night's battle was good, it was also one-sided. Fuller is game and good, as fighters go these days, but in my inexpert opinion, he wasn't in the same class with Petrolle. They both had two arms and two legs and used them, but there all resemblance between the two ended.

"Most of the boxing writers say that the decision was akin to robbery, but I wouldn't know about that. I imagine there are many ways of scoring boxing bouts, and it takes long practice and great technical knowledge to score them correctly. After the first couple of rounds, when Petrolle was moving along a picture of damaging efficiency and rhythmic grace, there wasn't anything to it.

"You could see Petrolle building up his openings with all the skill and science of a master swordsman, and then delivering the crushing climax blow. Everything he did had a purpose, and cause and effect followed one on the other like it does in chemistry, mathematics or some other exact science.

"Not once in the course of the bout did Petrolle hold. He didn't have to. A twist of his head, a roll of his shoulders, and Fuller's hard-swing punches stopped an inch from Petrolle's clipper nose or slid harmlessly off his ribs, like spent bullets off steel armor plate. It was fascinating to watch, this flawless control, this exact timing, this lightning shift from slashing attack to canny defense, a pattern so subtle that it approached fine art.

"I am wondering if our fighting has degenerated to a point where even the more capable officials can't tell good fighting when they see it. Referee Johnny Brassil voted for Petrolle which proves he knows good fighting. The experts were unanimous in calling it a bad decision, like many another rendered of late. As I say, I wouldn't know about that, but if fighters like Fuller can get draws with fighters like Petrolle, that's another thing that's the matter with boxing."[7]

Afterward, Hurley inquired, "What, might we ask, must a man do to win a verdict here? Fuller didn't win a round. While those gonifs were at it they should have given it to Fuller and made a good job of it." When somebody asked him on his way to the dressing room if he was going to pick up his

---

[7] Jones, Victor, O., "Found – A Clever Boxer; Self Defense an Art; Petrolle Scientist of Ring," *Boston Globe*, September 9, 1933, sports section.

money at the box office, an anguished Jack was heard to say, "For the lov'a Mike, they're not going to steal that too, are they?"[8]

In the semi-windup bout, Charley Retzlaff defeated Gene Stanton in an uninspired contest which had the spectators jeering at the ineffectiveness of the action. Although Retzlaff was slow and wild in his attack, his aggressiveness and fighting effort earned him the decision. Overall, attendance for the show was a disappointing 4,827, with gross receipts at $6,784 and net receipts $4,768.

As a postscript to the Petrolle-Fuller fight, the Massachusetts boxing commission, in its next meeting at month's end, suspended John Glackin and Tom Brady indefinitely from acting as boxing judges for any future bouts. In taking this almost unprecedented action, the commission was tacitly admitting that the votes rendered by these two judges at the end of the bout were unjustified.[9]

On September 12, 1933, three days after the Petrolle-Fuller bout, Barney Ross successfully defended his lightweight title against Tony Canzoneri at the Polo Grounds. The bout, promoted by Aram A. C. in conjunction with Mrs. William Randolph Hearst's Free Milk Fund for Babies, attracted a crowd of 36,000 and gross receipts of $114,000.

The next day, receipts after taxes were announced as $101,845. The Milk Fund received ten percent, Ross 40 percent or $36,668, and Canzoneri $13,750. After paying for the undercard and other operating expenses, the Aram A. C. was left with a nice profit in the range of $15,000-$20,000.[10]

Unfortunately for matchmaker Al Weill, Tim Mara decided that the success of the Ross-Canzoneri show was a good time to reevaluate his involvement in boxing. Mara was still seething about Dr. Sheridan's stoppage of the Petrolle-van Klaveren bout at its most exciting stage two months earlier. In his view, main-event boxers were paid to stand the gaff. If commissioners were "going to insist on fighters pelting each other with cream puffs at 20 paces" then the commission should stage its own shows.

Mara told Weill he had never encountered such interference in his other sports ventures, and he would rather get out of boxing altogether than stand for it now. Furthermore, the Petrolle-van Klaveren and Brouilliard-Jeby shows had been financial losers, and Tim's assessment of Al's future proposals gave him little hope they would be any different. As a result, he

---

[8] Hamilton, W. A., "Petrolle Wins Eight Rounds, But Fuller Receives Draw in 10-Round Bout at Garden," *Boston Traveler*, September 9, 1933, sports section. Hurley, Jack, "Ring Rations," *Fargo Forum*, September 17, 1933, sports section. "Gonif" is a Yiddish word for "thief, or dishonest person, or scoundrel." The word is often used as a general term of abuse.

[9] "Mitt Judges in Petrolle-Fuller Bout Suspended," *Fargo Forum*, October 1, 1933, sports section.

[10] Neil, Edward J., "Split Verdict Saves Laurels for Chicagoan" (AP), *Fargo Forum*, September 13, 1933, sports section. "Ross Is Hailed as True Lightweight Champion by Victory over Canzoneri" (AP), *Duluth News Tribune*, September 14, 1933 sports section.

decided the smart move was to take his profit from the Ross-Canzoneri fight and dismantle the Aram A. C. while he was ahead of the game.[11]

Mara's withdrawal left Al without a backer for the Petrolle-van Klaveren rematch. Weill was agreeable to assigning the contract to another club if the Petrolle and van Klaveren camps could agree on a promoter. Van Klaveren's manager, Theo Huizenaar, welcomed an offer from Madison Square Garden. Not so Hurley, who told all within earshot if Bep wanted the fight it would be at a club other than the Garden or not at all.

With this pronouncement Hurley took his grievance against Boy Bandit Johnston to a new level. Whereas at first the feud had been viewed as a private vendetta that would likely disappear at the first opportunity for mutual economic gain, it was now obvious the rift ran much deeper. Boxing experts, who previously saw Jack's position as an aberration from the norm, now viewed his defiance of the Garden boxing director as a harbinger of a much larger revolt that was spreading throughout the managerial fraternity.

Ed Frayne, sports editor of the *New York American,* was of the opinion that Hurley's stand was bringing into the open a conflict which had been simmering for quite awhile between the Garden and a loose-knit alliance of managers who were tired of Johnston's autocratic and egotistical policies:

> "The silent boycott of the Garden by boxers and managers flamed into outright rebellion yesterday. The Billy Petrolle-Bep van Klaveren rematch, the best welterweight attraction of the day, was signed by the Ridgewood Grove Arena, one of the smallest clubs in the city. It was just indignation on Hurley's part, for Petrolle had previously drawn $250,000 in fights for the Garden and the Garden refused to pay a mere $250 for training expenses."

What made Hurley's stance extraordinary was that it involved real monetary sacrifice. While during the summer rebellious managers like Jack and Barney Ross' pilot Sam Pian had been able to sign with other promoters at big outdoor arenas, their options in the fall were limited. Since the Johnstons operated the city's two largest and most centrally located indoor arenas, the Garden and St. Nick's, the only other available sites were small clubs like the Ridgewood Grove and the Broadway Arena.

The *New York Daily Mirror*'s Dan Parker explained the difference in potential revenues between the Garden and these smaller boxing clubs:

> "Because Jack Hurley, straight-shooting manager of Billy Petrolle, thinks more of a principle than he does of money, the Petrolle-van Klaveren bout is going to the Ridgewood Grove Club. At the Garden it would draw $25,000. At Ridgewood, the best it can do is

---

[11] Hurley, *op. cit.*, July 23, 1933, sports section.

$12,000 ... Hurley justly answers 'Petrolle not available' to all queries by the Garden for his fighter's services."

Wilbur Wood of the *New York Sun* echoed Parker's observations and contributed an additional comment offered by Hurley himself:

"The assumption that the fight would go to the Garden left out the undeniable fact that Hurley is a man of long memory and firm convictions. Hurley passed up a possible $25,000 gate for a $12,000 one at Ridgewood in this explanation: 'That's not the idea,' exploded Hurley, 'I would rather let Petrolle box the Dutchman under the Brooklyn Bridge with a free gate than to take him to the Garden.'

"... That's a sorry state of affairs for the world's largest boxing organization. But it is a fact and not a theory. Shades of Tex Rickard."[12]

The refusals of Hurley and other managers to box for Johnston made it difficult for the Garden to line up fighters for its main events. In addition to Jack and Pian, the managers of Max Baer, Max Schmeling, Tommy Loughran, Ray Impellettiere, King Levinsky, and Steve Hamas all preferred to box for someone other than Johnston. As a result, the Garden hosted an all-time low of nine shows in the months from April through December.[13]

Despite the controversy, the Petrolle-van Klaveren return bout never took place. In a training session six days before the rescheduled September 30th date, van Klaveren suffered a deep cut over his left eye (the previous injury had been over his right eye), and the fight was called off.

After this cancellation, a frustrated Hurley decided the bout was jinxed and vowed he was done trying to match Petrolle with van Klaveren: "We signed to fight that Dutchman three times and each time something happened. Well, enough is enough, and I had to convince the 'Old Man' that we'd never come back for van Klaveren. The time, money and effort we wasted trying to get that guy into the ring would amaze you.

"Look at some of our expenses on this trip. It cost over $300 for train fare, and we lived at a hotel for two weeks, Billy, his missus and me. This ran into a couple of 'C' notes, and where's our training bill? Add a couple

---

[12] Campbell, *op. cit.*, September 26, 1933, sports section. The foregoing quotes from articles by Frayne, Parker, and Wood, all came via "Cubby Campbell's Column."
[13] Hurley, *op. cit.*, December 10, 1933 (managers of Baer, Schmeling, Loughran, Impellettiere, and Levinsky), February 25, 1934 (manager of Steve Hamas), sports sections. Fleischer, Nat, "Garden Promotions under William F. Carey and James J. Johnston," *1957 Ring Record Book*, (Ring Book Shop, Inc., NY, NY, 1957), p. 75. To the eight indoor bouts listed on page 75 between April and December 1933, the author has added the Garden's one outdoor promotion, the Carnera-Sharkey heavyweight title fight, held June 29, 1933.

of more hundreds. Then there are the little incidentals, too, and no one to pay the freight. It's bad enough not having an opportunity to fight, but being without a promoter [to reimburse us for expenses] is worse.

"You know, Al Weill transferred the match to Johnny Attell of Ridgewood Grove, and he couldn't put it on because the Dutchman got his eye cut. I'm not squawking at Weill or Attell. It wasn't their fault. But that van Klaveren is absolutely poison to us. We won't touch him for anything. And that's a promise!"[14]

Hurley recovered part of his expenses when matchmaker Attell salvaged the date by rounding up Hans Birkie to face Retzlaff in a hastily arranged substitute for the Petrolle-van Klaveren affair. The match was a sequel to the draw the two men fought 15 months earlier on the Schmeling-Sharkey card. This time, Birkie won a decision in a dull ten-rounder booed by the crowd. Birkie earned the victory by furnishing a few offensive spurts which hurt Charley, forcing him to retreat and hold throughout the battle.[15]

Although Hurley's contract with Retzlaff still had five months to run, the Birkie fight was Charley's last for Jack. His record under Hurley ended with 49 wins, four losses, and two draws. Retzlaff resumed his career in April 1934 under different management and regained enough of his earlier form to garner a big payday against a young Joe Louis at Chicago in January 1936. Louis stopped Retzlaff in one round.

Retzlaff retired to his farm near Leonard, North Dakota, following the Louis fight. After a brief comeback in 1940, Charley left boxing for good with an overall record of 61 wins, eight losses, and four draws. He later moved to Detroit Lakes, Minnesota, where he operated a successful automobile dealership until his death in 1970.

On October 10, Hurley signed Petrolle to a rematch against Sammy Fuller at the Ridgewood Grove Arena October 21, 1933. As an incentive, the winner was promised a December fight against Barney Ross in a show sponsored by the Free Milk Fund for Babies. Since Ross was outgrowing the lightweight division, the bout was being touted as an elimination to determine the next challenger for McLarnin's welterweight title.[16]

One of the reasons Hurley chose the Ridgewood Grove as an alternative to Madison Square Garden was because the club had hired Billy McCarney as general manager. With the wholesale defection of star talent from the Garden, president I.T. Flatto and matchmaker Johnny Attell decided to capitalize on the situation by beefing up the Ridgewood's staff and enlisting McCarney to acquire some of the bouts the Garden was losing.[17]

---

[14] Gellis, "Around the Ring," *New York Evening Post*, October 3, 1933, sports section.

[15] "Birkie Beats Retzlaff in Slow Contest," *Fargo Forum*, October 1, 1933, sports section.

[16] "Petrolle-Fuller Bout Approved," *New York World-Telegram*, October 11, 1933, sports section. "Petrolle in Bid for Rematch with Ross," *New York World-Telegram*, October 17, 1933, sports section.

[17] Gellis, *op. cit.*, October 11, 1933, sports section.

McCarney had been a behind-the-scenes partner with Joe Jacobs in managing Max Schmeling, but had never bothered to reduce their partnership agreement to writing. Billy had recently fallen out with Jacobs and lost his position in Schmeling's camp. Jacobs refused to settle with the "Old Professor," and now he was experiencing hard times. By booking his fighters into the Ridgewood, Jack was helping his old mentor out.[18]

Promoting a major bout was an experiment for Flatto. The Ridgewood section of Brooklyn was in the center of a large German population accustomed to paying a top of $2 per seat for a standard club fight. For the Petrolle-Fuller show, Flatto raised the scale to $3, $2, and $1. House capacity of 4,400 at those prices would bring in a gate of about $10,000.[19]

To turn a profit, Flatto needed two sources of extra revenue. His first hope was that his regular Ridgewood patrons would pay the extra dollar to see a world-class fight. His second was that Manhattan fans would be willing to ride the subway an extra 30 minutes from the Times Square station on the Broadway line to the Myrtle Avenue Station on the Fourteenth Street line, a block from the arena. With advance sales heavier than usual, an average amount of walk-in trade would guarantee success.[20]

On the day of the fight, Petrolle was favored 8-to-5 in the betting. At the 2 p.m. weigh-in, Fuller tipped the scales at 140 pounds and Billy at 142-1/2.

Eight hours and 45 minutes later, Petrolle was awarded a ten-round decision over Fuller, erasing any doubt about his mastery over Sammy which may have lingered after their draw in Beantown a month earlier. Billy floored the Boston whaler for nine-counts in the second and seventh rounds. Even so, the bout was exciting as Fuller battled gamely and had the crowd on its feet several times with his brave rallies. Sammy's left eye was cut in the third round, and his right eye became swollen after the sixth.[21]

Unfortunately, the bout drew just 3,500 customers and receipts of only $5,000. While the $1 and $2 sections sold out, most $3 seats were vacant. Outside, "a couple thousand fans stood around, voicing their willingness to pay $2 but stubbornly refusing to part with three bucks." Afterward, Flatto admitted to an error in raising ticket prices and said the mistake cost him "around $2,500." He refused to sell the $3 seats for $2 during the show

---

[18] Hurley, *op. cit.*, August 13, September 24, and December 3, 1933 sports sections.

[19] Wood, Wilbur, "Sock Market Needs Leader," *New York Sun*, October 12, 1933, sports section. Other sources list arena capacity at 4,000 (Gellis), 4,500 (Sid Mercer and Harry Grayson), and 6,000 (Damon Runyon and James Dawson). The author has struck a middle ground by using Wood's estimate.

[20] "Ridgewood Grove Club Easily Reached from Times Square," *New York American*, October 21, 1933, p. 19.

[21] Dawson, James, "Petrolle Victor; Defeats Fuller," *New York Times*, October 22, 1933, sports section. "Scale Betwixt Ross, Petrolle," *New York Evening Journal*, October 23, 1933, sports section.

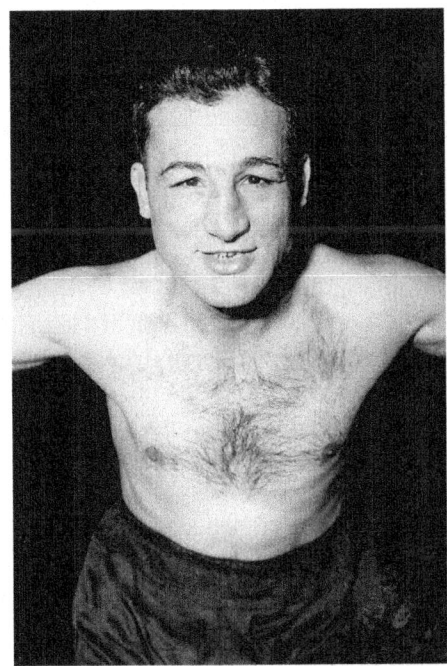

A smiling Billy prepares for Fuller. **Sammy Fuller, the Boston pride.**

Petrolle slips under Fuller's left in their New York rematch.

because it would have been "unfair to those who had paid $3."[22]

Although Hurley and Petrolle were guaranteed $2,500 on their end, they reduced their fee to $1,500 to help Flatto and McCarney out. Nonetheless, the club's management reported a loss for the evening.[23]

As expected, after the Fuller contest Hurley signed Petrolle to fight lightweight champion Barney Ross on the winter Free Milk Fund show. The bout was an overweight affair set for December 8, 1933, in the Bronx Coliseum, located at the Starlight Amusement Park (the arena was also known at the time as the New York Coliseum in the Bronx).

The Free Milk Fund for Babies was the pet charity of Millicent Hearst, wife of William Randolph Hearst, the owner of the largest newspaper syndicate in the country. The Hearsts had established the fund at New York in 1918 to provide free milk and food to the poor of the city on a year-round basis. To raise money, the fund sponsored many events in addition to boxing, including opera, art shows, wrestling and rodeo.

The Hearsts became publicly estranged in 1926 when Mr. Hearst's liaison with film star Marion Davies became intolerable. When he moved west with Davies, Mrs. Hearst chose to stay in New York where a long history of social activism made her a fixture in the city's social and political landscape. As part of his price for freedom to openly cavort with Marion in California, Randolph agreed to lend the full support of his journalistic empire to whatever political and charitable causes his wife pursued.[24]

As a result, the influence wielded by the Milk Fund in New York City's fight game was considerable. Beginning in 1922, the fund co-sponsored several important fights each year in partnership with an established boxing promoter. In exchange for the fund's share in the profits, the sports desks of Hearst's three New York daily newspapers, the *American*, the *Evening Journal*, and the *Daily Mirror*, delivered weeks of enthusiastic support and free publicity for whatever fight the promoter was presenting.

In 1933, the fund's boxing business was jointly administered by Damon Runyon, columnist for the *American*; Ed Frayne, sports editor of the *American*; and Bill Farnsworth, sports editor of the *Evening Journal*. While Runyon worked with the promoter to select the fighters on the card, Frayne and Farnsworth organized their papers' publicity campaigns for the show. Each of the men wrote articles on a daily basis leading up to the fight.[25]

In October, the three Hearst representatives asked Colonel John Reed

---

[22] Mercer, Sid, "Billy Floors Sammy Twice in Return Bout," *New York American*, October 22, 1933, sports section (attendance at 3,500 with receipts of $5,000). Wood, Wilbur, "Weight Holds Up Match" (subtitle – quotation just above subtitle), October 23, 1933, sports section (fans standing around outside, Flatto admitting to error).
[23] Wood, "Boxers Good Only in Ring," *New York Sun*, December 7, 1933, sport section.
[24] Proctor, Ben, *William Randolph Hearst, The Later Years 1911-1951*, (Oxford University Press, New York, 2007), p. 138.
[25] Nagler, Barney, *James Norris and the Decline of Boxing*, (Bobbs-Merrill Co., 1964), p. 8.

Kilpatrick, president of Madison Square Garden, about renting the Garden for the Milk Fund's 1933 Christmas show. Kilpatrick, who had succeeded William Carey as president two months earlier, replied by raising the Garden's fee ten percent over the amount the fund had been charged previously. To this, the Hearst triumvirate answered "No thanks," and instead decided to find a different backer to help them stage the fight.[26]

By raising the rent, Kilpatrick was reacting to what he believed to be the inequitable practice which allowed the Milk Fund to declare itself in on all the big money shows while leaving the Garden with all the losers. Since the beginning of 1933, the Garden had promoted 15 shows in New York, most of which had turned out to be losing ventures. Now, the fund was itself promoting the most profitable show of the winter season while at the same time trying to rent the Garden building at a charity rate to boot![27]

Kilpatrick was looking at a history where the Milk Fund had cut itself in on the last three heavyweight title bouts staged in New York without bearing any risk itself. In the most recent of these shows the fund's share in the Carnera-Sharkey fight had been 25 percent of the profit. Just a month earlier, the fund competed against the Garden when it joined with the Aram A. C. to put over the Ross-Canzoneri lightweight title card. The fund and Aram profited handsomely, while the Garden was left out in the cold.

All of this might have been fine in flush times when there was plenty of money and talent to go around. However, with the Depression causing fans to squeeze every dollar, and the manager's boycott depriving the Garden of the sport's premier stars, the Garden was feeling the pinch from all sides.

To fill the void created by Kilpatrick's rebuff, the Hearst triad engaged ticket broker Mike Jacobs as a partner to finance the pre-bout costs, advance the rent for the Coliseum, and assume responsibility for all the operative details connected with the Ross-Petrolle show. Uncle Mike, as he would come to be called, was a shrewd entrepreneur who had made much of his fortune buying up ducats for popular events of all descriptions at face value and then scalping them when the events became sellouts.

Although not widely known, Jacobs was the money man for Tex Rickard's biggest shows, fronting tens of thousands of dollars in exchange for choice tickets, which Mike sold for a huge profit. As the Garden's woes in 1933 mounted, Jacobs dispassionately followed the situation like the opportunistic businessman he was. Ever since Rickard's death, he had been waiting for the right moment to try his hand at promoting boxing. Now Hearst's Milk Fund was serving it to him on a silver platter.[28]

From Uncle Mike's perspective, a silent partnership with the fund was

---

[26] Durso, Joseph, *Madison Square Garden, 100 Years of History*, (Simon and Schuster, New York, 1979), p. 162.
[27] Borden, Eddie, "Broadcast from New York," *Ring Magazine*, July 1933, p. 40.
[28] Nagler, pp. 9-10.

Damon Runyon (left) alongside the *Journal-American*'s Bill Corum.

Mike Jacobs who stepped in to help Runyon and the Milk Fund.

Runyon discussing Milk Fund business with Jacobs in Florida.

the perfect situation to test the waters of the fight game. Ross-Petrolle was a solid attraction, the Hearst newspaper chain was a source of almost unlimited free publicity, and if everything went smoothly, the event would lay a foundation for the joint promotion of future topflight shows. Indeed, by aligning himself with the fund, Jacobs was bypassing boxing's minor leagues and gaining immediate access to the best talent the sport offered.

Before signing with the Milk Fund, Hurley met twice with new Garden president Kilpatrick. Although the public identified the Garden mainly as a boxing and wrestling arena, it also hosted hockey, the circus, trade shows, musical concerts, and political rallies. Since the colonel was hired for his overall management skill rather than his boxing knowledge, he sought out Hurley to discuss Jack's grievances and learn about the boxing business.

Kilpatrick confessed he knew little about boxing, but in his short time on the job he already was frustrated with the politicians on the commission who were trying to run the Garden's business. The colonel admitted he was disappointed with some of Johnston's tactics, and he was uncertain whether he would renew Boy Bandit's contract when it expired in October 1933.[29]

Hurley told the colonel patronage was so imbedded in New York's political system that he was wasting his time if he thought politicians would let a plum like boxing get away from them. Jack said that Billy McCarney was currently unaffiliated with any boxers and was a likely candidate to replace Johnston. Jack offered to set up a meeting for Kilpatrick with Billy.

Kilpatrick told Hurley the Garden was genuinely interested in promoting the Ross-Petrolle bout. The colonel argued the bout would draw twice as much at the Garden than at the Bronx Coliseum. As a peace offering, Kilpatrick offered to pay the $250 expense money which Jack claimed after the cancellation of Petrolle's bout with van Klaveren in January.

Hurley agreed the bout would gross more at the Garden, but his reply was unyielding: "You keep it. I asked for it once and didn't get it. As long as things are as they are at the Garden, I won't be asking – or taking – anything."[30]

As it turned out, Kilpatrick decided to straddle the fence when Johnston's contract as boxing director expired. Declining Hurley's offer to set up a meeting with McCarney, the colonel chose to neither fire the aging Boy Bandit nor offer him a contract renewal. Instead, he retained Johnston on a week-to-week basis, an arrangement which meant Jimmy had to either start delivering the goods or look for another job.[31]

Hurley's meetings with Kilpatrick were not his first with a Garden president. As discussed previously, former president William F. Carey had

---

[29] Hurley, "Ring Rations," *Fargo Forum*, October 1, 1933, sports section.
[30] Grayson, Harry, "Hurley Called by Bosses Determined upon Shake-up," *New York World-Telegram*, January 27, 1934, sports section.
[31] Hurley, *op. cit.*, October 8, 1933, sports section.

relied on Jack's opinion before reducing ticket prices at the Garden. Prior to that, Carey also had consulted Hurley about whether Garden investors should purchase the Chicago Stadium. Bill knew Jack was familiar with Chicago and would know why the Stadium had not been profitable.[32]

The fact that the Garden's officers sought Hurley's advice was evidence of his growing stature in the boxing business. Although Carey was no longer president, he was still on the board of directors. It was no secret he and other minority shareholders were working to have Kilpatrick and Johnston removed from their respective positions. It was also rumored Jack was the Carey faction's first choice as Johnston's successor.

In the meantime, a week before the scheduled December 8th fight, a doctor's exam confirmed Barney Ross had suffered "a muscle bruise between the second and third rib on his left side." As a result, Tom McArdle, the former Garden matchmaker who Jacobs had hired to handle the show's details, decided to postpone it until after the New Year.[33]

To keep Petrolle in fighting trim and at the same time recoup part of the extra expenses incurred because of the delay, Hurley presented McCarney and Ridgewood Grove matchmaker Johnny Attell with a proposal: "You lost some money on the Petrolle-Fuller fight. We don't like to leave any promoter we work for in the red. Why don't you get somebody for Petrolle to fight at your club while we are in the neighborhood?"[34]

In response, Attell signed Petrolle to face Stanislaus Loayza of Chile in a ten-round bout on December 12. Loayza had reached the "willing veteran" stage of his career where he could be relied upon to put up a good battle, but not upset the applecarts of the top contenders. His bout with Billy figured to be entertaining because Stanislaus had waged a surprisingly good fight against van Klaveren in his last New York appearance.

When Hurley made the Loayza match, Ross' co-manager Sam Pian objected. He feared a poor showing by Billy might endanger the bout with Ross. Jack did not take kindly to Pian's protest: "I didn't make any squawks when you jeopardized the Ross-Petrolle fight by letting Ross fight Sammy Fuller in November. If Petrolle can't lick Loayza, he doesn't deserve a shot at Ross. If Loayza licks Petrolle, you can call me all sorts of fool, but until that happens you look after Ross and I'll handle Petrolle."[35]

Loayza and Petrolle had met before in a short but torrid bout which Billy was happy to recall for reporters: "You know, I had a fight with Loayza five years ago in Detroit, and he almost got me. Late in the first round, he spun me around with a right hook to the jaw, and I was dizzy when I went to my corner. But I came out of it fast. When we began the second Loayza rushed,

---

[32] Hurley, *op. cit.*, January 22, 1933, sports section.

[33] Wood, "Ross Hurt, Fight Postponed," *New York Sun*, December 1, 1933, sports section.

[34] Wood, "Petrolle to Box Loayza," *New York Sun*, December 4, 1933, sports section.

[35] Wood, "Fight Managers a Scary Lot," *Fargo Forum*, December 8, 1933, sports section.

wide open, to finish me. He thought I was still dizzy. I nailed him on the chin with a right hand smash and it was all over."[36]

The bout did not begin as a body-punching affair, but it was Petrolle's shots to the midriff which eventually made the difference. For three rounds, they fought on even terms, going at it from crouched positions in the center of the ring. From the first bell, it was obvious Billy, apparently recalling the first fight, was out to end the bout quickly with a kayo punch to Stan's jaw.

At the start of the fourth, it looked like Petrolle's strategy was paying off as he landed a right to the jaw from long range which set Loayza down for a nine-count. After regaining his feet, however, Stan rallied with an assault that backed Billy around the ring, staggering and almost upsetting the Fargo scrapper. Rather than cover up, Petrolle met Loayza on his own terms and fought his way out of trouble. When the round ended, the battlers were going at it like a pair of dock wallopers, and the crowd was going wild.

In the fifth, Petrolle decided trading head shots with Loayza was too dangerous so he changed tactics. Billy found an opening to the body and sunk repeated rights into Stan's left side until he went on the defensive. Petrolle coasted for a while, peppering Loayza with jabs and hooks until late in the heat when Billy cornered him again and gave him a two-fisted battering. In the rest period between rounds, Stan told his seconds that his left leg was stiff, and his trainer massaged the afflicted limb vigorously.

Three more vicious rights to Loayza's left side in the sixth round sent him sinking slowly to the canvas. After he regained his feet at nine, Petrolle jabbed, took a left to the head from Stan, and dug another right to Loayza's body. This time he turned away from Billy, signaled that he had enough, and limped to his corner with his leg dragging. The time was 1:19.[37]

The sudden and anticlimactic ending stunned the crowd, leaving it undecided whether to applaud or boo. An examination of Loayza by two commission doctors after the fight revealed that blows below his left kidney had irritated Stan's sciatic nerve and produced a temporary and partial paralysis of his leg. Full recovery was expected in ten days.[38]

Billy's win was a good warm-up for the Ross bout, but the *New York Sun*'s Wilbur Wood noted "the customers ... stayed away in large numbers. So there was no joy for anyone. Petrolle received only a few hundred dollars in return for a fight that turned out to be anything but soft, Loayza finished with a paralyzed sciatic nerve, and the club lost more money. Also, fans who mistakenly figured Loayza to be a back number, and who therefore did not turn out, missed one of the best battles of the season."[39]

---

[36] Wood, "Petrolle Fears Big, Bad Wolf," *New York Sun*, December 12, 1933, sports section.

[37] Wood, "Loayza Is Stopped in Sixth," *New York Sun*, December 13, 1933, sports section.

[38] Grayson, "Doc Petrolle Sews Up New Tilt with Ross," *New York World-Telegram*, December 13, 1933, sports section.

[39] Wood, "Good Samaritan Role Risky," *New York Sun*, December 14, 1933, sports section.

Petrolle and Ross resumed serious training after the Christmas holiday when their fight was rescheduled for January 10, 1934. On December 27, Milk Fund matchmaker Tom McArdle announced a second postponement, this time until January 24. Although McArdle first gave the reason as a conflict with the date of a tennis match at Madison Square Garden, sportswriters soon learned the real reason was a "torn ligament in Barney's right shoulder" which was taking longer to heal than expected.

When the reason for the second delay came out, Hurley noted that Ross' complaints had changed from a bruised left side on December 1 to a sore right shoulder on December 27, and he immediately became suspicious: "Why don't they make up their minds? ... It was a queer thing that he first complained of one shoulder and then the other. He switched his pains. I don't think he was hurt at all. He just didn't think he could get right in the time left and ducked out on my old gentleman."[40]

With a week to go, Hurley went on record with a prediction of the bout's outcome, while at the same time challenging Ross to stand up and fight: "I want to say this, and you can make it as strong as you like. If Barney Ross stands up and fights any two rounds with my old gentleman, like he did against Tony Canzoneri, the old gentleman will knock him out ... If Ross gets on his scooter and races away like a deer, as he did in Chicago, well, I don't suppose that my old gentleman will succeed in tagging him.

"In any case, the old gentleman will win. You'll see a great fight, but a short and sweet one if this fellow Ross stands up for two rounds. It won't have to be two. Maybe my old gentleman will belt him out in one. All we ask is they take away the bike from Ross."[41]

Ross made no attempt to restrain his anger at the assault on his fighting spirit: "If Billy wants to gamble punches, he'll find me most agreeable ... I'm not one bit afraid of any of these promises that he's going to flatten me if I stand up and fight. What was I doing in Chicago in the last four rounds of my fight with him? I met him toe to toe and it was Petrolle who dropped out of the thick of it each time. He stopped fighting when I brought it to him, red hot and heavy.

"'Stand up.' I wouldn't be a world's champion, something he never has been, if I wasn't a stand-up fighter. What did I do in the Canzoneri fight when I was defending my title? Did I run in that fight, and who was it that backed away in every rally? Mr. Canzoneri, as you all saw. I like to fight. I would have knocked both Canzoneri and Petrolle out had I had my own way about it. Art Winch, my trainer and co-manager, and Sam Pian kept yelling for me to be careful and not lose fights that I had won ...

"I've improved since I met him the first time, to say nothing of picking

---

[40] Gellis, *op. cit.*, December 27 and 28, 1933, sports section. Igoe, Hype, "Chicago Boxer Petrolle Aversion," *New York Evening Journal*, January 18, 1934, p. 26.
[41] Igoe, *op cit.*

up a crown. I've never been on the floor, and this alone will make Petrolle wonder. If he sits me down, I'll get up and pat him on the back. But there'll be no back patting because he doesn't hit hard enough to bother me. He belted me before, and nothing happened. So what?"[42]

When told that Ross said he had made Petrolle back down in the last four rounds of their first fight, Billy laughed with disbelief and replied disdainfully: "How could that kid say such a thing? Why, he was taking fences, hedges and all the ditches in his hurry to get away from me. I never had to chase a fellow more than I did him. I hit him a couple of glancing left hooks as he was getting away and these scared him all the more.

"I don't question his right to run. I'd have knocked him out had he stood his ground. His business was not to get knocked cold. You can hardly blame him for taking it on the lam. But him, make me back away? Well, you watch Wednesday night. See who backs up. If he stands in there, I'll hook him cold in three heats. Get it? Any one of one, two, three (holding up three fingers in sequence)."[43]

Although it was hard to believe after reading the charges in the newspapers, the relationship between the Ross and Petrolle camps had been anything but contentious in the days before the two fighters became rivals.

Beginning in 1926 and for years afterward, Hurley had an arrangement with Ross' co-manager, Art Winch, in which he would send Petrolle on ahead before his Chicago fights to train under Winch's watchful eye. Jack told Billy to do everything Art said, and stay with him until Hurley arrived.

The first time it happened, Winch offered to get Petrolle a hotel room, but he refused, explaining that "Jack said for me to stay with you, and I'll sleep right here in your room." As Art told the story, the arrangement "would have been okay except there wasn't but one bed in the room, and Bill would go to bed at 9 o'clock and roll up in all the covers."

Five years later, Ross and Petrolle were both fighting on the undercard of a main event in Kansas City where Jack Dempsey was appearing in an exhibition. Barney as a kid was inclined to take the fight business lightly.

After the bouts, Billy came up to Ross and said: "You've got a fellow here (indicating Winch) who is heart and soul with any fighter he handles. You handle yourself like a good prospect. If you do what Art tells you, and keep yourself in shape, you might one day be the lightweight champion."

Winch later explained, "From that night on, Barney was more serious about his boxing and training and paid more attention to advice. I have always thanked Petrolle for it, and so does Barney."[44]

As the fight approached, oddsmakers made Ross a 2-to-1 choice over

---

[42] Igoe, "Chicago Mixing Recalled by Champion," *New York Evening Journal*, January 19, 1932, sports section.
[43] Igoe, "Kayo Seen by Billy if Rival Mixes," *New York Evening Journal* January 23, 1934, sports section.
[44] Corum, Bill, "Sports," *New York Evening Journal*, January 22, 1934, sports section.

Petrolle. The *New York Post*'s Ike Gellis wrote that although "it doesn't seem possible," every one of the 25 managers, promoters, and trainers he polled prior to the bout favored Barney. In addition, most of the New York-based writers also leaned heavily toward Ross. Only the *United Press'* Jack Cuddy, who picked Billy by kayo, and the *Associated Press'* Edward J. Neil, who gave him an even chance, went against the majority opinion.[45]

The reasoning by most of these experts was that Barney had defeated Billy in their first bout and was still improving with each fight. Petrolle, on the other hand, was not the fighter he had been even just six months earlier. Billy's most recent bouts at New York against Fuller and Loayza had been entertaining, but not impressive. The general belief was that while it would be a tough match, with Petrolle having a puncher's chance, Ross' youth, speed, and boxing ability would be too much for the fading Duluth veteran.

Two days before the contest, ticket sales reached $20,000. Although the Coliseum was located in the heart of the Bronx instead of Madison Square Garden, where most fans would have preferred, a sellout crowd of more than 12,000 and a gross gate of $36,000 was predicted. The last capacity show at an indoor arena in New York had been a year earlier for the ill-fated Carnera-Ernie Schaaf fight at the Garden on February 5, 1933.[46]

As New York City's second largest indoor arena, the Coliseum was not initially designed for spectator sports. Built to house exhibits at the 1926 Sesquicentennial Exposition at Philadelphia, the structure was bought for $11,000 by the owners of Starlight Amusement Park who shipped its steel framework to the Bronx. Re-assembly cost $100,000 and resulted in a building described as "cavernous, smoky, and poorly ventilated," especially in comparison to the more luxurious Madison Square Garden building.[47]

The week of the fight, Hurley was noticeably restrained in his remarks to the press, letting Billy take center stage and do most of the talking. To his friends, Jack confessed later he subsisted solely on a milk diet four days before and three days after the bout. Even beforehand, he admitted to a heightened state of anxiety when he told columnist Burris Jenkins, Jr.: "I'm all shaking inside, but I'll never let Bill know it ... I get sick ... whenever he fights. He can lick this Ross – but I wish it was over."[48]

---

[45] Gellis, *op. cit.*, January 24, 1934, sports section. Cuddy, Jack, "New York Sports Are Wagering 2 to 1 on Chicago Boy," *Duluth Herald*, January 24, 1933, sports section. Neil, "Petrolle and Ross to Draw Sellout Crowd," *Fargo Forum*, January 24, 1934, sports section.

[46] Gellis, "Chicagoan Scales 136-3/4, Heaviest of Boxing Career," *New York Evening Post*, January 24, 1934, sports section. Dawson, James, "Ross, Petrolle to Fight Tonight," *New York Times*, January 24, 1934, sports section.

[47] Gray, Christopher, "Streetscapes: The New York Coliseum; From Auditorium to Bus Garage to ...," *New York Times*, March 22, 1992, p. 10-7. Williams, "By Joe Williams," *New York Evening-World*, January 25, 1934, sports section.

[48] Jenkins, Burris, Jr., "A Fresh Slant," *New York Evening Journal*, January 23, 1934, sports section. "Frothy Facts," *New York World-Telegram*, January 31, 1934, sports section.

Petrolle was popular throughout his career. Fans admired his everyday, working-man approach to his craft. Above, he carries his own bags and bandages his own hands. Bottom, he models the Indian blanket he wore for all his fights and relaxes with a Reader's Digest.

In the final days before the contest, Hurley and Petrolle discussed the possibility the fight might be Billy's last. With purse sizes shrinking and no other lucrative matches on the horizon, they agreed a loss would take away Petrolle's only other reason to fight, a title bout with McLarnin. With this in mind, Jack reportedly gave Billy these instructions as he entered the ring:

"Billy, this will probably be your last fight. Naturally, I want you to win it in the worst way, for it may mean another shot at McLarnin and the welter title. But if it looks bad in there, and the going gets tough, I want you to go down fighting in the same way you've always fought – whether winning or losing. I don't want you to hold, grab or run. You've always been a fighter, and I want you to be remembered as a fighter. If this is our last fight, let's make it ring true like the others."[49]

Fulfilling in one fell swoop the prophecies of boxing's foremost experts and Hurley's worst fears, a dazzling Ross, 136-3/4, battered a game but old-looking Petrolle, 141-1/2, around the ring for ten rounds to earn the decision. Barney's victory was so decisive that not only did it end any doubt of his courage to "stand up and fight," but it confirmed that the time was right for Billy to hang up the gloves for good, as well.

From the outset, a swift and tireless Ross snapped Petrolle's head back with jabs and hooks which repeatedly upset Billy's rhythm as he moved forward. Employing a series of short, crisp left hooks to throw Petrolle off balance, Ross worked his way inside and whipped snappy two-fisted combinations to the head and body with dead-eye accuracy.

By comparison, Petrolle fought like a used-up warhorse whose every effort appeared slow and futile. Many of his swings were wild and without noticeable purpose, his footwork floundered awkwardly, and he sometimes fought as if befuddled and not sure about what to do. Now and then, he landed a right or a left to Ross' head or midsection, but the occasions were few and far between and never lasted long enough to do any real damage.

Except for the ninth round, which most observers gave to Petrolle, and flashes of the third and seventh rounds, which he won on a couple of scribes' scorecards, Billy was outfought at every turn. At the end, his eyes were swollen purple, and his lips puffed and bleeding. Even so, he was never knocked down, or ever in any real danger of a kayo.[50]

As predicted, a sellout crowd of 12,043 attended the bout, a figure which included 11,617 paying customers who contributed $36,522 to gross receipts and $33,212 to the net. Of this, the Milk Fund received $5,000, Ross $8,431, and Petrolle "about $7,000." Any remaining profit above expenses went to Mike Jacobs and, possibly, to the Hearst triumvirate.

---

[49] Campbell, "The Sports Mirror," *Duluth News Tribune*, January 28, 1934, sports section.
[50] Neil, "Lightweight Title-Holder Far Too Clever for Billy," *Duluth News Tribune*, January 25, 1934, sports section. Williams, *op. cit.* Cuddy, "Fargo Express Pulls Its Fire; Old Engine Makes Final Run on the Pugilistic Rails," *Duluth Herald*, January 25, 1934, sports section.

It was like old home week at the Pioneer Gym prior to the second Ross-Petrolle fight as rumors raged Petrolle would retire if he lost. Above, matchmaker Tom McArdle (left) & ex-referee Billy Roche (right) call on Billy to express their admiration for his ring work.

A tired Petrolle plods ahead against a young champion, Barney Ross.

Speed merchant Ross derails the Fargo Express with a stiff left jab.

With the air in the Bronx Coliseum filled with smoke, announcer Joe Humphreys raises Barney Ross' hand as a glum Petrolle watches.

The power of the Hearst newspaper syndicate to influence attendance at a fight was evidenced by the vast number of people who tried but were unable to see the bout. The crowd was the largest ever to attend a fight at the Bronx Coliseum. More than 6,000 were turned away when tickets sold out an hour in advance. The overflow crowd was so large the Bronx police had difficulty controlling pedestrian and vehicular traffic.[51]

When the bell ended the final round, Petrolle returned to his corner where Hurley performed the familiar ritual of draping Billy's Indian blanket around his shoulders. While announcer Joe Humphreys collected the scorecards, Jack and Petrolle held a short and subdued conversation as Billy paced back and forth in a circle near his corner awaiting the decision.

"Well, what do you say, Bill?" asked Hurley.

"Well, what do you say, Jack?"

"I say it's time to call it enough," was Hurley's response.

"O. K. You're the boss," answered Billy.[52]

Even before Humphreys raised Ross' hand, Hurley leaned through the ropes toward the press row and quietly announced: "Gentlemen, 'the Old Man' has made his last fight."[53]

Afterward writers packed the loser's dressing room to the rafters. Asked about Billy's retirement, Hurley said: "I made a lot of dough with the 'Old Man,' but I went through every dime. I am a sucker for a touch, and always will be, I guess. He gave me a chance to make more dough in the last year, but I have two bucks today. So why should he take the rap for me?

"... When he was a kid, beginning 11 years ago, he used to go in there looping right-handers, great caveman swings, which were loaded with TNT. I nearly fainted when I saw him reverting to his youthful days, to the homely, whole-hearted haymakers. He had tried everything under the sun on Ross and none was potent. He had only his heart left ... he went back to the primitive swings of 11 years ago in the last hope that these punches ... might fool Ross and turn the tables.

"I can't stand to see him get hit. It hurts me. I don't want to see him fight any more. I never felt that way about any other fighter, and I have had plenty. I probably never will feel that way about any other fighter. The 'Old Man' will live forever with me. I am happy in the thought that he has finished without a flaw in his physical makeup. Happy, too, that we wind up as we began – friends ... My 'Old Gentleman' will never want. He leaves

---

[51] Whether Frayne, Farnsworth, and Runyon profited from the first few Milk Fund promotions is a matter of conjecture. In 1935, Jacobs formed the Twentieth Century Sporting Club, Inc. in which these newsmen shared a silent interest. It is a safe bet that after the corporation was formed they did receive a share of profits from the Milk Fund shows. The subject of the corporation's formation will be addressed later in the Hurley story.

[52] Gellis, "Around the Ring," *New York Evening Post*, January 25, 1934, sports section.

[53] "Petrolle Retires with $200,000 after Dozen Years of Warfare," *New York World-Telegram*, January 25, 1934, sports section.

Another post-fight view. A bespeckled Jack Hurley is seen leaning on the top rope at the far right, a faint smile of relief on his face.

A poignant shot of Hurley and Petrolle in the dressing room after the "Kid's last fight."

the ring about $200,000 to the good. That consists of houses, a business, a little ornamental iron plant, and thanks to my advice, the rest in government bonds."[54]

Petrolle thanked the writers for all the nice things they had written about him. "If Hurley says I'm through, I'm through," he said. "I can't fight anymore, so I won't. Tell them that. I don't feel like quitting, but I guess my whiskers are getting a bit gray. Boxing has been mighty good to me and I want to thank the people who followed my career. I leave the game with the satisfaction of feeling that my supporters are certain that I always gave them the best I had.

"I'm glad I'm out of it while I still know east from west, and I don't hear bells that aren't ringing. I gave the fight game all I had and it gave me all I've got ... I quit once before – four years ago – and I came back after a rest because I knew that wasn't the real finish. I proved it wasn't. This time it is, and I know it. The old zip is gone. It had to go sometime."[55]

As the interviews ended and Hurley headed for the door, Petrolle called to him: "Hey, Jack. Any time you are broke and need work, there'll always be a job waiting for you at my iron foundry." Not sure if Billy was serious or not, Hurley snarled back: "You'll never get me working in an iron foundry or any other place for you. It is tough enough having you work for me!"[56]

The next day, while packing his bags, Hurley was interrupted by a phone call asking him to stop by Madison Square Garden before he left town. A faction of the Garden's board of directors, led by ex-president Carey, was upset about the lack of leadership shown by the corporation's boxing department and wanted to discuss how to remedy the situation. Specifically, the group wanted to know if Jack was interested in becoming the Garden's new boxing director were the position made available?"

After satisfying himself the call was not just a gag, Jack said he would be right over. Given that he was now an unemployed boxing manager without portfolio whose only standing offer for gainful work was a job in Petrolle's iron works, the position of boxing boss at Madison Square Garden sounded like a pretty good proposition.

---

[54] Gellis, *op. cit.* (first and third paragraphs). Igoe, "Boxing World Will Miss Petrolle," *New York Evening Journal*, January 26, 1934, sports section (second and fourth paragraphs).
[55] "Petrolle Retires with $200,000 after Dozen Years of Warfare, *op. cit.* ("If Hurley says I'm through, I'm through." and "I don't feel like quitting ... gave them the best I had."). Neil, *op. cit.* ("I can't fight anymore, so I won't. Tell them that."). Neil, "Glad to Quit, Warrior Says in Interview" (AP), *Duluth News Tribune*, January 26, 1934, p. 14 (last paragraph).
[56] Gellis, *op, cit.*

Afterword

The curtain draws to a close on Volume One of the Jack Hurley saga with the retirement of Billy Petrolle. From this point on, Hurley's life takes a new direction. Within a year, he will move to Chicago where he will develop a stable of fighters and find a niche in 1942 as matchmaker at the Chicago Stadium, then the country's largest sports arena. There, he will stage some of the decade's most important fights before a change in circumstances forces him to leave the Windy City in search of friendlier pastures.

Volume Two tells the story of those Chicago years.

BIBLIOGRAPHY

BOOKS

Ashbury, Herbert, *The Great Illusion*, in Perrett, Geoffrey, "America in the Twenties: A History," (Simon and Schuster, New York, NY, 1982)
Barton, George A., *My Lifetime in Sports*, (Lund Press, Minneapolis, MN, 1957)
Cass County, North Dakota, *"The Honor Roll in the World War—1917-1918-1919,"* (Buckbee-Mears Co., St. Paul, Minnesota, 1919)
Clark, Tom, *The World of Damon Runyon*, (Harper & Row, Publishers Inc., New York, New York, NY, 1978)
Collins, Mike, *Ring Battles of the Ages*, (Boxing Book Publishing Co., 1932)
Cooper, Jerry, *Citizens As Soldiers, A History of the North Dakota National Guard*, (The North Dakota Institute for Regional Studies, North Dakota State University, Fargo)
Davis, Charlie, *That Band from Indiana*, (Mathom Publishing Co., Oswego, New York, NY, 1982)
Dempsey, Jack and Cuddy, Jack, *Championship Fighting – Explosive Punching and Aggressive Defense*, (Nicholas Kaye, London, 1951)
Dempsey, Jack, with Barbara Piatelli Dempsey, "Dempsey," (Harper and Row, New York, NY, 1977)
Dent, Jim, *Monster of the Midway: Bronko Nagurski*, (MacMillan, 2004)
Durso, Joseph, *Madison Square Garden, 100 Years of History*, (Simon and Schuster, 1979)
English, T. J., *Paddy Whacked: The Untold Story of the Irish Gangster*, (Harper Collins, 2005)
Fargo-Moorhead City Directories of 1913, 1915, 1916, 1917, published by Pettibone Directory Company (each year is a separate volume)
Fleischer, Nat, "1958 Ring Record Book," Ring Book Shop, Inc., New York, NY, 1958)
Fleischer, Nat, "The 1957 Ring Record Book," (Ring Book Shop, New York, NY, 1957)
Fleischer, Nat, *1943 Ring Record Book*, (Ring Book Shop, New York, NY, 1943)
Fleischer, Nat, *50 Years at Ringside*, (Fleet Publishing Corp., New York, NY, 1958)
Fleischer, Nat, Nat *Fleischer's Ring Record Book and Boxing Encyclopedia, 1955 Edition*, (Ring Book Shop, New York, NY, 1955)
Fleischer, Nat, Nat *Fleischer's Ring Record Book and Boxing Encyclopedia, 1961 Edition*, (Ring Book Shop, New York, NY, 1961)
Gibbons, Mike, *How to Box*, Gibbons Athletic Association
Griffin, Marcus, *Wise Guy – James J. Johnston: A Rhapsody in Fistics*, (Vanguard Press, New York, NY, 1933)
Harding, John, with Berg, Jack, *Jackie Kid Berg, The Whitechapel Windmill*, (Robson Books, London, 1987)
Heinz, W. C., *Once They Heard the Cheers*, (Doubleday & Company, New York, NY, 1979)
Heller, Peter, *In This Corner*, (Simon and Schuster, New York, NY, 1973)
Ireland, Major General M. W., *The Medical Department of the United States in the World War*, (Washington Government Office, 1925)
Jerving, Ryan, contributor; Wintz, Cary D. and Finkelman, Paul, editors, *Encyclopedia of the Harlem Renaissance*, (Routledge, 2004)
Kahn, Roger, *A Flame of Pure Fire, Jack Dempsey and the Roaring -'20s*, (Harcourt Brace & Company, New York, San Diego, & London, 1999)
Kearns, Jack and Fraley, Oscar, *The Million Dollar Gate*, (Macmillan Company, 1966)

Kessler, Harry, *The Millionaire Referee* (Harkness Publishing, St. Louis, Missouri, 1982)
L'Amour, Louis, *Education of a Wandering Man*, (Bantam Books, 1989)
Legislative Assembly of North Dakota under direction of Brigadier General G. Angus Parker, *Official Roster of North Dakota Soldiers, Sailors, and Marines in the World War, 1917-1918, Volume 2*, (Bismarck Tribune Company, 1931)
Moline, Melva, *The Forum First Hundred Years*, (Fargo Forum, 1978)
Morgan, James, *The Life Work of Edward H. Moseley in the Service of Humanity*, (Macmillan Company, New York, NY, 1913)
Mullally, Frederic, *Primo, the Story of 'Man Mountain' Carnera*, (Robson Books, 1991)
Nagler, Barney, *James Norris and the Decline of Boxing*, (Bobbs-Merrill Co., Inc., New York, NY, 1964)
Paton, Bruce C., *Medical Aspects of Harsh Environments, Volume I: Chapter 10 – Cold, Casualties, and Conquests: The Effects of Cold on Warfare*, (Office of the Surgeon, Department of the Army, United States of America)
Proctor, Ben, *William Randolph Hearst, The Later Years 1911-1951*, (Oxford University Press, New York, 2007)
Roberts, Randy, *Jack Dempsey, the Manassa Mauler*, (Louisiana State University Press, 1979)
Samuels, Charles, *The Magnificent Rube*, (McGraw-Hill Book Co., Inc., 1957)
Scates, Shelby, *Warren Magnuson and the Shaping of Twentieth-Century America*, (University of Washington Press, 1997)
Stewart, Richard W., *American Military History, Volume II*, (Center of Military History, United States Army, Washington, D.C., 2005)
Sullivan, Russell, *Rocky Marciano: The Rock of His Times*, (University of Illinois Press, 2005)
Thompson, Gregory Lee, *The Passenger Train in the Motor Age: California Rail and Bus Industries, 1910-1941*, (Ohio State University Press, 1993)
Walker, Mickey and Reich, Joe, *Mickey Walker, the Toy Bulldog and His Times*, (Random House, New York, NY, 1961)
Watson, Emmett, *My Life in Print*, (Lesser Seattle Publishing, Seattle, 1993)

****

NEWSPAPERS

Associated Press
Biloxi Daily Herald
Bismarck Tribune
Boston Daily Record
Boston Evening American
Boston Evening Transcript
Boston Globe
Boston Herald
Boston Post
Boston Traveler.
Brooklyn Citizen
Brooklyn Daily Eagle
Brooklyn Daily News
Brooklyn Daily Times
Camp Dodger
Chicago Daily News
Chicago Evening American
Chicago Herald and Examiner

Chicago Tribune
Dallas Times Herald
Detroit Free Press
Detroit News
Detroit Times
Duluth Herald
Duluth News Tribune
Fargo Courier-News
Fargo Daily Tribune
Fargo Forum
Grace City Gazette, ND
Grand Forks Daily Herald
Griggs County Sentinel-Courier, ND
Hartford Daily Times
Havre Daily News
Houston Post
International News Service
Jamestown Daily Alert

Kansas City Journal
Lisbon Free Press, ND
Los Angeles Evening Express
Los Angeles Examiner
Los Angeles Herald
Los Angeles Times
Louisville Times
Mexia Daily News
Miami News
Milwaukee Journal
Minneapolis Daily Star
Minneapolis Tribune
Naples Daily News
New York American
New York Daily Graphic
New York Daily Mirror
New York Daily News
New York Evening Graphic
New York Evening Journal
New York Evening Post
New York Herald Tribune
New York Sun
New York Sun
New York Telegram
New York Times
New York World
New York World Telegram
Newark Evening News
Newark Star-Eagle
Northern News, Spooner, MN
Oklahoma City Times
Omaha World-Herald
Oregonian
Philadelphia Daily News
Philadelphia Evening Bulletin
Philadelphia Inquirer
Philadelphia Record
Prairie Press, Gwinner, ND
Schenectady Gazette
Seattle Post-Intelligencer
Seattle Star
Seattle Times
Sioux City Journal
Sioux City Tribune
Spokane Daily Chronicle
Spokesman-Review
Springfield Republican
St. Louis Post-Dispatch
St. Paul Daily News
St. Paul Pioneer Press
Sunday New York World-Herald Magazine
Syracuse NY Herald-Journal

****

PERIODICALS

Advances in Clinical and Experimental
Billboard Magazine
Boxing Annual–1953
Boxing Blade
Boxing Illustrated
Esquire Magazine
Frontier Times
Hong Kong Medical Journal
Medicine

Ramsey County History
Ring Magazine
Saturday Evening Post
Seattle Magazine
Self-Defense
Sport Magazine
Sports Illustrated
Time Magazine

****

UNPUBLISHED AND MISCELLANEOUS

"Canadian Northern Railway Claim Files," Central Regional Law Department, Library Archive of Canada
"Duluth Comprehensive Plan: Historic Development Patterns," Draft 1, October 21, 2005.
"Tales of Jack Hurley," KRAB-FM 107.7, Seattle WA, c. 1980s
1900, 1910, 1920, and 1930 U. S. Census
Coolidge, Calvin, "Patriotism in Time of Peace," (speech presented on October 4, 1924 dedicating the monument to the First Division A.E.F.)

Desmond Parry, "Remembering Max 'Boo Boo' Hoff," American Mafia.com, August 2006 (PLR International, 2006)
Dorgan, Ike, "Building Up Big Fights," (syndicated, copyright 1931)
Healy, Thomas, unpublished manuscript tracing Healy family lineage
Horton, Blaine A., "A Most Efficient Officer In Every Respect – George C. Marshall in World War I (1916-1919)," Shepherd College, Winner of the 2003 WFA-USA Phi Alpha Theta Undergraduate Essay Award, webpage: wfa-usa.org/new/geomarshall.htm
Kearns, "Life Story," Hearst newspapers, (copyright The Christy Walsh Syndicate 1926)
Kemp, David, "Northern League: Proud Tradition," northernleague.com (official website of the Northern League)
L'Amour, Beau and O'Dell, Paul J., "Biography," p. 2, *Official Louis L'Amour Website*
Lane, Andrew, "Weakened Immune System in Chronic Sinusitis Reveals New Treatment Targets," Johns Hopkins Medical Institutions Press Release, September 15, 2006
Last, Frank (edited by Rick Riehl), "My War Diary," webpage: fylde.demon.co.uk/riehl.htm
Marshall, Barry J., "Peptic Ulcers, Stomach Cancer and the Bacteria Which Are Responsible," *Heinekin Lectures 1998* (Royal Academy of Arts and Sciences, Amsterdam, 1999)
Marshwood School District and Old Berwick Historical Society, "Hike Through History, the Lure of Trains: Harry Ernest Adlington," Section 2.4.
Newman, Scott A., "Jazz Age Chicago – Urban Leisure from 1893 to 1945: Chicago Stadium," chicago.urban-history.org/ven/sas/chi_stad.shtm1.
Paradowski, Leszak; Blonski, Wojchiech; and Kempinski, Radoslaw; "Twenty Years After Introducing Proton Pump Inhibitors. What Have We Achieved in Peptic Ulcer Disease Conventional Treatment?" *Advances in Clinical and Experimental Medicine, 2004*, Volume 13, Number 5, pp. 737-747
Piehl, Mark, Clay County historian, interviewed by Dan Gunderson, *"The National Weather Service Predicts Red River Will Rise to 37.5 Feet in F-M,"* (Minnesota Public Radio, April 1997).
Quirk, Jim, "The Minneapolis Marines: Minnesota's Forgotten NFL Team," *The Coffin Corner*, Volume 20 (1998)
Staff of Kheel Center for Labor Management and Archives at Cornell University, "Abstract of Switchmen's Union of North America Arbitration Arbitration Proceedings, 1910," (Kheel Center for Labor-Management Documentation and Archives, Martin P. Catherwood Library of Cornell University)
University of Minnesota Extension Service,"Red River Valley Flooding During 1800s Was as Serious as 1997 Flooding," (University of Minnesota Extension Service, October 1997)
Unpublished Fargo Forum Biography Questionnaire filled out by Jack Hurley

Index of Names and Illustrations

Note: Illustrations and photos are referenced in bold italics

Abel, Barney, 429, 448, 459, 485
Adams, Johnny, 296, *298*, 308, 611, 614
Albertanti, Francis, 304, 607
Alvis, Ray, 197-8, 427, *428*, 429, 448-50, 454, 458, 461, *463*, 464, 468-69, 473-75, 478, 481, 485, 492-4, 516, 631, 635
Alvis, Crystal, 449
Aram A. C., 675-76, 678, 682, 684, 688-89, 695
Arcel, Ray, 371, 373, 375, 616
   on first Petrolle-Berg fight, 375
   on Jackie (Kid) Berg, 371, 373
   on Petrolle's punching power, 616
Attell, Abe, 451, 607
Attell, Johnny, 691, 698
Aurora, IL 420-21
Azzarella, Joe, 308, 353, 394
Backer, Les, 107, *185*, 186
Baer, Max, 30, 518, 557, 572, 574, 646, 661-64, 671, *672*, 673, 674-5, 690
Bailey, Jack (Hurley fighter), 110, *111*, 112, 118-19, 129-30, 140, 147-48, 150-51, 183
Baker, Sammy, ("Sergeant Sammy"), 325, 327, 410, 412-13, *414*, 423
Barnum, P. T., 99, 159
Barkley, Ralph (Slim), 122
Barton, George, 44, 102, 106, 132, 137, 187, 329, 378
Battaglia, Frank, 567, 575
Battalino, Bat, (Christopher Battaglia), 177, 271, 282-84, *283*, 515, 594, 602-605, *606*, 607-08, *609-10*, 611, *612*, 613, 617, 622-23, 625-26, *627-28*, 661, 667
Beery, Wallace, 663
Belanger, Charley, 571, 576
Berg, Jackie (Kid), ("the Whitechapel Windmill"), 371-76, *369*, *372*, 407, 420, 494-98, *499*, 500-01, 515, 524, 542, 614, 616, 648, 684
Bergomas, Giacomo, 568, 572-75, 623
Berlenbach, Paul, 274, 281
Bertazzolo, Riccardo, 566, 568, *570*, 575
Biddle, Al, (Hurley fighter), 126, 129
Biddle, Tony, 458-59, 536
Big Sandy Lake, 631, *632*, 633-35, 638, 641, 669
Birkie, Hans, 630, 659, 691
Bishop, Biddy, 193, 195, 368, *369*
Bismarck, SD, 108, 121-22, 130, 132, 144, 173, 228-31
Bismarck semi-pro baseball team, 108
Bliven, Perry, 121, 264
Blue, Earl ("Little Boy Blue"), (Hurley fighter), 143-44, 218, 221-229, *222*, 234, *257*, 259, 264-65, 293, 297, 299, 305, 309, *310*, *311*, 313, 316, 325-26, 329, 339
Blumenthal, Nessie, 439-40
Boehme, Eddie, 126, 129, 179
Bollin, Andy, (Hurley fighter), 143
Booth, Albie, 505-06
Borde, Jimmy, 394, 398, *395*, 446
Boston, MA, 203, 383, 421, 439, 441, 478, 572, 587, 622-23, 625, 648, 661, 684-88, 692
Boxing Blade (periodical), 137-38, 140, *194*
Braddock, James J., 448, 518, 622-3, *624*, 625, 659
Brady, Jack, 245, 255
Brady, Tom, 685, 688
Brady, William, 89
Brassil, Johnny, 625, 685, 687
Bricker, George, 440
Brisbane, Tom, (Sioux City promoter), 189

Broadway (New York street), 82, 269-72, *271*, 289, 318
Broadway Arena, 595, 689
"Broadway Breezes," (Hurley's newspaper column), 318-20
Bronson, Jimmy, 458
Bronx Coliseum, 683, 694, 697, 707
Brouillard, Lou, 602, 678, 688
Brown, Warren, 443
Buckley, Johnny, 383, *588*
Bull, Frankie, 235, *236,* 237
Bundlie, Gerhard J., 578
Burchard, Jim, coverage of Thompson-McLarnin fight, 465
Burnham Building, 427, 448, 450, 456, 485
Burns, Tommy, 27, 36
Byrne, Tim, coverage of Petrolle-Suarez fight, 548n
Callahan Andy, 659, 684
Callahan, Mushy, 218-21, *219*, 223, 226, 296, 318, 346, 373, 413, 497, 614
Camp Dodge, IA, 45, 69, 77, 102, 110
Camp Greene, North Carolina, 62
Camp Merrit, New Jersey, 63
Campbell, Cubby, 337, 339, 342-43, 354-55, 357-59, 377-78, 383, 389, 391, 396, 398, 405, 407, 408, 410-11, 419, 456, 459, 491, 496, 517, 525, 549, 629-30, 635, 643, 657
   coverage of
      Petrolle-Canzoneri I fight, 496
      Petrolle-Tut III fight, 378-79
Campolo, Victorio, 426, 558, 594
Canzoneri, Tony, 273, 281, 403-04, 416, 447, 484, 493-97, 500, 512, 515, 522, 524, 534, 541-42, 548-49, 594, 602, 604-05, 616-17, 630, 639, 641-42, 645, 647, 649-653, *651*, *664-65*, 656-57, 660-61, *666*, 667, 678, 683-84, 688-89, 695, 700-01
Capitol City Boxing Club, 566, 575
Carbo, Frank ("Mr. Gray"), *283*, 284-88
Carey, William F. (Bill), 418, 426, 583-85, 587, 589, 595, 658p., 662, 675, 695, 697-98, 710
Carveth, F. J., 346-47, 363-64
   coverage of

      Petrolle-Flowers II fight, 363-64
      Petrolle-Myers fight, 346-47
Carnera, Primo, 446, 450-51, *453-54*, 454-56, 474-79, 481, 493, 507, 515-16, 587, *588*, 589, 594, 645, 661, 663-64, 669, 674-75, 695, 702
Cassidy, Sergeant Major, 68
Castano, Andres, 489-90, 525
Cathedral Club, 41, 43
Ceccoli, Johnny, 289, 297, *298*
Chapman, Wilbur J., 12
Chevalier, Leon (Bombo), 478-79, 557
Chicago, IL, 11-12, 28, 31, 34-52, 54, 93, 99, 110, 130, 133-34, 142, 162, 183, 197, 200- 2, 212, 225, 231, 261, 265, 286, 290-91, 293, 296, 299, 301, 316, 318, 320-23, 329, 336, 346-47, 349, 353, 357, 361, 363, 371, 373-74, 376, 391-2, 403-06, 416, 419-21, 423-24, 426-27, 429, 431-32, 434, 439-40, 443, 447-51, 454, 456, 458-59, 464, 469, 474-75, 477-78, 481-85, 492-96, 503, 515, 541-42, 558, 562, 580, 595, 602, 604, 614, 616, 619, 621-23, 625, 630-31, 633, 635, 638, 641-43, 645, 647, 657, 659, 664-65, 667, 671, 678, 691, 698, 700-01
Chicago Coliseum, 321, 416, 423, 426-27, 443, 447, 464, 485
Chicago Cubs, 112n, 261, 262n, 301, 431-32 434, 477
Chicago Stadium, 246n, 403-04, 423-24, 426-27, 434, 443, 447, 451-52, 494, 496, 622, 630-31, 665, 667, 698
Chicago White Sox, 429- 431
Christner, Meyer (KO), 493, 531
Churchill, Frank, 478-79
Circus, 10-11, 80, 138, 201, 258
   A. G. Barnes Wild Animal, 11, 139
   Barnum and Bailey, 11, 258
   Ringling Brothers, 10-11, 258
   Sells-Floto, 11
Clark, Sheldon, 424, 426
Clememceau, Georges, 70
Clemmer, Jack, 119-20, 122-25
Clifford, Jack, 355, 357
Cobb, Walter, 671
Cochrane, Ed, 353, 479-80,
   coverage of Petrolle-Kane fight, 353

Colley, Reginald, Captain, (Fargo Company B recruiting officer), 59
Collins, Mike (Minneapolis promoter), 134, *135*, 137, 139-40, *141*, 143, 150, 178, 191, 343, 377, 454, 477-78, 667, 669
Comiskey Park, 421, 464
Commercial Club, 10-11, 14, 157
Coney Island Stadium, 262, 272n, 273, 277, 290, 292-93, 295
Conmy, Abigail Hurley, (Jack's second oldest sister), 4, 6, *7*, 20, *61*, 328, 365-66, 638
Comrie Bill, (Jack's brother-in-law), 116, 126
Comrie, Margaret Hurley, (Jack's oldest sister), 4, *7*, 116, 366
Conklin, Lester, 573
Coogan, Mel, 198-99, 233
Cook, George, 479
Cooney, Danny, 204, 206-07, *210*, 211, 217-18, 233, 264-65, 314
Cooperstown (town baseball team), 100
Corbett, James J., 582, 605, 611
  on Petrolle's fighting ability, 582
  on Petrolle-Battalino I, 611-13
Corbett III, Young (Ralph Giordano), 664
Cormany, Boyd, 58n, 60, 62, 64
Corum, Bill, 509, 535-37, 561, 582, *696*
  coverage of Retzlaff-Gallagher fight, 561
  opinion of Petrolle as a fighter, 582
Coulon, Johnny, 46, 314
Cox, Joe, 31
Criss, Battling, 439, 441, 443
Cuddy, Jack, 89, 702
Cullum, Dick, 346, 568
Cugat, Xavier, 633
Cunningham, Charles, 530
Cutler, Lou, (Oklahoma promoter), 474-75
Daly, Dan ("Dangerous Dan"), (Jim Gerry), 432, *433*, 440
Daniels, Dick, 671
Davies, Marion, 694
Dawson, James, 584, 608
  coverage of
    Petrolle-Battalino I fight, 608
    Petrolle-McLarnin III fight, 555
    Petrolle-Suarez fight, 548n
Dayton, Alfred,
  coverage of
    Blue-Okun fight, 305
    Petrolle-Martinez fight, 306-07, 568-69
    Retzlaff-Sekyra fight, 570-71
DeBeau, Eddie, 123, 129, 147n, 149-50, 162, *163*, 189
Debolt, Tiny, 558
DeForest, Jimmy, *92*
Delaney, Jack, 267, 274, 281
Delaney, Jimmy, 121n, 134, *136*, *141*, 144, 150, 305
DeMarco, Cuddy, 89, 234, 249, 322, *323*, 360
DeMave, Jack, 321, 325
Dempsey, Jack, (William Harrison), ("Manassa Mauler"), 33, *47*, 79-80, *84*, *87*, 89-98, *91*, *92*, *94*, *96*, 133, 153, 166, 218, 227, 274, 276, 290, 305, 314, 320, 333, 355, 357, 363, 402, 417-18, 423, 426-27, *428*, 429, 447-48, 450, 456, 458, 477-78, 482, 485, *486*, 487-92, 516, 522, 557, 562, 575-78, *579*, 580-81, 585, 645, 663-64, 669, 671, *672*, 673, 674, 701
Des Moines, IA, 77, 144, 153-54, 174, 184, 188, 191, 192
Detroit, MI, 421, 439-41, 455-56, 458-59, 469, 474, 483, 493, 501-02, 511, 516, 518, 524-25, 529, 537, 552, 558, 573, 625, 634, 691, 699
Dexter Park, 420-21
Diener, Franz, 485
Dillon, Jack, 51
Dilworth, MN, 145, 148, 150, 152, 162, 164, 365, 483
Doran, Jerk (St. Paul promoter), 329, 396, 516, 567
Dorgan, Tad, 308
  Hurley's discussion of Petrolle's "delayed knockout punch," 308
Doyle, Jack, (Los Angeles promoter), 38, 218, *219*, 221
Drukenbrod, M. F., 399

Druxman, Nate (Seattle promoter), 368-70, *369*
Duffy, Bill (Broadway Bill), 279-80, *303*
Duluth, MN, 365-66, 371, 374, 377, 380-83, 386, 388-89, 392, 294, 396, 401, 404-05, 408, 410-11, 413, 418-19, 424, 429, 439, 446, 456, 459, 483-84, 489-91, 515, 524-25, 557-58, 561, 563, 567, 569, 572, 575-76, 578, 580-81, 599, 621-22, 625, 629, 633, 635, 638, 641p., 645-46, 657, 659, 669, 671, 673-74, 702, 710
Dundee, Joe, 462, *463*, 469
Dundee, Vince, 447
Dunkley, Charles, 402-03
Dunn, Dick (Detroit promoter), *275*, 361-63, *362*, 376-78, 398, 401, 404, 456, 469, 625
Dunn, Edward L., 174, 179
"Eastern representative," 35, 277-79, 281-82, 287-88
Ebbets Field, 274, 281, 299, 456, 469, 625
Ehmke, Billy, (Hurley fighter), 143, 182-184, *185*
Ellis, Alfred (Al), 114, *115*
Epstein, Jack (Coney Island Stadium matchmaker), 273, 293
Erickson, John (Man Mountain), (the Big Swede), 458, 474-75
Ertle, Johnny (Kewpie), 133, *135*, 137-38
Faeth, Tony, 439, 441
Fagan Danny (Irish), 314-17, *315*, 355
Fargo, ND, 1-7, 10-11, 14-15, `17, 18, 20-28, 31, 33-34, 36, 37-38, 41-44, 46, 50-52, 54, 55, 59-60, 77, 99-103, 106-08, 110, *111*, 112-114, 116-17, 119-26, 129-31, 133, 143-45, 154, 156-57, 159-162, 164, 167, 169, 172-75, 177-85, 186-88., 190-93, 195, 197-200, 211-213, 216-18, 220-21, 224-28, 230-35 237-39, 241-44, 247, 249-50, 258-59, 262-65, 296, 301-02, 304-05, 312-14, 316, 318-19, 322, 326, 328, 332-334, 337, 339, 346, 364-66, 368, 374, 376, 381, 388-89, 392, 396, 401-02, 404, 417, 419, 460, 475, 482, 484-85, 487-89, 494-95, 497, 500, 505, 513, 515-17, 524, 536, 538, 541, 544, 552, 567, 574, 576, 578, 580, 582, 591, 594-95, 599, 605, 613, 617, 620-21, 629, 642, 646, 683, 699
Fargo Auditorium, 10, 60, 106, 123-24, *127-28*, 130, 156-57, 167, *168*, 173, 178, 183, 231, 235, 238, 247, 316, 332, 482, 488
Fargo Athletics, 52, 108
Fargo Cubs (baseball team), 51-52, 54
Fargo-Moorhead Graingrowers (baseball team), 8, 24, 51-52, 54-55, 114
Fargo-Moorhead Twins (baseball team), 216
Farley, William, 583
Farnsworth, Bill, *588*, 694-95
Farrell, Jack, 498
Fay, Al, 478-80
Feller, Bob, 216-17, *215*
Feller, Will, 216-17, *215*
Ficucello, Ralph, 562-64, *570*
Fields, Jackie, 447, 449, 462, *464*, 469-70, *471-472*, 506, 602, 659, 664
Fink, Lou, 647
First Division, 64, 66, 68-70, 74, 75
Fitger Brewing Company, 332, 334-36, *336*
Fitzgerald, Eugene, 217, 392, 487, 494, 642
   coverage of
      Dempsey's Fargo visit, 487-88
      Hurley- LeRoy reconciliation, 392
Fisher, Al (Big Hat), 139
Flaherty, Si, 562
Flatto, I. T., 691-92, 694
Fleischer, Nat, 444-45
Flowers, Bruce, 349, *350*, 353, 359, 361, 364, 366, 376, 542, 684
Flowers, Tiger, 272, 305, 457, 465, 468, 541
Flynn, Jim (Fireman), 25, 33, 36
Flynn, Leo P., 208, 313-14, *315*
Foster, Pop, 503, 552-53, *677*
Frayne, Ed, 501, 556, 563, 591, 596, 607, 658, 689, 694-95
   coverage of
      Hurley-Johnston feud, 689

Petrolle-Suarez fight, 547n
Free Milk Fund, 664, 688, 691, 694-95, 697, 700, 704
Friedman, Al, 478-79, 558
Friedman, Walter (Good-Time Charley), 451
Fugazy, Humbert (Jack), (New York promoter), 237, 273-76, *275*, 281, 291, 426-27, 585, ***588***
Fuller, Sammy, 648, 678, 684-85, 687-88, 691-92, *693*, 694, 698, 702
Fulton, Fred, 28, 137, 139, *141*
Furey, Barney, 432
Gagnon, Jack, 558
Galiano, Basil, 328,
Gallagher Marty, 558-59, 561-62, 564, 574
Gallico, Paul, 498, 535, 583, 598, 607, 649, 653
   coverage of
      Petrolle-Battalino I fight, 607
      Petrolle-Berg I fight, 498-500
   opinion of Petrolle as a fighter, 583
Gallop, Louis, (Hurley fighter), 413, *414*
Gans, Baby Joe, 659, 678
Gans, Dago Joe, 142, *185*, 186, *257*, 259, 264
Gans, Joe, (lightweight champion), 83, 85, 461, 605, 607
Garcia, Bobby, 207-10, *210*, 252n, 331
Gastanaga, Isadoro, 642, 671
Geiger, Ed, 434
Gellis, Ike, 674, 702
Gibbons, Mike, ("the St. Paul Phantom"), 44-52, *47-49*, 53n, 55, 69, 79, 102, 110, 119, 133-34, *135*, *136*, 137, 139-40, 142-44, 150, 165, 178, 191, 218, 516
Gibbons, Tommy, 46-7, *47*, 52, 133, *135*, 137, 143, 218, *222*
Gildersleeve, Vandes, 439-40, 443
Gill, B. K., (Billy Sunday's advance man), 14
Glackin, Jack, 685, 688
Goldfield, Nevada, 843, 85-86
Goldman, Sammy, 642, 645, 647, 660

Goldstein, Ruby, 189, 232, 273, 289, 291, 297-99, *298*, 325, 503
Goodrich, Jimmy, 173, 202, 207, 237, 249, 252, 255-59, *257*, 291, 299, 361, 404-05, 408, 483
Gorman, Steve, 200, 212-17, *214*, *215*, 246n, 261n
Gould, Alan, 462
Grace City Buckos (town baseball team), 100
Grand Forks, ND, 106, 108-09, 111, 121-22, 173, 177, 182, 225, 228-33, 241, 346, 394,
Grand Recreation billiard parlor, 212-16, *214*, *215*, 231, 241, 245n, 255, 261, 332, 365
Grayson, Harry, 497, 504, 561, 563-64, 571, 596, 599, 649
   coverage of Petrolle-Berg I fight, 497-98
   coverage of Petrolle-Ran fight, 599
Greaney, Art, (Holyoke promoter), 203, 207, 211
Great Depression, 514-15, 516, 538, 550, 580-81, 602, 650, 657-58, 664-65, 669, 674, 695
Greb, Harry, 468
Greene, Johnny,
   coverage of Petrolle-Smith fight, 246-47
Greene, Sam, 360, 401, 525
   coverage of
      Petrolle-Miller III fight, 401-02
      Retzlaff-Heeney fight, 525-26
      Petrolle-Suarez fight, 548n
Griffiths, Tuffy, 416, 426, 459, 485, 559
Grogan, Tommy, 295, 351-53, *352*, 359, 361, 376-67, 394, 399, 420, 630
Grossman, Morris and Sarah (Reggie Hurley's parents), 636
Gwinner Swedes (town baseball team), 108
Hafner, Gail Conmy, (Hurley niece), 638, ***640***
Hall, Charles R., 416, 427
Hall, Roscoe, 154, 162, *171*, 174-75, 178, 191-92, 353
Hamas, Steve, 563-64, 566, 572, 690

Hamilton, W. A., 625
Hammergren, W. Oscar (Swede), 186
Hanley, James, Major, (North Dakota National Guard), 60, 64
Harmon, Paddy, (Chicago promoter), 403, 405, 424, *425*, 426, 494-96, 647
Hart, Sig, 31
Harvey, Charley, 584
Hawkins, Dal, 88
Hayes, Teddy 480-81
Haymann, Ludwig, 484, 490
Healy, Cornelius, (Hurley's maternal grandfather), 4-6
Healy, Dan, (Hurley's Uncle Dan), 125-26
Healy, Margaret Scannell, (Hurley's maternal grandmother), 4-6, 7
Hearst, Mrs. Randolph (Millicent), 694, 707
Heeney, Tom, 417-18, 518, 525-26, 529, 558-59, 574, 625, *527-28*, 671
Heinz, W. C. (Bill), 51, 68, 205-06, 365-66, 518, 548, 596, 598-99
Helena, MT, 175, 184, 187
Herman, Jack, 485, 488
Herman, Tommy, 195, *330*, 331-32, 341, 381, 589
Herrera, Tony, 493
Heudicourt, 68-69, 166
Herrera, Tony, 493
Hoff, Max (Boo Boo), 199, 247, 249, *251*, 331
Hoffman, Ancil, 663
Hoffman, George, 479, 558
Hoke, Billy, 147, 180, 619, 669
Holland Hotel, *644*, 645
Houston, Robert, 620
Hoyt, Harry, 642
Hudkins, Ace, ("the Nebraska Wildcat"), 188-90, 192, *194*, 197, 212, 220-21, 273, *275*, 280, 296, 306, 325, 327, 374, 412
Hudson Arena, (Wisconsin), 137, *138*
Hughes, Ray W., (Duluth promoter), 336, 341, 343
Humphreys, Joe, 83, 611, *612*, *521*, *708*
Hurley, Henry J. (Hank), (Jack's brother), 4, *53*, 233, 365

Hurley, Jack, (entries chronologically arranged in order of first appearance):
  birth and christening of, 3
  marriage of parents of, 4
  settlement of family of, in Fargo, 4-6
  grade school years of, 6, *7*, 8, *9*
  influence of Billy Sunday on, 17
  move of, to Rainy River, ON, 17-19
  death of father of, 19-20
  reluctance of, to hold a regular job, 23-25
  pursuit of baseball by, as a career:
    as a teenager, 39, 42-43, 51-52, *53*, 54, 55
    as a semi-pro player, 100-01, 108-10, 112
    in minor-league tryouts, 38, 52, 112-16
  as an actor, 39-49
  as a gymnast, 24-25, 39
  as a bowler, 25
  introduction of, to Kossick's gym, 25-26
  early day jobs of, 23-24, 42, 51
  friendship of, with Billy McCarney, 30, 33, 35, 252, 272-73, 276-77, 287-88, 297, 313, 318, 692, 694, 697-98
  manages first fighter, 52, 54
  as a soldier in World War I:
    enlists in National Guard, 59, *61*
    postings of, in the U. S., 60-63
    voyage of, on S.S. Leviathan, 63
    mobilizations of, on way to Western Front, 63-68
    receives bayonet instruction from Sergeant Major Cassidy at Heudicourt, 68-69
    suffers from frozen feet, 73-73
    returns to U. S., receives disability rating and his discharge, *76*, 77,
  resumes managing in 1919 and signs Russie LeRoy to a contract, 107-08, 111
  discovers and signs Johnny Knauf and Jack Bailey to contracts in 1920, 11
  rivalry of, with promoter Frank

INDEX OF NAMES AND ILLUSTRATIONS

Sullivan, 119-20, 123-25,
  activities of, during the 1921-'22 boxing season, 118-31, *127-28*
  rivalry of, with Elks club, 130-31, 147-48, 150
  first promotions of, 122-26,
  lives in St. Paul, 131, 133-34, *141*, 143
  friendship of, with John Salvator, 140-42, 149, 186, 189-91, 239-43, 341, 396
  returns to Fargo from St. Paul, 150
  activities of, during the 1922-'23 boxing season, 144-53
    first sightings of Billy Petrolle by, 144-47, 148-49, 150-51
  dispute between, and Petrolle, 152-53
  activities of, 1923-'24 season, 156-77
    signs exclusive contract to promote at Fargo Auditorium, 156-57
    resolves feud with Petrolle and becomes his manager, 162-64
    method of training fighters by, 165-67
    opens his first gym at Tweeden Hotel in Fargo, 167-69
    relationship of, with Fargo city officials and businessmen, 168-73
    signs Battling Krause to a contract, 175-77
  activities of, during the 1924-'25 boxing season, 187- 224
    explores cities other than Fargo and considers moving his base to Sioux City, 187-89
    campaigns in Sioux City garnering LeRoy two wins over Ace Hudkins, 188-93
    leaves Sioux City and promotes three shows in Fargo, 194-200
    launches Eastern campaign of LeRoy and Petrolle at Holyoke and Philadelphia, 200-11
    physical ailments of, 205-06, 381-2, 332, 618-623
    returns to Fargo in April to promote two shows, 217-18
    signs Earl Blue to a contract, 218
    campaigns in California during summer of 1925 with Petrolle, Leroy, and Blue, 218-24, *219*
  activities of, during the 1925-'26 boxing season, 225-252
    opens new gym in Fargo at Equity Building and takes on Phil Terk as new partner, 230-32
    promotes title bout for LeRoy with Pinkey Mitchell, 234-43
    promotes breakthrough bout for Petrolle against Eddie (Kid) Wagner fight in Fargo, 247-51
    debuts as manager in New York in February 1926, 252-55
    matches Petrolle with Kid Kaplan in Hartford and LeRoy with Jimmy Goodrich in Fargo, 255-58
    promotes Lynn Nelson as Masked Marvel in Fargo, 259-62
    opens New York office to promote his boxers in the East, 270, *271*
  activities of, during the 1926-'27 boxing season, 290-333
    works to make Petrolle, LeRoy, and Blue New York attractions and world-class contenders, 290-301, 305-311
    works to make Petrolle and LeRoy Chicago attractions, 294-94, 296, 298-99, 301, 316, *317*, 318, 321-22, 371-76, 380-81, 403-05
    begins writing a weekly column for the *Fargo Forum*, 319-20
  activities of, during the 1927-'28 boxing season, 335-381
    leaves Fargo, moves to Duluth and opens Silver Spray gym, 332-34, 336, *340*
    promotes Wayne (Handsome) Pikka as Masked Marvel in Duluth, 337-39
    acquires National Athletic Club pro franchise in Duluth, 343
    lands Petrolle non-title bout with

Hurley, Jack (*continued*),
    Sammy Mandell, 343-46
    develops Petrolle as an
      attraction in Detroit, 346-47
      353, 361-63, 376-77, 398-408
    activities of, during the 1928-'29
      boxing season, 382-415
    develops several amateur
      prospects in Duluth, *387*
      388-92, 394-98, 410-415
    signs Charley Retzlaff to a pro
      contract, 392
    activities of, during the 1929-30
      boxing season, 404-59, 462-95
    retires Petrolle for the first time,
      404-10
    moves to Chicago in December
      1929, 419-19, 423
    works with promoter Jim Mullen
      to promote Art Shires, 429-39
    enters into partnership with Ray
      Alvis to book fighters, 448-49
    develops Retzlaff as an attraction
      in Detroit and Duluth, 455-61,
      484-85, 490, 493
    co-manages welterweight champ
      Young Jack Thompson, 461-70
    books opponents for Primo
      Carnera, 452, 474-479
    promotes Walker-Swiderski bout
      at Kentucky Derby, 478-81
    sponsors Jack Dempsey's tour as
      referee in the Midwest, 485-92
    activities of, during the 1930-31
      boxing season, 494-568
    breaks with Alvis to resume full-
      time management of Petrolle
      and Retzlaff in Duluth, 492-94
    guides Petrolle's comeback and
      develops him into a New York
      attraction, 494-513, 516-524,
      538-556
    promotes three shows in St.
      Louis, 529-32
    maneuvers Retzlaff into major
      bouts at Detroit and New York,
      524-26, 557-66, 623-25
    cultivates his relationship with
      sportswriters, 533-537
    stages Retzlaff-Bertazzolo card in
      St. Paul with Salvator, 566-68
    activities of, during the 1931-32
      boxing season, 569-645,
    witnesses Retzlaff's decline as a
      serious title contender, 568-74
    arranges Dempsey's exhibition-
      bout tour in Midwest, 574-81
    works with Garden director James
      J. Johnston to make Petrolle
      New York's No. 1 attraction,
      589-613,
    checks in for 40 days of treatment
      at the Mayo Clinic for sinus and
      stomach ulcer condition, 618-23
    takes up golf, 629-30
    courtship and marriage of, to
      Regina Grossman, 633-38, 643-
      45
    attitude of, toward women, 366,
      639-40
    activities of, during the 1932-33
      boxing season
    trains and handles Petrolle for title
      bout against Canzoneri, 647-58
    begins bitter vendetta with
      Johnston and Madison Square
      Garden, 658-61, 674-78, 697-98
    fails in efforts to help Salvator and
      Terk revive boxing in St. Paul
      and Duluth, 667-74
    boycotts the Garden and signs with
      Aram AC for Petrolle to box
      van Klaveren at Queensboro
      Stadium, 678-82, 689-94
    activities of, during the 1933-34
      boxing season,
    arranges a Boston bout for Petrolle
      against Sammy Fuller, 684-88
    terminates his relationship with
      Retzlaff, 691
    arranges two bouts for Petrolle at
      the Ridgewood Grove Arena,
      694-95, 698-700
    signs for Petrolle to box Barney
      Ross for the Free Milk Fund at
      the Bronx Coliseum, 694-97,

INDEX OF NAMES AND ILLUSTRATIONS

700-07
   advises Petrolle to retire from the ring, 704, 707-710
Hurley, John Albert, (Jack's father), 3-4, 16, 19, 20n. 23-24, 366
Hurley, Julia Healy, (Jack's mother), 1, 3-6, *8*, 11, 17-20, 24, 28, 41, 43, 99, 116, 119n, 125-26, 151, 200, 220, 366, *486*, 488, 638-39, *640*, 643, 645
Hurley, Katherine M., (Jack's youngest sister), 4, *9*, 366
Hurley, Regina Grossman, (Reggie, Rachel), (Jack's wife), 633-36, *637*, 638-39, 641-43, 645
Igoe, Hype, 254, 325, 462, 506, 536, 561, 599, 616, 649, 681
   coverage of
      Blue-LaRocco fight, 325-26
      Petrolle-Suarez fight, 548n
      Petrolle-Vogel fight, 254-55
Jacobs, Frankie, 375
Jacobs, Joe, 30, 270, *271*, 318, 662, 675, 692
Jacobs, Mike, 272, 286, 695, *696*, 704
Jadick, Johnny, 648, 659
Jamestown, ND, 59n, 102n, 106, 117-18, 119n, 212, 143, 153, 160-62, 181, 184, 241
Jawson, Joe, 233, *236*, 264, 613-14
Jeby, Ben, 678, 689
Jefferson Post, 478-79, 481
Jenkins, Burris, 702
Jennings, James W., coverage of Thompson-McLarnin fight, 465
Johnson, Charles, 346, 568
Johnson, Jack, 26, 31, 33, 80, 85
Johnson, Wesley, 60, 62, 64
Johnston, James J., 515, 561, 572, 581, 583-85, *586*, 587, *588*, 589, 594-96, 602, 617, 630, 642, 645, *651*, 658-64, 675-76, 678, 682, 689-90, 697-98
Johnston, Charley, 662, 664, 676
Jones, Victor O., coverage of Petrolle-Fuller I fight, 686-87
Kahler Grand Hotel, 621, *624*
Kahn, Harry, 331, *340*, 341, 358, 394
Kane, Eddie, 316, 345, *348*, 361, 375-75, 405

Kane, Jackie, 353, 357-59, 363, 374, 405
Kansas, Rocky, 202, 232, 237, 252, 258, 263, 291, 293, *294*, 296, 302, 361, 421, *422*
Kaplan, Louis (Kid), 207-08, 232, 249, 252, 253n, 255-56, *257*, 273, 325, 327, 347447, 506, 542, 596
Kearns, Jack (Doc), (John Leo McKernan), 79-80, 86, *87*, 88-90, *92*, 93, 98, 456-57, *458*, 459, 478-81, 536, 585, *588*, 602, 659
Kid Chocolate, (Eligio Sardinias Montalvo, Cuban Bon Bon), 418, 497, 594, 603, 642
Kilpatrick, John Reed, 695, 697-98
Kingsrud, Ralph, 629
Kirkenburg, Sigismund, (Jack Broad), 22, 23n
Kirkman, Boone, (Hurley fighter), 17
Knauf, Johnny, 101, 108, 110, 112, 117-221, 130, 147-48, 150, 154, 156, 173-74, 177, 182, 184, 225-28, 230, 232-33, 290
Knight Printing Company, 42
Kofoed, Jack, 503-04, 564, 607
   coverage of Petrolle-Battalino II fight, 607
Kohl, Louie, 439
Kolpack, Ed, interview with Hank Hurley, 365
Kossick, Leo, 22-23, 25, 27-28, 30, 38, 41, 46, *47*, 50-51, 59n, 101, 107n, 110, *127-28*, 200, 227, 241, 250, 258, 389
Krause, Jacob (Battling),121-22, 130, 151, 153-54, 156, 162, 164, 173-77, *176*, 181-84, 186, 228-30 232-33, 290
LaBarba, Fidel, 603
Kusy, Laddy, (Newark promoter), 272, 289, 297, 300, 313, 316, 322, 324-25
Lambert, Chuck, 124-25, 129-30 140, 142, 145, 148-49, *155*, 191, 227
L'Amour, Louis, 102n, 140n, 161-62, *163*
Landis, Kenesaw Mountain, 434, 443
LaRocco, George, 325-26
Larsen, Whitey, coverage of LeRoy-Hudkins I fight, 190

Lasky, Art, 580, 645, 671, *673*
Lassen, Leo, coverage of Petrolle-Snell fight, 370
Last, Frank, 60, 63-64, 66, 70, 72, 74
Laurel Garden (Newark boxing club), 272, 297, 299-300, 305-06, 320, 322, 324-25
Leonard, Benny, 46, 97, 195, 202, 237, 249, 328n, 421, 494, 585, 608
Leonard, Sammy, 187, *340*, 341-43
LeRoy, Russie, (Russell Miladore Backer), (Hurley fighter), 107-08, *111*, 112, 117-31, *127-28*, 140, 147- 54, 156, 162, 165-66, 173-75, 178 -84, 186-209, *194*, *196*, 211-12, 217-21, *219*, 223, 225-35, 237-39, 241-43, 245, 247, 255-56, 258, 258, 262-65, 290, 293, 299-301, 306 *309*, *310*, 311-14, 316, 320, 329, 336-39, *338*, 353, 365, 368, 382, 388-89, 392, 394, 401-02, 412, 419, 620
   fights of, against
      Ace Hudkins I, 190
      Ace Hudkins II, 192
      Pinkey Mitchell, 238-43
Leviathan S. S., 56, 63, *65*, *67*, *76*
Levinsky, King (Kingfish), (Harris Krakow), 479, 574, *670*, 671, 690
Lewis, Henry (Hen), 322-24, *323*
Lewis, Nate, *425*, 426, 494, 625, 630-31, 659, 664-65, 667
Lewis, Perry, 204, 206
   coverage of
      Petrolle-Garcia fight, 208-09
      Petrolle-Ruth fight, 204-05, 206
Light, Billy, 142, 341, 394, *395*, 396, 398, 410, 412-13, 516, 567, 634
Lindbergh, Charles, (Lucky Lindy), 327
Lindy's (Broadway restaurant), 269-70
Loayza, Stanislaus. 256, 273, 302n, 331, 363, 376-76, 497, 519, 542, 698 -99, 702
Locatelli, Cleo, 658
Lodge, Farmer, 474
Logan, Bud, 175-77, *176*
Lomski, Leo, 448, 455-56
Longfellow Grade School, 6, *8*, 17

Los Angeles, CA, 478, 482, 492, 580, 664
Loughran, Tommy, 418, 448, 518, 572-74, 690
Louisville, KY, 478-81, 484
Louisville Colonels (baseball team), 38, 113, 114n, *115*, 116
Lowery Hotel, 578, 645
Luvadis, Jerry (the Greek), 578, *579*
Macbeth, W. J., coverage of Petrolle-Battallino I fight, 607
Macdonald, Sandy, 337, 341-42, 353, 355, 378-80, 383, 389, 394, 396, 398, 404, 413, 459, 491, 558
   coverage of
      Petrolle-Tut III fight, 378, 379-80
      Puglisi-Light fight, 398
MacKenzie, Neil, 459
MacNamara, Harry, 431
Madden, Owney, 270, 279-81, 284, 286-87, 451
Madison Square Garden, 34, 97-98, 193, 202, 250, 252-53, 255-56, 258, 262-64, 270, 272, 277, 280-81, 291-97, 299, 303-06, 316, 318-322, 325, 349, 360, 363, 391, 398, 417-18, 423, 426-27, 451-52, 462-63, 497-500, 502, 540, 507, 515, 518-19, 522, 524, 532-33, 537-38, 542, 550, 556, 558-59, 562, 567, 572, 574, 581, 583-85, 587, 589, 594, 599, 602, 605, 607, 617, 630, 634, 645, 650, 653, 656-64, 675-76, 678, 682-83, 689-90, 692, 695, 697-98, 700, 702, 710
Magnuson, Warren G., *171*, 172, 287
Mahoney, Jim, 457
Malley, Hy, 605
Malloy, Andy, *92*
Malloy, Mique, 477-78, 631
Malone, Jock, *92*, 133, *136*, 139, 353, *356*
Malone, Joey, 457
Mandell, Sammy, 140, 195, 202, *222*, 262, 291, *293*, *294*, 296-97, 302, 304, 306, 313-14, 316, 321, 324, 343-47, *344*, 349, 353, 359-61, *362*, 364, 374- 77, 402-05, 410, 419-21, *422*, 432, 494-95, 503, 506, 515

INDEX OF NAMES AND ILLUSTRATIONS

Mara, Tim, 663, 675, *677*, 678, 688-89
Marciano, Rocky, 444-45, 562, 626
Marriner, Les, 630-31
Marshall, George C., Major, (acting chief of staff, First Division), 70
Martinez, Hilario, 306, *307*, 360, 582
Matthews, Harry (Kid), 17, 142, 172, 199n, 287, 370, 384, 444, 562, 619
Mayo Clinic, 489, 522, 617-18 621, *624*
McArdle, Tom, 496, 500-01, 515, 518, 542, 548, 550, 567, 572-73, 583-84, 589, 617, 698, 700, *705*
McCarney, Billy, 28, *29*, 30, 31, *32*, 33, 35-37, *38*, 39, 46, 142, 252, 270-4, *271*, 276-7, 287-8, 297, 304, 311n, 313, *315*, 318, 320, 691-92, 694, 697-98
McCarthy, Jack, 623, 625
McCarthy, Jim, 667, 669
McCarthy, Joe, 113, *115*
McCarty, Aaron P., (Chief White Eagle), 26-27, *32*
McCarty, Luther, (Lute, Luck), 26-28, *29*, 30-31, *32*, 33, *34*, 35-37, *38*, 39, 46, 77, 200
McCarty Marguerite, (Marguerite White Eagle), 26-27, *32*
McCarty, Rhoda Wright, 27-28, 37-38
McClelland, Elmer, 470
McGlynn, Stoney, coverage of Blue-Foster, 227
McGoorty, Eddie, 110, 137, 420
McGrath, Tim, 479
McKetrick, Dan, *588*
McLarnin, Jimmy, (Baby Face, "the Belfast Spider"), 15, 193, 277n, 295, 347-49, *348*, 360-61,*362*, 371, 376-77, 399, *400*, 413, 462, 465, *466*, 468-69, 501-503, *504*, 505, *506*, 507, *508*, 509, *510*, 511-12, 515-16, 519, 532-34, 536-38, *539-40*, 541-42, 547-50, *551*, 552-53, *554*, 555-56, 567, 71, 604, 634, 646-47, 664, *677*, 678, 691, 704
McLemore, Henry, 646
McMahon, Jess, 250-52, *251*, 256, 258, 263, 272, 306, 316, *348*
McPartland, Kid, 302n, *303*, 304
McTigue, Mike, 29, 320, 465, 585
Meade, Eddie, 440

Menke, Frank, 611
Miller, Freddie, 282, 284, 602
Miller, Ray, ("Chicago Knockout King"), 273, 280, 293-96, *294*, 377, 398-99, *400*, 401-403, 405, 407-08, 483, 501-02, 537, 541-42, 552, 667, 684
Minneapolis, MN 102, 106, 133, 138, 140, 164, 180, 187, 199, 326, 343, 345-46, 377-81, 388, 404-05, 452, 474, 477, 483, 516, 518-19, 524, 568, 575, 580, 666, 669, 671
Minneapolis Auditorium, 343, 377
Minneapolis Marines (football team), 102
Minneapolis Millers (baseball team), 8, 114, 302n
Miske, Billy, 133, *135*, 137, 142
Mitchell, Billy, 237-41, *240*, 243
Mitchell, Pinkey, 187, 221, 225, 237-43, *240*, 245, 247, 620
Mitchell, Ritchie, 97, *240*, 421
Mizner, Wilson, 82, 86, 88
Monahan, Walter, 31
Montgomery, Sully, 474, 477, 456, 493, 524-26, 529
Moore, Mark, 103, 151, *155*, 183, 234, 259
Moorhead, MN, 2, 4-5, 7, 14, 15, 22-25, 28, 38, 46, 50, 106-08, 110, 112, 114, 130, 148, 172, 181, 187, 212, 237, 250, 388, 410, 413
Montieth, Scotty, 232, 401, 404, 456, 495, 524-26, 529
Moose Jaw, SK, 181, 184
Moran, Frank, 30, 36, 80, 86, 139
Morgan, Tod, 262, 274, 319, 371, 377, 589
Morris, Carl, 30, 33
Morris, William, 634
Mueller, Freddie, 321, *323*, *371*, 419
Mullen, James C. (Jim), (Chicago promoter), 291, 293, 296, 299, 316, 416, 417, 419-21, *422*, 423, 426, 429, 431-32, 434-35, 439-41, 443-45, 456-57, 318, *317* (letter), 321-22, 324, 336 343, 349, 361, 371, 374-76, 391, 403

Murphy, Spud (Hurley fighter), 167, 237, 250, 410, 413, *414*
Murphy, Tommy (Kid), 237, 264, 312-16, *315*, 364
Myers, Spug, 299, 301, 311-12, 314-16, 315, 318, *323*, 324, 346-7, 349, 359, 363, 419, 493
Nardiello, Dr. Vincent, 678, 681
National Athletic Club (NAC), 336, 343, 355, 383, 394, 410, 412n, 415, 484, 575, 633
National Boxing Association (NBA), 439, 445, 462, 469, 475-76, 526
National Speedways, Inc., 631
National Sports Alliance, 421
Navin Field (Detroit), 382, 404
Neil, Edward J., 672, 702
Nelson, Lynn, (first "Masked Marvel"), 244-45, 259-62, *260*, 337, 389
Nelson, Oscar (Battling), 23, 83, 85, 195, 241
New York City, 29, 33-35, 44, 53, 56, 82, 98, 177, 189, 193, 198, 202, 232, 237, 252-55, 259, 264-79, 281, 285 93, 295-96, 299-311, 313, 316, 318-22, 325-27, 347, 349, 360-61, 392, 399, 412, 421, 426-27, 445, 451-52, 457, 462, 465, 469, 477, 485, 489, 494-95, 497p., 500-03, 505, 512-15, 518-19, 522, 533-36, 541-42, 547, 549-50, 552, 556-59, 561-64, 566-68, 571-73, 575-76, 581, 583-85, 587, 589, 591, 594-96, 598, 602-04, 613-14, 616-17, 623, 625, 630-31, 633-35, 639, 641-42, 650, 658, 661-65, 667, 671, 674, 676, 678, 681, 685, 689-90, 694, 697-98, 700, 702
Newark, NJ, 289, 296-98, 306, 313, 320, 322, 324-25, 372, 452, 536
Nichols, Jackie, (Hurley fighter), 143, 160, *163*
Neil, Edward J., 673, 702
Norris, Fane, coverage of California debut of Hurley's fighters, 223
Norris, James E., 424, 426
North Dakota National Guard 58-60, 75, 99
Northern League (baseball), 8, 54, 99-100, 114, 216

Noye, Johnny, 123-24, *128*, 129, 139
O'Dowd, Mike, 102, 133-34, *135*, 137, 516
Okun, Yale, 305, *307*, 316, 326
Olson, Carol Comrie, (Hurley's niece), 638, *640*
Olson, Floyd B., 575, 578
Olympia Stadium (Detroit), 346, 360-61, 363, 376, 396n, 455-57, 469-70, 524, 529, 625
Olympic Hotel, 618
Omaha, NE, 33, 188, 192, 262-63, 351, 353, 492, 577, 620
O'Neil, Frank, 254
Onken, Dick, 572
Osa, Mateo, 563-64
Owen, John, 169, 334, 620-21
Palzer, Al, 26, 30, 33, *34*
Pantaleo, Paul, 642, 645
Parker, Dan, 582-83, 689-90,
  coverage of
    Petrolle as a fighter, 582-83
    Hurley-Johnston feud, 689-90
Patterson, Floyd, 444-45
Pelkey, Arthur, 36, 37, *38*
Perry, Bob, 478-79
Peterson Big Boy, 451-52, 475, 477
Petrolle, Billy, (William Michael, "the Fargo Express"), (Hurley fighter), 15, 44, 69, 79, 102n, 132, 140-48, *146*, 150-53, 156, 160-67, *163*, 173, 180-93, *185*, 197-99, 211-12, *214*, 217-21, *219*, 223-29, 231-34, 245-50, *248*, 252-56, 258, 262-65, 270, 273, 289-93, 295-97, 300-14, *303*, *307*, *309*, *310*, 316, 318, 321-22, 324-29, 331-33, 336, 339-41, *340*, 343-47, *344*, 349-51, *350*, 353, 357-61, 363-68, *367*, 370-71, 373-82, 384, *387*, 388, 394, *395*, 397-99, 401-10, *406*, *409*, 417-20, 446, 483-85, 488, 493-98, *499*, 500-03, *504*, 505, *506*, 507, *508*, 509, *510*, 511-19, *520-21*, 522, 524, 530, 532-38, *539-540*, 541-42, *543*, 544, *545-46*, 547-50, *551*, *554*, 555-56, *565*, 567-68, 571, 574-75, 581-83, 589, *590*, 591, *595-93*, 594-99, *600-01*, 602-05, 607-08, *609-10*, 611, *612*, 613-14, *615*, 620-23, 625-26, *627-28* 629-30, 633-35, 639,

641-42, 645-50, *651*, 652-53, *654-55*
656-61, 664-65, *666*, 667, *668*, 678, *679*,
680, 681-92, *693*, 694-95, 697-702, *703*,
704, *706-706*, 707, *708*, 709-10
  acquires nom de guerre "Fargo
    Express," 246-47
  fights of, against:
    Battling Battalino I, 605-13
    Battling Battalino II, 625-26
    Jackie Kid Berg I, 373-74
    Jackie Kid Berg II, 374-76
    Jackie Kid Berg III, 497-500
    Tony Canzoneri I, 494-96
    Tony Canzoneri II, 650-57
    Bruce Flowers I, 349
    Bruce Flowers II, 363
    Sammy Fuller I, 684-88
    Sammy Fuller II, 692-94
    Bobby Garcia, 207-09
    Tommy Grogan I, 351-53
    Tommy Grogan II, 630
    Tommy Herman, 331-32
    Louis (Kid) Kaplan, 255-56
    Sammy Mandell, 345-346
    Hilario Martinez, 306-08
    Jimmy McLarnin I, 505-11
    Jimmy McLarnin II, 537-41
    Jimmy McLarnin III, 550-56
    Ray Miller I, 295-95
    Ray Miller II, 399-401
    Ray Miller III, 401-03
    Freddie Mueller, 321
    Spug Myers, 346-47
    Eddie Ran, 595-99
    Barney Ross I, 665-66
    Barney Ross II, 700-710
    Babe Ruth, 204-07
    Justo Suarez, 542-48
    Sid Terris, 291-92
    Billy Townsend, 589-94
    King Tut I, 329
    King Tut II, 331
    King Tut III, 377-80
    King Tut IV, 404-08
    King Tut V, 516-18
    King Tut VI, 519-24
    Bep van Klaveren, 678-80
    Sammy Vogel, 252-55

    Eddie (Kid) Wagner, 247-50
    Billy Wallace, 326-28
  first retirement of, 382, 408-10
  launches comeback, 483-84
  preparations and weight-making
    difficulties of, for Petrolle-
    Canzoneri II title fight,
    641-42, 647-50, 656-58
  punching power of, 613-617
Petrolle, Frank and Mary, (Billy's
  parents), 144-45, *146*, 162, 164
Petrolle, Frankie, (Billy's younger
  brother), 145, *146*
Petrolle, Pete, (Billy's older brother),
  145, *146*, 161
Phelan, John J., 660
Philadelphia, PA, 30, 33, 36, 38, 46, 79,
  93, 197-209, 211-12, 217, 247, 250, 261,
  264, 276, 325, 327-28, 331, 363, 402,
  429, 431, 648, 685, 702
Pian, Sam, 678, 689-90, 698, 700
Pierce Printing Company, 42
Pikka, Wayne (Handsome), (second
  "Masked Marvel"), 336-37, 339,
  340, 388
Pioneer Gym, 639, 641, 647
Polo Grounds, 274, 325, 327, 360, 418,
  584, 646, 675, 678, 681-82, 688
Potts, Jimmie, 23, 103n
Prohibition Era, 35, 247, 268-69, 279
Puglisi, Angelo, (Hurley fighter), 388-90,
  390, 394, 396, *395*, 398, 410-15, *414*,
  419, 423, 429, 432, 436, 567
Purcell, J. A. (Pat), 22, 129, 147-49,
  156, 162, 164-65, 174, 177-79, 187,
  192, 195, 199, 229-30, 232, 234, 237,
  242, 250, 258, 262, 264-65, 313, 316,
  318, 321, 339, 365, 380, 392, 394,
  401-02, 404, 613-14
  review of LeRoy's 1922 boxing
    season, 242-43
  review of LeRoy's 1923 boxing
    season, 151-52
  coverage of
    LeRoy-Coogan fight, 199
    LeRoy-Krause, 229-30
    LeRoy-Mars, 197
    LeRoy-Mitchell fight, 242-43

Purcell, J. A. (Pat), (*continued*),
   LeRoy-Ross fight, 234-35
   LeRoy-Shauers II fight, 179-80
   Petrolle-Wagner fight, 249-50, 252
   interviews with
      Hurley after Petrolle- Flowers II
         fight, 364
      Hurley after Petrolle-Tut IV fight,
         404-05
      Hurley after returning from his first
         trip to New York with LeRoy
         and Petrolle, 262-63
      LeRoy about Petrolle-Miller III
         fight, 402
      Hurley prior to Petrolle-Tut IV
         fight, 380-81
      King Tut prior to Petrolle-Tut IV
         fight, 380-81
   mediating Hurley-Sullivan
      promoters war, 156-57
Purvis, Jackie, 484
Queensboro Stadium, 562, 568, 642
Rabin, Lou, 324-5
Rademacher, Pete, 444-45
Rainy River, ON, 17-20, 23, 39, 220
Ran, Eddie, 567, 589, 595-99, *600-01*, 602-04, 616, 634-35, 646-47, 659, 661
Ray, Benny, 439
Ray, Tommy, (Hurley fighter), 123-24
Red River, 2, 5, 24-25, 145, 212
   Flood of 1897, 2-3
Reddy, Jack, (St. Paul promoter), 118, 120-21, *127-28*, 140, 200, 262-63.
Reilly, Pete, ("the Silver Fox"), 264, 267, 281-83, *283*, 284-87, 603, *606*
Reisler, John (the Barber), 562
Retzlaff, Charley, ("Smilin' Charley," "The Duluth Dynamiter"), 389-92, *390*, *393*, 412-13, 417-19, 423, 429, 432, 436, 455-57, *458*, 459-61, 484-85, *486*, 488-90, 493-94, 515, 524-26, *527-28*, 529, 536, 556-59, 561-64, *560*, *565*, 566, 568-69, 571-75, 580, 622-23, *624*, 625, 630-31, *632*, 642, 645, 660, *670*, 671, 684, 688, 691
   fights of, against
      Giacoma Bergomas, 573
      Ralph Bertazzola, 568

      Hans Birkie I, 630
      Hans Birkie II, 691
      James J. Braddock, 625
      Ralph Ficucello, 561-62
      Marty Gallagher, 558-61
      Isadoro Gastanaga, 642
      Tom Heeney, 525-26
      Art Lasky, 670
      Jack McCarthy, 623
      Mateo Osa, 562-64
      Johnny Risko, 524-25
      Tom Sayers, 493
      Joe Sekyra, 569-71
Rickard, Tex, 79-86, *84*, 88, 93, 95, 97-98, 120, 157, 159, 249, 258n, 272-76, *275*, 277n, 291, 311n, 314, 327, 334, 343, 347-49, *348*, 360-61, 363, 398, 417-18, 426, 429, 485, 583, 683, 690, 695
Ridgewood Grove, 689-92, 698
Riley, Don, 636
Ring Magazine (periodical), 37, 164, *309*, *310*, 311n, 402, 444, 526, *612*, 626
"Ring Rations," (Hurley's newspaper column), 622, 634-35, 671, 674
Rioux, Elizear, 451-52, *454*, 455, 474
Risko, Johnny, 418, 426, 524-26, 529, 557, 572, 625
Rivers, Indian Joe (Pedro Reyna), 575
Roaring-'20s, 80, 97-98, 268, 279
Roche, Billy, 663, *705*
Rojas, Quentin Romero, ("Lion of the Andes"), *356*, 357-59, 374, 382-83
Roosevelt, Franklin D., 664
Roper, Jack, 576, 580, 671
Rose Room gym, (St. Paul), 119, 131, 133, 140, 142-43, 149, 167
Ross, Barney, 665, *666*, 667, *668*, 678, 683, 688-89, 691, 694-95, 697-702, 704, *705-06*, 707, *708*, 709
Ross, Tony, 234, *240*, 353, 394
Rossi, Paul, 488
Routis, Andre, 277, 281-82, *283*, 603
Runyon, Damon, 177, 189, 269, 481, 535-37, 558, 561, 564, 572, 576, 581-82, *588*, 630-31, 643, *644*, 694-95, *696*
   coverage of Charley Retzlaff, 557-58, 564-66, 572

opinion of Petrolle as a fighter, 582
Ruth, Babe, (featherweight boxer), 204-08, *210*, 262, 321n, 351
Ryan, Joe, 193, 449
  assessment of LeRoy and Petrolle after their Sioux City fights, 193
Sachs, Leonard, 427, 448, 485, 577
Safro, Labe, 23, 50, 101-07, *104*, *105*, 161
Salvator, Bertha, *632*, 633-34, 638
Salvator, John II, 578, *579*, *632*, 634, 636, 638, *640*
Salvator, Johnny, (Johann Salwetter), 133, 140-42, *141*, 145, 149, 167, 175, 178, 182, 186, 190-91, 235, 239, 241, 243, 259, 341, 394, 396, 516, *521*, 566-68, 575, 578, *579*, 581, 631, *632*, 633-34, 645, 669, *670*, 671, 674
Sanders, Tony, 485, 488
Saumweber, George, 22, 25, 181
Saunders, Prince, 575, 631, *632*, 641
Sayers, Tom, 493, 524
Schaaf, Ernie, 518, 557, 572, 625, 642, 664, 702
Schauer, Johnny, *128*, 129, 178-80, 187, 191, 226
Schmeling, Max, 30 418, 426, 491, 515, 558-59, 561, 564, 569, 576, 581, 583, 585, 587, 630, 661-64, 671, *672*, 673, 675, 690-92
Schrankel, Lee, 153, 161-2, 164
Schroeder, Fred W. (Fritz), 42, 44, 52-53, 55
Schwabel, Len, 120-23, *128*, 129, 151, 181
Schwake, John, 529, 531
Scott, Phil, 418, 426, 485, 559, 585
Seattle, WA, 1, 4, 15, 86, 88, 99, 113, 169, 172, 217, 285, 366, 368, 370, 444-45 488, 577, 618-19
See, Leon, 451, 479, *588*, 591, 701
Sekyra, Joe, 568-69, 570, 571-73, 660
Self-Defense Magazine (periodical), *309*, *310*, 311, 318
Shanley, Bishop John, 41
Sharkey, Jack, 274, 320, 357, 363, 402, 417-18, 426, 485, 491, 515, 558-59, 583, 585, 587, *588*, 589, 630, 661-64, 674-75, 691, 695
Sheridan, WY, 175, 183-84
Sheridan, Dr. Joseph, 678, 681, 684, 688
Shires, Art, 429, *430*, 431-32, *433*, 434-36, *437*-*38*, 439-41, *442*, 443-44, 516
Shubert, Al, 207-08.
Shure, W. H., 169
Sigman, Jim, 415, 474
Silver Spray Gym, 336-37, 339, 343, 354, 359, 382, *383*, 386, 388-89, 396, 410-11, 413, 419, 483-84, 635
Simmons, Alf, 173, 301-02, *303*, 304
Singer, Al, 418, 494, 497, 500, 503, 594, 603, 648
Sioux City, IA, 144, 188-93, 196-98, 264, 326
Sivertson, Alexander, 524
Skene, Don, 501
Slattery, Jimmy, 274, 305
Sloan, Alec, 631
Slotsky, Sam, 190, 326, 529-31
Smith, Gunboat, 35-36, *610*, 611
Smith, Jeff, 46, 51
Smith, Steve, ("the Hungarian Bearcat"), 234, 245, *248*
Smith, Roy (Submarine), (Hurley fighter), 25, 52, 107, 148, 151-52, 155, *156*, 167
Snell, Doc, (William A. McEachern), 368-71, *369*, 489
St. Denis, Walter, 536
St. Louis, MO, 474, 477, 529, 532
St. Louis Coliseum, 529
St. Mary's Cathedral, 20, 39
St. Nicholas Arena, 585, 587, 676
St. Paul, MN, 4-5, 38, 44-46, 51, 55, 59n, 109, 118, 120, 122, 124-26, 129, 131, 133-34, 137, 138n, 140, 142-45, 147, 149-52, 154, 157, 160-61, 165, 167, 173, 175, 178, 182, 186n, 189-90, 200, 218, 223, 226, 231, 235, 239, 250, 259, 262-63, 296, 311, 329, 343, 346, 354-55, 388, 396, 439, 441, 516, 518-9, 566-68, 575-76, 578, 580-81, 621, 631, 634, 636, 638, 645, 669-70, 673, 674
St. Paul Saints (baseball team), 109
Spohrer, Al, 439, 441, *442*
Stanton Gene, 572, 684, 688

Steele, Freddie, 285, 370
Stern, William (Bill), 27, 170-73, *171*, 213, 296
Stokes, Leo, 25, 118, 123-24, 182
Stone, Pete, (Pete the Goat), 279, *303*
Strachan, Scotty, 439
Stribling, William Lawrence (Young), 417-18, 426, *453*, 558-59, 561, 583, 585, 587, 630, 661
Suarez, Justo, 536, 542, *543*, 544, *545-46*, 547-48, 591, 604, 616-17, 646-47
Sullivan, Frank J., 46, 119-20, 122-25, 142, 149-50, 156-57, 396, 410
Sullivan, John L., 487, 576
Sullivan, My, 142, 235-37, *236*, 250, 341, 396, 410, 567
Sunday, Billy, 1, 11-15 *13*, *16*, 17, 304
Sweeney, Al, 631, *632*, 633, 638, 641, 643
Sweeney, Berenice Peltz, (Brunch), 631, 633
Swiderski, Paul, 479, 587
Talarico, Tony, 455-56, *458*, 576
Taylor, Bud, 416, 432, 447
Taylor, Seneca, 529-30
Tenorio, Lope, 399, 530
Terk, Phil, 99, 231, 255, 259, 293, 302n, 332, 334, 336-37, 339, *340*, 343, 354-55, 357-59, 383, 386, 388, 394, 410, 412, 439, 484-85, 488-90, 575, 581, 618, 629, 633, 643, 669, 671, 674
Terris, Sid, ("the East Side Phantom"), 202, 249, 265, 273, 277n, 290-95, *294*, 304, 306, 325, 327, 347-49, *348*, 361, 474, 503, 614
Thompson, Scipio, ("Slick," Bob Johnson), 461, 463, 468-70n, 470, 474
Thompson, Young Jack, (Cecil Thompson), 449, 461-62, *463-64*, 465, *466-67*, 468-70, *471-73*, 474, 492-94, 502-03, 505, 511, 602
Times Square Building, 269
Times Square Hotel, 318
Toledo, OH, 80, 93, 95
Townsend, Billy, 589, 590, 591, *592-93*, 594-96, 604, 616, 635, 646, 661
Trafton, George, 434-36, *437-38*, 439, 474
Trotter, Tex, (Grand Forks promoter), 228-29, 233
Tunney, Gene, 79, 218, 276, 290, 355, 357, 363, 402, 417-18, 491, 525, 558, 585
Tuttle, Henry (King Tut), 140, 321, 329-31, *330*, 353, 371, 377-82, 392, 394, 404-05, 407-10, *409*, 420, 483, 502, 516-19, *520-21*, 522, *523*, 524, 533-34, 567-68, 594, 604, 620
Underwood, George,
  coverage of
    Petrolle-Terris fight, 292
    Petrolle-Flowers I fight, 349
Uzcudun, Paolino, 418, 485, 572, 642, 657
Van Klaveren, Bep, 646, 658-59, 661, 665, 678, *679-80*, 681, 682, 684, 688-91, 697-98
Van Ryan, Al, 142, 148-49, 151, *171*, 175, 177-78, 182-83, 187, 329, 341-42, 355, *397*, 396
Vicentini, Luis, 237, 252, 542
Vidmer, Richards,
  coverage of Petrolle-Suarez fight, 547-48n
Vogel, Sammy, *251*, 252-56, 263-64, 270, 291, 299, 306, 314, 349, 614
Von Porat, Otto, 426
Wagner, Eddie (Kid), 173, 199, 237-38, 247, 249-52, *251*, 258, 302n, 314, 321, 364, 376-77.
Wallace, Billy, 156, 187, 325-28, *330*, 331, 347, 684
Wallace, Otto, *155*, 156, 187
Walker Law, 97, 585
Walker, James J. (Jimmy), (Mayor of New York City), 97, 327, 522, 583, 675
Walker, Mickey, *87*, 272, 274, 403, 456, 457, *458*, 479-81, 541, 585, 587, *588*, 662
Walker, Paulie, 589, 659
Wall, Harry, 427, 489
Wallace, Francis, 605-07, 653,
  coverage of
    Petrolle-Battalino I fight, 605-07

INDEX OF NAMES AND ILLUSTRATIONS

Petrolle-Canzoneri II fight, 653-56
Walsh, Davis J., 535, 537, 552
Walsh, Tom, 353, *356*, 357-58, 479, 567
Walthier, Paddy, 493-94
Ward, Bobby, 125, *127-28*, 129, 197
Watson, Emmett, 63, 621
Weill, Al, 562, 568, *570*, 571, 675-76, *677*, 678, 682, 684, 688-89, 691
Wells, Billy (Bombardier), 35-36
Welsh, Freddy, 23, 50, 202
White, Gaylord, 631
White City, 423, 429, 432, 434, 443, 457, 477, 645
Wiggins, Chuck, 474
Willard, Battling, *210*, 211
Willard, Jess, 36, 80-81, *84*, 86, 93-95, *94*, 139, 211, 452, 674
Williams, Jack, 8, 52
Williams, Joe, 504, 535, 582, 604, 684
   coverage of Petrolle-McLarnin III fight, 509n
   opinion of Petrolle as a fighter, 582
   pre-bout coverage of Petrolle-Battalino I fight, 604-05
Wills, Harry, 457
Wilson, Gus, 514
Wilson, Hack, 431-32, 434-36, *438*, 439, 441, 443-44
Wilson, Red Cap, 232-33, *236*, 249
Wilson, Woodrow, 53, 57
Winch, Art, 700-01
Wine, Frankie, 479
Wolfe, Eddie (Kid), 659
Wood, Wilbur, 252, 281, 295, 503, 518, 541, 547, 552, 564, 587, 596, 604, 607, 690, 699
   coverage of
      Hurley-Johnston feud, 690
      Petrolle-Battalino II fight, 604, 607
      Petrolle-Flowers I fight, 349
      Petrolle-Miller I fight, 295
      Petrolle-McLarnin III fight, 553-55
      Petrolle-Suarez fight, 549n
      Petrolle-Vogel fight, 252, 253-54
      Petrolle-McLarnin III fight, 552
      Petrolle-Tut VI fight, 518
Woodhall, Jimmy, 108, 112, 151
Woodman, Joe, 198
Woods, Joe, 574
World War I, 38, 45, 54, 57, 59, 80, 85, 93, 95, 99, 102, 121, 142, 166, 183, 212, 268-69, 366, 450, 620
   background of, and entry of U. S. into, 57-58
   country's lack of readiness for, when war declared, 58, 60-63, 66, 72
   drafting of soldiers for, under Selective Service Act, 58-59
   enlistment of North Dakota National Guard, 1st Infantry Regiment, Company B during, 59-62
      re-assignments of Company B troops during the war:
         U. S. Army 41st Division, 164th Infantry Battalion, 62-66
         U. S. Army First Division, 18th Infantry Battalion, Company D, 66-70, 74
         First Army Corps, 75
   Private Jack Hurley's postings during, (arranged chronologically),
      Fargo Armory, 60
      Camp Greene, North Carolina, 62
      Camp Mills, New York, 62-63
      Camp Merritt, New Jersey, 63
      S. S. Leviathan enroute to Liverpool, England, 56, 63, *65*
      Port of Liverpool, 63-64, *67*
      Camp Winnall-Down, Winchester, England, 64
      Port of Southampton, England, 64
      Port of Le Havre, France, 64
      "Forty & Eight" boxcars enroute to Western Front, 64, *67*
      La Courtine, France, 66
      Heudicourt, St. Mihiel Sector, 68
      Toul Sector, front lines, 69-70
      18th Infantry Battalion Aid Station in Beaumont, 74
      First Division Field hospital at Menil-la-Tour, 74
      S. S. Leviathan enroute to U. S., 75, *76*
      Fort Des Moines Hospital at Camp Dodge in Iowa, 77

World War I, (*continued*),
   Honorable discharge at Camp
      Dodge, Jan 12, 1919, 77
   First Division troop engagements
      after Hurley became disabled at
      Toul (arranged chronologically):
         German attack at Bois du
            Remieres, March 1, 1918,
            70, *73*
         at Cantigny to resist German
            offensive at Amiens, 74,
         in Soisson sector to attack
            the German front, 74-75
         at St. Mihiel for the first all-
            out American offensive
            against Germany, 75
         at Argonne Forest in the big
            push to Meuse River, 75
   risks of,
      American casualites at sinking of
         Luisitania, 58
      British casulaties at Somme, 57
      disability impairment, 75
      First Division casualties, 75
      rat and lice infestation, 70
      trench foot (frozen feet),70, 72, 74
      trench warfare, 57-58, 60, 69-70,
         71, 72, *73*, 74
         71, 73, 74,

Wright, Bearcat, 326, 478, ***486***, 576, 587
Yankee Stadium, 276, 361n, 417-18, 548, 550, 556, 584-85, 634, 663, 675
Yarwitz, Ted, 659
Zabuil, Szymka, (Ben Szymkowski, "the Polish Killer"), 354-59, *356*, 374, 382-84, 386, 389, 411, 580